Two-Gun Cohen

Two-Gun Cohen

A Biography

Daniel S. Levy

St. Martin's Press
New York

Design by Maureen Troy

Library of Congress Cataloging-in-Publication Data

Levy, Daniel S. (Daniel Saul)
    Two-Gun Cohen : a biography / by Daniel S. Levy.
        p.   cm.
    "A Thomas Dunne Book"
    Includes bibliographical references.
    ISBN 0-312-15681-2
    1. Cohen, Morris Abraham, 1887–1970.   2. Jews—England—
London—Biography.   3. Jews—Canada—Biography.   4. Jewish
generals—China—Biography.   5. China—History—Republic,
1912–1949.   I. Title.
DS135.E6C63   1997
909'.04924—dc21   97-7033
                                                                                    CIP

First Edition: September 1997

10 9 8 7 6 5 4 3 2 1

To my love, Lillie

Acknowledgments

There are hundreds of people whom I want to acknowledge for their help and patience, but I would first like to thank my friend and colleague William A. Henry III and Morris Cohen's sister Sarah Rich, both of whom tragically passed away before I completed this work. The writing of Morris Cohen's biography was begun during a lunch with Bill when I casually mentioned that I had always been interested in the life of a picaresque Jewish adventurer named "Two-Gun" Cohen. He suggested that I work on the book and encouraged me throughout the project. Sarah Rich was the first person to humanize Cohen for me. During our talks in Manchester, she helped me see her older brother as more than the two-dimensional character that he had seemed to be in the Charles Drage biography and the press. I would also like to thank her son, Dr. Josef Rich, O.B.E., and daughter-in-law, Jacqueline Rich, who throughout this project gave me tremendous help and access.

Other members of Cohen's family who shared material with me and encouraged this work include Joan Cooper, Victor and Sonia Cooper, Janet Gothelf, Dr. Cyril Sherer, and Michael Wallace.

A number of people graciously read through various stages of the manuscript, and I am grateful to them for their insights, thoughts, and corrections: Barbara Dudley Davis, Professor Arif Dirlik, Paul Gray, Professor Anne Kershen, Professor Abe Peck, Professor Gerald Tulchinsky, and Michael Walsh.

Having done work in numerous cities, I would like to thank those who put up with my extended visits: Jonathan Abbatt and Chiho Tokita, Nadine Epstein, Brett Gorvy, Jennifer and George Pradas, and Jonathan and Wendy Segal.

I was fortunate to receive two fellowships during work on this book. Abe Peck not only got me to start the actual writing and then read through the final work, but also enabled me to spend a year at Northwestern University's Medill School of Journalism, where I was part of the National Arts Journalism Program. I would like to thank my fellow fellows Tony Brown and Sharon McDaniel as well as Bryn

Wagner at NAJP, Michael Janeway at Medill, and Marian Godfrey at the Pew Charitable Trust. Dee Reid at Duke University witnessed the early phase of this project.

As I worked in the United States, England, Canada, and China, I had to rely on many people who tracked down records and documents around the world or sent me letters and other materials on Cohen. I am especially indebted to the efforts of Henrietta Harrison, who looked for material in China and England and translated all of the Chinese articles and documents used in this book. Rabbi Max Roth, Michael Roth, Yakov Rubinson, Kyoung-Hi Song, and Malgorzata Kot did various translations from Yiddish, Hebrew, Russian, French, and Polish. Others who helped include Hanoch Arnon, Robert Bickers, Terence Bown, Harold Davis, John Edwards, Brian Evans, Eiran Harris, Tim Hughes, Valerie Knowles, Allan E. Levine, Cliff Moore, Pan Guang, Randy R. Rostecki, Gena Rotstein, Mary Scoggin, Liudmilla Selivanova, Laurence Sharpe, Ken Soloway, Lawrence Tapper, Gary Touma, Professor Xu Buzeng, and Professor Yao Yi-en.

Most libraries, archives, and government agencies were happy to share their records. I cannot say the same for the staff at the Central Intelligence Agency, who absurdly claimed that even to divulge the existence or nonexistence of records on Cohen would compromise American national security. Hogwash. I was involved in a three-and-a-half year battle with the CIA over Cohen documents, and greatly appreciate the tireless work of Allison Zieve at Public Citizen, who valiantly tried during two lawsuits to wrestle material from that intransigent agency.

Certain historians, librarians, and archivists went quite far to find records or contacts: Kathryn Bridge at the British Columbia Archives and Records Service; Janice Rosen at the Canadian Jewish Congress, Montreal; Fred Gaffen at the Canadian War Museum; Bruce Ibsen at the City of Edmonton Archives; Anne Lindsay at the Edmonton Police Museum and Archives; Zhang Fu-qiang at the Guangdong Academy of Social Sciences; Carol Leadenham at the Hoover Institution Archives, Stanford; R.W.A. Suddaby at the Imperial War Museum; Zhang Xianwen at the Institute of History, Nanjing; Mo Shi-xiang at Jinan University; the staff at the Library of Congress; Rickie Burman at the London Museum of Jewish Life; Paulette Dozois, Andrée Lavoie, and George Bolotenko at the National Archives, Canada; John Taylor at the National Archives of the United States; Guy Robbins at the National Maritime Museum, London; Evelyn Cherpak at the Naval War College; Thomas Bourke in Special Collections at the New York Public Library; Ted Slate at the *Newsweek* library; Fred Wallace, Jennifer Dean, Carol Johnson, and Julie Borden at Northwestern University's Interlibrary Loan section; David Leonard and Keith Stotyn at the Provincial Archives of Alberta; the staffs at the Public Records Offices of Hong Kong and London; Ruth Millar, Ron Jaremko, and George Kovalenko at the Saskatoon Public Library; Cai Hongyuan, Li Yu Ming, and Wan Renyuan at the Second Historical Archives of China in Nanjing; Li Yihai, Professor Wang Yintong, and Yao Qing Hua at the Shanghai Academy of Social Sciences; Guo Xu-yin at Shanghai Normal University and Dina Abramowicz at YIVO.

For their help in various other ways: Dan-San Abbott, Dr. Wendy Abraham,

Carl Alpert, David Bjerklie, Dr. Gerry Black, Virginia Black, B.R., Michael Brunton, Robert Callin, Ming K. Chan, Oscar Chiang, Harry Cohen, Renée Cumberbatch, Fred Dahlinger, Harold Davis, Robert Dickson, Teck Dines, Marta Dorion, David Drapkin, Dr. Mark Erooga, Michael H. Evans, Abraham Fradkin, Bud Gibbs, Barry Green, Emily Hahn, Brian D. Hanning, Professor Charles Hayford, Christopher Horymski, Helen Huang, Richard Katz, Chung S. Kim, William Kooiman, Rena Krasno, Lisa and Daniel Kubiske, Professor Daniel Kwan, Masha Leon, Ronald Levaco, David J. Levy, Chris J. Lloyd, Professor Melissa Macauley, Scott MacLeod, Dr. Stephen J. Marks, Eric Marcus, R. Russell Maylone, Maisie Meyer, Morris Middleton, Lawrence Mondi, Lance Morrow, Ni Jun Min, Qian Jinbao, Aeri Pak, Yuri Pak, Joyce Playford, Christopher Porterfield, Paul Riebenfeld, Jonathan Rosenblum, Allen J. Ryan, Andrew Sadler, Betty Satterwhite Sutter, Cristina Scalet, Congressman Charles Schumer, Nomi Silverman, William Smiley, Tim Spindler, Marianne Sussman, Mia Turner, William Tynan, Wang Ganxiong, Professor Bernard Wasserstein, Betty Wei, Norman Weiss, Steve Wilson, and Congressman Sidney Yates.

I would like to thank Thomas Dunne, Melissa Jacobs, and Jeremy Katz at St. Martin's Press for getting Cohen's life into print, and my agent, Michael Carlisle, at the William Morris Agency for finding a publishing house willing to take a chance on a first-time biographer.

I would especially like to thank my parents, Alan and Esther Levy, and my mother-in-law, Soon Yung Kang, for their continued encouragement throughout this process.

Finally, I don't know how to begin to thank my wife, Lillie Pak, for her help and support throughout this ordeal. She navigated us through small Canadian towns and Chinese side streets, assisted me with the research in dusty libraries and archives, and tolerated the presence of a Cockney adventurer who seemed to take up residence in our apartment. Without her aid, insight, patience, and compass this book could not have been written.

Contents

Foreword

Morris "Two-Gun" Cohen was an anomaly, a squat, two-hundred-pound Jew who survived within the top ranks of Chinese society. He spoke little Cantonese, never having mastered the subtle nuances of the six-tone tongue or the written intricacies of the ideograms. His English had a heavy Cockney lilt with a tinge of a western Canadian twang that was incomprehensible to many Chinese. And his Yiddish and minimal Hebrew did him no good in the Orient. Even so, this Polish-born adventurer became a bodyguard to Dr. Sun Yat-sen, the father of modern China, and rose to become a general in the Chinese army in the years between the downfall of the Manchu Empire and the Japanese invasion of China during World War II.

Much has been written on Cohen. Most of it is wrong, which is unfortunate, because his real life story is much more fascinating than the myth that has evolved over the past half century. Part of the problem is that starting in the 1920s Cohen became the focus of often fanatical media attention. He made great copy for any journalist who needed a colorful tale. Yet the press generally rehashed old stories, most of them supplied by Cohen. Almost all the articles contained outlandish claims about his accomplishments, stating that he commanded the Chinese army or single-handedly controlled China's finances. In the early 1950s Cohen further nurtured this myth by dictating his memoirs. From his home in Montreal, he retold his well-oiled tales, mixed up many of the accounts, confused names, and gave the wrong dates. Charles Drage and others cobbled together his stories. It was published as *Two-Gun Cohen* and *The Life and Times of General Two-Gun Cohen*.

I, like most people, learned of Cohen through the Drage book. It paints Cohen as a mover and shaker of Chinese history who seemed rarely to make a mistake. I was intrigued by Cohen's seemingly mythic life, but confused by much of what I read. The book suffers from numerous narrative flaws. It is also missing a historical center. The reader doesn't quite understand Cohen's place in the history or the larger forces that are spinning around and out of control, the struggles and the battles that brought about modern China.

I am thankful that Cohen took the time to make the book. The chronology that he left behind has given me hints of places to look for clues to his journey. Yet when I decided to write his biography, I realized that I had essentially to ignore what Drage wrote. I needed to reconstruct Cohen's life from primary and secondary sources and place him in a historic setting. After making notes from the Drage book, I then only warily referred to anything that Cohen claimed.

As I researched Cohen's life, I wrote more than fifteen hundred letters, made countless phone calls, and tracked down and interviewed more than one hundred people who knew him. I contacted archives, libraries, and firms, and was often surprised to find Cohen mentioned in everything from Foreign Office accounts and reminiscences to prison logs and personal letters. In the process I amassed piles of documents and contemporary accounts. From them I established my own timeline for his life. When I used quotes from Drage, I only picked the ones that appeared reliable. As I worked, I also felt that I had to travel along the route Cohen took. During many weekends, vacations, and a one-year National Arts Journalism Program fellowship at Northwestern University's Medill School of Journalism, my wife, Lillie, and I set off to visit almost every place that Cohen passed through. This involved tramping around the East End of London, visiting small towns in Saskatchewan and British Columbia, getting into abandoned jails in Manitoba, walking down the back-streets of Canton and Shanghai, and strolling along the shoreline of a former Japanese prison camp in Hong Kong.

Throughout, I kept on giving Cohen the benefit of the doubt. I figured that when he dictated his life story he just got things wrong, and so I constantly forgave him for not properly remembering events in their proper place. While I knew that most of the Drage account was wrong, I never chalked it up to an outright fabrication on Cohen's part. It wasn't until late 1994 that I started to have serious doubts about the truthfulness of major parts of the book. Then one cold winter day as I sat at one of the long tables at Northwestern's Deering Library reading over an account of Sun Yat-sen's 1911 trip across North America, I had an almost epiphanous moment. I am not sure I remember the exact instant, but the light that shafted through the room's tall windows suddenly swept over me. Something, I thought, seemed wrong when I compared Sun's itinerary with Cohen's account of accompanying him as a bodyguard. I then checked Cohen's arrest record and realized that while Sun traveled in Canada, Cohen languished in a jail cell in Prince Albert.

Cohen could not have met Sun when he claimed. In fact, he would not meet him until 1922. Other doubts quickly became confirmed, as I matched Cohen's claims against the mounting historic record. The following is my attempt to correct his tales and to tell his unique story.

JANUARY 6, 1997
NEW YORK CITY

A Note on Chinese Names

Chinese names have been transliterated numerous ways over the past century. In order to prevent confusion, I have adjusted almost all names in the text to the modern Pinyin spelling. Only names that are in common usage like Sun Yat-sen, Chiang Kai-shek, Sun Fo, and Canton, or those for which I could not find Chinese characters, have not been changed; they retain the familiar spellings of the older Wade Giles system of romanization (or transliteration) or of the *Postal Atlas of China*. When Soong Qingling is referred to as Mme. Sun in a quote, her more western appellation has also been retained.

Romanization of Personal Names and Place Names

PINYIN	WADE GILES/POSTAL ATLAS
Anfu Clique	Anfu Clique
Baohuanghui	Pao-huang hui
Bai Chongxi	Pai Chung-hsi
Beijing	Peking
Cai Tingkai	Ts'ai T'ing-k'ai
Cao Juren	Ts'ao Chu-jen
Cao Kun	Ts'ao K'un
Chen Ce	Ch'en Ts'e (Chan Chak)
Chen Duxiu	Ch'en Tu-hsiu
Chen Gongbo	Ch'en Kung-po
Chen Jitang	Ch'en Chi-t'ang
Chen Jiongming	Ch'en Chiung-ming
Chen Lianbo	Ch'en Lien-po

PINYIN	WADE GILES/POSTAL ATLAS
Chen Mingshu	Ch'en Ming-shu
Chen Shuren	Ch'en Shu-jen
Cheng Qian	Ch'eng Ch'ien
Chongqing	Chungking
Cixi, The Empress Dowager	Tz'u-hsi
Cuiheng	Choyhung
Dagong bao	*Ta Kung Pao*
Dai Li	Tai Li
Du Yuesheng	Tu Yue-sheng
Fan Liang	Fan Liang
Feng Yuxiang	Feng Yü-hsiang
Fu Bingchang	Fu Ping-ch'ang
Fuzhou	Foochow
The Guangxu Emperor	The Kuang Hsu Emperor
Hankou	Hankow
He Xiangning	Ho Hsiang-ning
Hong Xiuquan	Hung Hsiu-chüan
Hongqiao	Hongkew
Hu Hanmin	Hu Han-min
Hu Lin	Hu Lin
Huan Xiang	Huan Hsiang
Huang Liang	Huang Liang
Huang Qixiang	Huang Ch'i-hsiang
Huang Shaoxiong	Huang Shao-hsiung
Huang Xing	Huang Hsing
Huangpu River	Whangpoo River
Kang Youwei	K'ang You-wei
Li Dazhao	Li Ta-chao
Li Fulin	Li Fu-lin
Li Jishen	Li Chi-shen
Li Yuanhong	Li Yuan-hung
Li Zongren	Li Tsung-ren
Liang Qichao	Liang Ch'i-ch'ao
Liao Zhongkai	Liao Chung-k'ai
Lin Wenqing	Lin Wen-ch'ing
Lü Yanzhi	Lu Yen-chih
Ma Xiang	Ma Hsiang
Mao Zedong	Mao Tse-tung
Nanjing	Nanking
Sanmin zhuyi	San-min chu-i

PINYIN	WADE GILES/POSTAL ATLAS
Shanwei	Swabue
Shen Qi	Shen Ch'i
Shilong	Sheklung
Song Jiaoren	Sung Chiao-jen
Soong Ailing	Soong Ai-ling (Mme. H.H. Kung)
Soong Meiling	Soong Mei-ling (Mme. Chiang Kai-shek)
Soong Qingling	Soong Ch'ing-ling (Mme. Sun Yat-sen)
Sun Chuanfang	Sun Ch'uan-fang
Sun Zuobing	Sun Tso-ping
Suzhou	Su-chou
Tongmenghui	Tung-meng-hui
Wang Jingwei	Wang Ching-wei
Wu Peifu	Wu P'ei-fu
Wu Tiecheng	Wu T'ieh-ch'eng
Xiaguan	Hsia-kuan
Xiamen	Amoy
Xingzhonghui	Hsing-chung-hui
Xu Chongzhi	Hsu Ch'ung-chih
Xu Qian	Hsu Ch'ien
The Xuangtong Emperor	The Hsuan T'ung Emperor
Yangzi River	Yangtze River
Ye Gongchao	Yeh Kung-ch'ao
Ye Jianying	Yeh Chian-ying
Yu Hanmou	Yü Han-mou
Yuan Shikai	Yuan Shih-k'ai
Zhabei	Chapei
Zhang Fakui	Chang Fa-K'uei
Zhang Tailei	Chang T'ai-lei
Zhang Xueliang	Chang Hsueh-liang
Zhang Zhizhong	Chang Chih-chung
Zhang Zuolin	Chang Tso-lin
Zhigongtang	Chih-kung t'ang
Zhili Clique	Chih-li Clique
Zhou Cheng	Chou Ch'eng
Zou Lu	Tsou Lu
Zhou Enlai	Chou En-lai
Zhu De	Chu Teh
Zhu Kuan	Chu K'uan

Two-Gun Cohen

orris Cohen stood on the southern bank of the Pearl River and gazed through his binoculars at the communist troops torching his adopted hometown. He had slept little since word of the Canton Commune Uprising reached him downriver in Hong Kong. Thick stubble covered his beefy boxer's face. He needed a bath, and his tropical-weight white suit, beneath which bulged his trusty pair of Smith & Wesson guns, needed changing. As the head of security at the recently established Central Bank and one of the few westerners to work his way into the upper echelon of the Nationalist Chinese leadership, Cohen had rushed back to this southern Chinese port city to check on the bank vaults containing the national reserves. But with bands of communists ransacking stores, setting houses ablaze, and slaughtering citizens, he could not reach his office. He could only helplessly watch as flames blew out the building's windows. "The Communists controlled Canton and the horrors they perpetuated hit an all-time high," Cohen said of the anarchy. "They slaughtered, they looted and they burnt; one tenth of the whole city went up in flames."

Cohen waited as Li Fulin and other assorted Nationalist leaders gathered on Henan Island to repel the attack. While the forty-year-old former bodyguard to Dr. Sun Yat-sen stood in Li's compound looking for something to do, the fires blazing in Canton reminded him of the pogroms that raged during his childhood in Poland and the tales his family told him of the attacks by their Christian neighbors. The communists across the river meanwhile took and destroyed all that they could. "One woman orator who was overheard haranguing a crowd promised every person who joined up twenty dollars and a gun," wrote the American consul Jay C. Huston of the carnage he witnessed. "She also stated that the people who joined the Reds could loot at their pleasure, would have plenty to eat and wear and would have houses to live in."

With the attack, the communists were hoping to reverse major setbacks from earlier that year. In April, the Nationalist troops of Chiang Kai-shek along with criminals from the dreaded Green Gang massacred communists in Shanghai. In the fall, a series of communist uprisings failed to seize power in several central Chinese provinces. Undeterred, the communists under directives from the Soviet leader Joseph Stalin decided to focus their efforts on the Guangdong province and its main city, Canton. They planned to seize military and police headquarters and distribute weapons to the workers. Peasants would then slaughter landlords and appropriate land, while factory laborers killed industrialists and took the tools of production. The spoils hidden in bank vaults would revert to the people. Once in power in Guangdong, the communists hoped the fires of revolution would spread beyond the province and engulf the nation.

In preparation, the communists stockpiled pistols, rifles, and grenades, but when word of their plans leaked out, police and armored cars took to the streets. Officers searched pedestrians, uncovered caches of weapons, and came across red guards. The communists then decided to quicken their grab for power. Starting at three-thirty on the morning of December 11, 1927, the revolutionaries seized many of the planned bases, but did not secure the arsenal and all the important military centers. Because of poor planning, the peasants did not rise up en masse. Many of those who joined lacked weapons and organization. Yet as they rampaged, iron-bar-and-dagger-wielding reds broke bones and smashed windows. Looters stocked up on chairs, electric fans, and household utensils.[1]

Soon tens of thousands of Nationalist troops, along with the naval forces of China and foreign nations, launched their counterassault. Gunboats lobbed shells at the reds to protect those crossing the water. Cohen sailed over with the soldiers. "We attacked in overwhelming strength," he recalled of the landing. "These Communists had had the full dose of indoctrination and they fought to the last man—and the last woman too."[2]

Fleeing reds fired machine guns and tossed bombs. They looted as they retreated before the avenging forces, torching more than a thousand houses. Along the way they killed old women who tried to save their homes. As Cohen neared the shore, snipers fired at his boat from windows. Ten Mauser-wielding women with bobbed hair and peaked caps then ran out of a nearby side street. The young women lined up along the Bund and started emptying their pistols at his boat. The troops with Cohen were initially too surprised by the appearance of the women to shoot back. But after a moment of indecision they pulled out their weapons and gunned them down. The last woman struck kept on firing as she tumbled to the ground.

Cohen heaved his hefty five-foot eight-inch frame over the bleeding bodies and headed to the bank. The building still burned, and he and the available soldiers set up a bucket brigade to quench the flames. Once they had extinguished the fires, Cohen checked the smoldering ruin and headed over to the Soviet embassy. Throughout the city the fleeing reds ripped off their red arm and neck bands, hoping to escape detection. But the weather conspired against them, too. "During the two or three days of the Red Rebellion, the weather was fairly warm," wrote Huston.

"The proletariat in their efforts to accumulate loot in a short space of time, perspired freely, generally leaving a red stain about the neck. Upon the collapse of the movement there was a wholesale discarding of red insignia. Unfortunately for the wearers, there telltale stains remained and when the oncoming soldiers, detectives and members of the fighting squad of the Mechanics Union began to make a house-to-house search of the city, the color of red on the neck of one of the inmates meant instant death not only for the marked man, but for many others in the building."

The communist atrocities that Cohen viewed earlier through his binoculars paled next to what the Nationalists were about to wreak. Troops arrested about a thousand members of communist-affiliated unions and herded them into a large theater. From there soldiers dragged the prisoners out in groups of fifty and shot them. "Most of the fighting was in the form of executions which began early that day and lasted for several days," wrote Earl Swisher, a history instructor at Canton Christian College. "The 'White Terror,' which followed the Red Occupation, was more than appalling." Killing went on all over. Piles of dead collected in the gutters as the Nationalists issued a manifesto, accusing the communists of being "guilty of murder, arson, robbery and looting of crimes unworthy of beasts . . . and everyone urges not only their death but demands that their dead bodies be torn in ten thousand shreds, and even this is not enough to expiate their sins. Therefore, we must completely eradicate them."

Crowds cheered as the police butchered people. An old merchant whose shops were burned to the ground and most of whose family had been killed walked down the street splitting open the heads of executed communists. He then grabbed warm handfuls of brain and flung the wet clumps down with a curse. Bodies choked the river. "Everywhere was the odor of fire and corpses, sickening sights to contemplate," wrote Frederick W. Hinke, the American vice-consul. "One picked one's way carefully around the corpses, skirted pools of blood, dodged overhanging electric wires, stopped over scattered bricks and passed trucks into which the police were directing coolies to throw the bodies of the executed. Some of the victims in the truck were still quivering."[3]

Expecting a raid of their consulate, the Russian Soviets stuffed bundles of letters and propaganda literature into a roaring stove. When the Nationalist soldiers arrived they discovered a cache of weapons and bombs. They marched part of the consulate staff off to their death. General Zhang Fakui then issued Cohen instructions to enter the consulate, and Cohen asked British Lieutenant Commander Cyril M. Faure and a senior French naval officer to help him inspect the building. The place was a mess. Faure noted that the troops "seem to have been intent on bursting open all the safes and distributing all the documents on the floor." Cohen's search party scoured the building. There they discovered maps and a radio transmitter. The men gathered up mounds of paper and maps, dumped them into a trunk, and carted the documents to Cohen's room at the Victoria Hotel. Cohen also wired the Hong Kong police force and arranged for a Russian sergeant on the staff to come by and translate the papers. The group accumulated so much material, more than they could hope to sort through, that sometime past midnight Cohen ran over to the nearby apartment of his friends Olga and Vivian Ferrier and their five-month-old child, Arthur Michael, to secure more help. He pounded on their door, woke up the family, and enlisted the Russian-born Olga. The American consulate also found a Russian speaker to join in the work.

As the hours passed, the band of translators drank tea Ferrier brewed in a samovar, sipped cognac, and discovered damning reports. "I found many documents to prove beyond the shadow of a doubt that they were responsible for the coup," Cohen wrote soon after. They even discovered a list of Soviet secret service agents and a Russian plan for an uprising in Indochina. "To sum up, there is undeniable evidence that the Communist party organised the agrarian revolution in order to take over power by disarming Government troops and arming the peasants," reported Faure. "The fact that large-scale maps were found, one of which by the position of the forces marked on it, could only have dealt with peasant forces, coupled with the fact that a secret transmitting set was found, indicate that the consulate was in all probability the headquarters of the revolution."[4]

Thousands died during the days of communist and Nationalist fury. It took weeks for stability to be restored to Canton and the bloated bodies to wash out to the South China Sea. Once things calmed down, Cohen decided to take a much-deserved holiday in Hong Kong. He brought along the Ferriers and repaid Olga's assistance by showing them a good time. He set them up in the finest suite at the Peninsula hotel, plied them with champagne, and threw what he modestly referred to as "a party or two."

Morris Cohen's shindigs were legendary, as was the life of this chunky battler. He lived within the flames of early-twentieth-century China, battling the military and diplomatic forces of Russia, Japan, Chinese warlords, communists, and mercenaries. He was used to those fires and would always know them, having been born in the inferno of the Polish pogroms.

CHAPTER 2

THE POGROMS,
1880S

On the eve of Greek Orthodox Easter, a number of weeks af-
ter the assassination of Czar Alexander II, the Christians in the city of
Ylizavetgrad gathered on the streets and in their stores and declared that "the Zhyds
are about to be beaten." The police and a small detachment of troops were called
into this important trading port of 40,000 in the Russian province of Kherson to
maintain order, and the first few days of Passover passed peacefully for the 10,000
Jews. But then on the fifteenth of April 1881, the horrors began. Troublemakers
who blamed the Jews for the czar's death sent a mean drunk into a Jewish-owned
bar. When the proprietor evicted the unruly customer the crowd yelled, "The Zhyds
are beating our people!"

A mob surged through the streets, assaulting Jews and attacking their homes and
stores. "The rioting . . . assumed a more serious character upon revolver-shots being
fired from some Jewish homes," reported a *Times* of London correspondent. "The
Christians then attacked the houses and shops of the Jews indiscriminately by smashing doors, breaking windows." Jews cowered in their rooms and cellars throughout
the night. Drunken neighbors clubbed and beat men and raped women.

At first the police and troops dispersed the crowd, but by the morning of the
sixteenth the pogrom had spread throughout the town. "Clerks, saloon and hotel
waiters, artisans, drivers, flunkeys, day laborers in the employ of the Government,
and soldiers on furlough—all of these joined the movement," a Russian report stated.
"The city presented an extraordinary sight: streets covered with feathers and ob-
structed with broken furniture which had been thrown out of the residences; houses
with broken doors and windows; a raging mob, running about yelling and whistling
in all directions and continuing its work of destruction without let or hindrance,
and, as a finishing touch to this picture, complete indifference displayed by the local
non-Jewish inhabitants to the havoc wrought before their eyes."

The mob gleefully interpreted the general inaction of the troops as tacit approval for their acts. "Toward the evening the disorder increased in intensity, owing to the arrival of a large number of peasants from the adjacent villages, who were anxious to secure part of the Jewish loot." The farm folk went wild, freely joining in the "general mêlée, sacked the houses of the Jews, destroyed their furniture, and spoiled or stole their wares." By eight that evening a cold wind began to blow through the battered community, and the falling rain dampened the ardor of this booty-heavy crowd. Soon troops arrived. By the following morning the infantry brought calm. Yet by then one Jew lay dead, two hundred were injured, and a synagogue and more than half the Jewish homes were in shambles.[1]

The Jews bore no responsibility for the death of Alexander. He was killed in March by a Polish student named Hriniewicki, a member of the revolutionary group Narodnaia Volia—People's Will Party—who heaved a bomb at him on an empty St. Petersburg street. When the authorities learned that a Jewish seamstress named Jessie Helfmann belonged to Narodnaia Volia, they singled her out as the architect of the heinous deed. Though only an inconsequential operative who maintained a secret residence for her comrades and acted as a messenger, Helfmann was a Jewess, the ideal scapegoat. Pogroms spread as rioters learned what an easy target the Jews made. By the seventeenth of April local peasants swarmed through Jewish agricultural settlements in the area surrounding Ylizavetgrad. A few Christians protected their Jewish neighbors, yet others noted the passivity of the police and troops and pillaged at will as talk circulated that the newly crowned Alexander III had issued a ukase calling upon his subjects to punish the Jews for the death of his father.[2]

These and other falsehoods ranged widely. The Russian press latched on to Helfmann's reputed role. They vilified the Jews and circulated rumors of proposed pogroms. And while not orchestrated, the attacks, the looting, the rapes, and the murders were encouraged by a myriad of anti-Jewish groups, fanned by disparate collections of agitators and carried out by lumpenproletariat who took advantage of a limited opportunity to grab free goods and to vent their frustrations over their brutish lives.

Almost every stratum of Russian society joined in some aspect of the attacks. For high-level officials the pogroms presented a convenient way to channel and defuse peasant tensions over the current economic depression. Governors-general like Alexander Romanovich Drenteln of Kiev persuaded pogromists that Alexander III thirsted for blood. Noblemen, rural bourgeois, labor leaders, and the intelligentsia disseminated anti-Jewish propaganda and toured cities to discuss possible "spontaneous" outbursts of fury. Local workers returned home frothing with tales of plunder they had seen and loot to be had. Itinerant farm and factory workers dubbed the "bare-footed brigade" roused the peasantry. Revolutionary groups even hoped that if the czar's troops defended the Jews, their actions would infuriate the masses and hasten the destruction of the monarchy.[3]

The Jews presented an easy, definable target. They dressed differently, spoke a foreign tongue called Yiddish, and clustered together in shtetls, small towns and cities initially established by Polish and Lithuanian nobility to which they invited

Jews to live and work. The communities almost never bespoke wealth. They generally contained unpainted wooden houses plopped alongside muddy roads. Beneath the thatched roofs there might be one, maybe two whitewashed rooms heated by a clay stove.

Radzanow was one such shtetl. Situated about fifty-five miles northwest of Warsaw on a peninsula near the confluence of the Mlawka and Wkra Rivers, it was surrounded by lush forests and many swamps. During the summer, beautiful blossoming gardens filled the town. In the spring when the snow melted, floods wiped out the bridges and dirt roads and inundated the fields. The local noble who founded Radzanow in the 1400s granted the citizens permission to hold a weekly market, along with two large fairs a year. By the sixteenth century Radzanow had developed into a wool-processing center and had many textile factories. In the 1760s the town could boast 586 Christian residents and five Jews. In the 1880s 1,258 souls lived in 106 houses in this bustling community. By then Jews made up about two-fifths of the population, and the town contained a church, a school, a city hall, a windmill, and two blacksmith shops.

While life was not easy in such a town, at least there the Jews did not have to endure the harsh rules and restrictions imposed on them in royal towns. The Jews of Radzanow worshiped in their temple and the boys studied the Bible and the Talmud. By the early 1800s the town had an organized Jewish community. Most of the Radzanow Jews lived close to the rectangular market in the center of town where they made a meager living. The men brought produce to nearby cities and towns and returned with finished goods to sell to the Gentile and Jewish peasantry, while the women and children worked at the stalls and bought and sold vegetables, cattle, salt, and household goods. Some manufactured oil or milled flour. A few led a more clandestine life smuggling goods across the nearby Prussian border.[4]

Josef Leib Miaczyn was a Radzanow wheelwright. His family moved to Radzanow from Miaczyn Wielki and Miaczyn Maly, tiny nearby sister hamlets that boasted a handful of people, calcium deposits, cattle grazing, extensive swamps, and bad farmland. Josef Miaczyn was a short, thick man with a wide, bearded face, strong nose, and small, penetrating eyes. He had three brothers, and married Sheindel Lipshitz from Biezun, a community of 2,500 people just to the west on the Wkra. Sheindel's town produced many rabbis and scientists, and like Radzanow was granted rights by the local nobility, first becoming a commercial center in the fourteenth century. During the first half of the nineteenth century a textile factory opened in Biezun, and soon tanneries, a glass factory, a brewery, wind- and water mills along with twenty-five shops and restaurants appeared. Biezun fishermen pulled fish from the Wkra that fetched a goodly sum in Warsaw. The first Jewish settlers made a living as merchants and shop owners, and founded a community center and a cemetery. Most worked as tailors and hatmakers and shoemakers, selling their goods at the weekly markets as well as at seasonal fairs. In the 1870s they built small factories and a sawmill. A few years later they erected a brick synagogue.

Sheindel had two brothers and two sisters. Her sister Malka married Miaczyn's brother Zelig. Like their Jewish neighbors, the Miaczyns were orthodox and observant. After her marriage to Josef, Sheindel followed tradition and covered her head with a *shaytl*—a wig—as a sign of modesty. They had a daughter named Rose, and soon after that, on August 3, 1887—the thirteenth of Av, 5647—Sheindel gave birth to a son whom they named Abraham. He would eventually assume the first name of Morris.[5]

Besides the daily hardships that the Miaczyns and their neighbors had to endure, the land seemed to attract both conquerors and villains. In the fifteenth century East Prussian crusaders pillaged Biezun, and in the 1650s the hard-living king of Sweden, Karl X, passed through and destroyed both Radzanow and Biezun. Karl's bid for domination of Poland failed, but in 1772 Russia, Austria, and Prussia started slicing up the militarily weak kingdom. Over the next two decades their three partitions consumed Poland. Radzanow, Biezun, and Miaczyn fell into Prussian hands, remaining there only until Napoleon claimed the area in 1807. His empire too crumbled, and in 1815 the Congress of Vienna set about establishing new boundaries for Europe. Russia took over the part of pre-partitioned Poland containing Radzanow, Biezun, and Miaczyn, and the Czar became hereditary ruler of the land.[6]

For the Russians this proved to be a valuable acquisition. It had, though, something they desperately did not want—hardworking, pious Jews like Miaczyn. Hundreds of thousands of them. Russian leaders had labored long and hard to wipe out all traces of Jews from their feudal empire. Few remained after Czarina Anna Ivanovna banished them in the early eighteenth century. When in the late 1730s a Jew named Baruch Leibov decided to construct a synagogue in the town of Sverovich and convinced a retired captain to convert to Judaism, officials carted the two men off to St. Petersburg and publicly torched them. In 1742 Czarina Elizabeth Petrovna decreed that "all Jews . . . be immediately deported, together with all their property, from Our whole Empire . . . They shall henceforth not be admitted to Our Empire under any pretext and for any purpose, unless they be willing to adopt Christianity. . . ." In the decade prior to 1753 Russia deported 35,000 Jews.[7]

Since Russians widely believed that the newly acquired Jews possessed powers that made them more competitive, and used their crafty ways to dupe the dim-witted and defenseless peasantry, the government decreed that they were to be isolated and regulated in the sparsely populated western lands. There they could act as a buffer against foreign enemies. Eventually this zone of restriction stretched from the Baltic Sea southeast to the Black Sea, a 386,100-square-mile swatch of territory that became known as the Pale of Settlement. By the last two decades of the nineteenth century the Pale contained 94 percent of the Russian Jewish population: 4 million souls whose numbers had mushroomed at nearly twice the rate of the general population, rising 150 percent from 1,600,000 in 1820. When Prince Demidoff San-Donato surveyed this overpopulated territory in the 1880s, he reported that 1,584 people lived per square mile. In some towns and villages like Radzanow, Jews made up a sizable percentage of the inhabitants. To the general Russian population of 86 million, they represented a potential and potent threat.

For the Jews, far-reaching restrictions hindered their access to work. Laws forbade them from owning farms, and the vast majority of Jewish craftsmen, tailors, shoemakers, bakers and butchers, grocers and buttonmakers, in towns like Radzanow worked hard to make a few coppers. Shtetl Jews without a trade ran taverns and stores, let rooms, collected farm rents, bought grain, and sold produce and goods. Officials accused Jews of taking advantage of peasants, selling them overpriced liquor, and living off usury. They were, in the Russian eye, what the future Czar Nicholas I scrawled on visiting the western provinces in 1816: "The ruin of the peasants of these provinces are the Zhyds. As property-holders they are here second in importance to the landed nobility. By their commercial pursuits they drain the strength of the hapless White Russian people. . . . They are regular leeches, and suck these unfortunate governments to the point of exhaustion."[8]

Yet despite their supposed success, they were not all as rich as the Rothschilds. Like Josef Miaczyn, most were more akin to Shalom Aleichem's Tevye; 40 percent of the Jews lived in poverty. Regular economic depressions, severe competition, and underbidding between tailors, shopkeepers, and shoemakers brought abject suffering and hunger. Alexander II's freeing of the serfs in 1861 made conditions worse for the Jews as the new freemen streamed into urban areas and competed for the few jobs. Jewish families shared rooms and houses in rural hovels and urban slums. In some areas, a family might simply live on a herring, a pound of bread, and a few onions a day. At midcentury the Jewish death rate stood at twice that of the Gentiles.[9]

Up till the start of the pogroms, the average Jew like Miaczyn maintained respectable though nonsocial relations with his Gentile neighbors. The mass of Russians, though, saw them as outsiders. As non-Russians. As strangers. As aliens who did not accept the deity of Christ. What better reason to demonize them and keep them apart? Christian rumors and superstitions concerning the Jews abounded. For centuries Christians had accused them of such preposterous crimes as causing the Plague, poisoning wells, stealing and urinating on communion wafers, and using and consuming the blood of Christian children in their "evil" rituals. Christians harassed, hounded, maligned, and killed them. Scant protection came from the authorities.[10]

Talk of Jews' predilection for Christian blood was widespread and unsquelchable. The czars tried many ways to restrict the Jews and force them to abandon their faith. None of the czars, though, could compete with Nicholas I in sheer doggedness. He forbade Jews to hire Christian domestics, outlawed the construction of synagogues in the vicinity of churches, and started censoring and burning Jewish books. Soon after taking the throne, Nicholas issued a ukase calling for the compulsory quarter-century conscription of young Jewish men. Jewish officials had to administer the program. They hired *khappers* (snatchers) to grab the poor and unemployed off of the streets and from their beds. They tricked the illiterate into signing up, and did not flinch from taking children as young as eight, even five, presenting them to induction agents with the claim that the lads were actually older and merely puny. *Khappers* destroyed exemption certificates, shanghaied the excused, and gladly accepted the bribes of the rich to overlook their sons. Boys mutilated their bodies in order to avoid service. Parents hid their sons in the surrounding woods, assaulted community leaders and *khappers,* and even attacked convoys of recruits to retrieve their children.[11]

Once the army took their boys, parents could do little but mourn their loss and recite the Kaddish—the prayer for the dead—over the departed. The military jammed the kids into livestock cars, quartered them in Gentile homes, and spoke to them only in Russian as they made their way toward decades of service in the barren stretches of Siberia. Soldiers beat all who refused baptism, fed them salted, nonkosher foods, and denied them water. Half the children died because of long marches during which soldiers flogged and tortured them. Many of the boys resigned themselves to an unpalatable fate. Others refused to submit. One group of children about to be baptized in the Volga in the presence of Nicholas decided to suffer death rather than sacrilege, and supposedly drowned themselves.[12]

The Jews hoped for a reduction of restrictions following Alexander's emancipation of the serfs. The czar ended the forced conscriptions, relaxed conversionist policies, allowed Jews to move out of their ghettos and attend some schools. Yet all hope of change ended with the Eastertime rioting at Ylizavetgrad. Almost two weeks after those disturbances a pogrom flared in Kiev after word spread that rioters would receive the aid of the military. Christians hung religious icons in their windows and painted crosses on their doors, almost as a biblical mark to implore the furies to pass over their homes.

"At twelve o'clock . . . the air suddenly resounded with wild shouts, whistling, jeering, hooting, and laughing," recalled an eyewitness of the troubles.

> The destruction of Jewish houses began. Window-panes and doors began to fly about, and shortly thereafter the mob, having gained access to the houses and stores, began to throw upon the streets absolutely everything that fell into their hands. Clouds of feathers began to whirl in the air. The din of broken window-panes and frames, the crying, shouting, and despair on the one hand, and the terrible yelling and jeering on the other, completed the picture. . . . Soon afterwards the mob threw itself upon the Jewish synagogue, which, despite its strong bars, locks and shutters, was wrecked in a moment. One should have seen the fury with which the riff-raff fell upon the [Torah] scrolls, of which there were many in the synagogue. The scrolls were torn to shreds, trampled in the dirt, and destroyed with incredible passion. The streets were soon crammed with the trophies of destruction. Everywhere fragments of dishes, furniture, household utensils, and other articles lay scattered about.[13]

Bands of thirty to a hundred men armed with choppers, hammers, and bludgeons carried out the work. "Their proceedings were watched by large crowds of spectators, and it was difficult to distinguish the rioters from the well-disposed public," reported *The Illustrated London News.* "A crowd of people would be promenading a thoroughfare. Suddenly a whistle would be heard, and in a moment men would issue from the crowd and form themselves into a band, and an attack would be made upon a house. . . . None were left unmolested. Warehouses were opened and sacks of flour poured out into the streets; tea-shops were entered, and the chests of tea emptied into the gutter; jewelers' shops were broken open, and gold watches and all manner of jewelry thrown by handfuls among the crowd."[14]

Pogromists donned layers of suits and dresses as they went, carrying and carting away with stolen horses and wagons what they could not wear. They torched and destroyed about a thousand Jewish homes and businesses, tossing sobbing men and women through flaming doorways. They raped twenty girls and women, murdered others. In April and May pogromists attacked more than fifty villages and hamlets. They ripped out the beards of old men, tortured women, killed boys who refused to make the sign of the cross. Police in many towns and cities forbade the Jews to defend themselves. In Berdychev Jewish residents had to bribe the police commissioner so that he would not raise an objection when a club-wielding band of Jews met a trainload of tramps itching for a pogrom.

The first series of pogroms ended in July, yet during the summer months fires consumed large Jewish swaths of Minsk, Bobruisk, Vitebsk, and Pinsk. Then during Christmas trouble broke out in Warsaw, not far from Radzanow. In the midst of services at the Church of the Holy Cross someone, possibly a pickpocket who hoped to lift a few wallets and purses during the ensuing confusion, yelled "Fire." Horrified worshipers trampled one another as they rushed and stumbled toward the doors. Congregants afterward set the twenty-nine dead on the ground outside. Word started that two Jewish pickpockets had set off the panic. Whistles then shrilled as thieves orchestrated the gathered crowd. They attacked passing Jews and looted stores, but avoided the denser Jewish sections of town for fear of possible resistance. One Russian former colonel even carried a list of Jewish stores to be visited. Governor General Albedinski meanwhile forbade the formation of a civilian guard to stop the pogrom.[15]

The archbishop called on the rioters to desist. Catholic priests marched through the streets with raised crosses, begging the crowds not to blacken the holy season. Local intellectuals implored crowds to go home. But the attacks stopped only on the third day, when the authorities intervened and arrested 3,000 rioters. By then the synagogue and 1,500 Jewish homes and businesses were sacked, and twenty-four Jews wounded.

By the end of the year more than two hundred pogroms befell towns and villages. Forty Jews lay dead, tens of thousands lost their homes and their livelihoods. When Alexander III assumed the throne he worked to stop the rioting and also brought a quick end to his father's liberal reforms. And in the tradition of blaming the injured for his woes, the government set out to "protect" the pogromists from the pogromed. In late August 1881, Minister of Interior Count Nikolai P. Ignatev issued a memorandum stating that the Jews brought the pogroms on themselves.

Further restrictions followed. On May 3, 1882, Alexander sanctioned "The Temporary Orders Concerning the Jews." They were forbidden to settle or even own land outside towns or other urban areas, and were more tightly packed into cities. Certain added professions now stood closed to them, and they were prohibited from working on the Christian Sabbath or any religious holiday. Peasants could even insist on the removal of Jewish neighbors. When Count Dmitrii Tolstoy replaced Ignatev on May 30, he promptly set about suppressing agitation, and issued a circular demanding the end of all pogroms. Trials began. Some of the convicted obtained free passage to cold penal colonies.[16]

Fearful that the pogroms would intensify general emigration, which the Russians did not want to encourage, Tolstoy wrote a circular on June 25, 1882, saying that those who promoted Jewish migration would be punished. Jewish leaders also worried that a mass exodus might ruin efforts to reform Russia's feudal policies. Nonetheless, the Jews looked for places to flee. Some called for the establishment of agricultural settlements in Canada. Others wanted to move to Palestine. Many followed the tens of thousands who had emigrated to the United States in the previous decade.

Jews like Josef Miaczyn in such towns as Radzanow and Biezun learned of the United States and England from newspaper accounts and through mail sent home from friends and relatives. They eagerly shared letters around the village and marketplace, and the accounts of golden streets and bountiful harvests whetted the appetite to sail to the lands of freedom and opportunity. Regardless of Tolstoy's efforts, enticements to leave abounded. The Russian Jewish press published dispatches from correspondents in America. Steamship companies ran ads in European newspapers and sent agents to convince Jews that plentiful jobs awaited them. In Radzanow hopes of leaving only increased in 1885 when a large fire roared through the town and burned down the wooden synagogue. When Miaczyn received a letter from a friend in America who wrote that he would help get him established in the New World, he decided to join the westerly flow. He planned to set off to America on his own. Once there and working he would send for Sheindel, Rose, and Morris.

News of pogroms frightened British and American society. The United States Congress asked President James Garfield to write the czar to protect the Jews. In England such notables as the archbishop of Canterbury, Cardinal Manning, the bishop of London, and the poet Robert Browning supported relief efforts. Prominent Jews like the Rothschilds and the banker and community leader Herman Landau actively raised funds. The Lord Mayor of London called for a public meeting at his residence at Mansion House, and the resulting letter bore the signatures of luminaries like the poet Matthew Arnold and the evolutionist Charles Darwin.[17]

At the start of the pogroms, 60,000 Jews lived in England, two-thirds of them residing in London. As the flow increased, sympathy on the part of English Jews turned into fear of inundation. They began sending reports to Russia that arriving Jews sheared off their beards and lived dissolute lives in a dangerous land. The British consul general in Odessa spread frightful accounts of overcrowding and unemployment. Nathan Adler, the Chief Rabbi of England, contacted his European colleagues, warning them of the dangers awaiting their flocks. Many "are lost without livelihoods," he wrote. Worse yet, it was not uncommon for them to "contravene the will of their Maker on account of poverty and overwork, and violate the Sabbath and Festivals. Some have been ensnared in the net of the missionaries and renounced their religion. . . . There are many who believe that all the cobblestones of London are precious stones, and that it is the place of gold. Woe and alas, it is not so. . . ."

Horror stories, though, could not compete with the glowing account of freedom gleaned from a few priceless sentences in a letter. Relatives sent home tickets. Others sold their meager possessions to put together the fare. So many left that in Kiev in late April 1881 the railroad lines added ten to twelve extra carriages to some trains. During the summer of 1882 more than 12,000 refugees in Brody jammed thirty or forty to a room and crowded the streets and synagogues.

While Russian society held no love for the Jews, officials made it both hard and expensive for them to depart. Bribes had to be liberally doled out to the mayor or local magistrate in order to acquire a free document called a "legitimation." This had to be endorsed, at a price, by the local police chief, confirming the applicant's existence. The emigrant then had to pay the Revenue Department for a passport, and mail all the papers to the provincial governor. Two or three months later the material, it was hoped, returned in care of the local police chief, who had once again to be paid off. If an applicant received permission to leave, he had three weeks to slip out of town.[18]

Many realized that it was actually cheaper just to sneak across the border with professional smugglers and guides. Coming from the area of Radzanow, one generally took a train or wagon to the frontier, boarded a train to Bremen, Rotterdam, or Hamburg, then took a ship to London. Once in England an immigrant journeyed to the west coast and sailed steerage-class to the fabled land of America. It was a heavily traveled route. Few failed to escape. Along the way hostel keepers, railroad workers, and ticket agents robbed them, charged them inflated prices, and even sold them tickets to New York that only went as far as London.[19]

Passengers to England suffered in appalling conditions. Josef Miaczyn and countless others packed below deck for forty to sixty hours, sleeping on rags in holds and eating salted herrings. "By the time I got on deck darkness had set in, and nearly all my fellow-aliens had stowed away the pocket-handkerchiefs or canvas-bags containing their belongings in one or other of the two holds, which were to form their place of residence for the next two nights at any rate," reported the special commissioner of the *Evening News and Post*, who took the boat from Hamburg to England disguised as an immigrant.

> I sat down in a dark corner and quietly examined my surroundings. The greater portion of the deck was taken up by large boxes covered with sheets of canvas, and extending to a height in some places of perhaps eight or ten feet. On top of these, and in the narrow passages between them, the emigrants sat or stood, breaking the stillness of the evening with the hollow laugh or clamorous chatter. . . . All, with few exceptions, were yellow with dirt, and smelt foully. . . . I thought it to be about time to go and look after my sleeping quarters. . . . I made my way to the larger of the two steerage cabins. When I got to the top

of the gangway, the stench which issued from the semi-darkness beneath was pretty nearly unendurable, and it was even worse down-stairs, when blended with the heat from the bodies of the emigrants. But the scene which the place presented was still more disgusting. The apartment was about the breadth of the ship near the narrow end in width, and scarcely so long. In the centre a single oil-lamp was hanging, which threw out a feeble, flickering light. On each side a couple of platforms were erected, one over the other, with about two and a half feet between them, divided into spaces in some places a little over two feet broad, and not divided at all in others. Here men, women, and children were lying on the bare boards partly undressed, some in one direction, some in another. Young men lay abreast of young unmarried women, chatting jocularly, and acting indecently, and young children were witnesses of all that passed. The greater portion of the floor was taken up with boxes, on which such of the emigrants of both sexes as had not been able to obtain the ordinary sleeping accommodation were reclining as best they might.[20]

As the steamships streamed along the Thames River toward London, Miaczyn and crowds of men, women, and children gathered on deck to gaze at the passing counties of Kent and Essex. Some sat on baskets containing their bedding, clothing, and family finery. Others clutched bundles of essential items tied in bright-colored kerchiefs. All scratched their unwashed bodies. At London the steamers dropped anchor in the middle of the river, and Miaczyn transferred to a small boat for the ride ashore. Along the way the waterman gouged the passengers for more than the fixed rate of three pence. British officials at the docks gave Miaczyn a cursory medical examination and checked how much money he had to ensure that he would not become a ward of the state.

Tired and hungry, Miaczyn tried to regain his legs after days at sea, and scanned the crowd and looming warehouses. Few welcoming smiles greeted him. He could only experience shock at what he saw. "There are a few relations and friends awaiting the arrival of the small boats filled with immigrants: but the crowd gathered in and about the gin-shop overlooking the narrow entrance of the landing-stage are dock loungers of the lowest type and professional 'runners,' " wrote the sociologist Beatrice Potter. "These latter individuals, usually of the Hebrew race, are among the most repulsive of East London parasites; boat after boat touches the landing-stage, they push forward, seize hold of the bundles or baskets of the new-comers, offer bogus tickets to those who wish to travel forward to America, promise guidance and free lodging to those who hold in their hands addresses of acquaintances in Whitechapel, or who are absolutely friendless. . . . For a few moments it is a scene of indescribable confusion: cries and counter-cries; the hoarse laughter of the dock loungers at the strange garb and broken accent of the poverty-stricken foreigners; the rough swearing of the boatmen at passengers unable to pay the fee for landing."[21]

Things only got worse. Rogues enticed the immigrants with promises of a reliable place to stay and help getting work. "They then conduct them to so-called lodging houses, one man conducting while the other takes the luggage either by hand or on a barrow," wrote the English financier Herman Landau.

> The carrier of the luggage who is one of the fraternity, then demands some exorbitant sum for his services and that in a manner well calculated to intimidate a poor stranger for not unfrequently any remonstrance on the part of the passenger is met by blows. The master and mistress of the lodging house then urge the passenger to settle with the porter immediately; pretend to make some compromise honourable to the poor victim, who in the end is mulcted in about five shillings in addition to the sum already paid by the ships side. The luggage is retained in the house and when the passenger asks why he is not taken to the address he had given, the landlord tells him the address is not in London at all but in the country and that it would cost from one to five pounds to take him there and they urge these strangers to take refreshments and rest awhile in their house. A large number fall into this trap and are even induced to deposit for "safety" with the landlord any valuables or money they may have which they never recover again. The landlord and his confederator having obtained as much money as they possibly could to purchase the ticket for this pretended long journey into the country (in the last case that has come to my knowledge the sum of fifty shillings was thus obtained) the victim is taken to Liverpool St. Station and sent to Tottenham or some of the Metropolitan Railway Stations.[22]

Those who decided to stay in London were told that they would be looked after. The landlord charged the immigrant from two to five shillings a night for a squalid bed. Each morning he was tramped around town, supposedly to look for work. At night he returned to the flophouse to try again in the morning. This went on until he had no money left. The landlord then loaned him some cash, kept his luggage as collateral, and turned out the unfortunate and now destitute man.

Like thousands of others, Josef Miaczyn never intended to stay longer than necessary. So determined was he to join his landsmen in America that he didn't even take along the address of an aunt and uncle who lived in town. By the time he left the docks he had no money to continue on his way. He also had no place to sleep. Respectable Anglo-Jewish society tried to aid those in Miaczyn's predicament, establishing soup kitchens, boot and shoe distribution societies and other relief organizations. The most visionary act of charity, though, came from Simon Cohen, a kindly and devout baker who founded the Poor Jews' Temporary Shelter, a safe house and temporary flop for those in need.

Located not far from the landing docks on the Thames, the shelter ended up aiding 1,000 to 4,000 immigrants a year. Miaczyn was one of those helped. A German-speaking member of the staff met every boat, and the shelter posted Yiddish-language placards at the docks and on the ships warning passengers to be wary of overly friendly porters. The staff also welcomed non-Jews, but few came. The shelter had a fair number of good-sized rooms with dormitory-style sleeping quarters, cloth curtains, and tiled walls as well as a shed out back for luggage. Residency lasted only two weeks, during which time guests had to acclimate themselves to London, get settled, and find employment. The shelter put its guests to work around the facility, chopping wood and generally helping out. Residents also attended afternoon and evening services, lectures on religion, and the essential English classes.

When Miaczyn arrived in the late 1880s, the staff registered him, asked his profession and how much money he carried. The shelter doctor looked him over, and the staff then marched him and the other new guests off to the Russian vapor baths for a thorough soaking. They also placed his clothes in a disinfecting chamber. Miaczyn ate his first shelter meal, and cried over his state. He quickly tracked down his aunt and uncle and took refuge with them. His uncle owned a tailoring workshop. Miaczyn showed him that he could work a machine. The uncle asked him to stay in London, offered him a job, and sent for Sheindel, Rose, and Morris. As he settled, Miaczyn realized that in his new land his surname was hard for others to pronounce. Since he was descended from the Jewish priestly class, the *kohens,* Miaczyn changed his name to the simpler sounding Cohen. Thus ended his plans to sail to America.[23]

Josef Cohen entered a profession dominated by the Jews. They had initially broken into dry goods in the secondhand clothes markets, and the plaintive calls of Jewish rag collectors were a mainstay of nineteenth-century London streets: "But as I write, floats on the ambient air, adown the quiet street in which I live, softly through the open window, gently to my pleased ears, a very familiar and welcome cry," wrote Charles Dickens. "I have always heard *that* cry, and always shall, I hope. It was cried in London streets years before I was born, and will be cried years after I am dead. It never varies, never diminishes in volume or sonorous melody, this cry; for, as the world wags, and they that dwell in it live and die, they must be clothed— and, amidst the wear and tear of life, their clothes are worn and torn, too;—so we shall always have old clothes to buy or sell; and for many a year, down many a quiet street, through many an open window, shall float that old familiar cry—'Old Clo'!' . . . Carrying the bag, and crying 'oghclo!' seems a sort of novitiate, or apprenticeship, which all Hebrews are subjected to."[24]

Rag dealers worked the streets, alleys, and courts, gathering shirts, dresses, frock coats, and assorted flotsam cloth for sale at rag fairs. With the midcentury invention of the Singer sewing machine, many Jews who had tailoring training in the old country easily made the switch to the burgeoning ready-made industry. By the time Cohen started at his uncle's workshop, nearly one-third of those arriving in England worked in some area of tailoring.

The working class and those in colonial markets eagerly sought the mediocre and ill-fitting garments that came out of these workshops. Different workshops handled specific sections of each garment, and workers performed individual chores. Some made buttonholes; others sewed on collars or did basting. "The coat hangs on its owner's back like linen on a clothes-line, at the mercy of every movement or gust of wind," wrote Potter of an average East End garment. "Clearly, then, the order of the gentleman who knows how to clothe himself, and is able to pay for it, cannot be executed by a Jewish contractor. In the making of hand-sewn garments the English journeyman tailor has no rival. On the other hand the English tailor cannot compete with the Jewish contractor in supplying wholesale houses with ready-made clothing."[25]

With the constant flow of immigrants, the garment industry could count on a large and continuously replenished pool of cheap workers. Those venturing into the glutted labor market earned two to three shillings a week to start. Sometimes they only received food—stale bread, bad coffee, a salted herring or a pickled cucumber— along with a space on the floor to rest. Those who did not do tailoring work made shoes, furniture, and cigars. As with Cohen's uncle's enterprise, most of the work-shops were small, only employing a few men and women on a seasonal basis. Within two months, workers could master the trade, and after a year they might command a poverty weekly wage of seventy-five pence to two pounds fifty. Women made less than men. If a worker scrimped and saved, he could survive. Maybe one day he might open his own workshop.[26]

Tailors worked twelve to eighteen hours a day in cramped, dark rooms, cellars and sheds lined with tables and piled high with pieces waiting to be finished. Little natural light reached inside. "I have myself seen these poor creatures at work up till two in the morning, and I have found that they were again at work, the same people in the same room, at seven o'clock in the morning," noted the bishop of Bedford. "You can tell work is being done on the Sabbath, by the blinds being drawn."

Laborers had to supply their own materials, and each morning English, Irish, and Jewish girls brought tobacco or candle boxes containing the cottons, twists, gimps, needles, thimbles, and scissors they needed to do the job. The day started by 8 A.M., often much earlier. The pressers lit their gas jets and prepared their irons. As they worked, the gas jets and coke fires heated up the rooms and filled the air with lint, dust, and grit. Workers crammed sideways on benches just to get a little elbow room, and exchanged lively gossip, flirted with the pressers, sang new tunes from the music halls, or whispered about the latest Jack the Ripper murder, all to the monotonous whirling accompaniment of the machines.

If they received a lunch break, some headed out onto the streets and mingled with machinists, pressers, and sewers from competing workshops. Others pulled baskets from under tables, and spread out on soiled newspapers wedges of bread and butter, cold sausage, or salted fish. At night they headed home, their backs hurting from hunching over the tables, their fingers pricked sore from needles. They were a pallid, sickly crowd. Many came down with pulmonary tuberculosis, pneumonia, pleurisy, and bronchitis. Women had miscarriages, developed malformed vertebras and swollen veins, and suffered from tumors and eczema.[27]

Josef Cohen learned to slave in this world. He brought his family there. And while he might not be free from the grinding poverty he grew up with, in London he was far from the oppressions and violences of the czar and his former Polish neigh-bors. In England he prayed his family could live safely. In the East End he believed he and Sheindel could properly impart their values and beliefs to Rose and Morris.

orris Abraham Cohen settled into a world of both dire poverty and devout piety. In the early 1890s the Cohens moved into an eight-room building at 68 Umberston Street in the St. George's in the East district of London. Twenty-six-odd people jammed into No. 68, a building little different from the other squat, sooty structures in the heart of the East End. There Morris grew up on a block where women leaned from second- and third-floor stone sills and surveyed the comings and goings at the Umberston Street butcher shop, chandler shop, confectioner, cowkeeper, butter factory, baker, tobacconist, and grocer.

With 252 people per acre and 54.5 percent of its residents living in poverty, St. George's in the East was one of the most densely packed and impoverished parts of London. It was a district almost entirely inhabited by Jews. The earthen-and-reddish-colored neighborhood, with its blue or black bands of bricks and simple corbeled cornices, had the unenviable distinction of possessing the fewest public works of any section of the capital. It also had the city's highest birth and death rates. The urban sociologist Charles Booth might have clinically described St. George's in the East as having a "great deal of poverty in this district mixed with many queer characters," yet it contained immeasurably real suffering. Large numbers of women and children as young as seven sewed sacks for only a farthing apiece. The boxer Ted "Kid" Lewis, who grew up alongside Morris Cohen at 56 Umberston Street, recalled, "Often as a child I lived a hard day on a cup of water and a slice of bread covered thinly in sugar." But with all its problems, it took a visit by Jack the Ripper to make this area truly infamous. On September 30, 1888, he skulked down Berner Street, four blocks to the west of Umberston. There he grabbed Elizabeth "Long Liz" Stride, a forty-five-year-old prostitute, and according to the *Times* of London, "in the dark shadow near the entrance to the court he threw her to the ground, and with one gash severed her throat from ear to ear."[1]

Not far to the south stood St. Katherine's Docks, a tar-smelling stretch of warehouses lining the Thames River where disheveled emigrants disembarked. It was a dank place inhabited by a floating population of stevedores, ship's clerks, and dock laborers, as well as prostitutes who wore enticing scarlet and blue frocks to catch the eyes of the Scandinavian, Indian, African, and Chinese sailors whom they serviced and afterward rolled for their money. The press ran lurid tales of Morris's dockside neighbors, of Chinese gamblers and opium smokers. Even Arthur Conan Doyle helped immortalize this image when Sherlock Holmes, in "The Man with the Twisted Lip," investigated a cavernous den where he found "a long, low room, thick and heavy with the brown opium smoke, and terraced with wooden berths, like the forecastle of an emigrant ship. . . . Out of the black shadows there glimmered little red circles of light, now bright, now faint, as the burning poison waxed or waned in bowls of the metal pipes."

Two blocks to the east of Umberston Street ran Cannon Street, on the other side of which Jewish tailors, boot makers, laborers, cigar makers, and dock employees settled in small two-room houses, a family in each room. To the west were Polish tailors and boot and cigar makers. To the north beyond the heavy flow of mud-encrusted wagons, coal carts, and tramcars on Commercial Road was an area Booth called "abjectly poor," where more Jewish tailors and cigar makers, as well as furriers, leather workers, boot makers, hawkers, and casual laborers lived.

In the late 1880s, 908,959 people packed into the East End. Most of the Jews settled with fellow Jews in Whitechapel and St. George's in the East near where they landed. As more arrived, they spilled into Stepney, Mile End, Bethnal Green, and Spitalfields. Wholesale razing of buildings in the 1870s to make way for railway facilities, warehouses, offices, and needed street improvements made housing especially dear. Landlords shirked upkeep responsibilities, and critics railed that the thousands of Jews who sailed in each year inhabited hovels that no "God-fearing Christian" would occupy. Slum owners jacked up the rents and gouged the poor for key money. Those who could not meet the rent bill found themselves summarily tossed out onto the street. "The predominant idea was paying the rent," recalled the East End criminal Arthur Harding of his childhood. "That was the first and last duty of everybody, to pay that rent, 'cos you knew how damned hard it was to find another room."

Jumbles of clotheslines from which fluttered the day's wash seemingly wove together the crooked alleys, darkened courts, and rookeries of the East End. The formerly fine homes might have once enlivened the district with their fluted stone pilasters, dancing rooflines, and erratic, almost jagged coursing of dormers and chimney spouts, but the area had become a hard, mean place to survive. Blood-bathed animal organs and trash littered streets in Aldgate, to the west of Umberston, over which men and dogs herded sheep to slaughterhouses. Costermongers and merchants kept their donkeys, ponies, and cows in back-alley sheds. In the 1890s, old crones and swarthy men drank their meals in an area awash with one pub for every 393 people—basking at their bar stools beneath elaborate chandeliers of Potemkin pretensions. Women in soiled aprons, their hair askew, hunched upon the pavement clutching and breast-feeding babies. Ragged toddlers danced alongside blue-nosed monkeys to the music of organ-grinders.[2]

Writers painted gruesome pictures of East End conditions, of cramped warrens and airless hovels dimly lit by paraffin lamps, permeated with the acrid smell of stale fish and rotting vegetables. Broken chairs, tables constructed from rough wood and bricks, beds made from heaps of rags or straw shavings filled apartments. Whole families wedged into single rooms. Clean water had to be purchased from sellers or gathered from standpipes on the street. Many houses had cracked, mildewed walls, uncleaned water closets, and untrapped sinks. Rags stuffed in windows kept out the cold. In Andrew Mearns's 1883 study of London's abject poor, he noted that vermin flourished in dank courtyards that reeked "with poisonous and malodorous gases arising from accumulations of sewage and refuse scattered in all directions and often flowing beneath your feet."

In order to make extra cash just to survive, people had no choice but to work at home. Residents gagged from air thick with "particles of the superfluous fur pulled from the skins of rabbits, rats, dogs and other animals in their preparation for the furrier . . . the smell of paste and of drying match-boxes, mingling with other sickly odours. . . ." In one house a sanitary inspector discovered a father, mother, three children, and four pigs. "In another room a missionary found a man ill with small-pox, his wife just recovering from her eighth confinement, and the children running about half naked and covered with dirt. Here are seven people living in one under-ground kitchen, and a little dead child lying in the same room."[3]

Thieves, dragsmen who pilfered from carts, pickpockets, magsmen who cheated at games of chance, sharpers, forgers, and beggars filled the East End maze. It could be a dark and violent place. "Most of the inhabitants of my new division considered that they had a natural right to get fighting drunk and knock a policemen about whenever the spirit moved them," recalled Chief Constable Frederick P. Wensley. "Bruises and worse were our routine lot. Gangs of hooligans infested the streets and levied blackmail on timorous shopkeepers. There was an enormous amount of personal robbery with violence. The maze of narrow ill-lighted alleys offered easy ways of escape after a man had been knocked down and his watch and money stolen."

The Jews were involved in assorted criminal activities. They committed petty thievery, forgery, and illegal distilling of booze. Some sailed to eastern Europe and convinced young girls that jobs and bachelors awaited them in England, only to ship them off to Indian or Argentinean white slave markets. Occasionally there was a more notorious crime like the murder of Miriam Angel, a pregnant landlady poisoned by her tenant, Israel Lipski. The case became a cause célèbre. Many thought him innocent, and thousands signed petitions calling for Lipski's release. Even Queen Victoria took an interest in the plight of the Polish walking-stick maker. The day before he climbed the scaffold, though, Lipski confessed, and on the morning of August 22, 1887, a crowd gathered outside Newgate Prison and cheered when they learned of the successful hanging.[4]

With all its poverty, the area was a hotbed of union activity. On November 13, 1887, strikers in Trafalgar Square clashed with police. Three picketers were killed and seventy-five landed in jail in a failed confrontation that became known as "Bloody Sunday." Some protests succeeded. In June 1888 Bryant and May match girls staged a walkout in disgust over their supposed eight to nine shillings a week pittance pay; in reality they made less, since the firm fined them for petty errors. The women petitioned Parliament and marched through the West End wearing their ragged work garb. Their efforts so embarrassed the company that the owners settled after a mere two weeks. From August 29 to October 3, 1889, Josef Cohen's colleagues tried their luck. Ten thousand tailors walked out for a twelve-hour day, meals off premises, wages at trade-union rates, and no home work. They received the support of other unions, printed up flyers, issued manifestos in English and Yiddish, and tramped each day to Victoria Park for demonstrations. Eventually a compromise was negotiated, but the workers could not enforce the agreement. Those who insisted on the terms were often fired.[5]

A shock awaited all who hoped to have escaped anti-Semitism. While London Jews might not have experienced the violence they once encountered in Eastern Europe, the dearth of jobs meant resistance and resentment on the part of Christian laborers. Irish Catholics in particular saw the Jews as direct competitors. "Foreign paupers are replacing English workers, and driving to despair men, women, and children of our own blood," wrote Arnold White in the *Times* of London. In his 1892 book *The Destitute Alien in Great Britain,* the social reformer and one of the nation's most vocal anti-Semites further vilified the Jews, whose "alien looks, habits and language, combined with their remarkable fecundity, tenacity and money-getting gift, make them a ceaseless weight upon the poor amongst whom they live. . . . The alien . . . seems to bring a sort of social contagion with him, which has the effect of seriously deteriorating the life of those of our own people who are compelled to be his neighbour. . . . Their very virtues seem prolific of evil when, like some seed blown by the winds, they fall and fructify in English soil."

While the Ripper bloodied the dimly lit back lanes, rumors spread that a man wearing a leather apron was responsible for the black deed. The police subsequently arrested a Polish Jewish boot finisher named Jacob Pizer and discovered assorted long knives in his home. He was cleared after proving that the knives were part of his trade, but talk circulated that a "true Englishman" could never have committed such vile acts, of Jewish love of ritual murder and sadism, of reputed Talmudic invocations for killing Christian women with whom Jewish men had sex, and of a crazed *shochet*—Jewish butcher—working after hours.[6]

Yet despite its squalor and intolerance, dirt and oppression, the East End somehow also proved to be a vibrant area as the Jews transplanted and nurtured their culture in a land with a more agreeable social and political climate. They founded Yiddish papers and drama societies, attended night school, and played cricket. Here Josef Cohen and others could openly belong to synagogues and study the Talmud. On the Sabbath Josef groomed his beard and turned out in his Saturday best. Morris then accompanied his father to synagogue. "It was a sin for grown-ups to carry anything on the Sabbath," recalled Morris, "and so I would walk beside him with the velvet bag that held his tallis; and when he met his friends and said 'Shalom' in his deep voice, I felt very proud."

For the Sabbath women set candles in windows, and families went to the vapor baths, put on freshly pressed clothes, polished shoes, sang hymns, drank wine, and feasted on chicken, soup, fish, and stewed prunes. Saturday night they promenaded along the main streets. On Purim residents dressed up as their favorite characters from the Book of Esther and went from house to house socializing and drinking. Prior to the start of Passover, bonfires lit up the roadways as they burned leavened bread to purify their homes in preparation for the festival celebrating deliverance from Egyptian bondage.[7]

This was the world that Morris first knew, one of poverty and freedom. He had arrived from Poland as a babe in arms, and the first home he recalled was on Umberston Street. From there he ranged freely with his next-door pal Yutke Klein through a land within hearing range of the famed Bow Bells at St. Mary-le-Bow Church in Cheapside. These Cockney youths made mischief, disobeyed their mothers' pleas to stay inside, and hung out at markets where they watched the crowd. Josef was not elated with his son's ramblings, and Morris's earliest memory was of his disciplinarian father punishing him for not staying inside. The child's sense of independence only hardened with each blow. He received an even harder beating the following day when he slipped out again.

Why stay in a cramped apartment with so much to see in the spacious outdoors? The markets were a scene of frantic activity, a place where Morris and Yutke joined the shifting street theater. "There was plenty to look at, too," Morris said. "Jews from everywhere; *Hasidim* in their loose black coats shuffling along to the *Yeshivas;* Pollacks and *Litvoks* and Russian and Dutch and Spanish Jews." Machinists and pressers strutted by in new suits and flirted with full-figured Jewish maidens. Peddlers and costermongers battled with sticks over road turf in Petticoat Lane, Wentworth Street, Watney Street, and Chrisp Street so they could sell their pencils, birdcages, musical instruments, sheep's heads, lace, toys, bottled potions, rattraps, and books. Some stands remained open until midnight, lit with flaring naphtha lamps, greasy oil burners, and candles. The thick smell of fried fish, onions, roasted coffee, fat, and the biting traces of not-too-fresh meat wafted through the air. Thousands flocked in from all parts of London to sift through barrows and pushcarts piled high with coats and dresses. Brine oozed from the base of herring barrels. Cutlery and wares dangled from awnings. Pallid, fringe-shawled women, their hair pulled tight into buns, haggled over glistening heaps of whitefish, haddock, kippers, and smoked mackerel. Young girls hawked flowers. Men sold pornography on the sly. Street urchins and guttersnipes begged for anything. Acrobats and street entertainers performed. For a charge one could gaze through a telescope at the moon.

Morris loved food. He was a porky boy with a wide face and thick fingers. A cloth cap was scrunched down over his dark brown curly hair. To him, not having pocket pence to buy pies, baked potatoes, and assorted snacks from the stalls and shops was perceived as a hardship. Morris was, though, a quick learner and started to realize the ways he could make a little spare change. "Orange boxes were in great demand then," recalled Harding of one of his own early moneymaking ventures. "Cost nothing—they were only too glad to give 'em to you." Children tied the boxes in bundles and dragged them from house to house, calling out, "firewood for sale." A bundle could fetch a half pence or more. When Morris and Yutke were five, they decided to establish themselves in the fuel business. Morris swiped Sheindel's meat cleaver and the two boys hiked to the Billingsgate fish market to chop up fish crates. "It was heavy and awkward to handle and greasy with fish-scales and slime," said the neophyte Artful Dodger, "but somehow we'd drag it to a quiet corner and chop it into strips. Then we'd cart it from door to door—anywhere but down our own street—and shout 'Firewood oh! Firewood oh!'" The two boys could make up to twelve pence for their troubles.

Children regularly stole coal from delivery vans, grabbed butter, eggs, and cheese from barrows, snatched washerwomen's clothes, lifted luggage from carts, even whisked combs out of women's hair. The more daring swiped the wig. "If they could pinch anything, they'd pinch it," said Harding. "If they had anything over they'd sell it to the neighbours. A tin of blacking, that'd be 2d—they'd sell it very likely for ½d. They'd steal fruit—anything to eat. . . . A pair of shoes, hanging up outside a bootshop, was easy to cut down. . . . They'd bring back what they could lay their hands on, wrapped in a roll of paper—anything that was worth money."

There were countless other ways to make a few pence. Glaziers were a regular East End sight. They tramped up and down the streets and alleys lugging large panes of glass and other items strapped to their backs and scanning the buildings for damaged windows. Morris, with his endearing hazel-green eyes, must have seemed an enterprising young man, for one glazier hired him and Yutke to heave rocks through good windows. Prior to the deed, the boys flipped a coin to see who would do the honors, and once the projectile hit its mark they bolted around the corner. The glazier then innocently strolled by, ringing his handbell and chanting, "Shtick it in mit putty for sixpence." For each window mended the boys received a halfpenny.[8]

They lived a life of freedom, adventure, small change, and food. Then, as Morris and Yutke had feared, "the blow fell." Kindergarten. At the Jews' Infant School, Morris, Yutke, and other youngsters took their first steps toward what the Jewish establishment who founded the institution in 1841 hoped would be assimilation into British society. Morris started there in 1896, and on his first day of school his then stronger sister, Rose, firmly squeezed his hand and dragged him the eight blocks west to the school's new £7,000 mansard-roof facility on Buckle Street and Plough Square, just off of Leman Street. Teachers taught Morris and his fellow nine hundred classmates using the then innovative Froebelian teaching methods; they learned their letters, sewing, proper manners, and discipline through play. But courses in the classrooms with their twelve-foot-high ceilings, games in the adjoining playground, and the regimented schedule did not appeal to this freewheeling child of the streets.

"When I got there they patted me on the head and gave me a needle and thread and told me to sew two pieces of cloth together," he said. "It was a cissy sort of job and I felt awful." By the third day the two friends had had enough of it, and slipped through the back door to continue their cobblestone education.

Ah, but what to do about the parents? Fearful of going home to a beating, the truants passed a cold night in a vegetable warehouse. Morris then made one crucial mistake. The following morning he should have waited for his father to go to the tailor shop before he set foot again on Umberston Street. He didn't, and rudely met up with Josef, who had spent the night searching for his wayward son. Punishment was swift. A child whose family came from a town renowned for scholarship had better learn the rewards and hardships of an education. If he didn't want to be any better than the doltish hordes that rampaged through the shtetls, then he would pay the penalty. Afterward, Rose clenched Morris's hand and took the smarting penitent back to school. It must have been quite a beating, for Morris started attending classes.

The Jews' Infant School was used as a conduit to the famous Jews' Free School at Bell Lane to the northwest. Three-quarters of the Infant School graduates went there. Rose started in 1896, and Morris joined her on February 4, 1897, finding the school with its seventy-one well-lit rooms an "impressive and awe-inspiring place." Enrollment was highly competitive, and on days when there were openings, police bobbies had to control the crowds of child applicants and eager parents that packed the streets. According to government reports starting from the time when Matthew Arnold made his first official inspection in 1853, it was the best-run school in the realm.

Moses Angel, a rigid disciplinarian who sported a close-trimmed beard and wire-rimmed spectacles, ran the school for five decades. Angel believed that the children needed not only to be educated and protected from Christian missionary groups who hoped to ensnare the innocents with offers of food, coal, and clothes, but to be molded into good Englishmen. Angel arrived each day at eight-thirty, personally wound all the clocks, forbade corporal punishment, and trained all the school's teachers. The staff kept the place cozily warm, stoked fires in each hearth, daily swept classrooms, and liberally doused surfaces with disinfectant.

By the middle of the 1890s the school had 3,500-odd students. Children of all description attended. Morris belonged to the nearly 39 percent of the students who were foreign-born. Since most of the boys and girls started work at age thirteen or fourteen, much had to be learned quickly. Morris attended weekdays from nine through four and Sunday mornings, wearing to school a corduroy suit and pair of shoes courtesy of Lord Rothschild. Each morning Angel and the staff served him a free breakfast of fresh bread and hot milk. Morris studied at a small desk. Thirty-five certified teachers and twenty-five governesses taught him and his classmates everything from English and Hebrew, physics, and drawing to cabinetmaking and French polishing. Rose and the other girls received domestic training in baking and sewing. At breaks Morris and Rose played catch and did calisthenics in the stone courtyard.[9]

Morris had a longer walk to the Free School than he did to Buckle Street. He hiked west on Commercial Road, made a left on Whitechapel High Street, and then turned north up to Bell Lane. He could also take side-street shortcuts. Whichever way he went, it was a route fraught with dangers, filled with heckling Christian boys who called the Free School students "dirty Jews," "sheenys," and "Christ murderers." "When it was time to go to school in the morning, my best friend Curley would be waiting for me on the corner with the rest of the Jewish neighbourhood boys, to lead them and run the gauntlet through the 'Goys' that waited for the Jew boys," recalled Lewis. "I would wrap my belt around my hand and we marched through as one, defying any attack. If they did chance their arms, we would usually drive them back running to their parents."

Free School attendance hovered at 96 percent, and parents like Josef and Sheindel who wanted their children to receive additional secular and religious training sent their kids to evening courses. Josef gave a penny-a-day bribe to Morris as an incentive to attend classes. But as part of the 4 percent of the Free School student body that tried hard not to go to school, the money turned into a poor investment. Too many other noneducational East End enticements vied for Morris's attention. He joined the long lines of music hall goers queuing for performances on Whitechapel, envied the smart young set that showed up with flashy jewelry, and laughed at the street urchins and guttersnipes begging and performing for a few pence. "At the 'Standard,' " said Harding, "the queue would stretch right round from Norton Folgate into Great Eastern Street. There was a little short turning in Great Eastern Street where the crowd lined up for the gallery, and the kids used to do their little acrobatic tricks there. Somersaults and jumping over each other, leap frog—anything to attract attention." With the pennies he earned from Josef and his assorted ventures, Morris bought cheap gallery seats and watched the likes of Marie Lloyd and Little Tich.[10]

The Royal Pavilion Theatre was the most popular house in the East End. Nicknamed the Drury Lane of the East, its owners advertised it as "the people's own theatre, built for the million." Morris entered through terra-cotta arches and Doric pilasters off of Whitechapel, and strode down a long tunnel to a classical playground for the masses containing a stately auditorium of stalls, boxes, and a grand circle. Beneath a ceiling covered with cavorting cupids in seats awash in the light of incandescent gas burners, he marveled at English melodramas, Yiddish operettas, Christmas pantomimes, Shakespeare, and West End stars. Audience members spat, smoked, and scuffled, yelled vulgarities, pelted entertainers they did not like, or showed their appreciation by showering the stage with coins. Gangs of kids, many of whom stole money for admission, practiced chirruping, an unsubtle form of blackmail where an actor would have his performance heckled unless he paid a fee for which he was guaranteed a resounding ovation. As this circus of acts whirled before them, the audience feasted on and littered away the cakes, apples, oranges, chicken, fish, hot peas, monkey nuts, beer, and spirits they brought with them or bought in the hall.

One of Morris's other favorite hangouts was the Paragon Theatre of Varieties on Mile End Road across from Stepney Green. Opened on May 21, 1885, this was a truly imposing hall with an auditorium sixty feet wide by one hundred feet deep and a sixty-foot-high cupolaed ceiling. The Paragon had acres of crimson velvet, pale blue and cream walls with gold trim, oriental doorways, marble bars and grills, a conservatory, and twelve private boxes. Morris sat in the roomy upper gallery, where he watched an eclectic, almost schizophrenic program of entertainment. "The fun must be broad and old-fashioned; no one is more conservative than your music-hall-goer, so the jokes must centre round the stale old topics of the drunkard, the henpecked husband, and the mother-in-law," wrote the *Echo*. "The sentiment must be pronounced and stagey; the sketches must boast the most heroic of heroes, the most Satanic of villains, the most inane of heroines. And there must be at least one sample of blatant Jingoism. Throw in, as an appeal to Whitechapel instincts for beauty, a couple or two of shapely girls to warble love ditties and to prance in nicely-embroidered skirts, and, with sketches, gymnastics, dances, the inevitable comic songs, and a possibly realistic presentation of the coster and his 'donah,' you have the main constituents of the bill of an East-end hall, and a skeleton outline of the Paragon entertainment."[11]

When Morris found the music halls too tame he could watch gangs of teenagers nicknamed the Monkey Parade harassing walkers, intentionally knocking people off of the sidewalks, and pushing lampblack into the faces and the backs of young girls. Or he could frequent the penny gaffs, popular freak and music shows. Gaff proprietors were essentially carnival talkers, attracting audiences with garish posters and small bands into empty shops, stables, and warehouses that passed as theaters. There for a pence or two Morris and two or three hundred others crowded on benches, whistled, goosed the girls, and enjoyed an hour of broad, rowdy performances, vulgar songs, comedy, magic-lantern shows, and Shakespeare performed on a makeshift stage in a smoky room lit by wavering gas jets. Here they viewed the real outcasts of British society, the shunned, the crippled, sideshow oddities like an armless man who played a violin with his toes, or a "two-headed" lady.

In one such abandoned greengrocer shop not far from Umberston Street, Dr. Frederick Treves in November 1884 paid Tom Norman a shilling for a private viewing of Joseph Carey Merrick, the Elephant Man. "The shop was empty and grey with dust," wrote Treves. "The light in the place was dim, being obscured by the painted placard outside. The far end of the shop—where I expect the late proprietor sat at a desk—was cut off by a curtain or rather by a red tablecloth suspended from a cord by a few rings. The room was cold and dank. . . . Locked up in an empty shop and lit by the faint blue light of the gas jet, this hunched-up figure was the embodiment of loneliness. It might have been a captive in a cavern or a wizard watching for unholy manifestations in the ghostly flame."[12]

Such places horrified proper society. To counter their ill-effect, Queen Victoria kicked off her Jubilee Year with the May 14, 1887, opening of the People's Palace, a complex that she hoped would bring the light of culture to the darkened East End. It became the area's first center for intellectual and material advancement. Yet even with its literary club, fencing classes, swimming, art shows, organ recitals, flower shows, and debates, it just couldn't counter the neighborhood's allures.

There was no competition. Tastes in the East End simply ran toward the pedestrian, the base. The area east of Aldgate Pump and Shoreditch was dubbed the "cradle of pugilism." Noisy crowds packed theaters, clubs, and shops to watch boxing matches. On Whitechapel Road and Mile End Road promoters set up boxing booths for fans to spend twopence to see a bout. Sometimes beefy female brawlers took on all challengers. Theaters staged regular tournaments and Saturday afternoon matches. Swarms gathered to follow and bet on the rounds, and owners warned pugilists that if they didn't draw blood they wouldn't be rehired. A frenzy of slugging and pushing even reigned in the audience.

Morris loved the fights. The mixing-up. His hero was Thomas "Pedlar" Palmer, the unbeatable bantamweight from Canning Town. Like Morris, Palmer was not large, standing five-three and weighing in at 115 pounds. Yet when Palmer debuted in London in 1893 he dazzled audiences with the accuracy of his blows, along with his seemingly effortless bobbing and weaving. Palmer quickly won fans and earned the nickname "Little Box o' Tricks." Groupies flocked to Covent Garden to watch him dance, and in the mid-1890s Palmer turned the New East London Theatre into a boxing saloon.

Morris started his pugilistic career in 1896, the year after his idol beat Billy Plimmer in fourteen rounds for the British bantamweight title. Morris was not the ideal pick for a fighter. He was a clumsy, tubby child with a massive head, weighing in at a scale-tipping ninety-two pounds. It is not surprising that he had already earned the nicknamed "Fat Moisha." Yet his heft and stamina proved two useful attributes for a mug. When not roaming the streets he hung out in the pit of the Pavilion. Fights constantly broke out there as theatergoers quibbled over trivialities. One evening Morris started cuffing with an older and taller boy over his place in the crowded line. "I was quick on my pins and even then I packed a pretty good punch and I liked a fight." Other patrons turned to watch the brawl, and a man in a derby bet ten bob that Morris would wallop his opponent. Once Morris flattened the other boy, the wagerer and part-time thief asked the young bruiser if he wanted to climb into the ring. A dream come true. The following weekend Morris premiered at the People's Arcade in a smoke-filled room packed with two hundred touts and gamblers. "Cockney Cohen" came out swinging against "Battlin' Murphy," a.k.a. Izzy Fink. Afterward, as Morris washed the blood from his swollen nose, his derbied backer gave the triumphant nine-year-old the princely sum of two shillings. "That was the biggest money I'd ever made," said the fledgling professional. He slugged it out six times at the Arcade. Morris always beamed at seeing his name on posters, and nursed the first of many broken noses. He also fought in blacksmith shops in the midst of rampant betting, fighting any day except the Sabbath, when his father stayed home on Umberston Street.[13]

The money only helped further his delinquency. Morris got into trouble with the police and dropped boxing for what he jokingly deemed the more "respectable" occupation of shilling for Harry the Gonof. In the East End, "Gonof" was a common nickname for Jewish and Christian thieves. Harry the Gonof was one such criminal. He managed a purse stall at Petticoat Lane and ran a profitable scam to attract customers. To entice the curious he would put a shilling in one of the purses, telling the gathered that one "lucky" sixpence-paying customer would walk off with the treasure. In actuality Harry simply palmed the coin and slipped it into his pocket instead of the purse. "Once in a while, to whip up interest and attract customers, he would actually put the shilling inside and give me a nod to show what he'd done," said Morris. "This was my cue to push forward and buy the purse quickly before anyone else could. Then I'd hold it aloft, turn it upside down, catch the shilling as it fell out, pocket it and walk off. I had to bring the purses and shillings back that night, but I got tuppence a time for my trouble."

Morris soon graduated to the lucrative art of wallet lifting, becoming like Dickens's Artful Dodger, "as roystering and swaggering a young gentleman as ever stood four feet six, or something less, in his bluchers." He kept good company. Pickpockets were generally young, and they worked train stations and the ubiquitous markets. If the police grabbed them they played on their youth, lied about their names and ages, and embarrassed the officer by feigning tears so that they would be let go. "The other fellows were much older and took a real pride in their work," recalled Harding of his early career. "Women were the easiest to take from. They didn't have handbags then, but used to have pockets at the back of their skirts. It was easy to cut them away—they didn't even notice what had happened. Whoever invented these pockets must have been a whizzer. Wallets were more difficult because they were kept in breast pockets, and shoot-flying [grabbing a watch chain and pulling] you had to be ready to run. Pickpocketing men and women were two completely different lines. The Jewish boys, down in Whitechapel, were very good whizzers, but they only went in for women." Children posed an especially easy mark. "The kinchins, my dear, is the young children that's sent on errands by their mothers, with sixpences and shillings," noted Dickens's Fagin, "and the lay is just to take their money away—they've always got it ready in their hands,—then knock 'em into the kennel, and walk off very slow, as if there were nothing else the matter but a child fallen down and hurt itself. Ha! ha! ha!"[14]

Who needed to learn tailoring or their letters at the Jews' Free School? Morris was studying the art of the con, and his education was coming along nicely. Unlike Oliver Twist, he would have fit in well as one of Fagin's enterprising apprentices. It was a learning experience that would last him throughout his life.

CHAPTER 4

REFORM SCHOOL,
1900–1905

On Friday evening, September 16, 1898, a Jewish boy "whose
head did not reach the top of the dock" was dragged into the Thames
Police Court and charged with placing his hand in the pocket of Laura Briggs and
stealing her purse during rush hour at the Aldgate tram terminus. "I have very little
doubt this lad is an expert thief, and am sorry to say these cases of theft by little
Jewish boys are becoming sadly numerous," commented Magistrate John Dickinson
on the nine-year-old felon who was little different from Morris. "It is a crying
shame there is no industrial school to receive these boys, and I have to discharge
them. Their parents know that and so do the boys themselves, for there are none
sharper. . . . I cannot send the lad to a reformatory, for he is far too young. . . . I
have protested time after time respecting this serious state of things, and still nothing
is done. I shall remand the boy to the workhouse for a week, and suppose at the
end of that time I shall have to discharge him."[1]

As one of the few sympathetic magistrates in London, Dickinson's admonish-
ment stung the Jewish community, which was acutely sensitive to bad perceptions
and publicity. During most of the nineteenth century, the community had established
service programs, foster homes, and apprenticeship positions to channel bad seeds
like this nine-year-old pickpocket and Morris into safe, regenerative places. Yet as
more immigrants streamed in and the Jewish population swelled, these lads turned
into an embarrassment. The belief grew within the community that more institu-
tional help was desperately needed.

Back then, children up to the age of twelve could be committed to industrial
school for a first-time criminal offense, and youngsters as old as fourteen could be
sent away as educational cases. Reformatories received the more serious miscreants.
In order to find a suitable place for their boys, the Jewish Board of Deputies in 1889
struck a deal with the East London Industrial School in Lewisham. The board paid
the school fifty pounds per child per year for room and kosher board along with an

additional shilling a week since the boys couldn't work on the Sabbath. In 1893 they secured the services of Israel Ellis, a progressive theorist and deputy headmaster from the Jews' Free School, and appointed him Hebrew Master. Ellis watched over and taught his new wards. Not surprisingly, regular complaints arose of anti-Semitic taunting and attacks by staff and fellow students, only fueling Ellis's and the Jewish community's fears for the boys' safety, from harm as well as from conversionist groups working on the unprotected souls of these impressionable lads.

In 1898 the Board ended the agreement, and Ellis accompanied his students to the County Council School at Mayford. Meanwhile, Lord Rothschild, Felix Davis, Louis Davidson, and other Anglo-Jewish leaders set about founding a Jewish facility. They raised £14,000—Rothschild himself chipped in £5,000—hired the architect Lewis Solomon, and began planning and construction of the Hayes Industrial School.[2]

Their timing proved quite serendipitous, at least for Morris, whose days of free ranging ended abruptly on Monday, April 30, 1900, when Officer Albert Spenceley—an eleven-year veteran of the Metropolitan Police Service—grabbed him for picking pockets. Morris, who was twelve at the time, told Spenceley that he was a mere ten, and aptly fit Magistrate Dickinson's maxim of "none sharper."

His cohort, Dickens's Artful Dodger, was similarly picked up for lifting a common silver snuffbox. Spenceley took Morris to the Thames Magistrate Court on Arbour Square, where Magistrate Frank Mead temporarily remanded him to a work-house. Then on May 9 the police carted the boy back to the imposing two-story limestone and brick building. Mead, who was not as lenient as Dickinson, summarily clapped him into Mayford for five years of rehabilitation.

Morris did not take well to confinement. Mayford authorities listed him as "slow," and he received more severe reprimands at Mayford than he ever got from Josef, having been "several times previously charged and twice birched." When Hayes finally opened in February 1901, headmaster Ellis, Morris, and twenty-six other boys made the trip to their new home. At the consecration of the site, fifteen boys turned out smartly in their new blue uniforms with jauntily cocked pillbox caps emblazoned in gold with "H.I.S." They recited a prayer, and Louis Davidson, chairman of the school, affixed a mezuzah—an encased parchment scroll—to the door-jamb at the main entrance. The group then moved to the schoolroom, and Ellis read the service for the Dedication of a House, and the boys recited an appropriately chosen portion of Psalm 119, which begins, "Blessed are the undefiled in the way, who walk in the law of the Lord./ Blessed are they that keep his testimonies, and that seek him with the whole heart." Davidson then reminded the boys that they were "young, and had everything before them, and that they were Jews," and therefore should be credits to their community.

Morris was the eighth student listed on the rolls of the new school, and had four years of discipline before him. Others soon joined him from London and the provinces. By the end of the first year, school enrollment rose to forty-four. Like Morris, most were there because they had committed a crime. Quite a few of them attended simply "for being beyond the control of their parents."[3]

For boys like Morris, who grew up in hundred-square-foot hovels that housed entire families, the twelve-acre site with its 16,000-square-foot red brick building seemed palatial. After spending a life sleeping on straw or piles of old clothes, they could relax on individual metal-frame beds, each with a basket nearby for clothes and personal belongings. Morris ate in a spacious dining room, took classes in a large schoolroom on the ground floor, played in the gymnasium, and read in the library.

Ellis was a thoughtful yet severe educator, and he imposed a strictly regimented schedule on the boys. Morris woke at six-thirty, washed in a state-of-the-art bath-room, and dressed. He and his industrial-school mates then wrapped cloths around their knees and hands, kneeled in rows of twelve on the dormitory's pitch-pine floor, and followed Ellis's polishing directions: "Ready, begin. Left, right, left, right, left, right, up, down, up, down, up, down." After they completed the dormitory they moved through the dining room to the other rooms. "They did that until the floor was cleaner than clean," said Harry Cohen, who took over as headmaster in 1937. "You could eat from the floor."

Ellis, his wife as matron, two schoolmasters, a gardener, carpentry instructor, needle mistress, gymnastics instructor, cook, laundry maid, doctor, and dentist kept them busy. The boys prayed in the morning, took classes in history, arithmetic, English, Hebrew, geography, penmanship, algebra, and singing—to the accompa-niment of Ellis at the piano—and learned good posture and teamwork through regular military drills and exercises. Ellis put a special importance on the study of Shakespeare, and Morris spent hours learning passages from *Richard III* and *Henry VIII*. He loved the plays, having seen some in Whitechapel, but as a Cockney he had particular trouble with his "h"s and "g"s. It didn't matter. Ellis drilled him hard.[4]

Teachers determined each child's propensities and directed them toward the appropriate trade of joinery, metalwork, or tailoring. The boys also helped with laundry and mending, and even sewed their own suits. Outside of classes, Morris worked the land and helped tend a ten-acre plot of carrots, cabbage, and potatoes, keep a poultry farm, and maintain a plum orchard. The food raised supplied the school kitchen, and boys in white smocks loaded baskets and cartons of vegetables onto a cart and delivered the fresh cargo to market for sale to shops and wholesalers. In 1905 they made the princely sum of £160. Kosher food was brought in from the East End. It was all more nourishing than what they were used to, and Morris, who entered at a stout four feet five and a quarter inches, started to put on additional heft.

The staff encouraged the boys to write home, and all of the lads received weekly pocket money, which they could spend during supervised football matches as well as outings to London and Margate. Good work was rewarded, and the boys earned two pence a week through a Mark and Reward system. Since no gate stood around the complex, a boy could theoretically run off, though that rarely happened; at night a schoolteacher slept in a cubicle at the end of the dormitory to keep an eye on them. When Morris slipped out in March 1905, the staff set off the electric bell and rang up the local police to make pursuit.

If someone broke into the stores and stole food and no one admitted to the crime, Ellis would order all the boys to stand at stiff attention in the yard and watch them from his upstairs window to see when the guilty party broke down and confessed. Early on, the school instituted the somewhat revolutionary system of trial by peers. Each year the boys elected a judge and clerk to handle many of the offenses. Ellis left the proceeding up to the boys, and only took part when the crime called for corporal punishment or a boy made an appeal.

Ellis did not tolerate infractions: he never shirked from delivering punishment, which might mean learning a large tract from a play like *A Midsummer Night's Dream* or not being allowed to play sports, both of which Morris dreaded. Some acts, like running away, could mean the end of monthly family visits. In June 1902 Morris was implicated in a theft; in November 1903 the jury convicted him of stealing sugar and potatoes; and in 1904 he was on the bad-conduct list for three months for pilfering food. Such crimes brought up to six flicks across the open palm with a forty-two-inch flexible cane. More serious misdeeds called for confinement to a cell or the burning lash of the tawse, a three-foot-long leather belt cut into thin strips. A boy destined to feel its bite was taken into the gym, where two schoolmasters held him down across a gym horse as Ellis flogged him over the seat of his pants. Those who could not be controlled were sent to reformatory, or even prison.[5]

As energetic former guttersnipes, most of the Hayes boys enjoyed sports, particularly cricket and football. While not the best athlete, even Morris won an Indian club–swinging contest. In 1904 the school took second place in the Home Office Schools Southern League's cricket, football, and general athletics matches. In 1905 it beat all other reformatory and industrial schools in cricket, and its efforts helped the Southern League defeat the combined Northern League.

Hayes quickly proved to be a model school and received good, regular reports from government examiners. On April 26, 1904, James G. Legge, His Majesty's Inspector, visited the school for his annual review of the fifty-six students and said that "the spirit of progress, which is everywhere in evidence, should ensure success in the future as in the past." The students, he noted, scored high in all their exams, excelled in singing, mental arithmetic, and geography, attended lectures on winter evenings, and did well in the joiner's shop and physical training. Very importantly, except for one boy who made two attempts to run home and the usual "deceit and similar boyish misdemeanours," there had been no serious offenses during the year. The boys often recited Shakespeare at the annual inspections, and one year Morris and his classmates had to read aloud from *Richard III*. When Morris's turn came he walked to the dais, recited two lines, and then closing his book impressed the inspectors by completing the passage from memory. Punishment and rote occasionally paid off.

Two months after Legge's visit, Leopold de Rothschild presided over the annual distribution of prizes, and Magistrate Dickinson came by to see the lads' progress. A squad of Hayes boys in white attire gave a demonstration of physical drill in the courtyard. Three boys then staged a scene from Shakespeare's *Henry VIII,* and one lad in the character of Cardinal Wolsey "displayed much histrionic ability."

In a speech to the boys, Rothschild referred to Dickinson by saying, "I believe I am correct in saying that this Institution was founded owing to some words which fell from the magisterial bench, and were very much taken to heart by several members of the community, among them Lord Rothschild, Mr. Davidson, and others. But it is satisfactory to learn that the same magistrates, who previously rebuked Jewish boys for getting out of bounds, have found several opportunities to say that the Jewish boys were well looked after and well-cared-for, and that this Industrial School was equal to, and, probably better than, any others of a similar kind in England." Morris and the others lazily applauded during the speech, but cheered when Rothschild asked Ellis to give the boys a holiday and said that he would organize a treat for them. The boys then did "some tuneful singing" and gave a gymnastics display.

By the time Morris graduated in July 1905, school enrollment stood at fifty-five boys. The day started with drills in the playground. Dickinson returned to encourage the boys "to be manly, and to go straight." He told them to be proud of being Jews and worthy of their heritage and to have ideals. "If they were sweeping a crossing they should see that it was the best swept crossing in the world. The moulding of their lives was largely in their own hands. Even the humblest might rise to the highest distinctions if they would only persevere and put their minds into it."[6]

Now that he had graduated, the question was what to do with Morris so that he could rise to "the highest distinctions." Some graduates went home. Others enlisted in the army or navy or found jobs. Many now had practice tilling the land, and were sent to farms in Canada and western Australia. Prior to Morris's release someone from the school visited the Cohens of Umberston Street and discussed with Josef and Sheindel what they could do with their wayward son. Life had been less eventful with him away, even if they had had to contend with an enlarged family. Besides Rose, they now had Nathaniel, Leah, Rachel, Benjamin, and Sarah. Neither Josef nor Sheindel were eager for Morris's return, for they feared he would take up his old ways. They discussed sending him abroad, and the school assured Josef and Sheindel that someone would watch over him. If Morris lost his job, was in want or in trouble, he could be brought back. Josef mentioned that he had a friend who belonged to a two-decade-old Jewish farming community in Wapella, Northwest Territories—soon to be christened the province of Saskatchewan—and was willing to put him to work. Morris's approval was sought and received.

The English had a habit of sending away their poor, homeless, and orphaned. Such a move was perceived as a useful and expedient way to rid the nation of its unwanted. Prisoners founded Australia, and many early settlers in colonial America arrived as indentured servants, working for a set number of years to pay off their passage. In the late nineteenth century, England viewed Canada as the fashionable spot to send the adventurous and the excess. It was seen as a country where faithful men and pious women turned the wilderness into a land of milk and honey, where outcasts shed their dwarfish natures as they redeemed themselves in the good earth and fresh air of the New World.

Boys were often dispatched to work on farms and girls sent to small towns as domestics. Yet despite what the Hayes officials told the Cohens, no one generally checked out those who agreed to take on the youngsters as workers, domestics, or apprentices. A child would only meet his or her new boss upon alighting at an isolated train depot thousands of miles from home. There were reports of city kids arriving in frigid Canada without sufficiently warm underwear and shoes. Some lost fingers, toes, and even feet. Still England sent about 80,000 children there from 1868 to 1925, 1,000 to 2,000 a year on the average. The philanthropic organization run by Dr. Thomas Barnardo sent the most children to Canada, for to the good Dr. Barnardo it was "a fair garden-like country, yielding abundantly."

Since Hayes was a small, new school it didn't have extensive contacts abroad. Fortunately it received the assistance of groups like the Salvation Army and that of Dr. Barnardo, which made the arrangements for Morris's ship and rail transportation across the Atlantic and Canada. Once the school formalized his trip, Morris had little to do but to pack his assorted clothes in a wooden trunk. He was given five sovereigns, said his good-byes to his family and Umberston Street, and was taken by the Barnardo group to catch the boat that Josef had planned to take years earlier. Thus started Morris's trek west to the unknown East.[7]

CHAPTER 5

THE NEW WORLD,
1905–1906

he hour of departure from Stepney was fixed accordingly for eight o'clock, and well before the hour the boys from the various Homes . . . had been 'loaded up' on the omnibuses, brakes and other vehicles provided for the journey through London," wrote Alfred B. Owen of the Barnardo organization. London was parched during the summer morning in 1905 when he led Cohen and the other children to Canada, yet a heavy morning shower unexpectedly drenched the group. As the Barnardo children's parade of vehicles flowed through London's streets, a band seated in the four-horse carriage at the head of the procession played; pedestrians stopped in the rain to watch and listen. Once at the station, the boys and girls climbed aboard the train for Liverpool. It continued to rain as they arranged their belongings, but as the train pulled out for the trip west, the sky suddenly cleared.

In Liverpool, Cohen received a medical exam and settled into third-class compartments, where he and the other youngsters slept to the heavy pulsing beat of the ship's engines. Each morning at six the husky, bullet-headed Cohen woke, washed, and donned his blue serge jacket and shorts. He and the other children stood through roll call and then eagerly lined up for breakfast. "How often, when the sea seemed rough, that line has seemed endless, and instead of under 200 boys there has seemed to be twice that number," wrote a Barnardo nurse of one such trip across the Atlantic. Once seated at the long wooden tables, the children were spoiled with hearty servings doled out by white-coated stewards. Sunday they received the biggest meals. The staff had long hours to fill, and between the morning and evening services and hymn singing, they supervised games and drills. Sunday everyone cleaned. "There is some extra cleaning up in the morning, and everybody is expected to appear at church parade well washed and with clothes brushed and boots polished."[1]

The staff knew little about their wards, so a few days out on the Atlantic they interviewed the children to learn what sort of work they might like to do and if they had friends or relatives in Canada near whom they wanted to settle. As the ship slipped past icebergs in the Atlantic, the rest of the passengers slowly learned of the presence of so many "unfortunate" children. A few of the men and women in first class arranged egg-and-spoon, sack, and wheelbarrow races for the boys and skipping competitions for the girls.

A week after leaving, the ship sailed along the St. Lawrence: "After the evening service we had a long talk with each section of the party, explaining to them fully the arrangements we were making for them and what they might look forward to," wrote Owen. The following morning the staff roused them early to prepare for landing in Quebec. The girls and boys began the day with a good wash and substantial breakfast. Stewards hauled on deck the hardwood trunks containing the children's meager belongings and the Bibles issued to all. Each child then changed into fresh clothes.

Officials processed the five-three, 126-pound Cohen through the immigration shed, one of the thirteen hundred Barnardo children and 189,000 immigrants who flowed into Canada that year. Doctors checked him for trachoma and stamped his landing card. Once cleared, Cohen idled on one of the long wooden benches in the corner until the other children made their way out. Barnardo supervisors then marched the group single-file to the waiting Canadian Pacific Railway cars.

By noon they were on their way west, traveling ultra-economy class in stripped-down sixty-seven-foot-long sleeper cars. Most of the children disembarked at Ontario. The rest traveled toward Winnipeg. One of Cohen's Hayes classmates destined for Montgomery, Northwest Territories, kept him company. The children were wedged seventy-two to a car, two to a wooden seat. Each seat was hinged at the bend. At night Cohen and his section mates pulled two seats together to form a hard bed that accommodated two. The others hitched themselves into the narrow overhead berths. There were no partitions, and privacy did not exist.[2]

As the train jarred along on bad suspensions the twelve hundred miles west to Winnipeg, Cohen and his companions passed the time talking, reading, sleeping, watching the land roll by, and eating the bread, corned meat, cheese, and hard-boiled eggs the Barnardo group supplied. "For four hundred miles there is hardly a sign that humanity exists on the earth's face, only rocks and endless woods of scrubby pine, and the occasional strange gleam of water, and night and the wind," wrote the English poet Rupert Brooke of the stretch Cohen would have seen traveling from Port Arthur to Winnipeg. It was a long way across, and took a few days. For Cohen it was an anxiety-ridden ride as he chugged farther and farther away from his beloved London and pondered what lay in store for him.

At Winnipeg, Edmund A. Struthers, the Barnardo superintendent for western Canada, met Cohen, his Hayes mate, and some of the others at the Canadian Pacific Railway station. Struthers ushered them beneath the grand barrel-vaulted ceiling and by the long wooden benches, green columns, and dark paneling of the city's new grand Beaux Arts terminal and out to the Barnardo distributing home on Pacific Avenue. There they slept a few impatient nights. Within a week Cohen and the others were scattered throughout the prairies to farmers and homeowners who answered the Barnardo ads in papers.

Arrangements were already made by Hayes to send Cohen to Saskatchewan. His train to Wapella fitfully rolled through an endless series of small towns with names like Bergen, High Bluff, Carberry, and Virden. He was but one of the 28,728 immigrants that year making their way to the province's farms, towns, and railroad and lumber camps. "Each village—I beg your pardon, 'town'—seems to be exactly like the next," wrote Brooke. "They differ a little in size, from populations of 100 to nearly 2000, and in age, for some have buildings dating almost back to the nineteenth century, and a few are still mostly tents. . . . These little towns do not look to the passer-by comfortable as homes. . . . A town dumped down, apparently by chance, on a flat expanse wears the same air of discomfort as a man trying to make his bed on a level, unyielding surface such as a lawn or pavement. He feels hopelessly incidental to the superficies of the earth."[3]

Within the 252,000-square-mile province of Saskatchewan, Cohen must have felt hopelessly superfluous. The new province—which was to come into existence in September from part of the Northwest Territories—was more than twice the size of the British Isles, yet contained a fraction of its population. Barely ten people lived per square mile; the amount was nothing compared to the Umberston Street section of St. George's in the East, which ached with 252 crowded souls per acre. Saskatchewan also lacked the mugginess of his home, along with the paved streets and brick-and-stone buildings carved and erected by London's monarchs, master builders, and entrepreneurs. Prairie grass and bluffs and groves of poplar, cottonwood, and maple covered the land south of the Qu'Appelle River, for which Cohen was destined. The ground possessed an undulating sag-and-swell terrain impressed by the ancient shifting of glaciers, aeons of movement that gouged out valleys, sheered off rocks, and smoothed plains. Water from these tectonic ice fronts and glacial lakes sliced spillways through the surface, littered the land with a jumble of soil and rocks, and pocked the earth with poorly drained shallow lakes and sloughs.

The Assiniboine, Blackfoot, Blood, Cree, and other tribes once hunted buffalo in Cohen's new home. Whites initially came out in search of fur, and in the nineteenth century western settlers realized that cash crops could grow on the tree-, grass-, and daisy-covered glacial deposits. Confederation of the British North American colonies came about in 1867, and the new government worked to promote settlement both as a way to consolidate its realm and to fend off American encroachment. In 1870 the government acquired Rupert's Land, a country-sized tract of land bestowed on the Hudson's Bay Company by Charles II. They rechristened the land the Northwest Territories. In that year Manitoba was established, and the following year the government induced British Columbia to join the confederation. With so much arable land in Manitoba, the Northwest Territories, and Assiniboia, the government in 1872 copied its American neighbors and enacted the Dominion Lands Act. Survey parties plotted land in grids, laying out townships six miles square, with each township sliced into thirty-six one-mile-square lots of 640 acres. Homesteaders could then pick out 160-acre quarter sections for ten dollars. Soon they were able to acquire an adjoining quarter section.[4]

Homesteaders accompanied Cohen out on the train, disembarking near the land they had chosen from maps at government or railway offices. They then trekked for days or even a week in search of the iron surveyor rods that marked their new home. Once there they set up tents, lived in or under their wagons, or erected crude wooden houses. Some arrived with store-bought lumber shed kits. If no trees existed they might excavate dugouts, or do as Norwegian-American immigrants did, cutting the sod and stacking the wedges. Once settled, a homesteader needed simply to live on the property for six months per year for a few years and start tilling and planting part of the land. "You filed your claim, got a job if you could for the summer, and just before freeze-up you would throw up a sod shack and live in it through the winter when jobs were scarce or perhaps nonexistent," wrote Walter Wiggins, who settled in Saskatchewan the year after Cohen arrived. "When spring came you would have spent your savings for food and a stove, such other furniture as you had being made by yourself from scraps of boards. Then you would again look for a job. . . . If all went well and your health held good you might survive three years of such effort and then you could apply for your patent or title to 'a hundred and sixty acres full of sunshine.' "

Many were ill-prepared for the hardships of homesteading, and the almost Biblical calamities: long, frigid winters, frost, hail, grasshoppers, wind, rust, and blizzards. Saskatchewan weather was not that dissimilar to that of settled central Siberia. The growing season was short and hot. Sloughs and creeks were parched by summer, and well water was often contaminated. Prairie fires scorched crops and homes. To make matters worse, some of the acreage advertised as the "best" farmland in the world did not sprout the fifty to one hundred bushels per acre advertised by itchy land agents. Nineteenth-century settlement progressed slowly. By 1881 only 118,000 people lived on the vast prairies. Because of a long drought, low grain prices, and the perception of better land in the United States, half of the homesteaders abandoned their land. "It's twenty miles to water and thirty miles to wood," wrote one young man who nailed a card on his farmhouse door as he departed. "I'm leaving sunny Alberta and I'm leaving it for good."[5]

To encourage western settlement, Prime Minister John A. Macdonald's government made a deal with the Canadian Pacific Railway in 1881 to connect the two coasts, and lavished upon the firm $25 million and 25 million acres of land in payment. As the "trail of iron" rolled across the land, homesteaders started to come. Robert Nicholson and his younger brother, William, initially ventured west from Ontario. They used Brandon, Manitoba, as their base, and around 1882 William took to the rich black soil and timber around the new town of Whitewood in the southeastern part of the district of Assiniboia. The brothers purchased building supplies and enough food to last until spring and headed south of the town to an area with rolling hills and swaying groves of white poplars. There they built a three-bedroom wooden house. Robert brought out his wife, Margaret, and their infant daughter, Cora. In the spring of 1883 he found some silver willow–covered property in the nearby Silverwood District, eight and a half miles southeast of Whitewood and nine miles southwest of Wapella, and set up his own farm. In June 1886 Margaret gave birth to a daughter, Ruby Willamena.

Other homesteaders carted their farm equipment to the Whitewood area. They set up tents, cleared the ground of rocks and boulders, furrowed the fields with oxen and walking plows, herded cattle down the town's dirt streets, and, initially, vacated their grubstakes before the forty-below winter temperatures and the ten-foot snowdrifts blew in. With the spring thaw they returned and planted wheat. They lived off produce raised in their vegetable gardens and potatoes stored in root cellars, as well as prairie chickens, rabbits, and deer they trapped and shot. For coffee they roasted barley or brewed herbal teas.

Whitewood incorporated in 1892. As the town grew, one- and two-story wood structures with brick fronts—many built by William Nicholson—rose along Main Street. Wooden planks served as sidewalks. Soon churches, a livery stable, a gristmill, hotels, a Chinese laundry, a piano shop, a Hudson's Bay store, a billiards parlor, a veterinarian, a bank, and a doctor's office rose along the streets. Robert Nicholson's farm prospered, and as work increased he regularly answered the Barnardo notices advertising farm laborers for hire.[6]

For those who ventured west, life was lonely. Farmhouses were scattered across the land. Homes were small, cramped, poorly insulated shacks. Water froze on tables in winter. Men labored in the fields with oxen, horses, and plows, chopped wood, pitched sheaves, hauled grain, and cleaned out the barn. Women assisted the men and did the cleaning and cooking, fed the animals, planted and tended the kitchen garden, bore and raised the children, made the butter, hauled water, and sewed. If a husband had to find a paying job, the wife took over all his responsibilities, too. Neighbors watched over one another's crops and health, helped build barns, assisted with pregnancies, sicknesses, and burials. Since congregations tended to be small, different sects shared churches. On Sundays people washed and attended services to thank God and to visit with others. Afterward they "went neighboring."

In 1891 only 250,000 people lived on the prairies. Finally, by the 1890s the Canadian economy improved. While plenty of land was still available in the United States, the perception was otherwise, especially after the historian Frederick Jackson Turner intoned in 1893 that the American Frontier was about to end. Homesteaders looked north, where new varieties of grain like the hearty, high-milling Red Fife yielded good profitable crops, new plows and binders made planting and harvesting more efficient, and transporting grain to market became simpler as easy-loading and -unloading vertical grain elevators sprouted in towns.

The government was obsessed with the idea of filling the prairies with farmers. "When I speak of quality . . . I think that a stalwart peasant in a sheepskin coat, born to the soil, whose forefathers have been farmers for ten generations, with a stout wife and a half-dozen children, is good quality," wrote Minister of Interior Clifford Sifton at the turn of the century. Pamphlets touting the virtues of the land flooded the United States and Europe. Journalists received tours of the West. Large numbers of Germans, Scandinavians, Ukrainians, Austrians, and others responded to the un-relenting ad campaign and headed across the ocean.[7]

It therefore only seemed natural that the government looked for Jews fleeing from the pogroms in Russia. On January 25, 1882, Sir Alexander Tilloch Galt, the Canadian High Commissioner in London, approached Lord Rothschild about settling Jews in Canada. "The Jewish persecution in Russia has induced me to write Rothschild sug-gesting that I would like to discuss with him the feasibility of removing the agricultural Jews to Canada," he wrote Macdonald. On February 3 Galt attended the Mansion House meeting called by the Lord Mayor of London to discuss the Russian situation. He was nominated to the Russo-Jewish Committee, and became excited about the prospect of Jewish settlers in Canada. "From what I learn these Russian Jews are a su-perior class of people, partly farmers, but generally trade people."

Few Jews lived in Canada at that time. Most crossing the Atlantic did what Josef Cohen had intended to do and sailed toward the United States. Some ended up in Canada because the London Jewish relief agencies had closer ties to Montreal than New York. At the start of the 1880s Manitoba contained only thirty-three Jewish families. Their numbers mushroomed in May 1882, when Mansion House started sending Russians to Winnipeg in order to settle them on farms. By the following month hundreds had arrived; most decided to stay in town.

Galt's agent, W. A. Thompson, eventually found land twenty-five miles south-west of the rail connection at Moosomin, NWT, for the two dozen families that wished to raise crops. A $15,000 Mansion House Fund loan enabled the new farmers to purchase needed cattle, stock, and equipment. On May 12, 1884, they headed west. They called their land New Jerusalem, built homes, broke the soil, and planted seeds. They worked hard, erected a synagogue and a Hebrew school. Conditions, though, proved brutal. Crops failed, and residents started to abandon the land. In December 1886 the rabbi had to have his feet amputated after being caught in a blizzard. In September 1889 a suspicious fire destroyed hundreds of tons of hay. Eventually the community abandoned New Jerusalem.[8]

Little came of large-scale plans for Jewish migration, but Jews still arrived. From 1881 to 1901 their numbers in Canada rose from 2,443 to 16,401. Herman Landau—who helped establish the Poor Jews' Temporary Shelter in London where Josef Cohen found refuge—saw Canada as an ideal place for them to build a vibrant society. In September 1886 he financed a Russian named John Heppner and sent him and a few others to Wapella, fifteen miles northwest of Moosomin and eighteen miles east of Whitewood. Locals opposed the idea of Jewish neighbors, and peti-tioned the Minister of Interior in Ottawa that "unless some action was taken at once it would fare hard with the Jews." The threats did not sway Heppner and the others. By the start of the following decade about twenty-eight Jewish families arrived, including that of the future liquor magnate Samuel Bronfman.

Slowly the tailors, shoemakers, and peddlers who made up this small community learned the backbreaking task of clearing the spear, wheat, and porcupine grasses and raising a few acres of barley, wheat, oats, and vegetables. They caught prairie chickens and fished in Pipestone Creek. Some made money carting wood to town and selling it for a dollar a load, or hauling grain for twenty-five cents a bushel. "Nobody claimed any taxes and there were no roads," recalled settler Solomon Jacobson. "But there were plenty of wolves and bears, which troubled us." Families lived in sod huts and dugouts or hollowed caves into hills. As they became more settled, they felled poplars and erected log cabins, mixing clay, manure, and straw with their feet to make plaster to fill the cracks. Residents covered their roofs with straw or sod and planted grass on them to shed the rain.[9]

About fifty Jewish families lived in Wapella when Cohen disembarked at the new hip-roofed station in 1905. As his trunk, marked "M. A. Cohen Wapella," was hoisted from the train he looked over the sparse, dirt-road village of wood and stone buildings. A granary stood nearby, as well as a hotel and a blacksmith shop. This was his exile. He found himself bereft in a place whose alien rhythms and pulses were determined by the weather and wind, not by familiar pushcarts and vendors.

Josef's friend collected him and took him out to his farm. Cohen, though, was not destined to stay. "Although he'd told my father he would look after me, he'd never planned to employ me himself," Cohen later recalled. Possibly with the help of Archibald Beaton Gillis, a local businessman and postmaster who represented the Whitewood constituency in the legislature, Cohen was fobbed off on Robert Nicholson. Farmer Nicholson came out to look over his newest hired hand. Cohen was a chunky, short lad. His face was soft from the extra weight that he carried, his nose appeared remolded from too many boxing matches, and his eyes had a sleepy, faraway look that could suddenly rivet upon those around him. Nicholson tested his muscles, and realized that below the bulk was strength. Except for some market-gardening background, Cohen lacked farming experience, yet the eighteen-year-old confidently told Nicholson, "I'm willing to learn." He was hired, and climbed into Nicholson's buggy.

The Nicholsons lived in a red-trim, white-frame house with a cedar roof. As the only home in sight, it stood on a slight rise near a row of maples and a lone crab-apple tree about an eighth of a mile above the dirt road. It contained four bedrooms, a large living room, and a parlor filled with a piano and dark, heavy furniture. Fireplaces fed into the two chimneys. Wheat stalks between the walls gave the structure extra insulation. Not far from the house stood the barns and a hand pump. Just to the southwest lay a large slough, one of more than a dozen found throughout the farm from which the cattle drank. "As soon as we got to his farm I knew that I was going to be happy," said Cohen. "The house was clean and cheerful and comfortable and I had a tiny bedroom to myself—for the first time in my life."

Nicholson set about teaching Cohen his responsibilities. "He was an honest, honourable, kindly man, a good husband, a good father and a good boss," said Cohen of his tall, lanky employer with the severe, Yankee-captainesque beard, who labored in the fields with a broad-brimmed hat that kept the harsh sun off his balding head. Meanwhile, his wife, Margaret, a slight woman who wore silver-rimmed spectacles and lacy Victorian collars, showed him around the house. Cohen woke at five each morning. He lit the fires, milked the ten cows, watered the horses and pigs, and split logs. When the sun rose he walked out into the field with Nicholson and the farm's cowhand, Bobby Clark. "I am earning 150 dols. a year with board and lodging," he soon wrote back to Israel Ellis at Hayes. "I am now busy at the fall ploughing, and am putting in twelve hours a day. I have bought a fur overcoat for winter, which cost me 30 dols. There is a Jewish settlement in the North of Wapella. In a few years I will be able to earn 3 dols. a day."[10]

Yellow flowers called lady slippers lined the ditches around the farm. Wild roses and daisies appeared in the unplowed sections. Out in the fields often all Cohen could hear was the wind as it blew from the north and the west over the softly undulating knolls and ridges. Languid, ragged clouds drifted across the overarching sky. The area lacked heavy rain, but its good groundwater attracted flocks of wild geese, prairie chickens, and grouse, which milled around the grass-lined and water-lily-filled sloughs and ate the currants, strawberries, raspberries, gooseberries, and saskatoons that stained Cohen's shoes as he walked. Antelope still roamed here, along with wolves, black bears, weasels, and snowshoe rabbits. Brown bats flitted about, as did yellow-shafted flickers, sharp-skinned hawks, and turkey vultures. Mosquitoes, "Canadian hummingbirds," fruitfully flourished in the stagnant sloughs and ponds.

On Sundays, Cohen hitched the horses and took Mrs. Nicholson, Cora, and Ruby to the Methodist service at the nearby school; the buggy kicked up dust as they drove past copses of poplars on their way. The Reverend J. H. Hodges and later the Reverend Harrison rode out from Whitewood to lead the worshipers. While the congregation prayed in the small, white clapboard building built by Robert and William Nicholson in 1894, Cohen stood out back and enjoyed the Christian hymns Cora played on the organ and Ruby and the other congregants sang. The Nicholsons might then visit their neighbors. "Back in those years the neighbors would come over on Sunday and they would sing hymns," recalled Douglas Callin, Nicholson's grandson. Occasionally one of the ministers visited with the family.

Cohen's parents and his teachers at the Jews' Infant School, the Jews' Free School, and Hayes had instilled within Cohen a deep sense of his Jewish identity. He was comfortable about his religion, and gladly talked with the visiting ministers about the Bible. Yet Cohen was far from an observant Jew. In London he had regularly avoided Hebrew classes, and instead frequented myriad food stalls on the streets of the East End. Once he was in Canada, newer, nonkosher foods like those whipped up by Mrs. Nicholson beckoned him. In Whitewood Cohen ate well, too well. "The food was a revelation," he said of the fares Mrs. Nicholson and her daughters cooked up. "The food at home and at Hayes had been wholesome and sufficient, but I'd never before been able to eat just as much as I wanted and of dishes that were always appetizing. . . . At first I shied off ham and eggs because of my orthodox Jewish upbringing, but when I saw how often ham turned up on the table, I began to weaken. After I'd once tasted it, all my scruples went by the board and I dug into it like the rest." Within five months he no longer fit into his blue Barnardo suit. One day Nicholson took him into town to buy a new outfit for $8.50.[11]

With free time on his hands he easily and willingly fell under the cowhand Bobby Clark's spell. He was a teacher in search of a disciple to whom he could impart the arts of dice, cards, and pistols he had learned during his years of rambling across the North American continent. What better student could he hope for than one who had already picked up shady practices from Harry the Gonof in London? Explaining to Cohen that he hoped to help protect him when he was older, Clark taught the eager lad how to roll dice, and to check if they were crooked by dropping them in water. He also showed him how to make sure he threw the numbers he needed. "Supposing you want to throw a seven, you pick the bones up and hold them in your hand with the three and four uppermost," said Cohen. "You pretend to shake them, but really hold them steady and make the rattling noise by knocking your cuff buttons against the buttons on your coat. Then you throw them on to the table with a twist so that they spin around but don't turn over."

When it came to card playing, Clark instructed Cohen in how to manipulate the deck. Clark first taught him how to deal from the bottom of the deck, how to deal seconds, and even harder moves like "bringing in a cooler," which entailed switching a complete pack after the cards had been mixed. "I've big hands and quick fingers and I'd always been fond of amateur conjuring, so I made an apt pupil and the keener I got, the more he wanted to teach me." Cohen soon graduated to "playing the glim," learning how to position an opponent so he could see his cards in a mirror. It didn't stop there. Clark even taught him how to dress for the part of a cardsharp and how to insert mirrors in signet rings, cuff links, even corncob pipes so he could spy the cards as he dealt them from the deck.

Playing cards and rolling dice, though, were child's play, for then came the real lesson in self-defense, using a pistol. With the little cash he earned, Cohen purchased cartridges in Whitewood. Clark then showed him how to care for and clean the weapon, load the shells into the chamber, and how to squeeze off shots with minimal kick. Cohen tramped out to the fields with loose cartridges in his pocket, and set up beef cans and other objects for target practice. Soon he worked his way up to moving targets. All the while Clark admonished him to follow a brass-knuckled golden rule: "Do unto others what they would do unto you—but do it first!"

Nights were long in Saskatchewan, especially as winter approached. Cohen had little to do once he completed his chores and ate dinner. He stayed up in his room shaking the bones, shuffling, dealing, and riffling through the cards with his hammed hands. He curled cards, retried moves, learned the feel and the bend of the laminated papers. Cohen's first Canadian winter was considered mild. January had a lot of sunshine. More than half the days reached up to forty-one degrees, dipping down as low as thirty-three below at night. February brought some light snow, and the evening temperature reached a frigid thirty-seven below. The weather was tolerable as long as the wind didn't act up. When it did, the powdery snow bit into exposed flesh. "If one stepped outside the shack on such occasions in cloth clothes and there happened to be a wind, it seemed to reach the skin like a touch of ice," wrote Edward West, who homesteaded in Saskatchewan soon after Cohen arrived. During the day the light reflecting off the snow blinded Cohen. And when a blizzard blew through, visibility could be so bad that they had to string ropes between the barn and the house so they didn't get lost along the way.

Wolves came down from the north in search of food, and coyotes slunk from coulee to coulee and tried to abscond with chickens. Cohen, Nicholson, and Clark could do little in the cold but lock the livestock safely away. Cohen tended to the barn-bound livestock, made repairs around the farm, and collected and split wood from the coulees, birch thickets, and scrub poplar so they would have a stockpile that could last into the year.[12]

By March spring birds and gophers appeared. The ground with its rich black loam finally thawed out the following month as high winds blew through, and melted water collected in the sloughs. In the spring of 1906 Nicholson started seeding in April. Leaf buds appeared in May. A decent amount of rain fell in 1906—20 inches—and June was especially cloudy and wet. In July dry, hot winds blew in and frequent thunderstorms erupted. Haying started in mid-July.[13]

Farmers often cut the wheat before it ripened. As the crops matured, Nicholson regularly walked out into the field, picked a few heads of wheat, and rubbed them in his hands, looking and waiting for the berry to be firm and the smooth side to show an amber or yellow tinge. "Sometimes a man's wheat will ripen overnight, and unless he has his workers on the spot he may lose the best of his crop," noted harvester Robert L. Yates. "Sometimes a farmer will delay his cutting by one day, and that night a storm will come and lay low the heavy stalks with their burden of golden grains—and all will be lost. It is a land where tragedies and blessings abound side by side, for the storm that destroys one man's wheat, which was too advanced, may hasten the growth of his neighbor's, which, owing to a late planting, has been retarded."

In many Saskatchewan districts harvest began on August 5. Nineteen hundred and six promised to be a bumper year—exceeding the province-wide take of 46,947,464 bushels of grain in 1905. While Nicholson, Cohen, and Clark could seed the land by themselves, they needed a group of at least eight men to harvest. Nicholson headed to Whitewood to see about hiring help to cut the crop.

Most of the men who came to harvest arrived from the east and from the United States, taking advantage of cheap railway fares offered at harvest time and the pay that in 1906 averaged $2.27 a day. Nicholson picked his men, and put them right to work each morning before dawn. To cut the wheat, Nicholson sat squarely on the four-horse binder and flicked the reins to encourage the team to strain up the rolling hills; on the way down he had to hold them tight so they did not run off. Cohen and the harvesters followed the binder, whose rolling reels sliced the wheat, bound the loose stalks into sheaves, and dropped the bundles as it advanced. Since they cut the wheat early, the unripened grain had to be stooked—gathered and piled with the butt ends down—to temporarily keep the grain, prevent injury from moist ground, and allow it to "sweat" or cure in preparation for threshing.

August was warm, and both the vegetation and the workers suffered from the excessive heat. When Cohen walked and gathered the sheaves, he had to watch out for the "tanglefoot" sheaves, the cuttings that stuck together and were not easily parted, thus making it difficult to keep pace with Nicholson on the binder. As the day advanced and the sun rose, Cohen's dew-soaked gloves dried and then cracked. The hot glare bounced off the grain, and he and the others stripped off their overalls and jumpers and worked in their flannels. "Come out at seven a.m. when the dew on the stubble gets into your shoes to mix with the dust and the gravel to make walking a trial by ordeal," wrote Wiggins. "Bend your back and bow your head, pick up two sheaves and lift them clear of the stubble before you set them down just so. Do this again and again and keep it up for ten hours each day under a broiling sun with the sweat dripping from every pore and into your eyes, while your tongue licks up the dust that never seems to settle. Drink warm water from an earthen jug once each time around a 160-acre field. Keep your sleeves buttoned to the wrist regardless of the heat or your arms will get unbearably chaffed by the straw. . . . There are other arduous jobs I know in farming, but stooking while it lasts is the one that calls for all you've got. After the stooking 'Bringing in the Sheaves' is a picnic. No wonder there's a hymn about that." All work stopped on rainy days and Saturday at six. The men could then head into town for a drink, to talk, and to smoke. Sundays they had free. They might go duck shooting, attend church, walk along the hills, or watch the new Whitewood Baseball Club in action.[14]

The harvesters ate hearty meals; the Nicholson women prepared pies, breads, and meats for the mass of men. There was breakfast in the morning. At ten they might have a sandwich and tea break. Lunch came at noon, and at four Mrs. Nicholson, Cora, and Ruby might bring out a snack of cake or pie to the field.

Once the wheat dried in early September it was ready for threshing. Like his neighbors, Nicholson hired one of the professional crews that traveled the province. Work began in the early morning. Horses pulled a wagon alongside the line of waiting stooks, as field pitchers forked the sheaves onto the wagon. When they filled a wagon it was brought to the mill. There Cohen jumped up on the wagon and helped the driver and others pitch the load into the threshing machine's steam-run separator.

When the grain bins brimmed, Nicholson and Cohen hauled it to the granary at nearby Burrows. There they lined up their cart with those of their neighbors, waiting for the dominion weighmaster to measure the haul and pay them in cash. It proved to be a bumper year in Saskatchewan, with 63,052,210 bushels of grain. Farmers in the Whitewood area alone raised 3,444,622 bushels of wheat, 1,779,826 bushels of oats, 142,500 bushels of barley, 2,634 bushels of flax, and 1,192 bushels of spelt.

At the end of the harvest, Josef Cohen's friend came by to see Cohen. A good worker was an asset in labor-strapped Saskatchewan, and Cohen had proven that he was not just some juvenile delinquent but a helpful hired hand. Josef's friend now wanted him back. It didn't matter that he worked for a neighbor. He offered Cohen $250 for the coming year. Cohen had enjoyed living at the Nicholsons', but the man appealed to Cohen's loyalty as a friend of his father's. Cohen had no choice but to go. He packed his trunk and headed back to the farm near Wapella. He did not stay long. Within four days he left. "For one thing his place was all farming and no ranching; and I was a cowhand, not a market-gardener. Besides his food was filthy, no better than his hogs were eating. Come to that, my room wasn't much better than the sties the hogs lived in. He promised to improve things, but I didn't wait to see . . . I didn't even pack. I left my clothes behind and walked the twelve miles to Wapella in my overalls."[15]

CHAPTER 6

"THERE'S A SUCKER BORN
EVERY MINUTE,"
1906–1909

ohen arrived in Wapella with $9.50 in his pocket. He got a hotel room and contemplated his next move. Room and board cost a dollar a day. With the harvest at an end, he needed a job and he needed it fast. In the hotel's saloon a fellow customer told him of work just over the Manitoba border. So when he had spent $6.50 of his wad, he and his new friend hopped an eastbound boxcar to Virden, and made their way a mile east of town to the banks of Gopher Creek. There Virden Brick Company manager C. W. Wainwright looked Cohen over and hired him for a dollar a day.

Virden Brick was a small setup, yet their cream-colored bricks were renowned as far away as Regina. "There was an office and a house for the manager and several smaller houses for the workers, as well as barns for the horses," recalled one early brickmaker. Cohen bunked with his coworkers, and started each morning at the sound of the eight o'clock whistle. Horses loosened and dragged mounds of clay out of the deep pit, and Cohen and the others deposited the haul on a level spot where it was left to weather. When it was ready, they gathered the clay and inserted it into a pug mill, where rotating blades churned the mass. As it mixed, workers added water to create a uniform plasticity. The molder then force-formed a few thousand bricks a day, impressing with an iron stamp on the exposed side of each the word "Virden." As he filled the molds, the off-bearer stacked them on a wheelbarrow and carted them off to the yard, where Cohen arranged the water-laden bricks on pallet tiers. There they dried for a few weeks under gable-framed coverings.

Once they were sufficiently aged, the wheeler carted the bricks to the long, updraft kiln. Cohen stacked the bricks, making sure the rectangular masses had spaces to allow the heat and gases to flow through. Blocks of hardwood were lit and the temperature slowly raised. When the cooled-down kiln was finally opened after about a week, Cohen sorted and graded the bricks by quality. The men then started the process all over again. Cohen did this backbreaking work for a few months. He even received a fifty-cent-a-day raise, yet soon the weather turned cold, and the plant closed for the season. By then he had saved forty dollars and decided to ramble on.[1]

The winter of 1906–7 proved to be the most bitter and brutal season in the region's history. Blizzards blanketed the prairies. Sheep and cattle perished from exposure. In some areas the number of prairie chickens declined by as much as 90 percent. Cohen headed back into Saskatchewan, taking a train to Moose Jaw, a Western boomtown of construction, bars, brothels, and gambling joints that was trying to put behind it its distinction as a major exporter of buffalo bones.

In early July advance men from the Greater Norris & Rowe Circus rolled into town in preparation for the arrival of the show. They pasted up Norris & Rowe posters, hung bunting, placed signs in merchants' windows, handed out free litera- ture, and arranged for the public ground and water supply, as well as food for the legions of workers and animals.

A few days later twenty-odd train cars pulled into town, and down the main street rolled an elaborate spectacle–cum–promotional campaign—glittering Roman chariots, carved cages filled with wild beasts, richly decorated tableaux wagons, a steam calliope, a dog-and-monkey fire department, and nearly seventy Shetland po- nies. Come one, come all! Everyone was invited to see the show. Cohen answered the call, and headed over to the circus grounds and asked Walter Shannon and his as- sistant, William Bradford, for work at their sideshow. At a bulky five feet eight, and with a brimming self-assurance to boot, the nineteen-year-old Cohen would do just fine for a sideshow. They trained him to be a talker—a carnival barker. Cohen stood in front of the sideshow tent festooned with signs and fluttering banners bearing such distorted images as a snake woman covered with writhing reptiles or a midget stand- ing in the palm of a hand. He enticed people with a whirling patter to step inside and see such attractions as Major Mite, the twenty-five-pound, thirty-one-inch-tall man whom he pitched as "the smallest comedian in the world." There were many other marvels to behold, all for a small admission price. There was Prince Mungo doing his Torture Dance. Or how about W. P. Doss, the human telescope? Nor was Major Mite the only midget one could see. Just buy a ticket and view the famed Princess Numa. And that was not all, for there was the magician and illusionist King Cole, Mrs. Cole with her snakes, sharpshooters, and don't forget the terrifying untamed lion act. For Cohen it must have felt like home at the penny gaffs of London.[2]

Locals entered the grounds, saw the caged animals in the menagerie, and then worked their way through Cohen's sideshow to the 150-foot-long big top. There they witnessed a whirlwind two-ring show of "100 Circus Champions and Celeb- rities." Norris & Rowe had 22 famous equestrians, 18 dancing aerialists, 10 reckless roughriders, 11 Arabian tumblers, 23 merry mirthful clowns, 20 astonishing acrobats, a complete Japanese circus, herds of performing elephants, and thundering Roman chariot races. Besides all that there was also Mlle. Rita with her lion, leopard, tiger, puma, and hyena, and one of the stars of the show, Pretty Edna Maretta, billed as "the only lady in the Entire World who throws somersaults on the naked back of a swiftly running horse." Moose Jawians couldn't pass up the show, and they snapped up the seventy-five-cents to one-dollar tickets. "The performance in the main tent was good," noted the Moose Jaw *Times*, "no one left the tent dissatisfied."[3]

As the circus traveled east, stopping in such towns as Indian Head, Moosomin, and Deloraine, Cohen started graduate-level coursework in the art of the con. The minor gaffing he had learned from Harry the Gonof and the card and dice presti-digitation of Bobby Clark were elementary studies compared to the subtle persuasion his sideshow colleagues imparted. At Norris & Rowe, P. T. Barnum's maxim that "there's a sucker born every minute" was alive and well. Cohen's colleagues taught him not only how to do unto others first, but how to maintain a true psychological edge over his bitter adversaries, the general public. For the circus crew it was an "us versus them" mentality. The "troupers," like Cohen, who were "with it," had to be prepared to do battle with the "Yokels" and naive "Rubes" found in towns like Moose Jaw, who ridiculed the nomadic lives of the circus. Part of Cohen's job included duping "marks" and "suckers." Within this fraternity of showmen and hucksters, such behavior was encouraged, even revered. Cohen watched and mimicked the wheeling and dealing, grifting and gaffing of his coworkers. He quickly learned all the right angles, all the right moves.

As a talker, Cohen had to lie. Misrepresenting a sideshow was an almost sacred practice. It was proper to tell tales, to give a man from Evanston, Illinois, an exotic garb and present him as a Bornean jungle man. Sideshow workers passed off young children as dwarfs. Tall men inserted lifts in their shoes. Talkers apprised the audiences of the exhibits' noble histories and why they ended up traveling the circus circuit. As Clyde Ingalls, manager of the Ringling Brothers, Barnum & Bailey sideshow in the 1930s, said: "Aside from such unusual attractions as the famous three-legged man, and the Siamese twin combinations, freaks are what you make them. Take any peculiar-looking person, whose familiarity to those around him makes for acceptance, play up that peculiarity and add a good spiel and you have a great attraction."

Cohen and the others used various methods to increase excitement and to "turn the tip." As people gathered near the entrance, shills rushed the ticket lines with the hope that others would follow. The shills pushed and distracted the townsfolk on line, making it easier for Cohen to shortchange or pickpocket the "towners." Once inside, the customers viewed the exhibits standing along the edge of a raised platform. Prince Mungo did his dance, and locals gawked at Princess Numa and Major Mite. It was a quick show; the crowd had to be gotten through to make room for the next bunch of suckers. Gambling was a lucrative sideshow sideline, as circus people further hustled locals with loaded dice, crooked dealing, marked cards, and rigged wheels of chance. Clark's training was being put to some practical use. "I was always in the middle of a mob and at quiet moments I could start shooting craps and make a bit more that way," said Cohen. "My bankroll got fat again in no time."[4]

After only three weeks of traveling, breaking down the tents every few days, living in close quarters, and bathing in water holes to rid himself of lice, Cohen tired of circus life. When Norris & Rowe reached Winnipeg on July 31, Cohen decided to take his chances in the "Chicago of the North." As he exited the Canadian Pacific

Railway station, a hotel tout grabbed his bag and directed him alongside the station's small fenced-in front lawn and around the corner to the nearby Maple Leaf Hotel. There he took a room. Winnipeg was a grand, bustling place. "It seemed like London to me," Cohen said. While not quite London, here was a metropolis that was a far cry from the one–grain elevator towns he had passed through; Winnipeg handled more grain than any other city in the world. Main Street, along which stood the Maple Leaf, elbowed 132 feet wide and trolleys plied past Greek and Roman-style banks and turreted towers.

The Maple Leaf was a simple two-story hotel recently bought by a Russian Jew named Nathan Rosenblat. The hotel was one of sixty such places along Hotel Row in Winnipeg's North End that catered to the city's single men who worked to bring wives, families, or girlfriends over. North Winnipeg was an area not unlike Cohen's home in St. George's in the East. Immigrants accounted for the vast majority of the city's growth. Eastern European Jews, along with Ukrainians, Slavs, Germans, Scandinavians, and Poles, helped push Winnipeg's population to 111,729, causing the North End to be disparagingly nicknamed the "Foreign Quarter" and "New Jerusalem." Flour and sawmills, ironworks, carriage and wagon makers, farm suppliers, and concrete companies filled this area. Heavy traffic clogged the streets and hundreds of freight and passenger trains chugged through.

Housing differed little from what Cohen grew up in on Umberston Street. Large numbers of people jammed into small homes and boardinghouses. "All the houses were small," said Jacob Freedman, who arrived from Russia in 1904. "Sometimes [the walls were black with] the cockroaches—and bedbugs." Sanitation was minimal. Citizens stabled their horses and cows throughout the area, and the neighborhood reeked. Few buildings had running water, and the city had 6,339 outside privies in 1908. "There was a toilet but no bath in our house, and on Saturday nights my mother would take the boiler, in which she washed clothes, fill it with water and heat it on the stove," recalled Sheppy Hershfield, who came to Winnipeg from the Ukraine. "That is how we obtained hot water for bathing."

Long wool coats hung outside shops along the streets. A cacophonous babble of Polish, Yiddish, Ukrainian, and Russian filled the air and mixed with the smell of foods. Junk men plied their wagons and collected clothes and rags. "Main Street was a most colorful street," wrote Hershfield. "Much drunkenness . . . existed along the entire street . . . each hotel had its own large saloon, its own character and characteristic. . . . There were immigrants from all over the world bursting their way out of the CPR station, and at harvest time, thousands of French Canadians would spill over the sidewalks onto the streets . . . and the clothing stores all owned by Jews, did a roaring trade. . . . Every block had its fake jewelry store and one or two liquor stores."[5]

At harvesttime the CPR waiting room bustled with men who had come from Ontario, Quebec, the Maritimes, and the United States to make good money in places like Whitewood bringing in the sheaves. An almost circus-like atmosphere prevailed near the Maple Leaf. Tens of thousands who came to Winnipeg in the spring and fall stopped at banner-draped employment agencies plastered with signs advertising: "100 Men Wanted," "1 Cook Needed," and "2 Teamsters Wanted."

When not working or looking for a job, the roving male population hung out at hotel poolrooms and "Free Admission Parlours" where patrons enjoyed some open space away from their crowded boarding rooms, played slot machines, shot targets, and found a prostitute in a back room. Pool sharks, booze, confidence men, and pickpockets abounded. "Sally Annies," women from the Salvation Army, meanwhile worked hard to save willing and unwilling souls. Presbyterian and Methodist social reformers branded the North End a Sodom of wanton "bestial orgies" and "unChristian activities." Those who passed through this Gomorrah, beware! As the *Commercial Traveler* warned in 1907, "The assertion [has] been made that some of the hotels in the vicinity of the C.P.R. depot at Winnipeg have been resorting to nefarious practices, using 'knockout drops,' etc., for the purpose of stupefying and reducing men to unconsciousness in order that they may be relieved of their money . . ."[6]

As Cohen checked out the town's teeming bars and pool halls, a man came out of a store and asked him if he would like to step inside and see some real bargains. "Feeling pretty flush just then, I went in and bought a whole lot of things I didn't need," he said, "including a gold ring, which I knew must be real gold because it was stamped on the inside '14 carat'; I paid one dollar fifty for it." But when the ring started to turn his finger green, Cohen figured that something was terribly wrong. Maybe, he suspected, it wasn't really gold. With no job and a marked tendency to spend all he had as soon as he had it, Cohen started running low on cash. He sold the "gold" ring for two dollars to a sucker he met in a bar, and boasted to Robert Harris, the bartender and a fellow resident at the Maple Leaf, how he made fifty cents on the deal. Harris just laughed and explained that he could get as many "14 carat" rings as he wanted for fifteen cents each at a wholesale jewelry store owned by Lazarus and Benjamin Levi.

Cohen ran over, snapped up twelve rings, and started his new profession as a hoop merchant. It was the same old con with a different spin. Instead of working at a pocketbook stall in the East End or regaling people with sideshow tales, he now ventured into bars and told inebriated customers how his luck had turned bad and he desperately needed cash. All he had of value, he mournfully pointed out to the kind gentleman who listened, was a ring. It was a truly sad tale he told in his Cockney brogue, recently softened by the flat Canadian accents he had been hearing around him. This was a performance that ranked with his histrionic Shakespearean turns at Hayes. "I never actually said it was gold," he said of his masterful act, "but just let them examine it and spot the fourteen-carat stamp. I'd ask two or three dollars at first and let them beat me down to one. It hardly ever failed."

From fake rings, Cohen made a short vertical career move and earned a large pay increase when he started selling "Pittsburgh Specials," faux twenty-one-jewel pocket watches. He told the same tragic yarn, informing the transient harvesters who jammed into the immigration sheds, hotels, and rooming houses how he had splurged $27.50 for the watch and chain. His mournful hazel-green eyes would mist as he begged the fellow to please give him $12.50 "because I gotta have the dough." His broken nose and the scars on his hands and face must have made him look in need of sympathy. It was a good regular job, bringing in twenty to thirty dollars a day. With his income secure, he passed his nonworking hours playing poker and craps, raking in even more. He claims he did not lose much.[7]

As Cohen seasoned into his trade, he decided he needed a more permanent flop. While living at the Maple Leaf he met Benjamin Zimmerman, a stout cousin of the writer Shalom Aleichem, whose family had come over with the Mansion House group in 1882. In 1887 Zimmerman's father, Nissel, opened a general store at 669 Main Street, next to the Maple Leaf. When Nissel died ten years later Benjamin took over the business. In 1903 Benjamin built a red brick and rusticated limestone building next door for his pawn- and jewelry shop. It contained mahogany-and-oak-paneled rooms with pressed metal ceilings and mirrors. Initially he rented the upstairs rooms out as offices, but within a few years he started taking in bachelors and transient workers. Cohen and Zimmerman became friendly, and Cohen rented one of the steam-heated rooms with his new friend and associate William Vine.[8]

With so many men in Winnipeg—six for every five women—prostitution was a growing problem. Skimpily-clad women solicited along the streets and called to pedestrians from their porches. In 1907 the police convicted seventy-one keepers of bawdy houses and 101 prostitutes. In 1908 double that number went to jail. Even so, prostitutes perceived "Winnipeg the Wicked" as a profitable place to flock to. As two of the young, unattached men about town, Cohen and Vine were not averse to taking advantage of the women's services. Vine ran a bawdy house, and when not gambling or selling fake jewelry, Cohen made extra cash as a pimp.

In late March 1909, the two friends paid a young girl to come up to their room. Someone tipped off the police, and on a mild but chilly March 30, Officer Charles H. Knox arrested Cohen and Vine and charged them with carnal knowledge of a girl under sixteen. Cohen was booked as Arthur Cohen, and relieved of the rings, dice, chain, knife, pencils, and pipe in his pockets. The police then placed the roommates in jail at the Rupert Street Station to await their fates. Crime and convictions were up in town, and the holding pens brimmed with people charged for everything from being drunk on railway duty, breach of the Lord's Day bylaw, assault and battery, keeping an opium joint, and refusing to pay a chimney sweep. "The cells at police headquarters were filled to their utmost capacity last night, no less than seventy men, besides a number of women, finishing up . . . behind the bars," reported a correspondent at the Winnipeg *Free Press* who visited the cells around the time of Cohen's stay. "A number of others were bailed by their friends, and judging from the number of battered and bleeding faces seen in the station duty office, there were others who ought to have been there and some of whom likely will be. . . . There are seventeen cells for male prisoners, and these were so crowded that many of the men were spending the night lying on the concrete floor, while others paced to and fro behind the bars like wild beasts in a cage."

Civic groups had mixed results in quashing the trade that Cohen and Vine were involved in. Reformers were especially concerned that young girls like the teenager the two friends brought to their room were being lured into this nefarious trade. In 1898 the Canadian government passed the Children's Protection Act, calling for punishment for anyone who "ill-treats, neglects, abandons or exposes such child, or causes or procures such child to be ill-treated, neglected, abandoned or exposed." The act was finally given some teeth in January 1909 when Magistrate Thomas Mayne Daly, a portly, fifty-six-year-old former Minister of Interior, was appointed the first judge of a juvenile court in Canada. The wax-mustached Daly pitied the young girls. After initially letting a number of offenders off with stiff warnings, he decided he had to make an example of someone. Unfortunately for Cohen, he was the test case. When Cohen and Vine appeared before Daly, they pleaded not guilty to the charges. Their trial went quickly. "The evidence showed that the offence of Vine and Cohen was an especially flagrant one," noted the Manitoba *Free Press*. On the afternoon of April 7, Daly sentenced them to six months at hard labor.[9]

The officers shackled Cohen and carted him right over to the Eastern Judicial District Gaol, a formidable beige-colored building on Vaughan and York Street. When the heavily rusticated limestone facility with its corbeled bricks and thick bars opened in 1883, officials touted it as an up-to-date jail. Turnkeys locked Cohen into a six-by-eleven-foot cell. There he slept on a hay mattress, and he and the nearly two hundred other prisoners were confined to bed from five at night until seven or eight in the morning. They could not have books or newspapers to while away the hours. The regular cells, though, were better than the five dark solitary areas in the basement. In these four-by-eight-foot unventilated boxes, guards chained prisoners to the walls and fed them only bread, water, and porridge.

Some of the regular cells contained women. Most were prostitutes, vagrants, and alcoholics. The insane also ended up here, as they awaited medical examination, as well as those due to be hanged. Only a few fortunate inmates got outside to do roadwork and earn twenty-five-cents a day. Those not so lucky exercised during warm weather in the two jail yards. Cohen could also unwind in a small common area on the third floor—an open space with a glass cupola and a tin-plated ceiling festooned with small fleurs-de-lis—that stood near where officials performed the indoor hangings. While the jail had bathtubs, there was little privacy. Ventilation was bad. It was especially uncomfortable for those preparing food. In hot weather it "must be a veritable Hades for those unfortunates who must work there," wrote a prison investigator. "The range is an old-fashioned affair, with two fire boxes, and is a miniature volcano when in full operation."

Cohen passed nearly six months at the jail; he had six days chopped off his sentence. On October 6, he was allowed to leave. Despite the food, he actually gained four pounds, filling out to a hefty 179 pounds. He had had enough of the "Chicago of the North," and decided to try his luck in Saskatoon, Saskatchewan.[10]

CHAPTER 7

THE CHINESE,
1909–1911

*T*he *Methodist members of the Temperance Colonization* Society who came to this undulating land of blue grama grass, willows, and aspen bluffs in the early 1880s were the antithesis of the twenty-two-year-old Cohen. They worked to make their community, named after the rich red saskatoon berry, a place "where temperance ideals might prevail *exclusively*." Soon they had a school, a newspaper, and a bridge spanning the wide and muddy South Saskatchewan River. By 1890 the first train pulled into Saskatoon, and within two years the bones of 200,000 buffaloes were shipped east from there. Each spring also brought trainloads of homesteaders who crowded the hotels and immigration halls and scrambled for supplies and horses. Some, like the fifteen hundred Barr colonists from England who pitched tents in 1903, used Saskatoon as a jumping-off point to land to the Northwest. Others, like the thirty-one-year-old John Duncan Ferguson of Kincardine, Ontario, who camped alongside the Barr group, came to Saskatoon to escape the life of an eastern lawyer, which consisted of "tennis, fishing, pretty girls, and not much law."

When the boom that attracted more settlers as well as Cohen arrived, land that sold for $900 in June 1905 went for $16,000 just seventeen months later. In 1906, 2,317 homestead entries were made at the local land office, and Ferguson kept busy as the dominion land agent, registering homesteaders and processing proof of tenure. His law practice grew. Soon he took Frederick Finlay MacDermid on as a partner. When MacDermid's brother John arrived in town around the time of Cohen's appearance, the population stood at 12,000, and there were, according to John MacDermid, "fifteen or twenty automobiles and . . . probably as many or more livery stables."[1]

Saskatoon had not, though, developed into the godly place the Temperance Colonization Society had hoped for. With liquor, gambling, and prostitution, it suited Cohen. Once he came to town, he joined a grown-up band of merry Faginites, and resumed the London pickpocketing trade that first got him in trouble with the police. Numerous other thieves drifted through Saskatoon, from a bank clerk who pocketed $5,000 to a smooth con man who slipped into town bearing a letter of credit from an English bank, arranged for a $2,000 loan, bought a manufacturing concern, and threw champagne-popping parties before slipping away with the loot he scammed. The police valiantly tried to control the place, arresting low-level criminals like Mamie Mason and fining her fifty dollars for selling liquor, and an additional $4.50 for offering herself.

In late September 1909, the police began surveillance of a gambling den run by Mah Sam, a fifty-two-year-old Chinese immigrant from Guangdong province in southern China. At his store on Second Avenue they observed whites and Chinese strolling in and out at all hours. When Constable George M. Donald snuck up to the store and looked through the peephole, he saw gambling going on. At 11 P.M. on the twenty-fourth, Chief Robert E. Dunning, his men, and members of the Royal North West Mounted Police rushed through both the front and back doors. Inside they found ten "Celestials" innocently sitting around. All acted unaware of the three tables laden with dice, dominoes, cards, and Chinese money. The police arrested the whole lot of them. When the case came before Magistrate Fred M. Brown, the Chinese claimed they were simply having a friendly game of dominoes. They did not exchange any money, and of course the cards had never been touched. Brown didn't buy the argument. Mah's defense improved when Mandarin Mark, the leading Chinese in town, pleaded that he would "impress upon Mah Sam and the others that the house must be conducted differently in the future." His promise suited Brown and the police. Mah then changed his plea to guilty. Brown fined him ten dollars and costs, and the police said they would be pleased if Mah ran the place in a more orderly fashion so as not to disturb the neighbors. "There were several mitigating circumstances," noted the Saskatoon *Daily Phoenix*, "and chief among these was the fact that these men had to live here without their wives and families, and it was only natural that they should want some social entertainment."[2]

Mah and the rest of the Chinese in Saskatoon lived far from their wives, families, and homes in a land that did not understand, let alone welcome them. They led solitary lives. Like many others settlers, they originally flocked to western Canada to make their fortune at the "Gold Mountain," sailing north from San Francisco in the 1850s and '60s with the hope of striking it big at the Fraser River and the Cariboo gold rush. Panning for gold was a hard way to make a living, but to the Chinese it was better than eking out an existence in mid-nineteenth-century China. Back then, China contained 430 million people. Most of the land was held by few. In early-nineteenth-century Guangdong, only 10 percent of the land was arable. The average peasant household cultivated less than an acre of rice and vegetables.

Turmoil beset the nation. Bandits and private armies pillaged. A weak and corrupt Qing Dynasty was thrashed and humiliated by the British in the Opium War of 1839–42, and forced by the Treaty of Nanjing to open up the ports of Canton, Xiamen, Fuzhou, Ningbo, and Shanghai to barbarian Western trade. At the time of the Fraser River gold rush the government was fumbling through the Taiping Uprising, a grass-roots revolt in which the followers of Hong Xiuquan, a self-proclaimed younger brother of Christ, sought to establish a heavenly kingdom of God on earth. Hong's social and nationalistic movement and anti-Manchu stance attracted widespread support, since a majority of the country resented the foreign Manchurians for driving south in the seventeenth century, conquering the Ming Dynasty, and establishing the Qing Dynasty. By the time imperial forces suppressed the Taiping Uprising in 1864, tens of millions of Chinese were dead.

Those who left home in their teens or twenties for North America were generally Cantonese men from Guangdong. By the early 1860s 4,000 to 7,000 Chinese lived in current-day British Columbia. Many came alone and then brought over relatives and friends. Others arrived as indentured servants for large companies or wealthy investors. Miners hoped to make big money, and some of the Gold Mountain men even bought claims from whites that the settlers viewed as unprofitable. "The Chinese are come up in great numbers, and spreading themselves over the Bars," wrote Bishop George Hills in June 1861 of the Asian miners. "They work over again the claims which have already been searched by the Europeans. They are content with a dollar or two dollars a day, and will frequently make much more."[3]

Towns around the mines often lacked women, and some of the Chinese worked as cooks, washed clothes, and ran bathhouses, restaurants, and general stores. They clustered together for protection and comradeship, raised vegetables, sent remittances home to their wives and families, and dreamed of the day their sojourn would end. Most never made their fortune, never saw home again. As a Chinese song warned:

> *If you have a daughter, don't marry her to a Gold Mountain boy.*
> *Out of ten years, he will not be in bed for even one.*
> *The spider spins webs on top of the bed.*
> *While dust covers fully one side of the bed.*

When gold fever cooled down in mid-decade and claims dried up, the number of Chinese dropped to an estimated 1,705. Those who stayed searched out new claims or took jobs as domestics, in coal mines, and in canneries. Some opened laundries, restaurants, planted vegetable gardens, cut wood, worked on roads, or laid telegraph cables. While they were good, reliable workers, the public perceived them much as the Russians saw the Jews, as a danger. Whites despised the Chinese, and viewed them as dirty, illiterate aliens who practiced a heathen religion, were morally corrupt, and spread leprosy and smallpox. They dressed and spoke differently, and it was believed that their propensity for gambling and opium threatened to ensnare white women and destroy Western morality. And as with the Jews, they made the ideal scapegoat. Hard workers were branded as being unfairly competitive, and though their numbers never constituted more than half of one percent of the population, the public believed that a yellow horde was descending on Canada.

British Columbians were especially alarmed in the early 1880s when plans for a transcontinental railway promised a new wave of Asian laborers. Yet the province only had 35,000 whites, not enough to fill the ranks of railway workers. Andrew Onderdonk, the contractor responsible for much of the British Columbian section, brought in more than 10,000 Chinese, defending his business decision by noting, "Ninety-nine percent of the Chinese are industrious and steady" and arguing that "development of the country would be retarded and many industries abandoned" if they didn't help out.

Whites insisted that the Chinese be booted out once the work was completed. For their labor the Chinese navvies received one dollar for a twelve-hour day—white workers could expect $1.50 to $1.75. Working in gangs of thirty, the Chinese built the railway through some of the most impassable terrain in the world. They cut passages, leveled grades, and dug ditches. It was dangerous work. Blasting powder on the hand caused severe burns. Flying splinters from explosions maimed and killed. Rock and mud slides buried people. By the time the last iron spike was driven at Craigellachie, B.C., on November 7, 1885, and the Atlantic and Pacific shores were joined, hundreds of Chinese were injured or dead from accidents, explosions, exposure, malnutrition, and scurvy.[4]

A depression then struck British Columbia, and the Chinese found themselves trapped without work or enough money to return home. Many starved. The idling Chinese had to be dealt with. "Would it not, therefore, be a wise scheme for our local Government to charter a few vessels and send the Chinese back to their native land, free," mused the Port Moody *Gazette* in 1885. "We believe very many of them would readily avail themselves of such an opportunity, now that work is scarce, and furthermore, that to return is the aspiration, if not the destination, of nearly every Chinaman in the country."

To rid the land of Chinese, the Canadian government, like its sister democracy to the south, started legislating against them. British Columbia disenfranchised the Chinese, and the preamble to the province's Chinese Regulation Act of 1884 stated that the Chinese were "governed by pestilential habits" and were "inclined to habits subversive to the comfort and well-being of the community." Federal head taxes were imposed on those entering Canada, beginning at ten dollars a person and soon rising to fifty dollars.[5]

Yet they continued to come. Between 1889 and 1900 Chinese immigration averaged about 2,000 a year. With the new rail system the Chinese headed east to prairie towns like Calgary, Edmonton, Saskatoon, and Moose Jaw. There they opened hand laundries, restaurants, and grocery stores, and worked as cooks, in canneries, and as domestics.[6]

Groups like the Knights of Labour, the Anti-Chinese League, the Provincial Federated Labour Congress, and the Anti-Mongolian Society called for restrictions on Chinese. "Chinese, when they come to reside in a place ought to be treated much the same as an infectious disease or an isolation hospital," wrote James Short, a well-known Calgary lawyer. "They live like rabbits in a warren and 30 of them crowd into where five white people would ordinarily reside. . . . They have not the first idea of cleanliness or sanitation. Everywhere they go they are undesirable citizens and furnish a problem to the municipality."

At the turn of the century, the federal government raised the head tax to one hundred dollars. A few years later it was pushed up to five hundred, which then briefly stopped migration. "We know we are not welcomed in Canada," said one Chinese octogenarian in response to his treatment. "We are hated. But, we have to make a living. We have a family to support in China. I still remember the song they [whites] sang when they saw us: 'Chink, Chink, Chink, fifteen cents, wash my pants; five cents, make a dance . . . ' We are just hated by the whites. . . ."[7]

Few Chinese owned houses. They settled on the fringes of downtown in rooming houses or in the back of or above their stores. These areas became the start of many a Chinatown. Social relations between Asians and whites did not exist. Whites ate at Chinese restaurants, dropped off dirty clothes at Chinese laundries, bought vegetables from Chinese market gardeners, but refused to mix with them socially. A white woman who married a Chinese or a Japanese immediately became an outcast. "They were the point at which the famous hospitality and neighbourliness stopped," wrote Heather Gilead of that period. "There was not a white remittance-man shiftless or unwashed enough not to receive at least one invitation to eat his Christmas dinner with a proper family, but thousands of Chinese must have lived in our midst decade after decade without ever seeing the inside of a white Christian's home."

The laundries they ran were small clapboard businesses. A counter stood up front, behind which they stacked tied parcels. The smell of starch and steam permeated the candle- or kerosene-lit back room. "Everything in the laundry was done by hand," said launderer Chow Yin Wong of the sorting, boiling, pressing, and drying. "We had one mangle, a small one, to press the sheets, and then we had to fold by hand. We just used the metal iron for the shirts, put it on the stove, and then pressed, like that, all by hand. We hung the stuff upstairs to dry—kept the stove so hot, in 2 hours it was dry." At night the owner and workers slept upstairs, on the ironing table or anywhere else available. Chinese cafés served Western fare—breaded veal cutlets, mashed potatoes, hot beef sandwiches, pork chops, apple pie, coffee, and rice pudding. Whites socialized there, often insulting and pushing around the owner between bites of food.[8]

The Chinese lived a precarious, often violent existence. On Christmas Eve, 1907, Harry Smith, the manager of a farm south of Lethbridge, Alberta, went with six friends to the Chinese-owned Columbia Restaurant. Smith ordered food and then yelled at the owner to hurry up. The farmer just laughed when the owner told him to leave. One of the Chinese then grabbed Smith. Another rushed from behind the counter and whacked Smith over the head with a claw hammer, and struck one of his friends in the arm. Rumor then circulated that the Chinese had killed Smith. "A gang went into the place, told the waitresses to vacate, went through to the kitchen and into the dining room and proceeded to demolish everything in sight," reported the Lethbridge *Herald*. "The Chinamen were roughly handled but finally escaped. In a few minutes the place was completely wrecked, dishes were a foot deep on the kitchen floor, tables and chairs were smashed, show cases overturned, goods littered about and general ruination carried the place." The mob of five hundred then brawled across the street and smashed the windows at the Chinese-owned Alberta Restaurant. The workers hid in the cellar. Rioters then attacked Joe Fong's restaurant. When the Mounties arrived, they arrested a mere four whites for drunk and disorderly behavior.

Thus isolated, the Chinese founded social, cultural, and political groups. The Chinese Benevolent Organization aided the sick and the poor, mediated disputes, and dealt with non-Chinese. Eventually the Chinese also established fraternal, district, and clan associations that did work similar to that of the Benevolent Organization, and held major feasts and parades as well as smaller dinner parties and teas. Most North American Chinese belonged to the Hongmen Society or the Triad Society, a secret political grass-roots organization committed to the overthrow of the Qing Dynasty. The supreme triad was the Zhigongtang. Contrary to legend, most North American lodges were not the fighting tongs, renowned and feared for their gang-style tong wars, opium dealing, prostitution, and gambling. The average tong member was more interested in social and economic advancement and belonged to an occupation tong. These tongs helped raise money to start businesses, supplied banking services, found individuals employment, smuggled Chinese into the United States, and arranged for legal help. To join, one had to undergo an initiation ritual, swear brotherhood and allegiance to the others, and promise to help end the Qing Dynasty.[9]

The booming Canadian economy caused Chinatowns to prosper. Two- and three-story brick buildings with upturned tiled eaves, latticed windows, and moon-shaped doors rose in Chinatowns. These labyrinthine places with enclosed courtyards and alleys filled with opium dens, laundries, brothels, and cafés catered to the all-male society. Restaurants did good business, and small groups gathered to gamble. "Merchants . . . have made gambling into a form of business," wrote the Chinese reformer Liang Qichao in 1903. "There's hardly a single shop that doesn't have gambling. In just the tiny community in Vancouver there are more than twenty fan-tan gambling houses and sixteen or seventeen lotteries."

Gambling was one of the few ways whites and Chinese mixed. "If a community had some questionable activities to perform it would quite likely 'requisition' the premises of the Chinese for that purpose," wrote Gilead. "Regalia's more or less permanent poker game lived in the back room of the Chinese restaurant. I don't know that gambling was illegal: it was most certainly furtive. Men found it easier to behave discreditably in the presence of the Chinese than in the presence of men they regarded as their peers. He was the outsider to whose judgment one might remain indifferent. In towns large enough to sport a red-light district it was often almost synonymous with Chinatown, not because the Chinese were actively implicated in prostitution, but because, given half a chance, a portion of the white population would cocoon the Chinese in their midst in their own more malodorous fantasies and practices."

As with the arrest of Mah Sam in 1909, the police and newspapers made a big deal out of raids on the Chinese. The Chinese therefore tried to hide their activities. "The gambling houses were illegal so they were usually behind storefronts which sold cigarettes and pop or fruit as a cover," said Yun Ho Chang, who came to Canada in 1908. "And the owners must have had connections, because they usually knew ahead of time when the police were going to raid." To thwart the police, the Chinese frosted windows, put up iron bars, drilled peepholes, and even installed ropes that released heavy doors to slow down the advancing officers.[10]

Even though he had been convicted for running a gambling house and warned to cease his illegal activities, Mah continued his lucrative sidelines in the Alberta Restaurant on Twentieth Street West. He wisely kept the regular card playing at the Alberta in the rear of the restaurant, away from prying eyes glancing through the two large plate-glass windows out front. Mah had quite a busy business in his one-story frame building across the street from the King Edward Hotel and James Anderson's poolroom. Some of the poker matches amassed huge pots, and the mostly white gamblers could win $800 to $900 in one night's worth of play. It didn't take long for Cohen to find out about the action at the Alberta. He quickly became a regular in the smoky, messy back den. There he would sit, cupping his cards, his eyes darting and taking in the room. At the Alberta he used his old friend Bobby Clark's techniques, the new scams he learned in Winnipeg as well as some fast moves acquired from Hunky—a solemn-looking fellow gang member who wore blue glasses that picked up phosphorus spots on the back of marked cards. "I started serious gambling and soon got in with a bunch of 'rounders' who would chisel suckers out of their cash quick enough," said Cohen.

Cohen relaxed at the Alberta on the edges of the quasi-fraternity of the expatriate Chinese society. Sometimes Mah even fronted Cohen extra money to help him parlay his daytime pickpocketing take into goodly nightly sums. He started to make strong personal attachments unlike any he had known since he left his family on Umberston Street in the fall of 1905. Here in the restaurant's back room, Cohen could be at ease with his life, far from the codes of behavior his parents, the Jews' Free School, and Hayes Industrial School had demanded of him. Neither Mah nor Cohen's new Asian brothers pressured him to conform to the ways of law-abiding society and unseen ancestors. Cohen had the freedom to do as he pleased, to gamble, to carouse, to make mischief, to see questionable women, to rob. This suited him. And even though Mah spoke only halting English, the lack of constraining expectations drew Cohen closer to him. These two men, each far from his home, understood each other and developed a close friendship. After the all-night games were over Cohen sat in the back of the Alberta, picked up bastardized Cantonese, and chowed down authentic Cantonese dishes as Mah regaled this rare, tolerant white man with tales of old China.

One evening Cohen came by Mah's for some poker and food. When he strolled in he saw one customer in the store, a stocky "tough sort of guy" with his hand ominously placed in his pocket. The stranger was looming alongside Mah at the counter. The man looked at Cohen, and Cohen saw that Mah was desperately trying to pull a diamond ring off his own finger. Cohen had walked into the middle of a robbery. "I wasn't heeled and I had to be careful," said Cohen. "I closed in till I was too near for him to use his rod and socked him on the jaw." Cockney Cohen clobbered his opponent, and the mug was kissing the canvas. Cohen relieved the thief of his ill-gotten gains and kicked him out of the store.

Such an act was unheard of. Few white men in early-twentieth-century North America ever came to the aid of the Chinese. Mah and the others embraced Cohen as an ally, and pulled him even closer into their fraternity. As they drew him in, Mah educated Cohen on China, and why Cantonese like Mah resented the brutish Manchurian northerners. And not only did the Manchus control their land, but they brought shame on China by how they ruled. At the turn of the century, Cohen was taught, the country was ripe for revolution. Hoping to improve the state of his nation, the Guangxu Emperor in June 1898 announced plans to liberalize and westernize China, but his evil aunt, the Empress Dowager, Cixi, thwarted his efforts. The hopeful 100-Day Reform failed, and the emperor was imprisoned. Reformers like Kang Youwei and Liang Qichao fled the country. Their movement for change, though, did not stop. Kang, Liang, and the more radical Dr. Sun Yat-sen started to court and raise funds from those like Mah in North America. In 1899 Kang went to Canada and founded the reform political party, Baohuanghui (Society to Protect the Emperor), eventually forming more than one hundred branches throughout North America. The reform party could not usher in change, though, and when the Empress Dowager had the emperor killed in 1908 the purpose of the party perished with him.[11]

As the other reformers faltered and failed, the Chinese soon perceived the constant Sun as a reliable leader. Sun was born two years after the defeat of the Taipings, and while studying medicine in Hong Kong, he became enamored of the life of the Taiping leader, Hong. In the early 1890s, Sun began the Xingzhonghui (Revive China Society). He cobbled together a band of men in Hawaii and Hong Kong, and planned to capture Canton on October 26, 1895, with the hope his uprising would spark others. The revolt came to little. The local governor-general discovered the plot, and Sun fled for Japan. His continued talk of revolution was not well received, and his lectures in the United States in 1896 drew little support. He then traveled to England, and inexplicably allowed himself to be captured on October 11 while visiting the Chinese legation in London. The staff planned to ship this rabble-rouser home for a painful execution, yet luck was on Sun's side. When the press learned of his imprisonment, he became a cause célèbre, and after twelve days of captivity the Manchus released him. In 1905 Sun consolidated various anti-Manchu groups into the Tongmenghui (United League). The group dedicated itself to nationalism, democracy, and socialism, and advocated everything from the overthrow of the empire to equalization of land and social revolution. Branches of the TMH soon appeared in Berkeley, California, and Chicago, and then across North America. Like many other Cantonese, Mah joined up.[12]

To Cohen, all Mah's talk of Sun Yat-sen, the Manchus, and revolution must have sounded like pure fancy. "I'd sit for hours in his back room eating Chinese chow . . . and listening while he talked about Chinese politics. You'd never have dreamt that such a quiet, peaceable, soft-spoken old chap could be a revolutionary," Cohen said. "I didn't quite swallow all he told me, but it stirred my imagination. I was young enough to like excitement, and his talk of soldiering and conspiracy and revolution was exciting. I'd known poverty myself and what persecution meant from things I'd heard my parents say. And though I'd never seen China, I could guess that the life of the under-dog would be a whole lot worse there than it was in the white man's world."

While Cohen was intrigued by the tales and sympathetic to China's plight, he had more pressing financial concerns. When not listening to Mah's histories, Cohen and his band of pickpockets searched the streets for easy marks to roll for added cash with which to gamble. The police were wise to all of Cohen's activities, and on August 5, 1910, Officer John J. James told him to clear out of Saskatoon. He didn't. Why should he? He earned a good living, and the twenty-fourth Annual Saskatoon Fair was opening in four days. A gang like his just could not pass up the opportunity for a windfall—22,300 well-padded citizens just waiting to be plucked. The pigeons flocked to Saskatoon to see the fair's "monster parade of livestock," the afternoon horse racing, and the new Machinery Hall. It was carnival style with large milling crowds, the ideal hunting ground for Cohen on the prowl.

Union Jacks fluttered from poles and cables around the fairgrounds. Red, white, and blue bunting covered the main building. From the tower visitors marveled at the view. There were baseball matches, judging of horses, cattle, and sheep, and a drummer's parade. Inside Al. G. Barnes's circus big top, the lion trainer Edwin Kelly handled the African and Nubian lions, and the sea lions balanced balls and furniture on their noses. Outside, dealers set up stands displaying parlor stoves, straw burners, and peaches and plums. Other stalls offered visitors local bread and free cups of tea. In the evening electric lights lined the walkways. All the while Cohen stalked, lifting wallets and purses at will.[13]

Business was all but suspended in town during the fair, but some activities did not stop. Gambling continued at Mah's place. The money Cohen made during the day at the fair along with what Mah gave him was proving a good investment in these popular evening games. Too popular. As Chinese and whites streamed in and out of the Alberta to take part in the action, the restaurant become the talk of the town, attracting unwanted police attention.

When the fair ended, Cohen went back to the streets of Saskatoon. Pity the meek. Ire Toder, a Viennese who worked as a railroad laborer, was one easy mark.

Several men cajoled and scammed him out of town during the late summer of 1910, convincing him that they were plainclothes mounted police and he was under arrest for gambling. The pseudo-cops took him by train and buggy to Prince Albert. Toder then returned to Saskatoon. Such a pigeon was hard to pass up. So on September 2, Cohen decided to have a go at him.

Cohen spotted Toder eating at Wilson's Café, a small luncheonette on Second Avenue that served "Meals at all hours. Oysters any style." They started chatting, and Cohen asked Toder if he needed a job. When Toder said yes, Cohen confided in him that his father owned a livery stable at Brandon and needed a good man. Toder admitted he had never worked in a livery stable, but said he would like to try. He finished eating and the two new chums walked around town, stopping along the way at J. F. Cairns's dry goods emporium so Toder could buy the overalls he needed for livery work. When Toder found a $1.25 pair that fit, he fished for the money from his black leather wallet. Cohen noticed he had more than fifty dollars on him. Leaving Cairns's they stopped at the Empire Hotel for a drink, and then strolled toward the new traffic bridge. As they walked Cohen reached in and deftly picked Toder's pocket.

Toder didn't even know what had happened. But when they separated Cohen couldn't wait to claim his money; from a distance Toder saw him rifle through the wallet and throw it into the street. Cohen then continued on his way, flush with his earnings, making plans for his hard-earned cash. At six that evening, Cohen was at Percy Woolhouse's jewelry store on Twenty-first Street when Toder walked in with Detective James. The officer arrested Cohen and found a hundred dollars on him. Cohen insisted the money was given to him by Mah. James knew Cohen all too well and tossed him in jail. When a few days later Chief Dunning handed Cohen a confession, he signed it, only to have second thoughts. Why give in so easy? He hired John Duncan Ferguson to defend him at the trial in Police Court on the sixth. There he simply denied all of Toder's charges. "No," he stated from the witness stand in his booming voice, he did not say his father owned a livery stable. "I told him I knew there was a job in a livery barn at Brandon, as I knew a man had quit there." He then adamantly denied he picked Toder's pocket, claiming that Toder helped him scam another stranger they met near the traffic bridge. As for the signed confession, well, Cohen only put his name to it because he thought it just meant he had to return the money and he would then be free.

Spectators filled the courtroom to hear Cohen's forceful and monosyllabic answers to all of Ferguson's questions. "You heard the story of complainant yesterday," said Ferguson. "What do you say as to that?"

"Lie."

"You heard the complainant state there was no third party. What about that?"

"Lie."

"He states further that after he missed his pocket book he saw you throw it into the road."

"Lie."

As the trial rushed along, the police contemplated issuing a warrant for Cohen's gang. At one point one of his comrades named Scott even glanced into the courtroom. What he saw did not look good, and he hightailed it for the Canadian National Railway station. When Dunning took the stand, Cohen became excited, and yelled "Liar!" whenever the chief said anything. He only calmed down when Magistrate Brown threatened to clap him back in his cell.

It was an open-and-shut case. The following day Brown sentenced Cohen to one year hard labor at Prince Albert, informing him that he "may consider himself leniently dealt with," since he hadn't received the fourteen-year maximum sentence. "When Cohen heard the sentence that was pronounced upon him he created a scene in the court and had to be forcibly taken to the cells," wrote the *Daily Phoenix*. The Royal North West Mounted Police shackled his feet, cuffed his wrists, and took him straightaway to Prince Albert, eighty miles to the north.

The police then went after Mah. Dunning pounced on September 14 when he learned there was a large gathering of Chinese and white gamblers dealing away through the night. It proved to be quite a raid. Detective James and other officers rounded up twenty-eight Chinese, three whites, and one black. Inside Mah's place they found money, opium, and liquor. "Two tables of cards were going, each having over $100 up for play," reported the *Daily Phoenix*. "Other dice games and six complete opium-smoking sets were in use and taken by the police. The filth and squalor of the dive could hardly be imagined, let alone described." When news spread of the arrests, hotel and restaurant owners rushed over to free their Chinese cooks. The police advised the whites and the black to leave town. Only Mah was denied bail. Ferguson returned to court, and Mah plead guilty. This time Brown did not just slap his wrist, but sentenced Mah to six months hard labor at Prince Albert and a hundred-dollar fine. If he didn't pay the hundred, he would then get an additional six months.[14]

When Cohen arrived at the forty-eight-cell provincial facility up the hill from the North Saskatchewan River, the staff shaved his head to prevent lice. After that he was thrown into a cell. Cohen's fellow inmates included lumberjacks, jockeys, bootblacks, hack drivers, and physicians who were in jail for such assorted crimes as attempted suicide, begging, attempted rape of a thirteen-year-old girl, giving liquor to Indians, exposing herself, and horse stealing. Both Jews and Chinese were looked down on in Prince Albert. While Mah had no choice but to list himself as a Buddhist, Cohen put himself down as Church of England. Every Sunday he had to attend compulsory services.[15]

At Prince Albert, as at the Winnipeg jail Cohen had lived in, prisoners were forbidden to talk. Even so, it probably wasn't all that quiet; during Cohen's stay more than twenty people were committed as insane, along with addicts going through the agonizing effects of withdrawal. Each morning Cohen and Mah donned their denim jackets and flannel clothes and went to the nearby 37.5-acre prison farm. The warden used tobacco as an incentive to get the prisoners to work, and there, as at Hayes, Cohen raised and harvested oats for use at the jail and for sale. In a small garden at the back of the building where the hanging scaffold stood, Cohen and the others raised potatoes, carrots, and cabbage. Those the warden thought might escape were shackled to a gravel-filled copper ball. Cohen and the others also built a large stable, granary, implement shed, and driving shed. During the winter they cut trees from the nearby forests for firewood and sliced ice blocks from the river. The women lived in a separate area, where the warden's wife watched over them. They cooked meals of potatoes, beets, porridge, turnips, and pork, washed the clothes, sewed, and made bedding, suits, shirts, and sacks.

In early November Mah appealed his conviction. When he lost, the authorities transferred him to the common jail at Moosomin. After that Cohen passed his time monotonously, rising early, doing his chores, possibly looking for a book in the prison library, being shut in for the night. At Prince Albert, inmates could be locked down in the punishment cells for long periods, and put on a diet of bread and water. During Cohen's stay, ten fellow inmates received dark cells and four inmates were deprived of light. Corporal punishment meant feeling the bite of a leather strap. Serious miscreants and those convicted of rape were lashed with a cat-o'-nine-tails when they arrived. At least three inmates died—by hanging, of heart failure, and of syphilis—while Cohen lived there. One prisoner even tried to escape. He used a knife to cut away the woodwork that was keeping the bars in place and filled the spaces with soap as he waited for an opportunity to make a dash for liberty. Jail keepers discovered his handiwork, and the unlucky inmate received three months hard labor.[16]

In September 1911, Cohen left the jail dressed in a suit stitched by one of the female prisoners. In his pocket he had a couple of dollars and a ticket to Saskatoon. Once back in town he hooked up with Mah. The two had lived through a good deal together, and Mah stepped up Cohen's casual indoctrination in the ways of Sun. These were heady times for the Chinese. While Cohen languished in jail Sun Yat-sen had arrived in Vancouver for the start of a triumphant North American tour. In mid-February 1911, the revolutionary made fiery, anti-Manchu speeches to thousands. The members of the Zhigongtang were so taken by his passion, they gave him money and presented him with a bodyguard named Xie Qiu to accompany him on his fund-raising trip. Sun headed east through British Columbia to Calgary, Winnipeg, Toronto, Montreal, and New York. Along the way, he won more followers with his promises of success. At this point, total world membership for the TMH might have reached 10,000.

As Sun raised money, a group of low-level subalterns and noncommissioned officers in Wuhan who were not aligned with Sun and his TMH were planning an uprising. A bomb they constructed accidentally exploded on October 9, 1911. The police started rounding up members, and the revolutionaries had no choice but to take action. They soon controlled the provincial capital at Wuchang. As the uprising spread it was coopted by an alliance of reformers like Sun, who decided to capitalize on the upheaval and left Denver for Europe to present himself as the head of the revolution. Meanwhile, the empire appointed one of its most able generals, Yuan

Shikai, Imperial Commissioner with the authority to crush the revolutionaries. Yet instead of snuffing out the discontent, he started to negotiate with the revolutionaries. In early December, delegates convened in Nanjing to establish a provisional republican government. There were two favorite contenders for president of the new government. Delegates could not compromise on a candidate, so they turned to Sun Yat-sen, who returned to Shanghai on December 25. Four days later the man who made ten attempts to spark revolution was elected provisional president of China. The republican alliance, though, was precarious, and to gain the support of Yuan, it was agreed that if the general threw in his support he could assume the presidency. On February 12 the child Xuantong Emperor abdicated. Sun then stepped down and Yuan became President.[17]

As the empire folded and a new government emerged, Chinese throughout Canada threw large celebrations. One evening Mah took Cohen to Calgary's new Chinatown to introduce him to other republican-leaning Chinese.

"That night we went to a grocery store in a back alley. There was nothing for the casual passer-by to see, but I noticed that there were men watching not only the door, but the street corners each side of it. Mah took me up the stairs; at the top there were more guards, but this bunch were armed and didn't bother to hide their rods . . . and after a while heavy double doors were thrown open and I found myself in the biggest room. . . . There must have been a couple of hundred Chinese there wearing their best suits and sitting silent and solemn. . . . The whole lot turned their heads as one man and stared at me. I stood there feeling kind of conspicuous while Mah took the floor and said his piece. I didn't understand Cantonese . . . but I could see that he was giving me a bit of a boost. When he'd finished there was some sort of a vote, and I was formally asked if I'd join the lodge."

Cohen took the oath. He was now a full member of the Tongmenghui, and one of the few whites in the organization. "I walked down those twisty, shabby stairs and out of that poor little grocery shop . . . pledged to devote my life to the service of Sun Yat-sen . . . and the liberation of the Chinese people."[18]

CHAPTER 8

LET THE BUYER BEWARE,
1911–1914

Cohen must have liked Calgary, for he decided to settle there. He was not the only one lured by the quick fortunes that could be made in this wide-open town. Cowboys tore down the main streets on their stallions. Opium and gambling dens flourished, as did questionable characters like Johnny Reid, who ran a bar while his wife conducted a brothel upstairs. One evening in 1911, Police Chief Thomas Mackie foolishly led a raid on the Reids' dual business. Inside Mackie and his officers stumbled on Mayor John W. Mitchell and two commissioners. The officials claimed they were just doing a late-night building inspection. Mackie did the only wise thing. He resigned.

But alas, the good times were not to last. The law-abiding citizens of Calgary brought in Alfred Cuddy, a stern ex-inspector from Toronto, and appointed him top cop. Armed with a mandate to make Calgary respectable, Cuddy declared war on vice. He upgraded and strengthened the force, organized raids on the red-light districts and cracked down on Chinese opium dens, pickpockets, and con men. The force also hired stool pigeons to snitch on those with Cohen's type of background. When a lead appeared, the ax-wielding Detective Inspector David Richardson then whacked his way into the dens of iniquity.[1]

How was a gambler to make a respectable living? Cohen and his fellow tinhorns realized they could not safely stay around. Luckily for him, during his various wanderings he had become chummy with a CPR dining-car attendant named Bert Finch. As Cohen contemplated his next move, he heard that Finch was making a decent living in Edmonton selling real estate. Edmonton would make as good a place as any to settle, so Cohen headed north and tracked down Finch. "There he was sitting in his own posh office with his name on the door as Manager of the local branch of the National Land Company," said Cohen. "He gave me a big hand and before I walked out again I was hired as a salesman."

Here at long last, on the banks of the North Saskatchewan, Morris Cohen found his calling. Boomtown real estate. What better way to combine his education as a pickpocket, carnival talker, con man, and gambler? All his grifting education at the best schools in London, Moose Jaw, Saskatoon, and Calgary would finally serve him well. Now he could legally and lavishly lift money from the pockets of unsuspecting rubes. Cohen got an apartment next door to Finch and settled into their office at 702 First Street. There he observed how Finch talked up customers: "I listened carefully to what Bert had to say, and soon learnt his line of spiel." Once Cohen knew all the right selling points, the buyer had better beware.

Edmonton was a boon for slick developers and brokers like Finch and Cohen. By the end of 1912 the city had 32 real estate brokers, 135 financial agents, and 336 real estate agents. The average Edmonton real estate office was a simple, stripped-down affair—a rolltop desk, a wooden counter, and blackboards listing "Specials Today." While one broker put a monkey in his window with a sign promising that there was no monkey business about the land he handled, most made outlandish claims, running newspaper ads that screamed, "Buy Immediately," "Rare Opportunity of a Life Time," and "Going Like Hot Cakes."

Edmonton swelled as those seeking their fortune streamed in. It was a city on the move, a prime player in the bull market prior to World War I. New industries, hotels, theaters, and businesses opened. Streetcars and automobiles rolled along paved streets, schools and churches rose, new train lines pulled in. Light and power plants and an automatic phone system wired the town. So many immigrants arrived that the city had to temporarily house some of them in school buildings as well as tents pitched alongside the river. When Edmonton and neighboring Strathcona merged in 1912, the population jumped from 31,064 to a staggering 53,611. Buildings popped up everywhere. "I can well remember when going to work in the morning hearing hammers pounding away on new buildings in every direction," recalled real estate agent John Niddrie.[2]

Canadian cities became intoxicated with the perception of growth as the West became a hot place for Canadian, American, and British investors to sink money. From 1900 to 1916 the population of the prairies quadrupled from 420,000 to 1,700,000. More than 600 new towns with populations of at least 600 were established. In 1911 Winnipeg predicted that within a decade its population would reach a million. Calgary, which in 1907 had formed a "Hundred Thousand Club," soon changed its name to the "Quarter Million Club."

Cohen could not have missed such a frenzy as he dealt cards in Saskatoon and Calgary or looked from his jail cells at Winnipeg and Prince Albert. In Edmonton downtown lots that sold for a mere $1,000 in 1900 went for as much as $200,000 in 1910. One 145-acre estate that cost $1,450 in 1898 reportedly sold in 1912 for $850,000. Salesmen made fortunes just on commissions, as barren twelve-hundred-lot subdivisions sold out in three days. Land purchased at noon for $1,800 sold by two for $2,000. People bought and sold on margin, as speculators became paper millionaires. When the Hudson's Bay Company decided to sell its 3,000-acre holdings in central Edmonton by lottery, 1,285 people formed a line before the official location of the lottery was announced. "Men came from every direction like a swarm of bees discovering an open honey hive and stuck to their places throughout the night, sitting on old chairs, nail kegs, inverted buckets, or anything else that would support their posteriors," wrote Niddrie.

For real estate agents the one and only thing required was to make a sale and get the cash. Cohen, a slouch felt cap firmly planted on his head, a loose suit hanging on his hefty frame, dragged customers down streets, unfolding maps as he went, sweet-talking his way to a deal. "There was good money to be made in city building lots at two hundred and fifty dollars a time," he said. "I often sold four lots in a day and once or twice I handled as many as twenty in a week; at ten per cent commission that made five hundred smackers for Morris." As he became more adept at reeling in customers he got Finch to let him sell lots on installment. "I had to see that the sucker—I mean the buyer—paid the rest when he said he would and till he ante'd up I only drew half my commission. But it worked well and I averaged three hundred dollars a week all the time." And if the sucker didn't make the second payment after realizing that a lot was not as great as advertised, all was not lost for Cohen. The purchaser simply forfeited the land. Cohen then sold it to the next rube who wandered through the National Land Company's door.

So much land changed hands so easily and so quickly in Edmonton, that sometimes all a broker need do was take a dollar option for a lot and then transfer the option to the buyer for one hundred dollars. Land sharks—"smooth-tongued, unscrupulous, land-selling parasites"—waded toward the smell of money intent on the kill. "In the doorway of each lounges a thin-chested, much-spitting youth, with a flabby face, shifty eyes, and an inhuman mouth, who invites you continually, with the most raucous of American accents, to 'step inside and examine our Praposition,' " noted Rupert Brooke.

Many lots lay in suburban subdivisions, barren land sold sight unseen from maps hanging on paneled office walls. Agents sold land that lay underwater part of the year, were situated miles from the closest sewer connection, and lacked roadways and shade trees. They also palmed off lots that were smaller than claimed. "And yet the plain unvarnished truth may be that the beautiful suburban park is a dreary, desolate bit of prairie," noted the Edmonton *Journal*, "without even a single wooden shack in sight, uncrossed by so much as a trail, and far from any probable highway and with miles of empty space between it and the edge of the city."[3]

Firms hung attractive and misleading paintings of subdivisions in their windows. When a passerby stopped to admire the picture, an agent—a "capper"—invited him to drive out and see the land. The broker would race to the land, thus making the distance from town appear shorter. "If a prospective buyer appears skeptical, a 'capper' is taken along, posing as a buyer, who also is accompanying the agent to the property," wrote *Saturday Night* of one fail-safe selling technique. "He sits in the rear seat of the car with the man who has the money to invest, while a representative of the company accompanies them as a guide. When the auto arrives at the property the 'capper' assumes the role of a disinterested person, who has seen real estate propositions in every town in the west, but has never seen any to equal this particular one. He finally selects two or three lots for himself, although he declares he did not intend to buy when he started from the office, and with this example before him the investor is convinced that the property must be a safe deal."

Some real estate outfits set up offices in Europe, where they peddled third-rate land as prime property. The National Land Company boasted a headquarters in Calgary, had offices in Detroit, Toronto, and Winnipeg, and sold lots in places like Tofield, Athabasca, Leduc, and Camrose, Alberta. The company did booming business in Cohen's old town of Saskatoon—"The future Metropolis of the Northwest"—where they successfully competed against the city's other 260-odd real estate firms. National Land had plenty of lots to unload around the planned Grand Trunk Pacific railway depot. Cohen wisely looked in on his Chinese brothers, and brought in record business for the firm: "If any Chinese in the West thought of a deal in real estate, he'd come and consult me about it." One of the country's wealthiest Chinese eagerly snapped up the twenty-four Saskatoon lots Cohen offered him in April 1912.

Soon after Cohen started work, National Land president Stanley Shepard arrived from Calgary to open an office at 827 ½ First Street in order to cope with the added business. He announced in the Edmonton *Capital* that their star seller, "Mr. A. Cohen," had been "placed in charge" of the new outlet. Cohen was a comer on a steep upward trajectory. His sales motto was "High, dry, level and a good building lot," and he now commanded a two-hundred-dollar-a-month salary and 12.5 percent commission on sales. "I put in a big, solid safe to hold the cash, and I recruited ten salesmen," he recounted. "They were all sorts, shapes and sizes. . . . Some of them I'd known as rounders and I was scared they might try to dodge vagrancy charges by working for me as an alibi and go back to their old games again." Knowing firsthand all their possible ploys, Cohen laid down the rules and told his salesmen that if they wanted to stay they had to work: "If you can't sell a coupla lots a day, I just don't want you around." Lots, subdivisions, and farms started to fly off the rolltop. Cohen made so much money—up to $1,000 a week—he couldn't spend it fast enough. Pretty soon he claimed to have amassed $20,000, and sunk some of his cash into a diamond ring for his finger.[4]

Yet even with all his real estate duties, he always made time for one extracurricular nocturnal activity: gambling. On May 31, 1912, Cohen, Morris Salway, Arthur Gouchie, Spence Murray, and John Chenowith were having a pleasant game of poker upstairs at Fred J. Caron's gambling house. The police had been keeping an eye on Caron's for some time. That evening they decided to visit the den at Jasper and Namayo Avenue. Inspectors John Wright and James Campbell, and Detectives John J. Burbeck, Ernest Seymour, and Leonard Lang tapped at the front door. Thinking the plainclothes detectives were additional cardplayers eager for some action, the doorkeeper threw open the entrance. The officers strolled in and looked over the extensive gambling setup. "Not until they were right at the table where the cards and the money were, did those in the room tumble to the fact that police officers were amongst them," noted the *Daily Bulletin*. Magistrate Myers fined Cohen and the other players twenty-five dollars each, while Caron was slapped with a hundred-dollar fine. They were all "given notice that Edmonton did not require their presence."[5]

The gamblers scoffed at the request. If one game folded, another always popped up elsewhere in town. On March 15, 1913, the police made their largest arrest to date when they interrupted sixty people—twenty-eight of whom were Chinese—playing fan-tan, stud poker, and other assorted games in the heart of Chinatown. It "was a red-letter day at the city police station," reported the *Daily Bulletin*. "Never before have so many arrests been made within the space of twenty four hours as on Saturday and Sunday night."

The police kept a special eye on Cohen's Asian brothers. In 1908 and 1909, about fifteen hundred Chinese arrived in Canada, and from 1910 to 1911 4,515 entered the realm. By 1911, 27,774 Chinese lived in Canada; 1,787 Chinese lived in Alberta, and 154 in Edmonton. Only four of the Chinese in Edmonton were female. The Chinese centered on Ninety-seventh Street and 102nd Avenue, making a living as most others, cooking, washing, working in hotels, and growing vegetables. The press catered to its readers' prejudices and fears by reporting all Chinese arrests and indiscretions, along with fanciful tales of opium, leprosy, smallpox, and diabolism.[6]

With their increased presence, the provinces started further restricting the Chinese. Fewer than a thousand Chinese lived in all of Saskatchewan, yet around the time Cohen became involved with them the province revised its Election Act and took the franchise in provincial elections away from them. In 1912 Saskatchewan prohibited Chinese owners or managers of laundries, restaurants, and other businesses from hiring white women. In 1914 the Ontario legislature followed suit.

After he arrived in Edmonton, Cohen started hanging out in the local chop suey joints, and acted as an advocate for the Chinese. When the police in August 1912 charged one of his chums, May Gee, with gambling, Cohen contacted the press in his defense. At this point the Tongmenghui was reorganized as the Guomindang (GMD). Soon local branches of the GMD—called the Chinese Nationalist League—appeared in all major and minor Chinese settlements in British Columbia and Alberta along with some out east. Cohen regularly attended league meetings, and gave fifty to a hundred dollars at a pop to various funds. Cohen also became a clearinghouse for information. The Edmonton press, which regularly wrote up events in China, didn't quite know what to make of this Cockney Jew best known for his gambling and real estate deals. They sought out his thoughts on China, and rightly noted that "Mr. Cohen is in close touch with Chinese affairs here and knows the men of the orient probably better than any man in Edmonton or in western Canada." They also started spinning fabulous tales relating to his background. Most were obviously encouraged by Cohen. One paper reported that he was "a highly intelligent American with a long residence in China, who speaks fluent Cantonese and is a mason of high degree. . . ."

Things were not going well for Sun Yat-sen once he stepped down from the presidency in favor of Yuan. While the GMD had captured a majority of seats in the National Assembly, Yuan used autocratic means to thwart nationalism and democracy, consolidate his power, and crush his opponents. He was even assumed responsible for the assassination of Song Jiaoren, the chief organizer of the GMD, in March 1913. The opposition organized a revolt, but the Second Revolution failed and Sun fled to Japan. Yuan soon outlawed the GMD, dissolved parliament, and started to reestablish the monarchy with himself as emperor.[7]

Besides spreading the word on Sun, Cohen had much to keep him occupied on the China front. Sun needed trained soldiers, and dispatched followers to Canada to organize squads of overseas Chinese. Brigades formed in Vancouver, Saskatoon, Lethbridge, and Victoria. The military society organized in Edmonton trained men, and one of Cohen's National League friends, Ma Xiang, a Guangdong native whose father, Ma Houshu, was a Vancouver triad leader, helped sign up five hundred men for indoctrination and training before they were to travel to China. Cohen pitched in with the drilling of the men. "Here I found my military training at Hayes, elementary though it may have been, came in handy. I might not know much about soldiering, but I knew more than any other guy on the ground," he boasted.

Having sway with Chinese in town, Cohen made his presence known in political circles. He became friendly with Charles W. Cross, a member of the Liberal Party and the province's first attorney general. On Cross's recommendation, Cohen with a slew of others was appointed on April 23, 1913, a Commissioner to Administer Oaths. He then helped Chinese get naturalized.[8]

In 1913 the National Land Company wanted to move tracts of fruit land in British Columbia's Okanagan Valley. Cohen saw the orchard land as a good investment and even snapped up some himself. The firm had an office in Brussels, and in June Shepard approached Cohen and asked if he wanted to go to Belgium to sell some crop land there. "I needed no time to think that over. The one idea in my head was that I hadn't seen my family . . . and now was my chance." Cohen contacted the press and announced that he was off to England to manage the firm's new Manchester business, augmenting their supposed recently opened offices in London, Paris, Brussels, and "other continental centres." He then rushed back to his new apartment on Sixth Street. "I packed my bags the next day, turned over the office and off I went."[9]

Cohen's trip home was much different from his departure in 1905. Back then he left town in disgrace, dressed in a donated set of clothes with five sovereigns in his pocket. Now the prodigal child returned much changed. He was fashionably turned out, weighed nearly two hundred pounds, and carried a $10,000 letter of credit. Cohen made his way in the rain unannounced to Umberston Street. When he showed up his mother, Sheindel—who now went by the more Anglo-sounding name Jane—cried.

The family was proud of how Cohen looked and of the success he told them of. Having had little as a child, Cohen now wanted those he knew to have things, and reveled in distributing presents to children. "He gave me my first toy," said his sister Sarah Rich. "My younger brother he gave a bicycle, and I had a doll." Josef wanted to show his son off, and asked him to come to Saturday services at the Cannon Street Road Synagogue and read from the Torah. Cohen agreed. Not having spent time in or anywhere near a synagogue during his time in Canada, he was quite out of practice when it came to praying. Cohen also had found little chance to use the Yiddish spoken at home or the Hebrew he learned at the Jews' Free School and at Hayes. Worse yet, Cannon Street Road, which Josef joined at the turn of the century and where he was now a *Gabbai,* was renowned for its cantor, choir, and school. All critical ears would be tuned to this dandyish visitor from the New World. "When I thought of all that, I regretted my promise. I didn't know the words and I didn't know how to say them and I just couldn't see myself doing such a thing." But Cohen had blustered his way through before. He asked a cousin to come to the Strand Palace Hotel and teach him how to say the prayers. He practiced in front of the large mirror in his room and got the gestures and intonations just right. When Saturday came he accompanied his frock-coat-and-top-hatted father to services. "I stood up and declaimed as if I was still in the Shakespeare Class at Hayes—and they weren't used to it. Anyway my father was happy."

Cohen renewed old friendships and made an outing to his alma mater. Israel Ellis still ran the school, and Cohen asked his former headmaster to let him do as Lord Rothschild and others once did for him. Here at Hayes the former truant was now the patron. It was a role he coveted, and Cohen took a group of boys to the King's Theatre, Hammersmith, for an afternoon of entertainment. Afterward he treated them to tea and treats. Back at home, this former black sheep turned into the family's guardian angel. With his newfound wealth he moved the family out of their St. George's in the East hovel east to Tredegar Square, a prosperous early-nineteenth-century Georgian square. And even if the area had declined somewhat and now contained a few home factories, this tonier part of the East End with its brick and stucco exteriors, ironwork, central park, lawns, and chirping birds was leagues from Umberston Street. There the Cohens settled into No. 7 on the southeast corner of the park, a stooped row house with internal shutters, two fireplaces per floor, a delicate curving staircase, and white molding. A number of trees grew in the narrow garden out back. Quite a change. His parents *kvelled.*[10]

Cohen continued on his way to the Continent, fooled around with the ladies, and charmed and conned the Belgians to buy orchard land. He soon returned to Edmonton, a city gripped by the jitters. Though the boom continued, not all was stable. The Canadian economy showed signs of weakening. Credit was tight. Interest rates were high. Real estate started to slow. Prominent real estate men nervously gathered at one of Cohen's hangouts, the Lewis' Cafe, to try and stabilize the industry by forming a real estate exchange.

During 1913 the value of Edmonton building permits issued was two-thirds that of the previous year. Continued immigration only made the employment problem tighter. At the end of harvest and during the winter stoppage of railway construction, hundreds of men drifted into the city. Edmonton started to have a noticeable amount of "idle men." In May Edmonton officials discussed having Boy Scouts plant flower and vegetable gardens in vacant lots so the stagnant construction field would not show. The city tried to be upbeat; people were told that belt tightening was good and the lull would quickly pass. "Further, it has done an extremely good turn in driving the majority of the 'wildcatters' of a year or two ago from the field," noted the *Bulletin*, "leaving in the end an even better field than before for legitimate lines of business."[11]

Business had to be drummed up at the National Land Company. Soon after Cohen returned from England he headed out to the coal-mining town of Fernie, B.C. to see if he could unload some lots in the new College Heights section of Moose Jaw, Sask. He made his way along the telegraph pole–lined streets of this "Pittsburgh of Canada," passed the new stone and brick buildings, the eight to nine hotels and assorted boardinghouses that held a polyglot community of Italians, Poles, and Russians along with Blanche Duboise, Mamie LaRush, and the other girls from the local cathouses. He headed right to the Chinese section, and started pitching land to the market gardeners and launderers. Land in Moose Jaw, Cohen told the Chinese, was hot. The College Heights subdivision, he said, was a sure buy that would only increase in value. They couldn't do better. On July 7 and 8 he visited Huang Liang at his laundry, talked him up, told him of his Chinese contacts, and assured him that "the street cars went past" the bargain land he offered. Cohen did such a good job that the poor launderer parted with fifty dollars. He soon went into Kowong Wing's store on Victoria Avenue. There he met Huang along with Zhu Kuan and Wong Lally. He turned on the charm once again. "Cohen was trying to sell me some lots in College Heights, Moose Jaw," recalled Zhu. "He told me [that] Moose Jaw College Heights was a mile and three quarters from the Moose Jaw post office. He said the street cars came in to College Heights and through my property. After he told me that I gave him money. I gave him $62.50. He gave me a receipt. . . . I bought the property because I believed what he said. He said he had been in Moose Jaw."

Even with Cohen's seemingly impeccable contacts, Zhu decided to ask the Fernie Board of Trade if they could find out more on his new dream acreage. The board cabled Moose Jaw, which responded that College Heights lay three to four miles from the station, had a "beautiful wheat crop growing on same. Farm house only building in sight. No prospects of a water system for the next twenty years." So much for fraternal loyalty. Zhu went right to the police and had Cohen arrested. "I started this case because I found the property no good . . . I feel very sore," he said. The police charged Cohen with false pretenses, and the judge allowed him free on bond. Courts generally decided cases of whites versus Chinese in the white's favor. Despite the fact that Cohen blatantly lied to Zhu, the court discharged him.[12]

Fleeing from Fernie, Cohen headed back to Edmonton, and with the lull in business he desperately needed other ways to make money. He and a number of his friends—Arnold Abrams, Myer Shapiro, Bert Finch, Percy D. Watt, A. Viner, and M. Louer—had an ingenious idea. Club charters were hard to come by, so why not start a social club and sell the license to the highest bidder? It seemed simple enough. To do the deal, Cohen retained the services of George W. Massie, a local lawyer and an acting police magistrate. Massie drew up a charter for the Eastern Club and shepherded it through the Alberta Legislature, which approved the charter on October 25. Cohen and his friends could now start a club and borrow up to $15,000 to buy a site and construct the building. So eager were they to sell the charter, they never completed the club organization, nor did they even apply for the available liquor license. Cohen soon started spreading the word that interested parties could have the charter and a liquor license for $3,000.[13]

As Cohen tried to unload the license, more trouble awaited him. Concerned by the idleness on the streets, the police started to clear the town of confidence men. Each week they escorted about six such questionable characters to the train depot; the accompanying officers waited while the men bought their tickets, and watched to make sure they stayed on the train when it pulled out. As Cohen's lengthening criminal record and shenanigans became better known to the police, he joined their list of tough characters to watch. On Saturday evening, November 15, Cohen was lounging outside the Lewis' Cafe. Detectives W. B. McIvor and C. P. Kroning were there, too, watching him. Cohen did not like their attentions. He felt they were staring too hard. At one point McIvor told him to move along. Cohen walked up to the two men and started arguing with them. He angrily waved his hands up and down and bluntly asked why they were bothering him. Why were they staring at him? When McIvor started to answer, Cohen struck the policeman over the head, knocking him to the ground. Kroning grabbed Cohen and put him under arrest. On the twentieth a judge convicted him of assault and fined him fifty dollars and costs.

Fortunately, Cohen could claim a real job, and the police didn't ship him out of town. Earning an honest living, though, was becoming more difficult. The boom ended, and like other real estate firms, the National Land Company had trouble moving lots. Commercial and residential buildings stood empty. Tax revenues fell. The city's tax arrears rose. The government started public projects, putting the unemployed to work paving and grading streets and sidewalks.[14]

Having worked on a farm and in a circus, manual labor did not appeal to Cohen as a way to make some cash. He continued flogging the Eastern Club charter. When Louis Christensen and I. Tunberg heard that Cohen had a charter to sell, the two men went to see him at the Queen's Hotel on Jasper Avenue East, where Cohen basked in dollar-a-day splendor with steam heat, electric lights, and baths. Christensen and Tunberg met him in the lobby. Cohen offered the charter for $3,000. They said that was more than they could afford for their planned Scandinavian Club, and finally negotiated the price down to $2,500. On January 9, 1914, they went to Massie's office and paid a $500 deposit. Other payments followed. Massie soon told them that Attorney General Cross had approved the deal. In mid-January, Massie transferred control and possession of the club to the two men. Christensen subsequently presented checks for the balance to Massie as well as an additional $400 for a six-month liquor license, which Massie assured them he could get. The men then waited for Cross to transfer the liquor license.[15]

News of the unusual license offering and sale made it around town. On February 23, Joseph Burgess, a reporter from the *Daily Bulletin,* went to see Cohen at the Queen's Hotel. There he told Cohen he was a "wealthy Calgary capitalist" who was interested in buying the license.

"Mr. Cohen, who has his headquarters at the Queen's Hotel, was in the rotunda when the *Bulletin* reporter called early yesterday evening," wrote Burgess of their meeting.

"That's him," said the bell-boy, in answer to an inquiry, pointing to [a] short, dark, thick-set man who was on the point of going out for a walk.

Could Mr. Cohen spare a few minutes for a private conversation? Yes Mr. Cohen could. He led the way upstairs, and wended his way to a writing table on the landing. "What can I do for you?" he asked, pleasantly enough, as he pointed out a chair for the visitor, and also seated himself near the table.

"I understand," remarked the visitor, after the usual conversational formalities had been complied with, "that you have a club license for sale."

Mr. Cohen directed an intent gaze at the questioner for a moment, and then nodded his head.

"Well, that subtleties matters, let's understand one another. I represent a number of Calgary capitalists who wish to obtain a club license and operate a club in Edmonton. From all accounts it will be pretty difficult to get a new charter owing to the opposition that has been displayed to the clubs lately. Are you willing to dispose of your interests in the license you now hold?"

Mr. Cohen thought a little while. His brows were puckered and he was evidently racking his brains in an endeavor to find out exactly what to do and what answer to make.

After a while he said, "Here's the trouble. I don't know you. I don't think I would care to make a statement unless I were absolutely sure of your identity. This is, as you know, a very ticklish matter."

"Well," replied the visitor, "I cannot disclose the names of my principals until I communicate with them. They want a club license, but they do not intend to pay through the nose for it. If you will set a figure I will let them know the amount and then, if they are agreeable, and they accept the offer, I will tell you who they are. Is that satisfactory?"

Mr. Cohen said it was. "Upon that understanding," he continued, "we will discuss the matter at length. I hold a club license for a club which was incorporated by the provincial legislature, and I am in position to sell it. Certain parties have been after it, and I have received a deposit from them, but that can be called off if I can make suitable arrangements with you."

A Cohen family wedding celebration from the 1890s. Morris is in the bottom row, second from the right. (COLLECTION OF VICTOR D. COOPER)

Israel Ellis and his wards at the Hayes Industrial School in 1902. (COLLECTION OF HARRY COHEN)

The successful boomtown real-estate broker stands for a portrait. (COLLECTION OF VICTOR D. COOPER)

Acting Sergeant Cohen *(middle)* and his comrades. (COLLECTION OF VICTOR D. COOPER)

BELOW: The sergeants of the 218th Overseas Battalion, known as the Edmonton Irish Guards, before they ship off to fight the Germans and build railway tracks in Belgium. (CITY OF EDMONTON ARCHIVES)

Benjamin Cohen after World War I. (COLLECTION OF VICTOR D. COOPER)

In August 1923, after months of work, Harry Abbott, Guy Colwell, and Arthur "Pop" Wilde complete the *Rosamond*. Sun Yat-sen, Cohen, and members of Sun's entourage pose with the builders at the christening. (COLLECTION OF DAN-SAN ABBOTT)

Cohen and others in a detail from a July 1, 1926, photograph of the festivities celebrating the first anniversary of the founding of the Nationalist Government. (COLLECTION OF JOSEF L. RICH)

Liao Zhongkai, Chiang Kai-shek, Sun Yat-sen, and Soong Qingling preside over the June 1924 dedication of the Whampoa Military Academy. Cohen looms at right. (COLLECTION OF JOSEF L. RICH)

Sarah Rich's passport photo, taken right before her trip to the Continent with her brother in 1928. (COLLECTION OF JOSEF L. RICH)

Jane and Josef Cohen always looked forward to their son's visits home. (COLLECTION OF VIC-
TOR D. COOPER)

Cohen and Judith after taking their vows on June 18, 1944, at Temple Emanu-el in Montreal.
(COLLECTION OF JOSEF L. RICH)

General Cohen. (COLLEC-
TION OF JOSEF L. RICH)

Judith Cohen. (COLLEC-
TION OF VICTOR D.
COOPER)

Leslie Cohen. (COLLECTION
OF VICTOR D. COOPER)

Cohen kept in touch with many of the people he worked with during his time with Sun Yat-
sen. After the war he visited with Ma Xiang. (COLLECTION OF VICTOR D. COOPER)

Cohen laying a wreath at Sun Yat-sen's tomb in Nanking. (COLLECTION OF VICTOR D. COOPER)

Cohen and Chiang Kai-shek at one of Cohen's few audiences in Taiwan. (COLLECTION OF
VICTOR D. COOPER)

Cohen and Soong Qingling in the 1950s. (COLLECTION OF VICTOR D. COOPER)

Cohen with a Chinese delegation at a Rolls-Royce plant during negotiations to buy British planes and engines. (COLLECTION OF VICTOR D. COOPER)

After Cohen decided to side with the mainland, the communists gave him exceptional, though limited, access to the powerful. (COLLECTION OF VICTOR D. COOPER)

"But," demurred the visitor, "if you have received a deposit how can you do business with me?"

"Oh," ejaculated Mr. Cohen, "it hasn't gone so far as that. I simply gave them my word of honor, but I can call the deal off easily enough."

"You are quite sure there won't be any legal complications?"

"No," returned the vendor, "you can rest easily on that score. If you decide to purchase the license you can take the money to a firm of lawyers and place it in escrow and then when the license is absolutely transferred to your name they can pay the money over to me. There will be no difficulty at all about that."

"But how do I know—what assurances have I got—that the license will be transferred?" was the next objection. "There may be some hitch about it. I do not want to go to the trouble of expensive legal negotiations and then find the affair result in nothing after all."

"Don't you worry," returned Mr. Cohen. "I can absolutely promise you that the license will be transferred. . . . If Mr. Cross had been in the city this other deal would have gone through before this. He is the only one we are waiting for."

"What consideration," asked the visitor, "do you require for the license?"

"Three thousand dollars," said Mr. Cohen, "and it must be in cash."

"You will get the transfer all right," he said repeatedly; "don't worry about that."

As Cohen showed the reporter out he reminded him: "Don't forget to let me know if the price is right."

At eight that same evening Burgess, still in the guise of a "Calgary capitalist," approached Christensen. He found him perched on a high stool at the Odin Cafe on First Street, chatting with a bunch of friends.

Christensen was not inclined to talk, but when Burgess mentioned the name Cohen "he pricked up his ears, moved slightly forward in his chair and was all attention." Burgess said he heard that Christensen was not going through with the deal and that Cohen offered the license to him for $3,000. Christensen quickly proclaimed: "No chance. I have paid over the money, and everything is now in readiness for the opening of the club. Didn't he tell you I had paid the money?" Feigning ignorance, Burgess replied that he had heard that he merely paid a deposit. Christensen got annoyed and retorted: "Well, the deal has gone through. All we are waiting for is the transfer of the license. I only wish Mr. Cross would come back. His absence is holding things up. I have been telephoning to the department for several days, but he doesn't seem to be back yet. There is one good thing, he cannot stay away forever."

Burgess continued trying to ferret out the tale, and went to see the license inspector, Edward H. Garrison, who denied ever meeting with Christensen. Little else was heard of the deal. Christensen regularly called Massie and Cross to see what was up. Both repeatedly assured him that the transfer would happen any day. Any day.

The recession worsened. By mid-February, Edmonton contained a reported 4,000 unemployed, many living in tents. Cohen turned his attention to the next deal. When high-grade oil was discovered in May in Calgary many citizens rushed off to try to get a slice of the money; forty new oil companies were floated in a week, and scores of oil offices opened in Edmonton.[16]

Even as most businesses in the city weakened, a few stayed strong—too strong for local officials. In mid-month, Police Commissioner Manville S. Booth sent a memo to Police Chief Alfred C. Lancey saying, "Please take this as positive orders that every house of prostitution on First Street and Jasper Avenue must be closed forthwith. There are over twenty-three such houses to my knowledge on these streets, and if your detectives don't know where they are, fire them and get some who can see past the end of their noses." That night two houses were raided. The police also planned to attack gambling dens.

Meanwhile, Cohen could still count on his nimble fingers to draw full houses and straight flushes. On the morning of May 17 he took part in a bit of gambling with hundreds of his closest friends on First Street. "Race horse men, restaurant keepers, hotel clerks, touts, bartenders, railway employees, barbers, and representative citizens of all classes were there, as well as the wastrels from below the deadline," reported the *Bulletin*. The den had been going since the fourteenth, run by Cohen's friend Fred Caron, with whom he had been arrested in 1912. "The stuffy little quarters into which almost 250 men were packed like sardines in a can resembled an honest-to-goodness gambling joint in Reno, Goldfield or Dawson in the palmy days when gold dust was more plentiful than at present in Edmonton," reported the *Journal*. Smoke choked the room as men pushed against the roulette wheel, faro bank, blackjack, and craps table. "In one room could be heard the droning notes of the croupier's voice as he called the numbers, the colors, and the even and the odd, the while the little ivory ball fell into its chosen place on the roulette wheel," reported the *Bulletin*.

Passing to the next room, one might have heard the rattle of silver dollars and the strident voice of the man making his point at the crap table. A visit to a third room would have revealed a big faro bank game in progress, with the more subdued sound of the slow shuffling of checks, and the soft click as the case keeper moved over the little tell-tale discs that told of the fall of the cards. In a fourth room King Black Jack had gathered his devotees, the sigh of a disappointed loser and the jubilant cry of an elated winner adding their picturesque touches to the revelry of the night.

Suddenly . . . some strange men moved stealthily into the room. The roulette wheel was coming to a stop, the little ivory ball was rattling from compartment to compartment, when a hand shot out over the table and grabbed the chips and cash.

A hush fell across the room. The gamblers froze, knowing that sure enough a "pinch" was about to be made. There stood Inspector Burbeck and Detectives Seymour and Robert Unruh. One of the gamblers made a move, and others followed. Players escaped by jumping or dangling out the windows by bedsheets. Most did not make it far.

The police knew a few of those taken. Cohen was a definite regular. The group included Montana gamblers who made Edmonton their headquarters, conveniently changing their names each time the police caught them. Oddly, the police did not back the patrol wagon against the front door and load up the mass of people as was the custom when raiding gambling joints and whorehouses. They simply kept the bettors there for more than an hour, wrote down their names—mostly aliases—and confiscated their booty. The police left behind the gambling equipment and paraphernalia. By two-thirty they had gone, and at three the games were in full swing again.

Many did not show up for their arraignment, but Cohen had too much at stake in Edmonton and so made an appearance with numerous others. Caron's solicitor, Henry A. Mackie, "entered a plea of leniency on the grounds that most of the men were visitors to the city in Edmonton for the purpose of encouraging horseracing. They were not local men and so were not a sore on Edmonton society. They merely gathered there to do what is sanctioned in other quarters. They were quiet at their game. They tried to conceal nothing. The doors were open and anyone could walk in. They were not attempting to deceive anyone." Magistrate Massie refused to accept Mackie's argument. Cohen paid his friend and judge the ten-dollar fine and the dollar-fifty costs and left the court.[17]

The arrest had no effect on gambling. When the police raided one place, the gamblers simply moved to a different address and were running again "full blast until the small hours . . . without interference from the police," reported the *Journal*. Despite Commissioner Booth's wishes, prostitutes openly continued soliciting. Newspapers started reporting payoffs by cathouses in exchange for protection. Police were also accused of soliciting other forms of payoffs from the women. The *Bulletin* proclaimed in banner headlines: "Carnival of Vice; Police Are Apparently Inactive" and "1,500 Disorderly Women Have Shamelessly Disregarded Laws of Decency. With 200 Resorts Running Full Blast—Young Girls Under Legal Age Victims of Traffic."

"For weeks and months," the article reported, "the lid has been off and the city has been wide open. Gambling resorts and confidence games, conducted by some of the worst crooks that have ever been outside the gates of a penitentiary, have been carried on at full blast. Houses of prostitution, already in marked evidence, increased so enormously in number that it is estimated by those who have made a thorough investigation of conditions that at least one hundred of these sink holes of

iniquity have hung out their shingles in all quarters of the city." Two to three
hundred "moral lepers, without other means of support have lived on the earnings
of the unfortunate women and girls. . . . In the face of this remarkable state of affairs,
the police department has apparently been inactive."

Reporters roamed the streets, coming back with tales of being accosted twenty-
five times by prostitutes in fifteen minutes. The papers told how patrolmen had seen
and ignored "houses of prostitution in full blast on their beats, with automobiles
constantly driving up, and discharging and taking up an endless stream of men and
women." Ladies of the evening "have sat close to the front windows of their houses,
and made open solicitation. Colored women have roamed the east end on the look-
out for men under the influence of liquor, whom they have made a practice of
rolling." To make matters worse, customers walked into the wrong "houses" and
harassed respectable Edmontonians. All this waywardness was too much of an embarrassment for the city, and Commissioner Booth on the twenty-fourth sent an
even terser note to Chief Lancey demanding his resignation. Lancey complied.[18]

The police had to crack down hard on all the miscreants. On July 1 Chief
Detective Kroning and Detective R. L. Fryant arrested Cohen. The officers charged
him with vagrancy, since he was deemed a gambler and an undesirable character.
They told him they wanted him out of town. Then Christensen tired of waiting for
his club license, and accused Cohen of obtaining money from him under false pretense with intent to defraud. The police grabbed Cohen again. Not being able to
raise the steep $6,000 bail, he languished in jail.

The case first went to a preliminary hearing, where his attorney stated that
Cohen never promised Christensen a liquor license. As the hearing progressed, the
case took on political overtones. The *Bulletin* claimed Massie unduly used his influence as a magistrate in Cohen's favor. The *Daily Capital* then countered that the
Bulletin was intentionally trying to frame Massie, who was only acting as a lawyer
for Cohen. "This money was received by Mr. Massie in the usual way as attorney
for Cohen and turned over to him. Subsequently a clerk in Mr. Massie's law office
received the balance of the purchase price agreed upon between Christensen and
Cohen and this also was turned over to Cohen in the usual way."

The trial before Magistrate George F. Downes in the South Side police court
made the front page every day. Christensen swore that Massie delayed giving him
the charter for three months. He said he originally understood that the $2,500 price
included the liquor license, but when Massie demanded an additional $400 he paid
it because "he did not know any better." Then in the midst of the trial it was revealed
that reporter Burgess had in 1912 acted as a stool pigeon, giving the police evidence
on prostitutes for planned raids in the East End of the city. At the time he also
blackmailed a prostitute by demanding twenty-five dollars in return for withholding
evidence. For the latter offense he served two days in jail.

As for Massie, he swore he had only acted as Cohen's solicitor, nothing more.
He denied he ever told Christensen or Tunberg that he had or could get them a
liquor license. All he claimed to have done was to try his best to obtain one: "I told

him I did not know whether he could get one or not, but that I would do the best I could. . . . Mr. Cohen was the promoter, and I was acting as his solicitor. . . . I never knew of Christensen paying money to Cohen, but heard of it afterwards. I was not consulted. To my knowledge he paid it deliberately."

At the preliminary hearings, Downes sent Cohen up for trial. The magistrate set bail at $1,000; four of Cohen's wealthy Chinese friends and clients paid the amount. "When the magistrate saw the bondsmen approach, he said: 'Are these Chinamen worth $1,000?' " reported the *Journal*.

" 'Me worth $75,000,' spoke up one, and another said he was good for half the amount. When it came to Pon Yen's turn he said: 'Me got property in Edmonton, Calgary, Victoria, Vancouver, Saskatoon and I can't remember the other places.' "

The case never went to trial.[19]

CHAPTER 9

THE GREAT WAR,
1914–1918

A s the economy continued to decline, Canadians had trouble finding work. "We were heading
into another depression in 1914," recalled Mark Tanner of Toronto of the growing
economic malaise. "I was working on the railroad then, and I'd see the lineups every
morning in the freight sheds of the Grand Trunk and the C.P.R. . . . Men were
looking for jobs at one dollar a day, to load freight cars and trucks with goods that
were in the freight sheds. The lineups were getting bigger and bigger."

Cohen's prospects appeared bleak. Land sales came to a halt, and the National
Land Company was in bad financial straits. So when Gavrilo Princip shot Archduke
Franz Ferdinand and his wife, Countess Sophie Chotek, in Sarajevo on June 28,
1914, his actions could not have come at a better time for Cohen and the rest of
Canada's unemployed. Over the next few weeks the great powers of Europe fumbled
and tumbled toward World War I. When news arrived that Britain had declared
war on Germany, 10,000 citizens marched down the streets of Edmonton. They
waved British Union Jacks and French tricolors. Bands played "La Marseillaise" and
"Rule, Britannia." "French and Russian marched side by side, and hand in hand
cheered and cheered again their national songs," reported the Edmonton *Journal*.
Traffic stopped and men stood on the roofs of automobiles and streetcars to watch
the procession and listen to the speeches that promised a glorious victory by Christmas. "All the upper windows of property along the route were filled with women,
who clapped their hands, waved their handkerchiefs, cheered and some were almost
hysterical as the patriotic cries and cheers reached their ears. . . ."

Neither Canada nor the rest of the British Commonwealth were prepared for
the hostilities. Nor did they realize that after some initial movement, the opposing
armies would be bogged down for four years in trenches that meandered from Switzerland to the Atlantic. At the start of the war, Canada had about 1.5 million men
of military age, yet the country had a regular army of a mere 3,110 soldiers and 684

horses. The navy could only claim 300 sailors. The response to the call for men pleased the nation's leaders. The British-born and the unemployed flocked to recruiting offices to "do their bit." Some were like John Kerr and his brother, who left their land in the Peace River District in northern Alberta, and tacked a note to their door, "War is hell, but what is homesteading?"[1]

Most gladly enlisted. "There were thousands of unemployed people that were happy to join the army," said Sam Beckman of Toronto. "They were dressed properly, they got their meals, their training camps, they enjoyed themselves. They had some purpose in living." Cities lavished benefits on those who enlisted. Edmonton offered free streetcar tickets to soldiers, half pay to the families of enlisted civic employees, and aid for those military families having trouble paying utility bills. Newspaper editors and religious leaders spoke of the need to fight for one's country, while patriotic groups and organizations like the Imperial Order of the Daughters of the Empire and the Women's Canadian Clubs raised money and put together packages and clothes for soldiers.

Those who didn't sign up were branded unpatriotic "slackers." Women publicly embarrassed men in civilian clothes by handing them white feathers. "It was rather annoying to go out at all because the men in uniform, when you would walk down the street, they'd come and tap you on the shoulder and say, 'Why ain't you in the army?'" said Martin Colby from the Toronto area. "And I used to have difficulty even when I told them I had bad ears because I'd had scarlet fever . . . Oh Jesus, they used to pressure the life out of you. It was hell."

Already established military regiments enlisted tens of thousands of men. Within a year's time citizens formed seventy-one new battalions, as well as scores of machine-gun companies, artillery batteries, bicycle units, and others. After August 1915, any person or group could apply to form a battalion, and recruiting leagues popped up all over. In Alberta at the start of the war, 4,000 men belonged to the volunteer militia groups. By February 1916 three different Edmonton battalions vied for men.[2]

Many such groups appealed to specific segments of society. Some battalions wore Highland dress. Others recruited Americans, Indians, those under five feet two inches, or those who did not touch alcohol. The officers forming the 218th Overseas Battalion wanted Irish citizens. They nicknamed their group the "Canadian Irish Guards" and ran newspaper ads, imploring, "Join them and win an honored place. . . . You'll be in good company, for the typical Irishman courts danger, laughs at hardships, and is at his best when doing the impossible." The appeal to join was contagious. On March 10, 1916, "Peace River" James Kennedy Cornwall, a tall, broad-shouldered man who went from selling newspapers on the streets of Buffalo to setting up fur-trading posts, staking oil claims, and amassing a fortune in the Peace River area of Alberta, enlisted. He immediately set about recruiting tough, hard-bitten fur trappers, lumberjacks, and river men from the north country. By April Cornwall held the rank of major. Soon after that, lieutenant colonel. On July 6, Cornwall commanded the 218th.

By 1916 the National Land Company's Edmonton offices had shut down, one of the victims of the depression. Cohen had no work, though he claimed to still be making six hundred dollars a month as a real estate broker. Most of his money came from gambling. With few other prospects, as well as a need to do something patriotic and to fight those who were bombing London near where his family lived, he, too, decided to do his bit, signing up with the Irish three days after Cornwall. While not a callused laborer from the north, at a stout 187 pounds and with small scars on his head, Cohen fit right in with Cornwall's rough-and-tumble group. On the twenty-seventh he was made an acting sergeant, joining a polyglot band of patriots from fourteen nations. Members of the 218th spoke so many languages that the battalion required sixteen interpreters. Cornwall himself spoke Cree, Chipewyan, Dogrib, and several Eskimo dialects, and translated for the battalion's fifty Indians. He started English classes to make sure that the soldiers understood his orders.

Derogatory remarks were made about the overwhelming number of Indians, Russians, Jews, Romanians, and other foreigners in the Irish Brigade. Some unfairly branded the battalion undisciplined. On April 14, a reporter from the *Bulletin* visited their barracks at the Canadian Consolidated Rubber Company's building on Fourth Street and helped polish their image. He noted that the brigade of 685 men was a fine group. "In the sleeping barracks, soldiers' kits are piled neatly and methodically in long rows. . . ." The tailor shop customized uniforms for free for the members. The canteen sold tobacco, soft drinks, and other goods. There were a brass and a bugle band. Cohen and his fellow noncommissioned officers attended daily lectures for instruction in the use and abuse of military power and training. When leaving, it was noted, "one may see seven or eight squads of men daily in the different stages of military drill and tuition. All of these squads are first drilled by the bluff Irish recruiting sergeant instructor, M. A. Cohen, whose excellent voice in giving the commands can be heard clearly and distinctly above the hum of the neighboring street traffic."[3]

Cohen and his men soon moved to the Edmonton Exhibition grounds, taking with them their mascot, a black bear named Teddy, from the Peace River District. "Having only had a few days at the grounds the Guards already are at home in their new quarters," wrote the *Bulletin* later that month. "The officer's mess . . . has assumed the appearance of a smart military home for the leaders of the battalion. On entering the building one confronts the staff orderly room where everything in business, military and clerical pursuits connected with the battalion is cared for." The noncommissioned officers and their men lived in six buildings. "The men sleep in clean neat appearing bunks arranged in such a manner as to allow for full ventilation and plenty of room. The bedding and soldier's equipment is piled neatly on each bunk, showing good order and regularity." Cohen and the other noncommissioned officers drilled and trained the men. After hours "the officers and men have separate billiard and pool tables where the game with the ivories can be indulged in at will," or they could head to the YMCA rest-and-reading building to pick up a magazine, newspaper, or book.[4]

At the end of May, Cohen started classes to learn to be a sergeant. Then on June 29, he and the 218th joined 10,000 men at the training grounds to the south of Sarcee City, a makeshift town of wooden buildings on the northern shore of the Elbow River, outside Calgary. A dozen-odd battalions filled the camp. The 218th pitched their snow-white bell tents in neat rows opposite those of the 137th and the 113th, bridging the spaces between the tents with slatted-board duckwalks. In front of their encampment they lined the ground with white painted stones, forming orderly walkways. At the entrance they elaborately arranged more stones to form their battalion's number. Teddy came south with them, and was chained to a nearby tree stump.

For breakfast the soldiers ate oatmeal, bacon, potatoes, and coffee. At eight-thirty each morning they fell in on the parade grounds. After roll call two hundred officers and noncommissioned officers from all the battalions conducted physical training, bayonet fighting, rifle and machine-gun shooting, and signaling. Constant explosions rebounded from the southeastern edge of the camp as men hurled six hundred to seven hundred "powder puffs" a day, practice bombs constructed from old cans packed with mud, black powder, and guncotton. Each battalion also spent six days at a stretch wallowing in a phony no-man's-land, firing from trenches and charging with drawn bayonets across a battleground made to resemble the killing fields of France. From twelve to two they ate and rested, followed by more training until five-thirty. They then scrubbed up or showered. From supper time until "first post" at nine-thirty, the men played sports or sat and relaxed in the cool evening air and gabbed. Some might head to the nearby hillsides to paint their battalion's numbers on boulders. Others went to the YMCA reading tent to pick a novel from the thousand-volume library, or to the YMCA's writing tent to use the free stationery and postage. The YMCA brought in entertainers from throughout the province, held concerts, social events, religious meetings, stunt nights, classes in French and German, offered refreshments, and encouraged the men to open savings accounts. "Last post" and "lights out" were called at ten. After ten-fifteen all that could be heard in Sarcee was the sound of "the calls of the sentries on their beats, or the clicking of some signalling lamp on the hills about the camp, when the 'signallers' are on a night shift."[5]

At the start of the war, the police announced with pride that the crime and vagrancy rate had dropped in Calgary. The Chinese also cut back on gambling. The Calgary News-Telegram optimistically noted in June that since not a single drunk had faced the magistrate in police court on Tuesday morning, "drunkenness appears to have become an offense of the past, so far as the police are concerned." The police hoped for a further reduction in arrests with the July 1 enactment of the Alberta Liquor Act. As with their sisters to the south, Canadian prohibition organizations like the Woman's Christian Temperance Union and the Dominion Alliance for the Total Suppression of the Liquor Traffic fought "For God, and Home, and Canada," and actively campaigned for the banning of "Demon Rum." Only through prohibition, they believed, could Canada rid itself of evil, reform society, and bring in a more godly and Christian nation. After Princip shot the Archduke and Countess in Sarajevo, prohibitionists succeeded in branding bars as traitorous dens where enemies of the nation plotted. They claimed that Canada needed liquor restrictions to protect the health of the soldiers and increase wartime productivity, and succeeded in ramming through the appropriate legislation. Yet, as in the United States, officials could not enforce the ban. Saloons shut down and blind pigs sprang up. Stills percolated and bootleggers prospered. And while the Calgary police might have been hopeful in June, by July they were overwhelmed managing a city with 10,000 parched troops living nearby. All Chief Alfred Cuddy could do was try to cope with the problem and plead for extra help.[6]

Cohen's battalion arrived as the law took effect. When Cohen had time off, he could head to the Pastime Billiard Parlor, the Gaiety Theatre and Lunchroom, the Sarcee Shooting Gallery, the Royal Theatre, and Turner's Billiard Parlor in Sarcee City. Or he could join the noncommissioned officers and soldiers loosely marching the eight miles to Calgary center for some more sophisticated fun. "My sister and I used to listen for the approaching column of uniformed men," wrote author Jack Peach of the ragged lines of troops he saw during the war. "On a hot summer evening they would appear from the southwest and head for the streetcar line by way of our back lane. Mary and I would lug small pails of cold water and a long-handled dipper out to the back gate where some of the dry-as-dust soldiers would break ranks to quickly drain the buckets. 'Drinking the soldiers' we called it, a privileged and jealously guarded task because the men in khaki were so appreciative."

Cohen ambled into Calgary on Saturday evenings and had a good time spending his $1.10-a-day pay drinking illegal hooch, carousing, or taking in the latest reels by Charlie Chaplin, Fatty Arbuckle, and Mabel Normand. Sometimes he had too good a time, and his presence once again became known to the Calgary police. On July 8 he was enjoying himself at the cabaret in the King George Hotel. At about 11 P.M. Detectives Tom Turner and Joseph Carruthers approached him with a warrant for using obscene language. Cohen turned on the officers. Why, he screamed and cursed them, were they looking for him? Why were they bothering him? "Cohen was throwing things around down in the grill and was wild with excitement," said Turner, and using some of the most obscene language the officer had ever heard. Turner told Cohen that he had a warrant for his arrest, but when Cohen asked to see the paper, Turner resisted handing it over. Cohen did not let up with his demand, insisting that he had to see the document. Turner only then reluctantly presented it. When Cohen read the paper and saw that it lacked a judge's signature, he ripped it up and tossed the shreds into Turner's face. He then raised his cane and shook it close to Turner's face, yelling that he was going to bust the officer's nose. Turner no longer needed a judge's warrant. He charged Cohen with disorderly conduct and resisting arrest. He gathered up the torn paper and dragged Cohen off to the station, booking him at 11:55 P.M. Cohen was released on twenty-five dollars bail.

When the case came to trial two weeks later, Cohen's attorney, Thomas M. Tweedie, made the claim that in enforcing the new Liquor Act, overzealous police unfairly targeted Cohen and other soldiers. Yet the unsuspecting officer, he noted, didn't realize that Cohen was no ordinary noncommissioned officer. He had once been an Edmonton commissioner for the taking of oaths and affidavits, and he could easily recognize a false document. At least he could see if it was signed or not. When Tweedie asked Turner to produce the shredded document, Turner once again balked and said he could not. Tweedie then accused the officer of trumping up false charges against his client and using them to blackmail Cohen into becoming a snitch for the police.

"Did you tell Cohen that you had a proposition for him by which he could make money?" Tweedie demanded to know. "Did you not tell Cohen that you had his past record down pat and that you wanted him to hunt up a few blind pigs for you or you would squeal to his commanding officer and he would lose the three stripes?"

No, Turner swore in response to the questions. He did not and would not make up the charges. "I certainly did not. In fact I have never brought a case before his worship in which I have utilized stool pigeons, and I know the magistrate will bear out my statement."

At that Tweedie stopped the officer's pronouncements of innocence. The attorney opened a book of criminal offenses and asked Turner if he recalled the case of *Rex vs. Marceau,* in which Turner had been subjected to very harsh reprimands by Judge Nicholas D. Beck for doing just that.

"You would never have thought of that case if I hadn't mentioned it to you in a privileged conversation in your own office," exclaimed the detective.

Cohen then took the stand in his own defense, and according to the *Daily Herald,* "carried on very spirited conversation." He claimed that on July 1 he heard from Charlie Bell at the King George that Turner was looking for him.

"So I went down to the station right away to find Turner and see what he wanted me for. I didn't see him at the station so I let the thing go until the following Saturday night, when I was at the hotel and going up in the elevator. I saw a fellow stick his head into the lift and I asked the elevator boy who he was. He told me that he was a detective by the name of Turner. I immediately went after him and demanded an explanation.

"Turner wanted me to help him round up a few of the 'joints' in town."

"Just what did Turner say to you?" asked Tweedie.

"Well, he said, 'How do you like the army? I don't suppose you're making very much money at it. I have a little proposition for you whereby you can make a nice bit on the side. All you have to do is tip me off to a few of these places selling booze on the side and I'll do the rest.' I asked him what kind of a dirty sneak he thought I was and called him everything I could think of. He also told me if I didn't come through with the deal he would squeal to the commanding officer about my past record and I would lose the stripes. On the way back to the hotel to talk the matter over with the clerk Turner tried to smooth things over and told me not to be peeved. I didn't threaten to fight, but I sure called him names. What Turner was trying to pull [with] my past record, which I admit is not that of an angel, and use it as a leverage to compel me to act like a snake [was wrong]."

And while Cohen might have shaken his cane at Turner, he said he had no intention of actually hitting him.

Cohen frankly admitted to some of his crimes and misdemeanors, along with the year at Prince Albert. Yet he lied about his conviction for assaulting Detective McIvor in Edmonton, claiming that the Edmonton police were no better than their comrades in Calgary: "I was caught in a dirty game the same as Turner there was attempting to pull on me. I was gambling in Edmonton at a club and was caught. I was indeed. I smashed a detective right on the nose for the same dirty snake game Turner wanted to play."

In Cohen's defense, an insurance agent named A. W. C. Scragg testified that he overheard the argument between Cohen and Turner in which Cohen yelled: "What kind of a sneak do you think I am?" A week later Cohen returned to the courtroom for what the *Herald* referred to as "his weekly appearance." On the morning of August 4, the city withdrew the case, and Police Magistrate Davidson discharged Cohen.[7]

Cohen continued to take advantage of all that Calgary had to offer during his leaves. On October 11, the Pantages Theater scheduled a lively lineup of entertainers. There was Leo–Jackson–Mae, the Wonders on Wheels, Weber & Elliott Comedians, George Primrose and his Seven Blackface Boys, as well as the famous "Resista. You Can't Lift Her!" Resista was quite an attraction, a slip of a woman that no one could hoist. Some claimed she hid magnets beneath her clothes and under the stage to prevent people from budging her. So to dispel the rumors and drum up publicity, Resista stopped by the office of the Calgary *Daily Herald*, where her manager proclaimed, "Bring down one of your strongest men from the mechanical room." Dan McFarlane, a stereotyper whose job entailed lifting and moving heavy metal plates, strode in. He grabbed hold of the little lady, but even this strapping hulk couldn't budge the ninety-eight pounder.[8]

The paper wrote up the visit in detail. For Cohen it sounded like the sort of entertainment he once enjoyed seeing in London, so he picked up a ticket for the opening-night show at 8 P.M. Yet he was not destined to attend. The police continued arresting drunken soldiers, and the day of the show Magistrate Davidson passed judgment on five soldiers Detectives Turner and John Burroughs arrested for drinking alcohol inside a barn. Davidson convicted all five of violating the Liquor Act and fined them fifty dollars each plus costs. None of the men could pay the fine, so they all received thirty days in the slammer.

For Cohen and the other men at Sarcee who believed that they were being unfairly harassed by the police, this last conviction was too much. At seven-thirty a large body of men from the 218th, the 211th, and other battalions gathered at the

CPR station. Cohen and other noncommissioned officers ordered their men to stand in formation. They then marched them in fours to police headquarters. There the troops packed Seventh Avenue and the side streets. Fearing that the soldiers would raid the four-story red brick station, the police came out and formed a semicircular cordon around the main entrance. Soldiers walked up to the police line and screamed and cursed at the officers. Turner wisely stayed inside, and the soldiers singled him out for special insults. Many yelled, "Come out, Turner" and "Why don't you join the army, Turner?"

Civilians gathered along the sidewalk. One group of young women called on members of the force by name, and accused them of "hiding in the cellar." Cheers rose from the crowd as the troops made speeches. One soldier-leader implored the crowd, "Join us in getting these men out. These men are brave soldiers and good citizens who have committed no crime. They were not even accused of being drunk. The only charge against them was that they smelled of liquor and for that they are treated as criminals and sent down for 30 days. Do you call that justice? These men have volunteered to fight for you: some of them have crossed the border to fight for you people, and is that the way they should be treated?"

Cohen greatly enjoyed the disorder and the yelling. He eagerly egged his men on. In the midst of the ruckus Cohen screamed, "Go ahead boys!" As the police nervously watched, someone heaved a stone through a window. Chief Cuddy frantically tried to calm the crowd. The soldiers yelled back, "Go to hell!" and "All we want are the prisoners!" Cuddy attempted shouting over the men, and tried to explain that the convicted soldiers were not in his cells. When a group of six men asked to search the building and sixteen cells, he let them in. The delegation did not find any of their comrades. Sergeant C. C. Campbell of the 211th then rang the Royal North West Mounted Police barracks to see if they were there, telling the Mountie who answered the phone that he was calling from the army recruiting office. When the officer confirmed their presence, a cry went up outside: "To the barracks!"

Word reached Sarcee of the mob's movements. Officers rushed to town to try to break up the gathering. The military Provost Marshal, Lieutenant Colonel George West Jones, begged the men not to disgrace their comrades in arms. It was in vain. About two hundred soldiers waved their hats and canes, shouted, sang, and blew their bugles as their noncommissioned officers marched them in formation over to Seventh Avenue and Fourth Street West. As they moved they gathered force, and were cheered on by a following mass of other soldiers and civilians. When they reached the barracks, West Jones and Captain Main of the 211th as well as the Mounties tried again to reason with the men. Their entreaties were met with jibes and taunts. Cohen commanded here. He ordered his men to act.

"They were surging all around," said Inspector Newson of the RNWMP. "The crowd extended, as far as I could see, filling up the space between the barracks and the fence. . . . They were in a very excited condition and appeared to be determined to release the soldier prisoners whom we held. . . . A number of them kept shouting,

'We want justice'; 'Our comrades are inside and we want to get them released.' "
Men rushed the building, tearing down the fences and gateways around the barracks.
They threw stones and pieces of fence through the windowpanes. One of the soldiers
yelled: "We don't want the window, we want the men."

"They seemed to be getting worse all the time," said Sergeant Major T. H.
Irvine. "They had sticks from the fence with which they went breaking furniture
and anything they could touch with them. They also tore down the steam radiator
in the passage. It was impossible to do anything with them at all. The men that were
doing all the bad damage were foreigners who spoke broken English." As they raged
and destroyed, Cohen stood down on the street, directing, shouting, and cheering
on his men, driving them on to do more and more damage. They followed his and
others' orders, destroying the piano, bandoliers, Colt revolvers, blankets, tunics, field
jackets, spurs, fur caps, chairs, knives, benches, documents, fire extinguishers, garden
hoses, gramophones, records, plants, and flowerpots. They smashed everything,
throwing pieces of flotsam through the broken windows. As they demolished they
called out the names of their jailed comrades, and screamed at each other, "Get them
out!" Those massed outside carried broken wicker chairs and rubber hoses to the
curb and set them ablaze. "It's worse than Prussia!" yelled one perspiring solider as
he dragged a table to the bonfire.

Constable A. Gamman had heard that soldiers were attacking the headquarters,
and rushed over to see what he could do. As he neared the building he heard a shot
fired; the bullet struck army Private Julio Peregrino in the left shoulder as he tried
to climb in from the barracks' fire escape. Soldiers saw Gamman approaching the
building and accused him of wounding Peregrino. "They said they'd show me,"
said Gamman,

and six or eight started to lead me onto the corner of the street. I heard someone
shout "He shot him, he shot him" and several more took up the cry and
knocked me down; I heard somebody yelling to "Get a club and kill him." I
finally got up on my feet . . . I broke away from them and ran up to the corner
of 3rd Street West, when a soldier tripped me, and I fell, and the soldiers piled
on top of me and somebody hit me over the head with a stick, and someone
else hit me on the jaw; I could feel the sticks pounding on my head. Someone
helped me up on my feet and was leading me across the street, when another
soldier reached through between two others and kicked me in the testicles. I
got across the street and backed up against an automobile that was beside the
road, and opened the door and got inside in the back seat, and there were two
or three civilians who kept the crowd off me, and I could hear someone on
the other side of the crowd shouting that I wasn't the man.

Some of the men broke off from their rampage and called for volunteers to help
round up weapons. A party of thirty to forty set off up Eighth Avenue, carrying
sticks, carbines, and a jug of whiskey, headed toward the Ashdown hardware and

the Martin Sporting Goods stores to steal rifles, pistols, and ammunition. There they came upon police inspector W. A. Nutt and an armed police squad. The officers charged with drawn batons and routed the soldiers.

By then Brigadier General Ernest A. Cruikshank and other officers had arrived from Sarcee. He ordered the troops back to camp. The Mounties transferred the five jailed men over whom the ruckus had been caused to a jail in Lethbridge. Cohen was arrested by Inspector Nutt and released on bond. The army made a list of the 147 men from ten battalions—29 of whom belonged to the 218th—who were not back in camp the night of the rioting. Officers ordered the accused to march in small groups in front of city and mounted police officers for identification. As they walked by the soldiers insulted the police. When Cohen saw Sergeant S. R. Waugh and Constable Robert Campbell he leaned forward and sneered: "You sons of bitches, we'll get you yet." By the end of the day four city police officers and two Mounties identified Cohen as being actively involved in the melee. Cohen and eight others were confined to the guard room.

At the Sarcee court of inquiry convened to investigate the incident, Constable Thomas Ward testified that at the riot he saw Cohen's back and heard his voice. As the court examined Ward, Cohen approached the judge and requested to ask the detective a few questions. The judge allowed it.

"What is the first time you ever heard my name, Cohen?" he asked Ward. "Did you ever hear my name before? Was the first time in connection with this riot?"

The court quickly stopped Cohen and pointed out, "What took place before has nothing to do with this matter."

"But I wish to establish a point now in connection with this case," Cohen answered, "which will have considerable bearing on the case."

The court allowed him to continue.

"When was the first time you heard my name mentioned regarding this trouble?"

"I didn't hear your name mentioned," Ward said. "I only said that I recognized the voice and you are the build of the man that formed up the squad outside the Police Station."

"What reason—what made you believe that it was me?"

"Because you look like the man at the back and your voice sounded familiar to me."

"Well wasn't it just outside here you were walking along and some person said to me 'Hello Cohen'?"

"No, I didn't hear that."

"What time was it you said they fell in and marched off from the station?"

"About 8:20 or 8:30, around there."

"What time did they arrive at the Police Station?"

"Around eight o'clock."

"And they marched away and I was at the head—"

The judge stopped Cohen again: "You are not on trial," he pointed out, "and will be given every opportunity to ask any fair question bearing on the immediate case."

Cohen tried again to find out when Ward first heard his name mentioned. "At this point," the court stenographer noted, "Cohen . . . entered into a tirade against the City Police and was ordered by the Court to discontinue and was warned as to the manner of his address."

Ward wasn't the only one Cohen grilled. On the afternoon of the thirteenth he questioned Detective Sergeant William Symonds.

"You know my name?" Cohen asked.

"Yes."

"And you say you saw me—my back—there."

"Yes, I think I saw you around the station."

"At the time the row was going on—what time?"

"Between eight and nine o'clock."

"What part was I taking?"

"I could hear your voice and I saw you as well."

"What was I doing?"

"Shouting and yelling like the rest of them—'Go ahead boys.' "

Other witnesses followed. All testified that they saw Cohen. When Waugh took the stand he pointed at Cohen and exclaimed: "That man there seemed to be the agitator in chief—yelling and shouting 'Come along boys' and things like that, but I couldn't say that I saw him up very close to the door." Cohen, he said, was "on the steps, yelling and shouting and all around." Campbell referred to Cohen as: "That man, he was the chief agitator." Captain Main said he might have seen Cohen at the riot. Private John McDougall of the 187th said that "he was kind of a leader among them . . . a ring leader among the men. . . ."

All Cohen could do was deny the charges and weave an elaborate alibi during his own testimony: "Well I went down that night to go to the Theatre and I was down to the corner of Ninth Avenue, that drug store just opposite the C.P.R. Depot and I heard a bugle go and then some men lined up and just as soon as I saw it I went away and then I went into the King George . . ."

"Had you heard any talk about any trouble?" he was asked.

"I had an idea—an idea that they were going to get a certain person named Tom Turner and knock his block off."

"Why?"

"Because he framed up with his stool pigeons to supply five soldiers with one bottle of whiskey and then went and got them all convicted—the whole five for one bottle of whiskey and a week before that I heard they were going to do this as this same man arrested a soldier of the 211th for drunkenness. He was brought up before the Magistrate and convicted and fined, I believe, Ten Dollars. Right after this conviction this same Tom Turner placed another charge against him for having liquor in his possession and got him convicted and fined Fifty Dollars. That started the whole scrap according to what rumors I could pick up around town."

"Where were you when this bugle blew that you speak of?"

"I was right opposite the depot—Center Street and Ninth Avenue, just opposite the station."

"Who blew the bugle?"

"I don't know," Cohen replied. "I saw a bunch of men run and I stayed there just about a second and then I went away as I knew if I stayed around there there would be a frame up against me. I had some trouble with this same Tom Turner and he arrested me on some charges and then he absolutely refused to bring them up."

"You had some trouble with Turner before."

"Yes, I did."

"Where did you go when the bugle blew?"

"I stepped into the King George right away and I wasn't there a minute and I went over to the Palliser Hotel and there our Colonel of the 218th came up and I spoke to him and he spoke to me and asked me if there was any trouble and I told him there was going to be trouble and he asked me if there were any 218th men in it and I said that I didn't see any. I was only there a second and I told him there was none of the 218th that I had seen."

"You were only there a second and you could tell . . ."

"I don't suppose you are going to keep me down to that second," Cohen snapped back, "you have allowed others from an hour to two hours."

"Well according to your own statement you had no opportunity of ascertaining what men were there and you make a report to your Colonel that no men from your Battalion were there."

"Oh well I just looked when they were lining up. I looked over there but I didn't see anybody—I didn't want to see anybody in fact. I didn't want to be there and I didn't want to take any part in it. I reported it to the Colonel and the Colonel told me I had better keep out of sight. I had a ticket to Pantages and I told him that I was going to the theatre. I left there and walked around and I spoke to Colonel Craig—I spoke to him for some time."

"Well—what did you do then?"

"I think I went into the King George Hotel and from there I probably went around. . . ."

"I want to know where you went—you certainly went somewhere."

"No I don't go any place in particular, I just . . ."

"You certainly went some place—where was the first place you went into?"

"Well when I got off the street car I walked up . . ."

"After you left the Colonel—where did you go after you left him?"

"I went into the King George Hotel."

"How long?"

"I couldn't say—not more than five or ten minutes."

"From there where did you go?"

"I walked up—I'm not acquainted with the names of the streets—I think it was

Eighth Avenue, it's up past the Palliser Hotel and I walked around for a few minutes and I run into a lady acquaintance of mine from Edmonton and in conversation with her I met a Sergeant from the 218th and I introduced him to this party."

"Who was the Sergeant."

"Sergeant Davey."

"Well I want to know where you went and how long you stayed. How long did you remain on the streets?"

"I was only on the street about twenty minutes all evening and I went to Pantages Theatre later."

"Did you get there before the performance commenced?"

"Yes, and there was a Major from Headquarters, I don't know as he knows me, but he is a Doctor and he sat next to me."

"And you remained through the whole of the performance."

"Yes, I did."

"What was the number of your seat?"

"The number—J. 11."

Cohen then handed over a ticket stub as evidence.

All those charged did as their sergeant had done and tried to show that they were far from the riot. One said he stopped at the barbershop, the library, and a restaurant and knew nothing of what happened until a policeman arrested him. Another said he attended a picture show from eight till ten; he only happened to come by after the ruckus and was arrested. One other insisted that he had dinner with various sergeants at the Empire Hotel.[9]

No one saw anything. It was dark out. They weren't around.

By the twenty-seventh, Cohen and more than a dozen men were arraigned for rioting before Magistrate Davidson. At the Friday morning session Cohen continued his self-advocacy. "The most interesting part of the cases is the active participation of Sergt. Cohen, of the 218th," reported the Calgary *Daily Herald*. "Sergt. Cohen, when identified now as having been seen in the crowd of rioters conducts a cross-examination of [a] very painstaking kind. He is watching every step and he is displaying a certain familiarity with court proceedings. He even makes use of the expression 'my learned friend,' when referring to the prosecutor. But this morning he so astonished everyone in the courtroom that even the court stenographer gasped and looked up his dictionary while Chief Cuddy reached madly and blindly for his smelling salts. Sergt. Cohen was cross-examining Detective Symonds. He did not want to call the witness, or any other witnesses plain liars, Sergt. Cohen informed the court, but he did think that they were displaying 'pulchritudinous terminological inexactitude.' "

When Ward retook the stand, Cohen set upon him. "In a voice of command," noted the Calgary *News-Telegram*, "Sergt. Cohen demanded to know if the officer on the stand had stated at a hearing in Sarcee camp some days ago, if he had recognized him. He questioned further if the witness could say positively that he recognized the questioner on the occasion of the riots.

"Officer Ward replied that his testimony at the Sarcee was very much the same as it was on this occasion, that he had seen a soldier in the crowd on the night whose back and voice resembled that of Sergt. Cohen, the questioner. The prisoner repeated his questions several times, but the officer's statements were very much the same."

The prosecution soon learned that having eyewitnesses was not enough if all they could do was say they saw Cohen's back and heard someone who sounded like him. On the morning of the twenty-eighth, his fancy footwork paid off. Because of the circumstantial nature of the evidence Davidson discharged him. The rest of the men were not so lucky. Davidson fined nearly all of them ten to a hundred dollars.[10]

Calgary was only too glad to be rid of Cohen and the 218th, which returned to Edmonton that same day. In January 1917 the army converted the battalion into railway troops, since as the Inspector General noted, "they are men used to outdoor labour and should be well adapted for construction work." On February 8, Cornwall issued orders for noncommissioned officers and men of the 218th to report to the battalion headquarters at nine the following morning for transport to Europe. As a going-away present, excited soldiers from the 218th attacked fourteen stores, restaurants, and cafés in town. By the time they returned to their barracks later that evening, shattered glass covered 101st Street. Only two men from the battalion, Privates John Terentiuk and Joseph Buiar, were charged with yelling in the street and creating a disturbance. They were slapped with slight fines. The next afternoon a large crowd cheered and waved as two trainloads of troops pulled out of the CPR station.

Cohen and the 218th traveled east for Halifax, Nova Scotia. On February 16 they boarded the SS *Southland*. The voyage was uneventful. No one spotted enemy submarines. At eight-thirty on the evening of the twenty-seventh they pulled into the military base at Purfleet, Essex. There the 218th and 211th amalgamated to form the 8th Battalion of the Canadian Railway Troops. At the start of March, Cohen instructed the army paymaster to send twenty dollars of his pay each month to his family. He subsequently received leave and went straight to London to see them in Tredegar Square. "It was my second return home. This time I came as a sergeant in the Canadian Army, proud of my stripes." Cohen saw relatives, walked around the East End with his father, and even attended services at the Cannon Street Road Synagogue. He also had time to slip away from Tredegar Square and visit some of the East End's ladies of easy virtue. On April 6 Cohen spent part of his army pay on one such gal.

As he strolled through London, he could not help but notice the grimness gripping his hometown. Shops with German-sounding names had been attacked and stoned. Basics were scarce. Like their neighbors, the Cohens stockpiled what they could and kept chickens in the yard. At night street lamps around Tredegar Square and throughout the city had to be dimmed and house draperies kept closed to make it more difficult for the German Zeppelin bombers to see the city. Captain Erich Linnarz made the first Zeppelin attack on London on the evening of May 31, 1915, when he dropped more than one hundred incendiaries and bombs on Whitechapel, Stepney, and other parts of the city around Tredegar Square. "London was all lit up and we enjoyed total surprise," Linnarz boasted of his run that killed seven and wounded thirty-five. "Not a searchlight or antiaircraft gun was aimed at us before the first bomb was dropped."

Other bombs soon fell from the sky. On September 8, 1915, four airships headed toward London. "We were at about eighty-five hundred feet when we released our 660-pounder, the largest anyone had ever dropped up to that time," wrote an assistant engineman in the attack. "It did not hit the intended target, but you could see a whole mass of structures and street paving swallowed up in a tremendous crater, even at our height. We were awestruck and frozen as we stared until all at once we realized that we were caught in the glare of what seemed like a dozen searchlights. In the bright light, I could look down and see black objects almost floating up toward us. Flak from the antiaircraft guns. Very close.

"We dropped the rest of our load over a railroad station and had the satisfaction of seeing rails and ties and pieces of a depot and two big buses spouting into the air and then dropping back in a mass of wreckage. It was easy to see all this because we had dropped so many incendiaries and there were pools and rivers of fire all along the streets below."

As Zeppelins, Gotha bombers, and other airships terrorized the city, parents sent their children to relatives out of town. The Cohens built a shelter out back, and they regularly took refuge with other families in the deep underground subway stations. The bombs especially upset Josef Cohen. "My dad was the nervous type," recalled Sarah Rich. "When the alarms used to go, and the Germans were over in the Zeppelins, he used to run to the tubes for shelter and we used to follow him."[11]

Soon after Cohen's visit, his family came out to see him at Purfleet. Benjamin Cohen was especially taken by the patriotism of his older brother, and up and enlisted, underage. As the 8th underwent their final training and prepared for the front, the army handed out battle gear and instructed the men on how to deal with gas attacks. For their work as railway troops, the army issued the battalion nine lorries, eight Ford boxcars, ten motorcycles, two Sunbeam motorcars, 260 mules, ten horses, sixty-four wagons, four field kitchens, two water carts, and eight bicycles.

At the end of the month part of the battalion came down with mumps and measles and had to be quarantined. Cohen then had his own bout of illness. On April 13 he experienced his first painful attack of gonorrhea, which he picked up from his date in London the week before. Fortunately for him, such a problem was not that uncommon in the army. "As for the diseases, there was regular inspection that kept them under control," said Private Ben Wagner of the treatment offered. "There you had regular inspection. Whenever you went sick, it was on your daily orders. . . . It was always public. I might say that perhaps 5% of the battalion had had VD. But they were immediately put in hospital and under treatment, so that there wasn't the bad effects of it."

Since he had to be cured, Cohen couldn't ship off with Cornwall and the 33 officers and 957 others for the front on April 17. He was also reduced in rank to sapper. Worst of all, he had to endure a long and trying pre-penicillin medical regimen. At the start of his treatment the doctors confined him to bed, and prescribed a diet of fluids such as milk and barley water. Slowly they worked him up to bland foods and some exercise. The doctors inserted catheters and syringes into his penis and twice daily flushed out his urethra with a solution of potassium permanganate. After getting him started on the cure, they trained Cohen to administer it himself. If his glands were swollen they were massaged. All the while the doctors were hopeful that he would not eventually develop gonorrheal arthritis. During his treatment, the army shuttled him to various military medical centers. It was not until June 27 that the doctors finally pronounced him cured.[12]

Finally on September 8, Cohen got to join his comrades in Belgium. His battalion worked in the northern sector of the British front, not far from Ypres, near the towns of Poperinghe, Neuve Eglise, and Ploegsteert. When Cohen arrived a month after the start of the Battle of Passchendaele—the Third Battle of Ypres—the small hills that rose from the flat plains of Flanders on which farmers once raised hops, beets, and corn were fields of mud, shattered trees, and death. Surprisingly, nightingales still sang here. This was a war of immobility. Except for a rare advance, troops hunched in long-term terror within hearing range of the enemy. Frontline infantry lived in a labyrinth of trenches that sometimes meandered over one-mile-wide areas. Men fought for clumps of dirt. Heavy artillery shook the ground, flicked stone homes through the air, and turned barns, orchards, and towns into fertilizer. The wounded drowned in the mud. The acrid stench of carrion filled the air. When the thick yellow-gray clouds of chlorine gas drifted over the land, men fumbled with gas masks or placed urine-soaked handkerchiefs over their faces to prevent the fumes from searing their lungs and burning their eyes.

"Going up to the line for the first time my first indication of the horrors to come appeared as a small lump on the side of the duckboard," observed Major George Wade of the Machine Gun Corps.

I glanced at it, as I went past, and I saw to my horror, that it was a human hand gripping the side of the track—no trace of the owner, just a glimpse of a muddy wrist and a piece of sleeve sticking out of the mud. After that there were bodies every few yards. Some lying face downwards in the mud; others showing by the expressions fixed on their faces the sort of effort they had made to get back onto the track. Sometimes you could actually see blood seeping up from underneath. I saw the dead wherever I looked—a dead signaller still clinging to a basket cage with two dead pigeons in it, and further on, lying just off the track, two stretcher-bearers with a dead man on a stretcher. . . . When the dead men were just muddy mounds by the trackside it was not so bad—they were somehow impersonal. But what was unendurable were the bodies with up-turned faces. Sometimes the eyes were gone and the faces were like skulls with the lips drawn back, as if they were looking at you with terrible amusement. Mercifully, a lot of those dreadful eyes were closed.[13]

The Germans at Passchendaele to the west held the higher ground, and as the British slowly advanced over the flat, rain-soaked surface, the Germans exacted a heavy toll. Winston Churchill aptly called the Battle of Passchendaele "a forlorn expenditure of valor and life without equal in futility." The 8th built and maintained the railway system that brought the wounded to field hospitals, hauled water, carried ammunition and big guns, conveyed road material, delivered supplies for the trenches, and moved large bodies of troops from one point to another, and thus, according to Lieutenant Francis McMahon of the 8th, "saved the men many a weary tramp." Because of the closeness of the enemy lines, the railway troops didn't use large-scale standard-gauge railway systems. Instead, chunky, toy-like tank locomotives chugged along at ten miles an hour on a light railway that ran parallel to the front line. Spur lines then connected up with a trench tramway system and the battery positions, dumps, and field dressing stations. At a certain point within easy sight of the Germans, troops transferred ammunition and other supplies for delivery to less visible petrol tractors, road vehicles, mules, and horses.

Forward work proved deadly. Some sections of railway had to be repaired scores of times. As Cohen worked, he made his way across a ground pockmarked by shell holes and laced with barbed wire entanglements and abandoned trenches. Cohen's gang labored in the chilled mist, grading roads and ditches with plows, wheelbarrows, and mule-pulled scrapers, building bridges, laying and ballasting tracks, and constructing breastworks. The heavy clay surface retained water since it lacked a gravelly topsoil, and the men had to haul bricks from ruined towns and villages and use the rubble as ballast beneath steel ties to prevent them from sinking into the mud. When the troops had no stones and bricks, they salvaged boards, planks, and sheets of galvanized iron. If that was not available, they had to try and use the clay. Despite their efforts, railway tracks and engines sank in the morass.

By October, Cornwall's men had constructed 150 miles of rails. Work became especially difficult when the October rains and subsequent flooding trapped horses and carts in the mud; Cohen and his comrades bailed water out of shell holes, and erected culverts so the tracks could pass over the soggy land. "The construction of these railways is carried on under great difficulty, as immediately after 'the push' the steel is laid on the ground the infantry have just passed over, and anyone who has not seen this cannot realize what it really looks like, especially under bad weather conditions," wrote McMahon.

> The ground is just one mass of shell holes, most of them filled with water and the mud is indescribable. . . . The ground we had to build on was in a terrible condition, having been pounded to a pulp and then a heavy rain for several days. Hundreds of dead horses and mules were lying round, the enemy dead had mostly all been buried or half buried, wagons, guns, ammunition and all kinds of material lying around stuck in the awful mud. I also noticed a tank stuck fast. . . .
>
> The men are shelled off the work quite often and have to get what cover

they can and wait there sometimes for hours until Frits directs his efforts to some other part of the front. In fact, sometimes a line has to be abandoned altogether, as Frits is very consistent and will hammer away for weeks on one particular spot.

Again, he accustoms you to a certain method of shelling and will commence at a certain time, every twelve hours, so that you will know at what time to expect his artillery fire and from which direction it will come. He will do this for days, then quite suddenly when least expected he will change his tactics so that you have to be constantly on the alert. Very often during the course of shell fire the line is blown up and has to be repaired. This sometimes happens as many as fifty times within twenty-four hours and has to be kept open day and night.[14]

Often the men had to work at night and on overcast, foggy days so as not to be seen. They had to be especially wary of the occasional airborne flares that cast flickering preternatural light and exposed their positions. When the Germans heard or saw them they started a barrage of artillery and bullets. A soldier would have to then quickly dive for shelter. "You'd be lying on the surface," said Private W. G. Bell of the 9th Battalion Army Cyclist Corps. "Any dent in the ground you'd stick your head down as far as you could ram it. There might be a shell-hole, there might not, but you had to lay flat on the ground when these creeping barrages came and they were terrible things. You don't think you're coming out of it. There's the blast of them, you know, and you can hear the steel, awful sound, piece of steel as it goes by you. It would cut you in half, a piece of that shell."

Unlike the front line troops who wallowed behind sandbags in water-logged trenches, most of the Canadian Railway Troops men lived in tents or collapsible huts back to the rear. Yet even here they had to be careful not to be seen. Shrapnel fire and gas shells even fell on the nearby town of Poperinghe. "You cannot even take a chance of going to sleep with a light burning without screening the window," wrote Cornwall. "If you don't, well, a Hun plane might come along and lay an egg on you."

Everywhere conditions were atrocious. As the poet Wilfred Owen wrote in his poem "Exposure":

> Our brains ache, in the merciless iced east winds that knive us . . .
> Wearied we keep awake because the night is silent . . .
> Low, drooping flares confuse our memory of the salient . . .
> Worried by silence, sentries whisper, curious, nervous,
>   But nothing happens.
>
> Watching, we hear the mad gusts tugging on the wire,
> Like twitching agonies of men among its brambles.

Northward, incessantly, the flickering gunnery rumbles,
Far off, like a dull rumour of some other war.
What are we doing here?

Cohen had no choice but to venture out to where the winds knived him. Many from the 8th were wounded and killed doing their jobs. On September 17, Sapper H. W. Kiernan had his left hand shot off and was struck in the base of his skull. On October 10, Corporal W. Lauder had two fingers on his left hand blown off when he tried to remove a trench mortar bomb. On the twenty-first, H. Cleaver died in action, and on the twenty-seventh an aerial bomb pierced Sapper U. Kolomeech's shoulder and broke his arm.

In early November, the Canadians finally reached the heap of bricks and mud that was once the town of Passchendaele. It took ninety-nine days to advance fewer than five miles. Sixty hours later a light railway brought stores in and took away the wounded.[15]

Besides battling the Hun, Cohen had to fend off the constant assaults of lice. He tried everything to rid himself of the hordes, from shaking out his shirts and sprinkling on disinfectant powder to running candle flames over his clothes seams. "They crawl all over you; the lice drop all over the place, you were just lousy with them," said Sergeant Wally Ross of the railway troops. Even worse than the lice were the brigades of rats that gnawed on rotting corpses. Men fought off those voracious rodents with planks or dropped sticks of cordite down rat holes.

The army converted the Poperinghe sugar refinery into a delousing station. When the troops moved away from the front they could bathe there and at a few other limited spots. Facilities, though, were sorely limited, and soldiers might have to wait weeks before they could clean up. Officers sometimes filled large ditches with water so the men could wash off.

The men passed their free time talking or playing their fiddles and harmonicas. The 8th's baseball and football teams played other railway units, as well as American and Scottish troops on Sundays. They had a strong baseball team and trounced all comers until the final championship of the railway troops, in which the 6th railway battalion beat them. There were also occasional concerts given by the Canadian and American concert troupes.

When Cohen had a few francs to spare he could head to Poperinghe or one of the other villages for some rest. There he could get something to supplement the regular rations of corned beef, bread or biscuit, tea, and jam, hear a concert or revue, and get a real bed for a night. He and the other soldiers packed the cafés, where they sang, wolfed down eggs, chips, and sweets, guzzled white wine at one franc a bottle, or nursed a cup of coffee. "We used to go into the Café des Alliés in Po-peringhe," recalled W. Worrell of the 12th Battalion Rifle Brigade. "It was a popular place because there was a little man with a squeeze-box there and he knew all the right tunes to play. He'd picked them up from the troops and some of them were pretty fruity."

Some of the men did not always take advantage of leave. Cohen often stayed behind with other eager gamblers. Card playing was rife throughout the forces, and though officers discouraged it, the men used their soiled, frayed decks whenever they could to play everything from poker and bridge to whist. When not shuffling cards, they even wagered on louse races to see whose was fastest.[16]

For Christmas Cornwall tried to make things merry, arranging a holiday meal with cockfight entertainment. "The boys scoured the country for game birds" and other supplies that they could find or take, he wrote. The gathered birds were kept in cages in a nearby barn "where they can look at one another from day to day and work up an appetite for a scrap." The gambling was planned and Major William Hanley handled the bets and profits, which would undoubtedly "go to help swell the revenue of the local brewery." Cohen must have come back with bags of booty for the feast, for Cornwall rated him "the best judge of steal in the battalion." The lightweight boxer Sergeant Louis "Kid" Scaler supplied Limburger cheese he found in June in an underground German cave at Messines. The other men turned up enough "real meat of high quality to give us about a pound and a quarter each for Christmas dinner." On Christmas they filled up on plum pudding, a mysterious rum omelet, cauliflower, baked potatoes, and mincemeat with hard sauce.

Part of Cohen's battalion wintered in captured German dugouts, finding shelter and rest in "some of the strongest concrete ones we could find as our boys have to live right up front," wrote Cornwall. "Some of the half breed boys, true to their Bush instincts, are wintering in a bush that we captured. They have built a log house, and put in a mud fireplace. . . . They have fifteen layers of logs and steel railroad ties over the hut, so that the shells bounce off, and they are as happy as beavers in a dam. We have plenty to read, and Movies back from the front line, an easy walk from the dug outs."[17]

During the war about 190,000 Chinese worked for the British and the French armies in France, Egypt, Palestine, Mesopotamia, and the French colonies. They, along with Indians, Egyptians, Fijians, and conscientious objectors, laid railway tracks, constructed roads, hauled dirt, built earthworks, cut timber, worked in mines, factories, and tank workshops, did artillery maintenance, and repaired trucks and motorcycles. "They were immensely powerful fellows," noted British Prime Minister David Lloyd George, "and it was no uncommon spectacle to see one of the Chinese pick up a balk of timber or a bundle of corrugated iron sheets weighing three or four hundredweight, and walk off with it as calmly as if it weighed only as many stone!"

The British controlled 190 labor companies, and the 8th first supervised 170-odd Chinese workers in late August. The Chinese assisted them in building a stretch of railway that ran from Hyde Park Corner through Ploegsteert Wood to Dead Horse Corner. They drained the swampy areas, cleared large trees, and widened and deepened the main drainage ditch. Just after Christmas a group of Chinese helped the 8th excavate a pipeline, and in early January 1918 the battalion and attached Chinese strengthened bridges and reballasted the tracks after a heavy rain washed out tracks and submerged about a mile of the line. Cohen started working with the Chinese around the time he became an acting corporal, on January 5, 1918. "These weren't the folks I'd known in Canada. There I met (besides the prosperous merchants), cooks, laundrymen, small shopkeepers and so on—men who had either some craft, or some trade, or a tiny bit of cash behind them. These were just plain coolies, illiterate, unskilled and completely ignorant. Still, I knew what I had to do and that was to appeal to their personal interest. A Chinese doesn't like work any more than we do, but if he is going to get something out of it—and if he can see what that something is—he'll work harder than anyone."

The troops soon learned that the Chinese completed their work more quickly when they were set a specific task. After that many of the Chinese were assigned piecework; when they finished they could knock off for the day. "They worked like beavers and it was completed soon after four o'clock," Cohen said. "They were pleased, the engineers were pleased; in fact everyone was pleased."

Chinese workers wore long brown cloaks over their blue cotton jackets and trousers. Many labored, according to Second Lieutenant Daryl Klein, "within sound of the guns, with 'planes droning overhead, not so far away from the wings of death." During German advances they sometimes ended up in the middle of battle. In one company two Chinese received the British Distinguished Service Medal for conspicuous bravery. Elsewhere some of the Chinese fought the Germans with picks and shovels. "During the fiercest fighting in Picardy a British officer commanding a Chinese labor unit was caught in a sudden advance by the enemy and badly gassed. Although they were hard pressed, the coolies grouped around him and fought with their crude weapons until relief arrived," wrote Captain Harry L. Gilchriese; 2,000 to 3,000 Chinese died during bombings near Calais alone. For their efforts, the Chinese earned a franc per ten-hour day, food, clothing, tobacco, a twenty-dollar bonus when they embarked, along with a ten-dollar allotment remitted each month to their families in China. The military discouraged fraternization between easterners and westerners. Chinese workers lived in segregated compounds, forty or more men to a hut, where they passed their spare time gambling, having tugs of war, boxing, playing baseball, and staging operas and plays.

Cohen was one of the few who did not mind working with the Chinese. He was especially stunned at how badly his comrades dealt with the workers. "They didn't know how to handle Orientals and they showed it. Some lost their tempers and tried to throw their weight about, others were frankly frightened." The noncommissioned officers treated the men roughly, didn't speak Chinese, and disparagingly referred to their workers as "Chinks." "There is rivalry among the officers in regard to the number of canes broken on the backs, legs and shins, not to speak of the heads of defaulters," wrote Klein. Some Chinese took special offense when the British would yell "let's go," which sounds like the Chinese word for dog, *Gou*.

As a result there were numerous incidents. "Much valuable language was wasted on both sides, and more misunderstandings resulted," wrote Gilchriese. "Strikes, and even riots, occurred with alarming frequency. . . ." To calm growing tensions, the Allies in 1918 engaged the YMCA, which went about organizing chess clubs, gave lectures, showed movies, started a theater club, and published a Chinese-language newspaper to make the Chinese feel more wanted.[18]

After all its rowdiness in Calgary and Edmonton, discipline in the 8th was not much of a problem. The only real incident occurred at the start of 1918, when the Russians refused to work following news of a Russian-German ceasefire, the subsequent Treaty of Brest-Litovsk, and the Russian withdrawal from the war. "It is doubtful whether or not the principles of Bolshevism had begun to take root among the personnel of this Battalion, but it can safely be said that when a very limited number of Russian personnel refused duty and were court-martialed and punished for their disobedience, there was no recurrence of insubordination," wrote Ian MacKenzie, a staff officer with the railway troops.

In February, Cohen developed arthritis of the right articulation of his jaw, possibly brought on by his bout of gonorrhea. The joint was sensitive to pressure and he was in constant pain. He soon lost partial use of his mouth. If he spoke too much, the area swelled and increased in tenderness. Any excitement brought on spasms that his doctor noted caused the "most unseemly jerking of the jaw." At the start, his attacks happened every week or so, lasting for two or three days. During an attack he could only open his mouth three-quarters of an inch. When not suffering he could open his mouth one and three-quarters of an inch before he had any pain. Chewing was extremely uncomfortable, and he had to subsist on hash and soft foods. Changes in the weather especially affected him.

In early March, Cohen took a two-week leave and headed back to England. By then the family had joined relatives in Manchester, having been driven from town in September 1917 following a German bombing attack. "A lump of shrapnel fell in our garden. We had a summer house, and it took the whole wall down and embedded itself in the ground," recalled Cohen's sister Leah Cooper of the damage done to a small structure behind their house at Tredegar Square. "It was from our own anti-aircraft gun . . . We never slept in that house again."

Cohen rejoined the ranks in mid-March, just in time for the start of a major German offensive. When in April 1918 the Germans started advancing near his area, the battalion had to retreat from a long stretch of the front from Steenwerck to Ploegsteert Wood, along through Wytschaete and Messines to Ypres. The Germans made quick progress, overrunning the communications system and the light railways. As the Allies retreated, Cohen and his comrades used a plow-like device to pull up and destroy the tracks. They carried off lathes and grinders from base areas and repair shops, and loaded howitzers on trucks. Before abandoning at least 189 light-railway steam locomotives and 136 petrol tractors, the men disabled them and removed all essential parts. They also torched 2,000 wagons.

During the retreat the troops scavenged for food and goods. One day Cohen and his fellow soldiers passed a deserted farm. In a sty alongside the tracks he saw three little pigs. "They were just the right size for a barbecue and I hadn't tasted pork for a long long time," he said. Cohen braked the train, hopped the fence, and slit the piglets' throats. He also made off with a gramophone and some records, which he found inside the house. The crew soon feasted.[19]

While Cohen worked, though, the pain in his jaw worsened. He probably should have known better than to crave hard-to-chew nonkosher meat. Cohen left his regiment in mid-June for treatment. On June 21, he went to the Southern General Hospital in Birmingham, followed by stays at various other hospitals. He received facial massages and in August doctors wired his mouth shut. "Getting my jaw right proved to be a slow business," Cohen said. "I was given electric treatment and my head was put in splints so that I couldn't chew and had to go on what they called a 'liquid diet.' It wasn't the right kind of liquid—not for me at any rate." He stayed that way for a month, and even went on brief leave. When the splint was finally removed his jaw appeared better.

On October 25, he was discharged from the hospital and sent to the base at Seaford. By November 11, the armistice was declared and the war was over. Then on November 20 Cohen went AWOL. "As far as I was concerned, I'd enlisted for the duration of the war and, as soon as the shooting stopped, my contract expired." He "set out for the Big Cities and the Bright Lights. I had a little money on me and I could borrow more from my buddies. For the next few weeks, I stayed 'AWOL' and made one big whoopee. As for the liquid diet, it just went down by the buck-etful." On December 1, after nearly two weeks of reveling, Cohen returned to his base. The army docked him twelve days' pay. Three days later he reverted to the rank of sapper. Then on the seventeenth he went AWOL again for three days and forfeited eight days' pay. He just could not wait to get away.[20]

On January 5, 1919, the military transferred the increasingly re-bellious Sapper Cohen to Kinmel Park in Rhyl, Wales. Kinmel Park, with its twenty subcamps, messes, theater, cinemas, Salvation Army, and YMCA build-ings, was an uncomfortable place. Soldiers relentlessly complained about the bad food, the chilly wooden huts, delays in getting paid, the lack of fuel, blankets, and bathing facilities. Most of all, Cohen and the others just wanted to return home. Yet there were snags in getting the men back. Only the Canadian ports of Halifax and St. John were not icebound. The news of the frozen harbors did not go over well with those who had spent long, frostbitten periods at the front. Small-scale riots, disturbances, and strikes broke out nearly every day.

Cohen often caught the narrow-gauge railway to Rhyl for some rest and mis-behaving. At the end of January, he received ninety-six hours' detention and forfeited five days' pay for his actions. Cohen was therefore quite relieved when his battalion left Liverpool on February 1 aboard the SS *Carmania*. He arrived in Canada on February 7, and proudly let Edmonton know that he was on his way home. While stationed in Ontario, "Sergeant" Cohen shot off a cable to his friend Mayor Joseph Clarke: "I have won the war and am arriving with my heroes." Clarke then shared the telegram with the *Journal,* which quickly published a small item on the return of the railway sapper and one of the paper's more colorful subjects: "That Sergeant Morris Abraham Cohen, the 218th Irish Guards boasted no smarter soldier, and many feminine hearts went pitter pat as the gallant non-commissioned officer marched away at the head of his platoon. But cheer up, girls, the sergeant is returning."

The following week the city feted its brave returning heroes. "When our train pulled into Edmonton . . . the flags were flying and the bands playing and the Mayor and Corporation and leading citizens were on the red-carpeted platform to welcome us . . . ," said Cohen. He and some of his comrades attended a reception in the Great War Veterans' Association club rooms. After lunch Cohen got a room at the Selkirk

Hotel on Jasper and 101st Street—hot and cold running water and a telephone in every room—all for as little as a dollar fifty a day. He then made his way to Chinatown to see his Asian buddies. "There were high festivities in Chinatown that first night home," reported the *Journal* of the return of the friend of the Chinese, "and Morris once more took up his role as friend and adviser to the little slant-eyed men that run laundries, chop-suey joints and lunch counters here."[1]

For war veterans, it was often difficult to readjust to peace. Many felt adrift after years of battle. "I just felt like a fish out of water," said Richard Mills of his return. "Nearly four years in the army . . . you feel strange." Cohen, too, experienced this sense of dislocation. On March 17, the army honorably discharged him as medically unfit. He had to figure out what he should now do. "The whoopee over, I sat down like many another man and wondered what to do next. . . . Somehow the war had unsettled me. I wanted to strike out a new line for myself, but what that new line was I'd no idea at all. I took stock of my assets. They came to more than I'd thought. I still had a little money in the bank from my prewar savings, and I had my war gratuity. I sold that four-carat diamond ring I'd been so proud of. . . . So I decided to look around for a while."[2]

The economy was still in bad shape, and Cohen's $420 war gratuity along with the money from his ring came in handy. The bustling Edmonton streets through which he once dragged eager investors past a frenzy of construction were now lined with empty lots. The National Land Company was defunct and Shepard and his brother were trying their hand at oil prospecting in Texas. Bad harvests and low wheat prices caused some farmers to abandon their farms. Unemployment throughout the land was high, as hundreds of thousands of munitions workers lost their jobs when the weapons factories no longer had to stoke the war.[3]

Selling real estate was what he knew best, so Cohen opened an office on the third floor of the Gariepy Block at 101st Avenue and 100th Street. It was a sparse three-room place, with a bed, writing desk, phone, table, dressing table, eight chairs, and coat hooks. He tacked maps and blueprints on the wall, placed ads in the *Journal*, and was back at work, answering his phone: "This is Sergeant Cohen's real estate office."

Some business came in. He sold a few farms, mining land, and whatever else people wanted to buy. Occasionally he cobrokered with other local real estate dealers like Thomas Dace and Frank Wilson. "I have made a real good living in selling farms," Cohen commented at that time. "I have made what the average man would consider a fairly good livelihood." The land moved slowly, but the old carnival talker barked up his successes, telling people that "I have been promoting companies," and boasting that he had formed a "syndicate" and sent some men out to file claims in the north woods. His counsel, he casually would mention, was also in communication with a firm of bankers for a concession in a foreign country. When in late 1920, Imperial Oil Ltd. discovered oil at Fort Norman on the Mackenzie River in the Northwest Territories, Cohen invested some money there. "I sent two men out to Fort Norman," Cohen said of his venture. "I have a number of oil leases up there in Fort Norman, with Mr. Rae, member of Parliament from the North country and several other gentlemen." He was not alone. Thousands flocked there. The flying ace Captain Wilfrid "Wop" May—who escaped becoming Captain Manfred von Richthofen's eighty-first victim when one of his comrades in another plane shot the Red Baron through the heart—even convinced Imperial Oil to allow him to fly in supplies on a pontoon-outfitted plane.

Cohen's oil and mining companies were at best loosely formed affairs. "They are companies to this extent: that we have invested money," he would clarify. "I have invested money in its promotion. I should call it—it is syndicates really. They are not incorporated at the present time." Whatever he earned from them was modest at best. It was not, though, as bad as Edmonton Detective Herbert B. Petheram's claim that "I haven't known him to do anything since he came back from overseas."[4]

Cohen was back to work, but he needed something that he had been trying for his entire life, respectability. He wanted to be taken seriously, to be seen as an influential person. One of the best ways to make and maintain contacts in Alberta after the war, and to advance socially and financially, was to join the Great War Veterans' Association. Veterans felt that Canada owed the 628,462 Canadians who had served in the armed forces—60,661 of whom had died—more than just the pay they received while they fought. Some soldiers were especially incensed that those who stayed at home during the war made a safe and profitable living while they had slogged through the European mud for a dollar ten a day. With about 250,000 members in 1919, along with its tremendous political and economic clout, the GWVA actively petitioned and won from the government veterans' benefits, gratuities for service, and widows' and orphans' pensions. They established a labor bureau and persuaded the government to offer soldiers 320 acres of land and loans of up to fifteen hundred dollars.[5]

While Edmonton business was glum, the city had occasional moments of lightness. In September 1919 the Prince of Wales whisked through Edmonton. He received an honorary degree at the university, visited military hospitals, was hosted at a luncheon at the Hotel Macdonald, took part in a duck shoot, had dinner at Government House, and went to the GWVA headquarters, where Cohen heard him deliver an address.

Cohen also kept his spirits up by pulling practical jokes on strangers. One possibly apocryphal tale of his exploits entailed finding a single, out-of-town man at night in a café, and staging a variation on the badger game con. Cohen and his chums would ask the visitor if he desired companionship. If he said yes they would suggest he go and see Marie, an attractive, lonely lady who craved company. Her husband, they informed the fellow, was a railroad man who worked far away from home. They also recommended that the fellow bring chocolates, since Marie liked sweets. The rube would buy a box of candies, and Cohen and his friends would run over to the vacant house where they had told the fellow to visit. One of Cohen's cohorts would then wait inside the house while Cohen and his chums hid in a junkyard across the street. When the out-of-towner knocked, the door would fly open and the man behind it would yell: "So you, sir, are the cad who's been hanging around my wife, while I, a poor but honest man, have been out working on the railroad. You, sir, are unfit to hold a place in human society." He would then pull out a pistol and shoot blanks, causing the frightened victim to bolt down the street and out of town. Cohen and his guffawing pals would then collect and eat the dropped box of chocolates.[6]

When he was not pulling jokes, Cohen still had poker. Locals as well as prominent gamblers like Chicago's "Bullface Bill" and Calgary's Timboli Storey were attracted to his office by the card playing and the takeout food. The game's popularity naturally attracted police attention. "I kept observation over men entering the premises and leaving the premises, early at night and late in the morning—between three and four in the morning—large bodies of men leaving the premises," noted Detective Percy Appleby of the coming and going of gamblers. Cohen did not try to hide his activities. He even told the officers to come up when they liked, since he never locked the door. When Cohen was away, he had his friend Fred Caron supervise the games. The police strolled in a few times, watched the men play, and wrote down their names. They saw no evidence that Cohen ran a real estate office, no documents, no ledgers, no books, just one map of Edmonton on the wall. On April 3, 1920, Officer William J. Gillam and Detective Archibald Connop stopped by. It was a busy day. Eight men played stud poker and a total of seventeen filled the three-room office, "lounging around, talking, sitting around; I couldn't say what they were doing beyond that," said Gillam.

After nearly half a year of watching, the police decided to shut the gambling den down. On September 25, Emily Murphy, the first female police magistrate in the British Empire, issued a search warrant, and at eleven-ten that evening Gillam and his men came a-calling. As Cohen promised, the front door stood open. There in the main room the police found seven men playing poker at a canvas-covered table. On a side table rested sandwiches and other food from the nearby Shasta Cafe. Poker chips were spread around the corner room and a few men played on top of a safe. Others strolled back and forth through the sitting room. "As I approached the accused, they started to deal cards, playing cards, at some game," said Gillam. The police then arrested Cohen, Caron, Henry Poland, Robert Clark, L. Cochrane, Duncan Munro, Walter Kelly, William Cherry, Sam Brest, Sam Tilley, Dan Toftland, Oscar Kessick, William Willie, and Robert Chisholm. As the officers started gathering up the evidence, Cohen piped up: "These are my friends. I want to cash in these chips they have. I have their money." Gillam allowed Cohen to pay them. But after he distributed $817.50, he realized he didn't have enough for everyone, and promised his mates he would get them the cash later. The police then confiscated green dealer shades, twenty-four packs of new cards, and the poker chips. Gillam started questioning the players and asked Poland why he was there. The gambler simply responded: "It was Saturday night. I didn't have nothing to do . . . and [I] like to play cards." Cochrane said he "came to play bridge, and then started to play stud poker." Cohen didn't like Gillam's questions and told his friends not to say anything unless advised to by their counsel.

The case of the gambling den was to go to trial a few days later, but on October 1 Cohen got a few days' reprieve by submitting a note from Dr. James McCormick saying that he was ill, and that it would be "a few days before he is able to leave the house." When the court finally convened, Cohen admitted that many men played cards in his office, but insisted he "never charged anything from any angle; in no manner, shape or form have I made a nickel from having a poker game up there." Some of the men present, he noted, came by just to play whist. "I don't suppose there is hardly a night that there may not have been somebody up there playing cards, bridge, whist, or maybe a little game of rummy. They are my friends. They are welcome up there. I never invite them. I might tell them to come any time . . . the door is open. . . . Anytime I can get into a real good poker game, I will do it, provided it is within the law." Look, he told the judge, I have nothing to hide. "I told Detective Gillam: 'Come up to my place any time. I like a little game of cards and I have my friends there with me, and walk up any time you like and you don't need a warrant.' "

All his friends swore that Cohen did not run a gambling den, and they only stopped by for a little convivial card playing. Chisholm said he was a farmer and had visited eight or nine times. The night of the arrest he was playing rummy on the safe with Kessick. Willie denied he was the notorious Bullface Bill, said he made money in the oil business in Wyoming and Montana and was trying to put together some "oil affairs" in the north. He said he came to Cohen's office almost daily. Cherry said he was a farmer, and had known Cohen for nearly a decade. He stopped by the office because he needed to see Clark about land and some money he had paid on a mortgage. Kelly was a rancher from British Columbia, while Toftland was a Saskatchewan farmer. Both spent afternoons and evenings at Cohen's.

It must have looked odd to the court that so many farmers spent so much time so far from their fields and livestock. On October 5, Police Magistrate P.C.H. Primrose convicted Cohen and subsequently sentenced him to four months hard labor at the provincial jail at Fort Saskatchewan. The others were more leniently handled, receiving twenty-dollar fines. Cohen was then released on his own recognizance, noting in his bail application that he was worth at least $1,000 and had land in Saskatoon and Moose Jaw worth $5,000. His parliamentary friend and associate William Rae put up the collateral.

Cohen's lawyer then tried to get the conviction reversed, since he claimed there was no proof that he kept a gambling house, there was no evidence that he took a rake-off, nor were the rooms being used for any sort of gain. On December 28, Judge Hyndman agreed and quashed the gambling case. Cohen then served Chief Constable Anthony G. Shute with an order to return all the confiscated poker chips and other paraphernalia.[7]

Around this time Cohen's brother Benjamin settled in town, and got a job at the Edmonton Clothing Company, where he became an assistant to the owner. Cohen's Chinese brothers in Edmonton fared as well as everyone else during and after the war. While the Canadian government did not draft the Chinese, a few did volunteer as enlisted men. Chinese-Canadians helped send relief money to China, purchased bonds, and took part in Canadian Victory Loan Drive parades. Unemployment among the Chinese during the hostilities reached a staggering 70 to 80 percent. The wealthy, the benevolent organizations, and the Zhigongtang helped the poor. During this period immigration from China slowed, and Chinese organizations even encouraged some to return to home.

Support for Sun Yat-sen was strong across the dominion. Cohen kept active with the Chinese Nationalist League and in local politics. "As soon as I was demobilized they came around asking me to go out on the stump and explain the situation in China to their lodges. Once again it was about as bad as it could be and once again it needed a whole lot of explaining." As the English secretary of the organization, Cohen protected and spoke up in defense of the Chinese. "In days gone by, when election time came around and one wanted to find out how the Chinese vote was going, there were always certain persons who could give the desired information," wrote the *Journal*. "After the war, it was Morris Cohen they went to for information. Morris had entered into the most absorbing interest of the majority of the local Chinese. He had become a member of the Chinese National League in Edmonton, and he was regarded almost as one of themselves by its native members. With the power to sway some six or seven hundred votes, practically all of them in the political riding of East Edmonton, Morris Cohen became a figure to be reckoned with at election time." Cohen's arrival at his old hangout, the Lewis' Cafe, was a tradition. There he would let it be known that he would sell the Chinese vote to the highest bidder. Whether Cohen actually had the power or just simply knew how the Chinese planned to vote was another story. "If there was anything that the Chinese of Edmonton wanted from would-be politicians, Morris Cohen let it be known in the right quarters. The Chinese quarter waited for word from Cohen as to how they were to vote."

To help Sun and his forces, Sun's Canadian followers started supplying pilots for the new republic. The Chinese raised about $50,000 for equipment—Cohen chipped in his share—and in May 1919 formed the Keng Wah Aviation school on prairie grassland in the northern outskirts of Saskatoon. There the Chinese built a hangar, and started training students from Canada, the United States, and China. Sun gave his blessing to the venture, and in late 1919 sent a commemorative good-luck scroll. Their first airplane was a surplus Curtiss Jenny biplane, the same type used to train Canadian pilots during the war. They hired Lieutenant Douglas Fraser of the Royal Air Force to conduct flying classes. The six students also attended courses in aeromechanics and maintenance. Soon Lieutenant Harry Lobb took over the teaching. He and subsequent instructors trained the men, and the school occasionally gave aerial displays, as in May 1921 when they went to Vancouver to fly at the Chinese Nationalists convention.[8]

As Cohen's position with the Chinese improved, so did his standing in Edmonton, where he was elected to the Executive Committee of the GWVA. In 1919
the Edmonton chapter went ahead with plans to build a new headquarters suited to
their growing stature. Cohen's real estate buddy Dace found the land for the building.
The $100,000 one-and-a-half-story Georgian-style building opened in mid-April
1920. With its deep red brick and stone, oak and maple floors, and plasterwork, it
was a fitting memorial to those who fought in the Great War. The barrel-vaulted
Assembly Hall with dark stained floors and large murals portraying battle accommodated seven hundred. The building contained meeting rooms, a lounge decorated
with battalion crests above the brick and birch fireplace, a library, a committee room,
and a canteen. Downstairs the men could wile away the hours at the four billiard
tables, along with two pool tables and two large tables for games. Upstairs there was
a dormitory with twelve beds and shower facilities for those staying overnight.

The night of the opening, the route to the structure down Macdonald Drive was
"gaily lit with colored bulbs and the building itself was outlined in a golden flood."
In an elaborate ceremony ex-mayor Harry Evans turned over the building's key to
President H. L. Collins. The GWVA and the Journal Newsboys band provided the
music. When Lieutenant Governor Robert Brett stepped out on the stage the band
struck up the national anthem, and Cohen and his buddies jumped to attention. Premier Charles Stewart and others noted that "the fifteen hundred and more veterans
that crowded the assembly hall to the doors and overflowed into the hallways, lustily
cheered their appreciation of the generosity of the people of Alberta and more particularly of Edmonton, that had provided them with such a magnificent headquarters."

For quite a few of the soldiers, the opening of such a grand edifice was a pleasant
diversion from the poverty of the economy. The building became the focus of
veterans' activities, as the GWVA organized evening dances, concerts, and soccer
and cricket teams. Edmontonians also came here to donate clothes, overcoats, even
old uniforms for out-of-work and destitute soldiers. From their new headquarters,
the GWVA lobbied politicians and businesses to find veterans jobs.[9]

Even though officials voiced optimism that the economy was moving ahead, it
showed no real improvement. The Edmonton Horticultural and Vacant Lots Association as well as the North West Biscuit Company inaugurated programs for the
cultivation of land and the beautification of the cityscape. By the winter of 1921
conditions worsened as outdoor work stopped. The GWVA had four hundred veterans who needed work, and the city council met with the GWVA, the Trades and
Labor Council, the Welfare Board, the Red Cross, and the Provincial Labor Bureau
to make arrangements for food and temporary shelters. The GWVA even appointed
two committees to deal with the growing problem.[10]

With work hard to come by, some unemployed whites naturally blamed new-
comers like the Chinese for all their woes. Immigration had picked up after the Great
War, and in 1919, 4,066 Chinese arrived in Canada. As immigration rose so did
resentment. It mattered little that a mere 37,163 Chinese men and 2,424 Chinese
women lived in all of Canada in 1921. Groups like the Asiatic Exclusion League,

the United Farmers of British Columbia, and the Disabled Soldiers' Association called for the restriction of Asians. Veteran Bruce Cole recalled that in 1921 "organizations sprang up against ethnic elements, particularly against Hindus in British Columbia and Greeks in Toronto. Restaurants were smashed. The soldiers that came back and the Anglo-Saxons generally took the attitude that they couldn't find work because of these ethnic groups. In British Columbia there was an organization called the Anti Asiatic Exclusion League."

Prominent officials like Police Magistrate Murphy further fanned anti-Asian sentiments. Her 1922 book *The Black Candle* warned of the dangers posed by drugs brought in by the Chinese. Unless this menace was stopped, she predicted, Asians and blacks would take over and bring down white society. In 1919 the province of British Columbia prohibited white women and girls from being employed in Chinese-owned or -managed businesses. The government soon ruled that laboring-class Chinese could not enter the country. By 1921 the Chinese lost the federal election franchise. In Alberta the talk was less severe than in British Columbia, yet its volume and fervor increased. It was especially tense between white and Chinese businesses, and the Trades and Labor Council in Edmonton called for the punishment of Chinese laundries that did not shut at six in the evening as required by law.[11]

In 1921, Edmonton workers started protesting the announcement that Chinese from British Columbia would clean and gut trout, whitefish, and grayling at the new Mackenzie Fisheries Company facilities at Lake Athabaska to the north. "It has been found that white men will not perform the unpleasant task of gutting and cleaning the fish," reported the *Morning Bulletin*, "the Indians are too easy going to take any interest in toil, so as is the case on the coast, the ubiquitous Chinamen will have to fill the breach." A letter of complaint published in the local press and addressed to the Alberta premier Herbert H. Greenfield demanded that he exert some leadership by "putting [his] foot down firmly and asserting that the fisheries of Alberta shall not become the property of Japanese and Chinese."[12]

The image of the Chinese needed polishing, and Cohen actively set out to help his friends. He continued his advocacy and public relations efforts, and kept in touch with Sun Yat-sen and other Chinese officials. When Chen Shuren, the president of the Chinese Nationalist Party of Canada, arrived in Edmonton during the winter of 1921–22, Cohen showed him around and introduced him to such supporters as Lieutenant Colonel George B. McLeod, George Massie, and A. McLaughlin. On February 27, 1922, Mayor and Mrs. David M. Duggan, McLeod and his wife, Mr. and Mrs. Mark Wright, Alice A. McConnell, and Patrick Fitter attended a large annual Chinese banquet. There they feasted on bird's-nest soup, fish, meats, fowl, and dried Chinese fruits, listened to Chinese music and saw a Chinese play.[13]

In June 1922, the GWVA announced that in the last two weeks it had placed 210 men in jobs. Even so, 132 still needed employment. At a general meeting of the GWVA on the twenty-fifth, the group wrestled with what to do about work. "Many hard-hitting speeches were made during the debate on the subject by prominent members of the organization, including Comrades Wilson, Lang, Mason,

Poole, Irwin, Hawkins and Cohen," reported the *Journal*. The subject of the ideal
scapegoat, the Asiatics, quickly became the main item. When a member tabled a
motion to endorse a petition for the exclusion of undesirable Asiatics, it found resounding favor in the hall. Some of the veterans spoke of the impossibility of assim-
ilating the various people of Asia, "stating that the white races could not compete
with the yellow in the labor market, due to their standard of living and that it was
in the best interests of Canada to close her doors to this class of immigrants." One
of the lone voices of opposition, noted the *Morning Bulletin*, was comrade Cohen,
who "objected to the motion, pointing out that the Chinese had been our allies
during the war, and that Japanese soldiers who had fought in Canadian battalions
were also members of the GWVA." It would be a "rank ingratitude," Cohen
pleaded, to treat them badly. Despite his objections, the motion carried.[14]

Even if his former comrades in arms opposed the Chinese, Cohen worked to
make sure businesses gave the Asians a fair shake. He saw to it that Chinese chefs
received the same pay as white ones. When veterans complained that the Chinese
stole all the good jobs at the meat-packing plant, Cohen went to work to protect
them. Since he and the Chinese knew that whites considered work at the plant base
labor, Cohen told the Chinese to resign their jobs with the hope that no veterans
would fill the vacant spots. The Chinese nervously took his advice and quit. Cohen
then visited the meat-packing plant manager the following day and told him why
they had decided to leave. The manager called up the GWVA and let the organization know that he had work available. No one reportedly came forward. "I sat
back for four or five days, and then it was the Manager of the packing-plant who
wanted to see me, please."

Cohen and the Chinese easily followed the ongoing struggle in China, which
was regularly reported in the local papers. Cohen also disseminated Chinese news
to the press. "The civil war in China is far from being ended according to a report
on the affair which has been sent officially to the Edmonton Chinese, through the
English secretary of the nationalists, Morris A. Cohen, who has held the position for
the last decade, and who is reputed to be in close touch with Dr. Sun Yat-sen. Mr.
Cohen has been an authority on things Chinese in Edmonton and Canada for many
years, and he has now received from . . . [the] Washington plenipotentiary for Dr.
Sun Yat-sen, a communication to all the Chinese of Canada, stating the case of
Southern China in the present war."[15]

There was much to report. Yuan had announced his plan to reestablish the
empire with himself as emperor, but when he died on June 6, 1916, Vice President
Li Yuanhong took over as president, and republican government was marginally
restored. China, though, was still in disarray. The country started to fracture as
generals carved up provinces into personal fiefdoms. In August 1917, Sun returned
to Canton by gunboat to establish his own government, and invited others to join
him. Militarists, politicians, and legislatures gathered in the city, where they formed
the Chinese National Military Government. When Sun lost control of the government, he left first for Japan and then Shanghai.

He subsequently allied himself with the southern warlord Chen Jiongming, a reform-minded militarist who first joined Sun's Tongmenghui in 1909. Hoping to establish a base and a southern republic in Guangdong, Sun urged Chen to drive out the occupying armies from neighboring Kwangsi. When Chen was victorious, Sun returned to the city in November 1920. The following year Sun got Chen to invade and conquer Kwangsi. As the new governor of Guangdong, Chen set out to modernize Canton, rip down walls, build roads, abolish gambling and opium smoking, set up dozens of primary schools, improve health conditions, and hire street cleaners. On February 15, 1921, he asked Sun Yat-sen's son Sun Fo to become mayor and carry out reforms.

Chen was pleased with his autonomous satrapy, but Sun Yat-sen had grander dreams. In April 1921 Sun was elected provisional President, and set about waging a northern expedition to conquer the entire country. Chen, though, did not want to waste men or money on such an adventure. When Chen did not back him, Sun dismissed him. In May 1922 Chen struck back, captured Canton, and burned down Sun's home.[16]

Like Sun, Cohen's own prospects were dimming. Back on the evening of March 5, 1922, Cohen and about fifteen others were at a gambling den run on 101st Street. The playing was raucous. A number of neighbors complained, and Chief Constable Shute, Inspector Jacob J. Shaw, and others backed a patrol wagon up to the front door. Unlike Cohen's office–cum–gambling den, access here was not easy. Locks and bars prevented swift entry through the front and back doors. As the police forced their way through, Cohen and the others ran, and according to the *Bulletin* "there was a scurry to the basement." When the police made it in, they discovered an underground passage to an adjoining Chinese café.[17]

Cohen succeeded in getting acquitted on that one, too. By that summer he had had enough of Edmonton. He had no specific plans, but since his return from France he had spoken about going to China. He had even applied for a passport in August 1920, saying he needed it to travel to Hong Kong and China. When his friend M. D. Hong, a wealthy local Chinese merchant, mentioned that he wanted to visit his family in Canton, the two decided to set off together. As Cohen made arrangements to sail to China, he was contacted by Sun and asked to see about arranging for a Canadian railway contractor to come to Shanghai to discuss construction of a 252-mile-long central section of the Canton–Hankou railway.

To Sun, the railways represented a major project that was needed to make China strong. When the Manchus fell, China had a mere 5,796 miles of railway. Soon after Sun stepped down as provisional president, Yuan appointed him director general of National Railways, with authority to contract loans and execute projects. Sun came to his new job with big plans, hoping to harness two million workers to lay 75,000 miles of new tracks in ten years. He foresaw networks of national lines lacing together the provinces, but with all the upheavals that beset China following the fall of the Manchus and Yuan's own demise, progress was slow. By 1920 China had 6,856 miles of tracks. Only 398 miles of the Canton–Hankou line stood completed.[18]

Having been dropped into the job cold, Cohen scrounged around for a contractor. Eventually he went to Vancouver. There he obtained an introduction to the new firm of Northern Construction & J. W. Stewart Ltd. John W. Stewart, the major general who commanded Cohen's railway battalion in France, ran the firm. "I had pull there because General Stewart . . . [had] been in charge of light railway construction in France during the war and known me there. I saw the president of the company and he was interested from the start." The talks went smoothly with C. V. Cummins, the firm's vice president, and both sides agreed that Northern Construction would undertake the work and Cohen would receive a hefty commission. It was then arranged that Cohen would head off to Shanghai, where he would wait for Cummins to meet with Sun and complete the agreement.

In preparation for his trip Cohen bought some business and formal clothes, shoes and hats, and renewed his passport on November 5. The Chinese threw Cohen and Hong a large going-away dinner, and friends gave Cohen letters to deliver to family in China. "All Chinatown took an interest in seeing to it that he was properly equipped for the visit and the presentation to Dr. Sun. Morris must do the honors for all the China-boys of Edmonton," wrote the *Journal.* "There were consultations, rush orders at the tailor's, messages to be carried to Canton, and finally a lengthy dinner in the Chinese style, at which the formal farewells were said and the last felicitations given."

Cohen packed his bags and the railway contract, and checked out of his room with the adjoining gambling den at the Hotel Macdonald. The two friends then took a train to Vancouver and boarded the Canadian Pacific's new *Empress of Australia,* with its ballroom and fine cabins. Like his departure from England seventeen years earlier, the move was a gamble. This time, though, it was his decision to go. As he sailed out of Vancouver on November 23, 1922, Cohen watched his adopted Canada slip over the horizon. He was finally on his way to the mysterious Orient that Mah Sam had first told him about.[19]

ohen had talked with his friends about returning to
Canada after completing the Northern Construction deal. Yet
deep down he hoped to stay and work for Sun Yat-sen. Just in case his dream came
true, he packed accordingly: "I set out on that voyage with eight guns in my luggage,
and when I landed in Shanghai I was so top-heavy with artillery, if you'd given me
a push I'd have fallen slap on my backside." When Cohen and his guns arrived in
Shanghai on December 12, they headed away from the stagnant, smoky docks to
the grand Astor House Hotel in the city's International Settlement. He made a good
choice of lodgings, for the Astor House with its palm court and French chef was the
place where high society played. Here Ferral in André Malraux's *Man's Fate* uncaged
parrots, cockatoos, and a kangaroo in his mistress's room. Tea and dinner dances
were a regular event at the hotel, while silk-suited newspapermen like Vincent
Sheean passed the time in the wood-paneled lobby drinking scotch whiskey, puffing
on Egyptian cigarettes, and expounding on the shortcomings of China. As one old
resident of Shanghai and veteran hotel lounger told the journalist John B. Powell,
"If you will sit in the lobby of the Astor House and keep your eyes open you will
see all of the crooks who hang out on the China coast."

The desk clerk placed Cohen in room 301, partway up the grand winding
staircase. His small room with the high ceiling and black fireplace contained a round
table, a wooden chair, and a soft easy chair. In the corner stood a dresser with a large
round mirror, and next to it a wooden wardrobe. As he unpacked his clothes and
weapons, he could hear the sounds of ship horns and arguing sampan navigators as
their thin boats banged and jockeyed under the Garden Street Bridge. "From the
city street . . . came the hum of traffic, the sound of bicycle and street-car bells and
the eternal chanting of the coolies," wrote Dora Sanders Carney, who arrived at the
Astor about a decade after Cohen. "I could hear too the cries of boatmen poling
their craft on near-by Suzhou Creek."

Through the tall windows hung with long strips of flowered cretonne, Cohen gazed across at the heavily fortified Russian consulate. South, beyond the embassy and across Suzhou Creek, stood the public garden. Farther on along the Bund towered Shanghai's majestic skyline with the marble and limestone piles that housed the mighty western firms that dominated the city's business. "The Bund was a hurly-burly of movement and bewildering noise," wrote Carney of the stately road bordering the Huangpu River and into which the boats on the Suzhou flowed. "Cars tooted, street-cars clanged, bicycle bells shrilled continuously." The International Settlement, like similar concessions throughout China, was western controlled, wrestled by the foreign powers from the weak Chinese government years before. Because of the rules of extraterritoriality, foreigners like Cohen who settled and worked there were free of the confines of Chinese law. In these fortified enclaves, westerners scorned their Chinese hosts and lived by the rules of their homelands. Foreign troops stood guard, children attended European-style schools, and firms practiced commerce free of the constraints that shackled their Chinese counterparts.[1]

Cohen might have just disembarked from a nearly three-week journey across the Pacific, but he was anxious to meet Sun, the leader of whom he had heard glorious legends for more than a decade. He needed to discuss with him the Northern Construction contract, but more than that, he hankered for a job. Yet to get to Sun Cohen required an introduction. Cohen had heard that one of the best routes to Sun was through George Sokolsky, the Utica, New York, born journalist who worked for Sun's English-language Shanghai *Gazette*. He hailed one of the rickshaws waiting at the Astor's entrance and nervously settled into the narrow seat. The driver tilted back his heavy load and rhythmically loped along to Sokolsky's.

Cohen picked the right man for access to Sun. Sokolsky had proven an invaluable source of information, gossip, and contacts for reporters, having arrived in China via Russia in 1918 after the Bolsheviks expelled him for covering the revolution. As a Jew and the son of a rabbi, many westerners in China viewed Sokolsky as a subversive. What better supplicant could there be than a Cockney Jew who eagerly sought the real China. Sokolsky welcomed Cohen, and arranged an interview for him with Eugene Chen, a lawyer turned Sun's overly emphatic English language secretary. "I remember the day he came to call on me and ask me how to get to Sun," said Sokolsky of Cohen's visit. "He came to see me . . . and asked me if I would fix it up for him to see Eugene Chen, which I did." Cohen set right off to see the sharp-tongued Trinidad-born secretary. Despite Chen's well-deserved reputation of being the bane of western powers—what Sheean referred to as his "instinctively antagonistic" manner coupled with a laugh that was "a singularly humorless, inhuman thing"—Cohen passed his interview. He secured the desired appointment.[2]

Sun resided at 29 Rue Molière in the French Concession, a popular neighborhood to the south of the International Settlement, where prominent political refugees lived protected by the western law they condemned. Sun had settled there a few months earlier after fleeing Canton following Chen Jiongming's coup. When Cohen arrived, one of Sun's bodyguards looked him over and ushered him into the modest, stuccoed home and introduced him to Sun. While they spoke, Sun's wife, Soong Qingling [Mme. Sun], came by. There before Cohen stood one of the legendary Soong sisters. He was smitten. "To tell the truth I didn't look at him for very long, because we'd hardly begun to talk when Mme. Sun walked in and after that I'd only got eyes for her," Cohen said. "That first interview didn't last long. Mme. Sun had come in to remind the Doctor that he had a string of appointments all the afternoon and so he told me I'd better come back and discuss the contract the following day."

Cohen returned to the Astor. He stopped by the bar for a drink. Bored and lonely in a new city, Cohen said he felt like "a stranger in a very, very strange land." He wandered out of the Astor, through the settlement, and south into the Chinese city's "narrow, twisty, filthy little back streets." He just kept on walking, passing buildings where he "heard that awful Chinese music—I've never got to like it even today—and the rattle of the mah jong pieces and I learnt after a bit to jump out of the way when I heard a shout of 'Ohé!' and heavy breathing behind me, because that meant porters on the march and they might be carrying anything from a giant jar of oil to a dead man in a basket." Cohen explored the city for hours, and even though he had been in the country for only a short while, "already China was beginning to get under my skin."

The next day Cohen returned to Rue Molière. Sun examined the railway contract. All appeared in order. When C. V. Cummins's ship docked a fortnight later, Cohen met him at the pier. Sun and Cummins signed the contract. The following day Cohen rode back to Sun's home to give Sun the hard sell. Cohen turned on his best salesman charm and snagged the job he wanted, that of a bodyguard to the man he revered as the leader of China and China's dispossessed. Sun bestowed upon Cohen the title of *fuguan*, adjutant. Cohen's plans were complete. He soon adopted the pidgin name of Kow-hen. Later he would be occasionally referred to as the more Chinese sounding Ma-Kun. Yet Cohen had little use for the new appellation or the brothel-type Cantonese he had picked up in Canada. Most of Sun's entourage spoke English. Sun had been educated in Honolulu and Hong Kong. His bright, beautiful wife and her sisters and brothers had studied in the United States, and many of Sun's underlings attended western-run Chinese schools.

Cohen fit in for other reasons, too. Sun must have seen his more youthful self in the rough Cockney to whom he entrusted his safety. Like Cohen, he was not quite what his parents had bargained for. At an early age, Sun's father sent him to school in Honolulu. When the teenage Sun returned to China in the early 1880s, he felt alienated and very much out of place in his home village of Cuiheng, thirty miles north of Macao. He flaunted his western learning and scoffed at the idolatry and superstitions he perceived. There he defiled two temple statues. Sun's father— just like Cohen's in 1905—had no choice but to send his wayward child away. He dispatched him to Hong Kong, where he entered the Diocesan School of the Church of England. From there Sun attended Queen's College, and following his father's death converted to Christianity. While at medical school in Hong Kong, he was introduced to the anti-Manchu triads and learned of his nation's decline and shame. When Sun failed to obtain an audience with the viceroy in Tianjin to discuss a medical position in that city and to suggest reform policies, his transformation and abhorrence of the empire was firmly cast. He became a small-time revolutionary. As he plotted and planned to end imperial rule, he made feeble grasps at power. All failed. Like Cohen, he started reinventing his past. Sun used fake birth certificates, traveled with forged documents and passports, and even married Soong Qingling, the daughter of his friend and fellow triad member Charles Jones Soong, without divorcing his first wife.[3]

And like Cohen, Sun was an egotist. He claimed credit for many of the changes in China, barely admitting the accomplishments and contributions of others. But Sun also had selfless dreams of national redemption and the deliverance of the masses from Manchu bondage. He believed that like his hero, the Taiping leader Hong Xiuquan, he was on an almost divine mission to forge a new China. Such a utopian pursuit, though, was antithetical to Cohen's lifestyle. It was therefore odd that Cohen the hustler would want to ally himself with Sun the visionary. Yet despite the fact that China in the 1920s stood wide open for westerners to do as they pleased, with countless ways to make a fortune in shady enterprises, Cohen's time with Mah Sam and the rest of the Edmonton Chinatown crowd made this con man an unlikely idealistic.

In the Canadian prairies, thousands of miles from the turmoil of the Chinese revolution, this Polish son of persecuted Jews had fallen under Sun's spell. "I have never met a man with blood in his veins who after having had contact with Dr. Sun Yat-sen, hearing him speak and been taught by him, would not wish to follow him in revolution," said Cohen of the effect this son of a Chinese farmer had on him. "Dr. Sun Yat-sen often said to me that his aim in revolution was to make China a country respected among the nations of the world, to establish a government of the people, by the people and for the people. He also wanted to ensure that everyone had food to eat, and that laborers would enjoy the fruits of their labor, and ensure that children were educated. What an aspiration this is!"

This mustached and meticulously groomed man had such a mesmerizing effect on people. Sun commanded a fanatical following. His magnetic personality united his disparate party. His theories attracted interest far beyond the confines of the Guomindang, securing for him the admiration of students, intellectuals, and other countrymen, and making Sun a leading moral force in China. "It is a remarkable fact," wrote Sir Ronald Macleay, the British Minister in Beijing in 1923, "that Sun Yat-sen is the only personage of any prominence in China who manages to hold his own without any troops attached to him personally and his continuance in power . . . is apparently due solely to the force of his personality."

Fealty to Sun caused his oldest followers to call him *Xiansheng*—master. Many like Cohen swore their lives and sacred honor to him. Malraux best summed up the passion of Cohen and Sun's other followers when one of his characters in *The Conquerors* noted that for those who "came along in Sun's time, 1921, 1922, to take their chances or stake their lives, and who have to be called adventurers; for them China's a great pageant that they play parts in. Revolutionary fervor does for these men what a taste for army life does for members of the French Foreign Legion— they're men who've never been able to conform in ordinary society, who've asked a great deal of life, who wanted to give some meaning to their own lives, and who now, coming out the other side of all that, *serve*."[4]

Cohen the gambler and the cynic had come to Shanghai to serve Sun. He packed a Smith & Wesson and soon joined the other guards lodging above the garage to the side of the house. When on duty, he screened those who came by to visit his *Xiansheng*. Visitors to Rue Molière would often find Sun in his office dressed in a traditional long gown. As they sat down in the dark, mission-style furniture, sur- rounded by his wood-and-glass book cases, Sun offered callers Chinese tobacco and cigarette papers, some fruit, as well as a pot of tea. Outside in the hallway, Cohen sat, his gun ready for trouble. "I was met at the door by a colorful character named Maurice Cohen," recalled Powell of a visit with Sun. "Cohen always sat on a bench in the front hall and carried a large revolver in his hip pocket, which caused the seat of his trousers to sag grotesquely." Many others came by. "Mr. Sun's custom with visitors was to see them at whatever time they called, and he never kept guests out because he was busy with public business or with any other reason," said bodyguard Bi Xi of the steady stream of callers.[5]

As time passed, Cohen settled into the routine of his job, learned about the different callers, and listened to the goings on in Sun's study. "Whenever a visitor was announced (and there were dozens a day sometimes) I'd study his face and his dress and his mannerisms so that I'd know him again," he said. It was a relaxing time. During the day, the household might play a game of croquet in the small back garden. At night, Soong and Sun sat together and read and chatted. Being a movie fan, Soong occasionally organized an evening screening.

Cohen was enthralled by Sun's wife. He watched over her as carefully as he did Sun. Soong appreciated Cohen's attentions. She trusted him and grew quite fond of him. Soong was a woman "with a childlike figure of the most enchanting delicacy. . . . She had a dignity so natural and certain that it deserved the name of stateliness," wrote Sheean a few years later of the attraction that ended up captivating the nation.

The same quality can occasionally be observed in royal princes or princesses of Europe, especially in the older ones; but with them it is a clear result of lifelong training. Mme. Sun's stateliness was of a different, a more intrinsic quality; it came from the inside out, instead of being put on like a harness. She also possessed moral courage to a rare degree, which could keep her steadfast in grave peril. Her loyalty to the name of Sun Yat-sen, to the duty she felt she owed it, was able to withstand trials without end. These qualities—dignity, loyalty, moral courage—gave her character an underlying strength that could, at times, overcome the impressions of fragility and shyness created by her phys- ical appearance and endow her figure with the sternest aspect of heroism. . . .

She was, in a truer sense than the merely physical one intended by the headline writers, "China's Joan of Arc," but you had to know her for a good while before you realized the power of the spirit beneath that exquisite, tremulous envelope.

For Sun, however, his time in Shanghai proved trying. He yearned to return to power in Canton, as well as to secure diplomatic recognition, yet the British, Japanese, and Americans paid him scant attention. The only nation mildly interested in relations with China was the likewise disdained Soviet Russia. Following the 1917 Russian Revolution, the Soviets started viewing China as fertile ground on which to spread international Communism. In 1919, Vladimir Ilyich Lenin founded the Communist International—the Comintern—to disseminate his radical cause. The following year, the Comintern agent Gregory Voitinsky arrived in China and met with the Chinese communists Li Dazhao and Chen Duxiu. The three organized a Socialist Youth League and formed plans for the Chinese Communist Party.

In the fall of 1922 the Soviet representative, Dr. Adolf Joffe, traveled to Beijing to seek recognition of his government. He was rebuffed in his advances, so the English-speaking Joffe headed to Shanghai and dined at Rue Molière in mid-January 1923. Sun appealed to the Soviets. He sympathized with their cause, took an interest in Lenin's revolution, and wanted to learn more about the organization of Soviet government, army, and education. The Soviets also saw him as a potential border ally. The two men discussed the state of China. The land, they agreed, was not ready for communism. It needed to be unified first. They established relations, and on January 26 issued the Sun-Joffe Manifesto, which recognized Sun's right to speak for the nation.[6]

As Sun discussed relations with the Soviets, forces from Guangdong, Yunnan, and Guangxi allied to him defeated Chen. Sun could now return south. On the morning of February 15, Sun, Cohen, and the rest of the entourage boarded the SS *President Jefferson*. As they sailed down the coast, Cohen started his China-based self-promotion campaign. "The debonair Canadian of unmistakable Jewish features, is perfectly at home among Cantonese members of Dr. Sun's 'inner circle,' " wrote the American journalist Junius B. Wood of Cohen, hinting at his important involvement in the Chinese revolution. "While other members of the Chinese party kept strictly to themselves on the ship which brought Dr. Sun to Hongkong, the 'man of mystery' made friends with everybody and discussed everything except why he is interested in Chinese politics."

Two days later the *President Jefferson* sailed into Hong Kong harbor. Launches carrying labor union deputations and other pro-Sun groups cruised the water beneath the lush peaks on Hong Kong Island to greet the famed leader. Along the pier in Kowloon on the mainland, excited knots of Chinese gathered to catch a glimpse of him as he disembarked. The police ushered Sun, his bodyguards and friends away from the crowds and into a special boat and escorted them across to the island. There waiting motor cars took the group to the guarded home of a Sun supporter. On the following day, "A procession of cars with little flags on their bonnets took us up the hill and swept through the gates of Government House," said Cohen. The president had to be defended, so while Sun met with Governor Reginald E. Stubbs, Cohen hopped out with the other bodyguards and cased the area. There was a commotion when Sun left the colony, too; a large crowd gathered and set off firecrackers at the Steamboat Company Wharf as he arrived just before eight in the morning. Decorated launches and motor boats then escorted Sun's ship partway toward Canton.

Sailing up the Pearl River to Cohen's new home, the SS *Heungshan* passed paddy fields, clumps of wavering bamboo stands, small villages, and temples. Submerged water buffaloes, their nostrils sticking above the muddy water surface, bobbed nearby. Occasionally, frightened ducks and kingfishers skitted though the cattail-lined shore. At Canton, Sun and Soong disembarked, preceded by Cohen and some of the other plain-clothed guards. The town gave Sun a hero's welcome. Flags of the different guest armies flapped above the road. Cars sported flowers, thousands of troops lined the streets with blue GMD flags fluttering from their rifles. As Sun drove by, firecrackers exploded and bands dressed in red velvet tunics struck up the "Presidential Salute."[7]

When Chen's men captured the city in 1922, they had destroyed Sun's head-quarters. Now back in town, Sun and his entourage took over a former cement factory building on Henan Island, across the river from Canton. Shaded by bou-gainvillea and palms, the structure to the south of the city was a strong, three-story building with arched terraces and balustrades over which small, nearly transparent lizards scurried. They set up their new base, and started reestablishing a command center. *Fuguans* at the headquarters were divided into three sections. The highest-ranking group included Huang Huilong, Deng Yanhua, Ma Xiang, and Cohen. They manned their post outside Sun's rooms on the top floor. There Cohen, wearing his customary light-colored suit, tie, and sun helmet, lounged in a wicker armchair set on the tile floor. "The four of them stayed on the third floor where Sun Yat-sen was living," said Fan Liang, who joined the bodyguard staff in the autumn of 1923. "They stayed there all the time. They were there every day. They didn't leave him even for one day. They were very strong and no one could overcome them."

As they resettled in Canton, Cohen helped train and increase the number of uniformed bodyguards. The men did target practice and drills. Most importantly, when they had night duty, the *fuguans* made sure they stayed awake till morning. Cohen also taught the men self-defense and boxing; his training at the People's Arcade made him a good teacher. "All the boxing I know I learned from him," said Fan. Cohen advised his men, "First fight your enemies with the fists, and if you can't get them that way, then you should use your gun. Never use the gun first. Don't just pull out the gun anytime." Innocent bystanders might be around and "if you pull out your gun you are going to harm other people." Cohen made a for-midable instructor and foe. "Of course I could never beat him, he was our teacher," recalled Fan.[8]

In early March Sun became Generalissimo of the military government. He also met with Sir James Jamieson, the British consul general. The two men discussed improving the nearby port of Whampoa and linking the existing railway from Canton to Hankou and Canton to Kowloon. Sun took the opportunity to ask Jamieson for British assistance in reorganizing his government's finances. But since British policy in China officially centered on the British Legation in Beijing and the government of the north, no money was forthcoming. At the same time, Cohen made regular visits to the various western consulates on Shameen Island, a cigar-shaped western concession along the banks of the Pearl River. There he got to know the staffs and handed out freshly printed cream-colored business cards with raised black letters reading "Morris A. Cohen A.D.C. to Dr. Sun Yat-sen."[9]

As in Shanghai, a constant series of visitors stopped by Sun's headquarters. As guests disembarked from their boats and walked up from the jetty into the compound, they passed troops working on equipment and training. At the building, smart-looking soldiers presented arms and offered the impression of strength. If the visitor carried a weapon, he had to surrender it at the door. Many Chinese and westerners came by to see Sun and discuss politics. "Rarely during our months in Canton was the 'Generalissimo' seen even in semi-public without Mrs. Sun the second at his side and the belligerent, or at least highly protective, face of Mr. Cohen in the immediate background," wrote the travel writer Harry A. Franck. "When we had the honor one Sunday morning to call upon Dr. Sun at his cement factory headquarters and residence, his Canadian shadow, tucked into a corner of the stairway at the entrance to the Doctor's study, scrutinized not only me but my wife as if to make sure that she had not come to wreak mischief on his chief."

Sun took an interest in all his guests. "He would ask about their families' situation, and inquire for news of other comrades, making everyone feel really close," said Cohen. "In his hard won free time, he often went to the countryside to talk to the farmers, asking in detail about the peoples' hardships. Once he also told his A.D.C. to write down the address of a poor peasant woman, and find someone to take her relief items. But whenever rich merchants and big businessmen, or so-called important people came to visit him, we all knew they would not talk for very long."[10]

With so little foreign or domestic support, Sun had a lot of work ahead of him. Following the fall of the Manchus and the fiasco of Yuan's rule, China splintered into rival military satrapies ruled by powerful military cliques and petty warlords like Chen who hoped to suppress Sun's upstart government. It took little to be a warlord, essentially a tax base, a reliable source of soldiers and arms, and the control of ports. Sun lacked these prerequisites. In Canton, he reigned as a paper Generalissimo, controlling the city and little more; only his 150 to 200 bodyguards could be deemed entirely subordinate to him. He therefore had little choice but to sanction the acts of the Yunnan, Guangxi, Hunan, Jiangxi, Guangdong, and Fujian guest armies who filled the town and on whom he depended.

Ex-bandits often ran these bands of undisciplined, inexperienced mercenaries. The strutting gangsters lived on bravado, riding around town with Mauser-toting guards standing on their cars' running boards. "They couldn't do much in the way of shooting; they were too busy clinging on for their lives; but their just being there discouraged assassins, and anyway their actual bodies gave some sort of protection to the occupants," said Cohen. The troops appeared everywhere. According to Franck, they were "ragged, lazy, destructive bums and ex-bandits, who were quartered in almost every temple, in confiscated factories, commandeered houses, in anything without foreign protection that was capable of holding a few of them."

It cost a lot of money to maintain the forces. In early 1923 supporting the 30,000 to 40,000 troops under his nominal control cost Sun tens of thousands of dollars a day in payments to the various military forces. Warlords also taxed heavily and forced merchants and banks to issue loans. The Yunnanese, for example, controlled the gambling tax and made money by licensing opium-smoking establishments. Commanders spent little of their ill-gotten revenues on the maintenance of their men. Officers regularly beat soldiers, and executed men for minor offenses. Military equipment was shoddy, supplies minimal, training haphazard. Most soldiers could not even shoot a gun.[11]

Needing to establish a reliable force, Sun started organizing his military. In 1920 he ordered the establishment of an Aviation Bureau. One of his Hawaiian supporters, Yang Xianyi, traveled through the western United States in search of aviators. In March 1922, at an air show in San Jose, California, Yang came across the traveling Abbott's Sky Demons Aerial Circus. Major Wayne Abbott and his son Harry W. Abbott ran the barnstorming, wing-walking, and stunt-flying troupe. Yang asked the elder Abbott to train Chinese students to fly and maintain their planes. He said no, but his son, who had fought in the submarine service during World War I and also held a parachuting record, was interested. Abbott signed a two-year contract, and started running a small air school in Courtland, California. There he, like Douglas Fraser and Harry Lobb in Saskatoon, trained students with two Curtiss Jenny biplanes.

Classes ended in October 1922, and Abbott and his wife, Mary, set sail for China. When Sun returned to Canton, the Abbotts settled in the cement factory headquarters. Yang also enlisted the help of Guy Colwell, an aircraft engineer from England, and Arthur "Pop" Wilde, an aircraft builder in San Francisco. The two aeromechanics arrived in Shanghai in April 1923. Working with the help of Abbott and the Courtland graduates, Colwell and Wilde constructed a light reconnaissance bomber made from spruce, birch, and spare Curtiss plane parts. When they completed the *Rosamond*—named for Soong's American appellation—Abbott took the plane sporting the twelve-pointed GMD sun for a test whirl. "It took off quickly," Abbott commented on the first flight from their forty-acre airfield, "was well-balanced, with light control forces and a delight to fly." On August 8, a beaming Sun invited guests to his airfield for a dedication. He smashed a bottle of champagne on the black plane's steel propeller hub and christened the birth of his air force. The crew soon started work on more aircraft.[12]

Sun needed many reliable planes and soldiers, for Chen still posed a potent threat. Sun occasionally visited the battleground to monitor the progress of his hired troops. What he saw he did not always like. "It must also be borne in mind that many of these troops are worthless from a military point of view and cannot be relied upon to stand under fire," wrote the American consul general Douglas Jenkins. "This is particularly true of the Cantonese, who broke and ran as soon as skirmish firing began in front of their positions . . . the defeat of Sun Yat-sen forces at Shilong is attributed to the cowardice displayed on that occasion by the Cantonese troops. As I have mentioned before, detachments of Yunnanese are kept behind the lines to force the Cantonese to remain on their positions. Some fighting between these factions has occurred from time to time. . . ."

Battles went so badly that Sun had to try to stop his troops from being routed. "Mr. Sun went several times to the front line to direct the troops," wrote bodyguard Ye Jianying. "The troops in the area of Huizhou and Boluo suffered a setback, and they retreated to Shilong. Mr. Sun had taken a specially chartered train for Canton to Shitan, and set up a large banner at Shitan station. This banner said: 'I am at Shitan, anyone who retreats will be shot. Sun Yat-sen.' " Even such efforts could not stop his men from turning tail. Not knowing that Sun rode on the train, the escaping troops fired on the locomotive and even tried to commandeer it.

Spies appeared everywhere, and military executions were frequent. Sun's body-guards constantly worried for their boss's safety. Once while they were out on an inspection tour, enemy troops with guns and long bayonets surrounded them. They were about to capture Sun when Cohen grabbed his boss and put him on a train that whisked him off to safety. "Most of my time was spent arguing with the Doctor about keeping under cover, which was something he would not do," said Cohen. "He wandered about talking to the troops in the front line—as far as there was any front line. . . . Why he wasn't killed, I don't know. Luckily the other side hadn't much in the way of artillery—mostly machine guns, rifles, hand grenades and maybe a few trench mortars. With the rifles they couldn't shoot straight enough to matter, and with the hand grenades they as often as not blew themselves up; but for the machine guns and trench mortars we had to watch out."

Occasional bullets found their mark. During one skirmish, a machine-gun bullet nicked Cohen's arm. Fortunately, a doctor on the spot treated him. The injury gave Cohen pause. "The bullet that caught me in the left arm had made me think. Supposing it had been my right arm and I carried my gun that side, I'd not have been able to use it. As soon as we got back to Canton I got me a second gun, another Smith and Wesson revolver, and I packed it handy to my left hand. I practiced drawing and soon found that I was pretty well ambidextrous—one gun came out about as quick as the other." He now had a heavy .45 caliber gun on the hip and another in a shoulder holster. His fashionable two-gun accessories attracted attention among the western community already intrigued by this Jewish Englishman who cavorted with the Chinese. They started calling him "Two-Gun" Cohen. A nickname was born.

On some outings, Sun set out to gingerly deal with the warlords he depended on. "The Doctor had decided impulsively to go in person and interview a certain warlord whose intentions, he feared, were not strictly honorable," wrote Emily

Hahn, a *New Yorker* writer who came to China in the early 1930s and subsequently wrote a biography of Soong and her two sisters. The warlord claimed fealty to Sun, yet kept his forces within the city. Sun hoped to convince him to remove his men. As Sun prepared to head out alone, he ordered Cohen to stay behind and protect his wife. Soong, fearful for her husband's welfare, demanded that Cohen accompany him. His loyalty in question, Cohen hesitated, but Soong stood firm. "He had to make up his mind quickly, and with her eye upon him he had only one choice. He hurried after his leader, catching up with him at a distance. The Doctor scolded him, but did not again send him back. And anyway the expedition was successful." The warlord tactfully withdrew.[13]

Despite the tension and the presence of the surrounding troops, Cohen had plenty of time to get to know his coworkers. He palled around with Ma Xiang—who had left Canada a few years earlier to work for Sun—and the other bodyguards, tried new foods like snake, and impressed the members of the headquarters with his card and magic tricks. "Those were happy peaceful months," he said. "I enjoyed a kind of family life that I'd not known since my boyhood." After the morning visitors left, the group would have lunch. During the steamy spring and summer they also took a siesta.

The city was muggier than anything Cohen recalled from his London days. Heavy downpours drenched the city. At night people slept on cots in the streets to keep cool. Nothing in town seemed to dry out. The hot dampness gave Cohen prickly heat and caused him to go through two suits a day. People suffered from athlete's foot, ringworm, and other ailments. "Even on open verandas rug matting would quickly mildew. Electric lights, burning night and day in closets and wardrobes, could not prevent clothing from hanging damp and limp or shoes from being covered with a white fungus within 24 hours," wrote the journalist Hallett Abend. Worse yet, nighttime brought insects. "Mosquitoes swarmed with the coming of dusk, and reading in bed at night was usually impossible because of the loud buzzing of these pests just outside the stifling nets. When we played bridge in the evening . . . we all sat with our feet and legs inside oversized pillowcases, and with punk rings burning at every corner of the table to keep the mosquitoes from feasting upon us at their will."[14]

Cohen started to call the humid, bustling, port city home. More than 200,000 boat people lived on the waters in the shadow of the city's concrete office buildings, fancy brick towers, grand roofed temples, and somber red-tiled homes. Luxury shops along Canton's main streets glittered with marvelous treasures. The badly paved side streets through which crowds jostled were claustrophobic. Advertisements for cure-alls plastered walls, rickshaws had trouble passing each other, and according to the journalist Aleko E. Lilius, "a dog fight is enough to stop the traffic." These small streets echoed with the sounds of bellowing fish peddlers. As pedestrians passed through, their wooden clogs clomped and silk slippers rustled over the flagstone surface. Ladles clinked against metal canisters as vendors doled out soup, and the thick smell of fats and the miasmic stench of the canals mixed within the air. At food stalls, shoppers bought smoked hams, silver swordfish, cages of snakes, pig carcasses, preserved ginger, purple chilies, and mud-coated hundred-year-old eggs. Street merchants hawked feather dusters, peanuts, boiling water, ear swabs, performing hummingbirds, and branches of fresh lichee nuts. Departing customers dangled frogs and chickens from hooks.

In countless small shops, men and young boys hunched over work, sawing, hewing, painting, and embroidering products. The poor, beggars and cripples, those suffering from elephantiasis, leprosy, and syphilis filled other parts of Canton. In back alleys, poor families lived in long wooden trunks lined with torn matting and old rags. These boxes rested on props that kept out the packs of rats that scampered along the streets, as well as the water that flowed in the lanes during tropical monsoons.[15]

Some afternoons, Sun and his entourage went out for a stroll through some of these crowded back lanes. "Those little expeditions were some of the happiest times we had," said Cohen. "He'd stroll through the city, look into a rice go-down or a little fire-cracker factory, start talking to the coolies and get them to tell him their troubles." Occasionally Sun might stop a family with children and "ask them how they were doing at school and if—as usually happened—they weren't attending school at all, he'd fix up somewhere for them to go and likely pay a year's fees as well. And, of course, if he saw a beggar he just sent me to give the poor bum a handout. . . ."

Occasionally Sun, carrying his walking stick and with bodyguards in tow, rode out of town and hiked along the nearby hills. The group stopped to read grave inscriptions and snack on wild berries, or picnicked on small roast pig and winter melon in rice gruel. "The Guangdong people have a custom of 'climbing up high on Double 9th,'" recalled Fan Liang of one such morning jaunt.

Sun Yat-sen accompanied by his bodyguard ADC Cohen and twenty or more of us guards, got on board a bus and drove towards White Cloud Hill. When the bus reached the foot of the mountain Sun got out and looked around in all directions. In early autumn in Canton the sky is clear and the atmosphere is bright, the fragrant scents are strong and heady, and Mr. Sun's spirits were very high. Following a narrow path in a ravine which Mr. Sun pointed out we climbed towards the top, but we had not gone far when a few brothers who appeared to be peasants met us coming in the other direction. Mr. Sun immediately stopped and called to Cohen to beckon these brothers to squat down on a mountain path beside a stream. After he had asked all sorts of questions, we then discovered that they were peasants from the village at the bottom of the hill which the bus had just driven through. With a heavy heart Mr. Sun said to them, "The houses you live in are thatched huts and rooms built of mud, your life is very hard. We must definitely bring down these dreadful feudal practices, and solve your land problem."

When the peasants knew that the man in front of them was the famous

President Sun, tears filled their eyes and rolled down their cheeks. One peasant immediately stood up and most respectfully bowed to Sun and said in an unsteady voice, "You, sir, are really someone who cares for us. We will never forget your kindness."

The visit moved Sun. His group then continued on its way. "In order to encourage everyone's enthusiasm for climbing up, Mr. Sun proposed making the Nengren Temple the object of this climb. He said teasingly to ADC Ma, 'ADC Ma, you bodyguards have a competition, to see who reaches the Nengren Temple peak first. The prize for the person who gets there first will be two bread rolls.'

"With this, we bodyguards were all full of energy, and climbed up to Nengren Temple with all our strength. In the end Cohen came second and Mr. Sun joked with him saying, 'You didn't have the good luck to eat those two bread rolls.' "[16]

While not winning the bread rolls, Cohen easily feasted on food and other pleasures. As one of the top guards, Cohen earned a salary of a few hundred kuai a month. He boasted of his good fortune and decent wages and went around the headquarters showing off his money, saying to Fan, "Look here, Fan Liang, I've got all this money!" Though well paid, Cohen did not know how to save. And as he had done in England and Canada, he regularly blew his salary. He had many ways to spend his hot cash. Life in China was easy for westerners with a little pocket change. "Even a junior clerk could keep his own pony and belong to two or three clubs," wrote Owen M. Green. Food was cheap and varied, with inexpensive beef and mutton, pheasants, bamboo partridge, snipe, and quail readily available. Drinks were plentiful.

Cohen was a broad man with a special weakness for eating, picking up food at the countless street stalls or taking a table at various restaurants where he could try Cantonese delicacies. "When Sun Yat-sen would go to a movie Cohen would be looking around for stuff to eat," said Fan. "When he went to a movie he would spend all his money in eating. His salary of several hundred a month would be entirely spent on food." Besides dining at restaurants, westerners—even those in the employ of the Chinese—had countless dinner parties to attend. Cohen joined the whirl. "In Canton one goes to dinner parties in sampans and then crawls up the sides and over the decks of half a dozen junks before reaching the jetty," wrote Elsie McCormick. "Torn lace and smudgy satin are the order of the evening at most Canton parties, unless the guests had sufficient forethought to bring their gowns in a suitcase."

Cohen also headed out for more illicit carnal treats. "I used to slip down to Hong Kong about once a month for a little fun and games," said Cohen. "Mme. Sun never much approved of my Hong Kong holidays. She must have guessed their main purpose." Not only could he relax in far-off Hong Kong, he also kicked back on the local flower boats, the sixty-foot-long floating brothels anchored along the Pearl River. "Off the Cantonese Bund one sees river junks bristling with stove-pipe cannon to intimidate pirates; flower boats rented out for feasts and lavishly decorated in red, with festoons of hanging kerosene lamps," wrote McCormick. These bobbing pleasure houses clustered by rank and class. Some, especially those with singsong girls, were quite lush. Outside the women sat on view for those sailing by. Inside guests of the better brothels generally found large compartments containing rosewood and ebony tables, couches and chandeliers. There Cohen threw large parties and feasts, or had more personal interaction with the women, spending the night in a loft or on a small boat anchored nearby as the women and servants tended to his needs.

Sun forbade his men to frequent the flower boats. He opposed Cohen's regular visits. "Our headquarters were located near a river, and there were always little boats ferrying about, inviting guests, customers, tourists, and young people on board," said Fan. "One time Cohen went aboard one of those boats. Someone told Sun Yat-sen about it and he was very disturbed." He lectured Cohen and warned him, "If you dare go on any of those little boats, I'll lock you up!"[17]

Cohen was in his element—a good job, plenty of money, and boatloads of women. He began puffing himself up, and his tales once again started getting out of hand. Since Cohen and Ma Xiang headed up the bodyguard units, they dubbed themselves Generals, and told all who would listen of their importance. "His title of 'General' . . . was the subject of frequent puns in the local English newspapers," noted Powell of Cohen's airs. His rumors quickly spread across the Pacific to Canada. In April 1923 the Edmonton *Journal* reported that Cohen's father held a consular post in Canton. Another story said that Cohen had met Sun ten years earlier and served as his bodyguard during Sun's cross-Canada and U.S. fund-raising trip. "Maybe Dr. Sun trust him and keep him with him," the paper quoted Edmontonian Charlie Wong, "but I wait until I get my papers from Canton next two three week. Then I know what happened to Morris."

Cohen's brother Benjamin still worked at the Edmonton Clothing Company, and unwittingly disseminated the information. He told the papers that his older brother planned to return to Canada once he had finished his work there. The *Journal* noted that Cohen was "sitting pretty in China" and "is not returning to Alberta for some time yet." The *Bulletin* let on that Cohen went by the Chinese name Kowhen, was "in charge of the republican troops in southern China," had been decorated, held a high place in the councils of the republican government, and was seeking concessions in China worth several million dollars for various development schemes. Soon word even arrived of Cohen's death. Benjamin quickly denied the report, stating that he had recently heard from his brother and reporting him to be in good health.

The papers were not the only ones trying to make sense of Cohen's activities. The Royal Canadian Mounted Police considered a white man in the employ of the Chinese suspect. "Cohen's real motive for the trip was to bring back Drugs," surmised Detective Sergeant W. A. MacBrayne. Officials started asking for information on his past. Not surprisingly, Cohen's shady Canadian friends did not cooperate with their investigations. "It is impossible for us here to get any definite information as to what Cohen's real object was in visiting China. None of Cohen's intimate friends knew much about him."[18]

Chinese-Canadians meanwhile faced continued restrictions, school segregation, and other problems. More troubling was a powerful movement throughout Canada to replace the dreaded Chinese Head Tax with an outright ban on new Chinese immigration. The Chinese community appealed to Sun and Cohen for assistance. Sun dispatched a telegram on May 17, 1923, to the Minister of Interior requesting that discussion of the bill banning immigration be suspended since his government had just signed an important railroad construction contract with Northern Construction. The agreement, he wrote, ushered in a new era of Chinese-Canadian cooperation. But one small train contract could not stop a country that reveled in its decades-old animosity to the Chinese. The act went into effect on Dominion Day, a day the Chinese fittingly dubbed "Humiliation Day." To mark the event, they flew Chinese flags at half mast.

Later that month, worse news arrived from Edmonton. On July 27, Benjamin took his own life, two weeks after being charged and released on bail for robbery and attempted rape. When Benjamin's boss, William Diamond, found his body in his apartment, Benjamin clutched a picture of his mother. Nearby lay three letters addressed to the police, Cohen, and Diamond. "In his letter to the police he stated his intention of doing away with himself, but protested his innocence of the charge against him," reported the *Journal*. "It would be impossible, he said, to produce the witnesses he needed in the case without causing them considerable embarrassment. . . . The letter to his brother Morris was addressed care of President Sun Yat-sen, Canton, China. In it the deceased declared that his life had been one of mistakes, but that he had tried hard to make good."[19]

During the summer and fall of 1923, relations with Russia moved ahead, and on October 6, the Soviet adviser Michael Borodin arrived in Canton. Born Michael Markovich Gruzenberg, Borodin was a thirty-nine-year-old Jewish Bolshevik, a charming dark-haired, gray-eyed bear of a man with facial scars, a drooping mustache, and a bass voice who easily put others at ease. Besides speaking Russian and Yiddish, Borodin spoke fluent English, having studied at Valparaiso University in Indiana.

The Russians did not send Sun a stereotypical Bolshevik. According to Vincent Sheean, he was "a large, calm man with the natural dignity of a lion or a panther." Borodin was an avid reader of poetry and detective stories, a good chess player, and a mediocre polo player.

Everything interests him; to everything he applies the patient, humorous, thoughtful processes of his philosophy. . . . Borodin has, indeed, the detachment which Lenin is said to have preserved to the last, a recognition of the littleness of men and things in the vastness of their ultimate intention. I am quite conscious that Borodin, like Lenin, would stop at nothing to achieve his ends; but at the same time he, like Lenin, has no illusions about the nearness of those ends. He does not believe . . . that the "world revolution" is just around the corner. He is thus in the position of devoting his life to a cause which cannot be victorious until long after his death; and, once that choice, that decision, has been made, matters which would be sword-wounds to lesser men are not even pin-pricks to him.

The Soviets dispatched this methodical man to bring new life to the GMD and to hasten the day of world-wide communism. Sun warmly greeted his newest ally, boasting to Americans that "his name is Lafayette." Borodin settled with his wife, Fanya, and their sons, Fred and Norman, into a two-story dark gray building with verandas and a flat roof alongside a parade ground where the police executed criminals. The two new partners then got to work revitalizing the GMD. They sought to instill in the party a more radical program and a stronger organizational form. Borodin instructed Sun in how to win mass support, and helped him refine his *Sanmin zhuyi* (Three People's Principles), impregnating Sun's credos of nationalism, people's rights, and people's livelihood with anti-imperialist and even anti-feudal trappings. On October 25, Sun appointed a nine-man temporary Central Executive Committee with Borodin as its adviser to make preparations for a National Congress.[20]

Besides needing structure for his organization, Sun required cash. Greedy warlords continuously drained his government's coffers. It was a precarious existence. Sun's son Sun Fo served as mayor of Canton, and because of the demands of various military leaders, he had little money to run essential city services. The constant unrest caused Guangdong's annual revenue to drop by 60 percent between 1921 and 1923. To raise more money, Sun Yat-sen increased taxes and license fees and forced restaurants, firecracker dealers, pawnshops, salt merchants, mutton vendors, hotel keepers, and building contractors to make loans to him. His heavy-handed tactics proved quite unpopular, and on September 22, assassins tried to kill Sun Fo while he rode along the Bund. The following month the government offered a reward of 20 percent of the sale price of land to informers who could point out public land occupied by private individuals. They then started confiscating property.

Yet even the money that land confiscation brought in was not enough. By January 1924, Sun Yat-sen could not pay salaries, and his government had to issue worthless military notes to the troops. Merchants refused to accept the play money. He lost more backing. "As a result of his rather questionable efforts to raise funds in Canton, it has become apparent that Sun Yat-sen has alienated the sympathy and support of many of the merchants and business men here and the prevailing opinion seems to be that he is now making his last stand and that the chances of success for his regime are extremely doubtful," wrote Jenkins.[21]

In desperate need of money and finding taxation nonproductive, Sun went after two foreign-controlled sources of provincial revenue, the Salt Administration and the Chinese Maritime Customs. Soon after his arrival in town, Sun had appointed his own commissioner for the Salt Administration and started to reap its revenues. Getting the customs revenues from the port of Canton would not prove as easy. While the Maritime Customs was technically a branch of the Chinese government, the British Inspector General controlled the collecting, remitting, and banking of the revenues. The income went directly to Shanghai custodian banks, which then administered the repayment of foreign loans and reparations. The diplomatic body in Beijing then decided how much should be turned over to the regime controlling Beijing. In September 1923 Sun's government claimed that surpluses from the customs should stay in Canton and be used for capital improvement. The money should not, they said, be turned over to their northern enemies. The western powers ignored his demands. He renewed his claim on October 23, following it up with the threat that he would seize the customs house and drive the British from Asia.

The westerners ensconced on Shameen Island replied that if Sun used force, they would respond in kind. They had no care for Chinese autonomy and democracy, and fervently planned to protect all they controlled, including their forty-four-acre spit of land. Access to the island—separated from Canton by a narrow canal wide enough for sampans and small junks—was restricted to two bridges guarded by khaki-clad British soldiers armed with rifles and broadswords. "The sidewalks and the broad streets, then bare of vehicles of all kinds, were shaded by giant banyan trees, peppers, and palms. Bougainvillea vines made great splashes of cerise blossoms against the walls of massive granite and brick buildings," wrote Hallett Abend of the concession that looked nothing like the rest of Canton. It was a quiet refuge, filled with gardens, western-style houses and villas, clubs, tennis courts, croquet lawns, foreign banks, businesses, a hotel, and a boathouse.

Since the West refused to talk with Sun about the customs, he headed to Shameen to negotiate. "One day, we ten or so attendants and bodyguards wearing uniforms and holding our weapons escorted Sun to the consulate," recalled Fan. "We took a steamboat to the Shameen Concession. It was no easy thing to enter the concession. The only way in was over a bridge, which was guarded by armed British guards who checked all those going in or out. Sun Yat-sen did not want to undergo the shame of being checked by a foreigner on the territory of his own land, so he decided not to enter by the bridge, but to disembark on the shore. When the concession people saw that it was Sun there was nothing they could do to prevent him. When he had disembarked, Sun ordered us to guard the boat, and with his secretary Huang Changgu and ADC Ma Xiang walked towards the British consulate only ten meters or so away."[22]

The two sides did not reach an agreement. The West feared a confrontation, and Canton's waters filled with foreign warships. "Parties of marines from the foreign gunboats anchored off Canton have taken possession of the Custom House there. The troops are equipped with machine guns," reported the New York *Times*. Even though they had a pleasant meeting earlier in the year, Governor Stubbs in Hong Kong disdained Sun's efforts to grab the customs. "What I know of Sun I dislike: what I know of his entourage I dislike even more," he wrote. "They are the cleverest and most amusing scoundrels in China and there my interest in them ends." On December 4, Sun sent a note to Stubbs condemning British threats of retaliation. "I am informed that if any action be taken to enforce my Government's claim for its share of the Customs revenues, 'forcible measures' will be adopted, presumably, in the nature of either a naval bombardment of Canton or an economic blockade of the City directed from Hongkong. This threat leaves me unmoved. I am resolved that nothing shall prevent me from securing my Government's just share of the Customs revenue of the country. . . . It is impossible to take seriously the threat to bombard an unfortified and defenseless city like Canton."

Hoping to diffuse the situation and get the revenues, numerous Sun aides visited diplomatic and military officials. British Consul General Jamieson and others remained unswayed. "His threat of reprisals is an empty one," wrote Jamieson. Cohen even joined the round-making, making his case with officials, stopping and chatting up members of the western flotilla like Charles Hardinge Drage, a twenty-six-year-old first lieutenant serving on board the HMS *Bluebell,* which left Hong Kong for Canton on December 5. Cohen had gotten to know the consulate staffs over the preceding year, and made numerous visits to the American consulate during the crisis. Despite Cohen's own opinion of himself, Jenkins remained unimpressed.

Cohen does not appear to be a man of very high type, but he is an adventurer and, I understand, a radical. . . . Vice Consul Collins, in this office, is on fairly intimate terms with Cohen and the Vice Consul tells me that since the present crisis developed Cohen has repeatedly said that Sun would not under any circumstances give up his determination to get hold of the customs. Cohen has intimated to Vice Consul Collins, however, that Sun "will not fire a shot." He seems to think that when the matter comes to the final step the powers will back down and Sun will walk off with the prize. As I said, Cohen is not a man of high type and I am not sure that he can be entirely relied upon. In view of his acquaintance with Vice Consul Collins, however, and the fact that he has frequently given Collins information that proved to be correct, I am inclined in this instance to rely to some extent on what Cohen has said.

In the end, Sun could not resist the West. He simply stood down. Yet while Sun reaped no cash from the customs, he gained much needed political mileage. At a time of increased tensions over taxes and guest armies, he took the opportunity to counter his negative press by vilifying the Americans and British and accusing them of continued support of northern warlords. His rising popularity and his tough stance even gained a realization from Stubbs that he was a growing force in the South: "The prosperity of this Colony is bound up with Guangdong. With a hostile Guangdong, the trade of Hong Kong, which means most of the trade of Great Britain with China, cannot be carried on and it is essential in the interests of this trade that we should be on as good terms as possible with the power that rules Guangdong, whether that power be Sun Yat-sen or another."[23]

Plans meanwhile coalesced for the ten-day National Congress. The congress opened on January 20, 1924, at the Guangdong Higher Normal School, and each day Cohen escorted Sun through the streets to the school's assembly hall. Along the way, he and the other bodyguards dispersed the gaping crowds. At the hall, the mostly handpicked delegates passed programs calling for social reforms and improving China's international status. Despite some opposition, the delegates approved Sun's decision to admit communists to the party, and nominated three communists to the Central Executive Committee. The congress also accepted Sun's *Sanmin zhuyi* as the basis for party policy.

In the new and improved GMD fashioned by Sun and Borodin, Sun retained control. The constitution called for a five-part government, with executive, legislative, judicial, censorate, and civil service examination branches. As in the Soviet Communist Party, power descended from Sun and the ruling Central Executive Committee. At this time, Sun also issued his "Fundamentals of National Reconstruction for the National Government of China," in which he explained his vision of the three phases of the Chinese revolution. According to his plan, the initial stage of military conquest was followed by a period of political tutelage, during which the people would learn about self-government. Once they completed their education, constitutional government would rule.[24]

The congress likewise called for the formation of the Whampoa Military Academy to train politically dependable officers to fill the lower ranks of Sun's new revolutionary army. Sun's young aide Chiang Kai-shek was confirmed as commandant of the academy and chief of staff of the GMD army. Liao Zhongkai was appointed the chief political officer. Zhou Enlai became the deputy political commissar and Li Jishen ran the Training Department.

Situated on Changzhou Island in the Pearl River, just south of Canton, the academy had docks, a fort, gentle sloping hills, and sparse trees. Sun—Cohen looming at his side—presided at the June 16 dedication. At Whampoa, cadets, many hailing from the criminal Green Gang with which Chiang associated, underwent a six-month training period. They woke at five each morning for a full day's worth of classes and instructions in artillery, engineering, and infantry. The staff not only taught them to be crack soldiers but also indoctrinated them as revolutionary troops. They learned Sun's *Sanmin zhuyi,* and that they could help reconstruct China through the party. "Now there's one thing I've learnt in all these Chinese wars, and that is that troops only fight well when they've had some political indoctrination," said Cohen of the academy's founding. "It doesn't much matter whether their cause is right or wrong . . . so long as they believe in it." The Soviets helped underwrite the academy's expenses, and sent General P. A. Pavlov to assume the post of chief military adviser. Pavlov arrived in June, but while on an inspection tour in July, he drowned in a river. Sun, Soong, and Cohen attended a subsequent memorial service in his honor. Vasily Blyukher, a broad, red-haired man who distinguished himself in the Russian civil war, took his place at the end of October. Other Russian military experts soon filled Canton.[25]

One of the big problems facing Sun's new forces was getting enough decent weapons. Up till then, they had depended on local arsenals for equipment. Many of the weapons were substandard. Sun had ordered three hundred guns for the opening of Whampoa, but only thirty arrived in time. The West fervently opposed the idea of a strong China, and had been trying to control the flow of arms into the fractured land. In 1919 the powers agreed to an Arms Embargo Agreement, yet weapons still poured in from countries that did not sign the agreement. Merchants shipped weapons in on German or Norwegian vessels, and smugglers brought small arms through Canton, Hong Kong, and Macao. Even sailors disembarking from ships carried weapons. They visited dockside grog shops or teahouses and easily sold thirty-dollar Mauser automatics for four times that amount.[26]

Sun was therefore relieved when the Soviets in October sent him a ship laden with thousands of rifles, artillery, and machine guns. Besides needing weapons to combat warlords, he also had to have armaments to contend with problems brewing in town. In May 1924 westerners instituted regulations forbidding Chinese from using the Bund as a shortcut. Then at eight-thirty-five on the evening of June 19, during a banquet on Shameen in honor of M. Merlin, the visiting governor of Indo-China, an assassin tossed an explosive-laden attaché case through the window of the Victoria Hotel. Merlin escaped uninjured, yet flying shrapnel and cutlery killed five people and wounded twenty-eight, splattering the walls with blood and blowing a hole in the ceiling. Guards chased and shot at the assassin, but he jumped off the French Bund and swam away.

The British accused the Canton government of harboring the murderer. Not to be cowed, Sun made a show of force with a grand review of 4,000 troops on the Northern Parade Ground. "Long before the appointed time, the streets were lined with spectators and the grandstand was filled with officials and foreign friends," wrote the Hongkong *Telegraph* of the display on June 29. "Excellent arrangements were made for the reception of visitors. The troops were all ready at 10 A.M. waiting for the arrival of the Generalissimo, Dr. Sun Yat-sen. Dr. Sun arrived at 10:30 A.M., accompanied by his personal bodyguard under the direct supervision of Mr. Maurice Cohen. The troops immediately presented arms while bands played the Chinese National Anthem." As planes circled above, Sun inspected the troops.

Foreigners anxiously noted recent developments and Sun's brazen tone. They instituted stricter security measures on Shameen. Starting on August 1, all Chinese entering the island after nine in the evening were required to carry photographic identification. Taking this as an affront to their dignity, Chinese workers struck; 2,000 men and 300 women who labored in the assorted consulates, banks, stores, and homes walked out. Strikers planned to isolate the island and cut off supplies. To prevent citizens from passing, the Chinese posted strike pickets at the island's bridges. The British and French responded by dispatching gunboats to Canton. Not surprisingly, the strike quickly took on an anti-imperialist tone, as pickets shouted their opposition to unequal treaties and foreign control of the customs. Strikers collected funds, and at least twenty-six unions allied themselves with the workers. The two sides soon settled, and most of the strikers went back to work without having their wages docked. The strike's success gave the Chinese new confidence. Cohen naturally took credit for the end of the action. "When the strike on Shameen took place I was the general A.D.C. to Dr. Sun Yat-sen," Cohen soon after told British officials. "I was successful in persuading . . . Dr. Sun Yat-sen to use his influence with the strikers to call off the strike."[27]

Now that he had a more rationally structured party and the start of an officers corps, Sun set about trying to get the government's finances in order. He asked his Harvard-educated brother-in-law, T. V. Soong, to reorganize the party's finances and the Guangdong economy. Soong called for austerity, and imposed duties on rubber, wood alcohol, and ammonium sulfate. He ordered Canton merchants to lend the government money in amounts of five dollars to five hundred dollars. Soon new taxes appeared on patent medicines, soft drinks, cosmetics, weddings and funerals, even rickshaws. By August 16, Soong opened a Central Bank, with a reported $10 million in capital. Silver made up 25 percent of the reserves. Russia provided some if not all of the financing.

Soong served as the manager of the institution and Minister of Finance. The new bank acted as the sole financial agent of the government and possessed the exclusive right to float foreign and domestic bonds, issue bank notes, and serve as the government treasury. There were doubts, though, as to whether the bank's bonds and notes—which Soong referred to as "my bank notes"—would be accepted by merchants and others. So to rehabilitate the government's credit, the bank called in and publicly destroyed the military notes it had issued at the New Year. Savings soon flowed in.[28]

Under Sun Fo's mayorship, Canton also became a modern city. He saw to the creation, widening, and cleaning of streets and the construction of a sewage system and public utilities. New buildings went up throughout town and older ones were repaired. Wu Tiecheng meanwhile ran a good police force. Not everyone, though, appreciated what Sun Yat-sen, T. V. Soong, and Sun Fo had wrought. Local merchants resented the continuous imposition of new taxes and surcharges. They worried about lawlessness, the enrichment of guest armies, the cost of establishing Whampoa, preparations for a northern expedition against Beijing, as well as what they perceived as GMD officials' sympathetic alliances with the communists. Merchants shut their businesses and placed their property under foreign registry.

Businesses soon strengthened the Merchants' Volunteer Defense Force, a private militia group. Merchants under the leadership of Chen Lianbo, head of the Chamber of Commerce, called for a joint-defense headquarters of all merchants corps. Needing to arm their men, Chen placed an order in Belgium for thousands of guns, rifles, machine guns, and artillery, along with more than 3 million rounds of ammunition. The arms arrived in Canton around August 8 on board the Norwegian freighter *Hav*. Even though the merchants properly applied for and received a gun-importation permit from Sun's headquarters, the weapons-strapped Sun decided to commandeer the guns. Chiang seized the vessel. In retaliation, the merchants corps threatened a general strike. On the advice of Borodin, Sun declared martial law and charged the corps with plotting to take over the city.

Resistance grew. Bankers refused to accept notes from the new Central Bank. Rice shops held back their stocks. Street committees threw up barriers. Conditions grew so bad that Sun even contemplated bombing and attacking the most congested and wealthiest part of Canton. By the end of the month, the two sides reached a compromise. The GMD agreed to return half the weapons without ammunition and rescinded the order for the arrests of the merchant leaders. The merchants then called off their strike.[29]

Yet all was not settled. Fearing that the government would renege on its promise, the merchants threatened to close the city's markets if they did not get their guns on October 10 as promised. The "Double Tenth" was the anniversary of the October 1911 revolution, and the merchants erected a cordon across the Bund where junks docked to unload the arms. At two-thirty in the afternoon, a Nationalist parade made up of slogan-shouting labor corps and students carrying banners marched along the Bund. Some of the laborers and cadets carried weapons. When they arrived at the point where the merchants were off-loading their weapons, the parade leaders demanded the right to march straight through. The corps refused. A gun went off, and the merchants opened fire. As laborers and cadets scattered, merchants hunted them down. One corpsman even cut the heart out of a dead laborer and triumphantly held it aloft. Sun then dispatched Whampoa cadets, Workers' Militia, Peasants' Corps, troops under Wu, and others to do battle. They poured oil around the corps' headquarters and set it on fire. Troops then looted freely. By the night of "Bloody Wednesday," flames engulfed much of the commercial sector of Canton.[30]

Following Sun's brutal suppression of the merchants, work around Sun's headquarters returned to normal. Cohen once again became overly cocky about his position, and boasted about his authority within the organization. When an adviser, Ma Su, visited the headquarters, he heard Cohen claim, "The headquarters enlisting office is run by me, the ADCs office is run by me, and the secretarial office is also run by me."

Such claims surprised Ma. He went to see Ma Xiang to find out if there was any truth to Cohen's pronouncements.

"Of course that's not true!" Ma Xiang told him. "Cohen is just a second-lieutenant ADC. . . . If he is boasting like that he definitely has ulterior motives and what is more I expect that he is swindling and deceiving people outside the camp. When you have time would you explain the situation to the Generalissimo."

"Shortly afterwards Ma Su brought up this matter with Sun," wrote Ma Xiang. "When Sun heard of it he did not show any reaction. The next day the quartermaster's office summoned Cohen, gave him 300 yuan and said to him, 'The Generalissimo tells you to find another job, you need not come to work again.'" Cohen's dismissal by his hero was a sobering shock. He had lost his dream job, the one he sailed across the Pacific for. Penitence was in order. Apologies were profuse. Cohen must have been completely obsequious, for he soon returned to work.[31]

As he pacified Canton, Sun decided to go ahead with his plans for a military expedition. On September 3, he began a Northern Campaign to conquer Beijing from Cao Kun and Wu Peifu of the Zhili Clique. Nine days later, Sun left Canton. He set up his command in the railway station at Shaoguan, two hundred miles to the north, taking with him his own bodyguards, the airplane unit, Wu Tiecheng's gendarmes, and a company of cadets. The various units of troops from Henan, Hunan, Jiangxi, and Yunnan gradually assembled nearby. Hoping to prevent added opposition, Sun dispatched Sun Fo to Manchuria, where he formed an alliance with Marshal Zhang Zuolin and the Anfu group. As battle started, the Zhili Clique initially won in the north, but in late October, Wu Peifu's subordinate and adopted son, Feng Yuxiang, betrayed him and seized Beijing in the name of the people.

With the coup and the head of state gone, Sun asked for talks. Those controlling Beijing accepted his offer and invited him to town to form a new government. Sun had long hoped for this moment. He had grand plans for the trip north. He proposed the convocation of a national assembly, the demobilization of many of the nation's troops, and the development of GMD work in the North. He returned to Canton to prepare for his triumphant entrance to Beijing.

On November 12, Sun started saying his good-byes. It was his fifty-eighth birthday. From a terrace on the upper story of the Guangdong Finance Office, he watched a parade of 20,000 labor unionists, students, and others march by carrying lanterns. The following day, he left Canton with Soong Qingling, Borodin, Wang Jingwei, Eugene Chen, and Cohen, stopping at Whampoa, where he reviewed the troops and addressed the officers and students. That evening they set sail for Shanghai.

Sun planned for this to be his crowning glory. Yet he was in pain. He had liver cancer. During part of the trip Sun had to stay in bed. He ate little, mostly fruit. Nonetheless, he persevered. When the ship reached Shanghai on the seventeenth, a crowd enthusiastically greeted him at the docks. As they accompanied him to Rue Molière they shouted anti-imperialist slogans. Cohen, meanwhile, headed to Canada to buy weaponry. By the time Sun reached Beijing on December 31, his condition had dramatically deteriorated.[32]

As Sun lay in bed in Beijing, the Chinese in Vancouver feted Cohen as a returning hero. "As soon as the Chinamen found out who he was, they certainly showered him with attention giving us a special dinner for which we were not permitted to pay," recalled Lee Sereth, who visited Chinatown that winter with Cohen. By January, Cohen the dandy, wearing spats and sporting the false title of "General" arrived in Edmonton. He regaled his friends with tales of the Orient, informing them that during the Canton Customs Crisis Sun wanted him to take over the running of the customs.

Back in Edmonton for a short visit to old friends here after more than two years in the storm centres of China, where he was a prominent figure in the government of the republic, Morris Abraham Cohen, now bearing the title of general and aide-de-camp to President Sun Yat-sen, arrived in the city this

morning. . . . General Cohen shows little physical change since he left the city
in the fall of 1922. . . . The right hand man of the president of the South China
republic, when seen by the *Journal,* was reticent in discussing conditions in the
Far East, pointing out that it would be improper for him in his official position
to discuss the political affairs of China. "You can say this, however," he told
the *Journal,* "that conditions when I left were very favorable for a unification
of the different political forces of the country. A conference was being arranged
and the feeling was very hopeful that it would result in success. At present I am
not in a position to give further information on the situation." . . . He will
remain in Canada about two months, but the diplomatic object of his visit
remains a secret. The only word that comes from the lips of the envoy of the
Chinese republic is that he is here to visit old friends and to enjoy a rest after
the labors of the past two years.

While Sun was dying, others scrambled for power. Sun issued a political and
personal will, and passed away at nine-thirty on the morning of March 12. When
news of Sun's death reached Cohen, he rushed back to China. "It was in the middle
of March . . . when I heard of his death. I took the next ship for China and on that
passage I played no poker, I spent no time in the bar and in fact I scarcely spoke to
a soul on board. I slept badly too and that's something that has never happened to
me before or since."

Trans-Pacific travel took about two weeks, and from Shanghai he took a train
to Beijing. Cohen missed the private funeral for Sun on March 19, and the public
funeral at the chapel of Beijing Union Medical College. Sun's body then lay in state
in an imperial pavilion inside Central Park for two weeks. Half a million people
walked by to pay their respects. When Cohen finally arrived, he went straight to see
Soong Qingling. "When I met Mme. Sun I just burst into tears." He remembered
little of those mournful days. "The bottom had dropped out of my world and I still
felt lost." On April 2, pallbearers carried Sun's casket through the streets to the
chamber of the Azure Cloud Temple in the Western Hills. "We left Dr. Sun in the
Western Hills, and for a while I felt that I'd left the best part of myself there too. I
just mooned about and thought how empty my life was now and how little I realized
my luck when he was still alive." His hero was gone.[33]

CHAPTER 12

LIFE WITHOUT SUN,
1925–1927

*Throughout his life, Sun single-mindedly pursued his vi-*sion of the Chinese revolution and the creation of a democratic nation. When he died in 1925, the party was adrift and rudderless, the country leaderless. Despite the reorganization called for by the National Congress the year before, the party had no standard administration and no easy way to settle internal party problems. Worse yet, the Guomindang still depended on warlord support.

Sun's followers immediately beatified him. His photo graced offices and buildings. His writings became enshrined, his words sacred. By the first anniversary of Sun's death, work began on a grand mausoleum in his honor in Nanjing. "It is hard for foreigners to realize, perhaps, the almost sacerdotal significance of Dr. Sun Yat-sen's name," observed Sheean. "He was always the greatest crowd-idol of China, and since his death his name and portrait have been a sort of *in hoc signo*." Leaders, heir apparents, and presumptives claimed that they stood at his bedside when he died. All wanted to attach themselves to his memory; all hoped to claim his mandate as their own. Three leading contenders vied for Sun's throne. The most prominent was the moderate Wang Jingwei, who first burst on the revolutionary scene when he attempted to assassinate the Manchu regent prince in 1910. For his crime, the Manchus sentenced him to life imprisonment. Following the 1911 revolution and his release, Wang worked with Sun. In 1924 he became the second-ranking member of the party's Central Executive Committee. The rightist Hu Hanmin—the first ranking member of the committee—was a close aide to Sun and assisted Sun with a number of revolts prior to 1911. As Sun prepared for his fateful trip to Beijing, Hu became acting Generalissimo of the headquarters. Liao Zhongkai was the party's financial expert. He served as governor of Guangdong and Soong Qingling and Borodin liked him. Since it was felt that no one could replace Sun, a triumvirate of Wang, Hu, and Liao assumed control.

It did not take long for a struggle to develop between the GMD and the Chinese

Communist Party. The Comintern wanted a radicalized GMD void of conservative members. Rightists meanwhile sought to stop the party's liberal leanings. Then on August 20, 1925, as Liao stepped out of a car for a meeting of the GMD Central Committee, five gunmen shot him dead. The police never solved his murder, but a cousin of Hu's was believed to have been responsible, and Hu retired. Wang became the head of the party, and Borodin and the then centrist Chiang expelled some conservatives from the party. But they could not so easily repair the growing rift within the GMD. In November, right-wing members of the GMD Central Executive Committee met at Sun's tomb. There they resolved that Borodin should be let go, the communists and moderates should be purged and Wang suspended. The Western Hills faction subsequently set up a rival GMD headquarters in Shanghai.[1]

The rising power of unions and the accompanying labor unrest within the region especially disturbed the conservatives. Hong Kong was a major center of world shipping and warehouses. From 1918 to 1924, its annual trade stood at £150 million. Thirty to forty percent of China's trade slipped through the island. In 1923 Hong Kong had 243 registered factories, and the following year, 57,765 vessels, junks, steamers, and oceangoing carriers slipped through the harbor. As the British writer C. A. Middleton Smith noted in 1920, "Capital is safe, labor is cheap, and there is a wonderful market adjoining." The colony's shipyards, repair yards, sugar refineries, cement and electric companies as well as cotton mills attracted countless laborers who had no choice but to accept low wages, horrid working conditions, limited housing, and high living expenses.

To the British, China was a sphere of influence. They had wrestled control of numerous of her ports, and gained sway over her industry and shipping. The 600,000 Chinese who lived in Hong Kong following the end of World War I resented the control that the 7,900 British commanded. Labor organized. In March 1920, mechanics, shipyard employees, and workers at sugar refineries and other essential industries went on strike. They demanded a 40 percent wage increase, and settled the following month for nearly that amount. With the strike's success, one hundred new unions sprung up. In January 1922 the Seamen's Union walked out over wages, and within two weeks 30,000 seamen, lightermen, stevedores, and coal carriers picketed. The British viewed these strikers through jaundiced eyes. It did not matter that the Chinese strikers and leadership wished to bring about a revolutionary change to their society, to rule their own economy and their political future. For the British, such a move seemed opposed to the order they had imposed. What they possessed they planned to protect and hang on to as tightly as they could. The strikers therefore had to be dealt with harshly. The Hong Kong government enacted martial law and called in military patrols and strikebreakers. Soon all of Hong Kong went on strike. Millions of dollars in shipping revenue evaporated as ships bypassed the city. By March 5, shipowners had no choice but to agree to the union's demands.

Japanese plants were some of the worst places to work. In the spring of 1925 Chinese workers, fed up with the beatings and mistreatment they received from management, went on strike. Sympathetic labor actions erupted at numerous other mills. On May 15, an argument broke out in one of the mills in Shanghai. Japanese guards responded by firing on the workers, killing one and wounding others. Protests followed, and the authorities arrested union chiefs. When 3,000 picketers marched on May 30 to the police station to demand the release of some of their leaders, the British captain in charge, fearing the crowd planned to rush the station, ordered his Sikh and Chinese constables to open fire. About a dozen people died and several dozen were wounded. Strikes spread across the country. Union organizers distributed photos of the dead workers from the now notorious "May Thirtieth Incident." By mid-June, strikes and protests had spread to about twelve cities.[2]

On June 18, Chinese seamen from the Hong Kong, Macao, and Canton steamers went on strike, and three days later workmen from Hong Kong and Shameen Island joined them. Then during the afternoon of June 23 a parade of 50,000 workers, peasants, merchants, students, and military marched toward the now sandbagged Shameen Island. As the strikers passed Shameen, one or two isolated shots rang out, followed by a barrage of bullets between French and British marines and protesting Whampoa cadets. Fifty-two Chinese died. Fleeing crowds trampled a third of the 117 wounded. Only one French merchant died and eight others were wounded.

As each of the two sides accused the other of firing first, the Canton–Hong Kong Strike began. It involved workers from all industries and trades in Canton, Shameen, and Hong Kong, and affected about 250,000 people. Strikers called for a boycott of British goods, an inquiry into the shooting, punishment of the guilty, compensation for those hurt or killed, the banning of foreign ships within the harbor, and the expulsion of foreign troops from Chinese soil. Whampoa cadets thirsting for battle against the imperialist dogs even agitated for the conquest of Shameen. Many workers abandoned Hong Kong for Canton. By the end of 1925, 135 sympathetic strikes raged, 104 in Shanghai alone. Trade fell, and a few Chinese banks went under. The anti-foreign hostility garnered needed support for the GMD and caused Communist Party membership to spiral from 1,000 to 30,000. In response, the Hong Kong government censored cables and letters to and from Canton, and offered rewards for reports that led to the conviction of those intimidating workers.[3]

Since strikers would not allow ships passing through Hong Kong to dock in Canton, ships started to bypass the colony. To insure the boycott's effectiveness and the isolation of Hong Kong and Macao, the Canton government hired thousands of strike pickets. These quasi-guards received military training at Whampoa, were organized in squads of twelve to 104, given blue uniforms, and stationed in as many as nineteen Guangdong ports. Some even received rifles. At a few ports the pickets were supplemented by gunboats.

Most of these pickets had no money. Up to 27,000 lived in Cantonese-administered lodging and ate in soup kitchens maintained by the government. The pickets and their families "huddled together in overpacked, ill-constructed barracks, slept right on the earth and received a daily pittance," wrote Vera Vladimirovna Vishnyakova-Akimova, a Russian translator who arrived in Canton in 1926. They searched for boycotted goods, preserved order, caught scabs, maintained food embargoes, and stopped ships that docked in Hong Kong or carried British goods from entering the port.[4]

This period of political and labor turmoil was a time of flux for Cohen. Following Sun's death, he lacked work and direction. Only four days before the Shameen Incident he had finally secured a job as a liaison officer for Police Commissioner Wu Tiecheng. He also did work for Sun Fo. While he perceived himself as a powerful force within the government—"My liaison job . . . suddenly became important. I bustled to and fro between the different Yamens and the Shameen, carrying messages from Sun Fo and T. V. Soong and Wu Tiecheng, explaining and complaining and arguing and trying to keep matters on an even keel"—he was still not as well received as he believed. His constant self-promotion and touting of his Northern Construction contract did not help his career or reception at the consulates. He even bragged of friendships with famous politicians like William Lyon Mackenzie King, but when Canadian officials contacted the prime minister in Ottawa, King said he had never met the man. Jamieson had serious doubts about Cohen. To Jamieson and the rest of the class-obsessed diplomatic staff, he was not the right kind of Englishman. In their eyes, Cohen was simply an uneducated, pushy Jew with a low-class accent from a poor family. Jamieson cabled to Canada to get "particulars as to his past record," noting that he "possesses all the characteristics of an adventurer, joined the Guomindang in Alberta and came over to act as self-constituted personal bodyguard to Sun Yat-sen, but I have a shrewd suspicion that smuggling of Chinese into the North American Continent was his real aim."[5]

Life went on in Canton despite the pickets. With tensions so high, and so many troops in town, the nervous foreign naval crews stood on heightened military alert and engaged in extensive friendly contact with the different ships. "*Pampanga* enjoyed fraternizing with the British gunboats and arranged rendezvous up-river as often as possible," wrote Wilma Miles, whose husband Milton was stationed on board the nearly hundred-foot-long yellow and white gunboat that the Americans used to patrol the Pearl and West Rivers. "The British ships weren't equipped with ice machines or refrigerators to store food. On the other hand the Americans were not allowed liquor aboard. The exchange was irresistible. In addition British officers were invariably good company. They read well, worked hard at their hobbies and had lots of time. Both American and British officers joined in sympathy for the French, who attempted to solve the problem of fresh food by carrying live chickens, pigs and even cattle aboard."

During the summer of 1925, the *Pampanga* was on station duty opposite Shameen. One day as Ensign Miles stood on the deck, he noticed a motor boat having trouble with its engine. The boat drifted toward the *Pampanga*'s gangway. Miles sent for the machinist's mate and some tools and told him to go help. When the boat pulled alongside, Cohen stormed on board the *Pampanga* and demanded both gasoline and a mechanic to fix his engine. His behavior and effrontery shocked the crew. They ordered Cohen off the quarterdeck and told him to fix it himself. He then stomped off the *Pampanga*, yelling at Miles, "I will get you for this!"

Cohen could not control himself. He had an overinflated view of his own importance, and did not like it when things did not go his way. His brusque manner and outbursts did not go over well in Canton. One British official noted that "he is a pure adventurer with an unsavoury record and is believed to be an active member of the I.W.W." Nor did he receive a welcome up north. In August Cohen traveled to Beijing with Sun Fo and stopped by the British Legation to discuss the shootings at Shameen. He blamed the French for opening fire without any justification. Yet while he threw around accusations, he also schizophrenically strove to project a pro-western front. Cohen seemed to want to please both his bosses and the foreign community. "Cohen was at some pains to impress upon me that he was pro-British and not 'red' and that he had been thanked by Sir James [Jamieson] for his services. I find this difficult to believe in view of the general tenor of Sir James' despatch," wrote the official. Not only did he discount Cohen's statements, but when Cohen failed to obtain an appointment with the chargé d'affaires, Cohen showed signs of paranoia. He said he had been falsely charged with an unspecified crime and would be arrested as an undesirable and deported if he set foot in Shanghai's International Settlement. Not to let the matter drop, Cohen "followed this up by a veiled threat that if this action were contemplated apart from its execution, he would be able, through his associations in Canada, 'to make it hot' for everyone concerned." Conning people and making up tales was not how to win friends in the British consular service. According to another official, "Mr. Cohen struck me as being of the type known in America as a 'saloon bum,' offensive both in appearance and manner."

In late August Cohen arrived in Shanghai. Despite his unfounded fears, no one arrested him. He visited the British consulate and then made a follow-up appointment but failed to show up. On August 31, he boarded the *President Cleveland* for Hong Kong. Wilma Miles sailed on board, having just arrived from the United States to marry her twenty-five-year-old ensign. To pass the time as she crossed the Pacific, she played bridge with Captain George W. Yardley and two other passengers. "For want of better, Mr. Mungo Park, whose famous grandfather explored in Africa, had picked me as a permanent partner to play nightly with the skipper," she recalled. "Since I wouldn't play for money, he carried my losses or gains and as I was phenomenally lucky he made out all right." When the *President Cleveland* arrived in Shanghai, Yardley's partner disembarked and Cohen came on board. Cohen knew Yardley, and the captain asked him to sit in on the game. While Miles did not yet know of Cohen's irascible reputation, others warily watched as he fanned and riffled through the cards. "I remember Captain Yardley playfully warning Cohen when we sat down that he'd have to watch his dealing habits. Cohen grinned and told us, 'I never cheat with ladies present.' " The foursome had a pleasant trip, and when the ship arrived in Hong Kong, Ensign Miles was horrified to learn that his intended had played against such a man. He warned her to stay away from him since "he was bad medicine."[6]

The strike dragged out. On November 20, twenty Cantonese merchants concerned about the effect of the labor stoppage went to Hong Kong to talk with the Chamber of Commerce and Assistant Colonial Secretary A. G. M. Fletcher about ending the action. Yet there was no ending the increasingly violent work stoppage. Herbert Cadman, the resident engineer of the Asiatic Petroleum Company, ran a side business ferrying passengers and stores from steamers on the Pearl River to Shameen. He occasionally conveyed Chinese who violated the boycott and traveled on Hong Kong boats. The pickets resented his business. During the afternoon of December 18, as Cadman's motor boat pulled away from the SS *Honam*, a strike picket steam launch cruised toward him. Pickets fired a dozen shots, boarded his boat, took him and his two Indian workers—Gajan Singh and Hira Singh—hostage, and stole a bag of coins.

When the men tried to escape, the pickets beat them. "They then took our turbans off and tied them round our necks with two men at each end pulling in opposite directions," said Gajan Singh. The pickets secured their hands behind their backs, and marched them six miles to the strike headquarters. A howling mob followed behind, kicking and beating them along the way. News of Cadman's arrest spread quickly, and Cohen rushed to the headquarters to pressure the strikers and obtain his release.

Gajan and Hira Singh were not as lucky. Their captors stripped them of most of their clothes and tossed them into a cell. At their "trial," the judge told them that since they had served on board a British boat they would be shot. "We were taken to the office and searched," said Hira Singh. "We were then bound in a squatting position for one hour in the office. One man then said 'If you go back to the English or Shameen we will shoot you.' I said 'Shoot me then' and they then kicked and hit me with their fists." The pickets fed them little. "We were given a small bowl of rice every day at about 9 A.M. When we were taken to the lavatory by the duty man, they struck us every time." During their captivity, the guards sometimes put beef in their rice, which religious dietary rules forbade the Sikhs from eating. More beatings followed, and according to Gajan Singh the guards forced them "to clean floors which were covered with all sorts of expectorated matter and filth." Whenever the British consulate and Asiatic Petroleum tried to get them out, the strikers simply responded that they needed to further question the men. Finally on January 6, they set them free.[7]

Negotiations to end the strike continued. T. V. Soong and other GMD leaders insisted that the strikers should be reinstated and paid their back salaries, and suggested that the foreign community provide the needed money. On the evening of December 20, Cohen stopped by Shameen with a note from Soong about further discussions. The consul asked Cohen his opinion of the strike. He was always eager to try to impress people with what he knew and thought, and gladly complied. In order to show his own importance within the Cantonese hierarchy, Cohen claimed that he was initially involved in enlisting instructors for Whampoa. He went on to say that after years of working with Borodin and the Russians, the government was now tired of them. It was quite possible, he hinted, that they might be gotten rid of soon.

Sun Fo, Cohen let on, hated the Russians and especially disliked Borodin. As for the strike, Cohen reported that the Cantonese wanted to settle soon. The following morning Wang Jingwei, C. C. Wu, T. V. Soong, and others came by to discuss the strike, and the British suggested that as an incentive the Hong Kong government might make a loan to the Cantonese government so that it could complete the Canton-Hankou railway.[8]

After many ham-handed public relations attempts, Cohen worked hard to improve his own standing in the eyes of foreigners. He could bluster but he could also charm. While he got into trouble for packing his guns when he went to the Canton Club, he successfully palled around with sailors on the western gunboats, doing target practice and demonstrating how he could easily shoot coins tossed in the air. In March 1926 Wilma Miles visited the Nanti Club. The club attracted students who had studied abroad, as well as such regulars as T. V. Soong and Chiang. Many of the members spoke English. There westerners could mix with the Chinese and their wives, have a drink, discuss current events, or see a movie. The club also had a gramophone, and members anxiously asked the Americans to teach them the latest dance steps.

"One gentleman in Chinese gown—Wu Tiecheng, Chief of Police in Canton—was particularly nice to me," recalled Miles of one visit to the club. "As we chatted, he asked what I was reading about China and I had to admit my sources were limited." Wanting her to have a better understanding of her new home, Wu told her that he would send her a copy of a readable book on China. "The very next day, Morris Cohen sent word out by a sampan to ask if he might come aboard the *Pampanga,* to deliver a package. . . . When he came aboard, this time welcomed with a cup of coffee and a bowl of rice and gravy, he brought McNair's *History of Modern China* with the card of Wu Tiecheng." Unlike his behavior during the last visit on board the ship, his behavior did not involve shouts or threats. No temper tantrums. No storming off the deck. Cohen instead acted like a gentleman. Ensign Miles and Cohen then "buried the hatchet."

The consulates even started asking Cohen his opinion of undesirables entering town. When Frank A. Graham, a plumber from Victoria, B.C., whom the Victoria police reported was "a Communist of the 'reddist type,' " arrived in Canton on April 21, 1926, he met with Cohen. As far as Cohen could tell, Graham was simply short of money and in need of a job. When asked by the British consulate to apprise him, Cohen readily complied. "Graham did not make a serious impression on Mr. Cohen, who thought his manner particularly quiet and inoffensive and expressed himself convinced that Graham had not the ability to be in any way prominent in Communist circles," wrote Acting Consul General John Brenan.[9]

As the strike intensified and opposition to the radicals grew, it became dangerous for the Russians to move around town. Borodin started screening movies in his house, and both he and Blyukher rode through Canton with armed soldiers. Westerners also further fortified all routes to Shameen. "On the island side were concrete blockhouses, barbed wire, sandbags, machine guns, and British and French sentries with rifles and hand grenades. Night and day since June of the year before, Shameen had lived under fear of new attacks," wrote Abend. "At the mainland end of the bridges were more sandbags, more armed guards, Chinese this time. They searched every person coming from the island. . . . I found sandbags and barbed wire along the entire shoreline of the island facing the city, and here and there were concrete pillboxes equipped with machine guns placed to sweep all approaches to the bridges. The shoreline facing the river was also protected by barbed-wire barricades, and the entire circumference was patrolled by guards night and day. There was occasional sniping from roof tops in the city and from Chinese launches far out in the muddy stream."

The Chinese desperately tried to maintain their boycott and regain control of their economy. Pickets indiscriminately searched Europeans, Indians, and Japanese. In March 1926 two Indians spent two nights at strike headquarters for attempting to bring silk shawls to Shameen. "The strikers had become so strong and so bold that they actually maintained their own courts and a prison," wrote Abend.

No striker could be tried for any offense before any of the regular Canton courts, and the strikers arrogated to themselves the right to try in their own courts all Chinese caught trying to smuggle goods in from Hongkong. Sentences ranged from small to huge fines, and even to long terms of imprisonment, and no appeals were possible. This situation led to frequent bloody clashes between Canton's police force and the strike pickets and patrols. . . . In all cases the strikers were the victors, and why not? They were never less than 40,000 strong, and at one time had exceeded 300,000 in number. Canton's police force consisted of 4,600 men.

Strike pickets acted with impunity. Just before noon on April 26, the strike picket launch *Nan Chuk* pulled alongside a lighter being towed toward Shameen. On board rested furniture belonging to a Mr. Quinn. When the launch neared, the White Russian in charge of the furniture jumped into the river. The pickets arrested those still on the boat and confiscated the launch. The British patrol boat HMS *Onslaught* spotted the pickets and set off in pursuit. The Chinese steered the boats to the electric company's jetty. There they brandished rifles at the British and then fled. The *Onslaught* took control of the boats and started to escort the vessels to Shameen. But as they set off, a large and threatening crowd gathered, accusing the British sailors of piracy. A few even started marching toward Shameen. "The usual crowd of longshore loafers were standing about shouting slogans and shaking their fists," said Cohen, who happened to be passing by at that moment. "That didn't worry me till I saw most of the mob suddenly scatter and run from one little group who were standing on the edge of the wharf close up to the ship." A picket on the pier was yelling and threatened to throw a bomb on board the *Onslaught*. Cohen bounded out of his car and grabbed the bomb-toter, heaving the explosive into the water before it did any damage. He then carted the miscreant away.

Cohen intentionally sought such visibility. He especially enjoyed the rumor-filled press. Wilma Miles was horrified to one day hear that Wu "had been arrested by the Borodin group for not being 'Red' enough," and that Cohen had been summarily decapitated. She quickly realized that it was not true. When she saw Cohen she asked about the astonishing report. "What a stupid thing," he replied. "I hope my parents don't see it and worry." When Cohen thought a minute about the story, he asked Miles, "Are you sure it said executed and not assassinated?" There was an important difference, noted Miles. "After all the latter has more status."[10]

Talk of people being arrested was only natural in such a climate. Besides tension between the British and the Chinese, internal rifts within the party and with the Soviets grew. The ever paranoid Chiang vied with Borodin for power and shifted more to the right. He perceived a conspiracy brewing against him by the Soviets and his rival Wang, so on the early morning of March 20, 1926, Chiang declared martial law. Whampoa troops arrested political workers and Soviet advisers, raided communist offices, and closed trade unions and strike committee headquarters. Within a few hours, Chiang controlled Canton. He then ordered the Soviets' banishment from town. Despite his bravado, Chiang still needed Soviet advisers to help plan his conquest of Beijing. He apologized for his actions and blamed the "misunderstanding" on his subordinates. He then agreed to Borodin's peace overtures.[11]

It was humid during the summer of 1926. Outbreaks of typhus, amebic dysentery, and typhoid fever raged in Canton, along with an especially bad plague of cholera. The crew aboard the *Pampanga* inoculated themselves with a new serum, and watched as bodies floated near their ship. They boiled all their drinking water and also poured scorching water over fruits and vegetables. When people washed they added a spoonful of Lysol to their bathwater. In May, Lieutenant Colonel Cecil John L'Estrange Malone, a former member of parliament, came to Canton for a week. While there, the Canton government entertained the communist legislator who had once advocated that Churchill be hanged from a lamppost. Malone visited the strike headquarters. Sun Fo also started his third term as mayor in June, continued to build asphalt-paved streets, planned a public hospital, and installed public telephones throughout the city.

Blyukher, who originally left Canton for health reasons, returned that summer as Chiang's principal military strategist. He coordinated plans for the Northern Expedition. The following month the GMD made Chiang commander in chief of the Northern Expedition, and he officially launched the campaign. Unlike Sun Yat-sen's battle arrangements two years earlier, Chiang's army set off prepared. The GMD had its own troops, a base in Guangdong, and allies. Chiang's troops marched quickly north. As his forces advanced, his propaganda troops stirred up the enemy and roused locals to greet their liberators. According to Akimova, they "arranged real welcomes for them replete with colored lanterns, music and singing." Hunan fell that summer, and soon Chiang's troops stood outside the Wuhan cities of Hankou, Hanyang, and Wuchang. Resistance crumbled in early October. By the fall of 1926, fifteen armies marched under the GMD's flag. At the end of the year, the GMD controlled 260,000 troops.[12]

As they marched, strike pickets in Canton become more militant. Not all Chinese supported the strike. Businessmen tired of pickets taking advantage of the strike, and Cohen even had a strike leader and two pickets arrested for making money off of the boycott. New negotiations began to end the action. The British offered up to a $10 million industrial loan for the development of the Whampoa Port, and brought up again the construction of a loop line connecting the Kowloon–Canton and the Canton–Hankou railways. Neither side could reach terms. As the Chinese made their rounds of negotiations, bodyguard Cohen naturally put in his two cents whenever possible. "I spoke in very strong terms with Eugene Chen and T. V. Soong, saying that I was positive that the British were going to take action unless the pickets were called off and the boycott stopped," Cohen told the consulate. "T. V. Soong telephoned to Eugene Chen, and I explained to Eugene Chen that I got this information from a source that I was certain was correct."

Chiang for his part just wanted the strike called off. He could not afford unrest and possible western military reprisals while he advanced north. He told Chen to stop the boycott. It ended on October 10. After sixteen months of often violent protests, the Chinese gained little from their action, except the knowledge that they could financially cripple Hong Kong, which lost $300 million in trade. Cohen took credit for the peaceful resolution: "I feel that my efforts in obtaining the unconditional calling off of the strike and boycott had done a little good. I might state that I was the only person besides the British and Chinese delegates who was present at the conference, where I had been detailed by the Chinese government to give them protection."[13]

With the strike over, the tense peace between Chiang and Borodin frayed. When Wuhan fell, the Chinese leadership decided to move the government there. An essentially all-English speaking group that included Sun Fo, T. V. Soong, Soong Qingling, Borodin, and Chen trekked up north. As the government settled in, it approved holidays celebrating the labor movement, the death of Lenin, and the birth of Karl Marx. Unions flourished. Workers paralyzed businesses and shut down factories. Peasants attacked landlords and other rural power holders.

The rise in labor and peasant militancy frightened Chinese conservatives and the military, making them even more fearful of the Communist Party. Foreigners nervously watched communist gains. Many of their concerns were realized when the Chinese seized concessions in Jiujiang and Hankou on January 3, 1927. Some saw it as the start of another Boxer-like rebellion in which Chinese would massacre foreigners. Western security increased. "I visited the men sitting behind their machine-guns and sandbags in the Asiatic Petroleum Company's dominating concrete building," wrote consular Sir Owen O'Malley. "From the windows of the Consulate-General I watched the mob painting insulting messages on the garden walls. . . ."

Chiang meanwhile continued his rightward drift. He also decided to establish the government in Nanchang, with the aim of moving it to Nanjing once that city fell. With the continuing labor problems, crackdowns were in order. When Cohen visited Hong Kong at the beginning of January 1927, he let on that a new police chief had been appointed in Canton with explicit instructions to get control over the unions. Cohen also escorted journalists like Arthur Ransome of the Manchester *Guardian* to Canton so they could see conditions in town and meet with Cantonese leaders. "As soon as the boat was along side there was a scuffling outside my cabin and I found two men who simultaneously held out letters and announced that they were from the Cantonese Government," wrote Ransome in his diary on the twenty-first.

They then engaged in a mild fight while I, being half naked, retired and shut the door to dress and shave. One was Mr. Szeyuan Ho, Schantong representative of the Sun Yat-sen University, a spectacled Chinese youth and quite decent. The other was a British subject, Jew, Canadian origin, called Cohen. . . . He had a letter from the Canton Foreign Office, to say that they had sent him to accompany me to Canton. I decided to postpone my visit to that city but agreed to meet the man at the Hong Kong Hotel, where I drank some beer and he spilt more over my hat and coat. He was inclined to minimise Russian help, but also urged that anyhow the Cantonese had only accepted Russian help after they had begged in vain for British. Convinced that the Cantonese would win, but uncertain whether they would bother about Beijing. He was very uncertain what line of talk to take with me and I did not help him. Escaping from him . . .

The rift grew within the party, and Borodin publicly denounced Chiang as a mere militarist. Chiang sounded out western powers to see how they might respond to a purge of the communists. Further aligning himself with his conservative bosses, Cohen in mid-February visited Jenkins at the American consulate in Canton and reported that Chiang and Borodin had "a serious disagreement" that resulted in a "more or less permanent breach" between them. Cohen told Jenkins "very confidentially as usual," that

if the Powers wanted to get the Russians out of China, they should now establish direct contact with General Chiang. He was sure Chiang hated the Russians and was only cooperating with Borodin because the Soviet Government was supplying arms and ammunition which were absolutely essential for the success of the Cantonese forces. Mr. Cohen expressed the opinion that if Great Britain or any other power would undertake to do the same as the Russians are doing, General Chiang would immediately break with Borodin and cease his violent anti-imperialist and anti-capitalist activities. While Mr. Cohen's statements cannot be accepted as entirely reliable, they are not without interest. This is not the first time he has stressed the fact that the Cantonese were working with the Russians simply because they were receiving military supplies from Moscow. Mr. Cohen ventured the opinion that there was nothing brilliant about Borodin and the other Russian advisers. They were doing what Moscow told them to do and the Nationalist Army was succeeding because it had a definite program, as well as a fairly dependable source of ammunition and supplies.

Besides acting as a courier to accompany important officials passing through Canton and Hong Kong, Cohen also worked at T. V. Soong's Central Bank. There he watched over the vaults and superintended the transfer of bullion and notes. His public relations for the government continued. He told Brenan that Eugene Chen had made arrangements for the dissemination of Nationalist propaganda in England, and hired Reginald Bridgeman, a former Foreign Office employee, to run a Chinese Information Bureau out of Malone's London home.[14]

On February 19, Chiang announced his plans to expel the communists from the GMD. In response the Central Committee in Wuhan stripped him of his special emergency powers. Chiang then resigned as chairman of the committee but continued his military campaign. As his troops neared Shanghai, leftists took the town, disarming the police and northern forces. Fearing an assault on the western settlements, foreign troops set out to fortify their concessions. Chiang marched on, and Shanghai fell to him on March 22. Nanjing followed two days later. On the morning of the twenty-fourth, Nationalist troops looted foreign properties in Nanjing, attacked the British, American, and Japanese consulates, and killed a number of westerners. British and American gunboats retaliated by firing on and killing fifteen Chinese troops and four civilians. Not wishing further confrontation with the foreigners, Chiang headed to Shanghai to calm their fears and curb the militant mass movement.

Chiang blamed the Nanjing Incident on the communists, thus giving him an excuse to take action. Repression soon began. Sensing an opportunity to rid Shanghai of undesirables, conservative business and military leaders gave Chiang millions of dollars to cleanse the city and suppress the unions. He readily accepted the bribe and the help of his friend Du Yuesheng, the head of the Green Gang and the most powerful gangster in Shanghai. Starting at 4 A.M. on April 12, Chiang's troops and 15,000 Green Gang members slipped into the Chinese section of Shanghai. A bugle sounded and the massacre began. Rightists brandishing guns and broadswords attacked communists and suspected reds. They tied men together, gunned them down, and lopped off their heads. Thousands died. On the thirteenth, 100,000 workers took to the streets to protest the killings. After the meeting, demonstrators marched though the city, only to be met by soldiers who opened fire on them. The White Terror quickly spread to other cities, with similar atrocities being carried out in Nanjing and Nanchang.

Anti-communists in the south supported Chiang's efforts. In December 1926 the GMD leader Li Jishen, who controlled Canton, forbade workers to make arrests, carry weapons when they demonstrated, and seize and boycott factories and shops. He also instituted repressive activities against labor unions. The British had warning of a coup in Canton. In March 1927 Robert Norman, who had been Sun Yat-sen's legal adviser, stopped by the British consulate with Cohen and said that Chiang had had enough of communist interference with his military plans and intended to get rid of the Russians. "Mr. Norman and Mr. Morris Cohen . . . have been to me and to the American consul-general, evidently on behalf of some of the local officials, to ask if the Powers cannot give Chiang Kai-shek some assurance of their support provided he eliminates the Russians," wrote Brenan. "I replied that His Majesty's Government declined to interfere in Chinese politics, but that they had already publicly made known to both Governments in China their willingness to alter the treaties and to do their best to meet the Nationalist aspirations, and that this offer would not be withdrawn whatever happened to the Russians."

The British braced for action. Military preparedness increased on Shameen. Lieutenant F.M.V. Tregear took his post to defend the western end of the island. Tregear dug a redoubt, but could only go down about two feet before hitting the water level. "We had little wire, or other materials, so I used the iron gratings over the storm drains much to the wrath of the local citizens, who fell in them!" he wrote. "I put one Lewis gun section and a rifle section in my redoubt; my second Lewis gun section was round the corner by the boat house, and my second rifle section was in reserve in a house overlooking the redoubt."[15]

Li extensively planned his purge. He even prepared a Doomsday Book listing people he wished eliminated. He gave orders at one in the morning on the fifteenth for his men to raid communist dens and arrest all red agitators; 10,000 to 15,000 troops set out along with naval forces to do battle. Fearing that attacks on westerners might bring retaliations, Li posted guards near Shameen and told foreigners of possible problems. "A few days after we arrived we were warned by Mr. Cohen . . . that the Communists were planning to attack us at 9 A.M. the next day," noted Tregear of the coming assault. Li's troops stormed the headquarters of the Hong Kong Strike Committee, seized ammunition and rifles, and killed more than one hundred communists. They wounded hundreds more. "A fierce resistance was put up by the 'Reds' and armed labour pickets who were attacked by troops under government orders," reported the Hongkong *Telegraph*. Troops disarmed the strike pickets. They raided Sun Yat-sen University and shut down the two leading GMD newspapers. To prevent reds from escaping, Li stationed guards at the steamship wharves.

The purge swept the town. "On the day of our arrival there were already mass arrests going on, and many trade unions were surrounded," said the Soviet trade union representative, S. A. Lozovsky. Martial law was decreed. "Down with the Chinese Communist Party!" "Down with the Wuhan Government!" "Long Live Chiang Kai-shek!" proclaimed posters hung in the streets. "The railroad workers resisted and there were many victims among them. On the following day, the city which was usually so lively, seemed silent and deserted. Only the sounds of military trumpets could be heard. Bound workers were led along the street under convoy. Canton was occupied by troops and police, arrests and roundups did not cease. More than two thousand people were arrested and several hundred communists were shot. A wave of arrests also occurred in Sun Yat-sen University. The Whampoa Academy was destroyed." Labor leaders were killed and troops disarmed strike pickets. Canton merchants were so overjoyed by Li's efforts, that they gave feasts at local restaurants to celebrate the murders.[16]

With the purge, the GMD's Central Executive Committee expelled Chiang. He immediately formed his own rival Nationalist Government in Nanjing and blockaded his enemies. The Wuhan economy stagnated. The government crumbled. Military commanders acted disloyally. Troops attacked communist organizations and schools. The violence spread across the province as the military crushed peasant groups. Hundreds died.

Fearing for its own survival, the Wuhan government in mid-July expelled communist members from its ranks, terminated the United Front, and told the Soviets to leave. As Wuhan collapsed, its leaders dispersed. Borodin went to Mongolia. Soong Qingling moved back to her home on Rue Molière. There her family pressured her to support Chiang. But the massacre of the communists and the destruction of the labor movement "were to arouse her indignation to such a pitch that she seemed, before one's eyes, to take on stature," wrote Sheean. "Without physical or intellectual power, by sheer force of character, purity of motive, sovereign honesty, she became heroic. In the wreck of the Chinese Revolution this phenomenon was one of the most extraordinary: generals and orators fell to pieces, yielded, fled, or were silent, but the one revolutionary who could not be crushed and would not be still was the fragile little widow of Sun Yat-sen." Soong publicly denounced Chiang and slipped out of Shanghai, taking a sampan early one morning to a Soviet steamer. Chen and his daughters joined her, and they sailed to Vladivostok and then took a train to Moscow.

Yet only three months after establishing the Nanjing government, a coalition in Nanjing forced Chiang from power. Now without the communists and Chiang around, the various Nationalist factions tried to reconcile their differences; Nanjing, Wuhan, and the Western Hills group formed a government. Yet it lacked stability since neither Chiang nor Wang belonged to it. Nor was it financially sound. By the end of the year, Chiang returned to power strengthened by a marriage to Soong's sister Meiling and links to brother T.V. and the banks.[17]

With strong leaders vying for power, some of the Western press astonishingly made Morris Cohen out to be the real leader of China. It was not possible, they obviously believed, for unification to be brought about by the Chinese. A westerner had to be behind it. The press touted Cohen as an active enemy of Moscow's Far East aims, and noted that "a recent erroneous report of his execution is now believed to have been spread by his associates in order to enable him to escape from his many enemies." Despite what the press wrote and Cohen thought, he was not an important force in southern Chinese politics to be reckoned with. In reality, Cohen simply aligned himself with his bosses in Canton, whether it was Sun Yat-sen or Wu Tie-cheng. He did their errands and delivered their messages. When Li Jishen needed supplies, Cohen headed to Hong Kong to buy two hundred to three hundred army mules from the British forces and arranged for the purchase of six-wheeled lorries from the Morris Motor Company in England.[18]

The power base of the communists continued to shrink. Hoping to reverse recent setbacks, the Soviet leader Joseph Stalin in August ordered the CCP to launch a series of revolts. They staged an uprising at Nanchang in August, and then tried an Autumn Harvest uprising in several central provinces. All their coups failed. Undaunted, they decided to focus their efforts on Guangdong. There they had a strong base made up of workers who had flocked to Canton during the recent strike. They planned to take the province, and once in power, they would launch a communist takeover of the nation.

In November Li headed to Shanghai for a plenary session of the Central Executive Committee to restore party unity. While Li kept busy in Shanghai and Cohen did work in Hong Kong for the bank, Li's subordinate Zhang Fakui staged a coup, capturing the Whampoa Academy, the arsenal, the forts, and other key spots. Li ordered loyal troops to oust Zhang, and Zhang's soldiers had to abandon Canton to repulse their attackers. As a power vacuum developed within the city, the communists decided to take advantage of the situation. They called for the disarming of the 7,000 remaining troops and police, the taking of key military, police, and government centers, and the distribution to workers' battalions of weapons from the captured arms depot and arsenal. From there they planned to overrun Henan Island.

The communists attacked in the early hours of December 11. As their troops spread through the Chinese city, they distributed guns and red arm and neck bands to like-minded revolutionaries. They also handed out pamphlets proclaiming, "The oppressed of China have risen up and seized power for themselves. . . . We swear to die in the protection of our power. We must break up all reactionaries and all anti-revolutionaries." They quickly captured most of the planned bases, but failed to take the arms depot and arsenal as well as some key military headquarters. They ransacked the police headquarters, killed about three hundred policemen, and set hundreds of prisoners free. Their forces besieged the Guangdong Labourer's General Union, which opposed the communists, torched the building, and burned to death more than one hundred laborers.

These new rulers called for an eight-hour day, increased pay, confiscation of capitalists' property, the turning of mansions into workers dormitories, state control of banks, railways, mines, factories, and steamers, and the return of goods in pawnshops. They also offered a $50,000 reward to anyone who brought them the heads of "opponents of the revolution and enemies of the laborers, peasants and soldiers" such as Li Jishen, Chiang Kai-shek, and Wang Jingwei.

The communists, though, foolishly did not organize the masses beforehand for a general strike. The majority of Canton's workers therefore did not take part in the uprising. Nor did the peasantry rise up against the capitalist oppressors and cut the transportation links to the city. Only some five hundred peasant activists entered the fighting. As the small force spread through the city, they set buildings on fire, looted, and killed.[19]

The streets near Shameen became quiet. "All the shops were closed and barred with heavy iron grating," wrote Earl Swisher. "We saw two buses which had been commandeered by the Reds, but there were neither rickshas, nor people on the road. We walked along a short way when we saw a group of armed peasants and laborers run out of one of the narrow alleys. They paid no attention to us but hurried up and down looking for some kind of conveyance. They had several coolies loaded with loot, which they had taken from shops or houses, and were leading a merchant by the collar, the latter being handcuffed. They took one of the buses, loaded it with their stuff, and sailed off down Shakee Bund." A French gunboat meanwhile evacuated their nationals. "While we were standing there we saw a fire start up farther on down the Bund. We found, on going down there, that it was the Central Bank of China . . . on fire. The Reds had the fire department and would not allow anything to be done to save the building." They ransacked the bank and torched the Japanese hospital. Soon fires burned throughout the city. Gun-toting girls as young as fifteen stood guard at the wharves and went through the luggage of people trying to flee by steamer.[20]

Upon hearing of the Canton Commune Uprising, Cohen rushed back to the city, mimicking his boss T. V. Soong as he went by proclaiming, "I'm just a poor, peaceable, bloody banker, but I've got to look after my ledgers!" When he returned, he went to Li Fulin's headquarters on Henan Island. "For two days they enjoyed themselves while we watched from across the river," Cohen said of the looting communists. "Through my binoculars I saw sights that made me sick." But what the Nationalists were about to do would disgust anyone. Soon after the start of the commune, the now united forces of Zhang Fakui, Li Jishen, and Huang Qixiang, along with naval forces of China and foreign nations attacked.

Once across the Pearl River, the Nationalists killed indiscriminately. "Lee and I went in early Wednesday morning and the streets were piled with dead then," continued Swisher. "Most of them had their hands tied and were plainly the victims of execution rather than fighting." Throughout the streets and avenues "there were literally heaps of dead. . . . Down here below our wharf at the college, a special form of execution was staged. Seven boatloads of 'Reds' were towed down to Ha To and the occupants pushed into the river. Four shots were plugged into each as he struggled in the water. There were a number of women shot also. Three Zhongshan University girl students were shot at Tin Tsz Matau and their stripped bodies exposed to public view for twelve hours." Soldiers wrapped female communists in cotton blankets, doused them with gasoline, and set them on fire. Any woman with short bobbed hair was killed.[21]

Reds fought back and killed as they retreated. Those fleeing discarded their arm and neck bands. But the heat and perspiration had stained their necks and arms, leaving telltale marks of their affiliation. "Many rickshaw coolies who had joined the Red Guards quickly reverted to their old profession upon the arrival of the Whites," noted the American vice consul Frederick W. Hinke. "I, myself, saw a rickshaw stopped, the coolie grabbed by the police, his shirt jerked from his neck disclosing the red stain from the neck band. He was rushed to the side of the road, compelled to kneel down and unceremoniously shot, while the crowd of people in the street applauded. His body was left in the gutter."

The city reeked of rotting flesh. Corpses bobbed in the water. The Nationalists blamed the Soviets for orchestrating the coup. Fearing a raid of their consulate, the Soviets destroyed papers and reports. "As we neared the Russian consulate, they burned their documents," said Zhang Fakui. There the troops uncovered a large quantity of arms, ammunition, and bombs, and a wireless set along with Chinese bank notes that were printed in Russia bearing the name "The Farmers and Labourers Bank." They shackled the consulate staff, threw them in jail, and seized the documents. The following morning, a military squad executed five Russians and six Chinese.[22]

Cohen headed to the Russian consulate. With the help of British Lieutenant Commander Cyril M. Faure and a senior French naval officer, he searched the building. "I got permission in writing from General Zhang Fakui to raid the Soviet Consulate, where I found many documents to prove beyond the shadow of a doubt that they were responsible for the coup," wrote Cohen two years later. The group gathered mounds of paper from off the floor and took the piles to Cohen's room at the Victoria Hotel on Shameen. British and French intelligence officers pored over the material, and Cohen enlisted the help of his Russian-speaking friend Olga Ferrier. "I then went to the Victoria Hotel to see Sergeant Koretsky. I found him waiting for Mr. Cohen and Lieutenant Commander Faure in order to continue examination of documents found in the Russian Consulate," wrote T. H. King, Director of Criminal Intelligence in Hong Kong of the team of translators. "Mr. Cohen and Lieutenant Commander Faure had been to the Russian Consulate yesterday . . . and taken back to the Victoria Hotel (I understand to a room engaged by Mr. Cohen) a large quantity of documents which had been left by the Chinese soldiers who carried out the first search. . . . He took Sergeant Koretsky with him."[23]

The translators deciphered the papers and found incriminating documents. Despite the evidence, the Soviets denied involvement in the uprising. Chiang condemned Soviet consulates as "hot-beds of Communist propaganda," and the Nationalists withdrew recognition of their consuls and suspended the functions of the Soviet commercial agencies.

When he finished with the documents, Cohen bathed, slept, and then rushed back to check on the charred remains of the bank. Branches of the bank soon reopened, and the various chambers of commerce sent out notices that Central Bank currency would be accepted at par. Yet the value of the paper money plummeted, as the heads of the bank refused to confirm how much silver remained in the vaults. Many shops stayed closed so as not to be forced to accept money that might prove worthless. "Instead of helping matters, the invitation which the Government had extended to the five Chambers of Commerce to send their representatives to witness the opening of the vaults, has resulted in the merchants being more uneasy than ever," wrote the *South China Morning Post*. "This is because of the failure of the Treasurer to permit the members of the Chambers of Commerce to look inside the vaults after they had gone to the Central Bank at the Government's request.

"One of those who was present has told the writer that he and his colleagues reached the bank about noon on the day appointed. It was 3 o'clock before anyone from the Treasury showed up. Then Wang Chung-chu appeared, but he had with him no key, and he had to send back for one, and had to procure flashlights also. When the key had been found, Mr. Wang suddenly remembered that one key was not sufficient. Two are necessary in opening the vaults. So more time was wasted. It was about 5 o'clock before the second key was found, and then the party entered the bank." There they met Cohen, who controlled security. "But the officer in charge of the soldiers on guard there would not permit the safes to be opened. A permit had first to be obtained at the Provincial Military Headquarters, and another precious hour was wasted. By the time it had been procured, it was dark.

"Wang Chung-chu then told the merchants that it must be remembered the city was under martial law; that those were not normal times. If by chance the Government should lose any of the money because of the opening of the vaults at night time, these merchants would have to bear the responsibility.

"This was too much for the Chamber of Commerce men. They bade Mr. Wang good-night and went their separate ways. They have not since been requested to return."[24]

Things did not calm down following the restoration of order. Cohen tried to protect the reserves. William Shenton even commended him, writing that "Maurice Cohen did great work during this period and deserves full marks." Yet the finance commissioner, the accountant of the Canton treasury, and the bank's briefly reigning general manager stole millions of dollars worth of silver that survived the torching. Chiang and T. V. Soong themselves absconded with $150,000 to $200,000, which they forwarded to their accounts in Shanghai.

Soong planned the draining of the funds as a way financially to paralyze Li's regime, with the intent of forcing Canton in line with Nanjing and consolidating the GMD and support for the Northern Expedition. While some of the money was recovered, the vaults stayed closed, and the bank continued to hide the theft from the public. "Li Jishen is at his wit's end to know how to carry on for the time being," wrote Shenton, "he is absolutely without funds, and the notes are depreciating daily."

Canton lay in shambles. Bodies drifted in the Pearl River. Hundreds of merchants were on the verge of bankruptcy. "Without fear of exaggeration it can be truly said that Guangdong had about reached the bottom of the curve in political and economic disorganization as 1927 drew to a close," wrote the American consul

Jay Huston. While Canton was a mess, the Chinese Communist Party was nearly extinguished. From April to December 1927, the CCP lost most of its members to death or abandonment. Some leaders and military bands tried to form military bases in the mountains and plains of central China, but they had a long road ahead of them.[25]

CHAPTER 13

THE SOUTH,
1928–1929

Sun Jo, Hu Hanmin, and C.C. Wu were unhappy with Chiang's restoration as commander in chief and election as chairman of the Central Executive Committee. So as not to provoke further schisms in the party, the three leaders left their posts in early 1928 and set off on a round-the-world trip. The junket, planned by Thomas Cook, included stops in Manila, Singapore, Penang, Constantinople, Paris, London, and Washington. The leaders embarked in style with a reported $50,000 each for expenses. Sun, Hu, and Wu did not set off alone. Family members and government workers traveled with them, as did Cohen as an escort, courier, and bodyguard.

Prior to leaving, Cohen stopped by the British consulate to fill Consul General Brenan in on their plans to investigate foreign countries, improve China's diplomatic relations, and invite experts to China to help with the nation's reconstruction. "Mr. Morris Cohen tells me that a party of some seventeen people . . . have booked their passages for Egypt and are leaving Hong Kong on the 29th January by the steamship *President Wilson*," wrote Brenan. The trip to England also gave Cohen a chance to see his family. "It was nearly ten years since I'd been home," he said. "My father and mother were getting old and wanted to see me again before they died, and I wanted to see my brothers and sisters—my nephews and nieces too—and find out how they were doing up in Manchester." The party received visas for England, via India, Iraq, Egypt, Palestine, and other ports on the understanding that while they traveled through those countries they would do nothing to make the various governments uneasy.

The trip attracted a lot of attention, along with Chinese demonstrations at each port. In February the Chinese community of Manila warmly greeted the three leaders, yet while in Singapore on February 8 the communist Cheong Yo-kai, acting on instructions from the CCP, took a shot at Wu as he walked out of the Chinese

Chamber of Commerce building. Cheong missed Wu but slightly wounded Dr. Lin Wenqing, the former principal of the University of Xiamen.

Despite the group's assurances of good behavior, India was reluctant to grant them entry to the subcontinent, especially after a Guomindang Central Committee text appeared in the Chinese press stating that the group planned to study the "emancipation movement among oppressed small and weak races. . . ." India also entertained suspicions of Sun because of his former relations with Borodin and the communists, his interest in Indian seditionists, and the fact that the group possessed letters of introduction to Mohandas Gandhi and other so-called extremists. The government finally advised them not to stop by.[1]

Partway into the trip, Cohen took leave of them. He sailed to Africa to see his sister Rose, who had moved there in 1912 following her marriage to John Bernstein, a Polish-born tailor. Cohen arrived in Salisbury, Rhodesia, on March 6, laden with presents for Rose, John, and their son and two daughters. "It was the first time we'd seen him," said Cohen's niece Queenie Cohen. "He brought a lot of dolls and toys. But he got a shock when he saw that we were big girls." Realizing that his nieces were much older than he had thought, Cohen quickly replaced the dolls with more appropriate bracelets. He then paid up the Bernstein's debts and arranged for passports and tickets to take the family to England. At the last minute, John decided to stay behind. "He brought us all to England for the first time," said Queenie of the vacation. "First class in the ship, which was wonderful. It was the first time we had seen the sea."

The Cohen family lived in Salford, outside of Manchester, in a simple row house with a bay window and numerous bedrooms filled with dark and heavy Chinese furniture. Lancashire County was a major textile center, and Josef had established himself in town as a rag merchant. Each day he carted home piles of clippings from the local mills, and loaded them into the cellar. The family then helped him sort through the cuttings. "He had a contract with firms that were making up clothes," said Cohen's sister Sarah Rich. "And the cuttings they used to put in a bag and then my dad used to collect them. We then sorted out the wools from the mixtures." When Cohen arrived, he mostly vacationed, rested, and took the family on outings. "He was a very generous, loving man," said Queenie. "He hired a bus and took all the family out. We all had a wonderful time. Money was no object with him when he came over." Cohen also visited relatives in London's East End, stopping by to see his cousin Leonard Nathan Sherer and his wife, Mary. "My mother prepared a mountain of latkes. I knew that something important was happening because we ate in the front parlor on a weekday, which never happened," said their son Cyril. "Moisha turned up. My memory was the latkes disappearing at a rather fast rate. Moisha had a huge appetite."[2]

Soong Qingling had recently arrived in Berlin following a trying exile in Moscow, and Cohen, who worried for her well-being, contacted the League Against Imperialism to try and get in touch with her through the league's secretary in Berlin. While Cohen relaxed, the Chinese delegation made its rounds. The group arrived in Constantinople on March 14. They had little luck setting up interviews with officials. From Constantinople they headed to Angora. As they continued their lobbying, Chiang in April launched the final phase of his Northern Expedition. Japan also sent troops into Shandong Province. The traveling entourage knew that the League of Nations would not come to China's assistance over the invasion, so Hu suggested that they work the diplomatic channels to air their grievances against Japan. Wu went to the United States, Sun headed to Germany, and Hu set off for France.

By June they regrouped in Paris. There Wu met with Philippe Berthelot, the secretary general of the French Foreign Ministry, to discuss the Japanese occupation, and Hu took part in the French National Day celebrations. The Northern Expedition meanwhile advanced quickly. When Beijing fell on June 8, Chiang and other officials visited Sun Yat-sen's tomb in the Western Hills to commemorate Chinese unification. A speech was made to tell Sun's spirit of the completion of the campaign, and Chiang sobbed loudly as a dirge was played and they presented wreaths and offerings. With the conquest of Beijing, the traveling group could now claim a greater right to speak for all of China. They picnicked in a suburban Parisian park and discussed the unification of China, Sun Yat-sen's revolutionary beliefs, and what to do next.[3]

Cohen meanwhile needed to head across the English Channel to rejoin the group. He decided to take with him Sarah, as well as his cousin Rose Brookarsh. His two wards needed travel documents, so on June 6 Cohen stopped by the London passport office to vouch for Rose's application, telling the officials there that he was a banker and financial adviser to the Central Bank of Canton. Despite the passport office and Scotland Yard's misgivings and concerns, they issued the documents. "He saw to everything, passports and everything," said Sarah of the trip later that month aboard an Imperial Airways passenger plane. "Rose came to chaperone me, because Morris had conferences in Geneva at the time. There was quite a few of the Chinese delegation that met the plane when we got off it. Morris had a few meetings and he spent the rest of the time with us. We went to the Follies, to the theater and restaurants."[4]

Upon meeting up with his bosses, Cohen learned of their disappointing progress. Cohen was eager for the group to be well received in London. After a few days on the Continent, he headed back across the Channel to see if he could arrange a receptive greeting. "I persuaded the party to allow me to go to London, as I believed and felt sure that they would be welcome, about which they had great doubts at the time." In England Cohen searched out sympathetic contacts. "I did proceed to London and got in touch with Sir John Thornycroft." Sir John, he said, "worked very hard to get some recognition for the party in the event of its coming to England, and he introduced me to many members of Parliament whom I did my best to convince that it would be a very good thing if the delegation would receive some official recognition if it came to England." William Shenton was also in town. Cohen tracked him down, meeting with him on July 10 and making his pitch for interviews with British Foreign Secretary Austen Chamberlain. "I had a communication yesterday from the representatives," wrote Shenton of the traveling group. "They want to know how they would be received here—whether on a friendly basis." Cohen's talk with Shenton appeared promising. "He did see me and assured me that Mr. Chamberlain, the foreign minister, would give an interview if the interview were made through the Chinese Legation," recalled Cohen. "I immediately sent a very strong wire to the party in Paris to come to England, and in reply I received a wire that it was leaving at once."[5]

The group arrived separately in London, taking rooms at the Savoy Hotel. They had meetings in mid- and late-July with Ramsay MacDonald, the leader of the Labour Party, David Lloyd George, the leader of the Liberal Party, and with prominent businessmen. Hu first met Chamberlain at the House of Commons on July 18. They had a friendly chat.

A luncheon was given on July 19 at Claridge's in Hu's honor, and included Sir John Thornycroft, Sir Newton Stabb, Sir Montagu Turner, and others interested in Chinese banking, commerce, and shipping. "Cohen accompanied them and appeared at the public entertainments offered to them in London," noted Brenan of the group's activities. "He was referred to in the press reports as General Cohen." They did a bit of sight-seeing, and Hu went to the Chinese embassy to visit the room where the Manchus held Sun Yat-sen prisoner in 1896. On July 20, they attended a reception in St. John's Wood. Sun Fo arrived in England that day, and he and Hu met the foreign secretary on the afternoon of the twenty-third. Sun warned that if Britain did not help China they might have to turn back to Russia. After his pleasant talk with Hu the previous week, Chamberlain was somewhat surprised by Sun's tone. He told him that he thought he heard belligerence in his language. Sun quickly apologized, and admitted that he was not versed in the ways of diplomacy. "He then became more subdued," noted Chamberlain. "I rather liked Hu Hanmin but was very unfavourably impressed by Sun Fo."[6]

After completing the main meetings, Cohen headed back to Salford for a brief final visit and to give his father a chance to show him off at his synagogue. As the delegation prepared to leave, the group split up. Sun left for America. There he arranged for a $700 million loan. He also met with Edwin Kemmerer, the famous Princeton University "Money Doctor," who had reorganized the currencies of such nations as South Africa, Poland, and Chile, and convinced him to come to China. Cohen traveled back to China with Hu via the Suez Canal and Saigon, arriving in Hong Kong on August 28. When their ship sailed in, practically all of Canton's prominent officials showed up to welcome Hu. Cohen proceeded to Canton the following day.[7]

The trip proved a success, paving the way for formal recognition of the new government. It also ended up being a coup for Cohen, both with his bosses and grudgingly in the eyes of the British consulate in Canton. He was now seen as an effective and somewhat reliable go-between. "From the very first day of Mr. Brenan's arrival in Canton as Consul General I kept him posted on everything that was going on in the government," wrote Cohen of his twice-weekly visits. "On many of the reports I made I believe he had his doubts, but I can look back with pride and claim that all the reports I made to him proved true and correct."

Brenan agreed, noting that "in spite of Cohen's unsavory record in Canada I have never had any reason to complain of his conduct in China." Brenan was especially pleased by Cohen's pro-British and anticommunist stance.

Although he is an uneducated and simple minded person, he takes himself very seriously as a politician in close touch with the inner intrigues and activities of his Guomindang friends. For the past two years he has regularly called on me and discussed at length on the political situation. His theme always was that the revolutionary movement in China need not necessarily be anti-British and that the British authorities could easily capture it and oust the Russians by sympathising with the South and giving them practical help. In other words, by allowing them to procure the arms necessary for their struggle, which they could at present only get from the Russians. I suspect that this was not disinterested advice, as he wished to act as the Chinese agent for the purchase of arms in Canada, which would have been a lucrative business. Although Cohen undoubtedly held quite an unusual place, for a foreigner, in the confidence of the Chinese authorities in the city, I imagine that they told him chiefly the things that they wanted passed on to me, and I, of course, used him for the same purpose. Nevertheless he has frequently given me valuable information and has on occasion been of assistance in arranging matters where the Commissioner for Foreign Affairs could do nothing. . . .

Cohen is an adventurer with a shady past, and in his endeavour to obliterate his early reputation he is inclined to exaggerate the importance of his present position and his influence with the Canton officials. But in spite of his Canadian record I have not found him untruthful or untrustworthy. . . . In fact, it is only fair to him to say that since I have known him he has used such influence as he may possess with the Chinese authorities in the direction of restoring friendly relations with the British and helping British trade. This is in accordance with his own financial interests, as he earns commissions on purchases of British materials for government purposes and had ambitious projects regarding railway construction to be undertaken by Canadian contractors.[8]

Canton and China had changed since the upheavals Cohen witnessed during the Canton Commune Uprising. As he resettled in the south, the Nationalist Government in Nanjing became the Nationalist Government of China. The government regained tariff autonomy, sponsored fiscal reform, centralized tax collection, and developed a uniform silver dollar. It encouraged the expansion of industry, started construction on a network of roads and railways, and established telegraph, phone, and airline systems. Yet as always, factional struggles pulled at the government; Chiang had to balance powerful cliques and divisions within the army and civil government. While the GMD touted itself as the party of nationalism, the conservative leadership had a limited sense of the concept of democracy. Instead of relying on Sun Yat-sen's five-part government, rule evolved through personal contacts and relationships. Graft was pervasive. And though the Northern Expedition had successfully unified China, in actuality it merely brought independent regionalists under the GMD's banner. This wary confederation prevented the GMD from effectively controlling the nation.[9]

Chiang was beholden to regional warlords like the Guangxi Clique who ruled Guangdong and Guangxi. In return for their and the other warlords' backings, Nanjing instituted Branch Political Councils, independent regional administrations that allowed warlords to work within the government. Numerous Branch Political Councils existed. Marshal Li Jishen chaired the Canton branch of the Guangxi Clique.[10]

Upon returning to Canton, Cohen hooked up with Li, whom he had first met during his time with Sun Yat-sen when Li ran the Training Department at Whampoa. The marshal actively sought to improve the Guangdong economy and relations with Hong Kong. A number of months earlier he had received an official visit from Governor Cecil Clementi. With Canton–Hong Kong relations stabilized, Cohen started buying munitions for his boss. Brenan was right when he said it was a profitable occupation for Cohen. Arms sales were big business in China, and while some warlords like Zhang Zuolin of Manchuria had their own arsenals and employed adventurers like the Englishman Frederick "One-Arm" Sutton to increase their stockpiles, most warlords had to rely on a loose collection of merchants and brokers to bring in European weapons.

Hong Kong was an especially convenient inlet for arms, with countless sources like Vickers and Jardine Matheson for Cohen to approach. "Arms smuggling facilities in China have been so perfected that business is transacted in arms almost in the same convenient way as other commodities," reported the *China Weekly Review*. "Any general who wants to buy can always get in touch with an agent, and there are so many foreigners and Chinese engaged in smuggling both in the treaty ports and in interior towns that one wonders how China can ever get her house in order."[11]

Cohen's sales training in Edmonton came in handy, and he easily moved business along. The nickname "Two-Gun" Cohen did not quite capture the image of someone who wanted to be an international arms merchant, so he coined a new moniker: "Five-percent Cohen." He made sure that he never got less. "Morris named himself 'Five Per Cent Cohen,' " wrote the Shanghai lawyer Norwood Allman. "His subsidies, grants or salary from the GMD were never more than nominal plus for a time room and board. He, however, played up and sold his influence, real or fancied, for all he could get out of it. High members of the GMD . . . winked at and tolerated this sale of influence as it was the cheapest way of paying him off for past services to Dr. Sun."

Li needed more than just a couple of pistols and rifles. He wanted heavy armament and patrol boats not only to guard against the lethal shifts of southern Chinese politics but also to clean up the pirates on the China Coast. Throughout the

1920s, pirates relentlessly preyed on the river steamers, cargo ships, and sampans plying the Canton Delta, the East and West River, and the coast to Hong Kong, Shanghai, and other ports. These brigands did not discriminate, picking on foreign shipping and local Chinese fisherman alike.

The most notorious pirate nest was Bias Bay, a major inlet about sixty miles northeast of Hong Kong. "It is inhabited by the most infamous gang of high-sea pirates that infest the South China coast," wrote Aleko Lilius, who sailed with the pirate queen Lai Choi San and others in the late 1920s. Some pirate ships were juggernauts. "There were twelve smooth-bore, medieval-looking cannons on board, and two rather modern ones. Along the bulwarks of the junk were bolted rows of heavy iron plates." Magazines and cabins brimmed with weaponry. Lai's crew were fearsome fellows, muscular, bare-chested men who wore wide-brimmed hats and tied red kerchiefs around their heads and necks. Pirating was so rampant that many merchants paid Lai and others protection money.

Attacks on foreign passenger ships especially worried the western powers. To protect their vessels, owners fortified bridges with gun slits, grills, metal shutters, armor plating, and heavy iron nets. They also hired Indian guards and called for the screening of passengers. Precautions often did not work. After carefully choosing their mark, pirates posed as first and third class passengers, and smuggled ammunition and arms on board. Once a ship sailed away from port, they stormed the bridge, overwhelmed the crew, and sailed to Bias Bay. The pirates then off-loaded goods and hostages into waiting sampans and junks. Afterward, the pirates sent ransom requests to the families of hostages. If a family did not pay quickly, the pirates tortured the poor fellow. If news of his suffering or the delivery of a severed ear or other body parts did not move them to fork over the full return price, they killed him. It was a lucrative enterprise. "You could never be sure that the last time you were in a cocktail party in Hankou that you wouldn't be rubbing elbows with a Chinese bigshot who had planned the thing and who knew what was on the ship and when it was going," said U.S. Rear Admiral Kemp Tolley, who served with the U.S. forces in South China. "You could hardly call it piracy. It was business, big business."[12]

During Sun Yat-sen's rule there had been attempts at Chinese-British expeditions to eradicate brigands, culminating in a joint effort on March 20, 1924, against a pirate lair near the mouth of the East River. Three Chinese gunboats and Chinese troops set off to do battle, with the HMS *Tarantula* giving backup support. The team captured dozens of pirates, destroyed several ships, and released more than twenty captives. Further piracy and counterattacks took place, yet following the shootings at Shameen and the subsequent strikes, cooperation tapered off.

That did not stop the pirates, who worked with impunity. They grabbed the SS *Tungchow* on December 18, 1925, shooting the captain and making away with $30,000 and luggage. The British started taking independent action. In November 1926, pirates snatched the *Sunning* between Shanghai and Hong Kong. Trying to regain control of the ship, the crew set her on fire. The HMS *Bluebell* then came along and arrested twenty-two pirates. Other piracies resulted in more British attacks, and the torching and scuttling of brigand ships.

Whenever the British objected to the Chinese about an attack, they were told that the pirates were not their responsibility, insisting that they made their bases in Manila, Singapore, and Shanghai's International Settlement. From there "they are able to plot their outrages," wrote C. C. Wu. To back up their claim, the Chinese presented the British with names of suspected pirates. But the much touted lists proved useless, since many of the leads were vague and old. "The meager nature of the information supplied was making investigation a matter of great difficulty," noted one British memorandum on piracy.[13]

Then in October 1927 a British submarine sunk the *Irene* following the refusal of the pirates in control to stop. The British arrested and executed seven of the brigands. On November 7, Lieutenant Commander Faure met with Li to try and resolve the ongoing problem. Faure told the marshal that the British would gladly back up the attacks he organized. The Royal Navy would station an officer and a pilot on board each Cantonese boat, and British artillery would fire cover as Li's troops advanced into villages and rounded up the pirates. Li grudgingly agreed. A new rapprochement seemed to have finally been reached. The exchange of visits between British officials and Li followed.[14]

In 1928 R. R. Roxburgh, the resident representative of Thornycroft boat manufacturers in Shanghai, visited Canton several times to profit from Li's weapon-buying spree. He tried selling motor launches, but whenever Roxburgh came by he had difficulty getting beyond Li's graft-minded aides. According to Brenan, Roxburgh attempted "to place orders through subordinate officials in the Naval department, who were merely concerned to make a squeeze." He was not getting anywhere until he "eventually was taken direct to Li Jishen by Cohen and succeeded in interesting the Marshal in a number of models of launches which he took with him."

Thanks to Cohen, Li ordered four patrol boats, ranging in size from sixty to ninety-five feet and requested permission from the western powers to buy tens of thousands of dollars' worth of weapons, including six-pound guns, machine guns, mines, water-cooled maxims, rifles, revolvers, and hundreds of thousands of rounds of ammunition. Cohen likewise helped speed along a deal for Li for motor vehicles. "Incidentally I may state that Mr. Roxburgh has also obtained from the Canton municipality an order for the supply of five Thornycroft motor omnibuses for which cash payment has been made, and there is an understanding that five more will be ordered in the near future," wrote Brenan. "Mr. Roxburgh mentioned that he was largely indebted for the motor bus contract to the good offices of Mr. M. A. Cohen." Despite the fact that the British found some of Li's requests suspect, they knew that they had to give in. "Aircraft guns and mines seem curious equipment for dealing with pirates and their inclusion in the list throws some doubt on the bona-fides of the Canton authorities," wrote an official earlier in the year. But "it seems also absurd to provide unarmed launches, knowing that they have got to be armed to be of any

use, and then treat the supply of armament for them as a highly immoral proceeding."[15]

Not quite sure that the weapons buying would result in prompt and thorough
antipiracy action, British general Charles C. Luard wrote in May 1928 that continued Cantonese inaction would offer justification to the British in occupying
Bias Bay and purging the area of brigands. On May 27, pirates commandeered the
British ship *Tean,* took it to Bias Bay, and made off with seven passengers and two
British officers. Much to the surprise of the British, Li ordered troops to the bay
and instructed Admiral Chen Ce to send a gunboat with soldiers. They captured
four pirates. Other expeditions were hatched. There was also a plan to station an
army force at the bay and to erect a shortwave wireless station for more rapid
communications.

Cohen boasted in town that he helped clean up the brigands in Bias Bay. Even
so, piracy remained a perennial problem. All the while, Li increased his military
stores. "The local authorities are always profuse in promises of this sort, but they are
incompetent, and where their own immediate interests are not concerned they do
very little," wrote Brenan of the area around Bias Bay. "The truth of the matter is
that the area . . . is in the hands of pirates, brigands and communists and the military
authorities seem unable to bring it under control. At all events they are moving very
slowly in the matter and for some time to come British shipping will have to rely
on its own efforts or on the British naval and military authorities for protection
against piracy."[16]

Cohen meanwhile moonlighted for Sun Fo, who in October 1928 was made
vice president of the Examination Yuan and Minister of Railways. As the new
minister, Sun wished to implement his father's railway plans. While his goal was not
as grand as Sun Yat-sen's 75,000 miles of rails, he did hope to construct 20,000 miles
in ten years. The younger Sun streamlined the department, repaired the rails, paid
off debts, and centralized control of construction. He also improved working conditions, and established schools and clubs for the men. Sun especially wanted an
independent budget for his department, and hoped to tap into Boxer Indemnity
Funds and money from the surplus of the Customs. The British suspected his motives. Besides being wary of Sun, they did not completely trust Cohen, who continued his promotion of what to them appeared to be a questionable railway scheme.
"This goes to confirm my suspicion that Sun Fo (who has a corrupt reputation) is
getting more and more involved with American (and Canadian) firms for railway
orders; and it becomes doubly necessary to get loan assurances from the Chinese
Govt. regarding our Indemnity Fund," wrote the consular in Shanghai, who learned
that the "Chinese minister of railways was anxious to place this contract with
Northern Construction Company partly because Doctor Sun Yat-sen intended to
give it to them and partly because Mr. Morris A. Cohen stands to benefit pecuniarily
if Northern Construction Company and Reiss Massey and Company are associated
with this contract."[17]

On January 14, 1929, Li appointed Cohen his special ADC to the Military

Headquarters in Canton. It was a tense time to join Li's staff. Chiang had set his sights on emasculating militarists like Li and the Guangxi Clique. He decided to eliminate the Branch Political Councils and slash the number of military leaders and troops in China. In January a National Reorganization and Demobilization conference convened in Nanjing. The militarists, though, feared losing their political and military power. They also did not trust Chiang. The meeting predictably failed. Nanjing then set out to crush these intransigent independent rulers and prove their fears true. Marshal Li and his Guangxi Clique became the first quarry. In his campaign, Chiang purchased the support of other militarists along with that of one of Li's subordinates, the ambitious anticommunist Chen Jitang. The Guangxi Clique broke from the national government. Troops massed for battle.

Hoping to settle their differences, Li headed to Nanjing to attend the Third National Congress of the GMD. Cohen preceded the marshal to Hong Kong to make arrangements for his arrival, landing in the colony on March 4. Li, his wife, and numerous Cantonese politicians pulled in aboard a special train the following evening. During his stay, Li visited the governor, gave a news conference, and went on a motor outing through the New Territories. On the seventh the entourage sailed for Shanghai. Cohen landed first, taking room 305 at the Astor House. Li spent a few days in Shanghai, and then arrived in Nanjing on the sixteenth for the start of the congress. Cohen stayed behind, and did not head up to Nanjing until the nineteenth. On the twentieth, Chiang announced that he refused mediation with his opponents. The following day, he arrested Li and imprisoned him at Tangshan Hot Springs.

His detention caused quite a commotion. Pro- and anti-Li factions formed in Guangdong. Chiang meanwhile allowed Sun Fo, Hu Hanmin, and Cohen to visit Li at his well-guarded prison. Li's release or escape did not look likely. The British liked Li, and the day after his arrest they even considered granting him refuge if he should elude his captors. "It is feared that the life of Li is in danger and it is requested that if Li can contrive to escape either to the British Consulate or British cruiser at Nanjing he should be given British protection," wrote Governor Cecil Clementi. Little came of these plans. On March 26, Nanjing declared war against the Guangxi faction. The government accused them of shattering the peace and branded them selfish opportunists who looted the government and conspired with enemies. The congress dismissed Li and the clique members from their posts and the GMD for life. The group collapsed. Cohen lost his job.[18]

Chiang then turned on his other opponents. As Chiang consolidated his realm, he wanted to sanctify his new capital. What better offering could he present than the body of Sun Yat-sen? The government held a design competition, and about forty Chinese and foreign architects entered plans for a grand mausoleum to house Sun's remains. The winning entry came from the Tianjin-born, Cornell-educated architect Lü Yanzhi, who had been with the New York architecture firm Murphy & Dana before returning home. Work began a year after Sun's death on Lü's grand complex. Situated on a knoll on the sloping side of a hill in the Purple Mountains,

Sun's new resting place near the tombs of the Ming rulers was imperial. Lü terraced the site with gray granite stairs and laid out a paved causeway approach lined with cypress trees. He covered the square tomb with upturned Chinese eaves, marble from Italy, black marble from Shandong, granite from Suzhou, bronze, and iridescent blue glazed tile. Quotations from Sun's writings decorated the walls, and a large blue and white mosaic of the GMD sun blazed from the ceiling. And since they wanted Sun to be remembered as one of the world's great leaders, Lü set up the inner chamber room so that the casket could be viewed from all sides like that of President Ulysses S. Grant or Emperor Napoléon Bonaparte.

The reinternment began during the summer of 1929 a few months after Lü's own death. Soong Qingling planned to attend, but fearing that her brother-in-law Chiang might try to capitalize on her presence to bolster his own standing, she pointedly announced prior to leaving Berlin, "I am proceeding to China for the purpose of attending to the removal of the remains of Dr. Sun Yat-sen to the Purple Mountain. . . . It must therefore be abundantly clear that my attendance at the burial will not mean and is not to be interpreted as in any sense implying a modification or reversal of my decision to abstain from any direct or indirect work of the Guomindang so long as its leadership is opposed to the fundamental policies of Dr. Sun; namely, the policy of effective anti-imperialism, the policies of cooperation with Soviet Russia and the Workers and Peasant policy. . . ."[19]

An official delegation that included Lin Sen, Zheng Hongnian, and Wu Tiecheng arrived to attend to the body. Ma Xiang led the bodyguards, and Cohen was invited to take part in the procession. "I'd hoped for an invitation to the funeral, in spite of being tucked away out of sight, so to speak, down in Canton. I wasn't prepared for what actually happened. I was summoned, not to Nanjing, but to go first to Beijing and accompany Dr. Sun's body all the way from the Azure Cloud Temple. I was the only European present. . . . I realized the extraordinary honour that was done me, but somehow I couldn't feel pleased as I ought to have done. On that journey there was no room in my heart for anything but sadness."

On May 20, Sun's body was transferred to a new coffin in Beijing for the trip south. From the twenty-third to the twenty-fifth family and citizens paid their respects. Flags lined Beijing's streets on the route to the railway station. "The procession, emerging from the thickly wooded grounds of the Temple of Pi Yunssu [Jade Cloud], passed through 500 marshalled school children holding lanterns," wrote the *Times* of London of the activities that started on the morning of the twenty-sixth. "The principal feature of it was a huge catafalque, the moving of which required several hundreds of carriers working in relays. Only members of the family of the late leader, officials, and guards took part in the first stage of the journey into Beijing, but the proceedings were none the less impressive as the procession slowly passed down the long avenues of trees, brightened by arc lights, and between double lines of troops, whose bayonets flashed as they presented arms." As the specially painted white, blue, and gold train pulled out, funeral music was played and soldiers fired a 101-gun salute. On the twenty-eighth, the train arrived outside of Nanjing.[20]

Soong watched as the carriers placed her husband's coffin upon a platform near a special altar for a brief ceremony. They then hoisted the precious cargo onto a gunboat and ferried it across the Yangzi River to the accompaniment of a 101-gun salute from the forts on Lion Hill and a twenty-one gun salute from foreign warships. The carriers set Sun's casket in the hall of the Central Party Headquarters before a large photograph of him, and replaced the lid with a glass top. As the band played dirges, dignitaries solemnly advanced up the gangway to the rostrum to present wreaths and to view the president laid out in his blue and black clothes.

Nanjing was decorated for the ceremonies. Soldiers warily patrolled the town for fear that communists or some other group might try to stir up trouble. Pailoos decorated with blue and white bunting stood at intervals along Zhongshan Road. Flags flew at half-mast from houses. On the day of the reinternment, crowds packed the streets. "An eerie sight it was, that highway in early morning with its crowding men and rearing horses," wrote the American newspaperman Randall Gould. "Motor horns honked and shrilled, guards with bayonetted rifles barked sharp 'Halt!' orders so that they might inspect motorcar pennants and be sure that free passage was given only to those which bore prescribed 'chops.' "

At 4 A.M. the ceremonies began. In the Central Party Headquarters incense burned as Sun's last will was read. Bearers in blue smocks lifted the casket and placed it in an American-made hearse, which followed behind Sun's portrait. Soong, wearing a simple black dress, and accompanied by Sun Fo, T. V. Soong, Meiling Soong, and Chiang Kai-shek, filed behind a black screen in front of the hearse. On the right side of the hearse walked members of the foreign missions, and on the left members of the Central Executive Committee. Both groups held blue and white ropes that were attached to the coffin. "At 4:30 the coffin was brought out and placed on a motor hearse and the whole effect of watching the dawn slowly breaking and the bright moon was weird," recalled British Consul General Meyrick Hewlett. "The members of the Chinese Government formed on one side and the Foreign Missions on the other, and we all held a rope to give the impression we were drawing the body to its resting-place."

Officials, cavalry, Buddhist monks, soldiers, Boy Scouts, Girl Guides, government workers, students, educators, farmers, laborers, and merchants followed the hearse. Airplanes circled overhead. During the procession, Cohen solemnly accompanied the sons of two of Sun's western friends. Ropes and armed police held back the mass of spectators. "The great road was lined throughout its length by hundreds of thousands of spectators, who were closely watched by troops with their fingers constantly on the triggers of their rifles," reported the *Times* of London. The relentless heat thinned out the procession. Boy Scouts and Girl Guides assisted many of the marchers. Others took refuge in their cars.[21]

The cortege finally reached the tomb at nine-thirty. Spectators filled the sides of the steps and the nearby groves of trees. The hearse arrived at the base at ten, and the carriers set the casket on a massive blue and white catafalque. The chief mourners resumed their places in front, shielded again by a black screen. Foreign ministers and representatives took hold of the ropes that they had dropped earlier. Thirty-two blue- and white-uniformed men from Beijing then heaved the casket up the stairs to the accompaniment of a funeral dirge. "They worked in relays of sixteen, to the timing of a foreman, who marked their shuffling steps by blows on a hollow bamboo," wrote J. M. D. Hoste of the *North-China Herald*. "In the last two flights the men showed signs of strain and several of the mourners bent their weight to the ropes they held and assisted in dragging the massive structure upwards."

Once up to the mausoleum, they set the coffin onto a pedestal in the center of the structure's outer hall. There, surrounded by the thick black granite pillars, mourners laid wreaths and flowers. A ceremony with speeches and the playing of a dirge followed. At the end, the crowd bowed three times. Finally, the men carried the coffin into the inner rotunda, where Fan Liang and eight of Sun's other bodyguards lowered his remains into the vault. The entire diplomatic corps then passed through to view Sun's final resting place. At noon there were three minutes of silence. Guns from Lion Hill then gave a 101-gun salute, and foreign warships also fired a salute. Cohen watched all this in silence as he said his final good-bye.[22]

CHAPTER 14

ARMS DEALINGS,
1929–1936

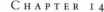

s *Chiang sanctified his capital with the re-*
mains of Sun Yat-sen, more and more of China
came under his control. Western powers started relinquishing a few of their concessions, the policy of extraterritoriality ended for some western citizens, and China
regained its tariff autonomy. Yet despite Chiang's efforts for unification and military
campaigns against the likes of Li Jishen, warlords under the Nationalist flag still
asserted their independence. In the south, Chen Jitang, the general who betrayed
Li, was one such a man. And since Cohen worked in the south for whoever was in
power, Chen was his new boss. "A new and rather different part of my life began,"
Cohen said of his employer. "It wasn't a very happy part either. Up till then I'd
served my chief whoever he was—Sun Yat-sen, Sun Fo, T. V. Soong or Li Jishen—
with my whole heart and without thought of personal gain. With Chen Jitang it
wasn't quite the same. . . . I never got very close to him."

The man he did not get close to had joined Sun's Tongmenghui just prior to
the 1911 revolution. But like most other militarists, Chen possessed limited appreciation of Sun's revolutionary ideas. He was also exceedingly greedy, an "avaricious
and ambitious, scheming and deceitful" man, according to Hallett Abend. In Chen's
regime, graft ruled. "Some of his followers squeezed immoderately," said Cohen of
his coworkers. "Their demands weren't reasonable. One of them made so much out
of bribery and polite blackmail that he had to found a real estate company to take
care of the proceeds. Another smuggled on a gigantic scale—he used to transport
his contraband in the gunboats of the Cantonese Navy."

Cohen kept busy during this period. He assisted missionaries beset by unruly
troops, dealt with western firms, and mostly stayed far away from Chen. "In the end
I kept away as much as possible and got myself sent off on detached duty whenever
I could think up an excuse." Cohen left his options open and maintained contacts
with Wu Tiecheng. He also assisted Sun Fo, who served as Minister of Commu-

nications. Cohen purchased materials for Sun's department, and dubbed himself "Adviser on Foreign Purchases."

Many other people called on him for odd chores. In August 1929 the British crown advocate sought the arrest and prosecution of three Sikhs in Nanjing on seditionist conspiracy and for publishing anti-British tracts. They wanted the men arrested and handed over to the Shanghai Municipal Police. "If we fail to do so, we must expect future expansion of Indian revolutionary organizations in China"—and elsewhere—wrote a British official.

On August 20, Captain Beatty, a former Shanghai assistant police commissioner, came to visit A. F. Aveling and the consul general at Nanjing. Beatty, who had been dismissed from his post, claimed to possess proof that the Sikh seditionists were really communists employed by Moscow. When Beatty arrived at the consulate, he said that he worked with Cohen. The consul told him that he would not help him until he presented verifiable instructions from Shanghai. Two days later, Beatty returned "saying that Mr. Cohen had received official instructions 'from the highest Chinese quarter' to approach me and asked whether under these circumstances I would receive them together," wrote Aveling. "Knowing Mr. Cohen's close relationship with certain prominent members of the National Government I acceded to this request and accompanied by His Majesty's Acting Consul General received them later in the day."

Cohen said he had known about the Sikhs from when they lived in Canton. Stressing his pro-British stance, Cohen said he had already made the necessary arrangements to raid the offices of the Indian Section of the Eastern Oppressed Peoples Association. "If he could help to effect their apprehension and deportation he would thus be rendering a good service both to England and to China." Aveling told Cohen that the consulate appreciated his help but wanted to make sure they had the right people. The consulate also worried about the awkwardness of raiding a building on British property without a warrant. But since Cohen had set the machinery in motion, Aveling asked him simply to delay action until they were sure that they were the right men. "My impression was that Mr. Cohen was acting in perfectly good faith and in the belief that Captain Beatty had approached him on behalf of the British authorities." Aveling then informed Cohen that Beatty no longer worked for the Shanghai police, had no official backing and "that the story which he had told me was nothing but a tissue of lies." Beatty did not even try to defend himself against Aveling's accusation. The news shocked Cohen, who declared that he had been "completely let down." He then announced that he wished to wash his hands entirely of the affair. Cohen returned later in the evening to announce that the Chinese possessed little evidence on which to arrest the Sikhs, and he had canceled the raid.[1]

During this time, Cohen was much let down. He had to keep on the move. He was in Canton in October, telling people that he was involved in the reestablishment of the Central banknotes for Guangdong. He then went to Hong Kong and negotiated with government officials for the importation of arms for Chen. Knowing of the growing desire of the south and others to buy weapons, manufacturers and merchants flocked to see Cohen. Ever ready to make a buck, Cohen showed Roxburgh of Thornycroft around and tried to interest T. V. Soong in a stockpile of Lewis guns, rifles, and ammunition from the Birmingham Small Arms Factory. He actively sought commissions, balancing and justifying his three-way loyalties to China, England, and himself. Roxburgh noted his buddy Cohen's multiple allegiances, and told Acting Consul General G. S. Moss that Cohen could be helpful in passing along useful information "culled from his Chinese official friends."

Cohen regularly stopped by the consulate in Canton to see Moss. While visiting the consulate, Cohen reported on gossip and current government activities. He made a point of promoting himself and his position, even justifying his tenuous claim to the title General. "He tells me that he is entitled to the title of 'General' as he was appointed General in charge of the 'late revered Doctor's' Body-Guard of 500 men. . . . He seemed very anxious to convince me that he is intensely British and anxious to do what he could to strengthen British influence in Nationalist circles, where he said pro-American sympathies ruled."

To disprove talk making the rounds in Canton, Cohen actively stressed his loyalties and usefulness. "He said that he had enemies who slandered him, alleging that he was pro-Soviet owing to his former connections with Borodin and Eugene Chen," wrote Moss. Cohen was so concerned about his image, that he even left a long statement at the consulate spelling out his pro-British activities "to counter-act some of the nonsensical rumors that have been circulated about myself." He told Moss, "I think that the above will show that in my humble capacity I have at least done a little for my country, and I hope that I will still be able to carry on the good work." According to Moss, "He evidently thinks he is entitled to good marks, if not open recognition."

Cohen's fears of enemies were proven two days later. Faure, Li Fang—a Chinese Nationalist officer—and an American "of very bad local reputation" known as Miske stopped by Cohen's hotel. They claimed they had come by to collect money that Cohen owed them, and Faure accused Cohen of being a Soviet spy. "Cohen was quite sober at the time," wrote Moss, "but recognized Miske (who is reputed to be a fighter) and jumping to the conclusion that the three men were intent on doing mischief, floored Li Fang and Faure before the Hotel Manager stopped the struggle. Li Fang, who was drunk, was rather badly hurt in falling. The result was that Li charged Cohen with assault and Cohen similarly charged Faure." At the court, Li withdrew the charge after Cohen apologized for belting him. The judge fined Faure ten dollars and bound him over for one hundred dollars to keep the peace. Faure also withdrew his spy accusation against Cohen.

Faure was typical of the arms merchants Cohen had to deal with as he bought weapons for Chen. He had left the navy following bitter differences with the consulate over the rounding up of pirates, and blamed the legation and members of the consul staff for his failures. By the time of the fight, Faure had almost no money and detested Cohen's arms sales successes. "It appears that Faure, who whilst acting as Intelligence Officer was much beholden to Cohen for information and later for business connections, resented Cohen's sudden appearance in the Canton field as an arms dealer," wrote Moss. Through his Equitable Trading Company, Faure worked as a customs broker for piece goods and as an agent for various companies selling boat engines, airplanes, arms, and jewelry. His business motto was, "It is business to be correctly informed yourself and misinform other people." Those who knew Faure did not trust him, and he had no capital with which to work. "He sometimes drinks to excess and consorts openly with undesirable foreign women. For these reasons he is untrustworthy as a confidential agent. . . . He is clever and knows the ropes of intrigue better than those of straight business. The more I learn of him and his friends the more I mistrust him."

As Chen expanded and consolidated his power base, he tried to maintain good relations with Nanjing. He feared that he, like Li, whom he had betrayed, would fall victim to Chiang's unification policy. In early 1931, Chiang ordered Chen to reduce the size of his armed forces. Chen refused. He likewise would not dispatch troops to suppress the communists in Jiangxi. Machinations continued throughout the country. Hu Hanmin and Chiang disagreed over the promulgation of a provisional constitution guaranteeing personal rights. On February 28, Chiang had Hu arrested. Outrage over the detention spread quickly. Anti-Chiang sentiment grew. On April 30, members of the supervisory committee of the Guomindang impeached Chiang. Chen quickly supported the charges.

Militarists and politicians as varied as Sun Fo, Eugene Chen, Zhang Fakui, Zou Lu, Wang Jingwei, and Xu Chongzhi as well as disparate cliques joined Chen in opposition to Chiang. They flocked to Canton and organized a United anti-Chiang front. The dissidents reorganized the Guangdong and Guangxi governments, and in late May formed the separatist Guangdong National Government in Canton.[2]

As tensions built, the south increased its stockpiling of weapons, with Cohen acting as a go-between for the government at his 5 percent commission basis. "When the rival provincial leaders began bickering again and the South started to re-arm and, particularly, to purchase munitions abroad, I was the obvious man for the job." Cohen procured tommy guns from the United States, Madsen machine guns from Denmark, "seventy-fives" from France, antiaircraft artillery from Britain, aircraft from Italy, and rifles and ammunition from throughout Europe. "The guy was a gunrunner," said Kemp Tolley, who in the mid-1930s was a lieutenant onboard the USS *Mindanao* in the South China Patrol. "When you say gunrunner, that doesn't mean anything disrespectful. After all, the Chinese needed guns. He was well versed in ways to do things. He was an ideal man for them."

Cohen had little trouble finding people who wanted to sell weapons to him. "My God, there were gun dealers everywhere," said Tolley. "All you have to do is put a call in the telephone. You can buy a shipload of guns tomorrow if you want to, just call up the right guy. There was no problem with that." When Cohen found the merchandise he desired, he discussed price. If they bargained, he dickered back. "They were trying that game on an old hand," said Cohen. "I'd learnt my bargaining as a boy back in Alberta. . . . If I couldn't beat their prices down by twenty or thirty per cent, I reckoned I was losing my grip. . . . The deals were nearly all put through in Hong Kong . . . and I became a bit of a landmark around the hotel lobbies.''

Besides being a fixture at the best hotels like the Hong Kong Hotel, Cohen dined at the homes of many of the colony's leading officials. ''As far as I can discover the Hong Kong Government now permits munitions and other military supplies to pass through the Colony almost without restriction and the most friendly relations seem to exist between Morris Cohen, the Colonial Secretary Mr. Southorn and others,'' wrote Consul General Jenkins in August 1931. ''Through a reliable source I have just learned that the Manager of the Hong Kong and Whampoa Dock Company recently entertained Morris Cohen at dinner at his residence. Among the guests were the Colonial Secretary and Mrs. Southorn and the Director of Public Works and Mrs. Creasy.''

When in town, Cohen also frequently visited the American consulate. He promised Jenkins and the staff that he would supply them with detailed information on arms shipments to the south. Cohen actively looked for deals, whether officials or merchants wanted his help or not. ''Cohen scouted around the Government bureaus, both provincial and national and smelled out negotiations that might be going on between foreign firms and these bureaus for contracts and then went to the foreign firm and sold his services for five percent of the contract,'' wrote Norwood Allman. ''He was very brassy about this and frequently admitted that though he sometimes cut this commission to 2 percent he raised it to 7.5 or 10% if the traffic would bear it. . . . Cohen's personal view was that the GMD owed him a living and his self appointed agency or intermediary 5% operations were a good way of collecting it.''

In 1930 and 1931 Cohen claimed to have bought 5,000 rifles, 200 machine guns, a couple of airplanes, and tons of explosives. Usually the weapons moved easily. Sometimes not. Once the Nanjing authorities seized a German vessel in Shanghai bound for Canton, since the Cantonese could not arrange for the transfer of the cargo at some intermediate port. ''Sometimes no arms were forthcoming, sometimes they were blocked, and sometimes the bulk deliveries were dud when we came to examine them,'' he said.

Some of Cohen's commissions were small. When he bought gunboats from Thornycroft in 1930, Cohen received only £2,931 from the firm. For other deals, he made much more. ''My biggest single deal was twenty thousand factory-new Mauser rifles from Germany with five hundred rounds apiece,'' he claimed. ''The price was a hundred gold dollars each, or a total of two million bucks, which made a nice little rake-off for Morris.'' He had many deals. ''We knew what was going on,'' said Tolley. ''He would make slight inferences from here and there whether he just got a shipload in or he was having a little problem getting the money out of Guangxi. That sort of stuff. Certainly never even the mildest aspects of details. We knew what it was and we felt that it was none of our business to inquire into the details.'' All the money that came pouring in, Cohen noted, went to start a retirement fund and to help his family. ''I was over forty, an age when a man's got to take a look at the future,'' he said of his plans. ''I had my father and mother back in

Manchester to think of, and, as well as them, a whole raft of relations who, without being in any way dependent on me, would certainly look to me for help if they were in a jam." Unfortunately, Cohen did not know how to save. When money came in he more than likely would spend it on frivolity.

Helping to arm Chen's forces was viewed as important work, and the south more than monetarily rewarded Cohen for his efforts. In June 1931 the press reported that the Canton government had made Cohen a Brigadier General. It was an honorary title. He did not lead any troops. But while he finally possessed a real rank, not a self-appointed one, westerners still questioned his position. Journalists continued using quotation marks around "General" when they wrote him up in the press.[3]

Besides having to contend with the rearming Guangdong separatists, Chiang also had the Chinese Communist Party on his mind. The communists were decimated in late 1927. Party membership fell from 58,000 in April 1927 to 10,000 in December. Prospects looked grim, and the party changed its tactics. Instead of trying to bring about an urban revolt as it failed to do in Canton, it decided to focus its efforts on the vast Chinese countryside. Needing territory from which they could expand, the communists established fifteen rural bases in central China. There troops trained and worked with the peasants and helped them acquire land. The most important of the soviets was the Jiangxi Soviet. In late 1931, representatives of a number of the soviets joined together to form the Chinese Soviet Republic, with Mao Zedong as Chairman.

Chiang despised the soviets. To him, "the Japanese are like a disease of the skin, but the Communists are like a disease of the heart." Cohen agreed, calling the soviets "a poisonous, dangerous growth slap in the middle of the country." Chiang needed to excise this cancer, and on the recommendation of the Hearst journalist Karl von Wiegand he sought out a series of German military advisers to direct his communist suppression campaign. The first such campaign set off in December 1930, yet Chiang's 100,000-man army, composed of warlord forces, did not fight well together. Communist guerrillas easily lured them into their territory and vanquished them. A second campaign in early 1931 started with more men, but did not fare much better.

By the time Chiang started his third campaign in July, he decided that once he defeated his enemy he would turn his attention to the Guangdong separatists. But as with his previous campaigns, the suppression did not go as planned. When Japanese troops staged an explosion on September 18, 1931, along the tracks of the Southern Manchurian Railway and started their conquest of Manchuria, Chiang had no choice but to postpone the communist liquidation. He offered no resistance to the quick Japanese advances, and simply asked the League of Nations to resolve the dispute. When the League condemned Japan's actions, Japan snubbed the organization and quit in early 1933. By then, they had long finished their campaign, renamed the land Manchukuo, and installed Henry Puyi, the last Manchu emperor, as the new head of state.[4]

The foreign threat caused Nanjing and the Guangdong seditionists to settle their differences. Yet divisions and mistrust still continued. The leaders of Guangdong and Guangxi reaffirmed their autonomy from Nanjing in January 1932 by organizing the Southwest Political Council and the Southwest Executive Committee of the GMD. In 1933, Chen started a series of programs to stabilize the province's economy and to increase economic development. Workers built roads and erected bridges. Canton's public utilities were improved and a network of sugar mills constructed. Private industry flourished. Chen called for land reclamation, established an agricultural research institute, began water conservancy projects, and started five model forestry centers and more than ten fish-breeding groups. By 1935, the province had succeeded at cutting its grain importation in half.[5]

To insure his security, Chen further expanded and modernized his army. He also created an air force. "He aims at a smaller army that will be mechanized. He is also forming two mountain divisions which are to be very mobile and efficient," wrote British Consul General Herbert Phillips in Canton. Weapons poured in. Arms dealers flocked to Canton to make sales and fortunes. Cohen's friend Henri Krebs, a Swiss representing the Belgium firm Fabrique Nationale, sold $2.3 million worth of arms, including Mauser carbines, rifles, pistols, and ammunition over a fifteen-month period. Mr. E. Ott, a Swiss representing Hotchkiss-Schneider, sold Chen four batteries of 75-millimeter mountain guns and 8,000 rounds of ammunition along with thirty Hotchkiss antiaircraft guns with 150,000 rounds of ammunition. Other armaments arrived in the province included 1,000 Czechoslovakian machine guns and twelve Thornycroft armored cars. The Cantonese even purchased Armstrong Whitworth pursuit planes, and fighter airplanes fitted with gun mountings, gun sights, and bomb racks.

During this time, Cohen searched out all his contacts. "I threw myself into the arms business with a new heart." As when he sold real estate in Canada, the commission was everything. If he did not get what he wanted, he was peeved. When Jardine Matheson in the mid-1930s refused to pay him the amount he felt he was due over the sale of Vickers tanks, he hired Eldon Potter, a King's Counsel in Hong Kong, and sued the firm. Cohen won the case. "He said he wanted to teach them a lesson since they tried to resist his 'assistance,' " wrote Allman.[6]

While he worked, more outrageous stories arrived in England of his activities. Reporters started comparing Cohen to Lawrence of Arabia, and calling him the Uncrowned King of China. They wrote that he was equivalent to the Chancellor of the Exchequer, "the financial and diplomatic force behind modern China," that "his financial and organising ability" made him "a powerful factor in the rise of the Chinese Nationalist Party . . . and, from being 'back-stage' assistant to the Chinese Nationalist leader he actually took on much of his political work." Some said he trained the Cantonese army, was one of the most closely guarded men in China, ". . . a war lord, diplomatist and power behind all the operations of the Chinese Nationalist party," quite simply "the real president of the country," whose "commands are said to be obeyed implicitly by Chinese." Others were understandably skeptical. "Edmontonians are not disposed to credit the report that he is supreme commander of the Chinese forces. Rather the belief is that Cohen is doing some romancing in letters to his parents in the old country."

While only in his mid-forties, Cohen was intent on perpetuating the myth he had carefully nurtured. It helped him in business. He started talking about issuing his memoirs, and took credit for some of the main events in modern Chinese history. His family unwittingly continued to spread these tales. "Mr. Cohen's astonishing career has just been revealed by his parents who live in Manchester," wrote the Edmonton *Journal*. "In letters to his parents in Manchester he constantly tells them that he hopes the day is approaching when all China will be united under a free government on the western model." His brother Leslie spoke to the paper, saying that they regularly received letters from Cohen, but since they contained references to official matters he could not discuss them. "My brother has warned us against divulging what he writes in his letters to us, because about three years ago an attempt was made on his life. It was during the civil war, but, fortunately, my brother escaped injury."[7]

With such advance press and much money in his pockets, he decided to head home. "By the autumn of 1932 I'd lined up some real big deals that involved visits to both Europe and the States. That suited me. I'd at last begun to save some of my money. There was enough in the bank to pay for a holiday in England and a little financial help for my family." Cohen returned to the West a hero bearing gifts for everyone and scorn for the press that published his tales. He had spent years courting the newspapers, but had a need to appear as if none of what they wrote mattered. His seeming nonchalance, even resistance, only added to his mystique.

He stopped in New York in early November 1932, where he found time to chat with a New York *Forward* reporter who revealed that Cohen was an ardent Zionist and a member of the Shanghai B'nai B'rith Organization. From there Cohen sailed for England. "I landed at Plymouth, and there waiting on the wharf were two of my brothers." Arriving in Manchester on November 10, he disembarked with two taxi loads of trunks. His parents and about a half dozen relatives met him. "When his train from Plymouth drew up at the platform a press photographer ranged his camera to take a photograph and the general called out, 'Lay off,'" reported the London *Daily Mirror*. "The photographer stepped into the background and while the general was being questioned by reporters, fired a flash." Cohen smashed the camera with his walking stick. "The general and the photographer then left the platform in the company of police officials to the railway police office, where the question of the disturbance was discussed." When local reporters asked him why he was in Manchester, Cohen indifferently responded, "I have not come on any official business in any shape or form. I have come to Manchester merely to see my relatives."

Back at the house, Cohen unpacked presents for everyone. He took his mother, aunts, and sister Sarah for an outing to Brighton, and kept mum on his activities. "He has had important work to do, but we know nothing about it," said his mother.

While he would not speak about whether or not he traveled to England on a trade mission, and refused to talk about his life among the Chinese, "including his escapes from assassination," he let slip tales, and then brushed off suggestions that he had led men into battle, only increasing the interest of reporters. He would simply tell them, "I am now a military organiser in the Cantonese forces, acting as liaison officer between the Southern Government and the Foreign Powers."

Despite his tales, he was a good promoter for China. Prior to World War I, the looms of the Lancashire cotton industry produced 65 percent of the world's cotton cloth. Its hold on the market started to slip with the start of the war as foreign competitors with cheap labor and new plants ate into the market. Prices fell throughout the 1920s, and the slump at the start of the Depression only worsened things.

Cohen pitched China as a burgeoning market for local textiles. He made sales plugs, speaking highly of the young men involved in the Lancashire cotton trade in the East. Cohen was hot on bringing back some commission-based deals. "I will . . . make contact with a few British firms with a view to developing trade between this country and China. China is just entering upon another stage of her evolution as a modern State—the age of machinery. I believe that there will be huge demands for machinery and other goods which British manufacturers can supply. I feel that conditions will improve in China and that she will eventually become the economic salvation of Europe."

Manchester feted him. The chamber of commerce and others held functions and lunches in his honor. Prominent members of the city's Jewish community entertained him at a Jewish folk song concert at Albert Hall. The local press duly picked up all the meetings and concerts. Cohen talked the talk, and he spoke it quite well. He chatted with the papers about meeting ancient orthodox Jewish "tribes" in China, and noted that China was "the only country in the world that has not at some time or other persecuted the Jews." He spoke knowingly about the Hong Kong and Shanghai Jewish community, telling the press, "In Hong Kong and in Shanghai I have been a constant worker for Jewish charities, and have long been connected with those interested in these things. Now I am in negotiation for the purchase of the site of the Jewish synagogue . . . in Kaifeng, now in the possession of a Canadian Christian Missionary organisation." When Cohen finally left Manchester, he said he was "loaded down with catalogues and price lists" as well as orders for merchandise.[8]

Cohen sailed into Shanghai aboard the *President McKinley* on March 31, 1933. A week earlier, Courtney C. Julian arrived in town on board the SS *Nagasaki*. Julian checked into the Metropole Hotel on Jiangxi Road, signing the register as T. R. King. He soon became friendly with Cohen. The following month, the press discovered Julian in "a well-appointed suite and well supplied with champagne." His presence created quite a stir, for in early February the forty-six-year old Winnipeg-born "Ace of Scamps" had fled Oklahoma City on the eve of his trial for mail fraud.

Julian had started as a clothing salesman, and subsequently worked in the California oil fields as a driller, manual laborer, and superintendent. He realized that there was more money in promoting wells than drilling for them. Most of his start-up ventures in Texas, California, and Oklahoma failed. Many small investors to whom he advised, "Mail that old check or run in and meet me personally" for "you'll never make a thin dime just lookin' on!" lost their savings. Julian consistently blamed his setbacks on double-crossing lawyers. But his schemes did not fail because of slick lawyers. It was the purported wells of the man who boldly told his salespeople, "Get the Money!," successfully conning legions of small investors to trade tens of millions of dollars' worth of high-grade bonds and U.S. Liberty bonds for worthless C. C. Julian Oil and Royalties Company stock.

When the press found Julian at the Metropole, he sought protection and hired lawyers, saying that his enemies might try to kidnap him. But Julian soon dropped the alias when he realized that he could not be arrested or extradited. As a Canadian citizen, the Shanghai police could not touch him since he had committed his crime in the United States. And because of the rules of extraterritoriality, he could not be thrown in jail by the Chinese. Western officials continued to try to find ways to arrest him. But with the loophole in place, Julian brazenly told the Americans to "go to hell."

Julian's post office wanted poster reported that he was "fond of liquor and women, lives at best hotels." He soon lived up to his reputation, moving into the Cathay Hotel on the Bund and Nanjing Road. From his suite he issued interviews and proclaimed his innocence. "I left the United States for only one reason; that reason being that due to the fact that I had created many powerful enemies in the United States, and being a Canadian, I felt that I could not receive a fair trial in America." All he said he wanted to do was make a fresh start, and he discussed plans to send geologists into the interior of China to find oil.[9]

Julian started looking for work. Not surprisingly, some of his schemes and associates proved suspect. In January 1934, he announced plans to form the American Stock and Bond Guarantee Company with James S. Dolan, a Bostonian who was once convicted in Hamburg of smuggling 457 tins of morphine in a cargo of tombstones. There were other purported and unusual associates. "Persistent rumours are in the air that a Chinese General is at the back of this new enterprise, but no confirmation of this has been received," noted the Shanghai Municipal Police. Julian and Dolan set up offices in the Continental Bank Building, and the partners also revealed plans to open a mausoleum in the city.

But it was not destined to last. Julian started drinking, his money ran low, and he argued with Dolan. He soon severed his ties with the firm. With money tight, he even had to pawn his typewriter. Julian then moved his twenty-one-year-old secretary and girlfriend Leonora Levy to the Weida Hotel and checked into room 300 at the Astor House under his T. R. King alias. He prayed that his luck would change. He had hoped for opportunities. Julian expected a $5,000 advance from his attorney, Dr. Oscar Fischer, for his exposé, *A Refugee from Justice*, and Cohen promised him $1,000. But then in March Julian heard from Oklahoma that his brother, C. A. Julian, and partner Samuel Mitchell had pleaded nolo contendere and received one-year suspended sentences for their dealings with the oil company. One night, Julian took out a razor and slashed his wrists. He did not die, and his former assistant Mary Cantorovitch confiscated all his razors.

Nothing improved. It soon ended. On March 24, Julian was at the Astor House with Levy. By eight that evening he was drunk. The couple headed up to his room and ordered dinner. Julian did not like to eat when he drank, but had some dinner to please and calm his jittery girlfriend. Levy phoned Cohen at his room upstairs, and asked if he wanted to come down for a visit. He passed. Julian continued to drink and then downed forty-eight Amytal tablets. "He had a drink that day on account of the terrible time he had had," Levy said. "He did not have a cent. He was teasing me with the contents of the bottle saying that it would not hurt a kid. He wanted to sleep and did not even know it himself that it was dangerous. He also said that he was as strong as a lion." Levy left the room for a while. When she returned, she found Julian in a stupor. She frantically called a doctor, and then fled. In the early hours of the morning she went to the hospital to visit him. But Julian had already died. Levy ran from the hospital, and was soon discovered overdosed on Amytal tablets in a telephone booth at the Shanghai Dispensary.

The British Police Court held an inquest on the twenty-ninth. Levy claimed that Julian had not intended to kill himself. "To emphasize her belief that Julian had taken the narcotic tablets with no thought of killing himself, Miss Levy excitedly related how he had told her how much he wanted to live and make good again," reported the *China Press*. "He had everything to live for," she testified. "He did not want to die. Only a few minutes before he became unconscious at the Astor House he told me that only cowards commit suicide." Cantorovitch then testified how he had tried to open his wrists earlier in the month. "With her evidence completed the silence of the court room was interrupted by General Cohen. 'May it please your honor,' he stated, but was told to keep quiet by the marshal." The court ruled Julian's death a simple suicide. Afterward, Cohen stormed up to Cantorovitch and accused her of deliberately not mentioning that Julian habitually popped Amytal tablets.[10]

Julian was not the only charlatan that Cohen knew. There were countless other shady acquaintances floating through Shanghai. Albert J. Avramow, a Jewish Bulgarian, first arrived in Shanghai in 1929. He came to the city to make business contacts for the large London-based printing firm of Thomas De La Rue and Company, Ltd. By the time he arrived in Shanghai, Avramow already had quite a notorious reputation. He had previously worked for the American Banknote Company and successfully bribed the Bulgarian finance minister to land a printing contract. The government subsequently executed the minister for corruption; Avramow escaped from the country unharmed. During Avramow's early days in Shanghai, he secured orders for De La Rue from the Bank of China. Avramow was quite full of himself. He steamed open his boss's letters and had clerks in the office photograph the contents. He also boasted that he could easily con the Chinese and would eventually control the whole Chinese market for De La Rue. Soon he landed the Chinese Post Office orders for the engraving and printing of new stamps. To further promote business, he bought fake banknotes from counterfeiters to show potential customers how easily their bills could be manufactured. But instead of proving the superiority of De La Rue's notes, his actions caused others to believe that he had ties with local criminals.

Avramow also lavishly entertained and unnerved friends and clients by plying them with opium and women. He cheated on his wife with numerous local Jewish and Russian girls. He spent money freely to win the women, set them up in apartments, and then doled out hush money to avoid scandals. He even had to hire a Serbian bodyguard to protect himself from threatened assaults stemming from his amorous adventures.

Avramow's reputation got in his way. It was soon discovered that he bribed a Chinese official to get the post office contract. The government dismissed the official and he fled from town. T. V. Soong then banned Avramow from receiving new orders from Chinese banks and government institutions. Avramow clumsily tried to win back Soong's favor, and asked Cohen and others to use their influence on his behalf. He also tried to obtain a letter of introduction to Soong from a high official. But his plans failed; while he attempted to regain Soong's trust, he told Chinese bankers that Soong would soon be removed from office and Avramow's assistant would become the new Minister of Finance. All his chatter did was increase Soong's dislike of him.[11]

Cohen also kept in touch with the armed forces throughout Hong Kong and Canton. In 1934 he regularly visited the *Mindanao,* a 560-ton American ship on which the then twenty-six-year-old Tolley sailed. Cohen became "sort of like a grandfather to the younger gunboat officers" aboard the *Mindanao,* said Tolley. To him, Cohen "was like one of the boys. He was like an old friend. A very amiable type. Down to earth. No pretense. No throwing his weight around or anything like that. I think that was why he and our people got along so well."

Tolley served as the Information Officer on the "Fat Minda" and gathered intelligence. "Information was wide-open as far as the Chinese were concerned." Cohen proved a reliable source. He would "say whose side is winning" and passed on information that "might possibly be useful in adjudicating some sort of a disagreement between the missionaries or Standard Oil and the Chinese. In that respect he was most useful to us. He kept us very well posted. We never pushed him. He dropped over for lunch just for fun." As far as Tolley was concerned, Cohen the gambler was improving his odds of survival. "I strongly suspect that he felt that there was some time or other when he was a refugee and that he could depend on us more than he could the British. I think that he trusted the Americans more. In any case, I am sure he had a foot in both camps. He kept his lines open all over because after all it was a dangerous game he was playing and it was always nice like a groundhog to have two entrances to your tunnel."

Cohen did more than just stop by. He also entertained the sailors. "Cohen . . . never seemed to lack for money; it was impossible to pick up a chit in the hotel lounge, and difficult to refuse his lavish dinner parties with top star Chinese actresses and local pols. It was in Hong Kong that the parties were held," recalled Tolley. The lounge of the Grips at the Hong Kong Hotel, "then the favorite watering hole for the upper crust other than the taipan club types," became a popular business hangout for Cohen. He hosted many parties at that hotel and elsewhere. When he had money, he spent it extravagantly. Cohen invited Tolley to a number of his culinary affairs. "He would have a very large room in a top flight Chinese restaurant in Hong Kong in a place thirty or thirty-five feet long and twenty feet wide and maybe twenty people present. It was the type of restaurants that foreigners would never go to," recalled Tolley. The meals served were endless feasts. "There is never a Chinese banquet without twenty courses. And of course you could guarantee a good case of indigestion after it was all over, unless you were a devotee or a veteran and you knew when to stop. The biggest actress in China at that time was Butterfly Wu. She was amongst the guests. She was a beauty. She really was. Of course once you sit down next to her you never forget her. She didn't speak any English, or if she did she didn't pretend to." As Cohen served his guests, he ate much, drank little, and regaled his guests with overwrought tales of his adventures. "I don't recall that Cohen was ever drunk or even giving the indication of being on the borderline," said Tolley. This was unusual in China, "an atmosphere reeking of alcohol."[12]

Cohen liked to live and eat well. Around 1931 he learned of David's Cafe in Kowloon, not far from the Peninsula hotel. The owner, David Gabruiler, a thickset man with a military mustache, served mounds of food prepared by his wife, Anna. "My father served some Jewish dishes that my mother used to make," said son Eric Gabriel. At least once a week for a year and a half, Cohen took one of the tables set with a large bowl of artificial flowers, scarfed down salted herring, borscht, latkes, beef stroganoff and chicken soup, and practiced his Yiddish with the Gabruilers. "General Cohen enjoyed home cooking. My mother used to make for him gefilte fish and things like that."

When not throwing his own parties or searching out meals that reminded him of St. George's in the East, he attended parties and celebrations. In the early 1930s the Shanghai Rotary Club organized an International Friendship Ball at the Paramount Ballroom. Representatives from Shanghai's different western communities attended. The highlight of the evening was a parade of nations in which young couples wearing their national costumes marched into the hall carrying their home flags. Israel did not yet exist, but the Zionist group Betar—an activist Jewish youth movement that advocated Zionist education, the teaching of self-defense, and called for emigration to British-ruled Palestine—sent Judith Ben-Eliezer and Leo Hanin to represent the organization and Jewish Palestine. "We were there and there was a parade with Americans and British and French. We went out with the white and blue ribbons on our chests and with the Jewish flag," said Hanin of the march. As the partners walked through the hall, they heard someone call out, "Hooray for Palestine." After they finished marching, Hanin and Ben-Eliezer settled at their table. "A man came up to us. That was Cohen, and he invited us to stay at their table," said Hanin. "There was the Chinese mayor of Shanghai and the Chief of Police."

Cohen and Ben-Eliezer became friends. He took a shine to her friends, too, and started to show them around town. "Cohen took me under his patronage and introduced me to everyone on the top rung of the ladder of important Chinese personalities," recalled Ben-Eliezer. They went to assorted functions, parties and lavish dinners in private homes and smart ballrooms and nightclubs. Cohen also threw parties at the Astor House with about twenty guests and countless courses of food. "It was a society of glitter and glamour. Suddenly I was hobnobbing with cabinet ministers, highest government officials and directors of banks. . . . My invitation into this new circle started with a whirl of parties that took my breath away. The parties were either given or attended by Cohen and his close Chinese associates."[13]

Shanghai was a city of parties and frivolities. "Such crowds at the night clubs! Such cocktail parties given! Such wine consumed," wrote Emily Hahn. Known as "Mickey" to her friends, the wonderfully outrageous cigar-smoking journalist from St. Louis—famous for owning gibbons with dinner jackets and fur overcoats—fit in well in the Shanghai nightlife and attended many such affairs. The city in the 1930s was a gay, bustling place. "For several blocks Nanjing Road was a crowded midway of flashing neon lights, fluttering banners, jostling Chinese pedestrians all over the street and vocal vehicles," wrote Dora Carney. By 1936, the foreign concessions had more than three hundred cabarets and casinos. Revelers like Cohen hopped among such nightclubs as the St. Anne Ballroom, the French Club, the Ambassador, the Vienna, the Casanova Cabaret, and the Venus Café. The famous Del Monte's only swung into action after three in the morning, and turbaned Sikh watchmen stood guard as tea-toting Russian dancing partners in satin or chiffon whirled with guests around the floor.

Shanghai's tree-lined Race Course had fields and courts for tennis, cricket, polo, and soccer. Racing could also be seen at the Canidrome in the French Concession, where dogs wearing silk coats chased after a small, white mechanical hare. The town even boasted a large foreign movie theater called the Nanjing, as well as the entertainment center called Great World, which the film director Josef von Sternberg noted was filled with "six floors to provide distraction for the milling crowd, six floors that seethed with life and all the commotion and noise that go with it, studded with every variety of entertainment Chinese ingenuity had contrived."[14]

About 100,000 prostitutes lived in Shanghai. Masseurs, waitresses, guides, and newspaper vendors engaged in the trade, working out of licensed and unlicensed establishments. Those running the brothels needed connections with the police, hoodlums, or gangs to open their houses. Occasionally the police rounded up the women, but like their sisters in Fernie, British Columbia, the law only slapped them with small fines. Upper-class houses were favorite places for Shanghai merchants to throw banquets, eat and drink, play mah-jongg, and close business deals.

While some prostitutes were treated as starlets, most were not so lucky. Poor families sold their daughters into slavery for a few dollars. Others were duped when they arrived in town and forced to work the streets. Streetwalking "pheasants" or "wild birds" made up the largest class of prostitutes. They donned excessively wide trousers and short jackets made of thick, bright-colored patterned brocade, and lined the streets waiting to snare passing customers. "They did not rely on beauty and charm exclusively or even on slim silken legs revealed by gowns slit almost to the thigh," wrote Percy Finch. "Congregating in bunches, they grabbed customers with the Chinese equivalent of an American football tackle. Kidnapped bedfellows were taken to small hotels around the corner."

Countless such women filled Shanghai, and it did not take long for Cohen's name to be attached to some of them, even if the connection was probably apocryphal. In the 1930s an American named Bellit brought a burlesque show called *Hello Shanghai* to China. Many of the girls doubled as prostitutes. It was a cheap affair. Admission initially started at two dollars, but soon dropped to fifty or thirty cents for the cheaper seats. Afterward, businessmen attended parties where they could meet the women. Some of the performers quit the show to become mistresses. The troupe then traveled to Manila, where it went by the name *Hello Manila*. After its run the entourage returned to Shanghai.

The women lived a precarious existence. "One night after I had retired to my room in the Palace Hotel in Shanghai and was about to fall asleep, I heard a sound as if someone was tampering with my door," said cast member Vivian Burke. "A moment later a faint line of white light flickered across the room and I knew that some one was trying to get in. . . . My screams soon brought help—help in the form of two burly north Chinese who soundly pummelled the intruder, a local Chinaman who had been annoying me for some days. The next day, somewhat over my ordeal, I made inquiries and discovered that my protectors were two of Cohen-Moische's men. The General was aware of the fact that Chinamen will stop at nothing to satisfy their crave [sic] for white women, especially blondes like myself, and he had stationed guards near my room."[15]

According to Sun Yat-sen's theory of the stages of government, China was in the period of political tutelage. The GMD had sovereignty over the nation and the party. It was supposed to follow Sun Yat-sen's principles and train the people in self-government. Despite Sun's wishes, Chiang showed scant respect for Sun's ideas and emasculated the party. He expertly dealt with factions and politicians, easily aligning himself with whatever group he needed. He balanced opposing camps, and made sure that only he maintained control. Chiang wanted a militarized society. He admired fascist Germany and Italy, and wanted a disciplined population. Essentially, Chiang wanted a subservient one. As he relied on bureaucrats and the army to run his government, corruption spread. Chiang countered protests by forbidding freedom of speech and assembly. He crushed student protests and had newspapermen arrested and opponents killed.[16]

Many politicians disgusted by Chiang's oppressive policies gravitated to Chen's southern domain. There they freely aired their antigovernment views. As the discontented gathered, the southern regime needed to strengthen its position. In March 1935 Cohen, representing Chen and other Guangdong officials, approached the British, telling them that the government wanted to form an Industrial Bank devoted to the promotion of Guangdong's industrial enterprises. Cohen said that a group of overseas Chinese wanted to invest in the bank, and if the government put in $2.5 million they would match that amount. But Guangdong did not have the money to spend, and were interested in using the Cement Works as security for a loan they hoped to get from foreign sources. Cohen did what he did so well, pitching the project, and asking the British consulate staff if they could help out. He wanted others to come on board and requested the consulate to approach wealthy Hong Kong investors for him. "General Cohen painted in glowing colours the profits which the Cement Works were making and said the loan could be paid back in monthly installments over 24 months with interest at 8%," wrote a member of the staff.

Cohen eagerly sought backing, and on April 1 he returned with a Guangdong official, Mr. Poon. "They said they were acting under the instructions of Marshal Chen Jitang who was anxious to encourage industrial development. They assured me that the money would be used for no other purpose whatever." When the consulate official noted that no loans could be made to the province without the approval of Nanjing, Cohen and Poon said that they could obtain that approval. But the project still sounded vague, and the official wanted more information on it. "I eventually stated that the scheme was in too nebulous a state to interest hard-headed business men and that to go further they would be advised to get a clear statement of the project on paper showing the overseas Chinese interests involved and quoting the Guangdong Government authority. A detailed and authoritative statement showing the value of the security and method of amortization was also desirable." Cohen and Poon left, stating that they would furnish the details in writing.

As he sought out such investments for his province, more respectability came Cohen's way. On April 18, 1935, Cohen was appointed to the rank of major general. While things were looking up for him in China, he was concerned for his aging parents back in Manchester. On October 2, 1933, a van struck his mother while she was crossing the street with her daughters Sarah and Leah. She hurt her back and head, and was taken to the Jewish Hospital, where she recovered. Worse yet, Josef suffered from diabetes. His health declined. So did that of his siblings. On April 30, 1935, Josef's brother Morris died of pneumonia and influenza. Josef made daily condolence calls to his brother's family, walking a few miles each way to their home. In the process he badly strained his leg. "From walking so much he aggravated it," said Sarah of her seventy-two-year-old father. Josef's condition worsened. "He came home one night and his toe was hurting him. So we gave him a bowl of water and he bathed his foot. He wasn't well. He wasn't healing. We had the doctor to come in to see. He said keep bathing it."

But the foot did not get better. Cohen heard of his father's declining health, and returned home in June. "My father was in bed at the time with his foot," said Sarah. "He wanted to greet my brother at the door with my mother. Soon as Morris saw my dad's foot, he got the doctor, who ordered him into the hospital. We got a specialist. Gangrene set in. They thought they could clear it, but it was too far gone. They took his leg off."

Josef did not survive the surgery, and died on July 13 with his famous son at his side. He had been prominent in the Manchester religious community, and as a special tribute prior to the burial his coffin was carried to the South Broughton Synagogue and placed on the synagogue's steps. Hundreds attended the funeral service, and a number of rabbis officiated. While standing at the graveside, Cohen became overcome with grief and wept. "We, in common with other synagogues, have lost a great supporter," said Rabbi M. M. Cohen. "We hope his famous son, the General, will carry on the traditions of his father." In Josef's memory, Cohen donated nearly one hundred guineas to various charities and synagogues.[17]

He had been away for a while, and as the new patriach Cohen decided to put family affairs in order and to take care of his mother. "In whatever part of the world I have been I have always carried a photograph of my parents," Cohen told the press the day of Josef's death. "I must remain in Manchester until my aged mother becomes reconciled to our loss." He had much to arrange, including the wedding of his sister Sarah. "Moisha was here and he wanted me to get married before he left for China again," she said. "He wanted to see me settled. He stayed to give me away." Cohen made arrangements for the ceremony, and cabled to China on July 24 for six and a half pounds' worth of silk gowns, slips, and other lingerie. "He sent over to China for a trousseau. The most gorgeous trousseau a girl could ever wish for. Pure silk handmade nighties. Everything you could think of," she said. "He took my measurements and sent them and everything was handmade of pure silk. He paid for the wedding and everything."

Much had to be done in a short time. Cohen even brought in two cousins to help with the preparations. Relatives came up from London, and Rose sailed in from Africa. The morning of the wedding, Sarah visited Josef's grave. The Cohens lived near the synagogue, and instead of hiring a carriage to take Sarah to the other side of the street for the ceremony they laid a carpet across the road. "They stopped the traffic for a little while until I crossed," she said. At the service Cohen sported a top hat, cane, and white gloves. A champagne dinner followed.

Cohen also spoiled his nephews and nieces while in town, buying them gifts and toys at local shops. "When he came over he took me there and said, 'Go ahead and get what you want,'" said nephew Victor Cooper. "He was generous to a fault." While Cohen passed his time, he tried to drum up some business for himself and China, once again promoting Lancashire trade in China. He went to Glasgow and visited local shipyards, and also went south to buy some weapons. In London an arms merchant introduced him to Captain John Ball, the director of the Soley Armament Company. Cohen told Ball that he wanted to buy tens of thousands of guns and other equipment for shipment to China, but the deal never went through. In mid-October Cohen headed home from Southampton on the Cunard White Star *Georgic*. Friends from Manchester were on board, and they threw him a feast on the twenty-fifth, complete with sausages, poached English fowl, lemon sorbet, roast chicken, green peas, broccoli, roast potatoes, globe artichokes, dates, figs, ginger, mixed nuts, and liqueur.[18]

Chiang meanwhile consolidated his control, and sought to conquer the communist-controlled land. Since his earlier efforts against the communists had failed, Chiang on the counsel of his German advisers finally changed his tactics. By the fifth annihilation campaign in October 1933, he had blockaded the Jiangxi Soviet. Three-quarters of a million troops surrounded the 150,000 communists with a series of blockhouses and trenches. His forces slowly tightened their military and economic grip. Hope appeared grim for the communists, and they decided to flee. In October 1934, 100,000 members of the Red Army, party administrators, and personnel headed out on the famed Long March. Over the next year they marched a grim 6,000 miles. Chiang's armies pursued them through the provinces of Hunan, Guizhou, Yunnan, and Sichuan. As the antagonists progressed, local militarists welcomed the Nationalist forces, since they feared the passing communists even more than they did Chiang. Once in a province, Chiang's followers took over the area.[19]

By the time the communists reached Shaanxi province in the fall of 1935 and set up their headquarters, fewer than 10,000 had survived. With the departure of the communists in the south, Chiang's control finally stretched to Chen's Guangdong borders. Chiang tried to negotiate with the south, but they rejected his offers. Treating them much as he had the communists, Chiang massed half a million men in an arc that stretched through Fujian, Jiangxi, Hunan, Guizhou, and Yunnan and called for Chen's surrender. Years of preparation and arms buying by Cohen and others meant that Chen was thoroughly prepared for this battle. He had a substantial army and a well-trained local militia equipped with tanks, antiaircraft guns, cruisers, large destroyers, swift torpedo boats, and airplanes.

As the two sides faced off, Japan started taking its own hard line toward China. The southern coalition asked Nanjing to mobilize against the true enemy, Japan. Nanjing refused, and in mid-1936 Guangdong and Guangxi troops organized the Anti-Japanese National Salvation Army. By June they began moving their forces north into Hunan to fight Japan. In actuality, they aimed at overthrowing Nanjing.

The planned war was not to be. Despite Chen's brimming armaments, Chiang simply bribed his forces and officials with well-aimed silver bullets. Generals and troops abandoned their posts for cash; the Guangdong general Yu Hanmou took with him the entire Canton air force. Chen's government collapsed. Tens of thousands of office seekers hoping to profit by Chen's downfall soon flooded Canton. "The good news had brought some 50,000 people to Canton—prospective candidates, their kinfolk and servants. The scrambling for hotel rooms was surpassed only by the scrambling for the highly desirable government jobs," wrote the journalist Ilona Ralf Sues. His empire gone, Chen left for Hong Kong on July 18, secure with tens of millions of dollars he had stocked away in the colony's banks.[20]

Sensing the coming downfall of his boss, Cohen left Chen's employ early in 1936 and reattached himself with Sun Fo. He also palled around with and worked for his old friend Wu Tiecheng, who had become mayor of Shanghai in 1932. Wu was a good municipal administrator. During his four years in office he streamlined the government, assigned new directors to almost all of the city's bureaus, and oversaw a period of urban modernization and the building of a new stadium, museum, library, hospital, and wharves. He worked hard for increased cooperation with foreigners. As Wilma Miles had learned the previous decade, the English-speaking Wu was quite sociable and cordial with westerners. Almost every day Wu and his wife held elaborate soirees and parties at their mansion on Avenue Haig. When Cohen started working for Wu, "he shuttled back and forth between Canton, Wu's headquarters, and Hong Kong, where he could mingle with visitors passing through," wrote Randall Gould. "He was a lively addition to General Wu's frequent and popular luncheons and dinners." Cohen "was otherwise an easy simple type seeming to need no visible means of support but wandering ceaselessly among foreigners and Chinese of all sorts. One wondered if maybe he didn't occasionally report the news to somebody."

Guests flowed into Wu's home, many of whom Cohen met. "A steady stream of visitors came to Wu's table," wrote Gould. "I recall how our host one day rallied Warner Oland, the Scandinavian actor who was Charlie Chan in the movies—'You look more like a Chinese than I do!' cried Wu laughingly. Another of his guests was ex-President Herbert Hoover, far more relaxed and happy than when I had seen him in office in Washington. . . . The procession of notables seemed endless—Col. McCormick of the Chicago *Tribune*, whom I had considered a reactionary ogre, turned out to seem mainly a pretty simple kindly soul when far from home."

Other guests included Max Malini, the Ostrov-born illusionist and master sleight-of-hand artist who was or had been on friendly terms with the likes of Theodore Roosevelt, King Edward VII, General John "Black Jack" Pershing, Sun Yat-sen, Al Capone, and Baron de Rothschild. While in Shanghai, both Malini and Cohen stayed at the Astor House. Cohen's reputation as a cardplayer was well-known throughout town, and one day two Americans asked Malini to introduce them to Cohen so they could cheat him at poker. They even offered Malini a cut of their take. Their request shocked Malini, and he just threw them out of his room. The gamblers soon found someone else to make the introduction. "They didn't know that Cohen was just as sharp with the cards as they were," said Malini's son, Oziar, of the Americans' attempt to cheat Cohen with marked cards. "They started playing. As soon as Cohen knew it was crooked he started serious playing, and he could read the cards as well as they, but they didn't know it. He took them for somewhere between $5,000 and $10,000." The failed cardsharps then wanted to play Cohen for credit. He said no, and told them that he was aware of their ploy. "You both better get out of town or I will put you in jail," he warned them. Cohen then found out from the men that they had tried to get Malini to set him up, but the magician flatly refused. "That is how Cohen became a great buddy of my father's, because my father wouldn't have anything to do with it."

Malini gave Cohen pointers on handling cards and doing magic. One afternoon, Malini lounged in Cohen's office. As they talked, Malini idly lifted a pencil off of

Cohen's desk and snapped it in two. He continued chatting and broke a second. Cohen watched Malini destroy the pencils and quietly moved the jar away from him, telling him that he had to have the Koh-i-noor pencils shipped in specially. Malini looked at Cohen, and feigning insult told him that he was hurt. Malini then lifted the four broken pieces, ran them through his hands, and plopped two restored pencils on Cohen's desk. In early 1937, Cohen threw a lavish Chinese New Year party in the Peninsula hotel's Roof Garden and Rose Room. He served trout from Japan, pheasants from Shanghai, mangos from Manila, and free-flowing champagne, and invited assorted guests along with Malini, who obliged by showing tricks to the guests, and Charles Drage, who was in town looking for intelligence information on the Japanese.[21]

Anxious to secure his own position in the new post-Chen south, Cohen visited R. H. Scott, the acting trade commissioner in Hong Kong, on July 30, 1936. He wanted to talk about plans by Nanjing for business in Guangdong. "It may interest you to know that 'General' Maurice Cohen ('Two Gun Cohen') called this morning and discussed the situation in Guangdong," wrote Scott. "In the course of the interview he told me confidentially that the Central Government was considering stimulating British interest in South China so that it should in time develop into, and be regarded by the British Government as, a special sphere of British influence." Scott found his scheme questionable. "Such an idea savours of the Victorian era and 'the partition of the melon,' and Cohen's record, which is doubtless well known to the Embassy, does not inspire confidence. Nevertheless, he is very closely in touch with Chinese official circles and there may be something in what he says." Others agreed with Cohen's usefulness. When a member of the British military who did not know Cohen surmised that he was suspect and should be watched, a colleague scribbled on the letter, "He is very useful in supplying information to certain branches of the Intelligence, and we don't want him molested if possible. I am personally on his visiting list!"

Cohen kept on the move. On the anniversary of Josef's death, he went to Bet Aharon Synagogue in Shanghai. Following Cohen's Aliyah—when he was called to the Torah to recite a blessing—he took out his wallet and placed a check for one hundred dollars on the table. Cohen must have cut the class at the Jews' Free School in London dealing with the biblical prohibition against handling money on the Sabbath. Not wanting to make an issue of his mistake, those running the service just left it on the table till after the day of rest was over. Two months later, Cohen attended Yom Kippur services at Ohel Rachel Synagogue. He once again plopped down one hundred dollars.

Now that Chiang had pacified the south, he made slight overtures to the anti-Japanese mood, but was still obsessed with the weakened communists holed up in Shaanxi. Many Chinese leaders believed that Chinese should not battle fellow countrymen but should fight the invading Japanese. In October 1936 Chiang visited Xi'an to confer with the Manchurian leader Zhang Xueliang about sending troops on a sixth communist suppression campaign. Zhang instead tried to convince him to resist

Japan and not resume the civil war. In December Chiang returned to Xi'an to order Zhang to continue the attack. Zhang had other ideas. Believing that Chiang's policies were harming China, Zhang and other commanders arrested Chiang on the morning of December 12. They demanded a reorganization of the government, an end to the civil war, and the start of active resistance to Japan. The communists naturally supported such a plan, and on the fifteenth Zhou Enlai arrived in Xi'an for negotiations. It took two weeks of confinement, but they finally coerced Chiang into calling off the civil war and forming a United Front with the communists. On the twenty-fifth, they released the cowered leader. China now attempted to prepare for the coming Japanese onslaught.[22]

he last thing Japan wanted was a stable China.
Chiang's pacification of the South and peace with the communists
jeopardized Japan's grand plan for regional dominance. If they waited and did not
gobble up more territory, unification would mean greater Chinese autonomy and
strength. They needed to act quickly. The Peace Protocol of 1901 allowed the
Japanese to keep 1,350 soldiers in the Beijing-Tianjin area. By 1937 they had 7,000
troops and regularly flaunted their power by conducting exercises in areas beyond
those proscribed by the agreement. In the midst of night maneuvers on July 7, 1937,
at the Marco Polo Bridge, near Wanping, southwest of Beijing, someone shot a
bullet at their forces. An exchange of fire followed, and a Japanese soldier was reported missing. The Japanese searched for their lost man. They knocked on the gates
of Wanping and insisted on the right to inspect the city. The Chinese refused them
entry, and even though the missing soldier turned up, the Japanese bombarded the
town. The Japanese then tried to settle the incident locally, but word arrived that
Chiang demanded the withdrawal of the troops, and had dispatched four army divisions. The Japanese then countered with their own reinforcements. Clashes broke
out and by the end of July the Japanese occupied Beijing and Tianjin.

Thus the Sino-Japanese War started, a petty act of aggression by a power-mad
nation. China geared up for battle. With the implementation of the new United
Front, the Chinese communists agreed to abolish soviet areas and suspend land confiscation. Their forces were also reorganized under Nationalist rule. Yet despite
peaceful overtures, the war with Japan only brought about minimal cooperation
between the former Chinese enemies. As the two partners flayed about, the Japanese
rolled across the land. Just before fighting started in Shanghai on August 13, Cohen
slipped out of town and headed south for Canton to join his boss Wu, who had
became governor of Guangdong. On August 14, two Chinese planes searching for
enemy targets mistakenly dropped bombs in Shanghai's International Settlement,

killing more than eighteen hundred people. "After the hundreds of corpses and maimed people had been removed the pavements and sidewalks had been sticky with clotting blood," wrote Abend of the senseless carnage. "Sand and disinfectant had been liberally sprinkled around, but the street still smelled like a foul charnel house, and little of the wreckage had been touched."

The devastation was widespread throughout the city. "Out near the race course conditions were still worse. Scores of bodies, and fragments of bodies, still lay about wrapped in cheap matting, and as yet the spatters of human flesh had not been removed from walls of buildings, billboards, or fences. The combination of the stench of unburied bodies and simmering August heat was unbearable." Both sides assaulted each other with land guns. The incessant rattle of rifle and machine-gun fire punctured the air. Occasional Japanese bombs fell near North Station. It was dangerous walking through the streets, as "the arrival of the Chinese planes brought the shore and ship anti-aircraft batteries of the Japanese into play, and the streets of Shanghai were made perilous by flying fragments of hot anti-aircraft shells."[1]

Shanghai fell on November 12. The Japanese then advanced on Chiang's capital. Nanjing had not yet become the grand city Chiang had hope for. While the government had recently constructed a few magnificent boulevards, the stately buildings that were to line them had not yet been built. Now Nanjing was a metropolis under siege. "The city was strewn with dugouts for the population and private shelters," wrote Sues. "At every few steps there were arrows pointing to the nearest place of refuge, in English and Chinese. Most houses were painted black, to prevent glare during raids. The Japanese raided the city practically every day. At the first sound of the sirens, the population would hurry to the shelters, but never have I seen any sign of panic. The usually so noisy Chinese talked in whispers. Somebody had circulated the rumor that the Japanese had such fine sound detectors in their planes that they could hear even a whisper. This absolute silence had something ominous in the dark shelters."

As the Japanese drew closer, their planes littered the city with pamphlets promising, "The Japanese troops exert themselves to the utmost to protect good citizens and to enable them to live in peace, enjoying their occupations." On December 10, Japanese general Iwane Matsui called on the Chinese to surrender, ensuring that "though harsh and relentless to those who resist, the Japanese troops are kind and generous to noncombatants and to Chinese troops who entertain no enmity to Japan." The Chinese did not believe Matsui's false promises. As Nanjing fell on the twelfth, civilians and soldiers fled. "There was panic as they made for the gate to Xiaguan and the river," wrote one foreigner. "The road for miles was strewn with the equipment they cast away—rifles, ammunition, belts, uniforms, cars, trucks—everything in the way of army impediments. Trucks and cars jammed, were overturned, caught fire; at the gate more cars jammed and were burned—a terrible holocaust,—and the dead lay feet deep. . . . But at the river was perhaps the most appalling scene of all. A fleet of junks was there. It was totally inadequate for the horde that was now in a frenzy to cross to the north side. The overcrowded junks capsized, then sank; thousands drowned. Other thousands tried to make rafts of the lumber on the river front, only to suffer the same fate. . . ."

But the tragedy of the fall of Nanjing paled compared to what the Japanese troops were to do. When the soldiers entered, they started a mindless orgy of rape and murder. They butchered as many as 200,000 people. "Any persons who ran in fear or excitement, and any one who was caught in the streets or alleys after dusk by roving patrols was likely to be killed on the spot. Most of this severity was beyond even theoretical excuse. . . . Some bayonet wounds were barbarously cruel," wrote another member of the Nanjing foreign community.

The Japanese lashed together unarmed groups of fifty, doused them with gasoline, set them aflame, and then machine-gunned their withering bodies. Troops held contests to see who could kill one hundred Chinese first with their swords. Many enjoyed exceeding the games' limits. One soldier boasted in his diary, "Today, we again beat the innocent Chinese half-dead, then pushed them into the ditch, and had their hairs lighted so as to see them lingering to die. For the sake of passing away time, everybody does the same to amuse himself. If this happened in Japan, it would have created a great uproar, but here at Nanjing it would be simply like killing a dog or cat."

Soldiers started destroying shops and looting, stealing such vast quantities of merchandise that they needed private carriers to move the spoils and load them into army trucks. Commanders encouraged their men to rape women. Soldiers assaulted tens of thousands of women. "Over a hundred women that we knew of were taken away by soldiers, seven of them from the University library; but there must have been many times that number who were raped in their homes," reported a foreigner. The rape and pillaging would not stop. "Robbery, murder, rape continue unabated. . . . One poor woman was raped thirty-seven times. Another had her five months infant deliberately smothered by the brute to stop its crying while he raped her. Resistance means the bayonet." As one soldier wrote home of the education he received from the Japanese Imperial Army, "in my half year at the front, about the only two things I have learned are rape and robbery. . . ."[2]

As the failing defense of China dragged on, Chiang followed his policy of biding his time. He avoided confrontation and built up his strength as he waited for help. The communists meanwhile fought in liberated areas and mobilized the population. Throughout, the Japanese advanced. By the end of 1937, they had reached the Yellow River. The Nationalists retreated first to Hankou. The city filled with refugees, and the Japanese greeted their arrival with almost daily bombing raids. "For miles up and down the Yangzi, the quais on both riverbanks were black with people living on the sidewalks for weeks, waiting for transportation," wrote Sues. "Foreigners complained bitterly of lack of butter, coffee, condensed milk, and other commodities, and when a shipment came, prices sky-rocketed and there was a mad rush on the two or three shops which still carried imported goods. But the worst thing was the lack of medical supplies and medicine." Instead of transports bringing in needed supplies, government officials and the wealthy bribed their way onto the planes. Wounded soldiers and civilians of the bombings had to then undergo surgery without anesthetics or bandages.

Cohen's family worried for his safety, and wished to keep track of his movements. His infrequent, once-a-year cables with such terse messages as, "Quite well; hope you are all well; love, Morris" did not allay their fears. With the start of the war, they did not know what had happened to him. The last the family had heard from him was when he wrote from Nanjing. "We don't even know where he is," said one sister in early September. "The only news we have had since the fighting broke out is that he is on active service. I think he will be all right. He has spent his life taking risks and always managed to come out with a whole skin." They put on a good British stiff upper lip. "Bad news travels faster than good news, and we keep on hoping that he is safe and sound," said brother Leslie on November 20. "Neither his mother nor we could tell where he is now. We should be glad to hear from him—but we are too used to his long silences to worry without real cause."

While used to his long silences, the Cohens eagerly tried to get in touch with him. Jane was not well. She suffered from diabetes, had heart disease, and had become senile. Knowing of her declining state, Cohen had recently arranged for Rose and Queenie to travel from Rhodesia to look after her. By November, her condition had deteriorated. As she worsened, the family sent Cohen cables. They did not hear from him, and on January 20, 1938, the seventy-eight-year-old Jane died in her bedroom on Bury New Road, surrounded by Chinese furniture and carvings that he had given her. "If the general can come we know that he will do so," said his sister Leah Cooper following Jane's death. "We all told my mother that he would come, and I am sure that the hope kept her alive. Whenever we mentioned Morris' name she would open her eyes and smile. She loved him so dearly."

Finally on June 6, a somber Cohen arrived in Manchester to take part in the unveiling of her tombstone. The war was a trying time for him. In preparation for battle, he had dropped fourteen pounds and got into shape, as he busily gathered instruments and maps from downed Japanese planes. While in Manchester, Cohen spoke of the problems facing his adopted homeland. China, he intoned, "will fight for her freedom to the last man. No doubt China will lose many battles, but it is the belief of all in close contact with the situation that she will win the final battle. . . . There is no dispute that to-day the Chinese people are unified. They obey the command of Military Council, of which that great man, Chiang Kai-shek, is head." Most of all, he told those who would listen, China needed weapons with which to fight. "If China had as much arms as she has sympathy the war would be over. She does not expect or wish for one foreign soldier to shoulder a rifle for her. China does hope that the nations that are friendly and that have signed treaties guaranteeing her integrity and sovereignty would help her in armaments. I don't want to give 'sob-stuff' accounts of the fighting. The Christian missionaries of Canton know how many children and others of the civil population have been slaughtered. Two days before I left China I visited the Hackett Hospital in Canton, and I saw many babies who had been wounded."

During his stay, Cohen headed to Paris for four days, and took Queenie along. He did his work and as always spoiled his niece. "Oh, he took me to Paris," said Queenie. "I stayed at the George V. He said go buy what you want. It was too wonderful for words. I used to go to the shops and say, 'Send it COD.' " Cohen also caught up on his patriarchal duties. During Queenie's stay in England, she had become involved with her cousin Harry Cohen. "I got very friendly with a relative. And he wanted to marry me," she said. Rose opposed the union. So did Cohen. "My uncle said, 'No, your mother says no and you can't.' " Cohen made Queenie go back to Rhodesia with her mother, but as an incentive he promised to send for her to join him in China. "He said in twelve months time I will send for you. I had no alternative. I had to go back to Africa with my mother."[3]

When Cohen returned to China, he took up his work for Wu. As in the past, he made his headquarters in the lobby of the Hong Kong Hotel, where the New York *Sun* noted that "his squat, powerful figure, bullet head and booming laugh have become an outstanding feature." He would chat up people, but regularly boasted, "I don't keep my job by talking." Soong Qingling meanwhile spent time in Canton, visiting local hospitals. She was the saintly Soong sister. While her two sisters fretted over power and wealth, she cared for the wounded and the survival of her homeland. When in town, Cohen looked after her. He escorted her on her rounds, doing what he could to drum up publicity for the war effort. He even ferried journalists like Israel Epstein of United Press Associations and *Time* to press conferences to hear her tell the latest news of the war front and the work of her China Defense League, a civilian and military relief organization.

During one meeting, Soong announced plans to organize a branch of the league in Canton. But she had little time to get it started. The Japanese massed troops nearby, and soon started bombing the city. "The weather had been overcast for almost a week and Japanese planes seemed to be taking off with a brief to bomb anything that looked like a building," wrote Charles Drage. "The noise of their engines as they flew lower and lower drowned ordinary conversation and was interspersed with uncomfortable thuds and rumbles as, one by one, they . . . unloaded their bombs at random before heading for home." Drage was around that October doing intelligence work for the British, and during the bombing, Cohen took him to destroyed sites where the two men gathered tail fins and bomb fragments for study. Cohen also sandbagged Wu's Yamen, mounting machine guns on the roof and preparing for their final stand.

But the battle never came. "On the morning of the 20th we heard their guns to the eastward and by the evening they sounded pretty close," said Cohen. The city could not be defended. They had no choice but to flee. The following day Canton fell. "During the day we loaded up a convoy of trucks with the government archives and office gear, and after dark we left. We'd cut it pretty fine too. . . . Actually they were in Canton just four hours after we'd gone." From there Wu's entourage trekked west, hiding from Japanese scouting missions along the way. "We were bombed most days, but there were some big caves in the mountainside where we could take shelter."

The fleeing Chinese government had relocated to Chongqing in Sichuan province. Wu's convoy joined the capital of Free China in January. The government made him Minister of Overseas Chinese, and he also worked as director of Guomindang affairs in Hong Kong and Macao. There Wu organized a new staff. Soong arrived too, as did Hahn, who was at work on an authorized biography of the Soong sisters. "I had got the Soong sisters' permission to write about them through Mme. Kung [Soong Ailing], who was on my side and told the other two they had to help me," she said. "She was the eldest and because they were Chinese in that respect they obeyed her." The sisters reserved oversight rights over Hahn's book, and at one point Soong Qingling dispatched Cohen to tell Hahn of her displeasure with part of the manuscript. He gladly did her bidding. "Mme. Sun sent him to see me, and he said 'Mme. Sun is disturbed because you say she is a *Commuuniist*. She ain't no *Commuuniist*.' She was, of course, but if that was what she wanted, I softened it. He did what she did. He was her mouthpiece, really. He was very devoted. Partly because of her dead husband and partly because of her. She could instill that sort of feeling in people." Cohen felt a loyalty to the whole Soong clan, having worked for numerous members of the family. He gladly ran their errands and did their bidding. Yet while Soong Qingling cared for Cohen and according to Hahn spoke about an "affection" that she had for him, the others were not as gracious. "Mme. Kung talked about him as if he were a sort of a family pet. She would talk about him as if he were a dog."[4]

The Chinese prepared for a long siege in this city alongside the Yangzi River where it meets the Jialing. They dismantled and moved whole factories there. Soon government officials, merchants, and peasants flocked in, filling large houses and living along the claustrophobic streets lined by framed buildings. Vendors clogged the roadways with stalls selling handmade combs, bags of candy, and peanuts. Pig, water buffalo, and cured chicken carcasses hung outside meat shops. Street dentists operated with crude hammers, chisels, and pliers, and professional writers composed letters with brushes. "The streets are narrow and lined on each side with rickshas, so automobiles can barely pass each other," recalled the American code breaker Herbert O. Yardley, who arrived in China in 1938 to work for Chiang. "The sidewalks, filled with Chinese in rags or long faded gowns, are brightened here and there by uniformed officers or prosperous civilians in new black or blue Chinese dress, followed by their wives or concubines clad in silk and furs."

During the winter the pale sun barely broke through the fog and overcast, making the city less of a target for the Japanese. In preparation for when the skies cleared and the Japanese dove from above, the government blasted and scratched air-raid shelters into the hills, honeycombing the ground with caves. Digging went on all the time. As the excavations progressed, the residents braced for the attack. "I sipped my gimlet and looked over at new China, waiting there in the night to be bombed again, a hopeless, battered mass of darker shadows in the dark," wrote Hahn.

Heavy attacks started in May 1939. When the sirens wailed and the swift planes carrying bombs neared, everyone fled for the caves and shelters. Chinese antiaircraft guns lacked range and their shells harmlessly burst beneath the overhead planes. Japanese bombs then fell. Incendiary lights shot through the shelter cracks and blanched the chambers. Doors groaned as flames pressed inward. Dugouts collapsed. When the planes departed, citizens dragged the rubble-covered dead into the streets and loaded them onto carts. "The planes seemed to be flying directly toward us over the lower part of the city, sowing bright seeds of death that flowered in red clusters of flame, flashing as a watch ticks," wrote Yardley. "Mushrooming geysers of smoke and debris leaped skyward, followed by the thunderous crashes of the exploding bombs. The earth heaved beneath our feet. . . . Throughout Chongqing a turbid wake of slow, creeping fires marked where they had passed." From January to October 1939, 785 planes unloaded 1,879 bombs, killing 5,247 people, wounding 4,196, and destroying 882 houses. Thousands more died in the 1940 "bombing season." As the bombing raids increased, long dusty lines of refugees streamed out of Chongqing to look for safer ground.[5]

After spending some time in Chongqing, Cohen flew to Hong Kong in mid-February 1939. There he established Wu's headquarters. Cohen meanwhile worked out of his own rooms, finding weapons and gasoline for the troops where he could. The war outwardly did not seem to have affected his life or activities in the colony. "In Hong Kong nothing had changed," said Cohen. "The last few months seemed like a bad dream. The hotels were full and the movies were full and the dance-halls were full." As the city continued on its merry way, Cohen tried to help friends. In 1939, Milton Miles arrived in town, following a tour of duty as a lieutenant commander aboard the USS *Black Hawk*. Miles wanted to do some reconnaissance work as he left China, and hoped to travel with Wilma and their sons, William, Murray, and Charles along the new 715-mile-long Burma Road. He could not, though, gain permission for the trip from Kunming, in Yunnan Province, to Lashio, Burma. Whenever he brought up the topic, Chinese and American officials advised him that the Burma Road was not a place for women and children. "The trip which you contemplate making will be difficult if not impossible to arrange for an independent traveler," advised American consul Paul W. Meyer. "Travel of foreigners in Yunnan has been restricted during the period of the war. . . . I think the trip unfeasible for the present and must advise you against it."

Prospects of making the trip appeared dim. One day, Wilma Miles and her three sons ran into Cohen. "We saw Morris on the street in Hong Kong," she recalled. "He was crazy about kids and he said, 'They have to come in and have a soda with me.' He squired us all into the Hong Kong Hotel to have a ginger beer soda." When they finished their drinks, Cohen insisted on buying her sons sweets. "He took them into the candy store, and said, 'Boys, you just pick what you want.' Well, that was bad for a ten-year-old and an eight-year-old and a five-year-old. I was a little worried about it. But the ten and the eight behaved very well, and they picked out something reasonable. The five-year-old looked at a great big red box. He said he wanted that.

Well it was almost too big for him to carry, and anyway, expensive." Even so, Cohen insisted on buying it for him: "Yes he has to have that. Of course he has to have that." When they left the store, Wilma filled Cohen in on their plans. Like the consul, he winced at the idea of her and the children tagging along with Miles on the Burma Road. "Oh, I am not going to help you do that. I'd help you, but that is no place for a woman and children." Not knowing what to do, Milton Miles finally approached Cohen's boss. Wu had no objections to the trip, and obtained for the family the official permission they needed.[6]

Soong soon returned to Hong Kong, and settled incognito as S. C. Ling in a two-bedroom apartment high up on the Peak. Cohen's work for her, Wu, and others in the anti-Japanese war effort attracted unwanted attention. Just before the war started and Cohen headed south, Max Malini was passing through Shanghai. Cohen heard of his arrival and asked him to disembark and come by for a visit. "My father sent word back," recalled Oziar. "You think I am crazy," he wrote. "That is all I need is to get off the boat on my way to Japan and let them know I am a friend of yours and I visited you there. They would crucify me."

The Japanese kept an eye on Cohen. On May 24, 1939, a Japanese cruiser flying a rear-admiral flag drew near the P&O liner *Ranpura* as she entered Hong Kong waters. The Japanese ship fired a blank shot to draw the *Ranpura*'s attention. The ship carried two hundred passengers, including Rear-Admiral A. J. L. Murray, the new Dockyard Commodore, Captain A. M. Peters, and Cohen. Three Japanese officers and a signaler boarded the ship and examined her papers, delaying her for thirty-five minutes. Meanwhile, the HMS *Duchess* arrived on the scene to see what was the matter. The British military also dispatched a seaplane from Hong Kong. After its brief delay, the Japanese allowed the ship to proceed. The stopping of such a passenger ship seemed odd. "The one obvious passenger in whom the Japanese might have been interested was 'General' Morris Cohen, formerly of Sun Yat-sen's bodyguard," surmised the *Times* of London. "It is believed here that the Japanese intended to make a gratuitous gesture of self-assertion."[7]

Besides his work, Cohen actively took part in the city's last gasp of frivolity, dressing in expensive clothes, carrying a walking stick, attending parties, or throwing his own. "He was strolling around, talking to people, acting out his part," said Hahn of Cohen the partygoer. "He was talkative and he was friendly to people. And one liked him. He was a character. It is hard to like a character, but I think you did like him. I have known people to groan and move away when they saw him coming, but they didn't always."

Cohen was quite the fixture at the city's celebrations. To many of the residents, he did not seem to have enough to keep him occupied. "The general was playing his role of Picturesque Old China Hand those days," noted Hahn. "He would sit in the lobby of the Grips day after day, slightly drunk, cheerfully ready to fasten on anyone who came by. He didn't have many troubles: Mme. Sun paid him a pension and he played a lot of poker, usually with Wu Tiecheng, and dabbled in various real-estate deals and so on just for the fun of it. It was a sort of hazard, getting through the Grips lobby around noon. If you didn't run into General Cohen you were apt to fall in with One-Arm Sutton." Cohen seemed to always be there. "I used to see him most Sunday nights in the Grips," said British wing commander Alf Bennett, who would stop by the hotel with his girlfriend. "We would sit at the table and he'd have a few drinks. He was living on his reminiscences by the time I met him."

Throughout, Cohen actively kept up the image of a mover and shaker. "Morris Cohen was unlike many of the would-be aviators and similar ornaments of the Hong Kong Hotel lobby in that he kept himself employed by and close to the Chinese," wrote Gould. "He took pride in this and was careful to preserve a sound professional status, though he didn't let that interfere with his being amusing company. One thing could make him huffy, and that was when some new acquaintance thought to display familiarity with his record by speaking of him as former bodyguard to Sun Yat-sen. It could be that his name of 'Two-Gun' dated from the Sun Yat-sen period, but Morris felt that such a role as bodyguard was far below the dignity of a general. I believe he preferred the designation 'aide-de-camp.' "

Cohen also passed time at the Jewish Club, whiling away the time playing poker with friends and showing magic tricks to children. "In Hong Kong I played poker with him and lost money," said Walter Citrin, an engineer who first met Cohen in the late 1930s. "He was there and he was showing card tricks. I think when he played with friends he was completely honest. He had a good sense of humor and was a first class bastard." Other members of the club agreed. "He was a very active and a very jolly one. He made people fond of him," said Dr. Solomon Bard, who used to visit the club with his wife, Sophie. "We all knew that he was a character, somewhat of a rogue with a somewhat unsavory past. It didn't somehow come through at all. Everybody was very fond of him. Morris was there right in the middle of everything and very much part of it. Very jolly, very benign, a very kind friend. He used to be very fond of children. He was very entertaining, showing card tricks. He could deal himself a full house quite easily without anyone knowing anything about it. He used to tell a lot of stories about his association as a bodyguard to Sun Yat-sen and his promotion to general, which really didn't mean much in China because you could buy a rank in those days. Most of his reminiscences were about China and how valued he was there." Cohen chatted and entertained, repeating the same old jokes and kidding with club members that he was just a "Yiddisha boy in the Edmonton Irish Brigade." Hahn especially remembered that "he was like a character out of a book. He was like something somebody wrote. I don't think he looked into himself very carefully. After all, I don't know what goes on in the mind of a bodyguard. I think he was a fairly typical bodyguard. He dramatized himself a lot. There was something childish about him. He was acting out this part to himself. That is boyish, isn't it?"

Cohen kept quite close to a few members of the club like Harry and Sophie Odell. He even attended one of their son David's tap dance class shows in the mid-1930s. "I was part of a tap dance school. Our class had our annual shows at one of the theaters in Hong Kong. After the show, parents sent up some gifts for their kids. In my case my parents didn't send anything. I was very upset. Morris Cohen could see after the show that I was crying. Everybody around me was getting flowers or presents and I got nothing. So he grabbed me and took me downstairs and walked me a block away on the corner to a candy shop called Bluebirds and he took me in there and bought me the biggest box of chocolates I could find."

During the day, Cohen took Soong around town as she conducted her relief work, collecting funds, foodstuffs, medical supplies, and clothing for the wounded and the needy; Cohen's guns bulged beneath his jacket as a warning to anyone who wished her harm. He knew that others could see his guns, and loved it, said Hahn. He worked hard at projecting a sense of menace. "There was about him always a faint glow of footlights. He was a pretty good new-world imitation of a gangster, and he wanted to be a gangster. I think he was living up to what he had always wanted to be as a child." Protecting Soong proved to be easy work. "Well, what work did he have to do? I don't think he worked much. He just protected Madame. Being a bodyguard means you just do whatever your boss does. He was supposed to be watchful and he was. Not that anybody would have tried to kill Mme. Sun. He did his job."[8]

It had been a year since Cohen left England, and he kept his promise to Queenie. "To the day at twelve months I was working in an office. I got a cable with a ticket, where to pick it up," said Queenie of how Cohen sent for her in Rhodesia. While she sailed to Hong Kong in the fall, World War II broke out in Europe. Queenie's sister cabled her to return, but Queenie was young and footloose and figured her uncle would watch over her during her six-month stay. "I went to Hong Kong. I had the time of my life there." At first he put her up at a residence for women. After that she stayed with the Odells. Cohen meanwhile went on with his work. "I didn't know his business. If he disappeared, nobody knew nothing. He would go away for a few days, and then came back. He would have appointments. He never spoke about his business or anything, whether hush-hush or not. I never asked him. He never told me anything. Nobody knows much about his business." While Queenie vacationed in Hong Kong, she heard regularly from her English boyfriend. "Harry Cohen in Manchester kept writing and said, 'When are you coming, when are you coming?' He drove me mad." Finally, in March Queenie returned to England. By then, the controversy over the relationship had passed; she carried with her a wedding trousseau courtesy of Cohen. Queenie and Harry married on June 9, 1940. "The only problem was that none of my family could come to the wedding, because they couldn't fly. The war was on."[9]

As the war began in Europe, the British in Asia evacuated women and children; in June 1940 Olga and Vivian Ferrier sent their sons, Arthur Michael and George Eric Serge, to Australia. In July the British formed the Special Operations Executive, a clandestine sabotage and propaganda organization under the Minister of Economic Warfare. Winston Churchill defined its purpose simply as "to create and foster the spirit of resistance" in occupied countries, and "to establish a nucleus of trained men who would be able to assist as 'a fifth column' in the liberation of the country concerned." SOE was quite active in Europe. It formed an Asian headquarters in Singapore. There they enlisted civilians, and trained them to use small arms, set explosives, operate a wireless, and sail.

Most of the British in Hong Kong felt threatened by the advancing Japanese, and businessmen released staff members for covert military operations and training. A local consulting mining engineer, Francis W. Kendall, went to the Japanese-controlled Hainan Island to form a clandestine group, sending back information on Japanese strength and training facilities. In Hong Kong, Kendall also commanded Force "Z." His small band of men held military exercises in secluded areas outside of Kowloon, stocked arms, materials, and medical stores in two natural caves, laid phone lines, and formed a training center. As they prepared, Kendall and his assistant, Michael H. Turner, enlisted people to supply the group with reliable intelligence. Cohen was friends with Kendall. He had also met two of the heads of SOE Singapore—Val St. John Killery and Lieutenant Colonel Alan Ferguson Warren—on a flight to Chongqing. Knowing of Cohen's extensive contacts, Kendall hired him at $1,000 a month to keep his ears open and report the news. "Cohen is a good tough determined sort of fellow . . . and suitable for such enterprises as resistance groups," wrote a member of the organization. "I do not know anything of his discretion. Some Chinese trusted him quite a lot."

In Hong Kong everyone prepared for the nearing war by drinking even more. "I was supposed to go to Mayor Wu Tiecheng's house for dinner and poker that evening, under the wing of General Cohen," wrote Hahn of one night of merriment. "I was to meet Morris Cohen on the Kowloon side at the ferry station at five o'clock. But I was still drinking at five o'clock, at Alf's flat, trying to talk sensibly with his French teacher. It was nearer seven when Alf drove me in his car over to the ferry. He was wearing his uniform cap, but no coat, and the general cocked a wise eye at him as I got out, full of apologies."

"Think nothing of it," Cohen said as he hailed a taxi. At the party, a lot of whiskey made the rounds, and Hahn imbibed way too much. "After dinner when the poker began, however, I wasn't sober enough to refuse to play, and I solemnly took my seat with the best sharks in the Far East. It was then that Morris Cohen won my everlasting gratitude. He let me play just one minute before he said, 'Get out of that chair and go upstairs, Mickey.'" Cohen then took her place. "I owe him a debt at that poker game."[10]

In 1940 Japan set up a rival puppet government in Nanjing with Wang Jingwei as the head. That October, the Free Chinese government in Chongqing dispatched Wu on a goodwill mission to build up support for the war effort. Cohen tagged along through the Philippines, Netherlands East Indies, and Malaya. On the way they collected large sums of money for the China Relief Fund. The British liked Wu, who had maintained good relations with the western powers during his four years as mayor of Shanghai. Unlike the reception given to Cohen and his group on their round-the-world trip in 1928, the British welcomed this Chinese entourage. "At first I wasn't keen on going," said Cohen of the trip. "It seemed like escaping from the real war to take a sort of tourist trip. But my arms-smuggling show was running itself by now and I couldn't pretend that I was really needed in Hong Kong." They stopped first in Manila. "For ten days we went speechifying all over the Philippines. My boss must have addressed upwards of half a million Chinese. Everybody was good to us. I was given so many presents that I couldn't possibly cart them along with me. I shipped the whole lot back to China."

Receptions were held in Wu's honor in East Java and at Batavia. The meetings proved quite profitable; Wu reportedly collected 260,000 guilders in East Java and 175,000 guilders in West Java. Since Wu's anti-Japanese stance was well known, his visit to the Netherlands East Indies was unofficial and he had to agree to avoid any public anti-Japanese activities along with publishing his political views. "The Dutch . . . had just seen their home country overrun and conquered and were taking things very seriously indeed," said Cohen of their wariness. Even so, the group cooperated with Dutch officials looking for intelligence information on warning systems and the construction of dugouts.

Wu also lunched with the heads of the local Dutch press. He discussed the recent United Front with the communists. Then on October 23 the Chinese consul general in Batavia held a reception in Wu's honor. Several hundred people attended the party, including leading members of the government, bankers and businessmen, a large number of local Chinese, and all the foreign consulars except for Japan's. It was a party, so throughout Cohen hobnobbed as Wu's personal adviser. The following day he stopped by the British consulate to discuss the trip, and willingly offered his opinion of relations between China and Japan. While Cohen said that China could not militarily beat Japan, he told the consul general that the nation did have capable allies such as malaria and dysentery, which he noted were taking a heavy toll on the Japanese. Following Batavia, the group headed to Singapore and on to Rangoon. Cohen and Wu then drove to Lashio and flew to Chongqing, arriving in the spring of 1941. In April Wu became secretary general of the GMD. Cohen stayed in town for a few weeks before heading back to Hong Kong, reportedly to discuss British-Chinese cooperation.[11]

As the war raged in Europe, Jews fleeing the Nazis flowed across Asia to Shanghai, the only place in the world for which a visa was not required. German, Austrian, and Polish Jews inundated the city's small Iranian, Iraqi, Russian, and Polish community. With Japanese controlling the surrounding territory, the International Settlement had become a hostage city. Japanese forces anxiously waited to enter. "On the other side of the Settlement is the Japanese sector, Hongqiao, separated by narrow Suzhou Creek, as smelly as Roquefort cheese," wrote the American journalist Gwen Dew. "When I arrived, soldiers with bayonets guarded each bridge, barricades choked every entrance, while Japanese gunboats controlled the Huangpu River and the Yangzi down to the sea. Shanghai was even then like a huge embryo concentration camp, where everyone was as yet free to act as he wished, but no one knew when the Tokyo trap would close its teeth. . . . On the streets more Chinese were dying daily as the Japanese hold grew tighter on the city's finances. Over 30,000 bodies were being taken from the streets every year, as many as 800 a night, ever since the beginning of the 'Incident.' "

In February 1939, 2,500 new Jewish refugees arrived in Shanghai. By the end of year the number had reached 17,000. Some found work. Many lived in Hongqiao. Most needed assistance. Shanghai's modest Jewish relief organizations could not cope with the influx of so many people, and the U.S. State Department wanted to process those heading for the United States. Hoping to smooth out the procedures, the State Department pressured The American Jewish Joint Distribution Committee to start sending money for relief. The AJJDC also dispatched the American social worker Laura Margolis to investigate and reorganize the relief for the refugees.

Margolis landed in Hong Kong in May 1941. She spent a week in the colony as she tried to secure a spot on a Dutch ship heading north. With time on her hands, she visited the offices of the Far East Rice Bowl Dinner Campaign. "When I got back to the hotel I found an invitation to dinner—at the home of Mrs. Sun Yat-sen. I would be picked up in the evening by a General Cohen," she said of the unexpected arrangements. "He picked me up and we got to her home for dinner. It was a delightful evening, with both foreigners and Chinese." Margolis was to see more of Soong and Cohen. "General Cohen and I became very good friends. He took me all over and became my Hong Kong escort. I became very good friends with Mrs. Sun Yat-sen as well, and she asked me again for dinner."

When Margolis arrived in Shanghai on the twelfth, she set up an office in her room at the Cathay Hotel. There she interviewed refugees. With funds supplied by the AJJDC, she successfully fed 8,000 refugees bowls of soup each day. When the Germans attacked Russia on June 22, the United States advised its nationals to leave, and Margolis received a telegram from her New York headquarters telling her to evacuate immediately for Manila. "The only transport available out of Shanghai by this time were troop ships for the Far East. I managed somehow to get on to one of these ships and cabled Soong Qingling immediately that when my ship stopped over in Hong Kong enroute to Manila I would like to visit her. Much to my surprise when we arrived in Hong Kong for a 24 hour stopover, no one was allowed off the ship . . . but suddenly I heard my name called, and there was General Morris Cohen to take me off to spend the day with Soong Qingling."[12]

The war had not, though, heated up as much as feared. By October, Margolis returned to Shanghai. Soong also continued her war work in Hong Kong. To help her raise money, Cohen arranged for the Manila-based Tait's Carnival to travel to the colony. On November 12, Soong along with Thomas Wilson—director of the American President Lines' Hong Kong operations—and Cohen officiated at the opening of the circus's sideshows, rides, and games.

The British were not strong enough to defend their reportedly impregnable fortress from the Japanese massing just outside Hong Kong territory. They positioned artillery and supporting units near the border and nervously waited. If the front lines failed, the British commander, Major General C. M. Maltby, planned for his troops to withdraw to the island. From there they would prevent the Japanese from using the harbor. As the wife of Sun Yat-sen and an outspoken opponent of the Japanese, Soong made an ideal target for the waiting enemy. At the start of December, Cohen went to see about getting her to safety before the Japanese came in: "If war was near and it obviously was, then it meant a siege. Mme. Sun must be got out." He went up to her home on the Peak, and tried to convince her to change her mind. "There I bumped up against the hardest of all brick walls—the obstinacy of a really good woman. Up to the day of the Great Doctor's death, she'd always done what he said was right. Since then she'd always done what she thought was right. She saw no reason to change now." Cohen therefore stopped by each day to see how she was getting on.

To all on the island, it was obvious that the Japanese were going to attack soon. "He was always gay, double chinned, with a loud voice and broken nose, and in the company of many Chinese, Canadian, and British friends," recalled Pierre Henkus, a purser-chief-steward, who first met Cohen during Wu's goodwill tour in the South Pacific. On the evening of December 5, Henkus had drinks with Cohen in the lounge of the Grips. There he listened to Cohen's dire predictions. "We had some Scotch, and that day he still believed that the British, Canadians, and Chinese, with his help and advice, were able to keep the Japs away from Hong Kong." Just in case, Henkus noticed that he carried "with him his Canadian passport and some fine guns."[13]

There was a ball to raise money for the Allied War Relief at the Peninsula hotel on the evening of December 6. Soong attended with her sister Soong Ailing. Dancers trying to block out thoughts of war packed the two large ballrooms. At one point, Wilson interrupted the party. Over a megaphone from the balcony above the dance floor, he instructed all men connected with ships in the harbor to return to their ships. "The last week has been a nightmare," wrote Phyllis Harrop in her diary on December 7. "Tension is almost at breaking point. Last week-end all the Colony's manpower was mobilised for emergency exercises . . . heavy troop movements were being carried out which did not strike me as being part of the exercise and looked very much more serious. . . ." To relieve the mounting nervousness, locals stopped by at Tait's Carnival. The fairground was "lit up like a Christmas tree," wrote George E. Baxter, bureau manager of the United Press Associations. There children amused themselves on the carnival rides and in the sideshows. "I took some Chinese children to the closing night of Tait's Carnival. . . . It happened to be a Sunday night, December 7, the last night that the city was to know any peace for months to come."[14]

In planning their assault, the Japanese decided to attack Pearl Harbor, Hong Kong, the Philippines, and Malaya simultaneously. As they awaited the expected attack, the British monitored the activities of the Japanese north of Hong Kong. On the evening of the seventh, Maltby had his battalions take up positions. He also had the antiaircraft batteries readied. That night, movie-theater screens flashed notices telling troops to report to duty. Then word arrived that the Japanese had attacked Malaya. On the morning of the eighth, the British saw Japanese troops moving near their border. At 5 A.M. the British demolished the frontier bridges and made connecting roads to Hong Kong impassable. At eight, as Japanese planes attacked American ships in Pearl Harbor across the international date line, a dozen Japanese bombers and thirty-six fighters swooped down on Hong Kong's airport, damaging and destroying the five RAF Walrus biplanes and Vickers Vildebeest torpedo bombers as well as the eight civilian planes on the ground. "Some of the Japanese came so low we could almost hit them with fly swatters," wrote Baxter. Tens of thousands of Chinese rushed to air-raid shelters. Merchants boarded up their windows and barred their doors.

Japanese troops quickly constructed temporary bridges and breached the border. Battle soon went into gear, and well-trained Japanese troops rolled over the outnumbered British. They advanced so quickly that they overran and passed Kendall's Force "Z." The group did not even have time to damage enemy communications, and only succeeded in carrying out a little sabotage. "In the city itself excited crowds milled about," wrote Gwen Priestwood, a nurse who worked as a driver for the Auxiliary Transport Service. "Soldiers, many of them recent arrivals, went to their battle stations, and soon our big guns were booming and our anti-aircraft trying to reach the far-away Jap bombers."

The British planned to blow up the airfield, but were persuaded to leave a three-hundred-foot-wide landing strip so incoming Allied planes could continue to land. Then soon after the war started a siren shrilled in the evening. "None of us, at that time, could understand an air-raid alarm which sounded at 11 pm that night. It was followed almost immediately by the all clear signal," wrote Baxter. "Information received the following day proved that it was due to the arrival of a couple of Chinese National Aviation Corporation (C.N.A.C.) planes which flew in from Chongqing to pick up the remaining members of the C.N.A.C. staff, the Clipper crew and several prominent Chinese officials including the widow of Sun Yat-sen, who were whisked away to safety before dawn."

Cohen escorted Soong Qingling and Ailing to their waiting plane. "I took the two sisters across to the mainland and saw them off," said Cohen of that long evening. "It was a pretty grim farewell. We all knew that it was likely to be our last. For once I found myself absolutely tongue-tied. I couldn't think what the hell to say. We shook hands, and I just blurted out, 'We'll fight to the bitter end, anyway.'" Soong Qingling stood on the ramp and gazed down at him. "We'll fight too, Morris," she told him, "but not to the *bitter* end. The end, when it comes, will be sweet!"

"The door shut behind her," he recalled. "They wheeled the ramp away, the plane taxied off across the tarmac, and I was left with just those words to hold on to for comfort."[15]

Those in Hong Kong had little comfort. "You would watch the Japanese planes drop bombs and return to Canton for more, with a feeling you were watching a newsreel," wrote Dew. "Then you would search for places where the missiles had fallen, and when you found them, and the masses of flesh left behind, you were sick with the reality of it." Work in the city came to a standstill. Ferries stopped crossing the bay. Bombs pitted the streets with craters. Buses and trams discontinued service. Many people on the streets wore helmets. Some carried gas masks. Air-raid wardens manned their posts. Street patrols kept the roads clear during raids, and rice-distributing centers were set up to feed the hungry. Places like the Jockey Club filled with camp beds containing poor Chinese patients evacuated from the better-equipped Donghua Hospital, which was being left open for the badly wounded. People tried to hoard food, and the Food Control office set out to make sure that the hospitals, air-raid shelters, and military posts received supplies.[16]

As bombs and artillery destroyed homes, nervous milling crowds camped out in hotel lobbies. At the Gloucester Hotel, troops and the police smashed all the windows with bamboo poles to prevent flying glass when bombs exploded nearby. They then sandbagged the openings. In the basement, the police stored weapons. Bombs rained continuously. "At regular intervals we could hear the swish of the shell, followed by the roar of the explosion as it struck, and then the distant boom of the gun," wrote Baxter of the attack on Castle Peak Road in the New Territories during the early hours of the eleventh. The order to retreat from the mainland was issued that day. As the British, Canadian, and Indian troops, police, firemen, and air raid wardens started the three-day evacuation of Kowloon, they destroyed the cement works, power station, and dockyards. Japanese-hired Chinese snipers fired at the retreating men. A stench of rotting bodies and seeping sewage filled the air of Kowloon. "Before morning all the ferries were scuttled and the dock floats on either side of the harbour were wrecked and sunk. A score or more large freight vessels were also scuttled. The harbour was devoid of anything afloat."

When Kowloon fell, organized gangs descended with shining axes and long staves. "Mad mobs of looters began to operate, moving systematically from house to house like locust scourges, leaving nothing but ruin in their trail," wrote Dew. "Anything they did not want they threw out of the window or destroyed. They broke windows, chopped up grand pianos, took food, bathtubs, clothes, money, and valuables." People were attacked. They stripped Chinese girls as they grabbed their purses and searched them for money.[17]

With Kowloon taken, the Japanese established their headquarters in the Peninsula hotel. A group of Japanese officers and British female hostages then sailed across the water in a small launch flying a white flag. They came to ask the British to surrender. Governor Sir Mark Young rejected their offer. On the seventeenth, another peace mission came across and Young said no again. Japanese planes then did as they had in Nanjing, and dropped thousands of leaflets on the island, imploring the Chinese to drive out their British exploiters and for Indian troops to kill whites. Fifth columnists also kept busy. As snipers terrorized troops and civilians, Japanese agents used lights to help direct enemy fire, filled fire buckets with kerosene, poured soapy water over engines, and added sand to rice.

Admiral Chen Ce, who had arrived in Hong Kong just before the attack, searched out and executed spies. Harrop spoke Chinese and she worked with the Chinese secret police responsible for the roundups. "Arrests of fifth columnists have been carried out all day," she wrote on the twelfth. "They are very active, many have already been executed." Cohen also kept busy. "It was now open war between my boys and the fifth columnists—and our hands were no longer tied," he said of his and the other anti–fifth columnist's activities. "They were in their element. They went around popping hand grenades through the traitors' windows while they were at supper. It was a good technique. We paid off some long standing accounts like that."[18]

When not attacking spies, Cohen checked on friends like the Odells. The family was housing Sophie Bard—who worked in one of the hospitals—while her husband served as a medical officer with the troops. "I remember meeting him very briefly during the actual hostilities, when there was a brief truce of a few hours," said Solomon Bard of his time with Cohen. "I came up to the Odells to see if my wife was there. He probably felt being with people during the actual fighting was more comforting. I remember one thing which in some ways contradicts his character. I found Morris Cohen rather frightened. Anybody would be at that sort of bombing and shelling. This man was used to personal kind of combat where he could see somebody with a gun in his hand. But when this big stuff going from somewhere miles away from guns and airplanes, it was a different story. He was just a very ordinary frightened man, as we were all. He was nervous. Very nervous. Morris was frightened, and I said to myself then that he wouldn't be if he had somebody in front of him with a gun. This thing was just beyond, distant, impersonal. You had no control."

The Japanese landed on the east side of the island during the night of the eighteenth. "Clerks and coolies were busy removing the stocks of goods from the shelves to be stored away," wrote Baxter. "Indian police were placed at strategic points with rifles, their bayonets glistening in the sun." As Japanese crossed in barges, they were so sure that they would not be attacked that they broadcast over loudspeakers "Home Sweet Home" and "The Last Rose of Summer." By the twenty-third, the Japanese destroyed the water system. The British opened disused wells. In the Hong Kong Hotel, a half dozen Chinese worked a large hand pump to draw brackish water from an abandoned well.[19]

Frightened citizens queued up for water on the shell-pocked streets or ran from cover to cover in their relentless search for food. There were no fresh vegetables. Meat was in short supply. "The faces of the women were white and drawn. . . . Rumors spread about friends and acquaintances who had been killed, raped, or even tortured. Husbands were missing, and homes wrecked, looted, or both," wrote John Stericker, a radio broadcaster for Radio Hong-Kong. The Japanese just kept on attacking. Fighting proved quite ferocious on the twenty-fourth. "The Japanese had the artillery range figured to a nicety and their planes swooped over the city, machine-gunning the streets with practically no ack-ack fire whatever," wrote Baxter. In the early morning they shelled the governor's home, and machine-gunned and bombed the central district. Hurricane lamps lit the main lounge of the Hong Kong Hotel. An emergency hospital operated on the second floor; casualties arrived on stretchers every few minutes. "In Mac's Cafeteria, meals of a sort were being served to service people only. The waiters had on dirty uniforms. Drinks were still being served, but only at the bar, and, strangest of all, the old-timers were still allowed to sign chits."

The British could not withstand the onslaught, yet Churchill sent a telegram to Governor Young imploring him, "There must however be no thought of surrender. Every part of the Island must be fought and the enemy resisted with the utmost stubbornness. . . . Every day that you are able to maintain your resistance you help the Allied cause all over the world, and by a prolonged resistance you and your men can win the lasting honour which we are sure will be your due."

Resistance, though, was futile. Early on Christmas Day there was an odd lull in the attack. "Something strange," wrote Harrop of the quiet. "After the first early morning bombing there has been a deathly silence, practically no shelling and no further raids." The battle was lost. Young and Maltby surrendered to the Japanese at Government House at three-fifteen that afternoon. "On Boxing Day we knew it was all over," said Cohen. "In the afternoon the news of our surrender was broadcast. There was nothing more for me to do. I sat in the lounge of the Hong Kong Hotel waiting to be picked up. I thought of all the different things the Japs might have against me. I began to feel frightened—more frightened than I'd ever been in my life."[20]

he British jewel of the Orient lay in shambles.
Burned vehicles and charred bodies littered the streets. Balconies, ripped from their facades, hung from buildings. Shell and rifle fire shattered walls. A few people ventured back to their houses, only to find their paths blocked and their homes destroyed. "A well-known lady resident, who had been cut off by the fighting, tried to get back through the lines," wrote Stericker. "She was accompanied by three R.A.M.C. men. Being held up by Japanese troops she was first of all robbed of her rings, then subjected to an undignified search, while her three companions were taken to the side of the road and disembowelled."

Japanese troops searched buildings, and posted sentries on street corners. They ordered all English signs removed from shops, hotels, and roads. Structures sprouted flags of the rising sun, and Japanese officers commandeered the best houses. The proud new homeowners then stood on their porches and grinned widely as they watched vanquished westerners creep along below. "It was a glorious day, and was the first time I had been out in the street for some days," wrote Harrop of the day following Christmas. "After the dark and gloomy corridors of the hotel I was almost blinded by the sun. Chinese were standing about Queen's Road in large groups, but seemed afraid to walk about or approach Pedder Street, and the lower roads. Steel helmets, gas masks, arm bands, badges and marks of identification were lying all over the streets, obviously discarded hurriedly when the news of capitulation was given out. . . . Damaged cars and trucks were also sprawled about the streets, exactly where they had been involved in accidents. The city was desolated and the scene in general was heartbreaking."

Banks stayed closed, and people couldn't get money to buy basic necessities. Some Chinese friends came forward and presented westerners with loans or parcels of food. Except for the money he had on him, Cohen possessed nothing. He did not even have identification. His $5,000 worth of Canadian fruit lands and $40,000 worth of stock in the China Power & Light Company could do him no good. Merchants kept their shops shut to avoid looting. A few set up baskets of goods on the streets, and the roads quickly filled with hawkers offering high-priced stolen goods as varied as American corned beef, peas, books for kindling, Singapore pineapples, canned duck, Scotch whiskey, English cakes, toothbrushes, silk dresses, men's suits, pots, and underwear. Supplies became so difficult to come by that it soon became a common sight to see Chinese walking behind Japanese horses, and picking through the manure for undigested grains of rice. The Japanese mocked attempts at survival. They grabbed an old man and woman and their child who tried to scoop up a few grains of fallen rice off the street, tossed them into the harbor, and used them for target practice.

Now that they controlled Hong Kong, the Japanese started finding out about their new tenants. They rounded up citizens for interrogation or worse. The Japanese took Cohen from the lobby of the Hong Kong Hotel to ask him a few questions. They then surprisingly let him go. Realizing that the Japanese were possibly setting him up so that he would lead them to his comrades, he quickly advised friends to keep away from him.

With the surrender, looting began. "Immediately after the fall of Hong Kong organized gangs of looters, like human tornadoes, had swept up and down the streets, breaking in store windows if they were not boarded up, spilling the materials on the street, taking what they wanted, leaving the rest," wrote Dew. Intent on maintaining order, the Japanese rounded up thieves, pierced their hands with bayonets, and slipped wires through their gaping flesh. They then lashed groups of looters to trees near the lower Peak tram terminus, and left them to die. Bodies of shot and bayoneted people filled the streets. The Japanese, meanwhile, flocked to cafés and toasted their own good fortune.[1]

The Japanese needed to celebrate their glorious conquest. A few days after the fall, they staged a victory parade, and ordered the Chinese to line the street, cheer on the soldiers, and wave Japanese flags. As 2,000 troops and brass bands strutted along, dozens of bombers and hydroplanes circled overhead. During the procession, soldiers solemnly carried several hundred small white boxes containing the ashes of dead comrades who had fallen in battle. The living were not to receive as much respect. Wounded western soldiers littered the hills of Hong Kong, but Japanese officers would not allow the British to collect them. As they died, their bodies decomposed in the sun.

Arranging things as they did elsewhere, the Japanese military authorities immediately started setting up brothels. Lieutenant Colonel Iguchi, the new Japanese Director of Medical Services, told Harrop "that he knew there were large numbers of 'girls' in the Colony, and that he wanted to organise a licensed quarter as quickly as possible. He went on to say that they would medically examine the girls and that they would be paid." Iguchi then ominously warned her "that there were 40,000 troops on the island, that New Year was coming on, and they were a victorious army, and that if some system was not started immediately there would be trouble for all of us. He would not be responsible for the safety of any woman, no matter what her nationality might be." Recalling Nanjing and other Japanese atrocities, western police and volunteers at the main hotels dumped all the alcohol down the drains. Since many of the pipes were blocked, the liquor flowed freely over floors and down staircases. Elsewhere on the island, the Japanese attacked people, dragging terrified nurses at Queen Mary Hospital from their hiding places under tables, beds, and in cupboards and raping them.[2]

Ten days after the surrender, the Japanese issued a directive ordering all enemy subjects to assemble the following morning on Murray Parade Ground. That evening, the journalist Joseph Alsop visited his friend Vaughn Meisling of the Associated Press at the Gloucester Hotel. They sat down to a final feast. "As the hotel food was uneatable and we had more canned stuff than we could carry, we all gorged ourselves on corned mutton and dill pickles and Vaughn's last bottle of whiskey, much in the manner of savages consuming their stores to keep them from the enemy." January 5 was warm and drizzling. The Japanese told people to come to the parade ground with what they could carry. Fearing that they would be shipped to Japan, some arrived wearing layers of clothes and lugging bundles of food and clothing. "You decided what you were going to carry. If you were very old you couldn't carry very much and if you were young like me you were a bloody Christmas tree," said George Wright-Nooth, an assistant superintendent of police.

Cohen showed up at the parade ground with a few piece of clothes and a padded silk coat, which he received from Soong's brother-in-law, H. H. Kung. About 3,000 men, women, and children gathered with him amid the bomb craters and burned-out autos, trucks, and gun carriers. Japanese guards clutching rifles and long bayonets forced the westerners to remove their pipes and cigarettes from their mouths, doff their caps, and bow low. "It struck me as being rather like Judgment Day," said Cohen. "All my past life in China seemed to be there, friends of yesterday and other friends I hadn't seen for years and had almost forgotten, business friends and wartime friends and drinking and poker-playing friends. One or two enemies too."[3]

The Japanese divided the foreigners into arbitrary groups and marched them off to native hotels and Chinese brothels along the waterfront. Men and women shared flea-infested spaces with only one narrow wooden bed, thin mattress, and soiled sheet per room. The dark rooms had not been cleaned since the occupants fled. Bathrooms were clogged and a foul stench permeated the structures.

Cohen and Alsop lodged in the Stag Hotel. The building had three toilets and no heat. Walls topped by chicken wire did not reach the ceilings of the partitioned cells. Spaces that once accommodated one Chinese prostitute now housed a minimum of three, generally four, or even five people. Cohen shared a cubicle with one cot with a woman and her child. All told, 140 people lived in the Stag. They had nothing to do. Inmates spent their time talking, walking on the roof, and lining up for the two daily issues of rice and gruel. Cohen fortunately received a care package from Sophie Odell and her mother, Rose Weill, both of whom were to avoid internment. He shared the food with the others, and gave a lot of thought to his life and his future. "They weren't particularly pleasant, but they were going to be mighty important for my future—that is, if I was going to have any future," Cohen said. "I realized only too well that the brief questioning I'd had on the night of the surrender had been only a preliminary in the hope of making some quick arrests. There was lots more to come. I just sat and sat in that tiny squalid room thinking of questions I was bound to be asked and working out plausible answers."

Finally, on the twenty-first, the Japanese herded Cohen and the others into an alley, organized them in columns, and marched them to the waterfront. The pier's entrance was shut, and the crowd milled about the street waiting for new orders. "A cretinous-looking gendarme suddenly dragged into the open an inoffensive Chinese who had evidently failed to understand a shouted order," wrote Alsop.

After giving the man two shattering blows across the shoulders with a heavy bamboo carrying pole, the gendarme tried to make him kneel for a formal beating. The Chinese, crazed by fear and pain, attempted to wriggle away. At that, the gendarme, who was plainly enjoying putting on a show for the waiting procession of British and Americans, gave way to a sort of frenzy, bringing the carrying pole crashing down on his victim's head and shoulder until be fell to the ground.

By this time a second gendarme, strangely armed with a steel golf club, had hurried up to help. Although the Chinese had fainted, they continued to beat him for five minutes, sometimes striking him across the face, and sometimes pounding him in the stomach and groin with the butt ends of their weapons. At last the Chinese gave a convulsive shudder, which could mean only one thing. Then the two gendarmes walked back to their stations, smiling proudly, leaving the broken body where it lay. All this had happened in a terrible silence, broken only by the grunts of the gendarmes and the moans of the Chinese.[4]

The Japanese formed camps for their western wards. Military personnel headed to Shamshuipo, North Point, and Argyle Street. Cohen, Alsop, and the other British, American, and Dutch civilian internees were packed onto buses, trucks, and cargo launches and sent to Stanley, an isthmus on the south end of the island. "The air soon became putrid with gas fumes from the creaking diesel engines," wrote Baxter of the ride that Cohen took on board one of the vessels. For some like Hannah Wittenbach, the change from the squalid brothels was invigorating. "It was pleasant to be out in the open air again—the first time for about six weeks for some of the people—but it was cold sitting on the deck of the small steamer by which we traveled."

An advance party headed by Dr. Selwyn Selwyn-Clarke, the director of medical services in Hong Kong, had ventured out to Stanley beforehand to clean the site for those destined to live there. The wooded hills flanked by Stanley and Datan Bay with its jail, college, school buildings, and apartments had seen heavy fighting. When the Japanese initially took the rocky peninsula, they tortured the British prisoners, blinded the men, and sliced off their tongues and ears. At St. Stephen's Casualty Hospital, they shot the doctors and then bayoneted them dozens of times. They likewise stabbed fifty-six wounded British and Canadian soldiers as they lay in bed and raped and murdered the nurses. Catholic Fathers at the adjacent Maryknoll Mission were tied together and left in a garage to starve. Their captors regularly came by to laugh at the prisoners and empty water bottles on the floor. Selwyn-Clarke's group found the buildings of the hospital and St. Stephen's College peppered with bullet and shell holes, and walls covered with Japanese characters written with the blood of humans. Grenade craters scarred the roadways. They cleaned as best they could, burned bloodied mattresses, and buried the dead beneath small, rough crosses. Hungry dogs later dug up many of the corpses. Unfortunately, some of the men in his party also grabbed good spots in the camp for themselves. "I fear that a small section behaved rather selfishly and, after completing the work, staked out claims in buildings which had been earmarked for families and elderly people," noted Selwyn-Clarke.[5]

When the launches pulled up to the tiny bathing beaches and overgrown cliffs, people rushed to find rooms. "The first night of our internment in Stanley will always be a nightmare," recalled auxiliary nurse Georgina Man. "Four of us were given a cold, grey cell with no beds or furniture. We huddled together and couldn't sleep, so we talked long into the night about our husbands and wedding days, and how wonderful life would be when we were released. I thought to myself, 'we can't live like this—we will die.' "

Internees tried to get organized. Internally there were three autonomous groups comprising 2,325 British, 290 Americans, and 60 Dutch. Each group had its own quarters and committees, and individually dealt with such issues as billeting, duties, medical clinics, and education. The Americans were the best organized, pooling their resources and working together as a community. The British meanwhile often descended into petty squabbling. The Japanese issued almost no supplies, so everything had to be improvised. Those who could help pitched in. Cohen, who was in his mid-fifties and out of shape, did little work. "I don't think he ever did any manual work at all in the camp there. He was a bit too old," said Wright-Nooth. Squads formed. Sanitation crews scrubbed pavements, walks, and hallways. One group chopped wood for the kitchens. The adventurer "One-Arm" Sutton worked on a wood crew, and wore a friend's gas mask when he cut wood to prevent sawdust from flying up his nose. Other groups kept water boiling all the time, fixed bathrooms, made crude utensils, planted gardens, and prettified the site with flower beds. Some constructed fireplaces and ovens using bricks and cinder blocks from collapsed walls and air-raid shelters, and formed new bricks with fresh clay.[6]

The buildings at Stanley were solidly built, styleless stucco-and-tile piles. Rooms were bare, with cracked and stained plaster, lit by exposed electrical lightbulbs. Some had charred holes in the floors from exploded grenades. A few had leftover mosquito netting or contained odds and ends or an old couch. New residents hung impromptu screens before windows as curtains and tried to settle in. "People were just bundled in anyhow; thirty to a flat and nearly fifty to a bungalow," recalled Jean Gittins. "Many slept for months and some even years on the floor. . . . Strangers of both sexes were pushed into the same cubicle."

There was much overcrowding. "I remember one medium sized room in the British married quarters which was shared by a businessman, his spoiled but orna-mental wife and two young children; a youthful Hong Kong civil servant, his wife and three babies—all suffering from impetigo contagiosus—and three unmarried girls," wrote Alsop. The most sought-after spaces were the tiny Chinese servants' rooms. A mother with a small child or an elderly couple generally occupied them. The classrooms at St. Stephen's College became dormitory spaces, with men sleeping on small army cots or improvised beds constructed from doors, boxes, and boards raised on stone and concrete blocks. The main idea was to keep away from the stone floors, over which scorpions crawled at night. Bedbugs were also a persistent prob-lem. The Japanese supplied no insecticide, and inmates regularly dragged their mat-tresses outside to examine them in the light for pests. They then doused the bed with boiling water. The blood of squashed bugs soon splattered the walls.

Wittenbach found herself living at the college. "We were not allocated to certain rooms, but just had to pack in as best we could in the buildings we were directed to. For the first three nights ten of us slept in a room measuring 12 feet by 15 feet. . . . There was hardly room to step between the various 'beds' but as it was cold weather we didn't mind huddling up. The electric sub-station had been damaged by a bomb, so we had no lights for about two weeks. . . . After the first three days one family left our room, so we were comparatively comfortable with only six. . . ."[7]

One of the worst places to live was in the Indian Warders' Quarters, ugly two- and three-story red brick buildings with malthoid-covered roofs. Constructed around a playing field that was dubbed the Village Green, the seven blocks numbered 12 to 18 alongside Datan Bay had been built to house 260 Indian civil servants. The Japanese humiliated rich internees by herding 780 British inside. Many of the other residents at Stanley took certain pleasure knowing that the wealthy from the Peak, whom they blamed for the fall of the city, lived there. Cohen occupied block 16. For his first six months, he slept on the floor. At one point ninety-three men and twenty-six women crowded into his building. Four internees, generally two married couples, lived in the larger rooms and three people in the smaller. Each flat had a washroom; there was a tap and a native-style bathroom with a hole in the floor—a luxury of one washroom for seven people, compared to other complexes, where thirty to fifty people shared facilities. "The rooms in the flats were so tiny that when four camp stretchers were set up there was barely the space to move, especially if the occupants happened to have purchased a table or chair from the departing In-dians," wrote Gittins. "Some folded their beds during the day. Strangely enough, in the smaller of the rooms . . . we were able to keep a small table under the shelves as well as two folding camp chairs." Balconies ran along the fronts of the Indian quarters from which Cohen and the other internees could see the high, bluish-green hills across the bay.[8]

Like most families of those interned, the Cohens knew nothing of his fate. In February 1942 the press reported that the Japanese had on the direct orders of Adolf Hitler placed Cohen before a wall and executed him. The Cohens panicked. "Since the news was cabled from Chongqing General Cohen's brothers and sisters, living in Broughton district of Salford, have been awaiting confirmation from the British Consul there," reported the *Sunday Dispatch*. His sister Leah Cooper sent a cablegram to Chongqing to find out about him. "If I thought he was dead I should go into mourning," said his brother Nathaniel, who adamantly demanded, "But what proof is there? Frankly, I do not believe the report—that he has been shot on the direct orders of Hitler. What has Hitler got against him?" It took an additional three months before they finally received a cable from British authorities telling them of his capture and internment.[9]

While Cohen settled in Stanley, the Japanese kept an eye on him. Nearly two weeks after he arrived, the Kempeitai, the Japanese secret police, carted him back to Kowloon for interrogation. "He got picked up by the Japanese Kempeitai quite early on," said Geoffrey Wilson, then an assistant superintendent in charge of the New Territory Police. "It was fairly obvious that he would be picked up." In Kowloon, the Japanese placed Cohen in a room with a few members of the Hong Kong police. There he languished for a number of days. Then on February 10 they transferred him to a basement cell with no furniture. From there they ushered him into a room for questioning by an officer and three Japanese soldiers. "I just denied everything and swore I knew nothing at all," said Cohen. The officer did not take well to his reticence, and kicked him in the ribs. His padded coat from Kung slightly softened the blow. One of the Japanese slashed him with a bamboo stick, and they kicked him some more. Cohen got up and slugged the officer in the jaw. The Japanese then stomped and punched away until they were exhausted, and tossed Cohen back into his cell. The following morning, he received a bowl of rice and a pad of paper to write down the work he did for the Chinese. Cohen wrote about his early years in China, but said that for the last few years he had been retired and lived on a pension. The next day they beat him some more. "They threw me back into my cell. I lay there weak and shivering. For the first time in my life I really wanted to die. Somewhere in his book Lawrence of Arabia tells how he felt after being beaten by Turkish soldiers: 'the citadel of my integrity had been irrevocably lost.' That isn't the sort of language I've ever learnt to use, but that was how I felt that day."

Soon Cohen rejoined the police officers. The group shared a few cigarettes that he had sewn into his coat. When Cohen heard a rumor that the Japanese planned to execute him, he distributed all the money he had. "A day or two later they took me out again to the interrogation room and made me kneel down. The officer who'd asked all the questions and was the biggest beast of the lot, jerked his great two-handed samurai sword out of its scabbard, swung it up and said, 'Put your head forward!'

"I muttered *'Shema Yisrael, Adonai Elohenu, Adonai Ehad.'* Aloud I said, with what I really thought would be my last breath, 'Get on with it, you lousy bastard!' "

Instead of beheading Cohen, the officer kicked him in the ribs and sent him back to Stanley. "He got a good beating up," said Wilson of how bad Cohen looked upon his return. "He didn't say much. When he came back, I asked him, 'Morris, how did you get on,' and he said, 'All I can say is those Japanese are lower than whale manure, that is what they are.'"

"He was beaten not all that badly but enough to put the fear of God into him," said Epstein. "He was an old man. He wasn't swathed in bandages or anything like that, but he had been kicked around." It took Cohen two weeks of rest to recover from his brutalization. He soon started to explore the hilly Stanley site. "I found myself taking pleasure in a whole lot of things I'd never noticed before. To be able to walk up and down in the open air, to sniff the smell of the sea, to have the sky overhead with clouds and rain showers and stars at night—even things like sunrise and sunset that had always seemed a bit cissy to me, now I found myself noticing them. Nobody could enjoy life in Stanley Camp. What I was enjoying was just being alive at all."[10]

The official supervisor of the camp was a Chinese Wang Jingwei supporter named C. L. Cheng, "a flabby, tubercular, grossly avaricious man," according to Alsop. "His object was to make hay while the sun shone, and besides taking bribes for special favors from the richer internees, Cheng and his gang chiseled on the rations, keeping back a portion of them and selling it on the rocketing Hong Kong food market. What the Japanese actually delivered was little enough—chiefly second-grade rice, with a tiny quantity of dead buffalo or half-putrid fish, and a few heads of wilted and flavorless Chinese cabbage. What we got after Cheng had taken his cut was close to nothing at all." Once when a block of 700 people got an allowance of 65 pounds of meat, only 15 pounds of it proved edible. The Japanese gave them so little food that doctors computed that the inmates received a mere thousand calories a day. "Even if the food had been all health-giving meats and vegetables, instead of soggy, second-grade rice, wetted with gruel, the quantity would have insured ultimate starvation."

The Japanese forbade the internees to cut down trees for fuel. Westerners therefore had to use grass, doors, and chairs for kindling. Cooks improvised with their limited supplies. When the inmates arrived at Stanley, they had no yeast with which to make bread, until Maryknoll Sister Teresa got a culture of yeast going from rice flour in water and a little sugar. Some like U.S. Navy commissary steward Ed Gingle learned to make conger eel and water buffalo meat edible. He also concocted endless rice variations. Internees had many words to describe the assorted rice medleys, but in the end they simply dubbed the shapeless mass of food "rice slum." "Serving soup to 536 people is no joke," wrote Frank H. Fisher in his diary. "Even the best cooking cannot make a satisfactory meal out of the rations supplied, certainly not sufficient for doing hard physical labour." Squads slaved at long tables preparing meals. Men manually turned a millstone to grind rice into flour, and passed the rice received from the Japanese through fine sieves to remove weevils. "Our men were unused to boiling rice, and overwhelmed by trying to cook the rations for three or four hundred people at a time, in such conditions," wrote Gittins. "Open wood fires on cold windy days are not conducive to good cooking, neither are used dustbins the best type of saucepans for boiling rice."

People came to meals armed with an odd assortment of old coffee and jam tins, cups with wire handles, and makeshift plates. Into their crockery the food staff ladled fish heads, buffalo bones, rice, stale pumpkin, and water spinach stews. Sometimes diners discovered a treat of alfalfa floating in the mix. Occasionally they received tea and sugar. "We queued up twice a day for cargo rice and thin stew which was sometimes close kin to sea water," wrote Marion Dudley of the YMCA. The fortunate like Dudley could also make their own meals with canned foods they carried in upon arrival. Those who could, saved food. Hoarding soon became so ingrained in the Stanley culture that people held supplies until they went bad. "I had some stocks of food left and was feeding all my room mates, but the question was how much to hoard for the future," wrote Dudley. "Would rations stop altogether? We meticulously divided the rice almost by the grain, we ate cooked dry rice and wished for more. Tiny half-slices of bread came from town spasmodically, sometimes whiskered with mold."

Cohen and the others obsessed over food and picked through garbage piles. Slowly they lost weight. Cohen's heft was starved away. Men averaging 160 to 180 pounds became gaunt shells, losing 40 to 50 pounds. Their ribs stuck through their chests. They all cherished small treats. A friend of Day Joyce invited her over to celebrate her birthday. The women shared curried bananas made from a pinch of curry powder and banana skins that the friend found in a dustbin. Those who kept diaries meticulously filled pages with descriptions of what they ate. "We managed to get hold of some Soya Beans which we ground down and now make Coffee out of," wrote Frederick Kelly of the Hong Kong police, who worked as a chief cook at Stanley. "Not at all bad either. They also make a good milk substitute. In making coffee you just roast them, in making milk use them as they are. Some queer things have to be done here."[11]

Stanley Pudding was made from peanut oil, rice, water, and sugar. The grounds of soybeans could be saved for a cake. Sifted wood ash or dried cuttlefish bones was used as tooth powder. Lye served as soap. People scratched tar or pitch from roads, using the material to repair leaks in pipes and watering cans. They scavenged for old lumber, convicts' uniforms, torn curtains, wardens' cast off boots.

Internees constructed hot plates from unglazed floor tiles and flower pots, inserting element wires for heat. When the wires burned out, they patched them with bits of tin. When their mini-stoves failed, they cooked over fires made of sticks or grass. Slowly, the Japanese reduced the camp's electric allowance, until there was almost no power even for lighting. With so little electricity, they could only run the water pumping stations every few days and had to carry water from a nearby stream. "We had no paraffin for lamps, but we contrived to make very small lamps which burnt peanut oil," wrote Wittenbach. "As peanut oil, or bean oil, was our only fat, we couldn't afford to use much for lights. . . . It is very trying to be completely without lights, for there are no long light evenings in the tropics. We just chatted or went to bed, or else attend talks and lectures which were given on the staircases, because they provided a fair amount of seating accommodations. Usually the speaker had a small light to read notes by, for the rule about not burning oil was not very strictly enforced, as long as the black-out was effective."[12]

Cohen woke to the sound of a gong at six-forty each morning, and rushed out for water and to join the meal queue. With so little food and so much empty time, tensions frayed and fights became common. "The lack of privacy was nearly as bad as the inadequate food. Except by sitting on a hillside for an hour, no one could hope to escape from incessant, intimate contact with others," wrote Alsop. "Old friends quarreled irremediably because one could not bear the other's habit of clearing his throat. Roommates whose mattresses perforce touched at night refused to speak all day. Men and women who were leaders of the community in the outer world wildly and publicly accused each other of petty pilfering. The most generous and sane developed the habit of mouth watching, as we used to call the envious glances everyone cast at the food of others. In the two daily ration line-ups every eye followed each plate as it was brought away from the rice bowl, as eyes follow the ball in tennis matches." Internees even rated arguments. Fisher ranked some of the best fights as those of a Dutchman smashing up a room with a golf stick, a woman professor of economics hitting and throwing water over another woman, and the almost scalping of a child by a stepfather.

People rumored that Eurasian women sold favors to the kitchen staff in exchange for food. A distinguished British barrister passed part of each day alongside the entrance to the British communal kitchen and hissed at the cooks, "Thieves, you're all thieves." When the Japanese issued an unexpected duck egg to each of the internees, they engaged in heated debates on how to prepare it. Some wanted to have their eggs fried while others wished to have it prepared with fried rice garnished with bits of egg and infinitesimal scraps of meat, bones, and vegetables. The fried eggers became so enraged when those opting for the fried rice received extra food that a mother of a large family hit the chairman of the kitchen committee over the head with her umbrella.

Cohen watched over many of the others in the camp, especially the young. "The worst of all our troubles was hunger, and the worst part of it was seeing the children go hungry and their mothers go hungrier still so as to give them a bit more to eat. It made me feel bad to watch them," he said. He did what he could to protect the children. "One day General Cohen felt there was some 'finagling' in one of the British kitchens, so he went and asked questions, which made the cook mad," wrote Dew.

" 'You're a fine one, Cohen, to say anything about stealing,' he blurted out. 'Your hands aren't reputed to be very clean.' "

" 'Maybe you're right,' the general replied. 'I've fought, I've maybe stolen, I've done things that probably were wrong. But, by God, I've never taken food from

hungry women and children under any circumstances, and you aren't going to now!'
With that he hit the cook in the eye, and a glorious fight ensued."

Others admired Cohen's kindness toward women and children. Louise Gill, who had worked for the Chinese Government Information Office in Hong Kong prior to the war and met Cohen at various official functions, recalled that one day the internees received seventy-five dollars with which they could order what they needed from town. People agonized over how to spend the money. "We took days and days of soul searching to know whether it was new teeth we needed or food we needed or whatever," said Mrs. Gill. "Morris didn't even need two minutes to make up his mind what he wanted. He ordered the whole amount in huang tang [Chinese brown sugar]. And when it arrived he gave it to all the children in the camp. The kids were just so grateful."[13]

It was cold in Stanley. In early 1942 the temperature dropped to the forties for days on end; frigid winds blew off the bay and through the nonsecure windows of the Indian quarters. Many people there and throughout the camp did not own heavy clothes, and possessed only one meager blanket. Some bundled themselves in old Hessian sacks to stay warm. Soap was scarce, and people tried not to dirty their clothes. The few items they had wore out quickly. Men cut off the bottoms of their trousers so they had material to patch the seats of their pants with. Women tailoring groups sewed shorts, pulled in waists, made wood- or tire-soled sandals, unraveled canvas gunnysacks, and crocheted the rough yarn with nails from shelled buildings. When holes appeared in shoes, they inserted cardboard.

With summer, cool breezes swept off the water, and the Japanese let internees bathe in the beach below the jail. Around the camp, women sported sun tops made from two pocket handkerchiefs. They fashioned hairpins out of wire, hats out of palm leaves. Most men went around shirtless and in khaki shorts. Some went without shoes. Cohen adopted the style and strolled bare-chested in dirty shorts with a towel tucked in his belt to wipe away his sweat. On his feet he wore a pair of shoes with the backs cut away. Despite his state, he tried to tend to his appearance. "He always looked like a reasonably well dressed man in the camp," recalled Wright-Nooth. "He never looked particularly scruffy."

Constant hunger caused inmates to bribe guards for food, or steal from several godowns stocked by the British prior to their defeat. They only stopped pilfering when someone got caught. Conditions became so bad and food so scarce that inmates tactfully complained about Cheng, telling Japanese officials that if the prisoners starved to death the officials would lose face. The Japanese dismissed Cheng in March 1942, replacing him with Yamashita, a former barber at the Hong Kong Hotel. Yamashita improved some conditions, and allowed friends in Hong Kong to send in packages.[14]

Internees slowly turned the large open space with its yellow clay and concrete chunks into vegetable gardens. To improve their planting beds, gardeners hauled topsoil from the hill next to the hospital. They planted tomato seeds and carrot tops from vegetables received in parcels from town. Some succeeded at growing quite a harvest. "I had a patch about eighty feet long by about twenty wide. I think I had eighty, ninety tomato plants growing," said Police Sergeant James Shepherd. Some used refuse from the kitchen as fertilizer. Others looked elsewhere. "For the communal gardens the sludge from the septic tanks was used, and for private gardens people used whatever they could get," wrote Wittenbach.

Those who avoided internment survived on an occupied island that was "dreary with little streaks of rage of helplessness," recalled Hahn. "You had to bow to these little bastards if they were in uniform." If westerners did not bow, they were slapped. The Japanese also regularly filled boats with Chinese, towed them out into the bay, and sunk or set the rafts on fire, killing all on board. To survive, Hahn sold belongings like her white rabbit coat. She also received money from Chinese friends to buy the high-priced foods and medicines for herself and her future husband, Charles Boxer, who had headed up British Intelligence in Hong Kong, and was interred at Shamshuipo. Looking for food became a routine joined in by many. "Shopping was our chief interest and it was becoming less and less fruitful, more and more of an ordeal," wrote Hahn. "Although Selwyn was mysteriously producing funds for this work, he didn't have much money, and Hilda [Selwyn-Clarke] had to go wearily all along the little side streets which were full of outside street-corner shops and were supposed to be comparatively cheap, haggling and searching and figuring, staying within the limits of the Japanese law on what could be taken in to Stanley and what couldn't, carrying backbreaking loads back to Happy Valley on the tram. After a week or so she asked us, her foreign friends, to help. Then she got the housework coolie to do some of it, for it was much too big a job for one woman. Then she hired an Indian besides."

In their search for food, they had to walk most everywhere. To the camps they carried boxes and bags of canned meat, vegetables, and fruit. Occasionally they risked slipping letters in the food. "I got so I could open a can and solder it back," said Hahn, who used to communicate via notes with Boxer. "I would take it to a man who had the tools. We would take the top off the can, and put the note in." She also used bottles. "Those were popular because the Japanese allowed the bottled goods to go in if they were sealed." At the camp gates, they handed the bags bearing prisoners' names over to the guards, who pilfered what they wanted before they turned over the remains. Rose Weill brought Cohen some supplies. He also received goods from Mr. Taketo, the manager of a Japanese bank, with whom he had maintained a friendship.[15]

For those in the camps, the care packages meant life. Most shared what they received. Supplies came from other sources, too. In April 1942 the Red Cross distributed shorts, shirts, basins, rubber shoes, soap, and grass mats. Other Red Cross supplies arrived containing meat, sugar, cocoa, tea, and dried fruits, as well as woolen cardigans. "The parcels have been issued at last, and, what a feast we have had," wrote Kelly on November 9, 1942, of one such parcel day. "They were not very big, that is the individual ones, but contained just what we were in need of. . . . Tea, sugar, bully beef, tinned stews, fruits, etc. are among some of the items. . . . Also, some clothes, khaki shirts, shorts, socks and underclothes have arrived which we are badly in need of."

People bartered for supplies, selling jewelry they brought into camp, even gold fillings. There was a weekly auction on the Village Green, and an infrequently held international canteen started by the Americans. The guards also bought merchandise in Hong Kong and sold it for a decent profit. Cohen purchased from some of them, and with one batch of flour from an Indian guard and eggs given to him by Taketo, he continued his reputation as a gracious host. "We'd fixed up a brazier in my room and I made pancakes—gave them plenty of fire so as to kill the bugs in the flour—and asked all those folk I reckoned needed a square meal the most. Forty of my friends ate my food that day. I was prouder of that party than of any I ever gave at the Peninsula hotel." His friend Olga Ferrier, who worked as a nurse's aide during the Japanese attack and whose husband Vivian was in Shamshuipo, lived nearby in block 15. Cohen fixed up fried eggs for her and a friend. He also bought her a half dozen packs of cigarettes.

Superior American cigarettes sold for as much as two dollars a pack. Occasionally the Japanese issued bad Chinese or Japanese cigarettes appropriately called "Horses," "Dogs," and "Pirates." Rolling paper was in short supply. Some internees attending religious services were so desperate for a drag that they ripped out the thin pages from prayer books for use afterwards as smoking papers. The desecration only stopped when guards started patrolling services. Tobacco was dear. People smoked cigarettes down to the last quarter-inch and saved the butts for rerolling. Those craving nicotine went "shooting snipes," searching the ground for discarded cigarettes. Cohen had a questionable way of getting a smoke. He walked around the camp with a small empty pipe in his mouth, and asked people if they could spare some tobacco. When they produced a packet, he put away the pipe and took out one twice the size and filled the bowl. When he couldn't get tobacco, he used pine needles as well as chrysanthemum and sweet potato leaves. Many had no choice but to cut down on their smoking. Prior to captivity, Alsop smoked fifty to sixty cigarettes a day. In Stanley he subsisted on eight a day, rolling the unappetizingly named Chinese tobacco "Eight Agricultural Smells" in toilet paper. Maryknoll fathers made "Padres Special" from collected butts mixed with pine needles and tea leaves.

Cigarettes were the main item of barter, and a Barter Board regularly listed the exchange rate for tobacco and other items. Nonsmokers made off well selling their issued cigarettes for other supplies. Chinese guards reaped an especially good profit selling eight-cent-a-pack Asian cigarettes for a dollar. The cigarette market was so lucrative that guards showed up at night with caps, shirts, and socks brimming with tobacco products. Eventually Japanese gendarmes shut down their enterprise. The Chinese wife of a British police sergeant also controlled a bustling tobacco monopoly. She shortchanged her customers by using a fine wire to fish out tobacco from closed packets. When two other policemen's wives started selling tobacco smuggled in by Chinese workers, she informed on the workers. The Japanese beheaded three of the

Chinese. As punishment, fellow police officers beat her husband, and female inmates whipped her.[16]

Under such horrific conditions, the health of the inmates naturally declined. "Slow starvation is not a pleasant experience," wrote Fisher. Conditions only worsened. Three weeks later he wrote, "Wet and dull. Nothing much doing and nowhere to do it. Beginning to find my bones and joints aching again, a sure sign that starvation is steadily making itself felt, we are promised more food . . . but its most likely to be only a minor increase."

The first signs of avitaminosis appeared in April 1942. Soon over 90 percent of the people suffered from some form of malnutrition and other diseases. Beriberi and the accompanying swollen ankles was the most common ailment, along with pellagra, rickets, scurvy, foot-and-mouth disease, septic sores, dysentery, malaria, diphtheria, typhus, intestinal worms, and typhoid. Cohen suffered from phlebitis. The strains of captivity caused bad dreams and garbled speech. "It was also interesting the number of wretched ailments an ordinary healthy person like me could suffer from," noted Joyce, "ulcerated ears again, ulcerated throat and nose, septic leg sores, septic 'Hong Kong foot', sore mouth and tail, feminine troubles, itch and toothache and dysentery." While many doctors and nurses lived in the camp, the medical staff was often too weak to care for the ill. They also lacked sufficient medicine or equipment, and performed few surgeries because of unsanitary conditions and a shortage of anesthetics. The Japanese would not even allow the doctors to take the operating and X-ray equipment from Stanley Prison Hospital. Many survived only through the tireless efforts of Selwyn and Hilda Selwyn-Clarke, who used cash received from friendly Chinese in town to provide medicine for the inmates. The doctor sometimes traveled to Stanley on Saturday afternoons to tend to the patients and see what else he could do to help.

When doctors ran out of medicine, they used such items as pumpkin seeds and garlic. They treated gastric complaints with alkali mixtures made from wall plaster, and calcium deficiencies with pulverized bones. Salt was at a premium, and after internees developed salt deficiencies the Japanese reluctantly allowed them to cook with water from the bay. Protein edema was treated with several cans of corned beef. To fight beriberi people initially ingested bran mixed with rice, and then tried yeast. Selwyn-Clarke finally stopped its spread when he got some thiamine. "Some individuals did, in fact, go temporarily mad," wrote Alsop. "There was, for instance, the faded, carefully genteel woman whose husband's beriberi was so severe that the camp council set aside for him the kidneys of the ration buffaloes. The woman had always been a model wife, yet after a couple of months it was found that the kidneys which were issued to her to take to the camp hospital were not reaching her husband. She was eating them, raw, in her room." A few did not survive. The first internee to die was an ex–British police inspector. His graveside service was short. Since the camp lacked coffins, they removed his body from the casket following the ceremony and buried him in a blanket. By the end of 1942, twenty-nine people aged two months to seventy-five years old had died.[17]

Assorted faiths held religious services. Once or twice water had to be used instead of wine during communion, and the first couple to marry knelt on sandbags during the ceremony. The Japanese did not interfere with these services but insisted that a notice had to be submitted to officials in advance of all private gatherings. "On one occasion permission was asked for a midnight Communion service—at Christmas, or New Year," wrote Wittenbach. "They wanted to know all about it, and when it was explained that at a Communion service bread and wine were used, they thought they had got the idea at last, and said 'Very sorry, cocktail parties not permitted.' "

All the children in the camp needed to continue their education. Many grew up not knowing about the outside world. Some forgot what a sheep or a train looked like. When a Japanese officer rode through the camp on a horse, a number of youngsters told their mothers that they had just seen a large dog. A professor of education and two of the headmistresses of local schools set up a kindergarten and primary and secondary schools. For writing paper, prisoners saved labels from tins, as well as the back of Red Cross parcels. Students used the American Club Library, which was sent to the camp, and the many university staff members in camp helped correct papers. There was a series of lectures given by assorted internees on various subjects for the general public. Adults attended classes in engineering, mathematics, history, economics, psychology, botany, English, literature, and languages. Teachers posted notices so the populace could choose from the offerings. "Economics this afternoon under paw-paw trees," "French class, east corner, cemetery, 4.30 PM," "Professor Smith will lecture on Bird Life at 5:30. Rendezvous on grass bank near septic tanks."[18]

A few tried to escape. Epstein decided to flee soon after he entered Stanley. "At first in the camp they didn't bother to check into who was who very much because they were winning victories all over the place, but we knew that sooner or later they would start combing through the camp," he said. "From very early on we thought we would like to get out and we were waiting for a chance to do it. One reason several of us wanted to get out of the camp was we had been very much involved with Chinese organizations, with anti-Japanese publicity and collecting money for the Chinese army. We didn't want to be singled out by the Japanese."

Four others belonged to Epstein's escape group. The only other person they asked to join them was Cohen. "We all had our various reasons why we wanted to get out. Cohen had helped with one of our affairs, collecting for the Chinese resistance, both refugee relief and medical supplies to the army. He had brought over a circus from the Philippines. He was quite a prominent figure in helping Mme. Sun, apart from his work against the Japanese with the Guomindang. We were young and vigorous and we had a chance to get out, so that was why we thought it would be a good thing to take this old man with us because he had already caught hell once. We trusted him enough to tell him. I knew enough about Cohen to know that he could keep it quiet. He thought about it for a while, but he wouldn't go.

He said it was too risky for him. We thought we might have to swim and so on. I don't think he was cowardly, but I suppose he was on the verge of his sixties. He had phlebitis. He looked more than his age. He had things to worry about. He had been kicked around. If they caught us after the escape he would have had a possibly harder time than we, though I think maybe none of us would have survived."

At first, Epstein did not know how they would get out. Then on the other side of the barbed wire they spotted a beached boat that the Japanese paid no attention to. "We found a derelict boat which we managed to rig up. It looked like nothing on earth. It had no rudder. It had no mast. It had no oars. The boards had dried out. You could see the air through its sides." One of his partners knew boats and looked it over a few times from the camp side of the wires. He determined that once they slipped into the bay, the water would tighten up the boat. On the night of March 18, 1942, the group headed out. "We had to get through the barbed wire to get to it. They didn't guard the camp very carefully because nobody had tried an escape and this was not a military camp. They had a patrol that marched around this camp, and you could tell exactly where they were going to be at any given time. They took about twenty-five minutes to march around the perimeter. So we crossed the street down through the barbed wire about two minutes after they passed. We had pliers. We cut through. We sailed to an island that was also occupied by the Japanese but not on that particular beach where we landed. The fisherman took us to Macao."

Another group coincidentally slipped out at the same time as Epstein's party. The Japanese held a major search, and for several days following the escapes the Japanese machine-gunned fishing junks that sailed too near the shore. A month later, four more inmates tried to flee. They were not as lucky as the Epstein party, and the Japanese paraded them through the streets of Hong Kong and clapped them into Stanley Jail. Whenever internees tried to escape, the wardens tightened rules, held morning and evening roll calls, and strengthened the fences. "Everyone had to be in his own building by eight p.m., and a roll call was taken at ten p.m.," wrote Dew of the crackdowns. "Lights had to be out at eleven, and when people were careless, shots were taken at them. No one could leave his quarters until eight in the morning." Roll call was arbitrary and petty. "They'd come around in the mornings sometimes early and say they wanted to search," said Kay Franklin. "There was nothing to search for. They would get us out and make us go down onto a piece of waste land and stand for hours. We were weak and we couldn't stand for long, but that used to amuse them. They were a bit sadistic like that."[19]

Inmates lived in fear of the arbitrariness of their Japanese captors. Soldiers amused themselves by rolling cans of food down the hills so they could watch internees scurry after them. One morning, the Japanese ordered inmates to gather in a field. There the westerners found soldiers with machine guns who directed them to line up according to housing blocks. "While this was going on, many of the officers and men broke ranks and, facing us, calmly unbuttoned their trousers and urinated in our direction," wrote Baxter. The group was casually frisked and forced to stand there in the cold and damp for two hours. On another occasion, thirty Stanley men were sunning themselves on a wall. A Japanese officer drove by, and his aide told them that it was not polite for white people to sit and look down on the prison. The colonel then ordered the aide to slap all the men. Besides the Japanese, inmates also feared spies. "We had a lot of informers in the camps," said Franklin of the Chinese wives of British soldiers. "They would do anything for extra food or money. So they'd keep their ears open to hear what was going on and then report to the Japs to get this extra food. So we had to be very careful."

After the inmates cleaned themselves and their rooms, found food, and completed their chores, they possessed little energy for much else. "The days passed in petty tasks, petty gossip and the exchange of rumors, which seemed, sometimes, to be the main industry in Stanley," wrote Alsop. Inmates lived on wishes of repatriation. Early on, arrangements were made for the exchange of American prisoners on board the *Asama Maru*. The fortunate like Thomas Wilson secured a spot. As they prepared to leave on June 29, 1942, some of the departing simply turned over all they owned to those staying behind. A friend gave Cohen a mattress. "Then down the hill from the camp came the long weary line of Americans, carrying children and bags—bags made from gunny sacks and broken boxes and pillowcases—wearing rough hand-made wooden clogs and cloth shoes, ragged dresses and torn shorts and threadbare trousers—the men shirtless, the women without hats in the blistering sun," wrote Dew. It was a hot, clear day, and from the beach the Japanese ferried them to the waiting ship. "We sat on the wall of the cemetery," said one internee who was left behind, "and with deep emotion watched them go. We had dreams of good food, of fruit and ice-cream for the children. In their departure there was promise that our reparation would follow. People were kissing each other goodbye and weeping. There was a shout, and a fresh burst of sobs and waves as the last boat pulled away."[20]

In July, Cohen prepared for the possibility of another prisoner exchange by receiving a written certificate verifying who he was from the Stanley Camp Commandant. He then had to wait. "I never ever saw him being miserable. He was a real optimist, he was," said Wright-Nooth of Cohen's manner around the camp. "He wasn't one of those chaps who was saying, 'Look how hard up I am and how miserable I am.' He was always a cheerful sight. Always had a friendly word. Gregarious. He could always make you laugh."

One could reach the farthest point in the camp in a brisk seven-minute walk. Cohen had a trusty walking stick and always found walking partners to while away the time with. He had many friends like Ferrier to visit, and enemies like Faure and Sutton to avoid. "They couldn't stand each other," said Geoffrey Wilson of Sutton and Cohen's mutual enmity. Shepherd took many strolls with Cohen. "We didn't walk, we doodled, because we were in each other's comforts," said Shepherd. "He was easy to get on with. There were times when we would walk around the perimeter of the camp at our leisure. At the back of the married quarters near the back of the jail there was a nice little hillock there. He and I would sit on that and look out to the east and we would be talking away on things in general, a good bit of humor in it. He knew my background better than I knew it myself."[21]

Cohen regularly stopped by friends' rooms to talk. "We didn't have much food, so it was just a question of wasting time. He would come up and have long chats with us," said Wright-Nooth of Cohen's visits with the members of the police. There Cohen regaled them with stories of China and his memories of Shameen Island. He also wowed them with card tricks. "All we had was one old pack of cards, which must have been two or three years old and were all broken up and greasy," said Wilson. "He used to do the most amazing tricks with these things with his great pudgy old hands. He was quite amazing. He was certainly very clever with cards." Seeing him handle the cards, no one dared play poker with him. "Oh God, no. Well, we didn't have any money anyway. I do remember that he used to deal poker hands. He would say, 'Let's sit down and pretend to play poker. Now what kind of hands would each of you like?' And you'd say, 'Right, I will have this and I will have that.' And then he would shuffle the cards in his pudgy old hands and he would deal the cards. You couldn't see what he did, but the hand you asked for you got."

In the early days while they still had energy, internees played football and softball. Sutton practiced his golf with a set of clubs he carried in with him. Many others passed their time reading. Alsop worked his way through the Chinese classics he found in the library of a young Chinese master at St. Stephen's College whom the Japanese had bayoneted. Inmates organized concerts, plays, musical comedies, ballets, revues, sing-alongs, and recitals. The assembly hall at the college had a gallery and platform that served as a stage. Sets and props were improvised. Dyed mosquito nets were turned into ballet costumes. Mercurochrome and Vaseline was used as rouge for performers.

Walter Frese of the U.S. Treasury Department and A. M. Fifer of the Red Cross played the piano most nights in the American Club. Dr. Harry Talbot and Elizabeth Drown might chip in by singing some Schubert. For an Easter sunrise service, worshipers played the piano, trombone, cornet, and violin and a soprano from Shanghai sang " 'O Sole Mio." The Japanese forbade them to celebrate patriotic holidays, so on George Washington's birthday the Maryknoll fathers set up a program featuring G. Washing Town. Gingle supplied a large tub of real coffee, baskets of doughnuts, and a sack of popcorn. Shepherd helped with the various plays. During the different shows honoring the various British saints' days, Shepherd played the appropriate saint. "I quite forgot to mention what a thrill I experienced last night, when at the conclusion of the St. Georges day concert, *God Save the King* was played," wrote Kelly on May 5, 1943. "The first time it has publicly been heard since we have been in here. It happened so unexpectedly, and the audience rose to a man, standing stiffly to attention. There were Japanese officials present, and what they thought of it I know not. . . . A lump came in my throat, as it must have done to many others."

There were also many informal get-togethers. "I used sometimes to be invited by a couple formerly celebrated for the sinister lavishness of their hospitality, from whose house it had once been difficult to escape sober and without indigestion," wrote Alsop.

> Four or five people, most of them dressed in rags and tatters, would gather solemnly in the couple's room and seat themselves on the remnant of a chair and the couch made of boards supported on concrete bombproofing blocks, which were the furniture. The host and hostess, still using the old lavish gestures and intonations, would produce a brew of tea leaves stewed for the third time and a little plate of cakes made of part of their luncheon rice sweetened with black-market sugar and roasted on the top of a biscuit tin over a fire of carefully collected twigs. The guests would compliment the hostess on the fare as though it had been the cocktails and rich sandwiches of the old days, and the meal would be consumed with immense attention to an exact division, down to the very last drop and crumb of the tea and cakes.[22]

Many journalists lived in Stanley, yet they like the others craved for even a little news. An occasional Red Cross postcard came through, though the Japanese often did not distribute letters or mail cards that the inmates wished sent. They did hand out copies of their own newspaper, the *Hong Kong News*, which inmates dubbed the "Daily Liar." They also screened propaganda newsreels. "We were herded into a large hall at St. Stephen's College, made to sit on a cold stone floor and look at films of Japanese soldiers triumphantly marching into conquered cities," wrote Priestwood.

Talk of a second prisoner exchange circulated for months, and people signed petitions to be included. On February 28, 1943, Fisher wrote, "The Canadians and those with wives and families in Canada have been called up. . . ." The following day he noted that "Pseudo Canadians getting quite frantic to get on the list." Claiming Canadian citizenship, Cohen got himself included on the departure list. Many who avoided the camps and stayed in town also found ways to get a spot on the *Teia Maru,* which set sail in the summer, picking up internees at various Japanese-controlled ports. Laura Margolis, who was trapped in Shanghai when it fell, embarked from that city on September 2. "Well, we got on that ship, and if camp was miserable, this was a real 'Gehinnom,' " she wrote. "There were two or three toilets on that ship for all of us; the weather was excruciatingly hot at that point in the Far East; and the women were bunked in bunkers. They had taken the big salons, emptied out the furniture and built stalls, so that there were rows of two, three, and four beds—wood with straw mattresses on them. We were like animals in stalls, really. The first night nobody could sleep because the mattresses were full of fleas, so we all took our mattresses out and dumped them overboard . . . it was impossible to sleep inside."[23]

The ship sailed to Hong Kong and anchored well offshore to await the prisoners. Cohen had little luggage to take with him, just a few possessions and the clothes he wore when the Japanese grabbed him. "A crowd gathered outside the prison wall on the western side of where we were," said Shepherd of the departure of the fortunate from Stanley. "The Red Cross ship was lying out in the bay right opposite Repulse Bay. We could see that and there was a launch there to take the people who were going away. They allowed everybody so far, then they called everybody out and into a circle who were going on board. I naturally walked with them, with Morris and another couple that I knew. I walked out part of the way with them." Soon, though, Shepherd could not advance any farther with his walking partner. He had to wish Cohen farewell.

When the *Teia Maru* left Hong Kong on September 23, Cohen weighed eighty pounds less than he did before his capture. Three days later they picked up people in the Philippines. From there they sailed to Saigon. Fifteen hundred people now packed onto a ship designed for seven hundred. Most of the men slept in the stifling hold. Hahn and her daughter Carola shared a cabin with another woman and her four children.

Cohen relaxed. "I just lazed around and reflected on my luck at being still alive," he said. People strolled the ship. "Uneasy and cramped, we wandered restlessly on deck, bumping into one another and stepping over stretched-out legs and stealing chairs and sitting on greasy machinery," wrote Hahn. "The custom of waiting in line had conditioned us for that aspect of communal life, and we stood patiently in long queues for our chance to buy coffee or liquor." At night large electric crosses shone from above the boat deck and elsewhere so that the vessel would not be mistaken for an enemy ship and sunk. One evening a young boy discovered a hidden stash of sake that the Japanese had stored for their own repatriates. Passengers quickly squirreled away the bottles.

At Goa in Portuguese India, the ship was scheduled to meet the *Gripsholm* bringing Japanese prisoners from America. Portuguese officials and troops waved at the *Teia Maru* as it pulled in, and small boats streamed around the ship to welcome its arrival. Telegrams and visitors awaited the passengers. Then on a fine, windy day the *Gripsholm* sailed into port. As the ship drew alongside, the generally noisy *Teia Maru* passengers fell silent. "We stared over at our Japanese opposite numbers," wrote Hahn. "The Japs, crowded along the rail, stared back at us, then suddenly burst into song. . . . We were dried out and grimy, on a filthy little ship. The Japs, standing on the bright, clean *Gripsholm,* sang loudly. We stood silent."

Officials tried to make the exchange go peacefully. "As our turn came we filed down from the deck, through the hold and out the gangplank," wrote Shelley Mydans in *Life*. "We all tried to comply with our committee's suggestion that we make our part of the exchange 'orderly, leisurely and dignified,' so we walked slowly in single line toward our ship. . . . The exchange was very orderly and quick. By 9:30 all 1,500 of us except the 17 stretcher cases were on board the *Gripsholm*. Despite our anticipations, none of us was quite prepared for the emotion that suddenly choked us as we stepped onto the deck. In one overwhelming moment we were free and on home territory, and among people who liked and wanted us. The Swedish crew helped us aboard and served us ice water in new paper cups. The American Red Cross gave each of us chocolate bars and American cigarettes."[24]

A huge meal awaited them. Missionaries sang "Praise God, from Whom All Blessings Flow." Many sobbed upon seeing food. "They couldn't feed us fast enough. They just loved it," said Hahn. "I turned around and saw Carola. She had never had chocolate in her life. Her face had chocolate all over it." All the food the repatriates had dreamed of was there: white bread, butter, tomato juice, cold ham, roast beef, turkey, vegetable salad, hard-boiled eggs, cheese, cucumbers, pickles, fruit salad, and iced tea with lemon. "The people cheered as the stewards set out each new dish," wrote Mydans. "They ate warily, mindful of the dangers of overeating. And they laughed all the time so that they wouldn't cry."

The *Gripsholm* was a much better ship than the *Teia Maru*. Passengers could go to the hairdresser, and use ironing boards, and had a seemingly unlimited supply of soap and towels. "When I got onto the *Gripsholm,* I had a steamed bath and the dirt rolled off of me," said Franklin. The crew distributed vitamins to help make up for dietary deficiencies. Passengers held lectures on child psychology, natives of Indo-China, the Bible, and cooperative economics. The American Red Cross distributed new clothes, and the Americans set up a hospital, kitchens, and schools. Passengers could watch movies and read current magazines. Everyone wrote reports for the U.S. State Department about their experiences and observations. People threw little parties in cabins and at the ship's bars. Most just sat on the sunny decks relaxing. "He just used to walk around and then sit for a while and chat with people," said Franklin of Cohen. "He was always smoking a cigar. He kept very much to himself. He didn't really bother to socialize."

On the first day out at sea, the crew handed out bundles of letters. Many finally learned of news from home. Cohen whisked off a telegram to his family in Rhodesia, asking them to meet him in Port Elizabeth. When the ship pulled into South Africa, people streamed off to see the city and to shop. Those who wanted to stay ashore were invited to do so by local families. The Chinese community held a picnic for the Chinese-Americans on board.[25]

"My mother went down there to see him," said Issie Bernstein of his uncle Morris's arrival. "He was wearing tennis shoes with toes sticking out. All his fat was gone. You can imagine all the loose skin hanging on him." The Jewish community put out a warm welcome. Several hundred guests were invited to a party in the home of Mr. and Mrs. A. Schauder to meet Cohen and twenty of the forty Jews on board the *Gripsholm*. "And resisting all attempts to persuade him to speak of the war situation in the Far East—for official reasons—he dilated instead upon the ancient and obscure Jewish connection with China," reported the London *Jewish Chronicle* of Cohen's brief talk. "The Chinese, he said, were the only people who had assimilated the Jews and who had never subjected them to racial persecution. Then, to the surprise of many, he spoke ardently in support of Zionism, of the necessity for a place to plant the Jewish flag and a seat at the Councils of the nations, and appealed to the gathering to do what they could in support of that ideal." Margolis also spoke of the plight of the 20,000 Jews left behind in Shanghai's crowded ghettos. She asked those at the party to help transmit funds to Shanghai through the Red Cross.

From there the *Gripsholm* sailed across the South Atlantic, arriving in Rio eleven days later. The ship spent two nights in the city, and passengers mobbed the distribution table to collect more mail. From Rio, it took two more weeks to New York City; the ship finally arrived in New York Harbor on the night of December 1. A few lights were lit onshore when they pulled in. "Then, somewhere out in the harbor, we dropped anchor," wrote Hahn. "It was cold, so everybody went to bed. In the morning I got up early and went out on deck. Everything was draped in a smoky blue light. There were a lot of ships around, and one came alongside us and tooted merrily four times; the men aboard her laughed and waved. They were all talking with American accents. Then the air came into my nostrils—the New York air, smoky and cold and tingling. I felt wonderful."[26]

Tight security prevailed at the pier, and officials reviewed passengers' papers before allowing them off. The crowd meeting the *Gripsholm* was ecstatic. Nuns and small children streamed off the boat and into the arms of waiting family members and friends. While the Americans went home, the Canadians had to await the Canadian authorities. "They kept us on board till the others had landed," said Cohen. Arthur Menzies, an Asian expert and then a junior officer in the Canadian Department of External Affairs, arrived with coworker Ralph Collins to meet the boat and usher the Canadians onto a special train the government had sent to New York. "They were supposed to be guarded by the RCMP and then interviewed in Canada," said Menzies. "We had one heck of a time getting through the various layers of U.S. security. The *Gripsholm* was not an American ship. It was an international arrangement, and because it put into New York the Americans had their security. They had I think seven layers of security, naval intelligence, army and air force and the FBI and narcotics bureau. A tremendous number. There were large numbers of the young intelligence officers and security officers who thought they would make their careers if they could catch a spy. There were a number in the Canadian list who were suspect as possible collaborators with the Japanese. We just had to get the people off that ship and move them across the dock and up to our train. It took about twenty hours to get them off the *Gripsholm* and onto a sealed train controlled by the RCMP. I think we left at one o'clock in the morning."

The Canadians were eager to hear what Cohen had to say. "The officials who dealt with him, although well aware of his tendency to over-rate his power in Guomindang circles, are satisfied that he was a sincere admirer of Sun Yat-sen and a devoted supporter of the Nationalist movement," wrote an External Affairs officer the day before his arrival. "Cohen is probably a mine of information, on conditions in China & in the Far East generally. It is noted that the FBI has been duly warned of his coming to America. He will be interrogated by their officers."

During his Canadian debriefings, Cohen told the officials about life in Stanley and his treatment at the hands of the Kempeitai. "They were debriefed by teams of people from the RCMP and other intelligence agencies of the Canadian government," said Menzies. "There was some debriefing on the train, but there wasn't much time. Some had pretty ordinary stories. Some of them were immediately sent on to their homes and then visited later to see if they had more information. Some were invited to stay a little while in a hotel where they could be further debriefed. That is standard procedure."

The train traveled north. "It wasn't till next day, when we pulled into Montreal, that I picked up my parcels and stepped down on the platform," Cohen recalled. Print press and newsreel photographers came to meet his train. Cohen allowed a Paramount newsreel reporter to interview him briefly, but told all there that he could not speak about conditions in Stanley "because any remark may influence the situation of people who are still prisoners." He was finally free.[27]

nce in Montreal, Cohen quietly slipped away from the train
station and registered at the opulent Edwardian-era Windsor Hotel overlooking Dominion Square. Dr. Yui Ming, the director of the Chinese Ministry of
Information stopped by to see him, as did the press. He told everyone who would
listen that he was relieved to return to Canada, and praised the government and the
Red Cross for their help: "I can tell you simply that I am very happy to be alive
and out of the Stanley internment camp at Hong Kong." He somewhat self-
effacingly downplayed himself: "One thing I wish to make clear. I am not a big shot.
People here have made a fuss over me, and I don't know why. It is true I was
appointed a major-general by the government of China. It is also true that I am a
friend of China. But really, I am the same Morris Cohen who came to Canada as a
Jewish immigrant when I was 16. Most of the things which have been written about
me were much exaggerated."

As a returning hero, Montreal insisted on feting him. On December 6, more
than five hundred members of the Jewish community gathered at the Mount Royal
Hotel to welcome Cohen. The head of the Canadian Jewish Congress, liquor magnate Samuel Bronfman, officiated at the dinner arranged by Montreal's Young Men's
and Young Women's Hebrew Associations. Cohen made a short address, rattled off
the highlights of his career, and told how the Rothschilds organized a club in his
old London neighborhood to provide recreation for local boys.[1]

Immediately after he returned, Cohen applied for a visa for the United States.
He wanted to tell the government his views on the war. The Americans thought
otherwise, and the FBI decided that "in view of the criminal record of Cohen,
Cohen would not be admissible to the United States." Later that month, he briefly
checked into the Chateau Laurier in Ottawa and sought out military officials in the
capital. Unlike the Americans, the Canadian government was interested in hearing
what he had to say. Cohen said he "gave them the true, ugly picture" of conditions

in China and the prison camp. His past, especially, intrigued the authorities. "While he is described as a notoriously unreliable gun-man, an opinion of Cohen expressed by one of our officers who knew him in Shanghai is to the effect that Cohen is probably loyal to the Allied cause," wrote Peter M. Dwyer of British Security Co-Ordination. "Incidentally it appears that a charge laid in Edmonton on July 3, 1914 against him for false pretenses and vagrancy has not yet been heard."

During his initial debriefing following his return, Cohen asked that the Ministry of Economic Warfare be contacted about his anti-Japanese work in Hong Kong and be informed that he wanted to get back to work. The Special Operations Executive looked over his case, and despite Cohen's view of himself, determined that they could not use his help. It was easier simply to pay him his salary covering his time in Stanley. They did, though, want to be kept posted of his movements just in case something came up. "Cohen is of the 'tough' variety, rather given to big talk; and though possibly not one hundred percent 'secure' was a suitable tool for the restricted enterprises upon which he worked for us," they noted in his file. Well aware of his tendency to spin fanciful tales, officials were especially eager that he be given "a talk upon 'security' and warned him strictly not to discuss aught of his recent work and experience on our behalf. He has plenty of good yarns to tell, and will be pressed to 'spill' them by others, if not by his own inward impulses. It can be pointed out to him that he has an ample fund of material if he confines himself to the other episodes of his career in China." They especially wanted him to be "advised or even instructed to be most strictly guarded in his references in conversation with others of 'Mike' Turner's activities in Hongkong and those of the resistance groups. Some of these men are still 'in the bag' and any lack of security might possibly result in leakages reaching the Japanese and prejudicing the fate of some of their activities."

In early March 1944, Sub-Inspector F. M. Brady of the RCMP and E. W. Bavin of British Security Co-Ordination stopped by the Windsor. They brought Cohen a check for his $6,118.75 back pay, and he acknowledged "that the work upon which I was recently engaged (in 1941/42/43) in Hongkong and China was of a confidential nature and I undertake not to reveal or discuss any of it with unauthoris [sic] persons either during or after the war." Brady and Bavin advised Cohen "that his services were much appreciated by his former employers and that there was no prospect of further employment for him on similar work in the Far East." Cohen did not like getting the brush-off, and told them that the SOE did not know and could not appreciate the value his work. He went on to say that he wanted to travel to England to offer what he knew to officials there. At the ripe age of fifty-six, he also wanted to start work on his memoirs, and told Brady and Bavin that he needed to contact Charles Drage, with whom he had discussed writing a biography. When Brady and Bavin filed their reports, they were informed that the head of the Secret Intelligence Service was not only not "interested in Cohen," but considered "him dangerous, if not suspect."[2]

Cohen had no choice but to sit out the rest of the war. As he settled into Montreal, he renewed acquaintances with western Canadian friends who had moved east. Samuel Vineberg, an old buddy from Edmonton who ran railway newsstands along the CPR, had retired in Montreal, where he helped his son Cecil in his flower shop. Cohen stopped by to chat and to catch up. One day during that winter, Samuel introduced him to Ida Judith Clark, a thirty-eight-year-old divorcée who owned a nearby swank dress shop. Cohen started courting Judith, taking her out to dinner and to meet friends. "I remember that after he did introduce them they came up to my house. They had dinner with us and then they got very friendly," said Frances Pascal of the budding romance.

Like Cohen's family, Judith's parents fled from Europe at the turn of the century. Her father, Samuel, left Galicia, stopping in Manchester to work in a clothing factory. There he met a fellow Galician, Polly Fink. In 1903, Samuel emigrated to Montreal, and found a job as a cutter and buttonhole maker. Polly soon joined him, and they started a family in the predominantly Jewish Main area. Judith was born on July 29, 1905, and Samuel and Polly raised her and her sister and two brothers in a kosher home. Samuel had a hobby of making violins, took night classes to learn pattern making, and soon started a small women's clothes company called Smart Style Cloak Company. Judith modeled his creations and acted as a salesperson. "She was very beautiful. And she was an excellent model and she also had a very winning personality," said Judith's good friend, Rose Klyne. "She had innately good taste."

As the Clarks advanced financially, they followed a set migration pattern, moving from the poorer Main area, drifting socially upward to such areas as Clark Street, Jeanne Mance, Hutchinson, and then Notre Dame de Grace in the West End, where Samuel worshiped at Shaare Zion Congregation. By the time Cohen arrived, Montreal's 64,000 Jews made up more than 5 percent of the population. The city had developed into a major Jewish center, with dozens of synagogues, the headquarters of such national Jewish organizations as the Canadian Jewish Congress, the Zionist Organization of Canada, Hadassah, Pioneer Women, and the National Council of Jewish Women. There was also a Yiddish theater, and a Jewish public library, which offered courses as well as lectures and readings.

In her twenties, Judith was briefly married to Leo Freudberg. During the Depression, she started her own couture shop, Judith Clark, with a two-hundred-dollar loan. It was a one-person operation. "She had absolutely nothing to back her in terms of resources or money, and built it up," said brother Harry. Judith made a success of it. By the time Cohen arrived from Hong Kong, Judith lived in the fashionable part of town, had a shop next door to the Ritz-Carlton Hotel, and employed numerous assistants. "She had very good connections," said Klyne. "Quebec people came into town and they went to 'Judith Clark.' It was one of the top stores."[3]

Cohen wined and dined Judith. They had a quick romance. "I can't say my people were happy about the thought," said Harry of his family's first impression of Cohen and the idea that he would marry Judith. "They figured he was a soldier of fortune and all the rest of it. They didn't know anything about him. My people were old-fashioned to that extent." Yet, Cohen as always won them over. "He sounded like a colorful person," said Ruth Field. "We thought he was too old for my sister, Judith. But she liked him. She always liked anything with glamour. They decided to marry." It was the old Cohen charm. "He wasn't a good-looking man," said Klyne. "An odd-looking man, but a charming style and blazing green eyes. He had penetrating eyes and a very warm, hearty laugh. Somehow there was something about his personality. When he spoke you listened, even though his English was abominable at times. He could capture attention." By the spring, Judith and Cohen announced their engagement. When asked why after spending decades in China he did not plan to marry a Chinese woman, Cohen would reply, "A good Chinese girl would never marry a foreigner and a bad Chinese girl I don't want!" He would also quip that Judith got him because of his weakened state following his internment.

As Montreal celebrated Cohen, Judith joined in the whirl. "My sister had a bit of flamboyance about her," said Harry. "She wore fancy hats and she liked the excitement of meeting important people. When she went out with the General she was well received. She had a glamorous view on certain things. She liked to be in his company because he was highly regarded and sought after in Montreal. The Jewish community was always approaching him for all kinds of information. They wrote about him. She was a participant."

That spring, Cohen went to visit his old western stomping grounds. He spent a few days in Winnipeg, where he was the guest of honor at a meeting of the B'nai B'rith. He then traveled to Edmonton and checked into the Hotel Macdonald. Throughout, he discussed his desire to return to the East. "I'm very happy to be back, and I'll be far more pleased when I can get back to China." And then promoting his adopted nation and positioning himself for the hoped for postwar boom, he predicted that "China will be the economic salvation of the American continent and Europe. The country is just entering the second stage of evolution, the machine age. It will require a great deal of machinery after the war, and Canada will be one of its main sources. Machinery, wheat, flour will be needed from Canada. . . . Generalissimo and Madame Chiang Kai-shek are doing a marvelous job in China, and I am glad to hear that Canada is doing a lot in supplying heavy war equipment to the Chinese." On his way back east, he stopped in Toronto for a few days and visited a few old friends, including Major William Hanley, his former commander in France. He also snagged a visa, and headed to the United States. The press covered his movements. He loved the accolade, but at the same time tried to brush off the attention, "I'm just a young fellow trying to get along." Then, in his oft-repeated phrase, he spoke a bit of truth. "My reputation, like the report of Mark Twain's death, is greatly exaggerated. So was the report of my own death as a matter of fact."[4]

Judith and Cohen married at Temple Emanu-el on June 18. They had a small ceremony within the synagogue's domed sanctuary. The distinguished Rabbi Harry Stern officiated. Judith wore a frock of pale orchid crepe, with hat and accessories to match. As she walked down the aisle, she carried a white Bible topped with an orchid and showered with streamers and small flowers. Her sister, Ruth, was the maid of honor, and Cohen's best man was David Druxerman. Harry Clark, Rose's brother Cyril Schwisberg, and others served as ushers. "I am sure he didn't go much to synagogue, but he insisted on a yamulka and a more Jewish type of wedding than was quite customary," said Klyne of the wedding. "It was not customary for that sort of a ceremony at the temple. But he insisted on a shawl. The ceremony was very simple and lovely, a fine Jewish ceremony." Afterward, the newlyweds hosted a reception at the Windsor Hotel.

The Cohens initially discussed a honeymoon in New Orleans and Miami, but decided in the end to head out to Lake Louise in Alberta and elsewhere west. They visited friends in Calgary, all the while promoting China. "The Chinese are waging a wonderful fight against the Japanese as they enter the eighth year of their war but what they really need for final victory is an increased air force and heavy equipment," he said. "Believe me, the Chinese are really strong. But there is no use kidding ourselves that they do not need more equipment. I believe, however, they will be getting it soon, and when they do there will be only one outcome of the conflict."

In late June, Judith and Cohen arrived in Vancouver. On July 3, they attended a packed meeting at the Vancouver chapter of the B'nai B'rith, where Cohen spoke on one his favorite topics, the Jews of China, and discussed the present situation of the Jewish refugees. He acknowledged the relief work carried out by Laura Margolis, the American Jewish Joint Distribution Committee, and the Chinese in keeping many refugees alive. All the while he told people his somewhat simplistic recipe for world peace. "I'd get Al Smith's brown derby and put in it the United States, Soviet Russia, Great Britain and China. I'd shake well, and I think they'd all come out a little pink." From there Judith and Cohen went to Victoria, before heading back east.[5]

Cohen became a doting husband. "When they were in shape he was very de-voted and loving. Very affectionate. She never complained about that at all. Always said he was wonderful," said a friend. Judith corresponded with her new family in England, and sent them clothes and hats. He palled around with his brother-in-law Harry. "He heard that I was playing at a four-wall handball championship, and he came up and went right through the series watching my games. We spent a lot of time together," said Harry of the matches at the YMHA and YWHA. "He was a very strong-willed man, a most generous kindhearted guy. He was empathetic to the extent that if I had any problem, he would sit down and talk it over with me. He treated me like a kid brother. I can't say that I ever thought of him as anything more than just a good big brother, and he treated me accordingly."

As a local Jewish celebrity, Cohen became friendly with some of the Jewish community's leading members like Bronfman. The Cohens socialized, and basked in the limelight. "He was very lavish and extravagant in a way," said Klyne. "It was his nature to enjoy himself, but with others. He liked others to share it. Very, very generous." The two spent a lot of time celebrating. "They didn't discourage it. I think that is a fair statement," said Judith's brother Gerald. Judith invited guests over and threw small cocktail and dinner parties. The couple attended concerts, and took friends and officials out for twenty-course feasts at local Chinese restaurants. "They very often had dignitaries from China, and people that were very prominent there. They would entertain them," said Pascal. At Montreal's Chinese restaurants, Cohen was an honored guest. "He was lionized here, at first," said Klyne. "When he took me into a restaurant, especially a Chinese down in Chinatown, oh my God, they didn't know what to do first. They bowed and kowtowed and served him like a King of England." Everything was grand. "It was real gala fashion. He loved it. Everybody was very, very nice to him. Judith liked that kind of thing, too. She was very good at it, too. Very good at arranging it. She always was quite the lady. Always. When he came up to ours for dinner one Friday night at my mother's, he was very gallant to older ladies. Very. He sent flowers."

Cohen also spent time at Judith's store, spoiling children who came in. He loved children, and couldn't do enough for them. "All the kids were crazy about him. He was like the pied piper," said Klyne. "My sister and I went to see Judith's store on Sherbrooke Street and he was there. My sister had her little girl, and Morris saw her and stuck ten dollars in her hand and hugged her and whatnot. My sister was a little annoyed and she said, 'Morris you can't do this ten-dollar business.' He said, 'She doesn't know how much it is. She just knows that I gave her something.' And she was very pleased and sang for him. She sang him a song." The Cohens took trips out to the countryside, driving to resorts in Lake George and elsewhere. Many excursions were on a whim. "It would be very impromptu," said Cecil Vineberg. "We would never ring them up in advance. All of a sudden he'd say, 'Let's go tomorrow.' That was the way he was. And we would go."

All the while, Cohen spent money quite freely. "While he had it he just splashed it," said the friend. "I always worried about the money he was spending, because I could see maybe in the future it wouldn't be so easy. I realized his age. He was much older than Judith." As a bridegroom, though, Cohen knew that he needed to bring home a salary and support his wife, so he looked for work. Montreal offered few suitable jobs for a man who spent his life as a go-between in China. He tried unusual ventures. Cohen became friendly with the Brooklyn-born Canadian moviemaker Arthur Gottlieb, founder of Film Laboratories of Canada, and the producer of such movies as *The King's Plate* and *Under Cover*. The two discussed forming a movie company. During the summer or early fall of 1944, Gottlieb tried to convince the journalist and publicist Ed Parker to help them with their project. "Gottlieb and Cohen confronted me one night with the staggering proposal that I become the head of their film company," wrote Parker. "At the time, I was earning about $3,000 a year. Here was a miracle proposition offering a starting salary of $14,000 a year." Parker's mind reeled with possibilities, but during a weekend away with Gottlieb, Parker saw the filmmaker and former boxer beat his mistress. He then knew that he did not want to work for him. Nothing came of the studio plans.[6]

As Cohen looked for work, he had to watch where he traveled. Despite the fact that he had escaped from Stanley by claiming to be a Canadian, he did not possess proper Canadian citizenship; he was only in the country on a "temporary" basis. Because of his precarious state, he constantly needed to extend his limited status. Working on one of his schemes, he told authorities soon after he returned to Canada that he had to travel to the United States in connection with his work for the National Film Board of Canada. Despite his empty boasts about work, the government started reviewing and approving his visa extension a year at a time. When the government finally checked with the Film Board, they learned from the board's personnel manager that Cohen had never been a staff member.

Nothing came of most of his ambitions. Cohen simply lived off Judith's salary, spinning yarns, looking for work, and biding his time for the war to end. He had promised to revisit his African relatives soon after his visit aboard the *Gripsholm,* but could not while the war continued. He wrote apologetically to his niece Evelyn Ferera that "circumstances and things moved very fast. Love, as you know, is very peculiar, and with my Chinese friends prevailing on me to write my autobiography, it upset my original plans." He had started gathering material for his memoirs, and asked her to send him full details of her work in Africa, especially for the promotion of the "Help China" movement, so that he could use the information in the manuscript. As with most wives of would-be authors, Judith eagerly awaited the book's completion. "Morris' book still needs working on but of course we shall send you a copy just as soon as it is published," she wrote Ferera. "Believe me, no one is more impatient than I to see it in print."[7]

During the fall of 1944, representatives from the United States, Britain, the Soviet Union, and China met at the Dumbarton Oaks Conference in Washington, D.C. There the Allies agreed to replace the much maligned League of Nations with a new and more effective organization. The United Nations' founding conference opened in San Francisco on April 25, 1945, thirteen days after President Franklin Roosevelt died, five days before Hitler killed himself, and two weeks before his thousand-year Reich unconditionally surrendered. Besides the representatives from four dozen nations, some forty nongovernmental organizations sent delegations. Jews were anxious about the future of the British mandate for Palestine. Representatives from the American Jewish Conference, the World Jewish Congress, the Canadian Jewish Congress, and the Board of Deputies of British Jews, as well as such prominent leaders as Rabbi Stephen Wise, Rabbi Abba Hillel Silver, Louis Lipsky, Eliahu Elath, Saul Hayes, and Samuel Bronfman descended on the Bay City to lobby their cause.

The Jewish group was especially concerned that Britain might abandon her commitment to establish a Jewish homeland. They wanted to make sure the United Nations did not reduce or eliminate Jewish rights in Palestine under the 1917 Balfour Declaration—which stated that the British "view with favour the establishment in Palestine of a national home for the Jewish people"—or the 1922 League of Nations–approved mandate over Palestine. They therefore sought the insertion of a clause within the United Nations charter that protected the rights of minority groups like those of the Jews living in Palestine. Yet they were not the only lobbyists. Arabs sent a delegation, too. Their group naturally wanted the council solely to recognize the rights of the single largest group in each trusteeship territory. In Palestine the Arabs made up the majority.

Starting each morning at eight in the offices of the local Jewish community building, the delegates held planning meetings and prepared for the day's formal sessions in the San Francisco Opera House. "The Jewish people, possessing no recognizable territory of its own, had no national status at the conference," wrote Rabbi Israel Goldstein. "Thus . . . the most that we could do was to hover about, talking to statesmen in the lobbies or seeing them elsewhere by appointment." Luckily for them, the powerful U.S., British, and French delegations opposed the Arab proposals. The Jewish delegates tried to line up further support from British commonwealth countries such as Canada, but Prime Minister William Lyon Mackenzie King headed the Canadian delegation, and he was unsympathetic to the Jewish cause. In the past he had opposed Jewish immigration to Canada, noting that "we must seek to keep Canada free from unrest and too great an intermixture of foreign strains of blood." From 1939 to 1945, Canada accepted only 500 Jews who escaped the Nazis and 2,250 German Jewish internees from Britain. The country was so hard to get into, so unreachable, that Jews in Auschwitz named the buildings in which the Nazis stored food, gold, diamonds, confiscated goods, and other luxuries "Canada." With the Canadians, the Zionist public relations attempts fell on deaf ears.[8]

National delegations agreed not to discuss the proceedings with the various nongovernmental representatives, and initially the Jewish delegation had little access or idea of what was going on in the various national groups. That did not stop them from trying. They wined and dined delegates, tried to find out advance positions, sought access to unpublished documents, and worked to ferret out inner debates. "Then you could go to them before they dug their heels in and try to convince them to do otherwise," recalled Hayes of the Canadian Jewish Congress.

One group the Zionists could not gain access to was the Chinese delegation. Then Goldstein remembered that Cohen had settled in Montreal. "As I sat in my hotel room, racking my brains to find some way of obtaining an interview [with] the head of China's delegation, I suddenly hit on a possible solution to our problem," recalled Goldstein. "While in Canada a year or two previously, I had met that picaresque character, Morris Abraham Cohen. . . . As a result of my brainwave, I wired 'Two-Gun Cohen,' urging him to fly out to San Francisco and assist us with an introduction. . . . He promptly obliged. . . ."

Cohen had an idea that the delegation might request his services. His yearly visa was coming up for renewal, and a week before the conference began he went to make sure that there would be no chance that his visa would expire while he worked in the United States. He repeated to officials details about his connections with the National Film Board, and mentioned how he had to go to San Francisco for the UN conference. He also let on that others would be calling on his services. "He spoke airily about another conference that would follow the San Francisco conference at which, if I can recapture his phraseology, 'the boys would want to have him around,' " wrote an official.

Others, besides Goldstein, had thought of contacting him. Cohen said he would be happy to help, though a few of the Canadian delegates were initially skeptical of his usefulness. "The general looked like a rough, tough prize-fighter or adventurer, and spoke like an illiterate," said Hayes. "But he was a kind man and he was fundamentally interested in the Jewish people. He wouldn't take a dime from us or a fee of any kind. He just couldn't afford to go to San Francisco on his own, so we sent him." In town, Hayes and Bronfman took him around to meet the other members of the lobby. "Cohen offered to introduce me to some of his friends in the Chinese delegation, to whom I'll be able to explain our problems," wrote Elath. "He knows that the Arabs are actively wooing the Chinese delegates; their propaganda stresses Asian solidarity, which 'obliges China,' so they claim, to support their campaign against Zionism. Cohen doubts whether the majority of the Chinese delegation have ever heard of Zionism; even among educated delegates knowledge of Jews and Judaism is very sketchy. He thinks that Arab propaganda can very well succeed if we do not take effective countermeasures."[9]

Cohen surprised the delegation with his contacts and usefulness. "It turned out that General Two-Gun Cohen wasn't kidding when he said he had influence with the Chinese," said Hayes. Not only did he know the Chinese leaders, but "he would get us the damnedest documents. I never asked how or why." While there, Cohen renewed his contacts with Wellington Koo and the others. "One day I was walking down the street with him to take him out to dinner and three other people were walking down the street—Ambassador Wellington Koo, the Chinese ambassador to the United States, a highly-polished and sophisticated gentleman . . . and H. H. Kung and T. V. Soong. And, by God, the first thing I know is they embrace the man, so this business of knowing them wasn't any put-on."

Cohen set up private get-togethers with different members of the Chinese delegation. On May 9, at seven in the evening, Koo had a meeting with Cohen, Bronfman, Hayes, and others. "Rec. deputation of the Jewish Agency in Palestine," scribbled Koo in his diary, "headed by Dr. Stephen Wise, Pres. World Jewish Congress, urging suitable provision in the trusteeship to protect the partition and rights of the Jews in Palestine, so as to make it their National Home." Other meetings followed. On May 22, Cohen got Elath an interview with Koo, and on June 5, he introduced him to Hu Lin, editor of the popular Chinese newspaper *Dagong bao*. "Cohen described him as one of the key men in the Chinese delegation and a personal friend of Generalissimo Chiang Kai-shek's," wrote Elath. The group's lobbying of all the national delegates paid off. Palestine remained a mandated territory, and Article 80—nicknamed the "Palestine Clause" of the UN Charter—protected the rights "of any states or any people" within such lands. "I am not suggesting that if we didn't succeed there'd be no state of Israel," said Hayes. "I am suggesting it would have taken a great many years of hard slogging if it had ever gone into the trusteeship division."

While in San Francisco, Cohen became friendly with Elath. He let on that his biography was to be published soon in London, and told him that he wanted to have it translated into Hebrew. Cohen also spoke to Elath about business opportunities in China, and about exporting Jewish goods there. He wanted to set up deals for when he returned. "Your uncle is beginning now to plan to return to China but he does not know just when that day will be," Judith wrote to Evelyn in August. "Most likely in the very near future." Cohen and Judith also discussed moving to China. They decided that he would head off first and get reestablished, "being as China is no place for us to make our home just yet." When the time was right, Judith would join him. Cohen was so eager to get back to work in China that in preparation for his return he had new business cards printed up that read "General Morris A. Cohen, Chongqing, China."[10]

Japan surrendered in August. By October Cohen was on his way home. He stopped in Manchester first. "He came loaded with presents for everybody," said Cyril Sherer, who had just finished medical school and worked in a local hospital. "Silk stockings, chocolate, chewing gum, a bit of perfume, cigarettes, a bottle of whiskey. England was starving in those days." The family greatly appreciated the gifts. Cohen also saw friends in London. "I remember how excited I was to see him again, all filled out standing there as jovial and happy as I remembered him prewar," said Mrs. Gill. "He was wearing a huge black sombrero hat. It was wonderful to see him because when we said good-bye in the internment camp my last vision of him was that of a skeleton. We were very excited. We hugged each other, and we raced through Piccadilly. Of course it was quite natural that we were heading for the first Chinese restaurant in order to celebrate. I remember that, as we were going along, there was a chap just by the rails of the underground, who was selling black market cigarettes. It was almost by second nature after all the black marketing that we had in Stanley, that I remember Morris belting down the stairs to get hold of those black market cigarettes. I said, 'Where on earth are you going?' And he said, 'I am after those black market cigarettes.' I stood there and I laughed and I laughed and I laughed and I said, 'Dear Morris, the war is over. We are free.' "

He told all who would listen about his plans to move to China with his bride, his treatment in Stanley, and how the Chinese had asked him to assist in the negotiations between the once again adversarial communists and Nationalists; the two sides severed relations in early 1941 when Guomindang forces attacked communist troops. "There will be unification in China in the very near future—provided there is no outside interference," he said. As always, he promoted business, desirous of picking up some commissions before he headed east. "I also hope to get into contact with a number of British firms with a view to buying industrial equipment." He even told people that he was considering an offer from Hollywood to make a movie on his life, and of the difficulty he was having writing his autobiography: "Hard work. I'd make a better mule driver than a writer."[11]

In January he was off for China. The old country was a mess. During the war Chiang's government became more dictatorial and repressive. The Chinese economy suffered from runaway inflation. Rampant corruption alienated intellectuals and the urban middle class. Chiang meanwhile blockaded communist areas. Instead of engaging the Japanese, he husbanded his 3 million troops, rifles, and heavy equipment in preparation for his final battle with the communists. Officers treated their troops poorly. Officials subjected citizens to involuntary conscription. Conditions became so bad that in areas like Henan some citizens even sided with the Japanese.

The communists, meanwhile, with their headquarters in Shaanxi Province, prospered. Party membership grew from 40,000 in 1937 to 1.2 million in 1945. Troop strength stood at 900,000, and a People's Militia claimed more than 2 million members. Many joined the communists as resistance fighters in response to the brutal Japanese "three-all" policy of "kill all, burn all, destroy all." While the Nationalists abused the peasantry, the communists won their admiration and support by instituting social reforms, reducing taxes, and confiscating the estates of traitorous landlords.

When the Japanese surrendered, General Douglas MacArthur designated Chiang to accept Japan's surrender in China. Chiang then invited Mao to Chongqing for talks. Despite Chiang's orders for the communists to stay put, the removal of the Japanese threat only caused the two sides to rush to grab Japanese-held territories. To help consolidate Nationalist positions, the United States airlifted and shipped about half a million Chinese troops to new positions in the north and east.[12]

Negotiations between the two sides began. The communists and the Nationalists agreed to call a multiparty Political Consultative Council with the aim of drafting a constitution and planning a government. On November 27, U.S. President Harry Truman made General George C. Marshall his special representative to China. Marshall arrived in China in December 1945, and a committee of three consisting of Marshall, Zhou Enlai, and Zhang Zhizhong for the Nationalists met the following month. It called for the end of hostilities, and a joint American-Nationalist-communist–supervised cease-fire. The communists called for a coalition government before turning over troops and land, yet Chiang insisted that they had to give up their army first. After that, he promised that liberalization would follow.

On February 25, the two sides agreed to the integration of their armies, with the cutting of communist and Nationalist forces to a one-to-five ratio. Despite their obvious advantages, the Nationalists feared losing power. The civil war started up soon afterwards. By late 1946, Chiang's army was winning battles. But not all went as planned. As the Nationalist forces advanced, they overextended themselves. Soon the communists started offensive actions.

Cohen arrived in China in the midst of this turmoil. He headed to Shanghai and stayed with his friend Wu Tiecheng. On February 14, 1946, Cohen and Sun Zuobing, the son of Sun Fo, went to see the Canadian ambassador. "There is nothing of the typical Jew (if there is anywhere a typical Jew!) in his voice, and little in his build," wrote the ambassador. "His laugh is as big and as hearty as are his frame and his voice. I am not surprised that he had quite a compelling affect on Dr. Sun Yat-sen and his entourage." Cohen let it be known that he was back in China to do business. He came bearing his decades-old contract for the construction of fifteen hundred miles of railway. He hoped to revive it. "Cohen gave me a fresh side-light on the Communist situation. . . . Rather oddly, he makes the same suggestion that I did—namely, that a rift *may* appear in the Communist ranks. He says, in effect, that the real, original Communists were not bad fellows and that they and Chiang Kai-shek might easily come together; but with them are the remnants of a Guomindang Army that was sent to round up the Communists. Instead of doing its duty, it double crossed the Generalissimo and joined his enemies. There are the ones who are keeping trouble alive—particularly in the field. They know, Cohen says, that there is no forgiveness for them. They are hang overs from the old 'war lord' type."[13]

The following day, Cohen headed to Macao to renew friendships with some of Sun's relatives. When he returned to Shanghai, he set off to see Soong Qingling. At her home he met such guests as the photographer Henri Cartier-Bresson who was in China to cover the civil war for *Life*. Cohen also started making his rounds of the Jewish Club and the city's plush hotel lobbies. He had no work and few prospects. Cohen sat around in his blue suit, looked for contacts, and tried to get back on his feet. "It was the custom of independent merchants in Shanghai who had the time to spare to come in at about 11 o'clock in the morning to have coffee at the Palace Hotel," said Ben Levaco, a local merchant who exported hog and sheep casings. "A regular visitor there was this chap Cohen."

His talks with Elath in San Francisco prompted him to try to arrange some business between China and Palestine. In early April 1946 the Far Eastern Palestine Office of the Jewish Agency for Palestine in Shanghai invited Cohen over to talk. He regaled officials with his tales of life with Sun Yat-sen. Cohen informed them how he had discussed with Elath and the Jewish statesman David Ben-Gurion the problems and possibilities of Palestine-China trade. Most of all, he spoke about the importance of importing Palestinian goods, and how he wanted to help open up Chinese markets to Palestinian chemicals and fertilizers. He seemed a commercial godsend, and "a good national-minded Jew." The group promised to refer the matter to the Jewish Agency, and sought information for Cohen on which chemical products could be exported to China.

In September 1946 Harry Clark joined Cohen for an eight-month stay in China. The brothers-in-law shared a suite at the posh Cathay Hotel. Cohen floated in and out of town on his countless projects and spoiled Harry. "When we were together in China, he would say, 'Harry I am going up to Beijing for a couple of weeks and you carry on and I will call you.' We never talked money. He always had enough when he was with me. He would never in China let me buy anything in the way of food, because he said, 'There is no argument here. If you give me a hard time I am going to give you a hard time. Don't try to pay for any food. And don't ever have any argument with me on the street because to the Chinese it is a terrible disgrace to lose face.' "[14]

As Cohen renewed old contacts, he saw Judith Ben-Eliezer. She was making plans to attend the twenty-second World Zionist Congress in Basel, Switzerland, and hoped to be elected as a Revisionist Party delegate to the December 1946 meeting. She filled Cohen in on the recent activities of Betar, and he assisted her with her campaign, stumping with her as she went around Shanghai. He was a well-known celebrity among the Shanghai Jewish population, always drew a crowd, and his remarks went down well. "He came on the stage with me a couple of times and he was saying that Eretz Israel should be as a Jewish state like Britain is for the British," she said. Abraham Fradkin, who was stationed with the U.S. Army in Shanghai and lived in the French Concession, was visiting his girlfriend Eve in Hongqiao when Cohen and Ben-Eliezer stopped by for one of their talks. "She told me that there was a gathering where Cohen was supposed to speak to the refugees," said Fradkin. "So we went to hear him." A few hundred other people collected as Cohen discussed the end of the war and current conditions in the Middle East. "Morris stated that no honorable person cares for violence as such, but the conditions in Palestine provoked it, and that he took his hat off to those who struggled in the name of freedom, national rights and dignity," wrote Ben-Eliezer. Afterward, Fradkin went up to talk with Cohen. "We had about a ten-minute chat. We talked about Zionism, about the problems in Palestine, about the refugees coming to Europe from all the different camps. He was a very keen Zionist."

Other Jewish groups sought out Cohen's help. In Tianjin, the merchant Moshe Triguboff had been charged with selling goatskin, kid leather, assorted leather pieces, and used military goods to the Japanese infantry during the war. His accusers also said he gave the Japanese money. Despite the fact that his leather goods had been confiscated by the Japanese, and like everyone else in town Triguboff was forced to hand over his money to the occupying forces, the Tianjin court convicted him of conspiring with the enemy.

In February 1947 Leo Piastunovich, Zelig Belokamen, and other leading members of the Tianjin Hebrew Association wrote to Cohen. They pleaded with him to use his influence to help their townsman: "Knowing your interest in the matters of Jewish life in China, we beg to approach you regarding the court case of our member Mr. M. Triguboff—who as you probably know—has been convicted by the Tianjin High Court. . . . The Council of the Tianjin Hebrew Association takes the liberty to approach you to intervene with respective higher Authorities that the appeal of Mr. M. Triguboff may be taken up for re-examination in shortest possible time. . . . We hope that you shall not decline your support in this matter." Cohen went to Tianjin to meet Triguboff's family and the Hebrew Association members, and to discuss what he could do to help. Triguboff even reportedly offered him a $200,000 reward if he could secure his freedom. Cohen's contacts paid off and he succeeded in getting Triguboff a new trial and a change of venue. On appeal, the court reversed itself. Triguboff's freedom and fortune were secure. He was quite grateful, and one of Triguboff's sons wrote Cohen a letter of thanks. But gratitude went only so far when it came to money. Even after Triguboff got the amount of the reward reduced to $100,000, he refused to honor his debt.[15]

While he could help a few people, things just did not work out for Cohen in China. He had limited influence, could not find employment or collect moneys owed him. He had also been away too long from his new wife, and soon returned to Canada. Cohen brought back gifts, and the apartment filled up with Chinese furniture, rugs, and porcelains. He tried to arrange work closer to home, and traveled to Ottawa to see about picking up some information. "During that time 'Two-Gun' Cohen came in and out of Ottawa quite a few times," said Menzies, who was now head of the Far Eastern section of the Department of External Affairs. "We talked about his very colorful career as a bodyguard to Dr. Sun Yat-sen and also his later somewhat more questionable life as an arms agent with the various warlords in China. He told a very good story with many expletives. For a young officer this was real romance. He liked to live well and he liked to get as close as he could to the seats of power. In the small world of Ottawa at that time, why, anybody who was sitting on the Far Eastern desk seemed to have power, even if he was only a junior officer." The two lunched at the Chateau Laurier, and Cohen told Menzies of his current deals and bragged of his importance. "Morris was a great name-dropper to indicate the influence he had with certain people and routes to get things done. But I don't think he ever got his hands on any big deal that I ever heard of. I don't think anybody would have trusted him. He was a person of great interest because of his previous role in China and his name-dropping and the color that he could add to what was often a rather dull day at the office."[16]

With no jobs coming his way, Cohen worked in earnest on his autobiography. Four or five days a week, Rose Klyne came by his apartment after a full day of teaching school to help him chronicle his life. Cohen sat in his living room, smoked his cigars, and did what he did best, he talked, rattling off tales about his adventures. Rose's younger sister Ethel worked as a legal stenographer, and she also stopped by to take down verbatim what he said. His yarns lacked order. "All he did was repeat orally stories to me," said Klyne. "He just reeled off stories of which he had experienced and episodes in his life. He was just clearing his mind of everything that occurred to him and that he was involved in. I used to tell him, 'Your English is lousy, you know,' and he would kiss me. 'I know, I know, that is why you are here,' he said."

Judith took care of the literary entourage during Cohen's late-night Scheherazade impersonations. "Judith, after a day's work in the store downstairs, had us for dinner every night through that. Here was a girl that was running a business and then after that having two people yakking away and serving them dinner and being so gracious about it. Now if that isn't devotion to help him to success with the book, I would like to know what is. It took a long time before he poured out all these different stories."

With Ethel's typed-up pages, they then started organizing. "My younger sister worked hard. She typed up the stories so that I could read them and look at them and see where the hell do they belong." Cohen told so many disjointed tales and jumbled reminiscences that it took a lot to make sense of it all. "I don't know if I got it in perfect chronological order. I am not at all sure. Oh, did I have a time. There was no time sense in any of it. I had to find out where they belonged, what part of history went where, and so I read a couple of books on China. Mind you I knew something about China. At least I made it a little coherent. Also his grammar was not all that good. He was not an educated man by a long shot. Then I said, 'Take it in and give it to a real writer now.' I am sure the editor in England must have done some research and checked it. But I did the best I could."[17]

Cohen still needed his visa status in Canada extended, and in 1947 he once again told officials that he was employed by the Canadian government. Of course, they could find no proof of his employment, but they still let him travel. He took trips with Judith to the United States to see about work and to meet up with friends. In New York, he ran into Israel Epstein. "I saw him more than once in New York," said Epstein. "I met him in one of those hotels in midtown. He was starting to go back to China and he was engaged in some sort of trade connected with surplus. The army was selling off jeeps and things like that. He was some sort of go-between. He proposed to me that I would get rich quick on one of those things. He said just fill a suitcase or two with nylons and what not and you will be OK, but I wasn't into that kind of thing." Cohen also saw Emily Hahn. They did not have as pleasant a meeting. "He accused me of having maligned him in my book *China to Me*. And he was going to sue me," said Hahn. "He said his piece and I said, 'Go ahead. I don't think that what I did was so awful, but you will have to sue me.'" Judith witnessed their mild confrontation. "Judith was with him. I was surprised that he married. He seemed to be too rough. She didn't look very angry. She didn't seem at all downtrodden. They seemed quite pleased with each other, because they hadn't been married very long."[18]

In 1947 the United Nations approved the establishment of a Jewish state in Palestine. The Arabs opposed the plan, and further fighting erupted between the Arabs and the Jews. Fearing that the surrounding Arab nations would attack once the British left in May 1948, many Canadian Jews bought rifles, machine guns, mortars, airplanes, and other war surplus for shipment to Jewish Palestine. They packed the cargoes in crates marked "machine tools" and sent them via front organizations to the Middle East. Sydney Shulemson, the most highly decorated Canadian Jew to fight in World War II, actively worked to round up troops and weapons for Palestine. In the spring of 1947 the thirty-one-year-old Montreal native and his friends acquired lists of Jews in Montreal and Toronto who had recently served in the armed forces. They sent out a mailing inviting the veterans to meet. "From that we got a number of recruits that we then had to process and eventually sent to Israel," he said. Other like-minded groups formed across the country.

Soon afterward Shulemson heard that China had purchased from Canada two hundred De Havilland Mosquito bombers. The legendary plywood and balsa "Mozzie" had a resilient fuselage and Rolls-Royce engines, which made it so fast and maneuverable that the aircraft distinguished itself in its sorties against shipping and V1 flying bombs. "The Canadian government had a large number of them at the end of World War II," said Shulemson. "I remember reading that these had all been test-flown, reconditioned and then disassembled, crated, and shipped to China. It occurred to me that I had never heard if China had ever used them. I wondered whether it might be possible to acquire these for Israel. That could have comprised the whole air force."

Shulemson looked for a contact. He was friends with Harry Clark and asked Clark to introduce him to Cohen. Clark quickly obliged. "The next day I met with him and told him about my problem," said Shulemson. "I told him that we would like to acquire these for Israel. He was very pro-Israel. He turned to me and said, 'Get me the Chinese ambassador in Ottawa.'" When Cohen hung up the phone, he asked Shulemson, "Do you like Chinese food?" Shulemson said yes, and Cohen then told him, "Well, we are having lunch with the Chinese ambassador in Ottawa tomorrow." Shulemson could not go, but one of his colleagues traveled west with Cohen. Despite their efforts, nothing came of the plane deal. The Chinese government was too corrupt to be bothered. "Eventually General Cohen told me not to pursue it. The planes had never been uncrated, but they could not be sold. Apparently the people who arranged the exchange were more interested in exchanging Chinese currency for Canadian currency."[19]

It was not long before Cohen left Judith again and headed back to China. Upon his return, more of China's Jews sought his help. Following the war, the Chinese government forced Russians in China to apply for Soviet passports. They then "invited" them to return to the Soviet Union. Before heading west, the Russian government told them to buy up refrigerators, cars, and other consumer products. When the expatriates entered their homeland, officials confiscated the goods. While not wanting to move back home, Russian citizens also lacked confidence in the disintegrating Nanjing government, and feared remaining in China. Many tried to emigrate to the West. The Tianjin Jewish community asked Cohen to assist them in their escape. In late September 1947 the assistant British air attaché and the Canadian military attaché had lunch with Cohen. During the meal, Cohen broached the possibility of a group of wealthy Jews settling in Canada. "Their characters as described by General Cohen were superlative. In fact, so much so, it was really quite amusing," wrote a Canadian official. "General Cohen stated that these people desired to retire and that they felt that in two or three years an international war would disrupt their declining days if they remained in China. I informed General Cohen that the subject was not within my sphere and that presumably any such people would make application to the Canadian Embassy in the normal way."[20]

While Canada welcomed other groups, it still would not let Jews in. And if Jews could not emigrate to Canada or other nations, there was always Palestine. Betar kept active in Shanghai anticipating the creation of a Jewish state. Young people joined up. The group ran meetings opposed to British policy in Palestine, petitioned the United Nations and assorted heads of state, and even got Sun Fo to issue a pro-Jewish statement.

Many Zionists realized that they needed to exert more than political pressure on the British to force them to leave. Betar members by then had joined the Irgun, a dissident underground military organization. The group advocated armed reprisals against Arabs in Palestine, and taught self-defense as well as the handling of weapons. Eventually, the British government's anti-Zionist policy caused various Palestinian Jewish factions to form a united front against the British. They sabotaged bridges, railways, and patrol boats and raided police stations for weapons. In October 1946 they bombed the British embassy in Rome. When the British retaliated, the Irgun kidnapped and even flogged British officers. Worried that the British might not withdraw from Palestine on May 15, 1948, as promised, the Irgun decided to stage simultaneous attacks on British military sites around the world. The Shanghai group headed by Ben-Eliezer, Anthony Gaberman, Harry Marinsky, Samuel Muller, and Yaacov Liberman joined in the plans.

But to make the attack, they needed weapons for their new members to practice with. "It was essential for us to get weapons for training," said the Harbin-born Liberman, who arrived in Shanghai in 1940. "That was where Judy was able to reach 'Two-Gun' Cohen. He believed in and accepted that that was the only way to go about getting a State, and he was prepared to help us." Cohen procured for them M-1 rapid-firing carbines, small arms, pistols, .45-caliber Thompson submachine guns, as well as lots of ammunition. The raw troops then headed out to the woods for target practice. The club's two-story red brick building stood next to the Jewish Club, and the grounds became a training center, where the recruits tossed faux grenades to get the lobbing movement down pat. They even drilled inside their club building. "On the upper floor of the building, we insulated a large room for small arms target practice, and we hid our weapons under the stage of the hall which was used for meeting or performances," wrote Ben-Eliezer.

"We were quite busy," said the then twenty-year-old Muller who had received Irgun military training in Italy, Germany, and Palestine. "These were six hectic months," he said of the period in early 1948 when he met Cohen. "Morris used to love to drive around in Judy's blue Chevrolet. He loved to go out on our nocturnal excursions where we would have a new recruit wait for us on a corner. We would grab the recruit, put a bag over his head, and put him in a car. He would then be taken to some place where he would swear his allegiance."[21]

As Cohen and the others drilled their men, they prepared for their part of the joint attack. "The movement basically was an underground movement," said Muller. "We were sent back because the headquarters of the Irgun at that time didn't completely believe that the British would end their mandate on the fifteenth of May. The idea was to take international action." They had plenty of military sites from which to choose. "The British destroyers anchored in the Huangpu River were good targets for us," wrote Ben-Eliezer of the ships in Shanghai. "Prospective action was likewise contemplated against British warships in the Hong Kong harbor as well as the sea-drome there. The dry docks in Singapore were also under consideration." Members of the group visited the waterfront to examine river traffic and determine the logistics of an attack. They decided to use innocuous-looking sampans in their assault. "One sampan would contain a large quantity of high explosives. . . . Upon contact the fuse would set off the explosion. Each pair of sampans would approach the designated destroyer anchored in midstream, and, when close enough, the sampan with the explosives would be set to drift with the current to reach the proximity of the destroyer and be pulled by it. After making certain that the objective was accomplished, the second sampan with the men, and positioned some distance away, would then disappear into the night."

Cohen prepared the plans for the Hong Kong and Singapore excursions. "He furnished us with detailed sketches and methods," recalled Ben-Eliezer. "In the straits separating the two sections [of Hong Kong] was anchored a flotilla of British warships, and, nestling against the shore, was a navy seadrome. These were our targets. Entry to and departure from Hong Kong was so restricted the General suggested that the persons involved in this action take a torpedo boat from Canton . . . to cross over to Hong Kong. After completing their acts of demolition they could speed back to Canton." Cohen "knew the territory very well. He knew all the ways in and out."

The group also intended to send one hundred trained men from Shanghai, the United States, and the Pacific Rim area to Palestine along with a stockpile of weapons on board a decommissioned American Liberty ship. Such mass-produced merchant cargo ships could be bought for little money, and wealthy members of the Jewish community promised them the necessary funds. "These ships were available in the Far East at a very low cost having been discarded by the U.S. navy after the war," wrote Ben-Eliezer. "A former Shanghai Betari, who had served as Captain in the U.S. Navy in the Pacific during the war, offered his services to captain this ship." Stockpiles of weapons could also be had cheaply. "At that time you could for $100,000 buy a whole depot of arms and munitions," said Muller. "These were the leftovers of the U.S. army after they left the Philippines. They didn't take the stuff back. The idea was to come on a ship and take as much as we could. We were of course looking for mostly light weapons. We weren't going after tanks or artillery pieces. The take was mostly rifles, submachine guns and heavy machine guns. I think there was some talk of three-inch mortars." Cohen and sympathetic Chinese friends contacted members of the military, and arranged to buy rifles, guns, and machine guns from the Chinese army. "He was close to the government and they were looking leftways to what we were doing."

Yet, surprising all expectations, the British withdrew from Palestine as promised, and the group called off their planned attacks. Independence, meanwhile, brought an immediate invasion by Jordanian, Egyptian, Syrian, Lebanese, and Iraqi troops. The Irgun went ahead with plans for the shipment of volunteers and weapons from China. A similar shipment of nearly 1,000 immigrants, 250 light machine guns, 5,000 rifles, and a large amount of ammunition sailed from France on board the *Altalena*. On June 20, in the midst of the first Arab-Israeli cease-fire, the *Altalena* reached Israel's coast. The new provisional government of Israel demanded the ship and its cargo. The Irgun insisted on keeping 20 percent of the weapons for its own units, and refused to hand over the material. Israeli soldiers then went to stop the supplies from being unloaded. Fighting broke out and the *Altalena* sailed away. When the ship appeared off Tel Aviv, the Israeli army shelled the renegade vessel. The Irgun immigrants jumped overboard before their ship blew up. With the demise of the *Altalena,* the Chinese announced that they were stopping delivery of weapons to the Shanghai group since they did not want to be implicated if a similar incident occurred involving their weapons. The group also received orders to cancel their Liberty ship plans.[22]

Cohen headed back to Canada in 1948. During what was becoming his infrequent time with Judith, he tried to be a good husband. "On a return trip from China he brought the family monogrammed silk scarves," wrote Harry Clark of one such return. "He couldn't remember Mother's first name (Polly). Hers was initialed 'M' for mother." He also regularly sent his mother-in-law flowers, and spent time sitting around Judith's store. Cohen maintained his friendship with Samuel Bronfman, and took Bronfman's teenage son Charles to hockey games. He naturally stopped by to see his friend Samuel Vineberg. "The general was always in there and up and down Peel Street," said Vineberg's grandson Michael Vineberg. "He knew my grandfather very well. The two of them just schlepped me around everywhere. Morris was like one of the family. He was always jovial but always unpredictable." Cohen played with the young Vineberg, and taught him songs. "He used to make me sing some silly song about a sampan everywhere we went walking. He had a very blustery voice, and it was always with a laugh. He had this incredible jovial big laugh."

He took Vineberg to baseball and hockey games. "Every time I saw him I knew something good was going to happen. And it was not as though he was going to buy me something. Just something good was going to happen. It was going to be fun. He knew I was interested in sports. On a whim, he walked by and said. 'Come, come let's go for a walk.' I can remember being six-years-old and fairly thin. He took me into a sporting goods shop and bought me this humongous catcher's mitt. He would buy me hockey sticks and skates, hockey equipment, baseball equipment." He even bought the lad a cocker spaniel puppy named Happy.

The Cohens and the Vinebergs socialized. "We went out a lot together," said Cecil Vineberg. "We went out eating to restaurants. Morris used to take us to the Chinese restaurants that he knew about. He used to call up in advance, and say, 'Have a meal ready for us. We will be four people or six people.' That was all he had to say." One of Cohen's favorite places was the Nanking Café on Lagauchetière Street West, opened in 1946 by Tan Wong, a local GMD leader. The bodyguard of Sun Yat-sen was always welcome at the Nanking. When Cohen and his guests arrived, a huge feast awaited them in private rooms behind the restaurant's wooden partitions. "He knew everyone in the Chinese section of town," said Michael Vineberg. "We used to go to Chinatown with him and just walk into any restaurant and it was like he owned the restaurant. It didn't matter how crowded they were. He always presented a grandiose figure with his spats and his bowler hat and his cane. He got this kind of respect from people. They would just bring food that nobody ever heard of."[23]

While food was abundant in North America, meat and other supplies were still rationed in England. Cohen airfreighted ten-pound slabs of kosher smoked beef, huge sticks of salami, and other foods to his family in Manchester. "When the family knew a delivery had just been made, they used to come down," said Victor Cooper. "On a large platter, mother used to make a huge pile of sandwiches, eight, ten inches high, and everyone used to dig in." During the summer of 1948, Cohen brought Judith and Polly Clark to England on a vacation and showed them both a good time. "He brought her mother over as well on a holiday," said Sarah Rich. "She went swimming. She was quite with it. His wife was a charming person."

The whole Cohen family was in awe of him, and they looked forward to his visits. "Even as a ten-year-old I realized that the rest of the family paid a great deal of respect to what he said," said Sarah's son, Josef. "My mother absolutely adored him. I think we all did. I remember he came and visited the house and asked me what I wanted as a present. I said I wanted a cricket bat. Later that day a large package arrived from a sports goods store in the city center, which contained everything for two teams to play the game, not just a bat." While in London, Cohen also rang up Charles Drage to introduce him to Judith and to discuss the reminiscences that Drage was going to form into a book.[24]

Life with Cohen was unpredictable and lonely for Judith. Barely had he returned to the West before he was out the door again toward the East. "Judith had only one worry, but it was well founded," noted Drage. "Those who have once served China can never feel free of her service. Black though the outlook was, her future remained unpredictable." Cohen just could not stay away from China. He was not the only one trying to get back there. Following the war, countless people were trapped far from home. When the Soviet forces left China, they shanghaied Russian citizens. Joseph Gleiberman was one of the people they took against their will. He had emigrated to China from Poland before the war, and with the fall of Japan the Soviets threw him into prison and labor camps. In 1947 they sent him back to Poland. For a long time his wife, Dinah, and the rest of the family had no idea where he was, and were frantic to find him. When his relatives, Raya and Benjamin Litvin, learned that Joseph was in Poland, they sent him some money to tide him over. He could not, though, secure a travel visa to return to China. They then asked Benjamin Litvin's brother-in-law Muller if he could help, and Muller passed on a message to Ben-Eliezer, who gave it to the visiting Cohen.

"He was at that time in Shanghai, and we were told that he was going to visit for a few days to Tianjin," said Raya Litvin. "We asked him to come and to meet us and to have dinner with us so that we could tell him about Joseph." She arranged a Jewish feast. As a wedding present they gave Cohen a silver rickshaw, purchased with the last of their savings. "It was a beauty. If we could have given him much more we would have given him everything we had so that we could get Joseph back." Cohen had a filling dinner, showed their three-year-old daughter magic tricks, and discussed Gleiberman's fate. "I told him that we were terribly upset and that it was a tragedy in our family that Joseph was taken away. I told him exactly as I felt it. I was crying, and he was very much touched. He said, 'Don't worry, I'll try and get him back to you.' He promised me that he would really manage to get a visa for him to get back from Poland to China." Cohen pulled some of the few strings he had left and obtained the visa. "What he did, I don't know," said Gleiberman, "but I got information that General Cohen arranged with the Chinese embassy in Warsaw, Poland, to give me the visa. Then I went to the embassy and they said, 'Yes, you have the visa.' "[25]

By the time Gleiberman returned, the United States was propping up Chiang's regime, offering him military aid at fabulous discount prices. Despite this support, Chiang's prospects looked dim. Inflation continued, and little came in in taxes. To meet expenditures, the government ran off paper money, and sold gold and U.S. currency. The black market flourished.

Chiang's army was on the defensive. Military leaders were often incompetent, corrupt, and selected solely for their loyalty to Chiang. U.S. Major General David Barr best summed up the problem with Chiang's forces when he noted, "Their military debacles in my opinion can all be attributed to the world's worst leadership and many other morale destroying factors that can lead to a complete loss of will to fight. The complete ineptness of high military leaders and the widespread corruption and dishonesty throughout the Armed Forces, could, in some measure, have been controlled and directed had the above authority and facilities been available. Chinese leaders lack the moral courage to issue and enforce an unpopular decision." While Nationalist officers abused their troops, their communist counterparts had learned well the lessons of Sun Yat-sen's Whampoa Military Academy. Officers cared for their men and enthusiastically indoctrinated them in the purpose of their struggle. Morale was high and esprit de corps stressed.[26]

Civil order under the Nationalists broke down. "Shanghai's police meanwhile set up a 'security system' in which the city population was divided into three classes of secret listings under 'excellent', 'normal' and 'suspicious,' " wrote Randall Gould. "Illegal raids of the last category began." Nationalist troops freely stole. Even worse, troops and police acted like Bias Bay pirates and kidnapped people and ransomed them off. "They were searching for people who had money," recalled David Vardi, who owned a taxi company in Shanghai and was held for ten days by Chinese troops who treated him "like a dog." All the soldiers wanted was "money, only money, and my cars they took from me. We had seventeen cars, they gave me back one car. They took all the money from my safe box. They took everything." Police grabbed many innocent people. "They were arresting people especially toward the end," said Citrin. "The gendarmerie worked on its own. Someone was kidnapped by the gendarmerie, by the police, and we had to get him out. It cost money and General Cohen handled that. It was all done through him. It was a lot of money."[27]

In the midst of the fall of China, Canadian Pacific Airways sought to establish air routes to Asia. In January 1949 the firm's general manager, Grant McConachie, arrived in Tokyo to see about obtaining an operating permit to start service from Vancouver to Tokyo, Shanghai, and Hong Kong. To fly there, McConachie needed the approval of MacArthur, Chiang, and Sir Alexander Grantham, the governor of Hong Kong. Cohen's old Edmonton friend Wilfrid "Wop" May, now Director of Northern Development for CPA, came along. It took two weeks to get MacArthur's approval to operate in Japan. When they arrived in Shanghai, May tracked down Cohen to see if he could tap his influence. McConachie meanwhile worked his way through the Canadian embassy. The ambassador, Tom Davis, invited McConachie to a reception to meet Soong Meiling. By that night Davis reported that Chiang had approved their application. "It was the easiest permit I ever got, but the least fruitful," McConachie later recalled.[28]

There was no point in establishing routes to China, as Chiang continued to lose battles to the communists. By early 1949 the road to Nanjing lay open. The economy plummeted. The black market rate for U.S. dollars had increased by more than fifty fold, and in seven urban centers the United States Economic Cooperation Administration fed 13 million people. Chiang begged for U.S. help and negotiations with the communists. Citizens panicked.

In Shanghai, women and children descended on the quays in search of coal, scraps of wood, even grains of rice or wheat. When the authorities announced that they would exchange paper money for forty grams of gold per person, citizens rushed to their banks. "Hordes of people queued up before the doors of the banks on the Bund, some waiting for 24 hours to exchange their paper money," wrote Henri Cartier-Bresson of the disorder in Shanghai. "As pressure built up, the line looked like a human accordion, squeezed in and out by invisible hands. Given the panic and hysteria, the police acted with leniency. To control and prevent riots, they only splashed cold dirty water from puddles or prodded the people with the rods used to clean their guns. Even as I watched, the gold-hungry crowd grew into such a mass that the police were immobilized, their arms pinned to their sides."

Nothing improved, and on January 21, Chiang retired from the presidency, yet retained control of the GMD. Beijing soon fell. "Today's big event has been the grand victory parade signaling the formal take-over of the city," wrote Professor Derk Bodde of the events on February 3. "Of chief interest was, of course, the Liberation Army itself . . . what I did see, lasting about an hour, I counted over 250 heavy motor vehicles of all kinds—tanks, armored cars, truck loads of soldiers, trucks mounted with machine guns, trucks towing heavy artillery. Behind them followed innumerable ambulances, jeeps, and other smaller vehicles. As probably the greatest demonstration of Chinese military might in history, the spectacle was enormously impressive. But what made it especially memorable to Americans was the fact that it was primarily a display of *American* military equipment, virtually all of it captured or obtained by bribe from Guomindang forces in the short space of two and one half years."[29]

By April 1949 communist forces crossed the Yangzi. "On hearing the rumor that the Guomindang government was being evacuated, I rushed to the airport just in time to photograph the exodus of the Legislative Yuan whose deputies wore their colonial hats and carried tennis rackets as though they were off on a vacation," wrote Cartier-Bresson, who was in Nanjing that month. "One or two promised they would return but their voices lacked conviction. The Nationalists' capital was crumbling." Once they left, citizens ransacked the homes of the officials and plundered rice shops. At seven on the morning of the twenty-fourth, Cartier-Bresson saw the first communist troops come into Nanjing. "Four days after 'Liberation,' the silk-brocade weaving looms, Nanjing's main source of trade, were back in business and so was the rest of the town. It was the day of the Water Dragon festival. The streets were gay, with herb doctors displaying their wares, vendors selling cigarettes and linen. The street-rental library was open for business and the opera was playing to an audience full of People's Army soldiers."[30]

With communist troops in Nanjing sporting fountain pens as symbols of their freedom from illiteracy, people panicked in places like Shanghai. Cities collapsed, Wuhan on May 17, Xi'an on May 20, Nanchang on May 23, and Shanghai on May 27. On October 1, 1949, Mao declared the establishment of the People's Republic of China. Two months later, Chiang, the Nationalists, 2 million troops, and all the Nationalist gold stocks made Taipei in Taiwan their new capital. Both groups claimed to be the sole voice of the nation. Only one controlled the mainland.

ith the fall of China to the communists, GMD leaders split between mainland and Taiwan. Soong Qing-ling became a vice chairman of the communist Central People's Government. Li Jishen, who had been expelled from the Guomindang in August 1947 following his call for communist-Nationalist rapprochement, also became a vice chairmen of the government. Many crossed to Taiwan. There Wu Tiecheng became a presidential adviser and an appraisal member of the Central Executive Committee, while Chen Jitang retired. Others like T. V. Soong, H. H. Kung, and Sun Fo left for the United States and France.

More than just the Taiwan Straits divided Cohen's friends and associates. All he could do was shake his head over the political and social rift as he bemoaned the nation's state. "Morris' problem was that he refused to recognize the change," wrote Gerald Clark. "He kept saying that communism was an aberration, that the Chinese would never accept it, that the Guomindang would regain power." Yet the change was here, and he had to learn to accept it. Trying to slip back into the loop, Cohen continued his hours-on-end lounging in the lobbies of the Hong Kong and the Peninsula hotel. There he rested in a high-back upholstered chair, smoked his cigars, and waited to snag friends and strangers to regale them with his well-tuned stories. No work came Cohen's way. He also possessed little influence. His breezy, back-slapping ways and well-known attachment to Sun Yat-sen did not count for much in post–civil war China. When Clark was in town on assignment to report on the changes going on in the mainland, Cohen could not even arrange a visa for him. "He didn't have any business, really, at that point. It was all finished. He was trying to recoup contacts."

Hong Kong, like Cohen, was still recovering from the war. "I don't think he was different from most people in that sense," said Clark. "Hong Kong at that point was a real meeting ground for all kinds of expatriates who had been thrown out of China. It was a real mélange of people just trying to regain the past."[1]

As expected, with the communist takeover, Mao and his underlings quickly instituted sweeping changes. They nationalized most of the urban economy, confiscating much private and foreign property. Families lost their farms, houses, draft animals, farm implements, and surplus grain. The communists convicted former businessmen of crimes against the people and exterminated millions.

They did allow some private ownership. Industrial and commercial firms flourished in 1950 and 1951, but their good fortune was short-lived. Hoping to stir up the masses, weed out corruption, as well as eradicate real and imagined counterrevolutionaries, the government in late 1951 instituted the Three-Anti Campaign. Mao called for a campaign to wash out the poisonous remains of the former society. This quickly led to the January 1952 Five-Anti Campaign to ferret out bribery, tax evasion, theft of state property, cheating on government contracts, and theft of state economic intelligence. Investigations began on hundreds of thousands of party members. Workers denounced managers and owners. The government stirred up labor troubles in foreign enterprises and drained their capital. Businessmen were terrorized, forced to author autobiographies listing their past transgressions, and made to pay taxes and penalties for income they did not earn or crimes they did not commit. Many businesses went bankrupt. Hundreds of people committed suicide. Cities like Shanghai that the communist leadership perceived as bastions of capitalist sin were strangled. In the process the government netted $1.25 billion, stabilized the currency, restored the communication system, brought agriculture and industrial production back to near prewar levels, and consolidated police control.[2]

Seeing the transformation, Cohen started to realize that the new unsettled China differed greatly from the old one he knew. His own life was also in turmoil. He had become an inattentive, unsupportive, and often verbally abusive husband. When he was home, it was for but an instant. Cohen returned to Canada in the fall of 1950 via Israel and England. He had a gall-bladder operation the following spring, spending almost four weeks in the hospital. When he arrived at their new apartment on Ridgewood Avenue, Judith tended to his recovery. She meanwhile worked hard, opening a plush new clothes store in March 1951. He on the other hand did not bring in a salary. Their marriage predictably deteriorated. "Of course he should never have married," wrote Charles Drage. "He was always shooting off to Formosa, or to Red China for indefinite stays; he never wrote letters (as a matter of fact, in his later years he actually couldn't write at all) and communicated only by rather expensive trans-world phone calls." The strain started to show. "It was just a story of his expectation to go back to China after the war," said Clark. "He was convinced that the communists would be overthrown, or if not, at least his life would return. My sister had expectations, too, of going back with him."

Throughout, Cohen desperately needed money. No longer having the seemingly bottomless coffers of prewar Chinese officials from which to draw, he did not know how to cut back and save. He survived by borrowing from Judith. His extensive travels cost her a lot of money. "Big money. Big amounts," said a friend. "He didn't know how to cut down for a long, long time. When he had the money he would just give it to you as well as spend it himself. Very generous. When they had money all was fine. It is what later happened when he didn't have it. He wouldn't start at rock bottom, it was just against the grain. There was nothing for him. That changed him a lot. He was still not unpleasant. It couldn't be good. He was unhappy, too, living like a parasite."

Cohen continued trying different schemes to make a living. He imported liquor cabinets from England, but did not market them well. Harry Clark had export companies and franchises dealing with such materials as pulp and chemicals, and Cohen occasionally passed on tips to him. When the information led to a sale, Harry gave him a commission. Cohen's profits were small, though. He only made a few thousand dollars, and told Harry simply to give the money to Judith. "He was into some pretty big things in China, but he did not have means after he was captured in Hong Kong," said Harry. "I don't think he ever had any means again. As far as my sister was concerned, she received nothing." Cohen also tried to collect the money owed to him by Moshe Triguboff. He had saved the documents and letters relating to the trial and their agreement, and asked friends to track down Triguboff's family. He even sought legal advice to see if he could force Triguboff to pay his debt. This constant lack of money irked him: "Next time I'd try to wind up with a little more money," he quipped about his somewhat impoverished state. "It's a damn good thing to have in older life."[3]

At one point, Cohen tried selling Chinese antiques. Sonny Booth owned the S. Breitman Antique shop near Judith's store, and Cohen convinced Booth to take a few pieces on consignment. The lacquered furniture with its carved animals, fish, and serpents was not quite the type of merchandise that Booth carried, but he agreed to display the items. "He had brought back from China a lot of beautifully carved furniture," said Booth. "It wasn't all that old. It was probably twentieth century. It was beautiful carving, but very, very black and heavy. They were big, huge sideboards and buffets. We had it in the back room set up against a wall, and it stood pretty high, one on top of the other." Cohen asked a lot for the furniture. "He had a highly inflated opinion as to the retail value. I got the impression that this was his own furniture, that it was given to him by various people. We tried to sell it for him. We were doing him a favor more than anything else. He was a nice guy, a very charming man." After a few months, no one bought the pieces, and Booth returned them.

Cohen's lack of stability and income was especially hard on Judith. "I personally think that he wasn't making enough money for her," said Cecil Vineberg. "Judith had a very successful dress shop in Montreal, and the poor General, he didn't have much to go on. He had little deals coming in, a little bit here and there, but it wasn't enough." As one friend noted, Judith was "very painstaking, very devoted and very long suffering. He was going here and yon and certainly no comfort, no comradeship, no nothing. What was the use of going on like this. She wasn't so young anymore."

Besides taking money from Judith, he also started borrowing from friends in Canada, from officials, even from people like Francis Kendall in Hong Kong, for whom he had been best man. His monetary demands proved so excessive that Judith even started borrowing money for him. "She must have found that out from some of their friends," said the friend of Cohen's debts. "I am sure he had to borrow, because he was broke. She would be generous for a long time, because she was generous. And she wouldn't have wanted him to go around shabby or lacking in something. For a long time she bore it well. And then I suppose like all people would be he even stopped feeling worried about borrowing from other people. I am sure what really disturbed her is that he borrowed money from other people without the hope of paying back. That would hurt her sense of honor."

Nothing worked out. "He just didn't find a base in our kind of environment in North America, and it just began to peter out," said Gerald Clark of the deteriorating marriage. The tension showed. Cohen started throwing domineering juvenile fits, often without cause. Judith's family called such outbursts his "tantrums." Cohen greatly embarrassed Judith, and she became more and more distressed. During a vacation trip to Sainte Agathe with her family, Cohen caused a major scene by attacking another man in the train. In restaurants he abused waiters and even tossed around dishes when he did not like the service. Once during a family game of cards at his mother-in-law's apartment, Cohen flipped over the card table and started screaming. Judith and her mother fled the room in tears. The strain affected Judith's nerves, and she became anxious and depressed. "She would lose weight like crazy," said the friend. Judith saw Dr. Louis Lowenstein about her nerves. She even confided in him about her treatment at Cohen's hands. Her condition worsened. By 1951, she made numerous appointments with Lowenstein over a period of only a few months. He prescribed sedatives and rest.

Soon the breakup started. "He was living the life of an adventurer," said Judith's sister, Ruth Field. "They weren't living a normal life." By the early 1950s, Cohen moved out of their apartment and back into the Windsor Hotel. "In the end Judith (who was the nicest of women) naturally got fed up," wrote Drage. The split greatly upset Cohen. "I know he felt badly about it, very badly," said the friend. "He had nothing to lose and all to gain. She really was very patient and very kind. He didn't even know what this could be doing to her. He wasn't aware of it. He really was down and out. That is enough to drive anybody crazy." Others were not surprised that they separated. "He was caught on the rebound, and he had to go over so often to China," said Sarah Rich. "No, I couldn't blame her. It was difficult, and he promised to be over at a certain date for their anniversary, and he had to make the effort, and he came over."[4]

Conditions also continued to decline in China. At the end of World War II, Catholics suffered severe persecution. In August 1945 communists killed Trappist monks, and during the "Bloody Winter" of 1947–48 they massacred one hundred priests, monks, and nuns. With the establishment of the People's Republic, the 3,295,000 Catholics in China faced new hardships. In December 1950 the government's Triple Autonomy Movement tried to force Catholics to create a reformed national church without financial or spiritual links to Rome. Missionaries had to give up religious work. Police helped form Committees of Reform to seize control of churches. People made public accusations against the clergy and the faithful. Those who opposed the movement were gotten rid of. Protestants were likewise attacked.

When the government realized that the Triple Autonomy Movement had failed to break the spirit of the faithful, they started the mass arrest of influential Catholics. Conditions turned especially bad in 1951. The government accused church members of collaborating with American imperialists and working to sabotage the nation. During that year, the communists expelled the papal internuncio, Monsignor Antonio Riberi, and nine foreign bishops, imprisoned nineteen foreign and Chinese priests, placed more than three hundred other priests under detention without charge, hounded nuns, and forced 1,238 missionaries to leave the country. Nine-tenths of the nation's Catholic buildings and institutions were destroyed or confiscated and turned into offices, meetinghouses, granaries, barracks, prisons, and theaters.

Many of those thrown in jail did not have trials, and the communists subjected those receiving a hearing to humiliating show trials in front of "People's Courts." Nuns received especially harsh treatment, being accused of neglecting and causing the death of orphans in their care. Police confiscated their habits, rosaries, and crosses. Guards beat them with rifle butts. In mid-1951 a People's Court sentenced a French and a Portuguese nun from the Sacred Heart Orphanage in Nanjing to ten years imprisonment for neglect and ill-treatment of their wards. Four other nuns were convicted without a trial and expelled after having "confessed their guilt."

On March 19, 1951, the Chinese announced the arrest of five nuns from the Canadian Les Soeurs Missionnaires de l'Immaculée-Conception. The Chinese charged that from October 1949 to February 1951 the nuns willfully murdered and maltreated orphans, causing the death and disappearance of 2,116 of their 2,251 wards. The church vehemently denied the accusations, stating that the nuns had set up the orphanage for stricken children and those abandoned on the streets by their parents. When brought to them by the police and concerned civilians, more than 2,000 of the children were dying of hunger and disease. Only about 200 could be nursed back to health. "We have been established in Canton for nearly 42 years, tens of thousands of babies have passed through our hands and this is the first time our work has been discredited," said an official of l'Immaculée-Conception.

Upon hearing of the nuns' arrest, Cohen shot off a cable to Soong Qingling, asking her to use her influence on behalf of the nuns. "If Mrs. Sun gets the cable she will do everything that is humanly possible for the Sisters," he said. "In the cable I told her that I had known three of the nuns a great many years. It is unbelievable they are guilty of anything as charged. . . . They have looked after tens of thousands of children from off the streets, and have saved many, many lives over the years. I, myself, can vouch for that."

His efforts were much appreciated. Sister Marie de la Providence at l'Immaculée-Conception convent in Montreal wrote him: "We were agreeably surprised and deeply touched to notice that you have so kindly taken the defense of our five Sisters arrested in Canton on a charge of manslaughter." She and the others in the convent were subsequently relieved when Soong wrote to let them know that the nuns were not being ill-treated and that she would use her influence to secure their release.

Yet, despite Soong's actions, the Chinese badly abused the women. In early December, they received a show trial in front of 6,000 spectators. The court then sentenced Sisters Antonette Couvrette and Germaine Gravel to five years imprisonment and ordered Sisters Germaine Tanguay, Imelda Laperrière, and Elisabeth Lemire expelled from China. After their sentencing, the court forced the nuns to walk round the courtroom bowing and apologizing for their crimes. They then paraded the women through the streets of Canton. Crowds stoned and spat upon them. The communists shuffled the three ordered expelled through various prisons before kicking them out of the country in early March 1952. When they arrived in Hong Kong, Sister Germaine Tanguay vehemently denied the charges and told the press how they had tried to save the newborn children. "Even with the best of care, most of them could not be saved because they had been delivered and handled by unsterile midwives. Mothers of many were opium addicts. . . . Many of the babies were premature because their mothers bore them while doing heavy coolie work. Many had congenital syphilis. Others were in the advanced stages of malnutrition and starvation."[5]

To bring about his socialist paradise, Mao believed that the compassionate, like the sisters of l'Immaculée-Conception, had to be done away with. Dreaming of even greater advancements, he focused his first Five Year Plan on industrial production. By 1957, workers constructed 2,532 miles of new railway. From 1953 to 1957 the annual rate of increase in the GNP was 7 percent. Steel production shot up 325 percent from 1952 to 1957, coal production rose 200 percent, and cities mushroomed as peasants streamed in looking for work.

Efforts to stride ahead of the West, though, failed. Product quality was shoddy. The plan all but ignored agriculture. Believing that farm consolidation and mechanization would create greater harvests, China in 1953 experimented with collectivization. Mao soon called for large cooperatives based on the Soviet kolkhoz. He hoped that the streamlined agriculture would provide for better marketing, mechanization, irrigation, and flood control. The government foolishly instituted changes too rapidly. Surpluses went to pay for urban industrialization and to feed the legions of factory workers.[6]

Cohen moved permanently to England in the early 1950s. He stayed with his sister Leah when in Salford and at the Mayfair Hotel in London; the Chinese reportedly paid his hotel bills. He tried to keep in touch with Judith. "I know that he wrote letters to Judith," said the friend. "He was very hurt about it. Of course he wasn't really justified being hurt. But he was very fond of her. He loved her and the loss he realized was a great one for him. I think he wrote her some very sad letters. I recall that she'd tell me once and a while. But I didn't pry. I was feeling sorry for both of them." His family knew of their problems, and Cohen accepted responsibility for the breakup. "He told us that it was no life for her. He couldn't blame her, but he told her when he married her that he would be traveling always," said Sarah. "It was the traveling. He said that did it. He kept going backwards and forwards to China from Canada. She didn't have much of a life really."

By the spring of 1952, he was again on his way to Asia. Cohen visited Taiwan during the summer, and even arranged a meeting with Chiang on June 6. After the get-together, he told the press that Chiang confidently announced that his forces would soon retake the mainland. The trip to Taiwan meant more hotel sitting. Henry Lieberman, a correspondent for the New York *Times*, stayed at the Friends of China Club in Taipei and saw Cohen constantly lounging around the facility. "I saw him practically every day," he said. "He would just hang around the lobby. I got tired of listening to his stories. In fact he was a goddamn pest. He was always the hero of these stories. To hear him talk he was responsible for the whole Sun Yat-sen revolution. So far as I could make out he had a minor role in the whole thing. He was just a .38-caliber bore. I certainly didn't socialize with him. I had to endure his stories, and endure is the word. I could not avoid him."

Judith meanwhile initiated a divorce. "It just was one of those things," said Frances Pascal. "People fall out of love." By 1953, Cohen was back in England and wrote to Rose Klyne's lawyer brother Cyril Schwisberg for legal advice. Schwisberg let Cohen know, "I am sure you understand in this matter what my own sentiments are, but in writing you, I am merely an instrument of Judith's will." They tried to work out the mechanics of the breakup. Cohen unhappily learned that in Canada the only ground for divorce was adultery. "That, of course, is out," wrote Schwisberg. But since Cohen was from England and was currently living there, the divorce could be processed in England, where he had other options for grounds besides adultery, such as desertion or cruelty.

In London Cohen and his brother Leslie started a furniture and carpet business. They opened a shop, and imported chairs and desks from China. As with the furniture that Sonny Booth tried to sell, no one bought the pieces. "A lot of houses at the time were very small. Some of this furniture was enormous. You needed a large house to show it off," said Leslie's son, Michael. After a while, the store closed. Cohen then tried to sell Chinese antique furniture and altarpieces from Chinese temples to friends and acquaintances. He likewise had little success.[7]

By early 1954, all appeared grim for Morris Cohen. He was out of cash and needed somehow to jump-start his career. Then, after years of preparation, his biography, *Two-Gun Cohen* (also issued as *The Life and Times of General Two-Gun Cohen*), hit the bookstores. His Montreal late-night musings compiled by Klyne, with information gathered in Canada and China by Gerald Clark, had been turned over to his old friend Drage, who bracketed Cohen's perky chatter with breathless empty prose about Two-Gun's legendary accomplishments. It was an amazing concoction. No one involved in the creation of the book seems to have questioned any of his outlandish tales. Since Cohen told unsequential and unrelated stories to Klyne—which she then valiantly tried to organize—the book rambles and lacks a historical sense or footing. Much like a postwar Soviet map of Russia, the book did not reflect reality. Instead, it twists and reinvents major segments of his history. As Lieberman and countless consulars had noted for decades, Cohen consistently placed himself in the center of the action, giving himself credit for events that he had little or nothing to do with. *Two-Gun Cohen* is essentially a piece of historic fiction.

Each page, like many of the stories that he relayed to the press over the preceding thirty years, contained inaccuracies and outright falsehoods. For the Cohen glorified in the book, all was possible, nothing was unsolvable, everyone loved him. All that was needed was a wink, a nudge, a slap on the back, and a round of pink gin. George Sokolsky might have overstated the fact, but he was not far off when he said, "He was not a big dealer and made no money, and rather was a rum figure around the place—unfortunately, because he could have done a lot of good had he not been what he was." As the Hong Kong *Standard* noted a year and a half following the book's publication, "When the Nationalists were in power on the mainland, 'Two-Gun' was a familiar figure in the entourage of the famed and powerful, but few knew whether or not to take him seriously."

But enough people took his stories seriously for them to become widely circulated. His tales were voluminous. In the book, he says that he was born in London. He brags that he could outquote seminary-educated Canadian ministers from the Bible. He only mentions one jail term in Canada—and fails to refer to the other ten-odd arrests. That pickpocketing confinement, Cohen claims, was on trumped-up charges; he says he only spent four weeks in jail and was eventually cleared of all charges. In actuality, he rotted in a Prince Albert jail for one year. Cohen says he met Sun Yat-sen in Canada, yet while Sun traveled across the country to raise money for his planned revolution, Cohen still languished in prison. He goes into detail about being badly wounded at the front in Europe, when he simply succumbed to a bad case of arthritis of the jaw. In the interest of self-promotion, he continued to use the title of sergeant following the war, when upon discharge he only held the rank of sapper. And since the book was written as his marriage was deteriorating as well as to stifle questions and curiosity about his frequent romantic liaisons with women—many of them of questionable character—he fabricates a story about falling madly in love with a Jewish girl in Edmonton.

Cohen boasts that he left China for America in the early 1920s to track down the pilots Harry Abbott, Arthur Wilde, and Guy Colwell and enlist their help in starting the Chinese air force and building the *Rosamond*. Abbott, though, arrived in Shanghai months before Cohen ever set foot on Chinese soil. Cohen goes on to claim that the government made him a general following Sun's death. Yet in actuality he had started telling people that he was a general prior to Sun's death. It was not until 1931 that reports circuited in the press that the Chinese had made him a brigadier general, and it was not until 1935 when the Chinese granted him the honorary title of Major General.

Following the destruction of the Canton Commune Uprising, there was a fear that the Central Bank of Canton's silver deposits might have been stolen by the communists. The Chamber of Commerce went to inspect the burned building so they could end speculations and stop the downslide of Cantonese currency. Bank officials did not want them to see the vaults, and Cohen claims in the book that he had to delay the members until the bank's director could think of how to handle the problem. In a typical passage of *Two-Gun Cohen*, he tells how he met the businessmen outside the bank and distracted them by chatting about the history of the institution and the beauty of the building. When he ran out of things to say, he began reciting the *Richard III* Israel Ellis forced him to learn back at Hayes Industrial School. The Chamber of Commerce listened politely and somewhat dumbfoundedly as Cohen stood on the smoldering Canton battleground and quoted Elizabethan passages about the final days of the War of the Roses and the rise of the Tudors. "Once you start Shakespeare you find that you can't damn well stop," he said. According to Cohen, his delaying tactics worked, and the director soon arrived and calmed the situation. Yet in reality, Cohen did not spout Shakespeare or have to entertain the Chamber of Commerce. It was an outright fabrication. The officials were simply held up as bank employees delayed their inspection by not producing the proper keys. Soon it got too late, and the businessmen left in disgust.

When it came to the problem of cleaning out the pirates in Bias Bay, Cohen boasts that he helped end the reign of the brigands: "We managed to corral most of the pirates either on land or sea. They put up surprisingly little fight. We took about seventy-five of them back to Canton where they were tried and condemned in batches of ten at a time." But efforts by the Chinese to combat piracy were minimal, and the pirates continued to be a problem. He fails also to mention that stories of valuable lists of pirates being handed over to the British proved apocryphal, since the names presented were essentially useless. In the book he does talk about his munitions purchases, but underrates his commission at 2.5 percent. In reality he earned a more hefty 5 percent. Sometimes he demanded more.

Following Li Jishen's arrest in 1929, Cohen says he visited Sun Yat-sen's mausoleum in Nanjing. There he met Ma Xiang and tried to arrange for a commando-style raid to free the marshal. But when Chiang had Li arrested, Sun's body still lay in Beijing, 550 miles to the north. And while Cohen was invited to Sun's reinterment two months later and did accompany his body down from Beijing, he was not "Marshal of the Diplomatic Corps," acting as the head of the delegation of foreign dignitaries, busily arranging dignitaries "in an order of march for the funeral procession." He was just one of a small group of foreign guests, and relegated to tending to a few westerners. The tales are countless. With the book's publication, Cohen secured his legend.[8]

Yet, even though Cohen might have been a blowhard, he was genuinely devoted to China and the memory of Sun. He went out of his way to make sure that others knew of Sun and learned of his accomplishments. Around the time of the book's publication, renovations began on the communist Chinese embassy in London. In the building's attic stood a shrine to Sun where the Manchus held him prisoner in 1896. The room still contained the original iron bedstead, broken chair, and barred window from the time of his captivity. Cohen and other friends of Sun feared for the sanctity of the site. They wanted the communist government to preserve the room, and perpetuate Sun's memory. When Cohen visited the embassy he told the consular of his concerns for the shrine. "He assured me that the room in which Dr. Sun was imprisoned would be maintained as a memorial in its original state," Cohen reported following his visit. Such an act, Cohen said, showed the mainland's recognition of Sun as a "stepping stone" to China's peaceful unification. "Although I am a member of the tribe of Israel I am not a prophet of Israel, but it is my belief that China will be unified a great deal sooner than the world at this moment believes."

While personally aligning himself with Taiwan, Cohen would not publicly choose sides in the split: "I am definitely refraining from taking part in this civil commotion. I have too many friends on both sides. . . . I want to maintain my neutrality, because some day I may be in a position to bring about a better understanding between the two sides." He repeated these sentiments wherever he went. During a visit with Rose in Salisbury in March 1954, he told a reporter that China was going through trying times, but felt that the country would right itself. "There is more going on inside China than the public know, and her people will do what they think is best."[9]

After the biography appeared, Cohen headed to Geneva, where Zhou Enlai attended the Indochina conference to end the French-Indochinese war. Cohen arrived in late April, bearing a copy of his biography, which he wanted Zhou to pass on to Soong. He contacted an official about arranging an interview. "I don't think Zhou will remember me," Cohen humbly said. "He was just a young student when I knew him." While there, Cohen expressed a simplistic way to negotiate an end to the hostilities between the communists and the Nationalists. "The only way to settle disputes is to go straight to the people and put the guns on the table. I believe the Communists want to enjoy life as much as we do. It just needs somebody to get the top men together and let them know the way to go about it."

He returned to Manchester soon after. Cohen and Drage then set out promoting the biography, having lunch with groups like the Anglo-Jewish Association. He also stopped by his alma mater to speak to the recent class of wayward boys. "He would come for tea," said headmaster Harry Cohen of the visit. "I would gather the boys together so that he could talk to them." Best of all, with the publication of the book, the press allowed him to pontificate on world events. But all he generally came up with were oft-repeated statements like "Politics are just *poisonalities*. Tell me who's behind a mob and I'll tell you what they're going to do. Tell me who's heading a movement and I'll tell you what's going to happen to it. If the guy's dumb, it'll break up on internal squabbles; if the guy's yellow, it'll fade out anyway. If he's smart *and* tough, someone's going to get hurt." Or when asked what he learned in life, he was quoted as saying, "Three things. First keep your mouth shut. Next, good things come slowly. Third, do unto the other guy as you'd like him to do to you."

Cohen loved receiving the attention he craved and felt he deserved. In 1954

Tina Dunn was on vacation with her parents in Blackpool, England. Cohen stayed at the same hotel. "He was very, very full of himself. He knew he was a sort of a celebrity and all he needed to do was click his fingers and people would come running," said Dunn of Cohen's manner. But it was not only nineteen-year-olds who noticed Cohen. Government officials started to take more of an interest in him because of the publicity surrounding the book. The Office of High Commissioner for Canada in London even contacted him at the Mayfair, and asked him "to drop into Canada House to talk about the Far East in light of your recent stay there."[10]

During that summer, his nephew Victor Cooper married in Manchester. Cooper and his bride, Sonia, arranged to take a train from Manchester to London and then catch a plane to northern France for their honeymoon. The day after the wedding, the newlyweds rushed to the station. There they were to meet Cohen, who was also traveling down to London. "We dashed onto the platform," said Cooper. "We had booked seats, but we had booked reserved seats in third class. We were in our compartment and there was a little fellow sitting in the corner." Cohen came into their car. "My uncle said, 'Come along to my compartment in first class.' The train was rather crowded and this fellow mumbling away, 'It is not right. If someone wants to sit on those seats, those are reserved, and you have gone elsewhere into another compartment, nobody will be able to use those seats.' So my uncle said to him in his booming accent, 'Get lost, small change, or I might spend you.' This fellow just sank into his seat and turned away."

Speech making and promotion of the book continued. A few year's earlier, the treatment of Catholic nuns and the religious in China had horrified him, yet he loved to note that "China is the only nation that has never persecuted the Jews. It is the only country that has ever assimilated our people, the reason being that it has always granted freedom of thought and of religion." His pronouncements on China started to change. While in the past he viewed the communists as "a poisonous, dangerous growth," he started speaking less harshly of the regime that was not going to be so easily dislodged from power and those he now needed to court. On March 1, 1955, Cohen spoke in Manchester, and somewhat wistfully noted that little fundamental difference existed between the principles of the Chinese communists and of the Guomindang. If only "the brains of China" could get together "irrespective of what they call themselves" and take the best principles of both parties. Cohen told the audience that he knew Mao and that he was "an idealist and a very honourable man," and that if he was able to carry out the manifesto that he issued when he came to power, it would be "a lesson to the universe." On Chiang, Cohen said that he was a very good soldier and at his best in adversity, and defended his military record during World War II.[11]

The talk of the divorce went on. "It took a long time for Judith to decide to divorce," said the friend. "Nobody here blamed her one iota. Nobody that I ever heard of ever said 'Why did she do that.' It took a long time and he wasn't here anyway, most of the time." Cohen and Judith legally separated in 1953. "I can no longer go on being neither married nor unmarried as in nearly nine years of married life he has been away more than half the time," Judith wrote. "That and a few other things finally made up my mind to make this decision. . . . I bear no ill-will towards Moisha. The worst I can say is that he was not a man who should have married—me or any one else. My family and I are fond of him—you know how wonderful he was to Mother—but they realize that I cannot go on this way any longer. He just never understood nor undertook the duties of a married man."

Cohen meanwhile delayed the divorce. "Its effect was disastrous," wrote Drage of Cohen's breakup with Judith. "Morris turned overnight from a genial, lovable old rough-neck into a morose, suspicious old horror. It is, for me, a very painful memory." Judith, her family, and lawyers wrote to him numerous times, but he did not answer them. "I am hoping your failure to reply is due to your consistent dislike of writing altogether and not a willful denial of co-operation," Judith wrote him. "Surely you must realize that my decision concerning us entails no malice nor ill will towards yourself—on the contrary—no matter what transpires, I hope that I will always regard you as a very good friend and I cannot bring myself to believe that you will do anything that would prove to the contrary." For the divorce to move forward, she needed him to return to Quebec, and understandably wanted to help him make the trip. "I realize that at the moment you may not have the necessary funds for this purpose and considering the end in view, I would cheerfully pay all expenses that the return fare and your stay here would involve. I know you are understanding and big enough to do the right thing and Morris, I count on it."

Steps for divorce finally started in seriousness soon after Judith swore an affidavit on March 4, 1955. In it she stated that Cohen had left his matrimonial home, acted cruelly, and had been unkind to her. He also had a violent temper, flew into fits of rage, abused her and her family, and threatened her with violence. All his actions made her quite ill. Cohen gave his own affidavit on June 23 at the office of his solicitors, Rowley Ashworth & Company, in London. And while he admitted to desertion, he denied the charge of cruelty, and asked that the court reject the petition.

On July 16, Judith sailed from New York to England aboard the SS *Liberty,* as part of a monthlong business trip to Paris and elsewhere in France and England. On the twenty-eighth, she visited her London solicitors, Barnett Janner & Davis, and swore an affidavit. She found it difficult to get away, Judith told them, but she wanted to put the divorce in order so she would not have to return to England. Her family had the unhappy task of testifying in the case. Harry was vacationing in Cannes and gave a deposition in Manchester on August 27. Others testified too. Once that was done, the divorce went quickly. Cohen was living at the Mayfair Hotel, and initially planned to defend himself. But when the case was called in London on December 16, there were no objections. Judith won a decree nisi, the penultimate phase of the divorce, for cruelty. On January 31, 1956, their marriage officially ended.[12]

Cohen did not wait around for the court to finalize the dissolution of his marriage. By the fall of 1955, he was making plans to return to China. On October 3, he received an invitation from Huan Xiang, the Chinese Chargé d'Affaires in London, to attend a reception at the embassy for the sixth anniversary of the founding of the new regime. Huan, possibly at the insistence of Soong, asked Cohen if he wanted to visit Beijing. He jumped at the idea, but told Huan that he would only go if the Chinese picked up his expenses. By late November, they extended him a full-paid invitation.

Cohen then contacted the U.S. embassy and told the Americans that when he exited China he would gladly report on the "true state of affairs" in China. The embassy staff was not that impressed either by him or his offer. "Discussions with him take the form of a disconnected monologue, dull and opaque for the most part, but occasionally illuminated by a casual quote from Borodin or Galen, or even Dr. Sun himself," wrote Arthur R. Ringwalt, the first secretary in the American embassy in London. "His present address is the Mayfair in the West End of London, a far from inexpensive hotel near Piccadilly. There seems to be little question, however, that he is in financial straits and that he hopes, through his visit to Beijing, to redress his fortunes. He seems to feel that he continues to enjoy the good-will of Mme. Sun Yat-sen, and perhaps he does. Although he is said still to be a member of the Guomindang, he claims to have friends on the mainland as well as on Formosa and to have refused to identify himself with one side or the other. He professes that his objective is to serve China by promoting an understanding between Beijing and Taipei. Conceivably he would be willing to work for both capitals." As an inducement for his offer, Cohen told Ringwalt that he was not planning to discuss the trip with the British or Canadians. "If he does get into contact with the Consulate General, it may be desirable to listen a while to what he has to say, especially with regard to such alleged intimates of his as Mme. Sun, Li Jishen and Cai Tingkai, but it is strongly recommended that members of the Consulate General *not* lend him any money."[13]

By the time the court had issued Judith her decree nisi, Morris Cohen was already back in China.

CHAPTER 19

*I*n late 1955 reports circulated of possible negotiations between
the Nationalists and the communists. Rumors even surfaced of the two
sides settling their differences. Zhou said that he would welcome discussions with
Chiang and offered him the title of Marshal if he surrendered. In Hong Kong talk
of a possible rapprochement centered around the journalist Cao Juren. Receiving
encouragement from Beijing, the anti-communist and anti-Guomindang Cao stated
that there was no future for an independent Taiwan. He wrote to Chiang's son,
Chiang Ching-kuo, to try to start a dialogue between the opposing sides, noting
that "in this time of emergency, I have something important to tell you." Cao even
implored Chiang, "Don't let this timely opportunity slip away."

The coincidence of the unsubstantiated reports proved quite fortuitous for Cohen, who needed something to take his mind off of his divorce. He landed in Hong
Kong in mid-December, and on the fifteenth he slipped into the mainland. News
emerged that he had arrived in China on a secret peace mission. The press quickly
lapped up the story of the sixty-eight-year-old Cockney Jew setting out to do what
others had failed to accomplish, bringing the two warring sides back together. *Time,
Newsweek,* the New York *Times,* the Hong Kong *Standard,* the *South China Morning
Post,* the Manchester *Evening News,* and other publications picked up the story.

Reporters had only scant leads on Cohen's activities. They even called on Judith,
who said that she was not aware of his movements, but was sure that he was working
for peace. "Close associates of the 'general' said he was 'on his way back to the old
country' and one intimate friend said Cohen had confided in him that he had been
invited to Beijing," wrote the *Standard.* "Cohen's visit to the Red China capital may
not be without considerable significance because it is known that he holds the view
that there are elements in the Nationalist regime [that] would not be adverse to
reaching some sort of understanding with Communist China."

As he traveled, Cohen openly hinted to friends that he was off to Beijing with the blessings of Taipei's leaders. "I may be able to get them together," he said in reference to his peace efforts. His old confidant, money lender, and SOE buddy Kendall even visited the U.S. consulate in Hong Kong to spread information on his visit. "Mr. Kendall said he asked Cohen whether Taipei knew about the trip," wrote U.S. Consul General Everett F. Drumright. "Cohen's reply was that he was making the trip with Taipei's 'knowledge and consent.' Mr. Kendall then inquired whether, in his words, Cohen was up to his old tricks as a go-between, to which the latter replied that 'this could be the case.' He said that he planned to remain indefinitely in Beijing if this proved feasible and that he would accept a position as an adviser to the Chinese Communist Government if one were offered to him. . . . Cohen also had some ideas about being able to do business in Beijing. . . . Mr. Kendall warned that it would be a mistake to underestimate the man. His impression was that Cohen, at least in his own mind, was probably proceeding to Beijing in the hope of acting as a bridge between Taiwan and the Communist regime."

Despite letting slip tidbits about his purported mission, Cohen assumed an air of secrecy about his movements. But just to drive home the image of a diplomatic wheeler-dealer, when Cohen set off for China he listed his occupation as "adviser to the Nationalist Government." The Nationalists denied that Cohen carried any "peace formula," calling the countless reports "too ridiculous to be dignified with a formal statement." Even Chiang Ching-kuo had enough of the various stories of rapprochement. He denounced them, saying "the rumors published this week are malicious fabrications. Communists are liars and devils. You cannot talk with the devil. It is my ardent belief that to solve the Communist problem, the only way is to eliminate Communism." Others quickly started to dismiss the rumors. "They realize that 'Two-Gun' is one of the China-coast's smoothest operators but believe that it would be the purest of fantasy to believe that he would be asked by anyone in authority in Taiwan to handle any contacting job with the Reds," wrote the *Standard*.[1]

"People were willing to make up romantic mysteries about him," said Israel Epstein of Cohen's masterful public relations campaign. The reports intrigued Cohen's fellow Stanley inmate Norwood Allman, with whom he did not get along: "He did not like me too well as I would never let my clients accept his 'assistance' even for free." After reading numerous stories on Cohen's activities, Allman decided to canvass a number of Cohen's American, British, and Chinese acquaintances to find out their thoughts regarding his reputed peacemaking overtures. None were flattering. According to the Americans: "Cohen has had no publicity for some time and probably needs to put his 'five per cent' moniker to work. So many trade missions have visited Beijing in the past two years it would be just like Cohen to constitute himself a one man trade mission from Canada in the hope of picking up a few orders. He probably will tell Zhou Enlai that he alone prompted the Canadian Government to urge Red China's admission to the UN. Maybe the only reason he did not also claim to be an emissary from Canada is that he wants to return to Canada."

"Well anyone who knows Cohen knows that he does not need any appointment from Chiang, or from anyone else, to speak for them," said the British. "For years he has claimed to speak for all members of the Guomindang especially if he could collect a commission. He frequently butted into negotiations between foreign firms and the Provincial and National Governments for contracts and insisted upon a commission on successful contracts whether he actually influenced the contracts or not. It is incredible that anyone would send a windbag like Cohen anywhere for anything."

Even the Chinese agreed: "Cohen is just trying to be sensational and mercenary. He probably told some naive, or maybe one not so naive, newspaper man in Hong Kong one of his tall tales and the latter relayed it to the London newspaper which gave publicity to the story which would of course please Cohen and might help him to sell something to the Reds. This kind of story would also be useful to the Chinese Reds as it would help to discredit the National Government and spread confusion about them in non-Red countries. Since Canada has been urging Red China's admission to the UN Cohen no doubt saw and seized an opportunity to ride on this wave."

"Strange things do happen in China," wrote Allman after gathering the responses, "but all of his acquaintances in New York who were canvassed claim that if he really has been authorized to speak to the Reds for anyone in authority in Taiwan it will be strange indeed. They all say this sounds more like another 'five per cent Cohen' operation."[2]

Despite the image he wished to project, Cohen basically went to China to see Soong. He would not miss a chance to see her, and waited for her to return from an extended tour of India and Burma. "Morris just worshiped Mme. Sun Yat-sen," said Gerald Clark. "She was a venerable old lady then." He also wanted to see old friends and to drum up business, telling people that he worked for a consulting engineer in London specializing in the erection of cement plants. But to get business he had to stay in the sort of limelight that rumors generated. On December 20, Cohen visited the British embassy in Beijing to try to keep the rapprochement rumor alive, and therefore make himself appear as an important diplomatic force. " 'Two gun' Cohen called here today and we had a long talk," wrote a British embassy staff member. "He dramatises everything and it is difficult to keep him to the point, but I think that it is clear that he has not come here with any mission from the Nationalists. . . . He still calls himself a Guomindang party member and claims that he has no sympathy with the Communists. He himself took the initiative in getting in touch with [the] Chinese Embassy in London and is now here as [a] guest of [the] China Committee for World Peace. He expects to see Mao Zedong, whom he knew in the old days, and intends to report to him on the attitude of overseas Chinese and of the Chinese in Formosa. He thinks that Chiang Kai-shek is ready to retire and that most of the Guomindang are prepared to do a deal with Beijing provided a face-saving formula can be found. He thinks he can help here with finding the formula."[3]

While in China, Cohen lived comfortably and well courtesy of the Chinese. He took a trip through Manchuria, and made other visits to the British embassy. "I enjoyed meeting him, since he is clearly a rascal of some distinction in that line, but everything he said strongly confirmed John Addis's impression that he has not come here with any mission from the Nationalists. . . . Like so many other visitors, he has been deeply impressed by what he has seen here," wrote C. O'Neill of Cohen's metamorphosing view of communist accomplishments.

> So much so that in describing his impressions he continually interrupts with the words "Mind you, I'm no Communist." He has also made up his mind that there is virtually no difference whatever between the programme of the Communists and that of Sun Yat-sen. . . . He did not claim to have met any of the present bosses (and I am sure if he had met them he would have told me), but he has had talks with some of his former friends who occupied high positions in the old days and are now doing nicely under the present régime. In particular he had a long talk with the former Marshal Li Jishen. . . . He apparently received highly favourable accounts of present conditions from him. . . . He says he intends to go to Formosa on his way back, and hopes to meet Chiang and at least tell him the truth about China and give him something to think about. But he was apparently, until I showed him a cutting from a Hong Kong paper, quite unaware of the rumours and suspicions his visit here has caused. . . . Meanwhile his presence here combined with the stories in the Hong Kong press have created much curiosity among my non-Communist colleagues, who frequently ask my opinion as to what he is up to. A more interesting question seems to me to be why the Chinese Government invited him to come here. I suppose the main answer is that they thought the kind of rumours his visit has in fact led to might contribute usefully to lowering morale in Formosa. A secondary consideration may perhaps have been that if he was suitably impressed, as he has been, he might perhaps act as a useful agency for spreading the gospel among his former influential friends now in Formosa or elsewhere outside China.[4]

Cohen did not leave right away to spread his newly discovered gospel. He just stayed on and tried to organize the export of Chinese handicrafts to Canada. The Chinese showed polite but unenthusiastic interest in his constant development talk. They tried to keep him busy, and bundled Cohen off to Tianjin, Hangzhou, Suzhou, Canton, Harbin, Shanghai, Chongqing, and other places. While in Nanjing, Cohen visited Sun's tomb and other memorial places. When his visa expired, the Chinese renewed it, and offered to extend it for as long as he wanted. They lavished him with gifts. Cohen mentioned to Chinese officials that he had carpets stored in Shanghai, and they gave orders for the rugs to be released through customs without charge. The Chinese even insisted on paying the $650 bill for storage and cleaning, and gave him the forty-two pounds freight cost for sending the carpets back to England.

Cohen had to wait longer to see Soong than planned, since she had headed to

Pakistan following her visit to India and Burma. When she finally returned, the two got together. He also saw Zhou. Cohen even told O'Neill that when he next saw the Chinese leaders, he would be delighted to put in a good word for the embassy, and asked if there were any difficulties he could help smooth out. "Being unable to imagine a less appropriate intermediary, I declined his kind offer and said we were doing very nicely," wrote O'Neill.

On the mainland, Cohen received much better treatment than he did in Taiwan. His conversion as an apologist for the Beijing regime was nearly complete. "His enthusiasm for the new China is now very great indeed," wrote O'Neill. "Apart from any genuine conviction he may have formed, I fear he has literally been bought. He repeated several times that the Chinese had not allowed him to spend a penny. Whenever he expressed admiration for any object it was presented to him. . . . He pulled a fat roll of £5 notes out of his pocket to testify to this generosity." Cohen, he continued, "frankly admits he is having a wonderful time and appears more or less to have told the Chinese that he will be happy to stay as long as they go on paying for his entertainment."

But there was a limit to how long they intended for him to remain, which according to Ringwalt, "may indicate that the Chinese reached the conclusion that Cohen was a man of limited value and that they had squeezed out of him the last ounce of whatever propaganda value he possessed." Cohen left Beijing on March 20. By then foreign officials had completely dismissed the notion that either of the sides intended to use him as a messenger. "It is unlikely that Cohen carries any weight at all but he is obviously useful to the Chinese Communists to cause doubt and confusion," wrote a British official. With his switched allegiances, Cohen's view of Taiwan severely dimmed. "He seems now to accept, as his new Chinese friends appear to have been telling him, that Chiang is a hopeless case; and he now himself believes that Chiang would be unlikely to receive him," wrote O'Neill. "He says however that he will take some soundings from a GMD friend in Hong Kong and will go to Formosa if Chiang will agree to receive him; not otherwise."[5]

Appearances, meanwhile, had to be kept up. When Cohen's train pulled into Hong Kong on March 22, he had what Drumright referred to as a "possibly calculated altercation" with a newsreel cameraman. Marvin Farkas, a twenty-nine-year-old UPI Movietone photographer, was waiting at the train station with about five or six journalists and photographers for a story to appear. "I used to go around to the railway station, because there were people coming from China every day," said Farkas. "On this particular day, I got there about an hour before the train came. One of the reporters said 'Two-Gun' Cohen was coming. I thought he was kidding me. I had never heard of him. So I waited around until he came out."

After a while, Cohen emerged wearing a gray felt hat and a double-breasted overcoat. When he saw the photographers, he pulled his coat over his face. As they snapped and filmed away, he flew into a rage and lurched at them. "He had this black cane with a silver knob on the top. I started shooting as he came out of the station. He said, 'Don't do that. You can't take my picture. It is an invasion of my privacy.' " Farkas kept on filming, and told Cohen that he had a right to record anything that comes into the public view. "He starts shaking this cane at me, and says 'Listen, young man, don't let this gray hair fool you. You better be careful.' " Uncowed, Farkas kept pace with Cohen as he walked out onto Salisbury Road. "I kept on walking in front of him. I kept shooting, and he was getting very threatening." Two police constables then passed, and Cohen shouted at them, "Arrest this man, he is invading my privacy. I want that film." Farkas refused to stop. "To me it was just like a joke. I wasn't going to give him the film. I didn't know how important a story he was or who he was." As the police grabbed Farkas, he clutched his camera and bag and yelled to his colleague P. C. Lee, "Get this picture, get this picture."

The police escorted Cohen and Farkas to the police station. Cohen angrily puffed on his Beijing-made cheroot and continued to demand the film. Farkas refused. Cohen then glowered, saying, "You will be sorry about this." At that, Cohen suddenly calmed down, and began to get friendly with Farkas, telling him, "After all, we are friends. You have nothing against me and I have nothing against you." He dropped the charges, and in a reversal of his earlier behavior, agreed to pose for pictures and talk about his mainland trip. "I didn't go to China on any mission whatsoever," he said. Reports of a peacemaking mission were a "Damn lie." All he wanted was to see old friends and tour the country.

Lee's photo made the *Standard* the following day along with a description of the fracas. When Farkas's film reached the UPI office in London, his boss asked him to get an on-film interview with Cohen. A few days later, Farkas headed to the Jewish Club. During his two years in Hong Kong, Farkas had become friendly with Cohen's pal Harry Odell. When Farkas entered the club, he saw Cohen and Odell together. Farkas went over and started talking to Cohen. "He was very jovial and friendly," said Farkas of the seemingly kinder Cohen. Farkas asked Cohen if he would sit for an interview, and Cohen then snapped, "Nothing doing. You are a rude guy. I have given the exclusive to N.B.C."[6]

Others in Hong Kong asked if Cohen had traveled to China with a message. He continued to violently deny the rumor, even at times slamming his fist on the table and bellowing "No, no, no. . . . Who the heck am I to go on peace missions. . . . I went on no secret mission—the Chinese are quite capable of handling their own affairs. How the heck could I go on a peace mission." His friend Kendall, though, visited the American consulate to let on that Cohen deliberately tried to mislead the press and was actually playing an intermediary role. "His story is he saw Zhou Enlai several times and has [an] important message to deliver to Taipei," wrote Drumright. "According [to] Kendall, he wants to go [to] Taipei if [he] can obtain entry and is seeing [a] Chinese Nationalist figure today in [an] effort [to] arrange [a] visit."

Taiwanese officials worried that all the talk of peace missions only created confusion in the press. They announced that the government still planned to reconquer the mainland. Cohen sent a telegram to a member of Chiang Kai-shek's personal staff asking for permission to visit Taiwan. Shen Qi, chief of the Government Information Bureau, said that a request for a visa would be viewed unfavorably. Cohen also tried to get in touch with Foreign Minister Ye Gongchao, but Ye replied that he had no interest in seeing Cohen. Most ignored him. As the *Standard* noted at the start of his trip, "The one man whom 'Two-Gun' never managed to get close to was Generalissimo Chiang Kai-shek and he always seemed peeved over the fact that in the latter years in his China-coast career he was left out of the limelight and merely hovered on the fringes of events and people." Others like the journalist Spencer Moosa reportedly agreed. "Cohen, who according to Moosa, has lived the life of a parasite for the last 20 years, used from time to time [to] touch Wu Tiecheng, when still alive, for money," wrote a Foreign Office official. "But with Wu Tiecheng gone, Cohen had no one he could any longer sponge on in Formosa." Cohen left Hong Kong for Britain on a British Overseas Airways flight at the start of April, booking his passage under the name M. A. Brown. He arrived in London on the evening of the third.

Being snubbed by the Taiwanese did not sit well with Cohen. He abandoned his pronounced neutral stance, and started promoting the mainland. Like many old China hands who recalled the hardships of prewar China, Cohen seemed genuinely impressed by what the communists showed him. He told people that Beijing only wanted peace, and announced from his room in the West End that "what I saw has convinced me that Red China today wants nothing but trade . . . with the world. They want to be allowed to get on with the job of building up Red China and believe me they are doing a great job. It is a new China today. . . . I went everywhere I wanted to go. I talked to whoever I liked. I talked with fountainheads of the government and I talked with peasants—and I liked what I saw. . . . The market is right before our eyes. It has the ability to trade and trade well. The fact that we are not taking advantage of this appears to me to be a matter for serious consideration."[7]

By this time, Cohen was ensconced in Salford with his now widowed sister Leah Cooper. Back in her large home on Broughton Lane, no one questioned his international position. Cohen was the undisputed patriarch of the family. "When he spoke in a room, you could hear a bloody pin drop. Even if people were chattering, if he opened his mouth he had such a powerful, wonderful heavy voice that people just shut up," noted his nephew Issie Bernstein. As the family head, he also spoiled his nephews and nieces. "He used to take me out and buy me toffees," said Michael Cohen. "He bought me my first set of lead British grenadiers. One of my earliest memories is him showing me how to set out these lead soldiers on the floor at Auntie Leah's." The two then had mock pitched battles.

Since much of the family lived in the Manchester area, they had regular late-afternoon and early-evening get togethers. On Sundays, Leah set out platters of chopped liver and onion, chicken, rolled meat, fish, salami, chicken soup, puddings, and cakes. When branches of the family came in from out of town they would screen home movies. "It used to be a sort of open house all day Sunday with buffet spread.

Everybody used to go. There was food on the table and people used to come and go during the course of the day," said Michael Cohen. All the while, Morris Cohen held court, chatting, laughing, and puffing away on his King Edward cigars. "She always kept a good table," said Sarah Rich of her sister's hospitality. "She used to make lovely meals. It was a real family. All the family used to go there."

Oddly, though, unlike his way of dealing with the press, whenever relatives asked Cohen questions about China, he was evasive, and would glare at the questioner. "I used to ask him questions and I never got an answer," said Victor Cooper. "I used to get either a dirty look or was just ignored. He just used to turn away. I was only a youth interested in world politics." Cohen told relatives that he could not say anything just in case his casual comments were reported in the press. He even warned that someone had tapped Leah's phone. "I think he was absolutely convinced of it."[8]

Not all was happy in the family. Cohen insisted on imposing his will on others. As a teenager, Leslie Cohen had fallen in love with Edith Conroy. She was not Jewish. Both families opposed a union. The couple nonetheless quietly married in October 1945 at the Salford Registry Office. A year and a half later they had Michael, and brought him up as a Methodist. "My father always said he would prefer me to be brought up as a good Methodist rather than as a bad Jew," Michael said. In the early 1950s Leslie came down with multiple sclerosis, but the doctors misdiagnosed him. "People genuinely didn't know what the problem was. They thought it was some sort of virus and then they thought it was a nervous breakdown. They really didn't know." Edith looked after her husband. His conditioned worsened. His speech slurred. By the end of the decade he had to spend a good deal of time in the hospital.

As Leslie's health declined, Edith went back to work, and established her own hair salon. The Cohens had difficulty accepting their brother's illness. Tensions heightened between Edith and the family, as some of them insisted that she bore responsibility for his condition and also improperly handled his treatment. And while part of his family regularly sent money, others were not that supportive. Cohen led the charge and friction. As some family members used to say, "You make your bed, and you have to lie in it."[9]

By the fall of 1956, Cohen prepared to return to China for the ninetieth anniversary of Sun's birth. He applied to the U.S. embassy for a visa to travel through the United States so he could see friends and promote his biography. When the embassy asked him for some biographical background, he balked. This did not sit well in the communist-phobic United States, especially from someone who was a personal friend of top communist officials. "He is now reported to have Communist sympathies or at least be favorably inclined towards the Communists and he apparently would like to engage in trade with the Chinese Communists," wrote a member of the embassy staff in London. They did not allow him into the country.

Despite the U.S. refusal to let him pass through, Cohen arrived in Canton on November 4. Many others gathered for Sun's birthday celebration. Officials from eight countries took part in the festivities in Nanjing. Cohen attended a large ceremony and wreath laying at Sun's mausoleum, and renewed friendships with Chen Mingshu and other members of the central party. He also did some sight-seeing.

The communists feted him as a celebrity. They showed deference to what he thought and said. Reporters interviewed him for the *People's Daily* and on Radio Beijing, and officials escorted him to countless factories and agricultural cooperatives. Cohen told all who would listen of how the Chinese were pooling farms, forming joint production units, and paying peasants according to their labor. "I see that everywhere the standard of living of the ordinary people is much much higher than before. I have never seen so many smiling faces. Here I have seen socialism. I am very glad to see in China many democratic parties working together under the leadership of the Communist Party, working hard to construct a socialist society. This has all broadened my horizons."

Cohen let friends know of his dealings with the China Association of the United Kingdom, which represented former large-scale British mercantile, industrial, and investment interests in China. He boasted that he played an instrumental role in arranging the sale of a thousand British tractors to China, and was in the midst of negotiating for the sale of two cement plants. He also indicated that he had been representing the trading firm of Jardine Matheson. "Cohen seemed to be playing his familiar role as go-between exploiting the many personal contacts which he had in the Chinese communist capital and his general soft-soaping ability," wrote the U.S. consul in Hong Kong, Thomas P. Dillon. Yet Cohen once again overstayed his welcome. "He seems to have made himself a complete nuisance to the Chinese authorities," wrote O'Neill. "Throughout his five-month sojourn he lived in the Beijing Hotel freely using cars and entertaining lavishly all at the expense of the Chinese Government. As his stay lengthened . . . his accounts of his activities became wilder. He apparently addressed several letters to Zhou Enlai offering to negotiate the sale of almost anything including whole factories for the manufacture of strategic items. I have no idea what came of all this but I think very little. My impression was that the Chinese became as tired of him as we did."

Prospects in China for business appeared good and Cohen simply wanted to be part of it. In May 1956 Mao called for increased intellectual openness and free discourse, launching his "Let a hundred flowers bloom, and a hundred schools of thought contend" movement. He hoped that the loosening of restrictions on political and social discussion would lead to increased support from intellectuals and others for his radical policies. The following February, Mao issued his "On the Correct Handling of Contradictions Among the People" speech, calling again for greater freedom for people to discuss politics. Initially there was little response to his call for openness, but when it came citizens spoke out against one-party rule, the lack of human rights, and voiced resentment over the way the government handled the economy. Strikes and demonstrations broke out, which shocked communist leaders. Some felt that the critics overdid their response. After a month and a half of freedom, officials started ripping out the "poisonous weeds" who betrayed their trust. The party and police made mass arrests of students, cadres, and intellectuals. More than 550,000 people were labeled rightists, lost their jobs, tossed in jail or carted off to reform labor camps. Many committed suicide.[10]

None of Mao's crackdowns affected Cohen's views. He seemed unaware of the turmoil. To pass the time when he was not schmoozing officials, Cohen continued his recreational hotel lobby lounging, smoking his cigars and waiting. "My meetings with him were mainly in the old Beijing Hotel, where he used to sit in the lobby in his fashionable threads from Bond Street and carried a malacca-headed cane," said Sidney Shapiro, a literary translator for the Chinese *Foreign Languages Press.* "He struck this fashionable, and elegant and refined pose. He used to sort of sit around there just waiting for someone that he could talk to because he didn't have much of a social life at that time. He seemed hungry for company, for people who could talk his language, who had somewhat similar backgrounds. My similar background was that we were both Jewish." Cohen had a limitless store of Jewish jokes to tell Shapiro. Many of his jokes were risqué. "He liked me because I was a receptive audience. We didn't have much of a joke-telling population among the foreign community." Despite his claims of major deals, Cohen obviously had too much time on his hands. "If he had business, if what he said was so, he would be meeting with officials of one ministry or another and talking on a formal basis. He wouldn't pick up any business in the lobby of the old Beijing Hotel."

Cohen basically sat there to be seen. "Do you know what a *luftmensch* is? Somebody who lives off the air," noted Epstein. In his pocket Cohen carried a key chain with a golden gun. When someone took an interest in his polished stories, and asked him how he whisked out his guns, he would oblige them with a mock demonstration. "He would usually be in one of the big overstuffed chairs that was fairly close to the reception desk," said Sidney Rittenberg, who had been released by the Chinese in 1955 after six years imprisonment on suspicion of being an American spy. "He would be there, very visible, a portly, affable-looking old gentleman with a big cigar and all the trimmings. He looked like he might be a traveling salesman who just dropped into town. He was a good storyteller. He would fasten you with his eye in a very genial manner. He knew just how much detail to go into without losing you or boring you. He was one of these people who is a very obvious sort of a faker, sort of a bluffer. And yet, you never felt that there was the slightest bit of malice in him. He would tell all these tall tales and he would swagger, but you always felt that he was a very decent man."

Westerners on the whole viewed Cohen as an entertaining oddity. "They liked him and they thought he was full of baloney, an eccentric old guy that had a colorful background. I never heard anyone say anything particularly bad about him. He was just a character," said Rittenberg. The more outrageous the story the better. "He said that while he was sitting in his chair in the lobby of the Beijing Hotel a party of about a half a dozen Saudi oilmen had come in. They were wearing their headdresses and long Arab gowns. 'I looked at them and I spotted one of them. I know a Jew when I see one,' he said. 'As they passed me by, I leaned over and I said to him in a low voice, *Was machta Yid.*' The man jerked upright and looked very frightened and leaned over and said to him, 'For God's sake, keep your mouth shut. You want to get me killed?' "[11]

As always, when Cohen returned to England, he came loaded down with furniture, tables, clothes, and other gifts. "The family used to come down when he used to come back from China," said Victor Cooper. "He used to open these bags upstairs and he used to bring down handfuls of things. Whoever happened to be in the house, he used to give something. Everybody. The cleaning lady, even." By then the former London guttersnipe and Jews' Free School truant had become an elder statesman of the Manchester Jewish community. In northern England he was viewed as an important diplomat. The Jewish press and congregations courted him as a celebrity, constantly calling on him to discuss the state of China as well as China-Israel relations.

In the fall of 1957 Cohen passed through Canada on his way to China. During the afternoon of September 18, he stopped by to see Menzies in the Department of External Affairs. "He is very fat, has a poor memory for names, and sweats profusely. He may not be pounding people's tables for much longer," noted Menzies. "He said that he had been offered a pension by the present authorities in Beijing . . . but that he had declined the pension and asked to be allowed to earn money as a commission agent." Menzies asked Cohen about the rumors of his involvement in peace negotiations a year and a half earlier. Cohen admitted that he had taken it upon himself while in Beijing to explore the possibility of a settlement. "He had been assured by Zhou Enlai . . . that if Chiang Kai-shek would recognize the indivisibility of China and the ultimate authority of the Government established in Beijing, he could have a high office in the state (possibly as Vice-President), could live on the mainland or in Formosa, as he pleased, and could maintain a government on the island together with a navy and an army."

Cohen told Menzies that he saw no prospect of Chiang accepting Zhou's offer, but stated that many people on Taiwan wanted to go to the mainland but feared seeking permission to leave the island. "Conversely he thought that there were many people on the mainland who would leave there if they could. He gave numerous examples of people on the mainland . . . who appeared to be content with their life there. He also said that although the Jews in China were being squeezed out of their sources of profit, they were, nevertheless, not being severely victimized. One suspects that there was a certain amount of rationalization in this statement."[12]

Cohen soon attended the eighth anniversary of the People's Republic in Beijing. He made a beeline back to the Beijing Hotel lobby, and waited for an opportunity to grab those who passed by. "Downstairs in the foyer, sitting away the hours and years, were two other characters, typical of this hotel's twilight world, General 'Two-gun' Cohen, who had once been bodyguard to Sun Yat-sen . . . and Rewi Alley, New Zealand Sinophile, poet and now propagandist," noted Desmond Donnelly, a British member of Parliament who was visiting the Chinese capital. While in town, Cohen attended a parade near the Tiananmen Gate. "Over half a million people had marched past the same spot in the October parade, with bands, tableaux and banners," wrote Donnelly. "Colorful balloons had drifted by in the breeze. Dancers, jugglers, athletes, and trick cyclists had followed the ranks of factory workers and the army. Aircraft had thundered past. For five hours without a break Mao Zedong had stood, waving and laughing." Yet, despite the festivities and Mao's cheerfulness, grimness had descended on China. With crackdowns on dissidents and turmoil within the economy, the flush of revolution had vanished. "In private conversation I found people afraid to commit themselves in a way that I had never encountered before."

Needing to bump up the economy, Mao in 1958 called for an explosion of economic output, technical innovation, and agricultural production. He wanted a Great Leap Forward, imploring the people to start "walking on two legs" instead of limping or hopping along on one appendage. Mao set insanely optimistic goals by which the nation would economically zip by the other powers. He called for a 19 percent increase in steel production in the first year, a 17 percent rise in coal output, and an 18 percent increase in electric power. Officials became intoxicated with predictions, and made even more outlandish promises.

To meet these utopian goals, party cadre swarmed across the land to stir up the people and encourage them to make Mao proud. The Chinese were called on to erect small workshops. Communities, cooperatives, and college campuses built pig iron ovens to produce iron and steel. People toiled sixteen or more hours a day, being told to use their free time for productive, socially conscious work. "In China, everyone has to be a 'volunteer' for work in fields or building roads," wrote Cartier-Bresson. "Thus I found little children laying sidewalks and young girls driving steam rollers, bureaucrats and intellectuals working on dams. Their production was perhaps minimal but I was told that this manual labor keeps the educated classes in contact with the peasants." Militia members even took breaks from their training to hoe fields. "The mobilization of so much energy gave me, at times, the impression that China had become a gigantic beehive: swarms of peasants building roads, factories, bridges, reclaiming arid fields, reforesting bare mountains."

The government called for the people's ownership of industry, commerce, military, and education. Cooperatives merged into People's Communes, autonomous communities that combined production with government administration. Peasants lost the little property they possessed. Members slept in dormitories and ate in mess halls. To increase agricultural production, the government called for the mobilizing of underemployed resources. More than 100 million people built water conservancy projects. Bureaucrats ignorant of agricultural techniques ordered farmers to plant crops closer together, and called for the extermination of grain-eating sparrows. "They're going to wipe the sparrows out of China because they eat too much," Cohen boasted of efforts in China. "The people are being urged to kill off all the sparrows because they eat seeds, grain, and so on. And they'll do it. They'll wipe them out. That's the kind of people the Chinese are." By 1959, 740,000 agricultural cooperatives consolidated into 24,000 rural communes. Each covered about 10,000 acres of land and contained 4,000 to 5,000 households. The Chinese showed Cohen the communes they wanted him to see. He quickly noted that many of the peasants were convinced that the communes were an improvement over the previous system. "I didn't only see the pretty ones, I went where I wanted," he said of his travels.

But the Great Leap was a grand flop. Reports of mass production and bumper harvests proved fraudulent. The peasants were overworked, morale was down. As discontent grew, work productivity decreased. Farmers furrowed too deep, digging up unfertile lower soil. With the extermination of a billion bug-eating sparrows, insects and other pests flourished. Much of the excessively hyped iron smelted in the backyard furnaces easily snapped in two. Soon the government had little choice but to return to simple collectivism and even smaller farming groups. Peasants got back their land, tools, and homes.[13]

By the summer of 1958, Cohen was safely settled in the Mayfair Hotel, far from the looming failures in China, touting his accomplishments and talking about how movie companies wanted to make a film on his life. "Maybe I should wait. After all, I'm only 71. I've a lot to do yet." He praised the communists no end.

What I'm going to tell you may make you think I'm a Communist. But I'm not. No, sir . . . I was over about four months ago. Went to Formosa first. Then to China, where they put the red carpet out for me. I saw anything I wanted, and I'm willing to go on record as saying China's in great shape. They've never had such a good Government. And that doesn't mean I'm a member of the Party, as I told you. They gave a big dinner for me. They were all there. Zhou Enlai. The lot. I stood up and told them I was proud of the new China. As a member of the Chinese Nationalist Party, the Guomindang. You know, they got up and cheered. What a lot of people here don't realise is that the Nationalist Party is still allowed to operate in China. The Commies are in power, but you can still recruit members for the Nationalist Party in Beijing. And several other parties. As Mao Zedong said "Let a hundred flowers blossom. . . ."

While talking up Mao's accomplishments, Cohen was appalled over China's continued exclusion from the United Nations. "It just don't make sense," he bellowed. "Personally I think it's the last stage of insanity. I've travelled the world a lot recently and I've never met a person yet who does not agree that it's a foolish attitude to take. I believe it is time now to 'forget, forgive; conclude and be agreed; Our doctors say this is no month to bleed.' That's Shakespeare. . . . To talk about any world conference without China just don't make sense."[14]

He occasionally heard from Judith. She had enlarged her new store on Peel Street to include bridal gowns, but the city in the spring of 1957 decided to widen the street by eleven feet. Customers had trouble getting to her shop and business dried up. "Peel Street was literally chopped up to pieces right in front of her store," said the friend. "Nobody could come and park. Nobody could do anything, so she

lost a lot of business. From that time and afterwards she started failing in health."
Judith became quite distraught. "I have been quite ill for the past year with a nervous
breakdown and I am just out of the hospital where I spent seven weeks," she wrote
Cohen. "This is all due to financial problems. I am allowed to work for only a few
hours a day and you can see how this affects my business. Under the circumstances,
it would be a God-send if you could see your way clear to repay me any part of the
large sums of money I gave you or paid many of your bills. These items ran into
thousands of dollars—$3,000 I borrowed for one trip back to England for you—to
mention just one item. I am sure that if you have it, you would do the fair thing
and this would go a long way to relieve my mind and help me regain my health."

Despite Cohen's boasts of big sales, he had no money to help Judith with. He
had no work, no prospects, and still could not get Triguboff to pay his debt. He
had even written to the Tianjin Hebrew Association in 1956 reminding them that
he "had worked for some considerable time at the request of the Hebrew Association of Tianjin for the release of and the return of all [the] property" of Triguboff. "I was successful in having Mr. Triguboff's previous conviction squashed
and all his property and goods . . . returned to him." In exchange it had been
agreed by Triguboff and the Hebrew Association that a "sum of money and the
Title Deeds of the Rich Hotel, Tianjin" would be given to Cohen. "Having not
received anything up till now, I would be happy if you could inform me now
what exactly is the situation."

While he could not assist Judith, he did occasionally see her family. He even
sent flowers to Polly. When Judith's sister Ruth Field visited London, she met with
Cohen for lunch. While they dined, she noticed that he still wore his wedding ring.
"I was at the Grosvenor House," said Field. "We had lunch, and he was wearing
his wedding ring and he said he would never take it off his finger." Such a move
did not shock those who knew Cohen. "Yes, I am not surprised. He had the most
unusual attachments to certain things. You would never have suspected it," said
Klyne.

Harry Clark ran into Cohen on the street in Montreal in the early 1960s. They
did not have a pleasant meeting. "He was rather indisposed towards me because my
name had been used in the divorce proceedings," said Clark. "He was a little mad
because my name was mentioned as having been a participant at a luncheon where
he got hot under the collar and bawled out a waiter. And I said to him, 'Morris,
you are the last person in the world I would say anything against because you are
my big brother and I would like you to feel that way towards me.' " In London,
Cohen also got together for an occasional lunch with Gerald Clark who was stationed
there for the Montreal *Star*. "Yep. I used to see him in London," he said. "I was on
good terms with him."

Throughout this period, tensions increased between the mainland and Taiwan.
The Nationalists made commando raids from their off-coast islands of Quemoy and
Matsu. They also did reconnaissance work and dropped leaflets on their enemy's
territory. After 1955, the communists started building up the area opposite Quemoy.

They stationed 200,000 troops there along with fighter planes, bombers, and a small navy. The Nationalists responded with nearly 100,000 troops and a much better navy. In August 1958 the communists started shelling Quemoy, and the United States dispatched planes, ships, and Marines. Gerald Clark wanted to visit China to cover the growing crisis for his paper. The Chinese, though, were not eager to have journalists running around the battle zone. No visa was forthcoming, so he got in touch with Cohen. "We got along well, meeting periodically for lunch," wrote Clark. "I called him and asked if he had any ideas on how I should apply for a visa to China. 'Cable Zhou Enlai and say you're my brother-in-law,' " Cohen told him. Clark took his advice. Much to Clark's surprise, he received a visa within five days.[15]

In April 1959 Cohen arrived in Hong Kong a few weeks after the Dalai Lama had to flee Tibet following anti-Chinese occupation protests. Eighty thousand Tibetans were subsequently massacred. Cohen made it known that he expected to be invited to attend the upcoming National People's Congress in Beijing. While in the past the Chinese had automatically granted him admittance, this time they did not issue Cohen a visa. He waited patiently for a number of weeks, and even made a side trip to Japan to visit Taketo, the banker who helped him when he was in Stanley. Despite his plans, he did not get into China, and told a Canadian newspaperman that the Chinese had advised him to apply again in August. "Cohen told this same newsman that he attributed his failure to receive either an invitation or a visa to visit the mainland to the fact that . . . Gerald Clark had been critical of the regime following his trip to Communist China last fall," wrote U.S. consul Harald W. Jacobson. It was also possible, Jacobson noted, that Cohen did not get a visa because the regime was reluctant to have too many visitors, even favorably inclined ones, wandering around China in the summer, when natural catastrophes might create a bad impression of the nation.

Cohen stayed in Hong Kong until June, visiting the Jewish Club, the Marco Polo Club, the Foreign Correspondents' Club, and the Cigar Smokers' Club. By November, he had a visa and returned for the anniversary celebration, praising the economic and industrial achievement of China. There was more hotel lounging and dirty jokes. To Cohen, all seemed fine in China. "It impressed me with the fact that the man was uneducated and you might say uncultured, but he was a very keen observer, very sharp," said Rittenberg. "I thought he was very good at encapsulating what he saw. It was the period of the Great Leap Forward in China, which turned out to be a total disaster economically, but which at the time looked wonderful. There were a lot of stories in the foreign press including the Hong Kong press about how bad things were in China. How short they were of grain and so on. I remember I went to lunch with Morris at the hotel, and he told me, 'Yesterday I had a talk with some Chinese business people, and they read me a whole list of statistics to show how good the economy is and how wonderful things are. I don't need all that bullshit. I don't have to listen to that stuff. I take a walk down the street. I just walk two blocks down the street, turn around and walk back again and I know the whole story. I notice that the Chinese walking along the street look me straight in the eye.

They don't avoid my face. Most of them smile a little or they get a light in their eye when they look at me. Any country where the people are walking along the street with their heads up and looking you right in the eye and smiling, you know damn well that they are not in bad trouble. Another thing that I notice was that many of the young people are humming a little tune, or they are talking excitedly with each other. I remember this country in the old days. People crept along the street, and nobody opened their mouth and most people looked down. Nobody would look a foreigner in the eye. I don't need the statistics. I look at the people and I make up my mind on what the state of the country is.' "

Cohen wished to show others the state of China. While visiting the Jewish Community Center in Hong Kong, he met Aaron Krauss, a twenty-eight-year-old American military chaplain on one-week shore leave. "He adopted me, to the point where he was anxious to take me anywhere I wanted to go. He could not have been kinder. He took me around and introduced me as his 'Marine Rabbi.' He acted as if the whole world revolved around our friendship. I asked him, 'Why did you stay in China all of these years?' His words were very clear, very plain. 'I wanted them Chinese to know what a Jew looked like.' " Cohen was anxious to take Krauss to China. "He wanted to show me China. He wanted to show me the Chinese people. He talked endlessly in a very plain, direct manner. He said the Chinese were better off with this government than they were under previous conditions. As bad as things were, as terrible as things are, the average Chinese was better off with this government. He thought Zhou was great. He was not thrilled with Chiang Kai-shek. He thought he was corrupt."[16]

Finally, after years of lobby sitting and endless talking, breaks came Cohen's way. The Chinese had realized that western planes and engines were superior to the various models of the *Ilyushin* they received from the Soviet Union. Following a visit by a delegation to the Farnborough Air Show, southwest of London, they approached Vickers and Rolls-Royce about buying Vickers Viscount passenger planes with Rolls-Royce engines. Figuring they needed some help in winning the Chinese over, Rolls-Royce turned to Cohen. On September 25, 1959, he landed a job as a consultant with Rolls-Royce. "Someone senior in Rolls-Royce found out about Morris's background, and took him on to help establish our credentials in the eyes of the Chinese," noted J. Peter Armstrong, who was then a technical service engineer with the firm. "It was not a very lucrative deal for Morris by the standards of his pre-war arms trading, as Rolls-Royce did not expect more from their advisors than general guidance, but he was always interested in helping improve Sino-British relations."

Cohen was not quite what the firm expected. "I was sorry I read the book," said then commercial director of Rolls-Royce, Sir David Huddie, of the Drage biography. "I got the impression from the book of a very rambunctious character. But he was really a very thoughtful character. I think he was proud of his ability to evaluate people."

Extensive discussions between the two sides followed. Cohen worked hard for his money. At a September 8, 1960, meeting with Chinese commercial attachés in London, Cohen helped the firm try to strike a deal. "The meeting was cordial, and was of a very preliminary nature, feelers being put out on both sides," wrote Gordon Scotter, who worked with the firm's export sales group. "The main message we got over to the Chinese was that if they were prepared to make an irrevocable deposit payable to Rolls-Royce of about one million pounds sterling, or some similar large figure, this would demonstrate the seriousness of their intentions and would enable further negotiations to proceed."[17]

Other deals came Cohen's way. Old contacts started to come through. Cohen's friend and former boss Li Jishen had a sinecure as chairman for the Revolutionary Committee of the GMD. The organization sought to convince those who had fled the mainland to return. Around the time of Li's death in the fall of 1959, his department gave Cohen an uncomplicated assignment in which he could tap his vast reserve of stories and anecdotes. Starting on November 1, Cohen, "a faithful assistant to Dr. Sun Yat-sen in his lifetime," was invited to be a special contributor for the Commission on the Collection and Edition of Historical Material of Revolution. All he had to do was "write for us from time to time memoirs of the life of Dr. Sun Yat-sen." As an incentive, they sent Cohen one hundred pounds a month for a term of two years. The media also courted him. In mid-May 1960, Cohen flew to Toronto to appeared as a "Secret Guest Challenger" on the talking heads show *Front Page Challenge*. The show paid him $923.60 as well as round-trip airfare. Better yet, in January 1961 Cohen finally received his certificate of Canadian citizenship because of his military service during World War I.[18]

The Vickers and Rolls-Royce negotiations took some time. When Rolls-Royce officials needed Cohen at their headquarters in Derby, they sent around a chauffeur-driven car. In September 1961 the Chinese had settled on buying six Vickers Viscounts powered by Rolls-Royce Dart 525F engines. More than 300 Viscounts had already been sold all over the world. A deal for six Viscounts was considered relatively small. But such a potential sale would mark the first time that China had bought aircraft from the West, and the British firms eagerly sought an agreement. A delegation of Chinese came to look over the Rolls-Royce factory, and Cohen and others escorted them through the manufacturing plant. As they worked out the plane deal, Cohen headed off to China in October to take part in the fiftieth anniversary of the 1911 revolution and to be on hand for the airplane negotiations scheduled in Beijing. On November 12, he actively took part in the rites for the ninety-fifth anniversary celebration of Sun's birth.

A business mission from Vickers arrived in Beijing first, followed by a team from Rolls-Royce. When the delegates landed, interpreters and officials escorted them in black Chinese limos to their hotel. There Cohen worked with the Rolls-Royce group to sell spare engines and a contract for ongoing support. Throughout, the Chinese insisted on complete secrecy, yet reports were leaked by Reuters, and Rolls-Royce reluctantly admitted that Cohen was their "consultant on commercial matters in China."

Cohen had no involvement with the day-to-day talks. While the two sides sat in discussions, he went around town and visited with Soong and others. "He came over to my flat two or three times," said Maggie Dean, who was head of the registry section at the British Chargé d'Affaires. "He would ring up and say he was bored. I said, 'Come to tea, come to tea.' So he used to come over for tea and tell me his Jewish jokes. He was very amusing." Cohen also whiled away his time at the hotel bar, fondling his silver-headed cane, drinking Shanghai beers and the local Chinese whiskey, and watching sportsmen play snooker. As he patiently waited for the Rolls-Royce group to finish for the day, he chatted with friends and even chuckled to Rewi Alley, "My God, I had an ejaculation last night in my dream."

In the evening, the Rolls-Royce crew discussed the talks with him. "We would go back to the hotel and he would be there and we would tell him how the day's negotiations had gone, and what the hard points were," said Armstrong. Cohen gave support, "simply acting as sort of a father confessor" to the group. According to Duncan Fraser, who was director and manager in Tokyo for Rolls-Royce Far East Ltd., Cohen "rather worked in the background. He wasn't necessarily a front-runner, but he did things on the wings." Besides helping Rolls-Royce, Cohen seems to have also received the good graces of his Chinese hosts. While in Beijing, he had an apartment and a driver who took him around. He never signed chits, and happily ordered anything he wanted. He also saw to it that the British guests had all that they needed.

The negotiations did not go as smoothly as Rolls-Royce had expected, so Cohen had to do some diplomatic greasing. "The people he was talking to there were not what I would call his Chinese," said Armstrong. "He was a little bit upset when we told him the sort of strong-arm tactics they were using in the negotiating table. They were being very hardheaded. Once in a while when there was something particularly difficult to shift he said, 'I will go and see what I can do about that.' He did help. We trusted him completely." When talks reached an impasse he even suggested waving his fee. "Typical Morris Cohen, at one stage when the price was being hotly debated, he dashed into the Chinese authorities and said, 'You can have all my commission if it will help.' He wanted the deal to go through. It was just the sort of a quixotic gesture that Morris would make." The two sides finally settled on a sale around Christmas. The Chinese agreed to buy the six planes along with twenty-four spare Rolls-Royce engines and a contract from the engine maker for ongoing support. Delivery of the planes was scheduled to begin in July 1963.[19]

In January 1962 Cohen arrived in Hong Kong, where he met with Israeli Foreign Minister Golda Meir. At the time Israel was diplomatically isolated. Cohen and Meir chatted on China-Israel relations. Meir told him of her country's desire to establish normal diplomatic links with China, and her own confusion over China's lack of response. Cohen excitedly said he would use his connections to bring about some progress. He promised speedy results. While in the colony, he visited old friends like Hans and Lala Diestel. "He was very friendly with the Diestels and he used to come there on Friday night for dinner when he was in Hong Kong," said

Roche Burgin, who moved to Hong Kong with her husband, David, the previous year. "On Friday nights Lala always had people to dinner. She very often invited us for a proper Shabbat meal. A very relaxed sort of evening. Nothing heavy politically." There the Burgins met Cohen. "He was quite a jolly old man and very sweet to the children. In fact, when I think of Moisha Cohen, I see him in my mind's eye dancing with my seven-year-old daughter, Suzanne. He was very gentle."

On January 31, 1962, the Central Committee of the Revolutionary Committee of the GMD renewed Cohen's contract for two more years, noting that, "The term can be extended on the agreement of both sides when it expires." He continued trying to drum up business. "China is a very big market, and the Beijing government is interested in businesslike trade." He boasted to the press how China entrusted him with £100 million to purchase English farm implements, but told the papers that the deal fell through because the British government refused to issue an export license. Throughout, he defended China. "It is not paradise—much is still to be done, and the government is fully aware of it. However, since my early days in China they have made great progress. If anyone in 1949 had told me that in five years there would be no opium smoking in China, I would have laughed up my sleeve; but they have done it."

He could not say enough nice things about the regime. "As far as the Government of China is concerned, the Chinese have never had a better one than that on the Mainland at the present time. Everyone is working and those who are over-age are cared for. I know that I may sound full of propaganda for China, but I am speaking of what I have seen and known of China and the Chinese people. If they have peace, they will be the mirror of what I call State Socialism. If I did not believe they were carrying out the fundamental approach and teaching of the late Dr. Sun Yat-sen, I would not be going to China as I do." And as for the Chinese who thought otherwise and left the country, "I believe, and I say this in perfect faith and not to create a false impression, that there are a few people in China today who would like to get out and live where there is a great deal of gaiety, opium and prostitution and 'good-time Charley,' instead of helping to build China into a real place to live in. There are some also who have finances abroad who would like to get out and live without any discipline."[20]

And while he would state that conditions in China were improving, life there was oppressively hard. Bad harvests and famines during the Great Leap Forward killed tens of millions of people. Cannibalism was not uncommon. By 1961, China was a dreary place. "I arrived in Beijing in the terrible winter of 1960–61," wrote Sven Lindqvist, who was studying at Beijing University. "The city seemed dead. The shops were empty, the restaurants closed. It was impossible to buy a nail, a piece of string or a sheet of paper. The streets were filled with endless queues, waiting outside the communal feeding centres. The dream of having just one good square meal hung over the city like a mirage over the desert. . . . The nation seemed to be holding its breath before a long scream."

Life in Taiwan was not much better. The Nationalists prepared to return across the Straits of Taiwan, if only they could. At the Historical Museum in Taipei, curators exhibited Tang-era horse statues in their packing crates. That way they could be shipped quickly when their troops retook the mainland, or sent elsewhere if the communists invaded. "In Formosa the myth of reconquest is maintained, and there is a peculiarly synthetic atmosphere of war," continued Lindqvist. "Before each film performance a plan is flashed on the screen, showing how the cinema is to be evacuated in case of an air attack—although Formosa has never been exposed to an attack of this kind."

Cohen made a point of speaking ill of the island's ruler. "We were talking about Chiang Kai-shek, whom he didn't like at all," said Cyril Sherer. "He had no respect for him. He thought he had no class. He said in the early to mid-1960s he was invited to a television program in New York. They asked him on the program what he thought of Chiang Kai-shek, and he said to me, 'Cyril, I couldn't say it, so I leaned forward to the camera and I said, "Tuches." ' "[21]

Following Cohen's return to England, he worked and lived out of a suite at the Park Lane Hotel. In July 1962 he had discussions with Decca Radar Ltd. By September he snared a contract with the firm as a commercial consultant; Decca hired him to advise the firm on the best way to export and sell various radar products to China. For his troubles, Cohen would receive a 5 percent commission on sales up to £100,000. After £100,000 he would receive 2.5 percent. "Most of the agents were companies, but we had a very few who were individuals like General Cohen," said Peter Daone, who dealt with Decca sales to China. Cohen was hired "because of his unique contacts and qualities. Clearly he had some very good contacts. We did attribute much of our great success in the sale, certainly of marine radar, to his own contacts and his own influence. It was through him that we became established there. I never had any doubt that his unique position and relationship was of great benefit. We worked on the basis—very, very much so—that it would have been most unwise for us to have terminated the relation in any way at all because of the high regard the Chinese had for him. Quite clearly he kept the name Decca quite well at the forefront."

His work also continued with Rolls-Royce. On March 12, 1964, the firm appointed Cohen "Commercial Consultant to Rolls-Royce (Far East) Limited," with territory covering all of China. He was to work at his "own expense to bring commercial persuasion to bear on all prospective purchasers in the Territory of Rolls-Royce Aero engine products." Rolls-Royce paid him an annual minimum retainer fee of five hundred pounds, and a commission on sales.

Cohen had met Golda Meir back in early 1962, and for one and a half years the Israelis heard nothing from him. They tried to keep in touch to see if he had made any progress opening up relations with China, and in August 1963 Yaacov Shimoni, the director of the Asian Department of the Ministry for Foreign Affairs in Jerusalem, wrote to Cohen in Salford. Then, on September 3, Cohen visited Ambassador A. Lurie in London. He told the staff that after talking with two high officials in Beijing, he felt that it was not a good time to accelerate relations with China. Nor had he brought up the topic with Zhou. Cohen promised, though, that when he returned to China, he would try again.

Nothing ever happened. In September 1965, Shimoni compiled a list of people who had good personal connections with Chinese officials, noting that one of them was a "somewhat strange character" by the name of General Morris Cohen whose true influence in China was doubtful. The Israelis once again wrote Cohen in England and asked him if he had taken any action with the Chinese. He answered that he had tried to make contacts but still felt that the time was not right to discuss it with Zhou.

Cohen was now in his late seventies, and divided his time between London and Salford. Back home, the family patriarch and his sister Leah fought with their sister-in-law Edith over the best way to care for Leslie. Cohen and Leah insisted that Leslie should not be in the hospital but resting at home. Once in the early 1960s Cohen and Leah actually discharged him without consulting Edith. At other times, when Edith would stop by the hospital to visit her husband and to talk to the doctors, she would be confronted by Cohen and Leah, who would start loud arguments with her about Leslie's treatment. In Manchester, statesman Cohen meanwhile met with Boy Scout troops to inspire them and to tell them about his adventures. He even chipped in to help the 401st scout troop buy an extension hut by donating an autographed copy of his biography for an auction. It netted a hefty twenty-five guineas.[22]

As Cohen entered his twilight days, Mao feared a loss of power, and decided to purge his enemies. As a way to rid himself of those he opposed, Mao began an ideological crusade to create more loyal leaders, to make society less elitist, and to improve the party. "Anyone who opposes Chairman Mao Zedong, opposes Mao Zedong's thoughts, opposes the party central leadership, opposes the proletariat's dictatorship, opposes the correct way of Socialism. . . ." Those who resist, warned the _People's Daily,_ "will be struck down by the entire party and by the entire people."

Mao decided that he would train a new generation of shock troops to revitalize the country's revolutionary values. His youthful Red Guards issued from high schools and colleges. They were dubbed "little generals" and commanded to rid the land of cadres who were responsible for past errors. In the spring of 1966 Red Guards attacked authors and officials as well as propagandists. They shut down schools. Students brandishing Mao's Little Red Book and clubs attacked and killed their teachers. By August, Mao launched the Great Proletarian Cultural Revolution. He directed the Red Guards to "dare to be violent" and that "to rebel is good." As he unleashed the furies, he implored them to attack the dreaded Four Olds: ideas, culture, habits, and customs. In a nation that once cherished tradition and age, children and teenagers abused the elderly and intellectuals, destroyed cultural relics, churches, temples, books, instruments, even jewelry. To help them wreak destruction, the guards received free rail passage. They stormed through cities, yanked leaders from their offices, planted tall dunce hats on their heads, and paraded the helpless through the streets. Red Guards acted as investigators, judges, and executioners. They even fought among themselves. No one was safe. They renounced politburo members, deputy premiers, and cabinet ministers. Reputed spies and traitors were killed. Soong was denounced as a bourgeois reactionary. Zhou tried to protect her. He ordered the Red Guards to leave her alone, but they would not even listen to him; on September 21, a mob stormed her house while she was away.[23]

The aim of this revolution was far from that of the one Sun Yat-sen was involved in fifty-five years earlier. That revolution promised democracy and freedom. This one bode terror. Cohen left England for China in the midst of this new revolution to celebrate the hundredth anniversary of his former boss's birth. He stopped along the way in Israel. In Tel Aviv three young foreign office men showed him around. "He wore them out sitting up all night with his stories, his *bubbe meisehen* [fairy tales], his cigars and whiskey. They were exhausted," said Sherer, who moved to Israel in 1961. When Cohen arrived in China, he figured prominently at the Sun celebration, appearing in an assemblage of dignitaries that included Zhou, Soong, and Mao. "This is the finest and best government that China has had in my experience," he once again intoned on the government of anarchy. "I know personally I have seen the results of what they have done and the happiness of the people as a whole."

With the Cultural Revolution brewing, Cohen was an odd reminder of the past. "His appearance seemed to denote a touch of sentimentality on the part of the Beijing rulers, who are striving to eliminate the Chinese equivalent of people like Cohen," wrote Stanley Karnow of the Washington *Post*. And while the Red Guards tortured and killed leaders and peasants, the Chinese spoiled Cohen. They treated him with great deference. Girl Guides and interpreters showed care and made a fuss over him, taking his arm and helping him in and out of his seat. At the celebrations, Cohen watched Red Guards march by. Despite the havoc they brought, he refused to speak badly of them: "I have seen millions of them. I think it is a wonderful thing. The spirit is wonderful. When it first started there was, as I understand it, a little over-enthusiasm with a few; very few. But now they are well disciplined." Not a bad word would be said.

At a state banquet for the "Double Tenth," Cohen sat at one of the long tables. During the dinner, Zhou walked over to him. He patted Cohen on the shoulder and raised his cup for a toast and said in English, "Morris, old friend." Cohen stood up, and Zhou then continued, "Long life." Cohen was overwhelmed by the attention. "I ran into him the next morning," said Rittenberg. "He was fresh from that experience. When he told me that he began to cry. I had never seen that kind of emotion from him. I said, 'What's the problem?' And he said, 'Well, I sat down after the toast and cried there at the table. Here I am, an old cocker. After all these years, and look at the things that I did to them in Shanghai. They ought to kick my ass and run me out of this country. Instead of which the premier himself comes over and honors me with a toast, which wasn't done to a lot of people.' He shook his head and he said, 'Nobody but the Chinese.' He was really very moved."

Before he left Beijing in late November, Cohen got a checkup from a local doctor. He traveled to Hong Kong and booked into a hotel under an assumed name.

Cohen then returned to the lobby of the Peninsula hotel, conjuring up prospects for selling everything from buttons to wheat, telling all who would listen, "I still have good contacts in Beijing." Karnow spent a few hours with him at the Peninsula. "He was not terribly interesting, a little bit of a letdown after all the publicity about him. I don't think he knew very much about what was going on in China at the time. We don't want to exaggerate this guy. He wasn't a neurosurgeon. He was representing some Canadian grain companies. He was playing it pretty close to the vest. The Chinese throughout the American embargo period didn't have enough grain to meet their needs, so they were importing from places that would sell to them, notably Argentina and Canada. He had gone there with this commercial mission in mind that he could act as an intermediary between the Canadian grain producers and the Chinese buyers. He was kind of secretive about it. He wasn't going to reveal the details of what they were to me. Maybe it was rather a gossamer, I don't know."[24]

Soon Cohen returned to England. As he lived safely in the West, the Red Guards he had watched march by were more than a little overly enthusiastic. By January 1967, the Chinese military had to be called in to quell riots and violence. Red Guards attacked foreign missions in Beijing. The Soviet embassy had to be evacuated. They accused the Indian embassy staff of espionage, tried the officials, and beat them as they waited at the airport to leave. When the chauffeur of the Mongolian ambassador refused to accept a portrait of Mao from the Red Guards, the guards dragged him from his car. They then set the car on fire, invaded the embassy, and assaulted the staff. Red Guards called for strikes against the British in Hong Kong, and at the end of August they burned the British chancery to the ground.

During the summer of 1967 they stormed the homes of journalists like that of the Reuters correspondent Anthony Grey. "Black paint was sloshed on me, soaking through my shirt and shorts and running down my bare legs into my socks and shoes," Grey wrote of his treatment after being dragged into his courtyard on the evening of August 18. "Glue was daubed on my back and a pink paper poster was slapped on it. I was tugged around with my head forced down among the crowd while they shouted and screamed slogans and pummelled me." The group forced Grey's tarred and feathered body into a jet plane position, with his head pushed down toward the ground and his arms pulled back behind him. The screaming crowd only quieted down as one of the Red Guards read Grey's "list of crimes," and cheered and jeered as such offenses as "You have drunk alcohol in your house" or "You have sneaked around in your house" were rattled off. When Grey tried to straighten out his body, he was struck hard in the stomach.

"The shouting and screaming of slogans was supplemented by the noise of other Red Guards rampaging through the house. Pictures were being flung to the floor and smashed. Typewriters, radios, and ornaments were hurled around, books were being scattered, curtains and furniture were being daubed with thick black slogans both in Chinese characters and English. Glass was breaking, nails were being hammered in and glue was dripping on me from a portrait of Mao that was being stuck up above the outside door of the house on the glass fanlight." When Grey was roughly told to straighten up, he saw his cat Ming Ming hanging from the balcony with a rope tied around its neck. The crowd then chanted for his lynching and took turns reading from Mao's Little Red Book. Instead of killing him, they imprisoned him in his home. They nailed wood across his doors and windows, and sealed his office and lounge with tape. Inside his new cell, they splashed paint on his sheets and walls, painted windows to block out the light, hung posters of Mao, dribbled Ming Ming's blood on his bunk, and put up such slogans as "Down with Grey." The Red Guards left him there for two years.[25]

Cohen did not talk of the Cultural Revolution. When he spoke to the Graduates Association at Hillel House, he discussed the Jews of Kaifeng, the discovery of Jewish scrolls in China, and complained that the United States forced Israel to vote against China's entry to the United Nations. "If Israel had not done what America wanted, the American Jewish community might have been unable to send money to Israel."

In mid-March 1967 Cohen visited relatives in Cape Town for the wedding of his great-nephew Adrian Wallace, and gave Adrian and his bride, Shelia, a ticket to London for their honeymoon. He continued to rave about the new China. "I must confess I was thrilled with what I saw."

His health started to decline. Around Christmas 1967, Cohen checked into the Salford Royal Hospital for a few weeks following a bout of influenza. Cohen also visited a health clinic in Bristol. While there, however, he refused to change his habits. "I didn't know who he was," said Rose Owen, who attended the clinic for treatment of her sciatica. "I went into the television room to watch television. I had some asthma. I suddenly smelt heavy cigar smoke at the back of the room. I didn't turn my head. I simply called out, 'No smoking allowed in this room.' Then the next day there was this big man, very big man, sort of obnoxious type of man, with a sister, glaring at me. I eventually found out that it was he who was smoking the cigar and had apparently been given permission to smoke this cigar. The other people said to me, 'Do you know who he is?' I said 'No,' and they said, 'He is 'Two-Gun' Cohen.' It meant nothing to me. He was a very self-important type of man. I found him most obnoxious. He went around smoking this vile-smelling cigar the whole time."[26]

In Salford Cohen took it easy, lounging in his favorite high-back leather arm-chair, smoking his King Edward cigars, and nursing a cup of black coffee. Each morning he headed out to the local news agent for his papers. "When he used to go in for the newspapers there were a lot of urchins there," said Cooper. "It wasn't an upper-class area. It was working-class. They used to come in to spend their five and ten pence on the sweets. When my uncle came in and there were three or four children in the shop, he would say to the news agent, 'Give them what they want.' " Cohen then bought for himself everything from the *Daily Worker,* the *Daily Herald,* the *Telegraph,* and the *Financial Times* to the *Times* of London. "He used to get an armful of newspapers," said Cooper "He just turned to the editorials and read all the editorials." His sister Sarah visited him regularly. Others stopped by, too. He enjoyed watching boxing on the television, and would sometimes invite passing garbage collectors into the house for a stiff glass of whiskey. On Saturdays, he attended religious services. He even donated a few carved blackwood chairs from China to the synagogue. He also took trips to London.

Occasionally he got his ire up. When in March 1969 a headline in the *Jewish Gazette* proclaimed, "Chinese a New Danger to Jews," and quoted a statement by a Glasgow rabbi warning of the threats of anti-Semitism coming from China, Cohen jumped to China's defense. He noted that even though many of the weapons used against Israel came from China and Russia, the Chinese had done more for the Jews than any other nation. He gave other talks. In May 1969 Cohen spoke at the annual luncheon of Southport WIZO.[27]

He had little else to do but to reflect on his improbable life. Despite the myth that he spent years nurturing, Cohen was not a force in Chinese politics, finance, or the military. Nor was he a grand strategist or political philosopher. His early years and predilections almost seemed to destine him for a life of crime. He ran with petty villains and could have easily graduated to being an enforcer, a rumrunner, or holding some other position within a large urban mob. He was never entirely to escape his shady past, his darker side as the gambler and charlatan, yet his makeup was thankfully tempered by an essentially generous soul. By chance or luck he fell in with a group of Chinese who, while engaging in the sort of nefarious practices that he gravitated to, also yearned for an overthrow of the imperial order in their homeland.

China between the wars was the Wild East. It was the last great frontier, filled with adventurers and fortune seekers, offering them the freedom to range and look for what they could take. Cohen seemed made for such a land. But as a Polish-born Jew who witnessed oppression in Poland and England, Cohen's past enabled him with the help of Mah Sam, Sun Yat-sen, Soong Qingling, and others to appreciate something larger than personal gains. From them he learned sacrifice. They tempered many but not all of his predilections, and gave him something to devote his life to. Cohen therefore did not take the easy route to wealth. He ultimately traveled the more rewarding path by working in his small way for China's development and quest for independence.

While in China he also matured. There as a means of survival Cohen learned to be effective. He figured out how to get things done, grudgingly earning the respect of a foreign diplomatic community obsessed with class, where a blue-collar accent and a non-Christian faith often meant little entrée.

His time with Sun and his reverence for the leader's name ultimately made Cohen's career. It guaranteed that he was always to be remembered as a loyal assistant to the father of modern China, and one of the rare white men who sided with the Chinese. With the communist takeover of the mainland and the Nationalists' departure for Taiwan, this link to the father of modern China gave Cohen rare though limited access to both camps. And when he took one of the last gambles of his life, and sided with the communists, they granted him an extended twilight during which he could nurture his myth.

In September 1970 Cohen attended a friend's wedding in Glasgow, and then returned home to Salford. "That day I went down to see him," said Sarah of her visit on the afternoon of the seventh. "He was in bed resting. He said he didn't feel well. He never used to say anything about himself like that. He said, 'Oh, I will just go into the bathroom.' " When he got up, Sarah and Leah changed his sheets. Leah also straightened the cushions on his chair. "When he came back he sat back in his chair," Sarah continued. "He sat down and I was next to him. He said he didn't feel well and my sister said she didn't like the looks of him." Cohen's head then dropped. "Oh, he is gone," Leah said. Sarah looked up at her brother, whom she held, and then turned to Leah. "What are you talking about," Sarah asked confusedly. "Well," she recalled later, "he died in my arms, in my arms!"

Cohen's battles ended that day in the year of the Dog. The man who lived through the turmoils of twentieth-century China, and was reported to have been killed numerous times, died peacefully in England surrounded by his sisters Leah and Sarah, but far from his adopted home and his Chinese comrades. After so many years and so many deals, he died with an estate worth less than £6,300. Yet he was to be well remembered. Morris Cohen was laid out in a coffin at the Broughton Lane house. He wore his tallith, his prayer shawl. His father, Josef, would have been pleased. "It was a clear day," said the Reverend Leslie Olsberg, the rabbi at the Headon Park Synagogue who officiated. "They all congregated at Broughton Lane. I remember remarking how the house was so beautiful with all the Chinese carvings and things on the wall. It was like a Chinese mausoleum."

Relatives, acquaintances, and the press came to pay their respects. So many people showed up at his funeral that the police had to control the traffic. The burial was marked by one of the few public occasions where Communist Chinese and Taiwanese officials appeared together in public. Even if these countrymen refused to accept each other's existence as they stood side by side above the grave, his old allies could not ignore their western brother. Soong could not forget Cohen either. Upon being contacted by his family, she sent a Chinese inscription to be carved alongside the English and Hebrew markings on his black granite tombstone. Then on September 12, 1971, two officials from the Chinese embassy in London traveled north for the memorial consecration. With them they brought a wreath of flowers, which they set by his stone: "This is the Tomb of Ma-Kun inscribed by Soong Qingling, Vice Chairman of the People's Republic of China Beijing." It was her final tribute to a faithful protector and friend.[28]

(AJJDC) American Jewish Joint Distribution Committee Archives
(BCA) British Columbia Archives and Records Service
(FBI) Federal Bureau of Investigation
(IWM) Imperial War Museum
(ISA) Israel State Archives
(NAC) National Archives, Ottawa, Canada
(NAUS) National Archives, Washington, DC, USA
(NWC) Naval War College, Naval Historical Collection
(PAHS) Prince Albert Historical Society
(PAA) Provincial Archives of Alberta
(PAM) Provincial Archives of Manitoba
(PRO) Public Record Office, London
(PROHK) Public Record Office, Hong Kong
(SAB) Saskatchewan Archives Board
(SMPR) Shanghai Municipal Police Records
(USSD) United States State Department

CHAPTER 1
Canton, December 1929

1. Interview with Victor Cooper, May 6, 1995. Cohen constantly stated that he was born in London. It was, though, an open family secret that he was actually born in Poland, and according to his nephew Victor Cooper and others, he arrived in England as a small child; "The Communists controlled . . ." from Charles Drage, *Two-Gun Cohen* (London: Jonathan Cape, 1954), p. 167. Pages 164–76 deal with Cohen's account of his activities during the uprising; Harold R. Isaacs, *The Tragedy of the Chinese Revolution* (New York: Atheneum, 1968), pp. 285–90; Edwin Pak-wah Leung, *Historical Dictionary of Revolutionary China, 1839–1976* (New York: Greenwood Press, 1992), pp. 12, 25; Thomas, S. Bernard, *Proletarian Hegemony in the Chinese Revolution and the Canton Commune of 1927* (Ann Arbor: Center for Chinese Studies, The University of Michigan, 1975), pp. 19–26; "One woman orator . . ." from Hoover Institution, Huston Papers, Part 2, Folder 5, p. 17. The uprising was covered extensively in the *South China Morning Post*, Dec. 12–31, 1927.

2. "We attacked in . . ." from Drage, p. 167.

3. "During the two . . ." from Huston Papers, Part 2, Folder 5, pp. 25–26; "Most of the fighting . . ." and "Guilty of murder . . ." from Earl Swisher, *Canton in Revolution, the Collected Papers of Earl Swisher, 1925–1928*, ed. Kenneth W. Rea (Boulder, Colo.: Westview Press,

1977), pp. 97–98, 115; "Everywhere was the odor . . ." from Huston Papers, report by Hinke, pp. 14–15.

4. "Seem to have been . . ." and "To sum up . . ." from PRO, FO371 13165 (F584/7/10), Dec. 28, 1927, enclosure by Faure; "A party or two" from Drage, p. 177; Interview with Arthur Michael Ferrier, June 5, 1995; "I found many . . ." from PRO, FO37113961 (F6976/6976/10), circa Oct. 1929. Statement by Morris Cohen.

CHAPTER 2

The Pogroms

1. "The Zhyds . . .," "Clerks, saloon . . .," and "Toward the evening . . ." quoted in S. M. Dubnow, *History of the Jews in Russia and Poland: From the Earliest Times Until the Present Day*, vol. 2 (Hoboken, N.J.: Ktav Publishing House, 1975), pp. 249–51; "The rioting . . ." and "general mêlée . . ." London *Times* piece quoted in the *Jewish Chronicle*, May 6, 1881.

2. E. M. Almedingen, *The Emperor Alexander II* (London: The Bodley Head, 1962), pp. 342–44; W. E. Mosse, *Alexander II and the Modernization of Russia* (London: I. B. Tauris & Co. Ltd., 1992), pp. 172–3; William J. Fishman, *East End Jewish Radicals 1875–1914* (London: Gerald Duckworth & Co. Ltd., 1975), p. 27; Dubnow, p. 251; Jonathan Frankel, *Prophecy and Politics: Socialism, Nationalism, and the Russian Jews, 1862–1917* (Cambridge: Cambridge University Press, 1981), pp. 52, 69.

3. *Encyclopaedia Judaica*, vol. 13, Encyclopaedia Judaica Jerusalem (New York: The Macmillan Company, 1971), p. 697; Saro W. Baron, *The Russian Jew Under Tsars and Soviets* (New York: Macmillan Publishing Co., Inc., 1976), p. 44; I. Michael Aronson, "Geographical and Socioeconomic Factors in the 1881 Anti-Jewish Pogroms in Russia," *The Russian Review* 39, no. 1 (January 1980), pp. 21–26; Dubnow, pp. 247–49.

4. *Roster of Communities*, Encyclopedia of the Jewish Settlements from the Day of their Establishment until the Holocaust of the Second World War, Poland, vol. 4, Warsaw and the Galilee (Jerusalem: Yad Va'Shem Publication, 1989), pp. 499–500; *Slownik Geograficzny Krolestwa Polskiego*, vol. 9 (Warsaw, 1888), p. 460.

5. *Roster of Communities*, p. 146; *Slownik Geograficzny Krolestwa Polskiego*, vol. 6, p. 290; *Slownik Geograficzny Krolestwa Polskiego*, vol. 1, p. 220; Interview with Leah Cooper, c. 1978, Manchester Public Library. Spellings for Josef and Sheindel are from a talk with their grandson, Victor Cooper. Spellings for Malka and Zelig are from a talk with their grandson, Monty Spiers; *Book of Remembrance*: The Martyrs of Biezun, (Tel Aviv: 1956), p. 103; Interview with Victor Cooper, May 6, 1995. Cohen consistently gave two different years of birth, 1887 and 1889. According to Cooper, the earlier date is the correct one.

6. Franklin D. Scott, *Sweden: The Nation's History* (Carbondale: Southern Illinois University Press, 1988), p. 208; Paul Robert Magocsi, *Historical Atlas of East Central Europe* (Seattle: University of Washington Press, 1993), pp. 70–76.

7. "All Jews . . ." quoted in Baron, pp. 10–11; Fishman, p. 3.

8. Fishman, p. 22; *Encyclopaedia Judaica*, vol. 13, pp. 26–28; Baron pp. 64–76; Albert S.

Lindemann, *The Jew Accused: Three Anti-Semitic Affairs (Dreyfus, Beilis, Frank) 1894–1915* (Cambridge: Cambridge University Press, 1991); "The ruin of the peasants . . ." quoted in Dubnow, p. 14.

9. Aronson, "Geographical," pp. 21–30; Baron, p. 95; *Encyclopaedia Judaica*, vol. 13, pp. 26–28.

10. Lindemann, p. 34.

11. Baron, pp. 29–35; Michael Stanislawski, "The Transformation of Traditional Authority in Russian Jewry: The First Stage," in *The Legacy of Jewish Immigration: 1881 and Its Impact*, ed. David Berger (New York: Brooklyn College Press, 1983), pp. 25–27; Lindemann, pp. 132–33.

12. Fishman, pp. 4–6.

13. Baron, pp. 39–40; "At twelve o'clock . . ." quoted in Dubnow, pp. 252–53.

14. "Their proceedings were watched . . ." from *The Illustrated London News*, June 18, 1881.

15. Dubnow, pp. 252–57, 280–81; Frankel, pp. 52–55; Baron, p. 45.

16. "The government will prosecute . . ." quoted in Frankel, p. 108; Baron, pp. 43–45; I. Michael Aronson, "The Attitudes of Russian Officials in the 1880s Toward Jewish Assimilation and Emigration," *Slavic Review* 34, no. 1 (Mar. 1975), pp. 1, 7; Lindemann, p. 138; Dubnow, pp. 312–16.

17. Frankel, p. 50; *Roster of Communities*, p. 417; Interview with Leah Cooper, c. 1978; Fishman, p. 69; Jonathan Frankel, "The Crisis of 1881–82 As a Turning Point in Modern Jewish History," in *The Legacy of Jewish Immigration: 1881 and Its Impact*, ed. David Berger (New York: Brooklyn College Press, 1983), p. 14; Harry Gutkin, *Journey Into Our Heritage: The Story of the Jewish People in the Canadian West* (Toronto: Lester & Orpen Dennys, 1980), p. 27.

18. V. D. Lipman, *A History of the Jews in Britain since 1858* (Leicester: Leicester University Press, 1990), pp. 12–14; Many "are lost without livelihoods . . ." quoted in Lloyd P. Gartner, *The Jewish Immigrant in England, 1870–1914* (London: Simon Publications, 1973), p. 24; Frankel, "Crisis," pp. 13–14; Frankel, *Prophecy*, pp. 58, 64, 73; Fishman, pp. 34–46.

19. Gartner, pp. 34–35.

20. "By the time . . ." from W. H. Wilkins, *The Alien Invasion* (London: Methuen & Co., 1892), pp. 40–41.

21. Wilkins, p. 42; "There are a few . . ." from Charles Booth, ed., *Labour and Life of the People*, vol. I, *East London* (London: Williams and Norgate, 1891), pp. 582–83.

22. "They then conduct them . . ." quoted in *A Documentary History of Jewish Immigrants in Britain, 1840–1920*, ed. David Englander (Leicester: Leicester University Press, 1994), pp. 19–21.

23. Wilkins, pp. 42–42; Manuscript, London Museum of Jewish Life, Memoirs of Abraham Mundy (Secretary of JTS), Jews' Temporary Shelter (1), 346–1983, pp. 1–36; Interview Leah Cooper, c. 1978.

24. "But as I write . . ." from Charles Dickens, "Old Clothes!" *Household Words,* no. 108, April 17, 1853, p. 108.

25. Gartner, pp. 81–87; "The coat hangs on . . ." from Booth, p. 212.

26. Lipman, pp. 51–57.

27. "I have myself seen . . ." from Wilkins, p. 45; Chaim Bermant, *Point of Arrival: A Study of London's East End* (London: Eyre Methuen, 1975), pp. 148–49; Robert Steven Wechsler, "The Jewish Garment Trade in East London 1875–1914: A Study of Conditions and Responses," Ph.D. diss., Columbia University, 1979, pp. 94–107; Beatrice Potter, "Pages from a Work-Girl's Diary," *The Nineteenth Century* 24, no. 139 (Sept. 1888), pp. 304–12; Gartner, pp. 160–61.

CHAPTER 3
London

1. 1897 Post Office London Street Directory, pp. 723–24; "Great deal of poverty . . ." from Booth, *Labour and Life of the People,* Appendix to vol. 2, pp. 29–30; W. J. Fishman, *East End 1888: Life in a London Borough among the Laboring Poor* (Philadelphia: Temple University Press, 1988), p. 42; "Often as a child . . ." from Morton Lewis, *Ted Kid Lewis: His Life and Times* (London: Robson Books, 1990), p. 3; Robin Odell, *Jack the Ripper in Fact and Fiction* (London: George G. Harrap & Co., 1965), p. 65; "In the dark shadow . . ." from *Times* of London, Oct. 1, 1888.

2. Fishman, pp. 6, 42, 183; H. J. Dyos and Michael Wolff, eds., *The Victorian City: Images and Realities,* vol. 1 (London: Routledge & Kegan Paul, 1973), pp. 162–75; vol. 2, p. 595; "A long, low room . . ." from Arthur Conan Doyle, *The Complete Sherlock Holmes,* vol. 1 (New York: Doubleday & Co., 1953), pp. 259–60; "Abjectly poor . . ." from Booth, p. 29; Bermant, pp. 190–92; "The predominant idea . . ." from Raphael Samuel, *East End Underworld: Chapters in the Life of Arthur Harding* (London: Routledge & Kegan Paul, 1981), pp. 2–5, 24.

3. Gartner, pp. 151–52; Aubrey Newman, ed., *The Jewish East End, 1840–1939* (London: The Jewish Historical Society of England, 1981), pp. 207–11; "With poisonous and malodorous . . . ," "Particles of the superfluous . . . ," and "In another room . . ." from Andrew Mearns, *The Bitter Cry of Outcast London: An Inquiry Into the Condition of the Abject Poor* (October 1883; reprint, the Victorian Library, Anthony S. Wohl, ed., New York: Humanities Press, 1970), pp. 58–60; Bermant, p. 149.

4. Odell, p. 23; "Most of the inhabitants . . ." from Frederick Porter Wensley, *Detective Days* (London: Cassell & Co. Ltd., 1931), p. 8; Gartner, pp. 183–84; *Times* of London, Aug. 23, 1887; Newman, pp. 110–12.

5. Anne, J. Kershen, *Uniting the Tailors: Trade Unionism amongst the Tailoring Workers of London and Leeds, 1870–1939* (Ilford: Frank Cass, 1995), pp. 134–36; Bermant, pp. 165–66; Alan Palmer, *The East End: Four Centuries of London Life* (London: John Murray Publishers Ltd., 1989), p. 93; Dyos, p. 594; Gartner, pp. 122–29.

6. Palmer, p. 100; "Foreign paupers . . ." from *Times* of London, May 19, 1887; "Alien looks, habits . . ." from Arnold White, *The Destitute Alien in Great Britain* (London: Swan Sonnenschein & Co., 1892), pp. 88–92; Bermant, pp. 115–17; Fishman, pp. 217–18; Odell, pp. 101–2.

7. "It was a sin . . ." from Drage, p. 12; Palmer, p. 103; Gartner, pp. 180–81; Samuel, p. 6; Fishman, p. 305; Lipman, pp. 95, 100.

8. "Orange boxes . . ." from Samuel, p. 22; "There was plenty . . ." and "It was heavy . . ." from Drage, pp. 12, 13; "Shtick it in . . ." from V. D. Lipman, "Trends in Anglo-Jewish Occupations," *The Jewish Journal of Sociology* 2, no. 2 (Nov. 1960), p. 202; Gartner p. 61.

9. Eugene C. Black, *The Social Politics of Anglo-Jewry 1880–1920* (Oxford: Basil Blackwell Ltd., 1988), pp. 109–11; *Jewish Chronicle*, March 8, 1889, July 2, 1982; "The blow . . . ," "When I got there . . . ," and "Impressive and awe-inspiring . . ." from Drage, pp. 13–14; Lipman, *History*, p. 106; S. L. Bensusan, "The Largest School in the World," *The Windsor Magazine*, 1896, p. 459; Jewish Free School, Admission Register.

10. "When it was time . . ." from Lewis, p. 5; Drage, p. 14; "At the Standard . . ." from Samuel, p. 49; Fishman, pp. 322–24.

11. *The Builder*, Dec. 22, 1894, p. 460, May 23, 1885, p. 748; "The people's own theatre . . ." quoted in A. E. Wilson, *East End Entertainment* (London: Arthur Barker Ltd., 1954), p. 80; Samuel, pp. 49–50; Odell, pp. 20–22; Fishman, p. 186; Palmer p. 90; *The Building News and Engineering Journal* 48, no. 1585 (May 22, 1885), p. 808; Drage, p. 15; "The fun must be broad . . ." from *The Echo*, Dec. 4, 1895; Paragon Programme, Jan. 25, 1894; Victor Glasstone, *Victorian and Edwardian Theatres: An Architectural and Social Survey* (London: Thames and Hudson, 1975), pp. 38, 57.

12. Fishman, pp. 185, 310; Millicent Rose, *The East End of London* (London: The Cresset Press, 1951), pp. 225–29; John Henry MacKay, *The Anarchists: A Picture of Civilization at the Close of the Nineteenth Century* (Boston: Benjamin R. Tucker, 1891), pp. 171–72; "The shop was empty . . ." from Sir Frederick Treves, *The Elephant Man and Other Reminiscences* (London: Cassell and Company, 1923), pp. 2–3; Michael Howell and Peter Ford, *The True History of the Elephant Man* (London: Allison & Busby, 1983), p. 54. Merrick's true first name was Joseph, not John as has been constantly misstated.

13. Deborah E. B. Weiner, "The People's Palace: An Image for East London in the 1880s," *Metropolis London: Histories and Representations Since 1800*, eds. David Feldman and Gareth Stedman Jones (London: Routledge, 1989), pp. 43–48; Fishman, p. 306; Lewis, pp. 6–11, 15; Samuel, p. 129; Bob Burrill, *Who's Who in Boxing* (New Rochelle: Arlington House, 1974), p. 151; *The Encyclopaedia of Boxing*, p. 161; Wilson, pp. 201, 205; "I was quick . . ." and "That was the biggest . . ." from Drage, pp. 15–16.

14. "Once in a while . . ." from Drage, p. 17; "As roystering . . ." and "The kinchins . . ." from Charles Dickens, *Oliver Twist* (New York: Bantam Books, 1981), pp. 54–55, 329; "I learnt about . . ." from Samuel, pp. 75–76; Kellow Chesney, *The Anti-Society: An Account of the Victorian Underworld* (Boston: Gambit, 1970), pp. 128–37, 146–47.

CHAPTER 4

Reform School

1. "Whose head did not . . ." from *Jewish Chronicle*, Sept. 23, 1898.

2. Dec. 29, 1906, paper by Israel Ellis, read at the Beth Hamudrash, collection Harry Cohen; Black, pp. 237–39; *Jewish Chronicle*, Feb. 2, 1901.

3. Dickens, *Oliver Twist*, p. 332; Greater London Record Office, PSTH/A1/63, PSTH/A1/62; Ellis paper; Research by Terence Bown, administrative officer at the Metropolitan Police Service; "Several times . . ." from Drage, p. 18; "Blessed are the undefiled . . ." from Psalm 119, *The Holy Bible* (Oxford: Oxford University Press, 1964), p. 646; "Young, and had . . ." and "For being beyond . . ." from *Jewish Chronicle*, Feb. 22, 1901.

4. Sales brochure for Sept. 26, 1935, auction, from Messers. J. Trevor & Sons, auctioneers; Ellis paper; *Jewish Chronicle*, Nov. 13, 1894, Feb. 22, 1901; "Ready, begin . . ." and "They did that until . . ." from an interview with Harry Cohen, Nov. 13, 1994.

5. Ellis paper; Harry Cohen interview, May 17, 1994, Nov. 13, 1994; *Certified School Gazette*, Sept. 1911; Drage, p. 19.

6. Ellis paper; Drage, pp. 19–20; "The spirit of progress . . ." and "Deceit and similar . . ." from *Jewish Chronicle*, June 17, 1904; "I believe I am correct . . ." and "some tuneful singing" from *Jewish Chronicle*, June 24, 1904; "To be manly . . ." from *Jewish Chronicle*, July 7, 1905; Report of the Sub-Committee on Finance. To the managers, Hayes Industrial School, collection of Harry Cohen.

7. *Jewish Chronicle*, July 7, 1905; Ellis paper; *Certified School Gazette*, Sept. 1912; Valerie Knowles, *Strangers at Our Gates: Canadian Immigration and Immigration Policy, 1540–1990* (Toronto: Dundurn Press, 1992), p. 69; "A fair garden-like country . . ." quoted in Joy Parr, *Labouring Children: British Immigrant Apprentices to Canada, 1869–1924* (Toronto: University of Toronto Press, 1994), pp. 46–47; Harry Cohen interview, May 17, 1994; *Certified School Gazette*, Sept. 1911.

CHAPTER 5

The New World

1. Shipping lists from England to Canada are not complete. A search of the lists has failed to turn up Cohen's name. In Drage, Cohen recalled being given a blue suit for his trip to Canada. Barnardo children were given blue suits before they left home. Cohen also said that it was raining when he departed. The summer of 1905 was quite parched in London. It likewise rained on Aug. 3, 1905, the date that Owen set off with one group of Barnardo children; "The hour of departure . . ." and "There is some extra . . ." from *Ups and Downs*, Jan. 1906; "How often, when the sea . . ." from Gail H. Corbett, *Barnardo Children in Canada* (Peterborough, N.H.: Woodland Publishing, 1981), pp. 33–34.

2. "After the evening service . . ." from *Ups and Downs*, Jan. 1906; Corbett, pp. 29–35; Kenneth Bagnell, *The Little Immigrants: The Orphans Who Came to Canada* (Toronto: Mac-

millan, 1980), pp. 205–7; Knowles, pp. 67, 84; Canadian Pacific Archives, RG-8 Public relations files; Gutkin, p. 43.

3. "For four hundred . . ." and "Each village . . ." from Rupert Brooke, *Letters from America* (New York: Charles Scribner's Sons, 1916), pp. 101, 123–24; Saskatchewan Department of Agriculture, *Annual Report, 1906*, published by Saskatchewan Department of Agriculture, 1907, pp. 54–55; John Herd Thompson, "Bringing in the Sheaves: The Harvest Excursionists, 1890–1929," *Canadian Historical Review* 59, no. 4 (Dec. 1978), pp. 467–89; Kenneth Bagnell, *The Little Immigrants: The Orphans Who Came to Canada* (Toronto: Macmillan, 1980), p. 207; James H. Gray, *Boomtime: Peopling the Canadian Prairies* (Saskatoon: Western Producer Prairie Books, 1979), p. 51.

4. John H. Archer, *Saskatchewan: A History* (Saskatoon: Western Producer Prairie Books, 1980), pp. 2–6; J. Howard Richards, *Saskatchewan Geography: The Physical Environment and Its Relationship with Population and the Economic Base* (Saskatoon: University of Saskatchewan, c. 1960), p. 5–8; J. Howard Richards and K. I. Fung, eds. *Atlas of Saskatchewan* (Saskatoon: University of Saskatchewan, 1969), p. 4; H. G. L. Strange, *A Short History of Prairie Agriculture* (Winnipeg: Searle Grain Company Ltd., 1954), pp. 7, 18; Donald G. Wetherell with Elise Corbet, *Breaking New Ground: A Century of Farm Equipment Manufacturing on the Canadian Prairies* (Saskatoon: Fifth House Publishers, 1993), p. 3.

5. "You filed your claim . . ." and "It's twenty miles . . ." from Walter Wiggins, "Hired Man in Saskatchewan," *The Marxist Quarterly* (winter 1964), pp. 77–78; Knowles, p. 49; Gray, pp. 52–62, 104; Richards and Fung, p. 17; C. F. Wilson, *A Century of Canadian Grain: Government Policy to 1951* (Saskatoon: Western Producer Prairie Books, 1978), pp. 3, 7–8; Simon Belkin, *Through Narrow Gates: A Review of Jewish Immigration, Colonization and Immigrant Aid Work in Canada (1840–1940)* (Montreal: The Eagle Publishing Co., 1966), pp. 1–7; Paul Voisey, "The Urbanization of the Canadian Prairies, 1871–1916," *Histoire sociale/ Social History* 8, no. 15 (May 1975), pp. 77–101; *Mingling Memories: A History of Wapella and Districts* (Wapella, Sask: Wapella History Committee, 1979), p. 61.

6. *Whitewood Centennial 1892–1992*, vol. 2, (Brigdens Printers, 1992), pp. 53–54, 63–66, 963; Strange, p. 22–23.

7. Voisey, pp. 78–82; Gray, pp. 19–21, 76–80, 84, 85, 101–2, 126–31; Archer, p. 161; David Spector, *Agriculture on the Prairies, 1870–1940* (Ottawa: National Historic Parks and Sites Branch, Parks Canada, 1983), p. 143; "When I think of quality . . ." quoted in Knowles, p. 64; Chester Martin, *History of Prairie Settlement: 'Dominion Lands' Policy* (Toronto: The Macmillan Company, 1938), pp. 116–17; Wilson, *A Century of Canadian Grain*, p. 10; Craig Brown, ed., *The Illustrated History of Canada* (Toronto: Lester & Orpen Dennys Ltd., 1987), pp. 383–87; Voisey, p. 83; Royal Commission on Agriculture and Rural Life, *Movement of Farm People*, Report No. 7 (Regina: Government of Saskatchewan, 1956), pp. 41–43; Richards & Fung, *Atlas*, pp. 17, 38; Strange, p. 11.

8. Gerald Tulchinsky, *Taking Root: The Origin of the Canadian Jewish Community* (Toronto: Lester Publishing Ltd., 1992), pp. 116–18; Jonathan D. Sarna, "Jewish Immigration to North America: The Canadian Experience (1870–1900)," *The Jewish Journal of Sociology* 18, no. 1 (June 1976), pp. 31–32; "The Jewish persecution . . ." quoted in Arthur A. Chiel, *The Jews in Manitoba* (Toronto: University of Toronto Press, 1961), p. 27; "From what I learn . . ." quoted in Gutkin, p. 30; Cyril Edel Leonoff, "Pioneers, Ploughs and Prayers: The Jewish Farmers of Western Canada," *Jewish Western Bulletin* (Sept. 1982).

9. "Unless some action . . ." quoted in Chiel *The Jews in Manitoba*, p. 47; Cyril Edel Leonoff, "Wapella Farm Settlement; (The First Successful Jewish Farm Settlement in Canada), A Pictorial History," (Historical and Scientific Society of Manitoba and Jewish Historical Society of Western Canada, 1970), pp. 3–20; Leonoff, "Pioneers," n.p.; Tulchinsky, pp. 109, 118–19; "Nobody claimed any taxes . . ." quoted in Michael R. Marrus, *Samuel Bronfman: The Life and Times of Seagram's Mr. Sam* (Hanover, N.H.: University Press of New England, 1991), p. 35; *Mingling Memories*, pp. 1–2; Richards & Fung, *Atlas*, pp. 73–4.

10. Cohen said that his father's friend was Abe Hyam, yet according to Cyril Leonoff, who studied the Wapella community, there was no Hyam present. Cohen must of misremembered the name. Leonoff, "Wapella Farm," p. 4; John Hawkes, *The Story of Saskatchewan and Its People* (Chicago: S. J. Clarke Publishing Co., 1924), p. 1736; "Although he'd told my father . . . ," "I'm willing to learn . . . ," "As soon as we got . . . ," and "He was an honest . . ." from Drage, pp. 22–24; "I am earning . . ." from a letter from Morris Cohen dated Oct. 21, 1905, in the possession of Harry Cohen.

11. Richards & Fung, *Atlas*, pp. 80–87; *Mingling Memories*, p. 229; "Back in those years . . ." from an interview with Douglas Callin, Apr. 9, 1995; "The food was a revelation . . ." from Drage, p. 23.

12. "Supposing you want . . . ," "I've big hands . . . ," and "Do unto others . . ." from Drage, pp. 25–27; *Saskatchewan Annual Report, 1906*, p. 15; "If one stepped . . ." from Edward West, *Homesteading: Two Prairie Seasons* (London: T. Fisher Unwin, 1918), p. 215; Robert L. Yates, *When I Was a Harvester* (New York: The Macmillan Co., 1930), p. 139.

13. *Saskatchewan Annual Report 1906*, pp. 7–8, 15–20; West, pp. 96–98.

14. Seager Wheeler, *Seager Wheeler's Book on Profitable Grain Growing* (Winnipeg: The Grain Growers' Guide, 1919), pp. 168–170; "Sometimes a man's wheat . . ." from Yates, p. 43; Wetherell, pp. 159, 175; John Bracken, *Crop Production in Western Canada* (Winnipeg: The Grain Growers' Guide, 1920), pp. 121–23; W. W. Swanson and P. C. Armstrong, *Wheat* (Toronto: The MacMillan Co., 1930), pp. 54–55; "Come out at seven . . ." from Wiggins, p. 83; Thompson, pp. 475–78, 482; *Saskatchewan Annual Report 1906*, p. 22.

15. Yates, pp. 82–88, 129; *Maclean's Magazine*, "Remember Those Harvest Excursions?" Sept. 1, 1954; "For one thing . . ." from Drage, p. 28; Thompson, pp. 478–79; Saskatchewan Department of Agriculture, *Annual Report, 1905*, published by Saskatchewan Department of Agriculture, 1906, p. 9; West, p. 138, 287; *Saskatchewan Annual Report 1906*, p. 11.

CHAPTER 6

"There's a sucker born every minute"

1. Lewis E. Aubury, "The Structural and Industrial Materials of California," Bulletin No. 38, California State Mining Bureau, San Francisco, Jan. 1906, pp. 233–40; Karl Gurcke, *Bricks and Brickmaking: A Handbook for Historical Archaeology* (Moscow, Idaho: The University of Idaho Press, 1987), pp. 5–35; "There was an office . . ." from *Anecdotes and Updates: Virden Centennial 1982* (Virden, Mani.: Empire Publishing Co. Ltd., 1982), pp. 29–30; Ida Clingan,

The Virden Story (Altona, Mani.: Friesen Printers, 1957), p. 57; Drage, pp. 28–9; "Michigan's Pioneer Brickmakers," *Journal of the IBCA* (Summer 1994).

2. In writing the biography, Cohen mistakenly put his time in Winnipeg before Moose Jaw. Archer, p. 141; Richards, *Saskatchewan Geography*, pp. 2–13; Saskatchewan Department of Agriculture, *Annual Report*, 1907, Published by Saskatchewan Department of Agriculture, 1908, pp. 94, 204–8; George L. Chindahl, *A History of the Circus in America* (Caldwell, Idaho: The Caxton Printers, Ltd., 1959), pp. 215–22; Leith Knight, *All the Moose . . . All the Jaw* (Moose Jaw: Moose Jaw 100, 1982), pp. 16–18, 60; Gordon W. Fulton, "Moose Jaw Main St. Project," 1984, unpublished paper, Moose Jaw Public Library; Moose Jaw *Times-Herald*, Sept. 21, 1989; Chang Reynolds, "The Norris & Rowe Show," part one, *Bandwagon*, Jan.–Feb. 1972, p. 8; Bob Taber, "The Greater Norris & Rowe Show," *Bandwagon*, Nov.–Dec. 1959, pp. 7–12; "The smallest comedian . . ." from a 1900 ad in the Circus World Museum collection; Robert Bogdan, *Freak Show: Presenting Human Oddities for Amusement and Profit* (Chicago: University of Chicago Press, 1988), pp. 3, 41, 45–46.

3. Taber, p. 9; Reynolds, "The Norris & Rowe Show," part 1, p. 4–13, and part 2, Mar.–Apr. 1972, pp. 4–7; "The only lady . . ." from Moose Jaw *Times*, July 5, 1907; "The performance in the main . . ." from Moose Jaw *Times*, July 12, 1907.

4. "There's a sucker . . ." the quote has been attributed to Barnum, and is quoted in John Bartlett, *Bartlett's Familiar Quotations*, 14th edition (Boston: Little, Brown and Co., 1968), p. 655; "Aside from such . . ." quoted in Bogdan, p. 95; "I was always in the middle . . ." from Drage, p. 32; Norris & Rowe 1907 Route List, collection of the Circus World Museum.

5. In Drage, Cohen says that when he left the station he was offered a room in both the Windsor Hotel and the Maple Leaf Hotel. In actuality, they were the same establishment. The Windsor Hotel was bought by Nathan Rosenblat in June 1907. He renovated the building and renamed it the Maple Leaf.; *The Commercial Traveler* 5, no. 4, June 1907, p. 7; "It seemed like London . . ." from Drage, p. 29; Gutkin, pp. 49–53; Alan Artibise, *Winnipeg: An Illustrated History* (Toronto: James Lorimer & Company, Publishers and National Museum of Man, National Museums of Canada, 1977), pp. 46–49, 64–66; Alan F. J. Artibise, *Winnipeg: A Social History of Urban Growth, 1874–1914* (Montreal: McGill-Queen's University Press, 1975), p. 130; R. C. Bellan, "Relief in Winnipeg: The Economic Background" (master's thesis, University of Toronto, 1941), pp. 55–56; "All the houses . . ." from *Personal Recollections: The Jewish Pioneer Past on the Prairies, Jewish Life and Times*, vol. 6 (Winnipeg: The Jewish Historical Society of Western Canada, 1993), p. 42; "There was a toilet . . ." and "Main Street was a most colorful . . ." from Sheppy Hershfield, "Growing Up in North Winnipeg," *The Jewish Historical Society of Western Canada*, second annual publication, selection of papers presented in 1969–1970, Apr. 1972, pp. 17, 24; J. S. Woodsworth, *My Neighbor* (Toronto: University of Toronto Press, 1972), pp. 138–39.

6. Artibise, *Winnipeg: An Illustrated History*, pp. 36–44, 62; Artibise, *Winnipeg: A Social History*, pp. 129–31, 159; "The assertion . . ." from "From Behind Hotel Registers," *The Commercial Traveler* 5, no. 10, December 1907, p. 7; Voisey, p. 91; Bellan, "Relief," pp. 46–55; *Winnipeg 100*, 100 Year Pictorial History of Winnipeg, compiled by Edith Paterson (Winnipeg: Winnipeg Free Press, 1973), p. 62; Gray, p. 93.

7. Historical research by Randy R. Rostecki; "Feeling pretty flush . . . ," "I never actually said . . .," and "Because I gotta . . ." from Drage pp. 29–31.

8. Chiel, pp. 16–20, 58–60; Sheila Grover, "669 Main Street, Zimmerman Block" (Winnipeg: City of Winnipeg Historical Buildings Committee, Mar. 10, 1986), unpublished at the Legislative Library; Sholom Aleichem, *From the Fair* (New York: Viking, 1985), pp. 38–41; Arthur Chiel, *Jewish Experiences in Early Manitoba* (Winnipeg: Manitoba Jewish Publications, 1955), pp. 9–12; *The Year Past, 1986*, Report of the City of Winnipeg Historical Buildings Committee, Department of Environmental Planning, Winnipeg, 1987, p. 39; Sheila Grover, "671–673 Main Street, 1903 Zimmerman Block" (Winnipeg: City of Winnipeg Historical Building Committee, Feb. 5, 1986), unpublished at the Legislative Library, Winnipeg, p. 3.

9. James H. Gray, *Red Lights on the Prairies* (Toronto: Macmillan of Canada, 1971), pp. 42–43, 46–50; Joy Cooper, "Red Lights of Winnipeg," *Transactions—Historical and Scientific Society of Manitoba* (Winnipeg) 3, no. 27, 1970–71, pp. 61–62; Artibise, *Winnipeg: An Illustrated History*, pp. 104–5; Artibise, *Winnipeg: A Social History*, p. 246; PAM, Archives Accession GR 651, "City of Winnipeg Police Court Record Book," Nov. 2, 1908–Sept. 30, 1909; PAM, Archives Accession GR1560, Eastern Judicial District Gaol, "Description of Prisoners Committed," Jan. 1908–Jan. 1912; "The cells at police . . ." quoted in Woodsworth, p. 140; "Ill-treats, neglects . . ." from *The Revised Statues of Manitoba* (James Hooper, King's Printer for the Province of Manitoba, 1903), p. 169; "The evidence showed . . ." from Manitoba *Free Press*, Apr. 8, 1909; Winnipeg *Telegram*, Apr. 8, 1909; Winnipeg *Tribune*, Mar. 31, 1909; Winnipeg Police Museum, *Winnipeg Record of Arrest*, 1909; Winnipeg Police Museum, *Jail Prisoner Book*, 1909; PAM, Archives Accession GR 1560, Eastern Judicial District Gaol, Return of Prisoner Committed, Jan. 1907–June 1915.

10. *Winnipeg 100*, p. 17; PAM, Archives Accession GR1560, Eastern Judicial District Gaol, "Description of Prisoners Committed," Jan. 1908–Jan. 1912; "Must be a veritable . . ." from "Special Commissioner Appointed to Investigate into the Management and Supervision of the Gaol and Prison Farm of the Eastern Judicial District of Manitoba," Printed by Order of the Legislative Assembly of Manitoba, Winnipeg, Manitoba, 1916, p. 5.

CHAPTER 7

The Chinese

1. The Saskatoon *Star Phoenix*, Oct. 10, 1953, Aug. 20, 1965; Don Kerr and Stan Hanson, *Saskatoon: The First Half-Century* (Edmonton: NeWest Press, 1982), pp. 69–78; Melville A. East, *The Saskatoon Story: 1882–1952* (Saskatoon: General Printing and Bookbinding Ltd., 1952), pp. 39–70; "Where temperance ideals . . ." quoted in John H. Archer and J. C. Bates, *Historic Saskatoon: A Concise Illustrated History of Saskatoon* (Junior Chamber of Commerce, 1947), p. 8; "Tennis, fishing . . ." and "fifteen or twenty . . ." quoted in Lorraine Blashill, *Legal Legacy* (Saskatoon: Core Communications, Inc., 1985), pp. 2, 17; Archer, *Saskatchewan: A History*, p. 162.

2. Kerr and Hanson, pp. 102–3; "Impress upon Mah Sam . . ." and "There were several . . ." from the Saskatoon *Daily Phoenix*, Sept. 28, 1909.

3. David Chuenyan Lai, *Chinatowns: Towns Within Cities in Canada* (Vancouver: University of British Columbia Press, 1988), pp. 15–20; Jin Tan and Patricia E. Roy, *The Chinese in*

Canada (Ottawa: Canadian Historical Association, 1985), pp. 3–4; Franz Schurmann and Or-ville Schell, eds., *Imperial China: The Decline of the Last Dynasty and the Origins of Modern China, The 18th and 19th Centuries* (New York: Random House, 1967), pp. 178–182; Edgar Wick-berg, ed., *From China to Canada: A History of the Chinese Communities in Canada*, (Toronto: McClelland and Stewart Ltd., 1982), pp. 6–20; "The Chinese are come up . . ." quoted in Richard Thomas Wright, *In a Strange Land: A Pictorial Record of the Chinese in Canada 1788–1923* (Saskatoon: Western Producer Prairie Books, 1988), p. 22.

4. "If you have a daughter . . ." quoted in Wright, p. 18; Knowles, p. 48; Tan and Roy, p. 7; Paul Voisey, "Chinatown on the Prairies: The Emergence of an Ethnic Community," Selected Papers from the Society for the Study of Architecture in Canada, Annual Meeting 1975 and 1976 (Ottawa: The Society, 1975–1983), pp. 33–34; Lai, pp. 31–32, 61; "Ninety-nine percent . . ." quoted in Lawrence Lam, *The Whites Accept Us Chinese Now: The Changing Dynamics of Being Chinese in Timmins*, York Timmins Project, Working Paper No. 4, York University, 1983, p. 12; Wickberg, pp. 20–23, 50; J. Brian Dawson, "The Chinese Experi-ence in Frontier Calgary: 1885–1910," in *Frontier Calgary: Town, City, and Region 1875–1914*, eds. Anthony W. Rasporich and Henry C. Klassen (Calgary: University of Calgary, 1975) p. 125; Wright, pp. 6–7; Pierre Berton, *The Great Railway, 1881–1885* (Toronto: McClelland and Stewart Ltd., 1971), pp. 182–202.

5. "Would it not . . ." quoted in Wright, p. 46; "Governed by pestilential . . ." quoted in Ban Seng Hoe, *Structural Changes of Two Chinese Communities in Alberta, Canada* (Ottawa: National Museum of Canada, 1976), p. 43; Tan and Roy, p. 8; Voisey, "Chinatown on the Prairies," p. 34; Wickberg, pp. 5, 67.

6. Wickberg, pp. 79, 84; Tien-fang Cheng, *Oriental Immigration in Canada* (Shanghai: The Commercial Press, Ltd., 1931), p. 208; Edmonton *Bulletin*, July 14, 1892; Hoe, p. 66; Daw-son, pp. 126–31; Lai, *Chinatowns*, pp. 87–89.

7. Lai, p. 54; "Chinese, when they come . . ." from Calgary *Daily Herald*, Oct. 4, 1910; Jack Peach, *Days Gone By* (Saskatoon: Fifth House Publishers, 1993), p. 55; "We know we are not . . ." quoted in Lam, p. 18.

8. "They were the point . . ." from Heather Gilead, *The Maple Leaf for Quite a While* (Lon-don: J. M. Dent & Sons Ltd., 1967), p. 18; Peach, p. 55; "Sing Lee Laundry" Proposal for 1905 Street Fort Edmonton Park. A Fort Edmonton Historical Foundation Project, p. 1; Voisey, "Chinatown on the Prairies," p. 36; Cheng, p. 201; Lai, pp. 34–35; Tan and Roy, p. 12; Lan Chan-Marples, "An Edmonton Chinese Project At Fort Edmonton Park: A Pro-posal," Fort Edmonton Historical Foundation, Feb. 24, 1983, pp. 2–3; Patrick John Day, "Wong Sing-Fuen and the Sing Lee Laundry," Historical and Natural Science Services, Edmonton Parks and Recreation, November 1978; "Everything in the laundry . . ." quoted in Daphne Marlatt and Carole Itter, eds., *Opening Doors, Vancouver's East End*, Sound Heritage (Victoria: Province of British Columbia, 1979), p. 46.

9. "A gang went . . ." from the Lethbridge *Herald*, Jan. 1, 1908; Wickberg, pp. 106–8; Cheng, p. 201; Lai, p. 55; Chuen-yan David Lai, "Contribution of the Zhigongtang in Can-ada to the Huanghuagang Uprising in Canton, 1911," *Canadian Ethnic Studies* 14, no. 3 (1982), pp. 97–98; Voisey, p. 38; L. Eve Armentrout Ma, *Revolutionaries, Monarchists, and Chinatowns: Chinese Politics in the Americas and the 1911 Revolution* (Honolulu: University of Hawaii Press, 1990), pp. 24–28.

10. Lai, *Chinatowns*, pp. 69–70; Cheng, p. 208; "Merchants . . . have made . . ." quoted in Wright, p. 56; "If a community . . ." from Gilead, p. 19; "The gambling houses . . ." quoted in Marlatt and Itter, p. 41; Voisey, p. 40.

11. Cohen claimed that a police chief Robinson had it in for him, yet there was no policeman in Saskatoon named Robinson. "I started serious gambling . . ." and "I wasn't heeled . . ." from Drage, pp. 32–33; Shih-shan Henry Tsai, *China and the Overseas Chinese in the United States, 1868–1911* (Fayetteville: University of Arkansas Press, 1983), pp. 130–36; Wickberg, p. 74.

12. Lai, "Contribution of the Zhigongtang," p. 95; Shelly Hsien Cheng, "The T'ung-Meng-Hui: Its Organization, Leadership and Finances, 1905–1912" (Ph.D. diss., University of Washington, 1962), pp. 19, 73, 102–126; Tsai, pp. 140–41; Harold Z. Schiffrin, *Sun Yat-sen: Reluctant Revolutionary* (Boston: Little, Brown and Co., 1980), pp. 116–18.

13. *Henderson's Saskatoon City Directory*, 1910, pp. 106, 202, 325; "I'd sit for hours . . ." from Drage, pp. 35–36; *Daily Phoenix*, Aug. 9–13, 1910.

14. Drage, pp. 33–34; "No, I told him . . ." and the rest of the testimony and coverage of the trial from *Daily Phoenix*, Sept. 7–9, 1910; Mah Sam's arrest and trial from *Daily Phoenix*, Sept. 15–16, 1910; *Henderson's Saskatoon City Directory*, 1910, pp. 71, 133, 155; "The Saskatoon Capital Anniversary Number," Saskatoon, May 12, 1909, pp. 29, 35, 36, 42, 61, 64.

15. PAHS, "Corrections Services (1886–1941), Documents, no. 308b"; Aug. 4, 1994, letter and research on the Prince Albert jail sent to the author from Cliff Moore, Assistant Warden, Saskatchewan Penitentiary; PAHS, "Murder Trials & Hangings Prince Albert Jail, no. 64b"; SAB, Records of the Department of Public Works, Collection no. R-195.2, file 112, Prince Albert Jail.

16. Letter and research from Cliff Moore to author; SAB, Records of the Department of Public Works, Collection no. R-195.2, file 112, Prince Albert Jail, Mar. 4, 1911, "Matrons Report," to Attorney General Alphonse Turgeon; SAB, Records of the Department of Public Works, Collection no. R-195.2, file 112, Prince Albert Jail, Mar. 4, 1911, "Gaolers Report," to Attorney General Alphonse Turgeon; SAB, Records of the Department of Public Works, Collection no. R-195.2, file 112, "Prince Albert Jail Paroles and Pardons"; PAHS, June 30, 1906, "Stock on hand in stores 30, June 1906," "Maintenance of Prisoners."; SAB, letter May 15, 1911, from gaoler C. F. McGregor to the Deputy Minister, Public Works, Regina; SAB, Records of the Department of Public Works, Collection no. R-195.2, file 112, Prince Albert Jail Prince Albert Gaol, Mar. 2, 1911, "Surgeon's Report," to Attorney General Alphonse Turgeon; *Canadian Criminal Cases* 19, Nov. 8, 1910, pp. 1–15.

17. Cohen was in jail during Sun's trip across Canada. Lai, "Contribution of the Zhigongtang," pp. 96–101; Cheng, pp. 127, 194; Tsai, p. 142; James E. Sheridan, *China in Disintegration: The Republican Era in Chinese History 1912–1949* (New York: The Free Press, 1975), pp. 40–43; Frederic Wakeman, *The Fall of Imperial China* (New York: The Free Press, 1975), pp. 226–27, 248–51; O. Edmund Clubb, *20th Century China* (New York: Columbia University Press, 1978), p. 42.

18. "That night we went . . ." from Drage, p. 37; Wang Gengxiong, "Sun Zhongshan yu Lin Baike, Ma Kun de jiaowang" (Sun Yatsen's Contacts with Paul Lineberger and Morris Cohen). Minguo chunqiu (Republican Annals) 1 (Jan. 25, 1988), pp. 3–5.

CHAPTER 8

Let the Buyer Beware

1. Margaret Gilkes and Marilyn Symons, *Calgary's Finest: A History of the City Police Force* (Calgary: Century Calgary Publications, 1975), pp. 47–57.

2. "There he was sitting . . ." and "I listened carefully . . ." from Drage, p. 40; J. G. MacGregor, *Edmonton, A History* (Edmonton: M. G. Hurtig Publishers, 1967), pp. 163–86, 189–98; Carl Frederick Betke, "The Development of Urban Community in Prairie Canada: Edmonton, 1898–1921" (Ph.D. diss., University of Alberta, Edmonton, 1981), p. 273; Edmonton *Daily Capital*, June 7, 1913; Edmonton *Journal*, Jan. 3, 1913; "I can well remember . . ." from John G. Niddrie, "The Edmonton Boom of 1911–1912," *Alberta Historical Review* (Historical Society of Alberta) 13 (Spring 1965), p. 2.

3. Voisey, "The Urbanization of the Canadian Prairies," pp. 83, 95; "Men came from . . ." Niddrie, p. 4; MacGregor, pp. 194, 197; *Saturday Night* (Toronto), Dec. 7, 1912; John F. Gilpin, "The Poor Relation has come into Her Fortune: The British Investment Boom in Canada 1905–1915," *Canada House Lecture Series*, no. 53. pp. 3, 6–10, 13–15; Voisey, "The Urbanization of the Canadian Prairies," p. 98; "There was good money . . ." and "I had to see . . ." from Drage, p. 40; "Smooth-tounged . . ." from *Monetary Times*, May 18, 1912; "In the doorway . . ." from Brooke, p.131; "And yet the plain . . ." from Edmonton *Journal*, Feb. 3, 1913.

4. "If a prospective . . ." from *Saturday Night*, Dec. 23, 1911; Edmonton *Capital*, Apr. 27, 1912; Archer, *Saskatchewan: A History*, p. 162; Archer, *Historic Saskatoon*, p. 30; "If any Chinese . . .," "High, dry . . .," and "I put in a big . . ." from Drage, pp. 41–42; "Mr. A. Cohen . . ." from *Edmonton Capital*, Apr. 27, 1912; *Henderson's Edmonton City Directory*, 1912.

5. Edmonton *Daily Capital*, June 1, 1912; "Not until they . . ." from Edmonton *Daily Bulletin*, June 3, 1912.

6. "Was a red-letter . . ." from Edmonton *Daily Bulletin*, Mar. 17, 1913; Cheng, *Oriental Immigration in Canada*, p. 78; Tan and Roy, p. 9; Day, pp. 6–7; Howard Palmer, *Patterns of Prejudice: A History of Nativism in Alberta* (Toronto: McClelland and Stewart, 1982), p. 32.

7. Clubb, pp. 47–60; "Mr. Cohen is in close . . ." from Edmonton *Daily Capital*, Aug. 8, 1912.

8. Hoe, p. 50; Wickberg, pp. 91, 104–5, 109, 148; "Sing Lee Laundry"; Betke, pp. 288–89; Chan-Marples, pp. 4–11; Day, pp. 4–11; Cheng, "The T'ung-Meng-Hui," p. 129; Edmonton *Daily Capital*, Aug. 8, 1912; Ma Xiang, "Gensui Sun Zhongshan xiansheng shi yu nian de huiyi" (Recollections of following Mr. Sun Yatsen for more than ten years), In Shang Mingxuan et al., eds., *Sun Zhongshan shengping shiye zhuiyilu* (Recollections of Sun Yatsen's life and work) (Beijing: Renmin chubanshe, 1986); Edmonton *Bulletin*, June 4, 1928; Edmonton *Journal*, Apr. 14, 1923; *Renwu shuangyuekan (People bimonthly)*, 1986, no. 5, pp. 83–85; "Here I found my . . ." from Drage, p. 42; PAA, *Commissioner of Oaths*, accession no. 70.427.

9. *Henderson's Edmonton City Directory*, 1913; Edmonton *Daily Capital*, June 12, 1913; "I needed no time . . ." and "I packed my bags . . ." from Drage, p. 46.

10. Millicent Rose, *The East End of London* (London: The Cresset Press, 1951), p. 157; Bermant, p. 132; "When I thought . . ." and "I stood up . . ." from Drage, p. 49; "He gave me my first toy" from an interview with Sarah Rich, Nov. 8, 1992.

11. Betke, pp. 306–11; "Edmonton Has Fortress . . ." from Edmonton *Journal*, June 7, 1913; Edmonton *Daily Capital*, June 14, 1913; *The Labour Gazette*, The Department of Labour, Dominion of Canada 13, no. 9 (March 1913); Voisey, "The Urbanization of the Canadian Prairies," p. 98; Edmonton *Daily Capital*, May 26, 1913; "Further, it has done . . ." from Edmonton *Bulletin*, Dec. 4, 1913.

12. *Backtracking with Fernie & District Historical Society*, Fernie and District Historical Society, 1977, pp. 17–73; Talk with Ella Verkerk, Fernie and District Historical Society, Fernie, B. C.; Knight, pp. 71–73; "The street cars . . . ," "Cohen was trying . . . ," and "I started this case . . ." from BCA, GR2422 file 32/13, July 22, 1913, Case files, Speedy Trials, Fernie. Information and Complaint for an Indictable Offense; "Beautiful wheat crop . . ." from BCA, GR2422 file 32/13, July 25, 1913, Case files, Speedy Trials, Fernie. Letter Frank Dubois to Gee Fun; FDHS, *Record of Arrests and Cases Tried*; BCA, GR2422 file 32/13, Case files, Speedy Trials, Fernie. Rex versus Cohen; Fernie *Free Press*, Oct. 17, 1913.

13. PAA, Accession No. Alberta Statutes 1914; Edmonton *Daily Capital*, July 6, 1914; Edmonton *Daily Bulletin*, July 8, 1914.

14. Edmonton *Journal*, Nov. 17–21, 1913. Cohen said he hit the policeman because the officer gave him a dirty look when he passed by with his girlfriend, Gladys Gardine. There was no family by the name of Gardine in Edmonton at that time.

15. Edmonton *Daily Bulletin*, July 2 and 8, 1914.

16. "Mr. Cohen, who has . . . ," "He pricked up . . . ," and the rest of the converstation from Edmonton *Daily Bulletin*, Feb. 24, 1914; *Edmonton 1910*, promotional booklet, p. 16; MacGregor, pp. 201–4; A. J. Mair, *E.P.S. The First 100 Years: A History of the Edmonton Police Service* (Edmonton: Edmonton Police Service, 1992), p. 35.

17. "Please take this . . ." quoted in Mair, p. 35; "Race horse men . . ." from Edmonton *Bulletin*, May 18, 1914. The *Bulletin* covered the story through the twenty-first; "The stuffy little quarters . . ." from Edmonton *Journal*, May 18, 1914. The *Journal* covered the story for the next few days, too; "Entered a plea . . ." from Edmonton *Bulletin*, May 20, 1914; Edmonton *Daily Capital*, May 20, 1914; POA, 1361/JP Massie, G. W., vol. 6 July 4, 1914; POA, 1361/JP Massie, G. W., vol. 7 Aug. 4, 1914.

18. Mair, p. 35; "Full blast . . ." from Edmonton *Journal*, May 23, 1914; "Carnival of Vice . . . ," "For weeks and months . . . ," and "Houses of prostitution . . ." from Edmonton *Bulletin*, May 23, 1914.

19. Edmonton *Bulletin*, July 6, 1914; "This money was received . . ." from Edmonton *Daily Capital*, July 6, 1914; "He did not know . . ." from Edmonton *Daily Bulletin*, July 7, 1914; "I told him . . ." from Edmonton *Daily Bulletin*, July 8, 1914; "When the magistrate . . ." from Edmonton *Journal*, July 8, 1914; Edmonton *Capital*, July 7, 1914.

CHAPTER 9
The Great War

1. "We were heading into . . ." quoted in Daphne Read, ed., *The Great War and Canadian Society: An Oral History* (Toronto: New Hogtown Press, 1978), p. 100; Leslie F. Hannon,

Canada at War (Toronto: McClelland and Stewart Ltd., 1968), p. 30; *The Armed Forces of Canada, 1867–1967: A Century of Achievement* Lieut.-Col. D. J. Goodspeed, ed. (Ottawa: Directorate of History, Canadian Forces Headquarters, 1967), p. 29; Desmond Morton, *A Military History of Canada* (Edmonton: Hurtig Publishers, 1985), p. 130; "French and Russians marched . . ." from Edmonton *Journal*, Aug. 5, 1914; MacGregor, pp. 209–10; "War is hell . . ." quoted in Howard Palmer with Tamara Palmer, *Alberta: A New History* (Edmonton: Hurtig Publishers, 1990), p. 168.

2. "There were thousands . . ." and "It was rather . . ." quoted in Read, pp. 101, 103; MacGregor, pp. 211–13, 224; Palmer, *Alberta*, p. 170; Morton, pp. 132, 135–36.

3. "Join them and win . . ." from Edmonton *Bulletin*, July 22, 1916; "In the sleeping barracks . . ." and "One may see . . ." from Edmonton *Bulletin*, Apr. 15, 1916; *Henderson's Edmonton City Directory*, 1915; Harold Fryer, *Alberta: The Pioneer Years* (Langley, B. C.: Stagecoach Publishing, 1977), pp. 85–90; MacGregor, J. G., *Peace River Jim Cornwall The Apostle of the North*, MSS Jim Cornwall, PAA, Acc. 84.378/39, pp. 146–47; NAC, RG 24, vol. 1646, H.Q. 683-284-1; NAC, RG 9, III, vol. 4704, folder 80, file 22; Biography of James Cornwall from the Peace River Museum.

4. Morton, p. 137; "Having only had . . ." from Edmonton *Bulletin*, Apr. 29, 1916.

5. "The calls of the sentries . . ." from Calgary *News-Telegram*, Aug. 21, 1916; Calgary *Daily Herald*, July 8, 21, 1916; Calgary *Daily News*, Aug. 1, 1916.

6. "Drunkenness appears . . ." from Calgary *News-Telegram*, June 11, 1916; Gilkes and Symons, p. 60; Palmer, *Alberta*, pp. 173–76; Richard Allen, "The Triumph and Decline of Prohibition," in *Documentary Problems in Canadian History*, vol. 2, *Post-Confederation*, ed. J. M. Bumsted (Georgetown, Ontario: Irwin-Dorsey Ltd., 1969), pp. 185–86; Ruth Elizabeth Spence, *Prohibition in Canada* (Toronto: The Ontario Branch of the Dominion Alliance, 1919), p. 457; MacGregor, *Edmonton*, p. 217; Marrus, pp. 59–63; Edmonton *Bulletin*, July 20, 1915; Edmonton *Daily Bulletin*, July 20, 1915; Calgary *Daily Herald*, Aug. 5, 1916.

7. Calgary *News-Telegram*, July 7, 1916; "My sister and I . . ." from Peach, p. 28; "Cohen was throwing . . . ," "Did you tell Cohen . . . ," and "What kind of a sneak . . ." from Calgary *Daily Herald*, July 21, 1916. Case also covered in July 28 and Aug. 4, 1916, edition.

8. "Bring down . . ." from Calgary *Daily Herald*, Oct. 11, 1916.

9. All the Calgary papers covered the rioting and the subsequent trials; "Come out, Turner" and "It's worse than Prussia" from Calgary *Daily Herald*, Oct. 12, 1916; "They were surging . . . ," "They seemed to be getting . . . ," and "They said they'd show . . ." from NAC, RG 18 vol 3274, 1916-HQ-1184-K-1 R.N.W.M. Police Barracks Attacked by Soldiers Calgary, Alta.; "Get them out . . ." from *The Daily Albertan*, Calgary, Oct. 12, 1916; Calgary *News-Telegram*, Oct. 12–31, 1916; Calgary *Daily Herald*, Oct. 12–30, 1916; "What is the first . . . ," "You know my name?," "That man there . . . ," and "Well I went . . ." from NAC, RG 24, vol. 1257, HQ593-1-108, vol. 1 13/6/18; Calgary Police Archives, FS Box 6, Charge Books, Item 28–29, Jan. 1914–Jan. 1916, Jan. 1916–Mar. 1917. Ident Acc. 91.30.

10. "The most interesting . . ." from Calgary *Daily Herald*, Oct. 28, 1916; "In a voice . . ." from Calgary *News-Telegram*, Oct. 27, 1916.

11. "They are men . . ." from NAC, RG 24, vol. 1657, H.Q. 683-284-7; Edmonton *Journal*, Feb. 9, 1917; Edmonton *Morning Bulletin*, Feb. 8, 10, 1917; MacGregor, *Peace River*, p. 147; "It was my second . . ." from Drage, p. 65; NAC, Morris Cohen Personnel Folder; Palmer, *The East End*, pp. 117–18; "London was all lit up . . ." and "We were at about . . ." from Wilbur Cross, *Zeppelins of World War I* (New York: Paragon House, 1991), pp. 27, 37; "My dad was . . ." from an interview with Sarah Rich, Mar. 14, 1993.

12. Cohen said he was reduced in rank because he got upset when he was transferred to the 8th. The 218th was simply subsumed within the 8th. Cornwall also continued to command. NAC, Confidential War Diary of 8th Battalion, Canadian Railway Troops; NAC, RG 24 vol. 1646, H.Q. 683-284-3; NAC, RG9, III, vol. 4462, folder 5 file 5; NAC, MG27 III-B-5 vol. 1, Ian MacKenzie Papers, file 2; NAC, RG 24 vol. 1646, H.Q. 683-284-3; NAC, RG 24 col. 1646, HQ 683-284-4; NAC, RG 24, vol. 1657, H.Q. 683-284-6; "As for the diseases . . ." quoted in Read, p. 145; Maj. General W. G. Macpherson, ed., *Medical History of the War*, vol. 2, HMSO (London: 1923), p. 150; N. P. L. Lumb, *The Systematic Treatment of Gonorrhœa* (Philadelphia: Lea & Febiger, 1918), pp. 38–47.

13. "Going up to the line . . ." quoted in Lyn Macdonald, *They Called It Passchendaele* (London: Michael Joseph, 1984), p. 187; Hannon, pp. 38–41; Goodspeed, p. 33; Morton, p. 138.

14. "A forlorn expenditure . . ." quoted in Hannon, p. 49; "Saved the men . . ." and "The construction of these railways . . ." from Edmonton *Journal*, Jan. 12, 1918; Goodspeed, pp. 51–54; Geoffrey W. Taylor, *The Railway Contractors: The Story of John W. Stewart, His Enterprises and Associates* (Victoria: Morriss Publishing, 1988), pp. 114–15; Macdonald, p. 185; Taylor, pp. 106–8, 113–14; *Canada in the Great War*, by Various Authorities, vol. 5., *The Canadian Railway Troops*, Roland H. Hill and H. L. Robertson (Toronto: United Publishers of Canada, 1920), pp. 308–14, 320–21; W. J. K. Davies, *Light Railways of the First World War: A History of Tactical Rail Communications on the British Fronts, 1914–18* (Newton Abbot, Devon: David & Charles, 1967), p. 21.

15. *Canadian Railway and Marine World*, Sept. 1917; "You cannot even . . ." from Edmonton *Journal*, Jan. 12, 1918; "You'd be lying on the surface . . ." quoted in Macdonald, p. 14; NAC, Confidential War Diary; "Our brains ache . . ." from "Exposure," *The Poems of Wilfred Owen*, ed. Jon Stallworthy (New York: W. W. Norton & Co., 1986), p. 162; Edmonton *Journal*, Jan. 12, 1918; Macdonald, p. 226; Davies, p. 67.

16. "They crawl all over . . ." from Read, p. 193; "We used to go into . . ." quoted in Macdonald, p. 80.

17. "The boys scoured . . ." from Edmonton *Journal*, Jan. 12, 1918; "Some of the strongest . . ." from Peace River *Standard*, Feb. 7, 1918.

18. "They were immensely . . ." from David Lloyd George, *War Memoirs, 1915–1916*, vol. 2 (Boston: Little Brown, and Company, 1933), p. 235; "These weren't the folks . . . ," "They worked like beavers . . . ," and "They didn't know how . . ." from Drage, pp. 67–68; *Times* of London, Dec. 26, 27, 1917; Judith Blick, "The Chinese Labor Corps in World War I," Harvard University Papers on China, vol. 9, August 1955, p. 117; "Within sound of the guns . . ." and "There is rivalry . . ." from Daryl Klein, *With the Chinks* (London: John Lane the Bodley Head, 1919), pp. 31, 257; *The North-China Herald*, Dec. 29, 1917; *Far Eastern Review*, Apr. 1918; Michael Summerskill, *China on the Western Front: Britain's Chinese Work Force in the First World War* (London: Michael Summerskill, 1982), pp. 90, 115–18, 135–42;

NAC, MG27 III-B-5 vol. 1, Ian MacKenzie Papers, file 3; "During the fiercest fighting . . ." and "Much valuable language . . ." from Captain Harry L. Gilchriese, "Managing 200,000 Coolies in France," *Current History* 11, no. 3, part 1 (December 1919), pp. 523, 525; Nicholas J. Griffin, "Britain's Chinese Labor Corps in World War I," *Military Affairs* 40, no. 3 (October 1976), p. 105; Charles W. Hayford, *To the People: James Yen and Village China* (New York: Columbia University Press, 1990), p. 24; Jean Chesneaux, *The Chinese Labor Movement 1919–1927* (Stanford: Stanford University Press, 1968), pp. 139–40; Summerskill, p. 69.

19. Interview with Sarah Rich Mar. 14, 1993; "It is doubtful . . ." from NAC, MG27 III-B-5 vol. 1, Ian MacKenzie Papers, file 3; NAC, MG30, E62, A. E. Nash Papers, "Reports"; NAC, MG27 III-B-5 vol. 1, Ian MacKenzie Papers, file 2; Taylor, pp. 117–118; "Most unseemly . . ." from NAC, Morris Cohen Personnel Folder; "A lump of shrapnel . . ." from an interview with Leah Cooper, c. 1978; "They were just . . ." from Drage, p. 69.

20. "Getting my jaw . . ." and "As far as I was concerned . . ." from Drage, pp. 70–71; NAC, Morris Cohen Personnel Record.

CHAPTER 10

Postwar

1. NAC, Morris Cohen Personnel record; Julian Putkowski, *The Kinmel Park Camp Riots, 1919* (Hawarden Desside Clwyd: The Flintshire Historical Society, 1989), pp. 8–13; Palmer, *Alberta*, p. 167; Desmond Morton, *Canada and War: A Military and Political History* (Toronto: Butterworths, 1981), p. 85; Morton, *A Military History of Canada*, p. 166; "I have won . . ." and "That Sergeant Morris . . ." from Edmonton *Journal*, Feb. 12, 1919; "There were high . . ." from Edmonton *Journal*, Apr. 14, 1923; "When our train . . ." from Drage, pp. 71–72. The notice in the paper about Cohen's arrival was not under a banner headline as claimed. It was just a small item at the bottom of the page.

2. "I just felt . . ." quoted in Read, p. 205; "The whoopee over . . ." from Drage, pp. 71–72.

3. MacGregor, *Edmonton*, p. 226; Palmer, *Alberta*, p. 193; Morton, *A Military History of Canada*, p. 166.

4. "This is Sergeant Cohen . . . ," "I have made a real . . . ," "I sent two men . . . ," "They are companies . . . ," and "I haven't known . . ." from POA, 83.1/774 (Middle Series), Papers relating to Morris Cohen's 1920 conviction; Palmer, *Alberta*, pp. 188–89; MacGregor, *Edmonton*, p. 229; Betke, pp. 469–72.

5. Edmonton *Bulletin*, Jan. 18, 1919; Morton, *Canada and War*, pp. 88–89; Palmer, *Alberta*, p. 187; Hannon, p. 70.

6. Edmonton *Morning Bulletin*, Sept. 15, 1919; "So you, sir . . ." from Tony Cashman, *The Best Edmonton Stories* (Edmonton: Hurtig Publishers, Alberta), 1976, pp. 73–75; *Henderson's Edmonton City Directory*, 1921.

7. *Henderson's Edmonton City Directory*, 1920; Edmonton Police Museum and Archives, Sept. and Oct. 1920 Edmonton Police Monthly Report; "I kept observation . . . ,"

"Lounging around . . . ," "As I approached . . . ," "These are my friends . . . ," "It was Saturday . . . ," "A few days . . . ," "Never charged anything . . . ," and "I don't suppose . . ." from POA, 83.1/774 (Middle Series), Papers relating to Morris Cohen's 1920 conviction; POA, Supreme Court of Alberta, King vs. Morris A. Cohen, Dec. 28, 1920; POA, accession no. 72.26/3130/c.

8. "As soon as I was . . ." from Drage, p. 76; Cheng, *Oriental Immigration in Canada*, pp. 182–88; Wickberg, pp. 118–19; "In days gone by . . ." and "If there was anything . . ." from Edmonton *Journal*, Apr. 14, 1923; Cashman, p. 73; Ray H. Crone, "The Unknown Air Force," *Saskatchewan History* 30, no. 1 (Winter 1977), pp. 1–13; Ray Crone, "The Unknown Air Force," Canadian Aviation Historical Society Journal 18, no. 2, 1980, pp. 42–46.

9. "Gaily lit . . ." and "The fifteen hundred . . ." from Edmonton *Journal*, Apr. 17, 1920; Edmonton *Journal*, Jan. 3, May 6, Oct. 22, 1921; *Henderson's Edmonton City Directory*, 1922.

10. Betke, pp. 463–65, 593; Edmonton *Journal*, Oct. 25, Nov. 28, 1921; Edmonton *Bulletin*, Nov. 23, 1921.

11. Cheng, *Oriental Immigration*, pp. 84–89; Palmer, *Patterns of Prejudice*, pp. 85–86; Lai, *Chinatowns*, pp. 55–60; "Organziations sprang up . . ." quoted in Read, p. 209; Emily F. Murphy, *The Black Candle* (Toronto: Thomas Allen, 1922); Palmer, *Alberta*, p. 180; Edmonton *Bulletin*, Sept. 28, 1920.

12. "It has been found . . ." from Edmonton *Morning Bulletin*, Oct. 19, 1921; "Putting [his] foot down . . ." quoted in Hoe, pp. 84–85.

13. Edmonton *Journal*, Feb. 28, 1922; Edmonton *Bulletin*, May 6, 1922.

14. "Many hard-hitting . . ." from Edmonton *Journal*, June 26, 1922; "Stating that the white races . . ." and "Objected to the motion . . ." from Edmonton *Morning Bulletin*, June 26, 1922.

15. "I sat back . . ." from Drage, p. 77; "The civil war . . ." from Edmonton *Bulletin*, May 13, 1922.

16. Clubb, pp. 60–67, 101–6; Jeh-hang Lai, "A Study of a Faltering Democrat: The Life of Sun Fo, 1891–1949" (Ph.D. diss., University of Illinois at Urbana-Champaign, August 1976), pp. 16–27, 32; Sterling Seagrave, *The Soong Dynasty* (New York: Harper & Row, 1985), pp. 167–68; Sheridan, pp. 69–70; Lyon Sharman, *Sun Yat-sen: His Life and Its Meaning, A Critical Biography* (New York: The John Day Company, 1934), pp. 159–65, 204–14.

17. Edmonton *Journal*, Mar. 6, 9, 1922; "There was a scurry . . ." from Edmonton *Bulletin*, Mar. 7, 1922.

18. NAC, RG 25, Volume 2251, File/Dossier 17-BVJ-40, July 13, 1925, Memorandum for the Prime Minister from the Office of the Under-Secretary of State for External Affairs. Ottawa; Toronto *Daily Star*, Apr. 25, 1927; Kia-ngau Chang, *China's Struggle for Railroad Development* (New York: The John Day Company, 1943), pp. 3, 46–54, 77; Seagrave, pp. 124–25; Sharman, p. 153.

19. "I had pull . . ." from Drage p. 79; "All Chinatown took . . ." from Edmonton *Journal*, Apr. 14, 1923; Geoffrey W. Taylor, *The Railway Contractors: The Story of John W. Stewart, His Enterprises and Associates* (Victoria: Morriss Publishing, 1988), p. 122; PRO, FO 371

13909, F2426/57/10; NAC, RG 25, Volume 2251, File/Dossier 17-BVJ-40, Dec. 20, 1922
report by C. A. Knight, "E" Division Royal Canadian Mounted Police.

CHAPTER II
Sun Yat-sen

1. The Shanghai Municipal Police had Sun under survelliance and noted Cohen's arrival in town. "I set out . . ." from Drage, p. 80; NAUS, SMPR, roll 59, file 9657; Vincent Sheean, *Personal History* (Garden City, N.Y.: Doubleday, Doran & Co., 1935), pp. 188–89, 230; "If you will sit . . ." from John B. Powell, *My Twenty-five Years in China* (New York: The MacMillan Company, 1945), p. 7; Elsie McCormick, *Audacious Angles on China* (New York: D. Appleton and Co., 1923), p. 43; André Malraux, *Man's Fate* (New York: Vintage Books, 1961), p. 231; Frederic Wakeman, Jr., *Policing Shanghai 1927–1937* (Berkeley: University of California Press, 1995), p. 106; "From the city street . . ." and "The Bund was a hurly-burly . . ." from Dora Sanders Carney, *Foreign Devils Had Light Eyes* (Toronto: Dorset Publishing, 1980), pp. 7, 10; Vera Vladimirovna (Vishnyakova) Akimova, *Two Years in Revolutionary China 1925–1927* (Cambridge, Mass.: East Asian Research Center, Harvard University, 1971), p. 147; Percy Finch, *Shanghai and Beyond* (New York: Charles Scribner's Sons, 1953), pp. 35–36; Nicholas R. Clifford, *Spoilt Children of Empire: Westerns in Shanghai and the Chinese Revolution of the 1920s* (Hanover, N.H.: Middlebury College Press, 1991), p. 62.

2. McCormick, pp. 52–53; Carney, p. 32; Malraux, pp. 79–80; The Reminiscences of George Sokolsky, Oral History Research Office, Columbia University, May 14, 1956, No. 219, Part II, Category IA, pp. 1–21; "I remember the day . . ." from The Reminiscences of George Sokolsky, Oral History Research Office, Columbia University, Part II, Nov. 29, 1962, No. 219, Category 1A, PRCQ, p. 49; Warren I. Cohen, *The Chinese Connection: Roger S. Greene, Thomas W. Lamont, George E. Sokolsky and American–East Asian Relations* (New York: Columbia University Press, 1978), pp. 71–76; *Tuanjie bao*, Oct. 31, 1992, p. 2; Sheean, pp. 205–6; Randall Gould, unpublished memoirs, Hoover Institution, Box 10, 69086-8.23, p. 28; "Instinctively antagonistic . . ." from Vincent Sheean, "Some People from Canton," *Asia* 27, no. 10 (Oct. 1927), p. 857.

3. "To tell the truth . . ." and "A stranger in a very . . ." from Drage, pp. 83–85; Schiffrin, pp. 25–28, 184; Sharman, pp. 15–29, 268; Seagrave, pp. 70–72, 92–94; David Clive Wilson, "Britain and the Kuomintang, 1924–28: A Study of the Interaction of Official Policies and Perceptions in Britain and China" (Ph.D. diss., School of Oriental and African Studies, University of London, May 1973), p. 23.

4. "I have never met a man . . ." from *Renmin ribao*, Nov. 19, 1956; James R. Shirley, "Control of the Kuomintang after Sun Yat-sen's Death," *The Journal of Asian Studies* 25, no. 1 (Nov. 1965), p. 71; "It is a remarkable fact . . ." quoted in Wilson, "Britain and the Kuomintang," p. 92; "Came along in Sun's time . . ." from André Malraux, *The Conquerors* (New York: Holt, Rinehart and Winston, 1976), p. 11.

5. "I was met at the door . . ." from Powell, p. 33; "Mr. Sun's custom . . ." from Bi Xi, "Ti Sun Zhongshan xiansheng dang weishi shi de huiyi" (My recollections of when I was a

bodyguard for Mr. Sun Yatsen). In Zhongguo renmin zhengzhi xieshang huiyi Zhejiang sheng weiyuanhui wenshi ziliao yanjiu weiyuanhui (Chinese People's Political Consultative Conference Zhejiang Province Committee Historical Materials Research Committee) ed., Sun Zhongshan yu Zhejiang (Sun Yatsen and Zhejiang). Hangzhou: Zhejiang renmin chubanshe, 1986, pp 145–48.

6. "Whenever a visitor . . ." from Drage, p. 89; Sharman, pp. 242, 253–60; Schiffrin, p. 234; Clubb, pp. 118–20; Roderick L. MacFarquhar, "The Whampoa Military Academy," Papers on China, vol. 9, East Asia Regional Studies Seminar, Harvard University, 1955, p. 149; Seagrave, p. 173; Wilson, "Britain and the Kuomintang," pp. 24–25; "With a child-like figure . . ." from Sheean, *Personal History*, pp. 208–29.

7. NAUS, SMPR, roll 59, file 9657; "The debonair Canadian . . ." from New York *Globe*, Feb. 19, 1923; *South China Morning Post*, Feb. 16, 19, 1923; Hongkong *Telegraph*, Feb. 19–22, 1923; "A procession of cars . . ." from Drage, p. 92.

8. *Tuanjie bao*, Oct. 31, 1992; "The four of them . . ." and "All the boxing I know . . ." from an interview with Fan Liang, Apr. 29, 1994.

9. *Tuanjie bao*, Oct. 31, 1992; Schiffrin, pp. 236–37; Seagrave, p. 174; Clubb, p. 120; Jehhang Lai, "A Study of a Faltering Democrat," p. 32; Wilson, "Britain and the Kuomintang," pp. 27–30, 86, 360.

10. *Renmin ribao*, Nov. 10, 1956; Drage, pp. 96, 123; *Tuanjie bao*, Oct. 31, 1992; Fan Liang, "Zai Sun Zhongshan xiansheng shenbian de rizili" (Days at the side of Mr. Sun Yatsen). Jiangsu sheng zhengxie wenshi ziliao yanjiu weiyuanhui (Jiangsu Province Political Consultative Conference Historical Materials Research Committee), ed., Zai Sun Zhongshan shenbian de rizi li (Days at the side of Sun Yatsen). Jiangsu guji chubanshe, 1986, pp. 149–58; *The North-China Herald*, Dec. 15, 1923; "Rarely during our months . . ." from Harry A. Franck, *Roving Through Southern China* (New York: The Century Co., 1925), p. 263; "He would ask . . ." from Morris Cohen, "Weida de aiguozhe, weida de gemingjia, weida de ren—Sun Zhongshan xiansheng" (A great patriot, a great revolutionary, a great man—Mr. Sun Yatsen), in Shang Mingxuan et al., ed., Sun Zhongshan shengping shiye zhuiyilu. (Recollections of Sun Yatsen's life and work). Beijing: Renmin chubanshe, 1986, pp. 113–15; *Wenhui bao*, Nov. 11, 1956.

11. "They couldn't do much . . ." from Drage p. 96; "These ragged, lazy . . ." from Franck, p. 275; Wilson, "Britain and the Kuomintang," pp. 21–23, 91–93; Martin C. Wilbur, "Forging the Weapons: Sun Yat-sen and the Kuomintang in Canton 1924" (Unpublished manuscript, Columbia University, 1966), p. 5; NAUS, USDS 893.00/5318.

12. "It took off quickly . . ." from Dan-San Abbott, "Rosamonde," *WWI Aero* 140, May 1993; Interview with Dan-San Abbott, May 22, 1996; Interview with Senator G. Patrick Abbott, Apr. 26, 1996.

13. "It must also be borne . . ." from NAUS, 893.00/5318, Nov. 24, 1923 letter from consul general Douglas Jenkins to Secretary of State; NAUS, 893.51/4516, Dec. 10, 1923 letter from Consul General Douglas Jenkins to Jacob Gould Schurman; "Mr. Sun went several . . ." from Ye Jianying, "Sun Zhongshan xiansheng de jianjun sixiang he da wuwei jingshen" (Mr. Sun Yatsen's ideology of military construction and fearless spirit), in Shang Mingxuan et al., ed., Sun Zhongshan shengping shiye zhuiyilu (Recollections of Sun Yatsen's life and work).

Beijing: Renmin Chubanshe, 1986, pp. 323–29; Interview with Fan Liang, Apr. 29, 1994; "Most of my time . . ." and "The bullet that caught . . ." from Drage, pp. 99, 103; *Daily Express*, Apr. 5, 1956; "The Doctor had decided . . ." from Emily Hahn, *The Soong Sisters* (Garden City, N.Y.: Doubleday, Doran & Co., 1943), p. 120.

14. "Those were happy . . ." from Drage, p. 138; "Even on open verandahs . . ." from Hallett Abend, *My Life in China 1926–1941* (New York: Harcourt, Brace and Co., 1943), p. 32; O. M. Green, *The Foreigner in China* (London: Hutchinson & Co., 1943), p. 9.

15. "A dog fight . . ." from Aleko E. Lilius, *I Sailed with Chinese Pirates* (London: Arrowsmith, 1930), p. 144; Ilona Ralf Sues, *Shark's Fins and Millet* (Boston: Little, Brown and Co., 1944), pp. 25–27; Victor Purcell, *The Memoirs of a Malayan Official* (London: Cassell, 1965), pp. 106–7; Akimova, pp. 178–180, 195–96, 199–201; *The North-China Herald*, Dec. 15, 1923.

16. *Renmin ribao*, Nov.10, 1956; "Those little expeditions . . ." from Drage, p. 131; "The Guangdong people . . ." from Fan Liang, "Zai Sun Zhongshan xiansheng shenbian de rizili."

17. "Look here, Fan Liang . . . ," "When Sun Yat-sen . . . ," and "Our headquarters . . ." from an interview with Fan Liang, Apr. 29, 1994; "Even a junior clerk . . ." from Green, p. 8; "In Canton one goes . . ." and "Off the Cantonese Bund . . ." from McCormick, p. 64; Sue Gronewold, *Beautiful Merchandise: Prostitution in China 1860–1936* (New York: The Institute for Research in History and the Haworth Press, 1982), pp. 6–10; "I used to . . ." from Drage, p. 136.

18. "His title of 'General' . . ." from Powell, p. 33; "Maybe Dr. Sun trust . . ." from *Edmonton Journal*, Apr. 14, 1923; "Sitting pretty . . ." from *Edmonton Journal*, June 23, 1923; "In charge of the republican . . ." from *Edmonton Bulletin*, May 9, 1923; "Cohen's real motive . . ." from NAC, RG 25, Volume 2251, File/Dossier 17-BVJ-40, Nov. 20, 1922 report "Morris Cohen," RCMP; "It is impossible . . ." from NAC, RG 25, Volume 2251, File/Dossier 17-BVJ-40, July 11, 1923, Report from W. A. MacBrayne, RCMP.

19. *Edmonton Bulletin*, Apr. 11, 1923; NAC, RG 76, vol 588, file 827821, pt. 7, May 17, 1923, Telegram from Sun Yat-sen to the Minister of Interior, Ottawa; Knowles, p. 100; Wickberg, pp. 135–44; *Hongkong Daily News*, June 16, 1924; Supreme Court of Canada, The King vs. Benjamin Cohen, Edmonton July 13, 1923; *Henderson's Edmonton City Directory*, 1923; "In his letter . . ." from *Edmonton Journal*, July 27, 1923.

20. Akimova, pp. 154, 221; "A large, calm . . ." from Sheean, *Personal History*, p. 203; "Everything interests him . . ." from Sheean, "Some People," pp. 813–14; MacFarquhar, pp. 149–51; Lydia Holubnychy, *Michael Borodin and the Chinese Revolution, 1923–1925* (New York: East Asian Institute, Columbia University, 1979), pp. 1–4; Seagrave, pp. 175–77; Schiffrin, pp. 240–243; Wilbur, p. 12; Leung, pp. 412–13.

21. Jerome Ch'en, "Dr. Sun Yat-sen's Trip to Peking 1924–1925," *Readings on Asian Topics*, Papers read at the inauguration of the Scandinavian Institute of Asian Studies, Sept. 16–18, 1968, Studentlitteratur, Sweden, 1970, pp. 78–79; Wilbur, pp. 5–9; "As a result of his rather . . ." from NAUS, 893.00/5318, Nov. 24, 1923, letter from Consul General Douglas Jenkins to the Secretary of State.

22. H. Staples Smith, *Diary of Events and the Progress on Shameen, 1859–1938*, 1938, pp. 1–26; Akimova, p. 193; Lilius, p. 150; "The sidewalks and the broad . . ." from Abend, p. 13;

"One day, we ten . . ." from Fan Liang, "Zai Sun Zhongshan xiansheng shenbian de ri-zili."

23. Sharman, pp. 254–56; Sheridan, pp. 92–93; Wilson, "Britain and the Kuomintang," pp. 31–39; Fan Liang, "Zai Sun Zhongshan xiansheng shenbian de rizili"; Schiffrin, p. 246; "Parties of marines . . ." from *New York Times*, Dec. 7, 1923; "What I know . . ." and "The prosperity of this Colony . . ." from PRO, CO129/481, Dec. 23, 1923 letter R. E. Stubbs to the Duke of Devonshire; "I am informed . . ." from PRO, CO129/481, Dec. 4, 1923, letter from Sun Yat Sen to Sir Reginald Stubbs; "His threat of reprisals . . ." from PRO, CO129/481, Dec. 13, 1923 letter from James Jamieson to Sir Edward; "Cohen does not appear . . ." from NAUS, 893.51/4516, Dec. 10, 1923, letter from Consul General Douglas Jenkins to Jacob Gould Schurman.

24. Sheridan, pp. 141–46, 216; Holubnychy, p. 266; Wilson, "Britain and the Kuomintang," pp. 40–41; Wilbur, pp. 15, 23–24, 27–28, 31–34; Shirley, pp. 71–73; Fan Liang, "Zai Sun Zhongshan xiansheng shenbian de rizili"; Schiffrin, pp. 253–56; Sharman, p. 272; *Renmin ribao*, Nov 10, 1956.

25. MacFarquhar, pp. 151–60; Gengxiong Wang, "Sun Zhongshan yu Lin Baike, Ma Kun de jiaowang" (Sun Yat-sen's contacts with Paul Lineberger and Morris Cohen). Minguo chunqiu (Republican Annals) 1. (Jan. 25, 1988), pp. 3–5; Akimova, pp. 177, 223–24; Holubnychy, pp. 414–16; Schiffrin, pp. 258–60; Sheridan, p. 157; Seagrave, pp. 184–87; Wilbur, pp. 13, 72–73; "Now there's one thing . . ." from Drage, p. 113; Leung, p. 18.

26. Sokolsky, Part II, 1962, pp. 52–53; *The China Weekly Review*, July 3, 1926; *Wenhui bao*, Nov. 11, 1956; Wilbur, p. 87.

27. Fan Liang, "Huiyi Zhongshan xiansheng" (Recollections of Mr. Sun Yat-sen). In Sun Zhongshan—Zhongguo renmin weida de geming de erzi (Sun Yat-sen—great revolutionary son of the Chinese People). Hong Kong: Zhonghua shuju, 1957, pp. 193–95; *North-China Daily News*, June 21, 1924; "Long before the appointed time . . ." from Hongkong *Telegraph*, June 30, 1924; Wilbur, pp. 41–43, 147–51, 692; Abend, p. 14; "When the strike . . ." from PRO, FO37113961, (F6976/6976/10), circa. Oct. 1929 statement by Morris Cohen.

28. Manchester *Guardian*, May 3, 1927; Sheean, *Personal History*, p. 233; Wilbur, pp. 69, 79, 83–84; Seagrave, pp. 189–93.

29. Leung, p. 392; Edmund S. K. Fung, *The Diplomacy of Imperial Retreat: Britain's South China Policy, 1924–1931* (Hong Kong: Oxford University Press, 1991), p. 83; Wilbur, pp. 69, 88–91; Wilson, "Britain and the Kuomintang," pp. 135–37; Schiffrin, p. 261.

30. Wilson, "Britain and the Kuomintang," pp. 166, 172–74; Schiffrin, p. 262; Wilbur, pp. 91–92, 100–4; Seagrave, pp. 193–96.

31. "The headquarters enlisting office . . ." from Ma Xiang, "Gensui Sun Zhongshan xian-sheng shi yu nian de huiyi" (Recollections of following Mr. Sun Yat-sen for more than ten years), in Shang Mingxuan et al., ed., Sun Zhongshan shengping shiye zhuiyilu (Recollections of Sun Yat-sen's life and work) (Beijing: Renmin chubanshe, 1986).

32. Schiffrin, pp. 262–64; Sharman, p. 301; Lai, *A Study of a Faltering Democrat*, p. 35; Holubnychy, pp. 464–69; Ch'en, pp. 76–77, 85–91; Wilbur, pp. 98–100, 109–10; Drage, p. 137.

33. "As soon as . . ." from *Time*, July 13, 1931; "Back in Edmonton . . ." from *Edmonton Journal*, Jan. 6, 1925; Schiffrin, pp. 265–68; Sharman, pp. 309–12; Seagrave, pp. 200–203; "It was in the middle . . ." and "When I met Mme. Sun . . ." from Drage, pp. 139, 143.

CHAPTER 12
Life Without Sun

1. Shirley, pp. 71–76; "It is hard . . ." from Sheean, "Some People from Canton," p. 852; Seagrave, pp. 205–7, 209–10, 257; Sharman, pp. 315–16; Schiffrin, pp. 3–5; Sheridan, pp. 158–59; Ch'en, p. 83.

2. "Captial is safe . . ." quoted in William Ayers, "The Hong Kong Strikes: 1920–1926," in *Papers on China*, Harvard University, Regional Studies Seminar, vol. 4, Apr. 1950, pp. 97–103, 109–14; Sheridan, pp. 150–53; Ta Chen, "Analysis of Strikes in China, from 1918 to 1926," *Chinese Economic Journal* 1, no. 11, (Nov. 1927), p. 947; Wilson, "Britain and the Kuomintang," pp. 198–99; Leung, p. 266.

3. Ayers, pp. 116–18; Chen, pp. 947–51; Wilson, "Britain and the Kuomintang," pp. 6–7, 212, 216–32, 270; Sheridan, pp. 154–55.

4. *The China Weekly Review*, Dec. 22, 1928; Ayers, pp. 119–21; Chen, pp. 951–52; "Huddled together . . ." from Akimova, pp. 232; *The China Weekly Review*, Dec. 12, 1925; Abend, p. 26.

5. NAUS, SMPR Box 2 File 101; "My liaison job . . ." from Drage, p. 151; "Particulars as to . . ." from PRO, FO 228 2952, Dossier 34K Vol V "Bad Hats (Sundry Suspects), July 14, 1925 letter from Jamieson to Peking; NAC, RG 25, Volume 2251, File/Dossier 17-BVJ-40, July 23, 1925 letter from O. D. Skelton to the Governor General's Secretary in Ottawa; NAC, RG 25, Volume 2251, File/Dossier 17-BVJ-40, Apr. 30, 1927 letter RCMP Office of the Commissioner to the Under Secretary of State for External Affairs.

6. "*Pampanga* enjoyed fratenizing . . ." from Wilma Sinton Jerman Miles, Biography of Milton Edward (Robbins) Miles, NWC, MS Coll., Wilma S. Miles, 26, Series 2, Box 2, Folder 6, Papers: Biography of Adm. Miles through 1939 written by Wilma S. Miles, p. 26; "I will get you . . ." from an interview with Wilma Miles, June 3, 1994; Evelyn M. Cherpak, "Remembering Days in Old China: A Navy Bride Recalls Life on the Asiatic Station in the 1920s," *The American Neptune* (summer 1984), pp. 179, 182; "He is a pure adventurer . . ." from PRO, FO 228 2952, Dossier 34K vols. 5, 6, "Bad Hats" (Sundry Suspects), July 24, 1925 letter to a number of people in British legation; "Cohen was at some pains . . ." and "Followed this up . . ." from FO 228 2952, Dossier 34K vol. 5, "Bad Hats (Sundry Suspects), Aug. 14, 1925, minutes in British Legation, Peking; "For want of a better . . ." and "He was bad medicine" from NWC, Miles Papers, MS Coll. 26, series 2, box 2, folder 1, Wilma Miles Papers: Vignettes on Canton 1925–1926.

7. Wilson, "Britain and the Kuomintang," pp. 54–55; Fung, p. 69; "They then took our turbans . . ." and "We were taken . . ." from PRO, FO371 11625 (F1790/1/10); PRO, FO371 11620 (F435/1/10); PRO, FO371 13234 (F5922/3145/10).

8. PRO, FO228 3153, Dec. 20 to 23, 1925, Diary of Visit to Canton by M. Fletcher; Fung, p. 69; Akimova, pp. 229, 280; Sheridan, pp. 159–60.

9. "One gentleman in Chinese gown . . ." from NWC, Miles Papers, MS Coll. 26, series 2, box 2, folder 1; Miles, *Biography of Milton Miles*, pp. 37–38; Lai, *A Study of a Faltering Democrat*, pp. 33–34; "A Communist of the reddist type" from PRO, FO228 2953, Dossier 34K vol. 6 (3113 /20 /32); "Graham did not make . . ." from PRO, FO228 2953, Dossier 34K, vol. 5 (4281/26/46).

10. "On the island . . ." and "The strikers had become . . ." from Abend, pp. 11, 26; Hongkong *Daily Press*, May 10, 1926; PRO, FO371 11625 (F1874/1/10); PRO, FO371 11627 (F2713/1/10); PRO, FO371 13961 (F6976/6976/10), circa. Oct. 1929 Statement by Morris Cohen; Drage, pp. 151–53; "Had been arrested . . ." from NWC, Miles Papers, MS Coll. 26, series 2, box 2, folder 1; "What a stupid thing . . ." from NWC, Miles Papers, MS Coll. 26, Series 2, Box 2, Folder 6; Miles, *Biography of Milton Miles*, p. 38; Montreal *Gazette*, Apr. 25, 1927; Toronto *Daily Star*, Apr. 25, 1927.

11. Clubb, p. 131; Sheridan, pp. 161–63; Seagrave, pp. 211–13; Hongkong *Daily Press*, Mar. 27, 1926.

12. *Who's Who of British MPs 1918–1945*, ed. M. Sterton, p. 235; Sheridan, pp. 165–67; PRO, FO228 2953 (4727/26/49) Dossier 34K vol. 6 (Bad Hats); Clubb, p. 134; Diana Lary, *The Kwangsi Clique in Chinese Politics, 1925–1937* (Cambridge: Cambridge University Press, 1974), pp. 67–74; "Arranged real welcomes . . ." from Akimova, p. 239; Lai, *A Study of a Faltering Democrat*, pp. 36–37.

13. Akimova, pp. 201, 252; NWC, Miles, Wilma J., MS Coll. 26; Wilson, "Britain and the Kuomintang," pp. 362–65, 372–83; *Times* of London, July 26, 1926; Ayers, pp. 120–21; "I spoke in very strong . . ." and "I feel that my efforts . . ." from PRO, FO371 13961 (FO371 13961, F6976/6976/10), circa. Oct. 1929 Statement by Morris Cohen.

14. Sheridan, p. 170; "I visited the men . . ." from Sir Owen O'Malley, *The Phantom Caravan* (London: John Murray, 1954), p. 109; Seagrave, p. 216; Wilson, "Britain and the Kuomintang," pp. 462–64, 484, 511; NAUS, 893.00/8502, Feb. 16, 1927, report from counsel general Douglas Jenkins; NAUS, 893.00/8427, Mar. 24, 1927, letter Minister MacMurray to State; Jonathan Spence, *To Change China: Western Advisers in China 1620–1960* (Boston: Little, Brown and Company, 1969), p. 197; Sheridan, pp. 171–73; Lai, *A Study of a Faltering Democrat*, pp. 70–76; Manchester *Guardian*, May 3, 1927; PRO, FO371 12474 (F1421/1421/ 10); "As soon as the boat . . ." from the Diary of Arthur Ransome, Apr. 21, 1927, University of Leeds, Special Collections; *Biographical Dictionary of Republican China*, Howard L. Boorman, ed., vol. 3 (New York: Columbia University Press, 1970), p. 163; "A serious disagreement . . ." from NAUS, 893.00/8502, Feb. 16, 1927, letter from Douglas Jenkins to Minister JVA MacMurray "Conversation with Mr. Morris Cohen"; *The Daily Mail*, London, Jan. 26, 1927; *Daily Mail*, Feb. 27, 1965; *Daily Telegraph*, Feb. 27, 1965; PRO, FO371 13234 (F5922/ 3145/10); PRO, FO371 12466 (F4172/801/10).

15. Nicholas R. Clifford, *Spoilt Children of Empire: Westerns in Shanghai and the Chinese Revolution of the 1920s* (Hanover, N.H.: Middlebury College Press, 1991), pp. 243, 251–54; Clubb, pp. 135–36; Sheridan, pp. 180–81; F. F. Liu, *A Military History of Modern China, 1924–1949* (Princeton: Princeton University Press, 1956), p. 41; "Mr. Norman and Mr. Morris Cohen . . ." from PRO, FO371 12405 (F4170/2/10), Mar. 21, 1927, letter Acting

Consul-General Brenan to Sir M. Lampson; "We had little wire . . ." from IMW, Papers of F. M. V. Tregear; *The Cambridge History of China, Republican China 1912–1949*, eds. John K. Fairbank and Albert Feuerwerker, part 2, vol. 13 (Cambridge: Cambridge University Press, 1986), p. 116.

16. Wilson, "Britain and the Kuomintang," p. 625; "A few days after . . ." from F. M. V. Tregear papers; Lary, pp. 73–78; S. Bernard Thomas, *'Proletarian Hegemony' in the Chinese Revolution and the Canton Commune of 1927* (Ann Arbor: Center for Chinese Studies, The University of Michigan, 1975), p. 20; "A fierce resistance . . ." from Hongkong *Telegraph*, Apr. 16, 1927; "On the day of our arrival . . ." from Akimova, p. 258.

17. "Were to arouse . . ." from Sheean, *Personal History*, pp. 210–11; Clubb, pp. 137–139; Wilson, "Britain and the Kuomintang," p. 578; Seagrave, pp. 219–29; Akimova, pp. 258–60, 336–37; Sheridan, pp. 174–76; Lary, pp. 78–81; *Cambridge History* part 2, vol. 13, pp. 118–119.

18. "A recent erroneous report . . ." from *Sunday Chronicle*, June 19, 1927; NAUS, SMPR Box 2 File 101; PRO, FO371 13234 (F5922/3145/10).

19. Isaacs, pp. 285–86; Leung, pp. 12, 25; Thomas, pp. 19–25; *Biographical Dictionary*, vol. 2, pp. 292–93; Hoover Institution, Houston Papers, Dec. 31, 1927, Despatch, Political Events of 1927; Lary, p. 84; Swisher, p. 101; "The oppressed of China . . ." from Hoover Institution, Huston Papers, Part 2, Folder 5, Enclosure 2, a handbill distributed in Canton on Dec. 11, 1927; "Opponents of the revolution . . ." from PRO, FO371 13164 (F357/7/10), translation of handbill distributed in Canton on that day, December 11, 1927.

20. "All the shops . . . " and "While we were standing . . ." from Swisher, pp. 90–91; *South China Morning Post*, Dec. 12, 13, 15, 19, 1927; Drage, p. 167.

21. "I'm just a poor . . ." and "For two days . . ." from Drage, p. 167; "Lee and I . . ." Swisher, pp. 97–98; *South China Morning Post*, Dec. 14, 1927.

22. *South China Morning Post*, Dec. 15, 17, 19, 31, 1927; Hoover Institution, Huston Papers, Part 2, Folder 5, pp. 25–26; report by Hinke, pp. 12–15; Isaacs, p. 290; "As we neared . . ." from Chang Fa-k'uei, Related Papers, Box 27, file 2a, Chinese Oral History Collection, Rare Book and Manuscript Library, Columbia University.

23. "I got permission . . ." from PRO, FO37113961 (F6976/6976/10), circa. Oct. 1929 Statement by Morris Cohen; "I then went to the Victoria Hotel . . ." from PRO, FO371 13199 (F927/84/10) Folio 196, Dec. 19, 1927, Enclosure from T. H. King; PRO, FO371 13165 (F584/7/10); Drage, pp. 168–71; Interview with Arthur Michael Ferrier, June 5, 1995; *South China Morning Post*, Dec. 16, 28, 1927, Jan. 3, 1928.

24. "Instead of helping . . ." from *South China Morning Post*, Dec. 27, 1927; The uprising and the following repression was covered extensively in the Dec. and Jan. issues of the *South China Morning Post*.

25. "Maurice Cohen did great work . . ." and "Li Jishen is at his wit's . . ." from PRO, FO228 3728 (3728 2CC 164620), Jan. 16, 1927, letter WEL Shenton to E. R. Hallifax; "Without fear of exaggeration . . ." from Hoover Institution, J. C. Huston Papers, 2/2/4,

Hoover, Dec. 31, 1927 Despatch, Political Events of 1927; Swisher, p. 98; *South China Morning Post*, Jan. 9, 1928.

CHAPTER 13
The South

1. *South China Morning Post*, Dec. 30, 1927, Jan. 30, 1928; *Times* of London, Feb. 9, 16, March 15, 1928; Lai, *A Study of a Faltering Democrat*, pp. 84–85, 108; "Mr. Morris Cohen tells me . . ." from PRO, FO371 13165 (F1148/7/10), Jan. 26, 1928, letter from Brenan to Lampson; Wilson, "Britain and the Kuomintang," pp. 641–42; New York *Times*, Feb. 18, 1928; "It was nearly ten years . . ." from Drage, p. 178; "Emancipation movement . . ." from PRO, FO371 13220 (F555/444/10), Feb. 2, 1928, World Tour of C. C. Wu and Party.

2. "It was the first time . . ." and "He was very generous . . ." from an interview with Queenie Cohen, Nov. 14, 1992; "He had a contract . . ." from an interview with Sarah Rich, Apr. 10, 1994; Interview with Leah Cooper, c. 1978, Manchester Public Library; "My mother prepared . . ." from an interview with Cyril Sherer, Dec. 20, 1993; Interview with Issie Bernstein, Nov. 14, 1992.

3. PRO, FO371 13220 (F1686/444/10); *Times* of London, May 5, July 7, 1928; Lai, *A Study of a Faltering Democrat*, pp. 86, 90.

4. NAUS, SMPR Box 2 File 101; PRO, FO371 13234 (3145/3145/10); PRO, FO228 3872 (Dossier 61H); "He saw to everything . . ." from an interview with Sarah Rich, Mar. 14, 1993.

5. "I persuaded the party . . ." and "He did see men . . ." from PRO,FO37113961 (F6976/6976/10), circa. Oct. 1929 statement by Morris Cohen; "I had a communication . . ." from PRO, FO371 13220 (F3689/444/10), July 11, 1928, letter from William Shenton to Mr. Pratt.

6. "Cohen accompanied them . . ." from PRO, FO371 13234 (F5922/3145/10), Sept. 24, 1928, letter from Brenan to Sir Miles Lampson; "He then became . . ." from PRO, FO371 13170 (F3881/7/10), July 26, 1928 telegram Foreign Office to Sir M. Lampson; Fung, p. 172.

7. PRO, FO371 13220 (F3819/444/10); Lai, *A Study of a Faltering Democrat*, pp. 90, 91; PRO, FO371 13170 (F3797/7/10); PRO, FO371 13220 (F3874/444/10); Jiang Yongjing, "Hu Hanmin xiansheng nianpu goa" (A draft chronological biography of Mr. Hu Hanmin), in Hu Hanmin shiji ziliao huiji (Collected materials on the life of Hu Hanmin) (Hong Kong: Dadong tushu gongsi, 1980), vol 1; Wilson, "Britain and the Kuomintang," pp. 652–56, 681, 694–95; Clubb, p. 159; Manchester *Guardian*, July 21, 1928; *Times* of London, July 16, Aug. 29, Sept. 11, 1928; Drage, pp. 178–81; PRO, FO371 13171 (F4515/7/10); NAUS, SMPR Box 2 File 101; New York *Times*, June 19, 1929.

8. "From the very first . . ." from FO37113961 (F6976/6976/10), circa. Oct. 1929 Statement by Morris Cohen; "In spite of Cohen's . . ." from PRO, FO371 13234 (F5922/3145/10), Sept. 24, 1928, letter from Brenan to Sir Miles Lampson.

9. Sheridan, pp. 207, 221–22; *The China Weekly Review*, July 27, 1929; Lary, pp. 16–20, 115; Clubb, pp. 144–51; Seagrave, pp. 302–3; Sheridan, pp. 208–9.

10. Lary, pp. 27–38, 34, 43–45, 49, 56–62, 115–18; Sheridan, p. 195; *Biographical Dictionary of Republican China*, vol. 2, pp. 292–93; *The Cambridge History of China*, pp. 13, 125.

11. Lary, p. 119; Wilson, "Britain and the Kuomintang," p. 650; Sheridan, pp. 95–96; "Arms smuggling facilities . . ." from *The China Weekly Review*, Apr. 18, 1925.

12. "Morris named himself . . ." from Hoover Institution Archives, Norwood F. Allman, Acc. No. 87042-8M.12, Box 12, file 2; "It is inhabited . . . " and "There were twelve . . . " from Aleko E. Lilius, *I Sailed with Chinese Pirates* (London: Arrowsmith, 1930), pp. 15, 41; Christopher J. Bowie, "Great Britain and the Use of Force in China, 1919 to 1931" (Ph.D. diss., Oxford University, 1983), pp. 151–53; "You could never be sure . . ." from an interview with Kemp Tolley, Nov. 24, 1993.

13. "They are able to plot . . ." from PRO, FO228 3682 (Dossier 75), July 21, 1927, letter from C. C. Wu; PRO, FO228/4053 (Dossier 75, p. 34); *South China Morning Post*, Mar. 25, 1927; Hongkong *Daily Press*, Sept. 3, 1927; PRO, FO228 3682 (Dossier 75, pp. 15, 17, 23); "The meager nature . . ." from PRO, FO228 3891 (Dossier 75), Nov. 22, 1928, A continuation of the Sept. 12, 1927, Memorandum on Piracy.

14. Cohen did not set up the first visit between Li Jishen and the British. Li made that visit prior to Cohen working for him. Bowie, pp. 169, 173, 181–87, 190–93 ; PRO, FO228 3891 (Dossier 75); PRO, FO228 3682 (Dossier 75); PRO, FO371 13225 (F1076/1076/10).

15. "To place orders . . ." from PRO, FO228 3891 (Dossier 75), Aug. 16, 1928, letter from Brenan to Southorn; "Incidentally I may state . . ." from PRO, FO228 3891 (Dossier 75), Oct. 30, 1928, letter from Brenan to Peking; PRO, FO371 13165 (F963/7/10); "Aircraft guns and mines . . ." from PRO, FO228/3890 (Dossier 75), Jan. 20, 1928, Suppression of Piracy by Canton Authorities; PRO, FO371 13961 (F6976/6976/10).

16. PRO, FO228 3891, (Dossier 75); "The local authorities . . ." from PRO, FO228/3892 (Dossier 75L), Oct. 4, 1928, letter from John Brenan to Minister Peking; Hongkong *Daily Press*, Oct. 18, 1928.

17. Lai, *A Study of a Faltering Democrat*, pp. 91–95; "This goes to confirm . . ." from PRO, FO371 13909 (F2318/57/10), May 10, 1929, Minutes.

18. *The Cambridge History of China*, part 2, vol. 13, pp. 125–27; Hongkong *Telegraph*, Jan. 16, 1929; "It is feared that . . ." PRO, FO228/3930, Mar. 21, 1929, telegram Clementi to Peking; Lary, pp. 138–44; *Biographical Dictionary*, vol. 2, p. 293; PRO, FO371 13889 (F1488/3/10); Clubb, pp. 152–56; *The China Year Book*, 1929–1930, H. G. W. Woodhead, ed. (Tientsin: The Tientsin Press, Ltd., 1931), p. 733; NAUS, SMPR Box 2 File 101; *South China Morning Post*, Mar. 6, 7, 25, 1929; *The China Press*, Mar. 12, 1929; London *Daily Telegraph*, Apr. 10, 1929.

19. *The China Weekly Review*, 1929; *North China Daily News*, Mar. 21, 1929; "I am proceeding . . ." quoted in Hahn, *The Soong Sisters*, pp. 157–158.

20. Xu Youchun, Wu Zhiming, eds., Sun Zhongshan feng'an da dian (The great ceremony of Sun Yat-sen's interment) (Beijing: Huawen chubanshe, 1989); "I'd hoped for an invitation . . ." from Drage, p. 197; "The procession, emerging . . ." from *Times* of London, May 27, 1929; London *Daily Telegraph*, May 22, 1929.

21. "An eerie sight . . ." from Bangkok *Daily Mail*, June 20, 1929; "At 4:30 the coffin . . ." from Sir Meyrick Hewlett, *Forty Years in China* (London: Macmillan & Co., 1944), p. 226; "The great road . . ." from *Times* of London, June 3, 1929.

22. "They worked in relays . . ." from *The North-China Herald*, June 8, 1929; *Times* of London, June 3, 1929; Fan Liang, "Wo wei Zhongshan xiansheng shou ling" (I guarded the tomb of Mr. Sun Yat-sen), Jiangsu sheng zhengxie wenshi ziliao yanjiu weiyuanhui (Jiangsu Province Political Consultative Conference Historical Materials Research Committee), ed. Zai Sun Zhongshan shenbian de rizi li (Days at the side of Sun Yat-sen), Jiangsu guji chubanshe, 1986.

CHAPTER 14

Arms Dealings

1. "A new and rather . . . ," "Some of his followers . . . ," and "In the end . . ." from Drage, pp. 206–07; "Avaricious and ambitious . . ." from Abend, p. 196; "If we fail to do so . . ." from PRO, FO371 13934 (F3583/350/10), June 28, 1929, telegram from Viceroy, Home Office to Secretary of State for India; "Saying that Mr. Cohen . . . ," "If he could help . . . ," "My impression . . . ," and "Completely let down" from PRO, FO371 13934 (F6160/350/10), Aug. 24, 1929, letter from A. F. Aveling to Sir Miles W. Lampson.

2. "Culled from his Chinese friends," "He tells me . . . ," "He said that he had enemies . . . ," "Of very bad . . . ," and "It appears that Faure . . ." from PRO, FO371 13961 (F6976/6976/10), Oct. 21, 1929, letter from G. S. Moss to Sir Miles Lampson; "To counter-act . . ." from FO371 13961 (F6976/6976/10), circa. Oct. 1929, statement by Morris Cohen; "It is business . . ." and "He sometimes drinks . . ." from PRO, WO106 5270, Document 1B, 1C, Dec. 31, 1929, "Canton Memorandum on Mr. C. M. Faure, late Commander R.N," by G. S. Moss; *The North-China Daily News*, Oct. 17, 1929; PRO, WO106 5269, Document 8D; *The Shanghai Times*, Nov. 21, 1929; Seagrave, pp. 274–75; Lai, *A Study of a Faltering Democrat*, pp. 119–37; Clubb, pp. 157, 160–61.

3. "When the rival . . . ," "They were trying . . . ," "Sometimes no arms . . . ," "My biggest single deal . . . ," and "I was over forty . . ." from Drage, pp. 213, 214, 217; "The guy was a gunrunner . . . ," "My God . . . ," and "We knew what was going . . ." from an interview with Kemp Tolley, Sept. 2, 1993; Southampton Archives, D/VT 2/8/3, John I. Thornycroft & Co. Ltd. Shanghai, Comparison of Yearly Results, Southampton Archives, D/VT 2/8/3; NAUS, 893.113/1327, July 30, 1931, letter from Douglas Jenkins to Trusler Johnson; "As far as I can discover . . ." from NAUS, 893.113/1336, Aug. 26, 1931, letter from Douglas Jenkins to Trusler Johnson; "Cohen scouted around . . ." from Allman Papers, Hoover Institution Archives, Box 12, file 2; NAUS, 893.113/1339, Sept. 10, 1931, Importation of arms and military supplies into Canton; NAUS, 893.113/1307, July 11, 1931, telegram from Secretary of State, Washington to Peking; *Time*, June 22, 1931.

4. Sheridan, pp. 244–51; Clubb, pp. 166–74, 185, 194–96; "The Japanese are like a disease . . ." from *The Cambridge History of China*, vol. 13, p. 148; "A poisonous, dangerous . . ." from Drage, p. 226; Lai, *A Study of a Faltering Democrat*, pp. 144–55; Augustus Tung Kwok

Leung, "A Study of the Relationship between Chen Jitang and the Nanking Government, 1929–1936" (master's thesis, University of Hong Kong, 1991), pp. 73–80; Leung, pp. 272–73.

5. Tung Kwok Leung, pp. 56–57, 65–66, 95–98; Sheridan, pp. 194–96; Sues, p. 31; Leung, p. 45.

6. "He aims at a smaller . . ." from PRO, FO371 17098 (F160/160/10), Sept. 29, 1932, letter from Herbert Phillips to E. M. B. Ingram; PRO, FO371 17098 (F223/160/10), (F315/160/10), (F5621/160/10); PRO, WO106 5269, Document 8A, 8B, 8C; NAUS, 893.113/1339, Oct. 23, 1931, telegram from Engert to the Secretary of State; "I threw myself . . ." Drage, p. 220; "He said he wanted . . ." from Allman Papers, Box 12, file 2.

7. "The financial and diplomatic . . ." from *Daily Mail*, Mar. 5, 1932; "A war lord . . ." and "Mr. Cohen's astonishing . . ." from *Edmonton Journal*, Mar. 5, 1932; "My brother has warned . . ." from the *Evening Chronicle*, Mar. 7, 1932; London *Sunday Dispatch*, Mar. 6, 1932; *New York Times*, Mar. 6, 1932.

8. "By the autumn of 1932 . . . ," "I landed at Plymouth . . . ," and "Loaded down with catalogues . . ." from Drage, pp. 220, 224; Alan Kidd, *Manchester* (Keele, Staffordshire: Ryburn Publishing, 1993), pp. 184–85; *Israelite Press*, Nov. 2, 1932; "When his train . . ." from London *Daily Mirror*, Nov. 10, 1932; "He has had important . . ." from London *Daily Dispatch*, Jan. 28, 1933; "Including his escapes . . ." and "The only country . . ." from Manchester *News Chronicle*, Nov. 11, 1932; "I will . . . make contact . . ." from London *Daily Mirror*, Nov. 11, 1932; Manchester *News Chronicle*, Nov. 11, 1932; Interview with Sarah Rich, Apr. 10, 1994; Manchester *Evening Standard*, Nov. 10, 1932; London *Jewish Chronicle*, Nov. 25, 1932.

9. "A well-appointed suite . . ." from Shanghai *Times*, Mar. 26, 1934; "Mail that old check . . ." quoted in Kenny A. Franks and Paul F. Lambert, *Early California Oil: A Photographic History, 1865–1940* (College Station: Texas A&M University Press, 1985), pp. 105–6; "Get the Money!" from *The China Press*, May 8, 1933; "Go to hell" from *The China Weekly Review*, May 6, 1933; "Fond of liquor . . ." wanted poster contained in NAUS, SMPR, Box 38 file 4806; "I left the United States . . ." from *The China Press*, May 7, 1933; *The China Press*, Apr. 27, 29, Sept. 4, 1935; *The Shanghai Evening Post & Mercury*, May 6, 1933, Mar. 26, 1934; *North-China Daily News*, May 1, 1933.

10. *The North-China Daily News*, Mar. 21, 1934; "Persistent rumours . . ." from NAUS, SMPR, Box 38, file 4806, Jan. 30, 1934, "American Stock and Bond Guarantee Company"; "He had a drink . . . ," "To emphasize her belief . . . ," and "With the evidence . . ." from *The China Press*, Mar. 30, 1934; *The China Press*, May 7, 1933, Jan. 4, Feb. 2, 1934; the Shanghai *Times*, Mar. 26, 1934.

11. NAUS, SMPR, roll 15, file 4961; Lorna Houseman, *The House that Thomas Built* (London: Chatto & Windus, 1968), pp. 168–69.

12. Kemp Tolley, *Yangtze Patrol; The U.S. Navy in China* (Annapolis, Maryland: Naval Institute Press, 1971), pp. 180, 184, 298– 99; "Sort of like a grandfather . . ." from *Reminiscences of Rear Admiral Kemp Tolley U.S. Navy (Retired)*, vol. I, U.S. Naval Institute, Annapolis, Maryland, 1983, p. 385; "Was like one of the boys . . . ," "Information was wide . . . ," and

"He would have . . ." from an interview with Kemp Tolley, Sept. 2, 1993; Interview with Kemp Tolley, Nov. 24, 1993; "Cohen . . . never seemed to lack . . ." from a letter Kemp Tolley to author, Aug. 28, 1993.

13. *The Critic*, Sept. 10, 1932; "My father served . . ." from an interview with Eric Gabriel, Feb. 5, 1994; Drage, p. 231; "We were there . . ." and "A man came up . . ." from an interview with Leo Hanin, Sept. 2, 1993; *Encyclopaedia Judaica*, vol. 4, Encyclopaedia Judaica Jerusalem (New York: The Macmillan Company, 1971); "Cohen took me under . . ." from Judith Ben-Eliezer, *Shanghai Lost, Jerusalem Regained* (Israel: Steimatzky, 1985), pp. 80–81.

14. "Such crowds . . ." from Emily Hahn, *China to Me: A Partial Autobiography* (Garden City, N.Y.: Doubleday, Doran & Co., 1944), pp. 3–4, 35; Gwen Dew, *Prisoner of the Japs* (New York: Alfred A. Knopf, 1943), p. 210; "For several blocks . . ." from Carney, pp. 15–16; Wakeman, *Policing Shanghai*, pp. 106–8; *The China Weekly Review*, July 27, 1929; "Six floors . . ." from Josef von Sternberg, *Fun in a Chinese Laundry* (New York: The Macmillan Co., 1965), p. 62.

15. Gail Hershatter, "The Hierarchy of Shanghai Prostitution, 1870–1949," *Modern China* 15, no. 4 (October 1989), pp. 463–73, 476–79, 483–86; "They did not rely . . ." from Finch, p. 11; "One night after . . ." quoted in Leang-li T'ang, *China Facts and Fancies* (Shanghai: China United Press, 1936), pp. 200–203.

16. *Cambridge History*, pp. 134–38, 142–46; Sheridan, pp. 213, 218–19; Seagrave, pp. 292–294; Abend, p. 222.

17. "General Cohen painted . . . ," "They said . . . ," and "I eventually stated . . ." from PRO, FO371 19284 (F3913/77/10), Mar. 30 and Apr. 1, 1935, minutes on Proposed Industrial Bank in Kwangtung; Liu Guoming, ed., Zhonghua minguo guomin zhengfu junzheng zhiguan renwu zhi (Directory of people holding official military or civilian positions in the national government of the Republic of China). Chunqiu chubanshe; "From walking so much . . ." and "My father was in bed . . ." from an interview with Sarah Rich, Mar. 14, 1993; "We, in common . . ." from news clip, paper unknown; Manchester *News Chronicle*, Oct. 4, 1933; London *Daily Telegraph*, Oct. 4, 1933; Death Certificate, District of Salford; London *Daily Telegraph*, July 15, 1935; *The Daily Herald*, July 15, 1935; Manchester *Daily Mail*, July 15, 1935; Manchester *Daily Dispatch*, July 15, 1935.

18. "In whatever part . . ." from Manchester *Evening Chronicle*, July 15, 1935; "Moisha was here . . ." from an interview with Sarah Rich, Mar. 14, 1993; "He sent over . . ." from an interview with Sarah Rich, Apr. 10, 1994; "They stopped the traffic . . ." from an interview with Sarah Rich Nov. 14, 1992; London *Daily Telegraph*, Aug. 7, 1935; "When he came over . . ." from an interview with Victor David Cooper, July 19, 1994; London Central Criminal Court, The King v. Montague Wentworth and Alexander Herbert Tucker, 1935; Gray Trading Company, Shanghai to Morris Cohen, Sept. 18, 1935, collection of Josef Rich; *North-China Daily News*, Feb. 8, Mar. 2, 1936; Manchester *Evening News*, Aug. 9, 1935; *New Chronicle*, Sept. 12, 1935; Letter M. A. Cohen to Jane Cohen, Oct. 19, 1935, collection of Victor Cooper; Letter M. A. Cohen to Jane Cohen, Oct. 1935, collection of Victor Cooper; Invitation for Special Dinner for Gen. Cohen by his friends on the MV *Georgic*, collection of Victor Cooper.

19. Sheridan, pp. 251–52; Tung Kwok Leung, pp. 129–36; Leung, *Historical Dictionary of Revolutionary China*, pp. 121–22; *Cambridge History*, p. 148.

20. Clubb, pp. 183–84, 204–5; Sheridan, pp. 194–97; Sues, p. 25; Lary, p. 197; Tung Kwok Leung, pp. 144–45, 149; PRO, FO371 20250 (F4446/166/10); "The good news . . ." from Sues, p. 25.

21. *Biographical Dictionary of Republican China*, pp. 450–51; *Oriental Affairs*, May 1937; Wakeman, *Policing Shanghai*, pp. 213–17; "He shuttled back . . ." from Randall Gould, *China in the Sun* (Garden City, N.Y.: Doubleday & Company, Inc., 1946), pp. 354–55; "Was otherwise an easy . . ." and "A steady stream . . ." from Gould, unpublished memoirs, p. 132; "They didn't know . . ." from an interview with Oziar Malini, Jan. 9, 1996; Drage, p. 233; Ricky Jay, *Learned Pigs & Fireproof Women* (New York: Warner Books, 1986), pp. 86–88, 90–91.

22. "It may interest . . ." from PRO, FO371 20251 (F6608/166/10), July 30, 1936, letter from R. H. Scott to R. G. Howe; "He is very useful . . ." from PRO, WO106 5269, Document 8A, Dec. 29, 1936, Secret and Personal; *Israel's Messenger*, Oct. 6, 1936; Interview with Rose Horowitz, Jan. 21, 1993; *Cambridge History*, pp. 160–63; Sheridan, pp. 250–56; Clubb, pp. 193–202, 207–9.

CHAPTER 15

The Japanese

1. Sheridan, pp. 256–57; Clubb, pp. 213–14; "After the hundreds . . . ," "Out near the race . . . ," and "The arrival of . . ." from Abend, pp. 254–55.

2. "The city was strewn . . ." from Sues, pp. 126–27; "The Japanese troops . . . ," "Though harsh and relentless . . . ," "There was panic . . . ," "Any persons who ran . . . ," and "Over one hundred women . . ." from H. J. Timperley, compiled and edited, *Japanese Terror in China* (New York: Modern Age Books, 1938), pp. 18, 26, 31–33; "Today, we again beat . . ." and "In my half year . . ." Leung, *Historical Dictionary of Revolutionary China*, pp. 279–80.

3. "For miles up and down . . ." from Sues, p. 293; *Sunday Express* (South Africa), July 18, 1937; "Quite well . . ." and "Bad news travels . . ." from Manchester *Sunday Dispatch*, Nov. 21, 1937; "We don't even know . . ." from *Sunday Referee*, Sept. 5, 1937; Death Certificate, District of Salford; "If the general . . ." from Manchester *Evening News*, Jan. 20, 1938; "Will fight for her . . ." from Manchester *Daily Dispatch*, June 7, 1938; London *Daily Mail*, June 7, 1938; "Oh, he took . . ." and "I got very friendly . . ." from an interview with Queenie Cohen, Nov. 14, 1992.

4. "His squat, powerful . . ." and "I don't keep . . ." from the New York *Sun*, Dec. 15, 1938; Clubb, pp. 222, 226; PRO, CO129/560; Interview with Abraham Bates, Sept. 16, 1993 ; Interview with Israel Epstein, Jan. 18, 1993; "The weather had been . . . ," "On the morning . . . ," and "We were bombed . . ." from Drage, pp. 237, 251; "I had got . . ." from an interview with Emily Hahn, Feb. 28, 1993.

5. "The streets are narrow . . ." and "The planes seemed . . ." from Herbert O. Yardley,

The Chinese Black Chamber; An Adventure in Espionage (Boston: Houghton Mifflin Company, 1983), pp. 21, 93; "I sipped my gimlet . . ." from Hahn, *China to Me*, p. 182; Emily Hahn, *Hong Kong Holiday* (Garden City, N.Y.: Doubleday & Co. Inc., 1946), p. 67; Randall Gould, *Chungking Today* (Shanghai: The Mercury Press, 1941), p. 22.

6. "In Hong Kong . . ." from Drage, p. 253; Cherpak, "Remembering Days in Old China," p. 185; "The trip which you . . ." from Hoover Institution, Miles Papers, Box 4, China-China-Burma Highway, Jan. 9, 1939, letter from Paul W. Meyer to Lt. Commander Milton Miles; "We saw Morris . . ." from an interview with Wilma Miles, June 3, 1994; Miles, "Biography of Milton Edward (Robbins) Miles," pp. 72–73; Miles Papers, MS Coll. 26, series 2, box 2, folder 1, Vignettes on Canton 1925–1926, pp. 2–3.

7. "My father sent word . . ." from an interview with Oziar Malini, Jan. 9, 1996; "The one obvious . . ." from *Times* of London, May 25, 1939.

8. "He was strolling . . . ," "He was a character . . . ," and "There was about him . . ." from an interview with Emily Hahn, Feb. 28, 1993; "The general was playing . . ." from Hahn, *China to Me*, p. 159; "I used to see . . ." from an interview with Group Captain HT (Alf) Bennett, Oct. 18, 1993; "Morris Cohen was unlike . . ." from Gould, *China in the Sun*, p. 354; "In Hong Kong I played . . ." from an interview with Walter J. Citrin, Dec. 9, 1993; "He was very active . . ." from an interview with Solomon Bard, Aug. 8, 1994; "Yiddisha boy . . ." from an interview with Israel Epstein, Jan. 18, 1993; "I was part . . ." from an interview with David Odell, Aug. 9, 1993.

9. "To the day . . ." and "I went to Hong Kong . . ." from an interview with Queenie Cohen, Nov. 14, 1992; Interview with Queenie Cohen, Apr. 13, 1994.

10. "To create and foster . . ." from Charles Cruickshank, *SOE in the Far East* (Oxford: Oxford University Press, 1983), p. 5; "Cohen is a good . . ." from PRO, HS1/112, Dec. 11, 1943; G. B. Endacott, *Hong Kong Eclipse* (Oxford: Oxford University Press, 1978), p. 78; Richard Gough, *SOE Singapore, 1941–1942* (London: William Kimber, 1985), pp. 42–45; "I was supposed to go . . ." from Hahn, *China to Me*, pp. 159–60; Interview with Arthur Michael Ferrier, June 5, 1995.

11. PRO, FO371 24704 (F4594/4594/10), (F4594/4594/10); *Biographical Dictionary*, vol. 3, p. 451; PRO, FO371 27824; "At first I wasn't keen . . ." and "The Dutch . . ." from Drage, p. 257.

12. "On the other side . . ." from Gwen Dew, *Prisoner of the Japs* (New York: Alfred A. Knopf, 1943), pp. 11–12; Sues, pp. 165, 313; "When I got back . . ." from United Jewish Appeal, Interview with Laura Margolis Jarblum by Menahem Kaufman, Apr. 26, 1976, AJJDC Archives, AR3344.130, pp. 14–15; "The only transport . . ." from "Remembering Soong Ching Ling," Laura Jarblum file, Joint Distribution Committee, Sept. 1986; *Newsview*, Dec. 1, 1981; Yehuda Bauer, *American Jewry and the Holocaust: The American Jewish Joint Distribution Committee, 1935–1945* (Detroit: Wayne State University Press, 1981), pp. 302–9.

13. Interview with Israel Epstein, Jan. 18, 1993; Rewi Alley, *At 90: Memoirs of My China Years: An Autobiography of Rewi Alley* (Beijing: New World Press, 1986), pp. 145–46; Leung, *Historical Dictionary of Revolutionary China*, p. 1; "If war was near . . ." from Drage, p. 261; G. B. Endacott, *A History of Hong Kong* (Oxford University Press, 1964), p. 299; "He was always . . ." from *Newsweek*, Apr. 20, 1942.

14. Letter from John Childs to author, Oct. 31, 1994; "The last week . . ." from Phyllis Harrop, *Hong Kong Incident* (London: Eyre & Spottiswoode, 1943), p. 66; "Lit up like a Christmas . . ." from *South China Morning Post*, Nov. 30, 1975.

15. Endacott, *Hong Kong Eclipse*, pp. 69–71, 78; "Some of the Japanese . . ." and "None of us . . ." from *South China Morning Post*, Nov. 30, 1975; "In the city . . ." from Gwen Priestwood, *Through Japanese Barbed Wire: A Thousand-mile Trek from a Japanese Prison Camp* (London: George G. Harrap & Co. Ltd., 1944), p. 10; Dew, p. 31; Montreal *Standard*, Dec. 4, 1943; "I took the two sisters . . ." from Drage, p. 262.

16. "You would watch . . ." from Dew, p. 23; Hahn, *China to Me*, p. 273; Priestwood, pp. 13–15.

17. "At regular intervals . . ." and "Before morning . . ." from *South China Morning Post*, Nov. 30, 1975; "Mad mobs . . ." from Dew, p. 42; Harrop, p. 78; John Stericker, *A Tear for the Dragon* (London: Arthur Barker, 1958), p. 127.

18. "Arrests of fifth . . ." from Harrop, p. 74; "It was now open war . . ." from Drage, p. 263.

19. "I remember meeting . . ." from an interview with Solomon Bard, Aug. 8, 1994; "Clerks and coolies . . ." from *South China Morning Post*, Dec. 7, 1975; Stericker, p. 127.

20. "The faces of the women . . ." from Stericker, p. 129; "The Japanese had the artillery . . ." from *South China Morning Post*, Dec. 7, 1975; "There must be no thought . . ." from Endacott, *Hong Kong Eclipse*, p. 85; "Something strange . . ." from Harrop, p. 85; "On Boxing Day . . ." from Drage, p. 264.

CHAPTER 16
Stanley

1. "A well-known lady . . ." from Stericker, p. 134; "It was a glorious . . ." from Harrop, p. 89; Priestwood, pp. 25–26; "Immediately after the fall . . ." from Dew, pp. 169–70.

2. Endacott, *Hong Kong Eclipse*, p. 118; *South China Morning Post*, Dec. 7, 1975; "That he knew . . ." from Harrop, p. 92.

3. "As the hotel food . . ." from *Saturday Evening Post*, Jan. 9, 1943; Stericker, p. 141; Dew, p. 146; *South China Morning Post*, Dec. 14, 1975; "You decided what . . ." from an interview with George Wright-Nooth, Mar. 10, 1993; "It struck me . . ." from Drage, p. 266; *Post Telegram*, Oct. 9, 1945.

4. Marion Dudley, *Hong Kong Prison Camp*, New York (no pub.), Letter dated Aug. 22, 1942, p. 1; "They weren't particularly . . ." from Drage, p. 267; A Cretinous-looking . . ." from *Saturday Evening Post*, Jan. 9, 1943; Dew, Gwen, p. 147; Jean Gittins, *Stanley: Behind Barbed Wire* (Hong Kong: Hong Kong University Press, 1982), p. 28.

5. Endacott, *Hong Kong Eclipse*, p. 105; *A Record of the Actions of the Hongkong Volunteer Defence Corps in the Battle for Hong Kong December 1941* (Hong Kong: Ye Olde Printerie, Ltd., 1953), pp. 54–55; "The air soon became . . ." from *South China Morning Post*, Dec. 14, 1975; "It was pleasant . . ." from H. G. Wittenbach, Notes on internment by the Japanese, in

Kowloon and in Stanley Camp, Hong Kong, written by Mrs. H. G. Wittenbach soon after her return to England towards the end of 1945. Department of Documents, IWM, 89/9/1, p. 2; Gittins, p. 1, 30; Stericker, pp. 151–56; "I fear that a small . . ." quoted in Oliver Lindsay, *At the Going Down of the Sun; Hong Kong and South-East Asia*, 1941–1945 (London: Hamish Hamilton, 1981), p. 34.

6. "The first night . . ." from Lindsay, p. 36; Jean Gittins, *I Was at Stanley* (Ye Olde Printerie, Ltd., 1945), p. 10; Day Joyce, *Ordinary People: The Sheet*, Account based on diaries kept at the time of her experience as a civilian internee of the Japanese in Hong Kong 1941–45, ca. 1974, IWM, Department of Documents, P324, p. 226; Lindsay, p. 37; "I don't think . . ." from an interview with George Wright-Nooth, Mar. 10, 1993.

7. "People were just bundled . . ." from Gittins, *I Was at Stanley*, p. 8; "I remember one medium . . ." from *Saturday Evening Post*, Jan. 9, 1943; Dew, p. 235; "We were not allocated . . ." from Wittenbach, pp. 2–3.

8. PROHK, *Stanley-Block Nominal Roll*, HKRS No. 170, D&S No. 1/573D; Dew, p. 235; Envelope to Cohen in Stanley, collection of Victor Cooper; "The rooms in the flats . . ." from Gittins, *Stanley: Behind Barbed Wire*, p. 52.

9. London *Daily Express*, Feb. 14, 1942; *Newsweek*, Mar. 16, 1942; PRO, WO106 5269, Telegram, Feb. 26, 1942; "Since the news . . ." and "If I thought . . ." from *Sunday Dispatch*, Feb.15, 1942.

10. "He got picked up . . ." and "He got a good . . ." from an interview with Geoffrey Wilson, Apr. 29, 1993; *Post Telegram*, Oct. 9, 1945; "I just denied everything . . . ," "A day or two . . .," and "I found myself . . ." from Drage, pp. 269, 273–75; "He was beaten . . ." from an interview with Israel Epstein, Jan. 18, 1993.

11. "A flabby, tubercular . . ." and "Even if the food . . ." from *Saturday Evening Post*, Jan. 16, 1943; Lindsay, p. 42; *South China Morning Post*, Dec. 21, 1975; "Serving soup to 536 . . ." from Frank Hastings Fisher, *The Diary of F. H. Fisher in Hong Kong 1942–1945, Written in the form of a letter to his wife*, Department of Documents, IWM. 67/191/1; Stericker, p. 159; "Our men were unused . . ." from Gittins, *I Was at Stanley*, p. 9; "We queued up . . ." from Dudley, p. 6; Joyce, p. 5; "We managed to get hold . . ." from F. H. J. Kelly, Typescript of Part of Diary Kept in Stanley Civilian Internment Camp 1942–1945, IWM, Department of Documents, 84/59/1.

12. "We had no paraffin . . ." from Wittenbach, p. 4; *South China Morning Post*, Dec. 21, 1975; M. L. Bevan, *Diary and Album of Sketches of Stanley Gaol*. Hong Kong, 1941–45, Department of Documents, IWM, London, 69/6/1; Stericker, p. 166; Gittins, *I Was at Stanley*, p. 14; Gittins, *Stanley: Behind Barbed Wire*, pp. 78, 135; *Saturday Evening Post*, Jan. 9, 1943; Dew, p. 251.

13. Gittins, *I Was at Stanley*, p. 17; "The lack of privacy . . ." and "Thieves, you're all thieves . . ." from *Saturday Evening Post*, Jan. 16, 1943; Fisher Diary; "The worst of all . . ." from Drage, p. 278; "One day General Cohen . . ." from Dew, pp. 244–45; "We took days . . ." from an interview with Louise Gill, Sept. 7, 1993.

14. Stericker, pp. 162–63; Drage, p. 279; "He always looked . . ." from an interview with George Wright-Nooth, Mar. 10, 1993; Priestwood, p. 56; *Saturday Evening Post*, Jan. 16, 1943.

15. "I had a patch . . ." from an interview with James Shepherd, Sr., Mar. 15, 1994; "For the communal . . ." from Wittenbach, p. 5; Gittins, *I Was at Stanley*, p. 15; *South China Morning Post*, Dec. 21, 1975; "Shopping was our chief . . ." from Hahn, *China to Me*, p. 359; Hahn, *Hong Kong Holiday*, p. 253; George Wright-Nooth, *Prisoner of the Turnip Heads, Horror, Hunger and Humor in Hong Kong, 1941–1945* (London: Leo Cooper, 1994), p. 69; "I got so . . ." from an interview with Emily Hahn, Feb. 28, 1993.

16. "The parcels have been . . ." from Kelly Diary, p. 14; "We'd fixed up . . ." from Drage, p. 279; Gittins, *I Was at Stanley*, pp. 10–11; Dew, pp. 253, 267; Stericker, p. 166; Wright-Nooth, p. 220; *Saturday Evening Post*, Jan. 16, 1943; *South China Morning Post*, Dec. 21, 1975; Lindsay, pp. 41–42.

17. "Slow starvation . . ." from Fisher Diary; Gittins, *I Was at Stanley*, p. 13; Hahn, *China to Me*, p. 354; Stericker, pp. 190–93; "It was also interesting . . ." from Joyce, p. 230; Geoffrey Charles Emerson, "Stanley Internment Camp, Hong Kong, 1942–1945: A Study of Civilian Internment During the Second World War" (master's thesis, University of Hong Kong, 1973), p. 271; Wittenbach, p. 6; Hahn, *Hong Kong Holiday*, p. 120; *South China Morning Post*, Dec. 21, 1975; "Some individuals did . . ." from *Saturday Evening Post*, Jan. 16, 1943; Stericker, p. 194.

18. "On one occasion . . ." from Wittenbach, p. 5; Stericker, pp. 165–66, 185; Gittins, *I Was at Stanley*, p. 13.

19. "At first in the camp . . . ," "We all had various . . . ," and "We found a derelict . . ." from an interview with Israel Epstein, Jan. 18, 1993; Gittins, *Stanley: Behind Barbed Wire*, p. 49; "Everyone had to be . . ." from Dew, p. 255; *South China Morning Post*, Dec. 21, 1975; "They'd come around . . ." from an interview with Kay Franklin, Dec. 1, 1993.

20. "While this was going . . ." from *South China Morning Post*, Dec. 21, 1975; "We had a lot . . ." from an interview with Kay Franklin, Dec. 1, 1993; "The days passed . . ." from *Saturday Evening Post*, Jan. 16, 1943; "Then down the hill . . ." from Dew, p. 290; "We sat on the wall . . ." quoted in Lindsay, p. 48.

21. Stanley Identification, July 24, 1942, collection Victor Cooper; "I never ever saw . . ." from an interview with George Wright-Nooth, Mar. 10, 1993; "They couldn't stand . . ." from an interview with Geoffrey Wilson, Apr. 29, 1993; "We didn't walk . . ." from an interview with James Shepherd, Sr., Mar. 15, 1994.

22. "We didn't have much food . . ." from an interview with George Wright-Nooth, Mar. 10, 1993; "All we had . . ." from an interview with Geoffrey Wilson, Apr. 29, 1993; Joyce, introduction, p. 2, 129; Stericker, p. 167; Gittins, *I Was at Stanley*, p. 14; Dew, p. 248; B. C. Anslow (Then B. C. Redwood) *Extracts from Diaries Kept During Japanese War on Hong Kong*, IWM, Department of Documents, 73/67/1 (P), p. 108; *South China Morning Post*, Dec. 21, 1975; Interview with James Shepherd, Sr., Mar. 15, 1994; I quite forgot . . ." from Kelly Diary; "I used sometimes to . . ." *Saturday Evening Post*, Jan. 9, 1943.

23. Gittins, *I Was at Stanley*, p. 16; Stericker, p. 173; "We were herded . . ." from Priestwood, p. 50; "The Canadians . . ." from Fisher Diary; "Well we got on . . ." from Laura Margolis Jarblum, United Jewish Appeal, Interview with Laura Margolis Jarblum by Menahem Kaufman, Apr. 26, 1976, AJJDC Archives, AR3344.130, p. 30.

24. "A crowd gathered . . ." from an interview with James Shepherd, Sr., Mar. 15, 1994; "I

just lazed . . ." from Drage, p. 283; "We stared over . . ." from Hahn, *Hong Kong Holiday*, p. 292; "As our turn came . . ." from *Life*, Nov. 29, 1943.

25. "They couldn't feed us . . ." from an interview with Emily Hahn, Feb. 28, 1993; "The people cheered . . ." from *Life*, Dec. 20, 1943; Hahn, *Hong Kong Holiday*, pp. 279–82, 294; Telegram Morris Cohen to Evelyn Wallace, Oct. 24, 1943, collection of Michael Wallace; Reuters, Nov. 4, 1943; London *Daily Telegraph*, Nov. 4, 1943; Manchester *Evening News*, Nov. 4, 1943; "When I got onto . . ." and "He just used to . . ." from an interview with Kay Franklin, Dec. 1, 1993.

26. "My mother went . . ." from an interview with Issie Bernstein, Nov. 14, 1992; *The Zionist Record*, Nov. 12, 1943; "When he was prevailed . . ." from London Jewish Chronicle, Nov. 12, 1943; Jarblum UJA interview, p. 30; "Then, somewhere out . . ." from Hahn, Hong Kong Holiday, p. 305.

27. Jarblum UJA interview, p. 30; "They kept us . . ." and "It wasn't till . . ." from Drage, p. 284; "They were supposed to . . ." and "They were debriefed . . ." from an interview with Arthur Menzies, Mar. 25, 1994; "The officials who dealt . . ." from NAC, RG25, vol. 2251, file/dossier 17-BVJ-40, Nov. 30, 1943 Memorandum for Mr. Stone, Ottawa; "Because any remarks . . ." from the Vancouver *Daily,* Dec. 4, 1943; NAC, RG25 vol. 2251 file / dossier 17-BVJ-40, Nov. 10, 1943 letter from S. T. Wood, RCMP to Under Secretary of State for External Affairs; Paramount Newsreel segment on Morris Cohen, Dec. 1943.

CHAPTER 17
Judith

1. "I can tell you . . ." from *The National Jewish Monthly*, Jan. 1944; "One thing I wish . . ." from Montreal *Standard*, Dec. 4, 1943; Montreal *Star,* Dec. 7, 1943; Montreal *Herald*, Dec. 8, 1943.

2. "In view of the criminal . . ." from Federal Bureau of Investigation Morris Cohen folder, 100–244116; "Gave them the . . ." from Drage, p. 284; The actual date of Cohen's arrest was July 1, 1914; "While he is described . . ." from NAC, RG25, vol. 2251, file/dossier 17-BVJ-40, Dec. 8, 1943, letter from Peter M. Dwyer to T. A. Stone; "Cohen is of the 'tough' . . ." and "That the work . . ." from PRO, HS1/112, Feb. 11, 1944; "That his services . . ." and "Not interested in Cohen . . ." from PRO, HS1/112, Mar. 4, 1944.

3. Interview with Harold Vineberg, Feb. 25, 1994; Interview with Cecil Vineberg, Aug. 25, 1993; "I remember that after . . ." from an interview with Frances Pascal, Aug. 20, 1993; Gerald Clark, *No Mud on the Back Seat, Memoirs of a Reporter* (Montreal: Robert Davies Publishing, 1985), pp. 30–31; Gerald Tulchinsky, "The Third Solitude: A. M. Klein's Jewish Montreal, 1910–1950," *Journal of Canadian Studies* 19, no. 2 (summer 1984), pp. 97, 106–7; "She was very beautiful . . ." and "She had very good . . ." from an interview with Rose Klyne, Jan. 19, 1994; "She had absolutely . . ." from an interview with Harry Clark, July 23, 1993; Interview with Gerald Clark, Jan. 21, 1993.

4. "I can't say . . ." and "My sister had . . ." from an interview with Harry Clark, July 23,

1993; "He sounded like . . ." from an interview with Ruth Field, July 26, 1993; "He wasn't a good . . ." from an interview with Rose Klyne, Jan. 19, 1994; "A good Chinese girl . . ." from Drage, p. 137; Clark, p. 126; "I'm very happy . . ." and "China will be . . ." from news clip 1944, no paper listed; " 'I'm just a young . . ." from Toronto *Daily Star*, Apr. 5, 1944; Winnipeg *Free Press*, Mar. 16, 1944; Montreal *Gazette*, Apr. 6, 1944; Toronto *Globe and Mail*, Apr. 5, 1944.

5. Letter Harry Clark to author, Oct. 9, 1993; Montreal *Gazette*, May 20, 1944; Edmonton *Journal*, June 27, 1944; *Daily Province*, Vancouver, Mar. 24, 1944; "I am sure he didn't . . ." from an interview with Rose Klyne, Jan. 19, 1994; "The Chinese are waging . . ." from a 1944 Calgary news clip; The Vancouver *Sun*, June 27, 1944; *Jewish Western Bulletin*, Vancouver, July 7, 1944; "I'd get Al Smith's . . ." from Toronto *Globe and Mail*, June 20, 1944.

6. Letter Judith Cohen to Evelyn Ferera, Mar. 14, 1949, collection of Michael Wallace; Letter Harry Clark to author, Oct. 9, 1993; "He heard that I . . ." from an interview with Harry Clark, July 23, 1993; "He was very lavish . . . ," "He was lionized . . . ," and "All the kids . . ." from an interview with Rose Klyne, Jan. 19, 1994; "They didn't discourage . . ." from an interview with Gerald Clark, Aug. 13, 1993; "It would be very impromptu . . ." from an interview with Cecil Vineberg, Aug. 25, 1993; Interview with Frances Pascal, Aug. 20, 1993; "Gottlieb and Cohen confronted . . ." from Ed Parker, *I Didn't Come Here to Stay: The Memoirs of Ed Parker* (Toronto: Natural Heritage/ Natural History, Inc., 1993), p. 128; *Variety Obituaries, 1957–1963*, vol. 5 (New York: Garland Publishers, 1988); D. J. Turner, *Canadian Feature Film Index, 1913–1985* (Canada: Public Archives, 1985).

7. NAC, RG25, vol. 2251, file/dossier 17-BVJ-40, June 15, 1944, letter from A. L. Jolliffe to Mr. Kennlyeside; NAC, RG25, vol. 2251, file/dossier 17-BVJ-40, June 23, 1944, letter from A. L. Jolliffe to Mr. Kennlyeside, Ottawa; NAC, RG25, vol. 2251, file/dossier 17-BVJ-40, May 1, 1945, letter from R. M. Macdonnell to Morris Cohen; NAC, RG25, vol. 2251, file/dossier 17-BVJ-40, Nov. 19, 1945, letter from A. L. Jolliffe to the Under Secretary of State for External Affairs; "Circumstances and things . . ." from a Dec. 18, 1944, letter from Morris Cohen to Evelyn Ferera, collection of Michael Wallace; "Morris' book . . ." from an Aug. 26, 1945, letter from Judith Cohen to Evelyn Wallace, collection of Michael Wallace.

8. Marrus, pp. 338–39; David J. Bercuson, *Canada and the Birth of Israel; A Study in Canadian Foreign Policy* (Toronto: University of Toronto Press, 1985), pp. 30–33; "The Jewish people . . ." from Israel Goldstein, *My World as a Jew: The Memoirs of Israel Goldstein*, vol. 1 (New York: Herzl Press, 1984), p. 148; "We must seek . . ." from Irving Abella, *A Coat of Many Colours: Two Centuries of Jewish Life in Canada* (Toronto: Lester & Orpen Dennys, 1990), p. 200; *Anatomy of the Auschwitz Death Camp*, eds. Yisreal Gutman, Michael Berenbaum, Yehuda Bauer, Raul Hilberg, and Franciszek Piper (Bloomington: Indiana University Press, 1994), pp. 250–251.

9. "Then you could go . . ." and "The general looked . . ." from the Montreal *Star*, May 5, 1973; Marrus, p. 340; "Cohen offered to introduce . . ." from Eliahu Elath, *Zionism at the UN: A Diary of the First Days* (Philadelphia: The Jewish Publication Society of America,

1976), p. 111; "As I sat . . ." from Goldstein, pp. 151–52; "He spoke airily . . ." from NAC, RG25, vol. 2251, file/dossier 17-BVJ-40, Apr. 17, 1945, Memorandum for Mr. Norman.

10. "It turned out . . ." and "I am not suggesting . . ." from the Montreal *Star*, May 5, 1973; Goldstein, pp. 148–52; "Rec. deputation . . ." from Columbia University Libraries Manuscript Collections, Diary of Wellington Koo, No. 17, Apr. 5–June 27, 1945. Box 216; "Cohen described him . . ." from Elath, p. 251; "Of any state . . ." from Thomas Hovet, Jr., and Erica Hovet, *Annual Review of United Nations Affairs. A Chronology and Fact Book of the United Nations, 1941–1985* (Dobbs Ferry, N.Y.: Oceana Publications, 1986); "Your uncle is beginning . . ." from Aug. 26, 1945 letter from Judith Cohen to Evelyn Wallace, collection of Michael Wallace.

11. "He came loaded . . ." from an interview with Cyril Sherer, Dec. 20, 1993; *Post Telegram*, Jan. 20, 1946; "I remember how excited . . ." from an interview with Louise Gill, Sept. 7, 1993; "There will be unification . . ." news clip, Nov. 9, 1945, no issue listed; "Hard work . . ." from London *Evening News*, Nov. 7, 1945.

12. "Kill all . . ." quoted in Sheridan, p. 264. Other material from pp. 259–82; Clubb, pp. 252–59, 263.

13. Sheridan, pp. 269–76; Clubb, 264, 277–80; "There is nothing . . ." from NAC, RG25, vol. 2251, file/dossier 17-BVJ-40, Feb. 14, 1946, Confidential Memorandum entitled, "General Morris A. Cohen."

14. John F. Melby, *The Mandate of Heaven: Record of a Civil War, China 1945–49* (Toronto: University of Toronto Press, 1968), p. 121; "It was the custom . . ." from an interview with Ben Levaco, Sept. 2, 1993; Chester Ronning, *A Memoir of China in Revolution: From the Boxer Rebellion to the People's Republic* (New York: Pantheon Books, 1974), p. 99; "A good national-minded . . ." Central Zionist Archives, S8/635, Apr. 10, 1946, letter from the Far Eastern Palestine Office of the Jewish Agency for Palestine in Shanghai to Emil Schmorak at the Jewish Agency for Palestine; Central Zionist Archives, Z410153, Apr. 10, 1946, letter; Central Zionist Archives, May 7, 1946 letter Emil Schmorak to The Far Eastern; "When we were together . . ." from an interview with Harry Clark, July 23, 1993.

15. "He came on the stage . . ." from an interview with Ben-Eliezer, Oct. 25, 1993; "She told me . . ." and "We had about . . ." from an interview with Abraham Fradkin, May 23, 1994; "Morris stated that no . . ." from Ben-Eliezer, pp. 295–96; "Knowing your interest . . ." from Feb.18, 1947, letter from Tientsin Hebrew Association to Morris Cohen, collection of Victor Cooper; The Criminal Decision of the Nanking Higher Court, collection of Victor Cooper; Oct. 3, 1951, letter Morris Cohen to Max Seligman, collection of Victor Cooper.

16. "During that time . . ." from an interview with Arthur Menzies, Mar. 25, 1994.

17. "All he did . . . ," "Judith after a day's . . . ," and "My younger sister . . ." from an interview with Rose Klyne, Jan. 19, 1994.

18. NAC, RG25, vol. 2251, file/dossier 17-BVJ-40, Apr. 15, 1947, Memorandum for Miss H. Reid; NAC, RG25, vol. 2251, file/dossier 17-BVJ-40, from Apr. 24, 1947, letter from S. T. Wood to the Under Secretary of State for External Affairs; "I saw him more than . . ."

from an interview with Israel Epstein, Jan. 18, 1993; "He accused me . . ." from an interview with Emily Hahn, Feb. 28, 1993.

19. Abella, pp. 227–29; Jerusalem *Post*, Nov. 29, 1991; "From that we got . . . ," "The Canadian government . . . ," and "The next day . . ." from an interview with Sydney Shulemson, Oct. 1, 1993; *Jane's Encyclopedia of Aviation*, vol. 3 (Danbury: Grolier Educational Corporation, 1980), pp. 458–59.

20. "Their characters as described . . ." from NAC, RG25, vol. 2251, file/dossier 17-BVJ-40, Oct. 10, 1947, confidential letter, The Military Attaché Nanking, China.

21. *Encyclopaedia Judaica*, vols. 4, 8; Ben-Eliezer, pp. 304–11, 317–19; "It was essential . . ." from an interview with Yaacov Liberman, Sept. 2, 1993; "On the upper floor . . ." from *Betar in China: 1929–1949*, p. 90; "We were quite busy . . ." from an interview with Samuel Muller, Nov. 18, 1993.

22. "The movement basically . . ." and "At that time . . ." from an interview with Samuel Muller, Nov. 18, 1993; "The British destroyers . . ." and "He furnished us . . ." from Ben-Eliezer, p. 319; "Knew the territory . . ." from an interview with Judith Ben-Eliezer, Oct. 25, 1993; "These ships were available . . ." from *Betar in China*, p. 90; *Encyclopaedia Judaica*, vols. 8, 9.

23. "On a return trip . . ." from an Oct. 9, 1993, letter from Harry Clark to the author; Feb. 7, 1994 letter from Charles Bronfman to the author; "The general was always . . . ," "Every time I saw him . . . ," and "He knew everyone . . ." from an interview with Michael Vineberg, Sept. 28, 1993; "We went out eating . . ." from an interview with Cecil Vineberg, Aug. 25, 1993; Montreal research conducted by Eiran Harris.

24. "When the family . . ." from an interview with Victor Cooper, July 22, 1994; "He brought her mother . . ." from an interview with Sarah Rich, Nov. 14, 1992; "Even as a ten-year-old . . ." from an interview with Josef Rich, Nov. 8, 1992.

25. Mar. 14, 1949 letter from Judith Cohen to Evelyn Ferera, collection of Michael Wallace; "Judith had only one . . ." from Drage, p. 286; "He was at that time . . ." from an interview with Raya Litvin, Dec. 27, 1993; "What he did . . ." from an interview with Joseph Gleiberman, Dec. 17, 1993.

26. Sheridan, pp. 259–82; Gould, unpublished memoirs, p. 389; Sheridan, pp. 272–73, 286–89; "Their military debacles . . ." from Clubb, p. 295; Other material, pp. 276–84.

27. "Shanghai's police . . ." from Gould, unpublished memoirs, p. 392; "They were searching . . ." from an interview with David Vardi, Feb. 22, 1994; "They were arresting . . ." from an interview with Walter J. Citrin, Dec. 9, 1993. Citrin would not go into any further details on the case, or say who was kidnapped.

28. "It was the easiest . . ." from Ronald A. Keith, *Bush Pilot with a Briefcase: The Happy-Go-Lucky Story of Grant McConachie* (Ontario: Doubleday Canada Ltd., 1972), p. 266; Dale M. Titler, *The Day the Red Baron Died* (New York: Walker and Company, 1970), p. 290; Eugenie Louise Myles, *Airborne From Edmonton* (Toronto: The Ryerson Press, 1959), pp. 196, 257.

29. "Hordes of people . . ." from Henri Cartier-Bresson and Barbara Brakeley Miller, *China* (New York: Bantam Books, 1964); "Today's big event . . ." from Derk Bodde, *Peking Diary: A Year of Revolution* (New York: Henry Schuman, 1950), pp. 103–4; Clubb, pp. 248, 291, 295–97; Sheridan, p. 271.

30. "On hearing the rumor . . ." from Cartier-Bresson, *China.*

CHAPTER 18

The Myth

1. Clubb, 310; *Biographical Dictionary*, vol. 2, pp. 292, 294; vol. 3, p. 451; "Morris' problem . . ." from Clark, p. 129; "He didn't have any . . ." from an interview with Gerald Clark, Aug. 13, 1993; "I don't think he was . . ." from an interview with Gerald Clark, Jan. 21, 1993.

2. Clubb, pp. 312–14, 318–19, 324–25; Leung, *Historical Dictionary of Revolutionary China*, pp. 120–21, pp. 411–12.

3. Apr. 22, 1951, letter from Judith Cohen to Rose Bernstein, collection of Michael Wallace; Oct. 9, 1993, letter from Harry Clark to the author; Oct. 3, 1951, letter from Morris Cohen to Max Seligman, collection of Victor Cooper; "Of course he should never . . ." from Oct. 2, 1981, letter from Charles Drage to Allan Levine; Divorce Affidavit of Ida Judith Cohen, High Court of Justice, Probate, Divorce and Admiralty Division. 2425/55, filed Mar. 22, 1955; "It was just a story . . ." from an interview with Gerald Clark, Jan. 21, 1993; "He was into some pretty . . ." from an interview with Harry Clark, July 23, 1993; "Next time I'd try . . ." from *Evening Standard*, Apr. 14, 1954.

4. "He had brought back . . ." from an interview with Sonny Booth, Sept. 21, 1993; "I personally think . . ." from an interview with Cecil Vineberg, Aug. 25, 1993; "He just didn't find . . ." from an interview with Gerald Clark, Jan. 21, 1993; Divorce Affidavit of Louis Lowenstein, High Court of Justice, Probate, Divorce and Admiralty Division. 2425/55, filed Dec. 9, 1955; "He was living . . ." from an interview with Ruth Field, July 26, 1993; "In the end . . ." from an Oct. 2, 1981, letter from Charles Drage to Allan Levine; Interview with Sarah Rich, Nov. 14, 1992.

5. *New Catholic Encyclopedia*, vol. 3 (San Francisco: McGraw Hill, 1967), pp. 598–99; "We have been established . . ." and "If Mrs. Sun gets . . ." from Montreal *Gazette*, Mar. 20, 1951; "We were agreeably . . ." from a Mar. 21, 1951, letter from Sister Marie de la Providence, to Morris Cohen, courtesy of Les Soeurs Missionnaires de l'Immaculée-Conception; "Even with the best . . ." from Keesing's Contemporary Archives, Mar. 29–Apr. 5, 1952, p. 12117.

6. Clubb, pp. 321–22, 328–33, 347–48.

7. "He told us that . . ." from an interview with Sarah Rich, Mar. 14, 1993; *Chicago Tribune*, June 7, 1952; "I saw him practically . . ." from an interview with Henry Lieberman, Dec. 3, 1993; "It just was one . . ." from an interview with Frances Pascal, Aug. 20, 1993; "I am sure you understand . . ." and "That of course . . ." from a Dec. 8, 1953, letter from Cyril E. Schwisberg to Morris Cohen, collection of Victor Cooper; "A lot of houses . . ." from an

interview with Joseph Michael Cohen, Dec. 28, 1993; Interview with Sarah Rich, Mar. 14, 1993; Interview with Phyllis Horal, Dec. 6, 1994.

8. "He was not a . . ." from Sokolsky, part 2, p. 49; "When the Nationalist . . ." from *Hong Kong Standard*, Jan. 4, 1956; "Once you start . . .," "We managed to corral . . .," "Marshal of the Diplomatic . . ." from Drage, pp. 175, 196–97.

9. "He assured me . . ." from a United Press clip, 1954; *Evening Standard*, Apr. 14, 1954; *The Rhodesian Herald*, Mar. 2, 1954; 1954 Invitation from the Chinese Association of Salisbury, collection of Michael Wallace.

10. Dick Wilson, *Chou: The Story of Zhou Enlai, 1896–1976* (London: Hutchinson, 1984), pp. 193–94; "I don't think . . ." from Associated Press, May 1, 1954; "The only way . . ." from Manchester *Evening News*, Feb. 6, 1956; Manchester *Jewish Gazette*, May 14, 1954; *The Jewish Chronicle*, June 18, 1954, Jan. 28, 1955; "He would come for . . ." from an interview with Harry Cohen, May 17, 1994; Invitation for luncheon at the Wingate Park Club, 1954, collection of Michael Wallace; *Newsweek*, June 28, 1954; "Politics are just . . ." from Manchester *News Chronicle*, Mar. 30, 1954; *Daily Express*, Apr. 6, 1954; "He was very, very . . ." from an interview with Tina Dunn, Nov. 1992; "To drop into . . ." from a Jan. 4, 1955, letter from B. Margaret Meagher to Morris Cohen, collection of Victor Cooper.

11. "We dashed onto . . ." from an interview with Victor Cooper, July 19, 1994; China is the only . . ." from *The Jewish Chronicle*, May 7, 1954; "A poisonous, dangerous . . ." from Drage, p. 226; "The brains . . ." from Manchester *Guardian*, Mar. 2, 1955.

12. "I can no longer . . ." from a letter from Judith Cohen to Leah Cooper, Mar. 21, 1953, collection of Victor Cooper; "Its effect was . . ." from letter from Charles Drage to Allan Levine, Oct. 2, 1981; "I am hoping . . ." from a June 20, 1953 letter from Judith Cohen to Morris Cohen, collection of Victor Cooper; Divorce Affidavit of Ida Judith Cohen, Mar. 22, 1955; Divorce Affidavit of Morris Abraham Cohen, High Court of Justice, Probate, Divorce and Admiralty Division. 2425/55, filed June 27, 1955; Divorce Affidavit of Judith Cohen, High Court of Justice, Probate, Divorce and Admiralty Division. 2425/55, filed July 30, 1955; Divorce Affidavit of Harry E. Clark, High Court of Justice, Probate, Divorce and Admiralty Division. 2425/55, filed Sept. 10, 1955; Decree Nisi—Dissolution, High Court of Justice, Probate, Divorce and Admiralty Division, Def. 460, Dec. 16, 1955; *Evening Standard*, Dec. 16, 1955.

13. "True state of affairs . . ." and "Discussions with him . . ." from USSD, 100-244116-10, Dec. 6, 1955, letter from Arthur Ringwalt, Embassy in London to Washington.

CHAPTER 19
Twilight

1. "In this time . . ." and "The rumors published . . ." from *Time*, Jan. 16, 1956; Decree Absolute; "I may be able . . ." quoted in a January 1955 Norwood Allman note, Allman Papers, Box 12, file 2; *Daily Mirror*, Dec. 29, 1955; *Chicago Tribune*, Dec. 29, 1955; "Mr. Kendall said . . ." from USSD, 100-244116, Dec. 20, 1955, letter from Consul General

Everett F. Drumright to Dept. of State; "Adviser to the Nationalist . . ." from Manchester *Guardian*, Mar. 24, 1956; Too ridiculous to be . . ." from New York *Times*, Jan. 4, 1956; "They realized that . . ." from Hong Kong *Standard*, Jan. 4, 1956; Hong Kong *Standard*, Dec 25, 1955.

2. "People were willing . . ." from an interview with Israel Epstein, Jan. 18, 1993; "He did not like . . ." and "Cohen has had . . ." Allman Papers, Box 12, file 2.

3. Montreal *Gazette*, Feb. 3, 1956; "Morris just worshiped . . ." from an interview with Gerald Clark, Jan. 21, 1993; " 'Two gun' Cohen called . . ." from HKPRO, Dec. 20, 1955, confidential telegram from Peking to Foreign Office.

4. "I enjoyed meeting . . ." from HKPRO, Jan. 17, 1956, confidential letter from C. O'Neill, Peking to C. T. Crowe, Foreign Office, 1632/2/56.

5. "Being unable to imagine . . ." and "His enthusiasm for . . ." from HKPRO, Mar. 6, 1956, confidential letter C. O'Neill, Peking to C. T. Crowe, Foreign Office. 1632/2/56; *South China Morning Post*, Mar. 24, 1956; "May indicate that the Chinese . . ." from USSD, 100-244116, Mar. 28, 1956, letter from Arthur R. Ringwalt to the State Department; "It is unlikely . . ." from HKPRO, Mar. 25, 1956, confidential telegram Secretary of State to Governor of Hong Kong.

6. "Possibly calculated altercation . . ." from USSD, 100-244116, Mar. 23, 1956, letter Drumright in Hong Kong to the Secretary of State; "I used to go . . . ," "He had this black . . . ," and "He was very jovial . . ." from an interview with Marvin Farkas, May 22, 1995; "I didn't go . . ." from Hong Kong *Standard*, Mar. 23, 1956.

7. *Evening Chronicle*, Mar. 22, 1956; *Times* of London, Mar. 23, Apr. 3, 1956, Dec. 7, 1966; "Who the heck . . ." and "What I saw . . ." from Hong Kong *Standard*, Apr. 6, 1956; "No, no, no . . ." from Manchester *Guardian*, Mar. 24, 1956; London *Daily Telegraph*, Apr. 3, 1956; "His story is . . ." from USSD, 100-244116, Mar. 23, 1956, note from Drumright in Hong Kong to the Secretary of State; "The one man whom . . ." from Hong Kong *Standard*, Jan. 4, 1956; "Cohen, who according to . . ." from PROHK, Apr. 16, 1956, letter from British consulate at Tamsui to Far Eastern Department, Foreign Office, London, 1001/56; PROHK, Mar. 29, 1956, confidential telegram, from Secretary of State to Governor of Hong Kong; *China News,* Taipei, Mar. 26, 1956; *Times* of London, Apr. 4, 1956.

8. "When he spoke . . ." from an interview with Issie Bernstein, Nov. 14, 1992; "He used to take . . ." and "It used to be . . ." from an interview with Joseph Michael Cohen, Dec. 28, 1993; "She always kept . . ." from an interview with Sarah Rich, Apr. 10, 1994; "I used to get . . ." from an interview with Victor David Cooper, July 19, 1994.

9. "My father always . . ." from an interview with Joseph Michael Cohen, Dec. 28, 1993; Interviews with various family members.

10. "He is now reported . . ." from USSD, 100-244116, Aug. 29, 1956, letter from U.S. Embassy, London to the Department of State; *Wenhui bao*, Nov. 7, 11, 1956; *Xinhua ribao*, Nov. 14, 1956; "I see that everywhere . . ." from *Renmin ribao*, Nov. 19, 1956; Nov. 9, 1956 letter from Tso Mu-yeh to Morris Cohen, collection of Victor Cooper; Zhou Daochun, Zhonghsan lingyuan boji (Various notes on the Sun Yat-sen Mausoleum Park), Jiangsu renmin chubanshe; "Cohen seemed to be . . ." from USSD, 100-244116, Apr. 16, 1957, letter

Consul Thomas P. Dillon to the Department of State; "He seems to have . . ." from HKPRO, Apr. 25, 1957, letter from G. O'Neill to P. G. F. Dalton, Foreign Office; "Let a hundred . . ." and "Poisonous weeds . . ." quoted in Clubb, pp. 349–50; Leung, *Historical Dictionary of Revolutionary China*, pp. 10–11.

11. "My meetings with him . . ." from an interview with Sidney Shapiro, Jan. 20, 1993; "Do you know . . ." from an interview with Israel Epstein, Jan. 18, 1993; "He would usually be . . ." from an interview with Sidney Rittenberg, Oct. 15, 1992.

12. "The family used to . . ." from an interview with Victor Cooper, July 22, 1994; Manchester *Jewish Telegraph*, May 3, 1957; *The Jewish Chronicle*, April 26, 1957; "He is very fat . . ." and "Conversely he thought . . ." from NAC, RG25, vol. 2251, file/dossier 17-BVJ-40, Sept. 20, 1957, memorandum, "Interview with General Two-Gun Cohen; The Ming Sung Loan," by A. R. Menzies.

13. *Daily Victoria*, Sept. 21, 1957; "Downstairs in the foyer . . ." and "Over half a million . . ." from *The Observer*, Dec. 1, 1957; "In China, everyone . . ." from Cartier-Bresson, *China*, 1964; Clubb, pp. 355–58; "They're going to wipe . . ." from Manchester *Daily Mail*, Apr. 5, 1956; "I didn't only see . . ." from *Far East American*, Feb. 16, 1962; Leung, *Historical Dictionary of Revolutionary China*, pp. 96–97, 140–41; Clubb, pp. 359–64.

14. "Maybe I should wait . . ." and "What I'm going . . ." from *Daily Express*, Nov. 21, 1958; "It just don't . . ." from *China Mail*, July 23, 1958.

15. "I have been quite . . ." from letter written in the mid to late 1950s from Judith Cohen to Morris Cohen, collection of Victor Cooper; "Had worked for some . . ." from Feb. 20, 1956, letter from Morris Cohen to the Tientsin Hebrew Association, collection of Victor Cooper; Oct. 9, 1993, letter from Harry Clark to the author; "I was at Grosvenor . . ." from an interview with Ruth Field, July 26, 1993; "Yes, I am not . . ." from an interview with Rose Klyne, Jan. 19, 1994; "He was rather . . ." from an interview with Harry Clark, July 23, 1993; "Yep, I used . . ." from an interview with Gerald Clark, Aug. 13, 1993; "We got along well . . ." from Clark, pp. 155–56; Clubb, pp. 369–72.

16. London Sunday *Times*, Apr. 26, 1959; "Cohen told this same . . ." from USSD, 100-40-246-82, July 13, 1959 letter from Harald W. Jacobson, to Department of State; Dec. 24, 1994, letter from Michael Alderton to the author; "It impressed me . . ." from an interview with Sidney Rittenberg, Oct. 15, 1992; "He adopted me . . ." from an interview with Rabbi Aaron Krauss, Oct. 7, 1994.

17. Rolls-Royce Contract, Mar. 12, 1964, letter from F. T. Hinkley to Morris Cohen, collection of Victor Cooper; "Someone senior in Rolls-Royce . . ." from a letter from J. Peter Armstrong to author, Dec. 28, 1995; "I was sorry . . ." from an interview with Sir David Huddie, Mar. 12, 1993; "The meeting was cordial . . ." from Sept. 8, 1960 notes on Meeting Rolls-Royce with Chinese Commercial Attaches, London, collection of Victor Cooper; Interview with Duncan Fraser, Apr. 17, 1996.

18. *Biographical Dictionary*, vol. 2, p. 292; "A faithful assistant . . ." from Nov. 3, 1959 letter from Mei Kung-ping to Morris Cohen, collection of Victor Cooper; May 3, 1960 contract Canadian Broadcasting Corporation, Casting Department with Morris Cohen, collection of Victor Cooper; Jan. 19, 1961, letter L. Thompson to Morris Cohen, collection of Victor Cooper.

19. Sept. 29, 1961, invitation from Huan Hsiang to Morris Cohen, collection of Victor Cooper; Interview with Josef Rich, Nov. 8, 1992; *Tuanjie bao*, Nov. 19, 1961; "He came over . . ." from an interview with Maggie Dean, Dec. 15, 1995; "My God . . ." from an interview with Cyril Sherer, Aug. 17, 1994; "He would go back . . ." and "The people he was . . ." from an interview with J. Peter Armstrong, Jan. 4, 1996; "He rather worked . . ." from an interview with Duncan Fraser, Apr. 17, 1996; *Far East American*, Dec. 15, 1961; Topic, Dec. 16, 1961.

20. Aug. 19, 1963 letter from Yaacov Shimoni to Morris Cohen, collection of Victor Cooper; ISA, 3426/17; "He was very friendly . . ." from an interview with Roche Burgin, May 25, 1994; "The terms can be . . ." from a Jan. 31, 1962, letter from Mei Kung-ping to Morris Cohen, collection of Victor Cooper; "China is a very big . . ." and "It is not paradise . . ." from *Far East American*, Feb. 16, 1962; *Far East American*, Feb. 16, 1962; "As far as the Government . . ." from *South China Morning Post*, Feb. 17, 1962.

21. "I arrived in Beijing . . ." "But in Formosa . . ." from Sven Lindqvist, *China in Crisis* (London: Faber and Faber, 1963), pp. 73, 108; "We were talking . . ." from an interview with Cyril Sherer, Dec. 20, 1993; "Tuches" means ass.

22. Sept. 20, 1962, letter from Decca Navigation to Morris Cohen, collection of Victor Cooper; Sept. 24, 1962, letter from Decca Radar Ltd. to Morris Cohen, collection of Victor Cooper; "Most of the agents . . ." from an interview with Peter Daone, May 11, 1995; Hongkong *Tiger Standard*, Nov. 28, 1962; Mar. 12, 1964, letter from F. T. Hinkley of Rolls-Royce to Morris Cohen, collection of Victor Cooper; Aug. 19, 1963 letter from Yaacov Shimoni to Morris Cohen, collection of Victor Cooper; "Somewhat strange . . ." from ISA, 3426/17, Sept. 22, 1965, letter from Y. Shimoni to the Prime Minister; Interviews with various members of the Cohen family; Manchester *Jewish Telegraph*, Oct. 22, 1965, Nov. 18, 25, 1966.

23. "Anyone who opposes . . ." and "Dare to be . . ." quoted in Clubb, pp. 404, 406; Clubb, pp. 400–417; Seagrave, pp. 459–60.

24. "He wore them out . . ." from an interview with Cyril Sherer, Dec. 20, 1993; "This is the finest . . ." and "I have seen millions . . ." from *Times* of London, Dec. 7, 1966; *The Journal*, London, Dec. 8, 1966; "Morris, old friend . . ." and "I ran into him . . ." from an interview with Sidney Rittenberg, Oct. 15, 1992; "I still have good . . ." from *Washington Post*, Nov. 20, 1966; "He was not terribly . . ." from an interview with Stanley Karnow, May 26, 1994; London *Daily Telegraph*, Nov. 27, 1966.

25. Clubb, pp. 443–49, 454; "Black paint . . ." and "The shouting . . ." from Anthony Grey, *Hostage in Peking* (London: Michael Joseph Ltd., 1970), pp. 100, 102.

26. "If Israel had not . . ." from Manchester *Jewish Telegraph*, Feb. 17, 1967; Interview with Issie Bernstein, Apr. 13, 1994; "I must confess . . ." from *South African Jewish Times*, Apr. 14, 1967; "I didn't know . . ." from an interview with Rose Owen, Apr. 9, 1995.

27. "When he used to . . ." from an interview with Victor Cooper, July 19, 1994; Interview with Sarah Rich, Nov. 8, 1992; *Jewish Gazette*, Sept. 18, 1970.

28. *The Sunday Mail*, Rhodesia, Nov. 30, 1969; Manchester *Daily Mail*, Sept. 8, 1970; Manchester *Jewish Telegraph*, Sept. 11, 1970; "That day I went . . ." from an interview with Sarah

Rich, Mar. 14, 1993; "It was a clear . . ." from an interview with Rev. Leslie Olsberg, May 22, 1995; Interview with Josef Rich, Nov. 14, 1992; The presence of both Chinese delegations was confirmed during a talk with Josef Rich; Interview with Queenie Cohen, Apr. 13, 1994; Manchester *Jewish Telegraph*, Sept. 17, 1971; *Calendar of All Grants of Probate and Letters of Administration Made in the Probate Registries of the High Court of Justice in England, During the Year 1970* (London: Her Majesty's Stationery Office, 1972).

Bibliography

ARCHIVES, LIBRARIES, COLLECTIONS, AND PRIVATE PAPERS

Alberta Corporate Registry
Alberta Legislature Library
American Jewish Joint Distribution Committee Archives
   Laura Jarblum file
Bancroft Library, Local History Library & Archives
British Columbia Archives and Records Service
Brooklands Museum
   Vickers Archives
Calgary City Archives
Calgary Police Archives
Canadian Jewish Congress
Canadian Pacific Archives
The Canadian War Museum
Circus World Museum
   Norris & Rowe Collection
City of Edmonton Archives
Harry Cohen, Personal Papers
Columbia University Libraries Manuscript Collections
   Papers of Chang Fa-k'uei
   Papers of Wellington Koo
   Reminiscences of George Sokolsky
Victor Cooper, Personal Papers
Edmonton Police Museum/Archives
Federal Bureau of Investigation
   File on Morris Cohen
The Fernie and District Historical Society
Glenbow Archives
Greater London Record Office
The Hertzberg Circus Collection & Museum
Hoover Institution Archives, Stanford
   Norwood Allman Papers
   Randall Gould Papers
   J. C. Huston Papers
   Milton Miles Papers
Imperial War Museum
   B. C. Anslow Papers

M. L. Bevan Papers
Frank Hastings Fisher Papers
Day Joyce Papers
F. H. J. Kelly Papers
F. M. V. Tregear Papers
Israel State Archives
Legal Archives Society of Alberta
Legislative Library, Winnipeg
Library of Congress
The London Museum of Jewish Life
   Papers on the Jews' Temporary Shelter
Manitoba Provincial Archives
National Air and Space Museum
National Archives, Ottawa, Canada
   External Affairs Papers
National Archives, Washington, D.C.
   Shanghai Municipal Police Records
National Maritime Museum, Greenwich
Naval War College, Naval Historical Collection
   Papers of Wilma Miles
   Papers of Kemp Tolley
Peace River Centennial Museum
Prince Albert Historical Society
Provincial Archives of Alberta
Provincial Archives of Manitoba
Public Record Office, London
   Colonial Office Papers
   Foreign Office Papers
   Military Intelligence Papers
Public Record Office, Hong Kong
Josef Rich, Personal Papers
San Francisco Maritime National Historical Park, Maritime Museum Library
Saskatchewan Archives Board
Saskatoon Public Library, Local History Room
Southampton City Records Office, Archives Service
   Records of John I. Thornycroft & Co.
Theatre Museum, London
United States Holocaust Museum
United States State Department
   File on Morris Cohen
University of Leeds, Brotherton Library, Special Collections
   Papers and correspondences of Arthur Ransome
Michael Wallace, Personal Papers
Winnipeg Police Service
YIVO

INTERVIEWS

Abbott, Dan-San, June 22, 1996
Abbott, Senator G. Patrick, Apr. 26, 1996
Armstrong, J. Peter, Jan. 4, 1996
Bard, Solomon, Aug. 8, 1994, Aug. 11, 1994
Barnett, Doak, Aug. 18, 1994
Bates, Abraham, Sept. 16, 1993
Ben-Eliezer, Judith, Oct. 25, 1993
Bennett, H. T., Oct. 18, 1993
Bernstein, Issie, Nov. 14, 1992, Apr. 13, 1994
Booth, Sonny, Sept. 21, 1993
Burgin, Roche, May 25, 1994
Callin, Douglas, Apr. 9, 1995
Chalmers, Margaret, Feb. 27, 1995
Citrin, Walter J., Dec. 9, 1993
Clark, Gerald, Jan. 21, 1993, Aug. 13, 1993
Clark, Harry, July 23, 1993
Cohen, Harry, May 17, 1994, Nov. 13, 1994
Cohen, J. Michael, Dec. 28, 1993
Cohen, Queenie, Nov. 14, 1993, Apr. 13, 1994
Cooper, Leah, c. 1978
Cooper, Victor, July 19, 1994, July 22, 1994, May 6, 1995
Daone, Peter, May 11, 1995
Dean, Maggie, Dec. 15, 1995
Diestel, Lala, Aug. 17, 1994
Epstein, Israel, Jan. 18, 1993
Fan Liang, Apr. 29, 1994
Farkas, Marvin, May 22, 1995
Ferrier, Arthur Michael, June 5, 1995
Ferrier, George Eric Serge, June 5, 1995
Field, Ruth, July 26, 1993
Fishman, Leonard, May 27, 1995
Fradkin, Abraham, May 23, 1994
Franklin, Kay, Dec. 1, 1993
Fraser, Duncan, Apr. 17, 1996
Gabriel, Eric, Feb. 5, 1994
Gill, Louise, Sept. 7, 1993
Gleiberman, Joseph, Dec. 17, 1993
Hahn, Emily, Feb. 28, 1993
Hanin, Leo, Sept. 2, 1993
Heath, Henry, Apr. 29, 1993
Hillaly, Estelle, Dec. 13, 1993
Horal, Phyllis, Dec. 6, 1993
Horowitz, Rose, Jan. 21, 1993
Karnow, Stanley, May 26, 1994
Klyne, Rose, Jan. 19, 1994

Krauss, Rabbi Aaron, Oct. 7, 1994

Landau, Leo, Dec. 3, 1993

Levaco, Ben, Sept. 2, 1993

Liberman, Yaacov, Sept. 2, 1993

Lieberman, Henry, Dec. 3, 1993

Litvin, Raya, Dec. 27, 1994

Malini, Oziar, Jan. 9, 1996

Marks, Irene, Apr. 9, 1995

Menzies, Arthur, Mar. 25, 1994

Miles, Wilma, June 3, 1994

Muller, Samuel, Nov. 18, 1993, Dec. 15, 1993

Odell, David, Aug. 9, 1993

Odell, Jack, Aug. 8, 1993

Odell, Molly, Aug. 9, 1993

Odell, Yvonne, Aug. 8, 1993

Olsberg, Rev. Leslie, May 22, 1995

Owen, Rose, Apr. 9, 1995

Pan Jing-qing, Dec. 13, 1994

Pascal, Frances, Aug. 20, 1993

Piastunovich, Teddy, May 30, 1996

Reifler, Henriette, Oct. 11, 1993

Rich, Josef, Nov. 8, 1992, Nov. 14, 1992

Rich, Sarah, Nov. 8, 1992, Nov. 14, 1992, Mar. 14, 1993, Apr. 10, 1994

Rittenberg, Sidney, Oct. 15, 1992

Rome, David, Sept. 22, 1993

Shapiro, Sidney, Jan. 20, 1993

Shepherd, Sr., James, Mar. 15, 1994

Sherer, Cyril Dec. 13, 1993, Dec. 20, 1993, Dec. 22, 1993, Aug. 17, 1994

Shulemson, Sydney, Oct. 1, 1993

Spindel, Dinah, July 26, 1994

Tolley, Kemp, Sept. 2, 1993, Nov. 24, 1993

Vardi, David, Feb. 22, 1994

Vineberg, Cecil, Aug. 25, 1993

Vineberg, Harold, Feb. 25, 1994

Vineberg, Michael, Sept. 28, 1993

Wilson, Geoffrey, Apr. 29, 1993

Wright-Nooth, George, Mar. 10, 1993

Zarinski, Victor, Aug. 12, 1993

NEWSPAPERS AND PERIODICALS

Alberta History

Alberta Historical Review

Associated Press

Bandwagon

Bangkok *Daily Mail*
The Builder
The Building News and Engineering Journal
Calgary *Daily Herald*
Calgary *Daily News*
Calgary *Herald*
Calgary *News-Telegram*
The Canadian
Canadian Aviation Historical Society Journal
Canadian Jewish News
Canadian Railway and Marine World
Certified Schools Gazette
The China Critic
China Mail
China News (Taipei)
The China Press
The China Weekly Review
Chicago Tribune
The Commercial Traveler
The Critic
The Daily Albertan, Calgary
The Daily Phoenix, Saskatoon
The Daily Mail, London
Daily Province, Vancouver
Daily Telegraph
East End News
The Echo
Edmonton *Bulletin*
Edmonton *Capital*
Edmonton *Daily Bulletin*
Edmonton *Daily Capital*
Edmonton *Journal*
Edmonton *Morning Bulletin*
Entracte
Evening Chronicle
Evening Standard
Family Herald
Far East American
Far Eastern Review
Fernie *Free Press*
Hongkong *Daily News*
Hongkong *Daily Press*
Hong Kong *Standard*
Hongkong *Telegraph*
Hongkong *Tiger Standard*
Honolulu *Advertiser*
The Illustrated London News
Israelite Press

Israel's Messenger
Jerusalem *Post*
The Jewish Chronicle
Jewish Western Bulletin, Vancouver
The Journal, London
The Journal of Asian Studies
Lancashire *Evening Post*
Lethbridge *Herald*
Life
London *Daily Dispatch*
London *Daily Express*
London *Daily Mail*
London *Daily Mirror*
London *Daily Telegraph.*
London *Evening News*
London *Jewish Chronicle*
London *Star*
Maclean's
Manchester *Daily Dispatch*
Manchester *Daily Express*
Manchester *Daily Mail*
Manchester *Evening Chronicle*
Manchester *Evening News*
Manchester *Evening Standard*
Manchester *Guardian*
Manchester *Jewish Gazette*
Manchester *Jewish Telegraph*
Manchester *News Chronicle*
Manitoba *Free Press*, Winnipeg
Military Affairs
The Monetary Times
Montreal *Gazette*
Montreal *Herald*
Montreal *Standard*
Montreal *Star*
Moose Jaw *Times*
Moose Jaw *Times-Herald*
The Morning Albertan, Calgary
The National Jewish Monthly
New York *Globe*
New York *Herald Tribune*
New York *Post*
New York *Sun*
New York *Times*
Newsweek
The North-China Daily News
The North-China Herald
Novosti Dnia

The Observer
Oriental Affairs
Ottawa *Journal*
Peace River *Record*
Peace River *Standard*
Renmin Ribao
Reuters
Rhodesian *Herald*
Saturday Evening Post
Saturday Night, Toronto
The Shanghai Evening Post & Mercury
Shanghai *Times*
The Sketch: The English Illustrated Magazine
South African *Jewish Times*
South China Morning Post
The Star Phoenix
Sunday Chronicle
Sunday Dispatch
Sunday Express, South Africa
Sunday Graphic and Sunday News
The Sunday Mail, Rhodesia
Sunday Referee
Time
Times, London
Topic
Toronto *Daily Star*
Toronto *Globe and Mail*
Tuanjie bao
Ups and Downs
Vancouver *Sun*
Washington *Post*
Wenhui bao
Winnipeg *Evening Tribune*
Winnipeg *Free Press*
Winnipeg *Telegram*
Winnipeg *Tribune*
Xinhua ribao
The Zionist Record

UNPUBLISHED DISSERTATIONS, THESES, AND PAPERS

Andrews, G. "Moose Jaw—1882–1914: A Summary of Early Development," Moose Jaw, Growth of, file, Moose Jaw Public Library.

Anslow, B. C. Extracts from Diaries of B. C. Anslow (Then B. C. Redwood) Kept During Japanese War on Hong Kong, Imperial War Museum, Department of Documents, 73/67/1 (P).

Bellan, Ruben C. "The Development of Winnipeg as a Metropolitan Centre." Ph.D. diss., Columbia University, 1958.

Bellan, R. C. "Relief in Winnipeg: The Economic Background." Master's thesis, University of Toronto, 1941.

Betke, Carl Frederick. "The Development of Urban Community in Prairie Canada: Edmonton, 1898–1921." Ph.D. diss., University of Alberta, Edmonton, 1981.

Bevan, M. L. Diary and Album of Sketches of Stanley Gaol. Hong Kong, 1941–45, Department of Documents, Imperial War Museum, London, 69/6/1.

Bowie, Christopher J. "Great Britain and the Use of Force in China, 1919 to 1931." Ph.D. diss., Oxford University, 1983.

Cheng, Shelly Hsien. "The T'ung-Meng-Hui: Its Organization, Leadership and Finances, 1905–1912." Ph.D. diss., University of Washington, 1962.

Dudley, Marion. Hong Kong Prison Camp. New York (no pub.), Letter dated August 22, 1942.

Emerson, Geoffrey Charles. "Stanley Internment Camp, Hong Kong, 1942–1945: A Study of Civilian Internment During the Second World War." Master's thesis, University of Hong Kong, 1973.

Fisher, Frank Hastings. The Diary of F. H. Fisher in Hong Kong 1942–1945, Written in the form of a letter to his wife, Department of Documents, Imperial War Museum. 67/191/1.

Fulton, Gordon W. "Moose Jaw Main St. Project." Moose Jaw Public Library, 1984.

Gould, Randall. Unpublished memoirs, Hoover Institution, Box 10, 69086-8.23.

Grover, Sheila. "669 Main Street, Zimmerman Block." City of Winnipeg Historical Buildings Committee, Mar. 10, 1986, The Legislative Library.

———. "671–673 Main Street, 1903 Zimmerman Block," City of Winnipeg Historical Building Committee, Feb. 5, 1986, The Legislative Library.

Jarblum, Laura Margolis. United Jewish Appeal. Interview with Laura Margolis Jarblum by Menahem Kaufman, Apr. 26, 1976, AJJDC Archives, AR3344.130.

Jarblum, Laura. "Remembering Soong Ching Ling," Laura Jarblum file, Joint Distribution Committee, September 1986.

Joyce, Day. "Ordinary People: The Sheet." Account based on diaries kept at the time of her experience as a civilian internee of the Japanese in Hong Kong 1941–45, ca. 1974. Imperial War Museum, Department of Documents, P324.

Kelly, F. H. J. Typescript of Part of Diary Kept in Stanley Civilian Internment Camp 1942–1945. Imperial War Museum, Department of Documents, 84/59/1.

Lai, Jeh-hang. "A Study of a Faltering Democrat: The Life of Sun Fo, 1891–1949." Ph.D. diss., University of Illinois, 1976.

"London County Council, Minutes. Industrial & Reformatory Schools Committee. Commencing 16th January 1899 ending 18th December 1900."

MacGregor, J. G. *Peace River Jim Cornwall the Apostle of the North*. Provincial Archives of Alberta, MSS Jim Cornwall.

Miles, Wilma Sinton Jerman. *Biography of Milton Edward (Robbins) Miles*, Naval War College, MS Coll., Miles, Wilma S., 26, Series 2, Box 2, Folder 6, Papers: Biography of Adm. Miles through 1939 written by Wilma S. Miles.

Tolley, Kemp. *Reminiscences of Rear Admiral Kemp Tolley U.S. Navy (Retired)*, vol. I. U.S. Naval Institute, Annapolis, Maryland, 1983.

Tung Kwok Leung, Augustus. "A Study of the Relationship between Chen Jitang and the Nanking Government, 1929–1936." Master's thesis, University of Hong Kong, 1991.

Wechsler, Robert Steven. "The Jewish Garment Trade in East London 1875–1914: A Study of Conditions and Responses." Ph.D. diss., Columbia University, 1979.

Wilbur, Martin C. "Forging the Weapons: Sun Yat-sen and the Kuomintang in Canton 1924." Unpublished manuscript, Columbia University, 1966.

Wiley, James Hundley. "A Study of Chinese Prostitution." Master's thesis, University of Chicago, 1928.

Wilson, David Clive. "Britain and the Kuomintang, 1924–28: A Study of the interaction of official policies and perceptions in Britain and China" (Ph.D. diss., University of London, May 1973).

Wittenbach, H.G. Notes on internment by the Japanese, in Kowloon and in Stanley Camp, Hong Kong, written by Mrs. H. G. Wittenbach soon after her return to England towards the end of 1945. Department of Documents, Imperial War Museum. 89/9/1.

Books and Articles

Abbott, Dan-San. "Rosamonde," *WWI Aero* 140, May 1993, pp. 17–26.

Abbott, Senator G. Patrick. "China's First Military Airplane," *US-China Review* 11, no. 4, (July–August 1987).

Abella, Irving. *A Coat of Many Colours: Two Centuries of Jewish Life in Canada.* Toronto: Lester & Orpen Dennys, 1990.

Abend, Hallett. *My Life in China 1926–1941.* New York: Harcourt, Brace and Co., 1943.

Abrams, Gary W. D. *Prince Albert: The First Century, 1866–1966,* Saskatoon: Modern Press, 1966.

Akimova, Vera Vladimirovna (Vishnyakova). *Two Years in Revolutionary China 1925–1927.* Cambridge, Mass.: East Asian Research Center, Harvard University, 1971.

Alderman, Geoffrey. *London Jewry and London Politics 1889–1986.* London: Routledge, 1989.

Aleichem, Sholom. *From the Fair.* New York: Viking, 1985.

Allen, Richard. "The Triumph and Decline of Prohibition." In J. M. Bumstead, ed., *Documentary Problems in Canadian History,* vol. 2, *Post-Confederation.* Georgetown, Ont.: Irwin-Dorsey Ltd., 1969.

Alley, Rewi. *At 90: Memoirs of My China Years: An Autobiography of Rewi Alley.* Beijing: New World Press, 1986.

Almedingen, E. M. *The Emperor Alexander II.* London: The Bodley Head, 1962.

Anecdotes and Updates: Virden Centennial 1982. Virden, Manitoba: Empire Publishing Co. Ltd., 1982.

Archer, John H. *Saskatchewan: A History.* Saskatoon: Western Producer Prairie Books, 1980.

Archer, John H., and J. C. Bates. *Historic Saskatoon: A Concise Illustrated History of Saskatoon.* Junior Chamber of Commerce. 1947.

Aronson, I. Michael. "Geographical and Socioeconomic Factors in the 1881 Anti-Jewish Pogroms in Russia," *The Russian Review* 39, no. 1, January 1980.

———. "The Attitudes of Russian Officials in the 1880s Toward Jewish Assimilation and Emigration," *Slavic Review* 34, no. 1, March 1975.

Artibise, Alan. *Winnipeg: An Illustrated History.* Toronto: James Lorimer & Company, Publishers and National Museum of Man, National Museums of Canada, 1977.

Artibise, Alan F. J. "The Urban West: The Evolution of Prairie Towns and Cities to 1930," *Prairie Forum* 4, no. 2, Fall 1979.

————. *Winnipeg: A Social History of Urban Growth, 1874–1914.* Montreal: McGill-Queen's University Press, 1975.

Aubury, Lewis E. "The Structural and Industrial Materials of California," Bulletin No. 38, California State Mining Bureau, San Francisco, January 1906.

Ayers, William. "The Hong Kong Strikes: 1920–1926," *Papers on China,* Harvard University, Regional Studies Seminar, vol. 4, April 1950, pp. 94–130.

Backtracking with Fernie & District Historical Society. Fernie and District Historical Society, 1977.

Bagnell, Kenneth. *The Little Immigrants: The Orphans Who Came to Canada.* Toronto: Macmillan, 1980.

Baron, Salo W. *The Russian Jew Under Tsars and Soviets.* New York: Macmillan, 1976.

Bartlett, John. *Bartlett's Familiar Quotations,* 14th edition. Boston: Little, Brown and Co., 1968.

Bauer, Yehuda. *American Jewry and the Holocaust: The American Jewish Joint Distribution Committee, 1935–1945.* Detroit: Wayne State University Press, 1981.

Baureiss, Gunter. "The Chinese Community in Calgary," *Alberta Historical Review* 22, no. 2, 1974.

Baureiss, Gunter, and Leo Driedger. "Winnipeg Chinatown: Demographic, Ecological and Organizational Change, 1900–1980." *Urban History Review* 10, no. 3, February 1982, pp. 11–24.

Beahen, William. "Mob Law Could Not Prevail." *Alberta History* 29, no. 3, 1981.

Belkin, Simon. *Through Narrow Gates: A Review of Jewish Immigration, Colonization and Immigrant Aid Work in Canada (1840–1940).* Montreal: The Eagle Publishing Co., 1966.

Ben-Eliezer, Judith. *Shanghai Lost, Jerusalem Regained,* Israel: Steimatzky, 1985.

Bensusan, S. L., "The Largest School in the World." *The Windsor Magazine,* 1896.

Bercuson, David J. *Canada and the Birth of Israel; A Study in Canadian Foreign Policy.* Toronto: University of Toronto Press, 1985.

Bermant, Chaim. *Point of Arrival: A Study of London's East End.* London: Eyre Methuen, 1975.

Berton, Pierre. *The Great Railway, 1881–1885.* Toronto: McClelland and Stewart Ltd., 1971.

Bertram, James. *Beneath the Shadow: A New Zealander in the Far East, 1939–1946.* New York: The John Day Co., 1947.

Betar in China: 1929–1949.

Bi Xi, "Ti Sun Zhongshan xiansheng dang weishi shi de huiyi" (My recollections of when I was a bodyguard for Mr. Sun Yat-sen). In *Zhongguo renmin zhengzhi xieshang huiyi Zhejiang sheng weiyuanhui wenshi ziliao yanjiu weiyuanhui* (Chinese People's Political Consultative Conference Zhejiang Province Committee Historical Materials Research Committee) Ed., Sun Zhongshan yu Zhejiang (Sun Yat-sen and Zhejiang). Hangzhou: Zhejiang renmin chubanshe, 1986, pp. 145–48.

Biographical Dictionary of Republican China. Howard L. Boorman, ed. Vol. 3. Columbia University Press, New York, 1970.

Black, Eugene C. *The Social Politics of Anglo-Jewry 1880–1920.* Oxford: Basil Blackwell Ltd., 1988.

Blashill, Lorraine. *Legal Legacy.* Saskatoon: Core Communications, Inc., 1985.

Blick, Judith. "The Chinese Labor Corps in World War I," Harvard University Papers on China, vol. 9, August 1955.

Bodde, Derk. *Peking Diary: A Year of Revolution.* New York: Henry Schuman, 1950.

Bogdan, Robert. *Freak Show: Presenting Human Oddities for Amusement and Profit.* Chicago: University of Chicago Press, 1988.

Book of Remembrance: The Martyrs of Biezun. Tel Aviv: 1956.

Booth, Charles, ed. *Labour and Life of the People: Appendix to Volume II*. London: Williams and Norgate, 1891.

———. *Labour and Life of the People, vol. I, East London*. London: Williams and Norgate, 1891.

———. *Labour and Life of the People: Appendix to Volume II*. London: Williams and Norgate, 1891.

Bracken, John. *Crop Production in Western Canada*. Winnipeg: The Grain Growers' Guide, 1920.

Brooke, Rupert. *Letters from America*. New York: Charles Scribner's Sons, 1916.

Brown, Craig, ed. *The Illustrated History of Canada*. Toronto: Lester & Orpen Dennys Ltd., 1987.

Burrill, Bob. *Who's Who in Boxing*. New Rochelle: Arlington House, 1974.

The Cambridge History of China, Republican China 1912–1949, part 2, vol. 13, eds. John K. Fairbank and Albert Feuerwerker. Cambridge: Cambridge University Press, 1986.

Cameron, Nigel. *An Illustrated History of Hong Kong*. Oxford: Oxford University Press, 1991.

Canada in the Great War, by Various Authorities, vol. 5., "The Canadian Railway Troops," Hill, Roland H., and Robertson, H. L., United Publishers of Canada, Toronto, 1920.

Canadian Criminal Cases 19, November 8, 1910.

Carney, Dora Sanders. *Foreign Devils Had Light Eyes*. Toronto: Dorset Publishing, 1980.

Cartier-Bresson, Henri, and Barbara Brakeley Miller. *China*. New York: Bantam Books, 1964.

Cashman, Tony. *The Best Edmonton Stories*. Edmonton, Alberta: Hurtig Publishers, 1976.

Chan, Anthony B. *Arming the Chinese: The Western Armaments Trade in Warlord China, 1920–1928*. Vancouver: University of British Columbia Press, 1982.

Chan-Marples, Lan. "An Edmonton Chinese Project at Fort Edmonton Park: A Proposal." Fort Edmonton Historical Foundation, Feb. 24, 1983.

Chang Kia-ngau. *China's Struggle for Railroad Development*. New York: The John Day Company, 1943.

Ch'en, Jerome. "Dr. Sun Yat-sen's Trip to Peking 1924–1925." *Readings on Asian Topics*. Papers read at the inauguration of the Scandinavian Institute of Asian Studies, Sept. 16–18, 1968, Studentlitteratur, Sweden, 1970.

Chen Shuyu. *Song Qingling zhuan* (A biography of Song Qingling). Beifang funu ertong chubanshe, 1988.

Chen, Ta. "Analysis of Strikes in China, from 1918 to 1926." *Chinese Economic Journal* 1, no. 11, November 1927, pp. 945–62.

Cheng, Tien-fang. *Oriental Immigration in Canada*. Shanghai: The Commercial Press, Ltd., 1931.

Cherpak, Evelyn M. "Remembering Days in Old China: A Navy Bride Recalls Life on the Asiatic Station in the 1920s." *The American Neptune*, Summer 1984.

Chesneaux, Jean. *The Chinese Labor Movement 1919–1927*. Stanford: Stanford University Press, 1968.

Chesney, Kellow. *The Anti-Society: An Account of the Victorian Underworld*. Boston: Gambit, 1970.

Chiel, Arthur. *Jewish Experiences in Early Manitoba*. Winnipeg: Manitoba Jewish Publications, 1955.

———. *The Jews in Manitoba*. Toronto: University of Toronto Press, 1961.

The China Year Book, 1929–1930. H. G. W. Woodhead, ed. Tientsin: The Tientsin Press, Ltd., 1931.

Chindahl, George L. *A History of the Circus in America*. Caldwell, Idaho: The Caxton Printers, Ltd., 1959.

Chipman, George Fisher. "The Refining Process." *The Canadian Magazine* 33, no. 6, Oct. 1909, pp. 548–54.

Chittenden, Newton H. *Travels in British Columbia*. Vancouver: Gordon Soules, 1984.

Clark, Gerald. *No Mud on the Back Seat, Memoirs of a Reporter*. Montreal: Robert Davies Publishing, 1985.

Clifford, Nicholas R. *Spoilt Children of Empire: Westerns in Shanghai and the Chinese Revolution of the 1920s*. Hanover, N.H.: Middlebury College Press, 1991.

Clingan, Ida. *The Virden Story*. Altona, Mani.: Friesen Printers, 1957.

Clubb, O. Edmund. *20th Century China*. New York: Columbia University Press, 1978.

Cohen, Morris. "Weida de aiguozhe, weida de gemingjia, weida de ren—Sun Zhongshan xiansheng" (A great patriot, a great revolutionary, a great man—Mr. Sun Yat-sen). In Shang Mingxuan et al., ed., *Sun Zhongshan shengping shiye zhuiyilu* (Recollections of Sun Yat-sen's life and work). Beijing: Renmin chubanshe, 1986, pp. 113–15.

Cohen, Warren I. *The Chinese Connection: Roger S. Greene, Thomas W. Lamont, George E. Sokolsky and American–East Asian Relations*. New York: Columbia University Press, 1978.

The Community of Shrensek and Surroundings. A Memorial Book, Jerusalem, 1960.

Cooper, Joy. "Red Lights of Winnipeg." *Transactions—Historical and Scientific Society of Manitoba* 3, no. 27, 1970–71, pp. 61–74.

Corbett, Gail H. *Barnardo Children in Canada*. Peterborough: Woodland Publishing, 1981.

Cowen, Anne and Roger. *Victorian Jews Through British Eyes*. Oxford: Oxford University Press, 1986.

Crone, Ray. "The Unknown Air Force." *Canadian Aviation Historical Society Journal*, 18, no. 2, 1980.

Crone. Ray H. "The Unknown Air Force." *Saskatchewan History* 30, no. 1 (winter 1977).

Cross, W. K. *The Charlton Prize Guide to First World War Canadian Infantry Brigades*. Toronto: The Charlton Press, nid.

Cross, Wilbur. *Zeppelins of World War I*. New York: Paragon House, 1991.

Cruickshank, Charles. *SOE in the Far East*. Oxford: Oxford University Press, 1983.

Davies, W. J. K. *Light Railways of the First World War: A History of Tactical Rail Communications on the British Fronts, 1914–18*. Newton Abbot, Devon: David & Charles, 1967.

Dawson, J. Brian. "The Chinese Experience in Frontier Calgary: 1885–1910." In *Frontier Calgary: Town, City, and Region 1875–1914*, edited by Anthony W. Rasporich and Henry C. Klassen. Calgary: University of Calgary, 1975.

Day, Patrick John. "Wong Sing-Fuen and the Sing Lee Laundry." Historical and Natural Science Services, Edmonton Parks and Recreation, November 1978.

Dew, Gwen. *Prisoner of the Japs*. New York: Alfred A. Knopf, 1943.

Dickens, Charles. "Old Clothes!" *Household Words*, no. 108, April 17, 1853.

———. *Oliver Twist*. New York: Bantam Books, 1981.

Dickinson, F. L. *Prairie Wheat: Three Centuries of Wheat Varieties in Western Canada*. Winnipeg: Canada Grains Council.

Doyle, Arthur Conan. *The Complete Sherlock Holmes*. Vol. 1. New York: Doubleday & Co., 1953.

Drage, Charles. *Two-Gun Cohen*. London: Jonathan Cape, 1954.

Dubnow, S. M. *History of the Jews in Russia and Poland: From the Earliest Times Until the Present Day*. Vol. 2. Hoboken, N.J.: Ktav Publishing House, 1975.

Dyos, H. J., and Michael Wolff, eds. *The Victorian City: Images and Realities*. 2 vols. London: Routledge & Kegan Paul, 1973.

East, Melville A. *The Saskatoon Story: 1882–1952*. Saskatoon: General Printing and Bookbinding Ltd., 1952.

Elath, Eliahu. *Zionism at the UN: A Diary of the First Days*. Philadelphia: The Jewish Publication Society of America, 1976.

Ellis, Anthony L. "The East-End Jew At His Playhouse." *Pall Mall Magazine* 35, 1908, pp. 173–79.

Ellis, Frank. *Canada's Flying Heritage*. Toronto: University of Toronto Press, 1954.

The Encyclopaedia of Boxing. Compiled by Maurice Golesworthy. London: Robert Hale Ltd., 1988.

Encyclopaedia Judaica. Encyclopaedia Judaica Jerusalem. New York: The Macmillan Company, 1971.

Endacott, G. B. *A History of Hong Kong*. Oxford: Oxford University Press, 1964.

———. *Hong Kong Eclipse*. Oxford: Oxford University Press, 1978.

Englander, David, ed. *A Documentary History of Jewish Immigrants in Britain, 1840–1920*. Leicester: Leicester University Press, 1994.

Eyges, Thomas, B. *Beyond the Horizon: The Story of a Radical Emigrant*. Boston: Group Free Society, 1944.

Fan Liang. "Huiyi Zhongshan xiansheng" (Recollections of Mr. Sun Yat-sen). In *Sun Zhongshan—Zhongguo renmin weida de geming de erzi* (Sun Yat-sen—great revolutionary son of the Chinese People). Hong Kong: Zhonghua shuju, 1957, pp. 193–95.

———. "Wo wei Zhongshan xiansheng shou ling" (I guarded the tomb of Mr. Sun Yat-sen), Jiangsu sheng zhengxie wenshi ziliao yanjiu weiyuanhui (Jiangsu Province Political Consultative Conference Historical Materials Research Committee) ed. Zai Sun Zhongshan shenbian de rizi li (Days at the side of Sun Yat-sen). Jiangsu guji chubanshe, 1986, pp. 220–24.

———. "Zai Sun Zhongshan xiansheng shenbian de rizili" (Days at the side of Mr. Sun Yat-sen). Jiangsu sheng zhengxie wenshi ziliao yanjiu weiyuanhui (Jiangsu Province Political Consultative Conference Historical Materials Research Committee) ed. Zai Sun Zhongshan shenbian de rizi li (Days at the side of Sun Yat-sen). Jiangsu guji chubanshe, 1986, pp. 149–58.

Farson, Daniel. *Marie Lloyd & Music Hall*. London: Tom Stacey, 1972.

Finch, Percy. *Shanghai and Beyond*. New York: Charles Scribner's Sons, 1953.

Fishman, W. J. *East End 1888: Life in a London Borough among the Laboring Poor*. Philadelphia: Temple University Press, 1988.

Fishman, William J. *East End Jewish Radicals 1875–1914*. London: Gerald Duckworth & Co. Ltd., 1975.

Foran, Max. "Land Speculation and Urban Development: Calgary 1884–1912." In *Frontier Calgary: Town, City, and Region 1875–1914*, edited by Anthony W. Rasporich and Henry C. Klassen. Calgary: University of Calgary, 1975.

Franck, Harry A. *Roving Through Southern China*. New York: The Century Co., 1925.

Frankel, Jonathan. "The Crisis of 1881–82 As a Turning Point in Modern Jewish History." In *The Legacy of Jewish Immigration: 1881 and Its Impact*, edited by David Berger. New York: Brooklyn College Press, 1983.

———. *Prophecy and Politics: Socialism, Nationalism, and the Russian Jews, 1862–1917*. Cambridge: Cambridge University Press, 1981.

Franks, Kenny A., and Paul F. Lambert. *Early California Oil: A Photographic History, 1865–1940.* College Station: Texas A&M University Press, 1985.

Fryer, Harold. *Alberta: The Pioneer Years.* Langley, B.C.: Stagecoach Publishing, 1977.

Fung, Edmund S. K. *The Diplomacy of Imperial Retreat: Britain's South China Policy, 1924–1931.* Hong Kong: Oxford University Press, 1991.

Gartner, Lloyd P. *The Jewish Immigrant in England, 1870–1914.* London: Simon Publications, 1973.

Gieysztor, Aleksander, Stefan Kieniewicz, Emanuel Rostworowski, Janusz Tazbir, and Henryk Wereszycki. *History of Poland.* Warsaw: Polish Scientific Publishers, 1979.

Gilchriese, Captain Harry L. "Managing 200,000 Coolies in France." *Current History* 11, no. 3, part 1, December 1919.

Gilead, Heather. *The Maple Leaf for Quite a While.* London: J. M. Dent & Sons Ltd., 1967.

Gilkes, Margaret, and Marilyn Symons. *Calgary's Finest: A History of the City Police Force.* Calgary: Century Calgary Publications, 1975.

Gilpin, John F. "The Poor Relation Has Come into Her Fortune: The British Investment Boom in Canada 1905–1915." Canada House Lecture Series, no. 53.

Gittins, Jean. *I Was at Stanley.* Ye Olde Printerie, Ltd., 1945.

———. *Stanley: Behind Barbed Wire.* Hong Kong: Hong Kong University Press, 1982.

Glasstone, Victor. *Victorian and Edwardian Theatres: An Architectural and Social Survey.* London: Thames and Hudson, 1975.

Goldstein, Israel. *My World as a Jew: The Memoirs of Israel Goldstein.* Vol. 1. New York: Herzl Press, 1984.

Goodspeed, Lieut.-Col. D. J., ed. *The Armed Forces of Canada, 1867–1967: A Century of Achievement.* Ottawa: Directorate of History, Canadian Forces Headquarters, 1967.

Gough, Richard. *SOE Singapore, 1941–1942.* London: William Kimber, 1985.

Gould, Randall. *China in the Sun.* Garden City, N.Y.: Doubleday & Company, Inc., 1946.

———. *Chungking Today.* Shanghai: The Mercury Press, 1941.

Gray, James H. *Boomtime: Peopling the Canadian Prairies.* Saskatoon: Western Producer Prairie Books, 1979.

———. *Red Lights on the Prairies.* Toronto: Macmillan of Canada, 1971.

Green, O. M. *The Foreigner in China.* London: Hutchinson & Co., 1943.

Grey, Anthony. *Hostage in Peking.* London: Michael Joseph Ltd., 1970.

Griffin, Nicholas J. "Britain's Chinese Labor Corps in World War I." *Military Affairs* 40, no. 3, October 1976.

Gronewold, Sue. *Beautiful Merchandise: Prostitution in China 1860–1936.* New York: The Institute for Research in History and the Haworth Press, 1982.

Gurcke, Karl. *Bricks and Brickmaking: A Handbook for Historical Archaeology.* Moscow, Idaho: The University of Idaho Press, 1987.

Gutkin, Harry. *Journey into Our Heritage: The Story of the Jewish People in the Canadian West.* Toronto: Lester & Orpen Dennys, 1980.

Gutman, Yisreal, Michael Berenbaum, Yehuda Bauer, Raul Hilberg, and Franciszek Piper. *Anatomy of the Auschwitz Death Camp.* Bloomington: Indiana University Press, 1994.

Hahn, Emily. *China to Me: A Partial Autobiography.* Garden City, N.Y.: Doubleday, Doran & Co., 1944.

———. *Hong Kong Holiday.* Garden City, N.Y.: Doubleday & Co. Inc., 1946.

———. *The Soong Sisters.* Garden City, N.Y.: Doubleday, Doran & Co., 1943.

Hannon, Leslie F. *Canada at War*. Toronto: McClelland and Stewart Ltd., 1968.

Harrop, Phyllis. *Hong Kong Incident*. London: Eyre & Spottiswoode, 1943.

Hayford, Charles W. *To the People: James Yen and Village China*. New York: Columbia University Press, 1990.

Henderson's Edmonton City Directory.

Henderson's Prince Albert City Directory.

Henderson's Saskatoon City Directory.

Hershatter, Gail. "The Hierarchy of Shanghai Prostitution, 1870–1949," *Modern China* 15, no. 4 (October 1989), pp. 463–98.

Hershfield, Sheppy. "Growing Up in North Winnipeg," *The Jewish Historical Society of Western Canada*. Second annual publication, selection of papers presented in 1969–1970, Apr. 1972.

Hewlett, Sir Meyrick. *Forty Years in China*. London: Macmillan & Co., 1944.

Hoe, Ban Seng. *Structural Changes of Two Chinese Communities in Alberta, Canada*. Ottawa: National Museum of Canada, 1976.

Holubnychy, Lydia. *Michael Borodin and the Chinese Revolution, 1923–1925*. New York: East Asian Institute, Columbia University, 1979.

Houseman, Lorna. *The House that Thomas Built*. London: Chatto & Windus, 1968.

Hovet, Thomas, Jr., and Erica Hovet. *Annual Review of United Nations Affairs. A Chronology and Fact Book of the United Nations, 1941–1985*. Dobbs Ferry, New York, Oceana Publications, 1986.

Howell, Michael, and Peter Ford. *The True History of the Elephant Man*. London: Allison & Busby, 1983.

Isaacs, Harold R. *The Tragedy of the Chinese Revolution*. New York: Atheneum, 1968.

Jane's Encyclopedia of Aviation. Vol. 3. Danbury: Grolier Educational Corporation, 1980.

Jay, Ricky. *Learned Pigs & Fireproof Women*. New York: Warner Books, 1986.

Jiang Yongjing. "Hu Hanmin xiansheng nianpu goa" (A draft chronological biography of Mr. Hu Hanmin). In *Hu Hanmin shiji ziliao huiji* (Collected materials on the life of Hu Hanmin). Hong Kong: Dadong tushu gongsi, 1980. Vol 1, pp. 321–end.

Johnston, Tess, and Deke Erh. *A Last Look: Western Architecture in Old Shanghai*. Hong Kong: Old China Hand Press, 1993.

Jones, Gareth Stedman. *Outcast London: A Study in the Relationship Between Classes in Victorian Society*. Oxford: Clarendon Press, 1971.

Keesing's Contemporary Archives, Mar. 29–Apr. 5, 1952.

Keith, Ronald A. *Bush Pilot with a Briefcase: The Happy-Go-Lucky Story of Grant McConachie*. Ontario: Doubleday Canada Ltd., 1972.

Kerr, D.C. "Saskatoon 1910–13, Ideology of the Boomtime." *Saskatchewan History* 32, 1979, pp. 16–28.

Kerr, Don, and Stan Hanson. *Saskatoon: The First Half-Century*. Edmonton: NeWest Press, 1982.

Kershen, Anne J. *Uniting the Tailors: Trade Unionism amongst the Tailoring Workers of London and Leeds, 1870–1939*. Ilford: Frank Cass, 1995.

Kidd, Alan. *Manchester*. Keele, Staffordshire: Ryburn Publishing, 1993.

Klein, Daryl. *With the Chinks*. London: John Lane the Bodley Head, 1919.

Knight, Leith. *All the Moose . . . All the Jaw*. Moose Jaw: Moose Jaw 100, 1982.

Knowles, Valerie. *Strangers at Our Gates: Canadian Immigration and Immigration Policy, 1540–1990*. Toronto: Dundurn Press, 1992.

The Labour Gazette. The Department of Labour, Dominion of Canada. Col. 13, Mar. 1913, and col. 14, Jan. 1914.

Lai, Chuen-yan David. "Contribution of the Zhigongtang in Canada to the Huanghuagang Uprising in Canton, 1911," *Canadian Ethnic Studies* 14, no. 3, 1982, pp. 95–104.

Lai, David Chuenyan. *Chinatowns: Towns Within Cities in Canada.* Vancouver: University of British Columbia Press, 1988.

Lam, Lawrence. *The Whites Accept Us Chinese Now: The Changing Dynamics of Being Chinese in Timmins.* York Timmins Project, Working Paper No. 4, York University, 1983.

Lary, Diana. *The Kwangsi Clique in Chinese Politics, 1925–1937.* Cambridge: Cambridge University Press, 1974.

Leonoff, Cyril Edel. "Pioneers, Ploughs and Prayers: The Jewish Farmers of Western Canada." *Jewish Western Bulletin* (September 1982).

———. "Wapella Farm Settlement; (The First Successful Jewish Farm Settlement in Canada), A Pictorial History." Published by Historical and Scientific Society of Manitoba and Jewish Historical Society of Western Canada, 1970.

Leung, Edwin Pak-wah. *Historical Dictionary of Revolutionary China, 1839–1976.* New York: Greenwood Press, 1992.

Levy, Abraham B. *East End Story.* London: Constellation Books, 1951.

Lewis, Morton. *Ted Kid Lewis: His Life and Times.* London: Robson Books, 1990.

Li, Peter S. "Chinese Immigrants on the Canadian Prairie, 1910–1947." *The Canadian Review of Sociology and Anthropology* 19, no. 4, November 1982, Univ. of Toronto Press, pp. 527–540.

Lilius, Aleko E. *I Sailed with Chinese Pirates.* London: Arrowsmith, 1930.

Lindemann, Albert S. *The Jew Accused: Three Anti-Semitic Affairs (Dreyfus, Beilis, Frank) 1894–1915.* Cambridge: Cambridge University Press, 1991.

Lindqvist, Sven. *China in Crisis.* London: Faber and Faber, 1963.

Lindsay, Oliver. *At the Going Down of the Sun, Hong Kong and South-East Asia, 1941–1945.* London: Hamish Hamilton, 1981.

———. *The Lasting Honour: The Fall of Hong Kong, 1941.* London: Hamish Hamilton, 1978.

Lipman, V. D. *A History of the Jews in Britain since 1858.* Leicester: Leicester University Press, 1990.

———. *Social History of the Jews in England 1850–1950.* London: Watts & Co., 1954.

———. "Trends in Anglo-Jewish Occupations," *The Jewish Journal of Sociology* 2, no. 2, November 1960.

Liu, F. F. *A Military History of Modern China, 1924–1949.* Princeton: Princeton University Press, 1956.

Liu Guoming, ed. Zhonghua minguo guomin zhengfu junzheng zhiguan renwu zhi (Directory of people holding official military or civilian positions in the national government of the Republic of China). Chunqiu chubanshe.

Lloyd George, David. *War Memoirs, 1915–1916.* Vol. 2. Boston: Little, Brown and Company, 1933.

Lumb, N. P. L. *The Systematic Treatment of Gonorrhœa.* Philadelphia: Lea & Febiger, 1918.

Ma, L. Eve Armentrout. *Revolutionaries, Monarchists, and Chinatowns: Chinese Politics in the Americas and the 1911 Revolution.* Honolulu: University of Hawaii Press, 1990.

Ma Xiang. "Gensui Sun Zhongshan xiansheng shi yu nian de huiyi" (Recollections of following Mr. Sun Yat-sen for more than ten years). In Shang Mingxuan et al., eds., *Sun Zhongshan shengping shiye zhuiyilu* (Recollections of Sun Yat-sen's life and work). Beijing: Renmin chubanshe, 1986, pp. 116–161.

Macdonald, Lyn. *They Called It Passchendaele.* London: Michael Joseph, 1984.

MacFarquhar, Roderick L. "The Whampoa Military Academy." Papers on China, vol. 9, East Asia Regional Studies Seminar, Harvard University, 1955, pp. 146–72.

MacGregor, J. G. *Edmonton, A History*. Edmonton: M. G. Hurtig Publishers, 1967.

MacKay, John Henry. *The Anarchists: A Picture of Civilization at the Close of the Nineteenth Century*. Boston: Benjamin R. Tucker, 1891.

Macpherson, Maj. General W. G., ed. *Medical History of the War*. Vol 2. London: HMSO, 1923.

Magocsi, Paul Robert. *Historical Atlas of East Central Europe*. Seattle: University of Washington Press, 1993.

Mair, A. J. E.P.S. *The First 100 Years: A History of the Edmonton Police Service*. Edmonton: Edmonton Police Service, 1992.

Malraux, André. *The Conquerors*. New York: Holt, Rinehart and Winston, 1976.

———. *Man's Fate*. New York: Vintage Books, 1961.

Marlatt, Daphne and Carole Itter, eds. *Opening Doors, Vancouver's East End*. Victoria: Sound Heritage, Province of British Columbia, 1979.

Marrus Michael R. *Samuel Bronfman: The Life and Times of Seagram's Mr. Sam*. Hanover, N.H.: University Press of New England, 1991.

Martin, Chester. *History of Prairie Settlement: 'Dominion Lands' Policy*. Toronto: The Macmillan Company, 1938.

Mazower, David. *Yiddish Theatre in London*. London: The Museum of the Jewish East End, 1987.

McCormick, Elsie. *Audacious Angles on China*. New York: D. Appleton and Co., 1923.

McGinnis, J. P. Dickin. "Birth to Boom to Bust: Building in Calgary 1875–1914." In *Frontier Calgary: Town, City, and Region 1875–1914*, edited by Anthony W. Rasporich and Henry C. Klassen. Calgary: University of Calgary, 1975.

Mearns, Andrew. *The Bitter Cry of Outcast London: An Inquiry Into the Condition of the Abject Poor*. October 1883. Reprint, the Victorian Library, Anthony S. Wohl, ed., New York: Humanities Press, 1970.

Melby, John F. *The Mandate of Heaven: Record of a Civil War, China 1945–49*. Toronto: University of Toronto Press, 1968.

"Michigan's Pioneer Brickmakers," *Journal of the IBCA*, Summer 1994.

Mingling Memories: A History of Wapella and Districts. Wapella, Sask.: Wapella History Committee, 1979.

Morton, Desmond. *Canada and War: A Military and Political History*. Toronto: Butterworths, 1981.

———. *A Military History of Canada*. Edmonton: Hurtig Publishers, 1985.

Mosse, W. E. *Alexander II and the Modernization of Russia*. London: I. B. Tauris & Co. Ltd., 1992.

Movement of Farm People. Royal Commission on Agriculture and Rural Life, Report No. 7. Government of Saskatchewan, Regina, 1956.

Murphy, Emily F. *The Black Candle*. Toronto: Thomas Allen, 1922.

Myles, Eugenie Louise. *Airborne from Edmonton*. Toronto: The Ryerson Press, 1959.

New Catholic Encyclopedia. Vol. 3. San Francisco: McGraw Hill, 1967.

Newman, Aubrey, ed. *The Jewish East End, 1840–1939*. London: The Jewish Historical Society of England, 1981.

Niddrie, John G. "The Edmonton Boom of 1911–1912," *Alberta Historical Review* (Historical Society of Alberta) 13 (spring 1965).

Nordstrom, Byron J., ed. *Dictionary of Scandinavian History*. Westport, Conn.: Greenwood Press, 1986.

Oakley, Stewart. *A Short History of Sweden*. New York: Frederick A. Praeger, 1966.

Odell, Robin. *Jack the Ripper in Fact and Fiction*. London: George G. Harrap & Co., 1965.

O'Malley, Sir Owen. *The Phantom Caravan*. London: John Murray, 1954.

Palmer, Alan. *The East End: Four Centuries of London Life*. London: John Murray Publishers Ltd., 1989.

Palmer, Howard. *Patterns of Prejudice: A History of Nativism in Alberta*. Toronto: McClelland and Stewart, 1982.

Palmer, Howard, with Tamara Palmer. *Alberta: A New History*. Edmonton: Hurtig Publishers, 1990.

Parker, Ed. *I Didn't Come Here to Stay: The Memoirs of Ed Parker*. Toronto: Natural Heritage/ Natural History Inc., 1993.

Parr, Joy. *Labouring Children: British Immigrant Apprentices to Canada, 1869–1924*. Toronto: University of Toronto Press, 1994.

Peach, Jack. *Days Gone By*. Saskatoon: Fifth House Publishers, 1993.

Personal Recollections: The Jewish Pioneer Past on the Prairies, Jewish Life and Times. Vol. 6. Winnipeg: The Jewish Historical Society of Western Canada, 1993.

The Poems of Wilfred Owen. Edited by Jon Stallworthy. New York: W. W. Norton & Co., 1986.

Potter, Beatrice. "Pages From a Work-Girl's Diary." *The Nineteenth Century* 25, no. CXXXIX, September 1888.

Powell, John B. *My Twenty-five Years in China*. New York: The MacMillan Company, 1945.

Priestwood, Gwen. *Through Japanese Barbed Wire: A Thousand-mile Trek from a Japanese Prison Camp*. London: George G. Harrap & Co. Ltd., 1944.

Purcell, Victor. *The Memoirs of a Malayan Official*. London: Cassell, 1965.

Putkowski, Julian. *The Kinmel Park Camp Riots, 1919*. Hawarden Desside Clwyd: The Flintshire Historical Society, 1989.

Read, Daphne, ed. *The Great War and Canadian Society: An Oral History*. Toronto: New Hogtown Press, 1978.

A Record of the Actions of the Hongkong Volunteer Defence Corps in the Battle for Hong Kong December 1941. Hong Kong: Ye Olde Printerie, Ltd., 1953.

The Revised Statutes of Manitoba. James Hooper, King's Printer for the Province of Manitoba, 1903.

Reynolds, Chang. "The Norris & Rowe Show." Part one. *Bandwagon*, January–February 1972.

———. "The Norris & Rowe Show." Part two. *Bandwagon*, March–April 1972.

Richards, J. Howard. *Saskatchewan Geography: The Physical Environment and Its Relationship with Population and the Economic Base*. Saskatoon: University of Saskatchewan. c. 1960.

Richards, J. Howard and K. I. Fung *Atlas of Saskatchewan*. Saskatoon: University of Saskatchewan, 1969.

Ride, Edwin. *British Army Aid Group: Hong Kong Resistance 1942–1945*. Oxford: Oxford University Press, 1981.

Robinson, William J. *The Treatment of Gonorrhea and Its Complications in Men and Women*. New York: Critic and Guide Company, 1915.

Ronning, Chester. *A Memoir of China in Revolution: From the Boxer Rebellion to the People's Republic*. New York: Pantheon Books, 1974.

Rose, Millicent. *The East End of London*. London: The Cresset Press, 1951.

Roster of Communities. Encyclopedia of the Jewish Settlements from the Day of their Establishment until the Holocaust of the Second World War, Poland. Vol 4. Warsaw and the Galilee, Jerusalem: Yad Va'Shem Publication, 1989.

Salford, A City and its Past. Edited by Tom Bergin, Dorothy N. Pearce, and Stanley Shaw. The City of Salford, 1975.

Samuel, Raphael. *East End Underworld: Chapters in the Life of Arthur Harding.* London: Routledge & Kegan Paul, 1981.

Saskatchewan Department of Agriculture. *Annual Report,* 1905. Published by Saskatchewan Department of Agriculture, 1906.

———. *Annual Report,* 1906. Published by Saskatchewan Department of Agriculture, 1907.

———. *Annual Report,* 1907. Published by Saskatchewan Department of Agriculture, 1908.

"The Saskatoon Capital Anniversary Number," Saskatoon, May 12, 1909.

Schiffrin, Harold Z. *Sun Yat-sen: Reluctant Revolutionary.* Boston: Little, Brown and Co., 1980.

Schurmann, Franz and Orville Schell, eds. *Imperial China: The Decline of the Last Dynasty and the Origins of Modern China, The 18th and 19th Centuries.* New York: Random House, 1967.

Scott, Franklin D. *Sweden: The Nation's History.* Carbondale: Southern Illinois University Press, 1988.

Seagrave, Sterling. *The Soong Dynasty.* New York: Harper & Row, 1985.

Sharman, Lyon. *Sun Yat-sen: His Life and Its Meaning, A Critical Biography.* New York: The John Day Company, 1934.

Sheean, Vincent. *Personal History,* Garden City, N.Y.: Doubleday, Doran & Co. 1935.

———. "Some People from Canton," *Asia* 27, no. 10, October 1927.

Sheridan, James E. *China in Disintegration: The Republican Era in Chinese History 1912–1949.* New York: The Free Press, 1975.

Sherson, Erroll. *London's Lost Theatres of the Nineteenth Century.* London: John Lane the Bodley Head, 1925.

Shirley, James R. "Control of the Kuomintang after Sun Yat-sen's Death." *The Journal of Asian Studies* 25, no. 1 (November 1965), pp. 69–82.

"Sing Lee Laundry" Proposal for 1905 Street, Fort Edmonton Park. A Fort Edmonton Historical Foundation Project, n.d.

Slownik Geograficzny Krolestwa Polskiego. Vol. I, VI, IX. Warsaw, 1880.

Smith, H. Staples. *Diary of Events and the Progress on Shameen, 1859–1938.* 1938.

Spector, David. *Agriculture on the Prairies, 1870–1940.* Ottawa: National Historic Parks and Sites Branch, Parks Canada, 1983.

Spence, Jonathan. *To Change China: Western Advisers in China 1620–1960.* Boston: Little, Brown and Company, 1969.

Spence, Ruth Elizabeth. *Prohibition in Canada.* Toronto: The Ontario Branch of the Dominion Alliance, 1919.

Stanislawski, Michael. "The Transformation of Traditional Authority in Russian Jewry: The First Stage." In *The Legacy of Jewish Immigration: 1881 and Its Impact,* edited by David Berger. Brooklyn College Press, 1983.

Stericker, John. *A Tear for the Dragon.* London: Arthur Barker, 1958.

Strange, H. G. L. *A Short History of Prairie Agriculture.* Winnipeg: Searle Grain Company Ltd., 1954.

Sues, Ilona Ralf. *Shark's Fins and Millet.* Boston: Little, Brown and Co., 1944.

Summerskill, Michael. *China on the Western Front: Britain's Chinese Work Force in the First World War.* London: Michael Summerskill, 1982.

Swanson, W. W. and P. C. Armstrong. *Wheat.* Toronto: The MacMillan Co., 1930.

Swisher, Earl. *Canton in Revolution, The Collected Papers of Earl Swisher, 1925–1928*, edited by Kenneth W. Rea. Boulder, Colo: Westview Press, 1977.

Taber, Bob. "The Greater Norris & Rowe Show." *Bandwagon*, November–December, 1959, pp. 7–12.

Tan, Jin, and Patricia E. Roy. *The Chinese in Canada.* Ottawa: Canadian Historical Association, 1985.

T'ang Leang-li. *China Facts and Fancies.* Shanghai: China United Press, 1936.

Taylor, A. J. P. *The First World War: An Illustrated History.* New York: Perigee Book, 1980.

Taylor, Geoffrey W. *The Railway Contractors: The Story of John W. Stewart, His Enterprises and Associates.* Victoria: Morriss Publishing, 1988.

Thomas, S. Bernard. *'Proletarian Hegemony' in the Chinese Revolution and the Canton Commune of 1927.* Ann Arbor: Center for Chinese Studies, The University of Michigan, 1975.

Thompson, John Herd. "Bringing in the Sheaves: The Harvest Excursionists, 1890–1929," *Canadian Historical Review* 59, no. 4 (December 1978), pp. 467–89.

Timperley, H. J. compiled and edited. *Japanese Terror in China.* New York: Modern Age Books, 1938.

Titler, Dale M. *The Day the Red Baron Died.* New York: Walker and Company, 1970.

Tolley, Kemp. *Yangtze Patrol: The U.S. Navy in China.* Annapolis, Maryland: Naval Institute Press, 1971.

Treves, Sir Frederick. *The Elephant Man and Other Reminiscences.* London: Cassell and Company, 1923.

Tsai, Shih-shan Henry. *China and the Overseas Chinese in the United States, 1868–1911.* Fayetteville: University of Arkansas Press, 1983.

Tulchinsky, Gerald. *Taking Root: The Origin of the Canadian Jewish Community.* Toronto: Lester Publishing Ltd., 1992.

———. "The Third Solitude: A. M. Klein's Jewish Montreal, 1910–1950." *Journal of Canadian Studies* 19, no. 2 (summer 1984).

Turner, D. J. *Canadian Feature Film Index, 1913–1985.* Public Archives, Canada, 1985.

Usiskin, Roz. "Continuity and Change: The Jewish Experience in Winnipeg's North End, 1900–1914." *Canadian Jewish Historical Society Journal* (Toronto) 4, 1980, pp. 71–94.

Variety Obituaries, 1957–1963. Vol. 5. New York: Garland Publishers, 1988.

The Victorian City: Images and Realities. Vol. 2. Edited by H. J. Dyos, and Michael Wolff. London: Routledge & Kegan Paul Ltd., 1973.

Voisey, Paul. "Chinatown on the Prairies: The Emergence of an Ethnic Community." Selected Papers from the Society for the Study of Architecture in Canada, Annual Meeting 1975 and 1976. Ottawa: The Society, 1975–83.

———. "The Urbanization of the Canadian Prairies, 1871–1916." *Histoire sociale/Social History* 8, no. 15 (May 1975), pp. 77–101.

Von Sternberg, Josef. *Fun in a Chinese Laundry.* New York: The Macmillan Co., 1965.

Wakeman, Frederic. *The Fall of Imperial China.* New York: The Free Press, 1975.

Wakeman, Frederic, Jr. *Policing Shanghai 1927–1937.* Berkeley: University of California Press, 1995.

Wang Gengxiong. "Sun Zhongshan yu Lin Baike, Ma Kun de jiaowang" (Sun Yat-sen's contacts with Paul Lineberger and Morris Cohen). Minguo chunqiu (Republican Annals) 1. (Jan. 25, 1988) pp. 3–5.

Weiner, Deborah E. B. "The People's Palace: An Image for East London in the 1880s." In *Metropolis London: Histories and Representations Since 1800*, edited by David Feldman and Gareth Stedman Jones. London: Routledge, 1989.

Wensley, Frederick Porter. *Detective Days*. London: Cassell & Co. Ltd., 1931.

West, Edward. *Homesteading: Two Prairie Seasons*. London: T. Fisher Unwin, 1918.

Wetherell, Donald G., with Elise Corbet. *Breaking New Ground: A Century of Farm Equipment Manufacturing on the Canadian Prairies*. Saskatoon: Fifth House Publishers, 1993.

Wheeler, Seager. *Seager Wheeler's Book on Profitable Grain Growing*. Winnipeg: The Grain Growers' Guide, 1919.

White, Arnold. *The Destitute Alien in Great Britain*. London: Swan Sonnenschein & Co., 1892.

Whitewood Centennial 1892–1992. Vol. 2, Brigdens Printers, 1992.

Who's Who of British MPs 1918–1945. ed. M. Sterton.

Wickberg, Edgar, ed. *From China to Canada: A History of the Chinese Communities in Canada*. Toronto: McClelland and Stewart Ltd., 1982.

Wiggins, Walter. "Hired Man in Saskatchewan." *The Marxist Quarterly* (winter 1964).

Wilkins, W. H. *The Alien Invasion*. London: Methuen & Co., 1892.

Wilson, A. E. *East End Entertainment*. London: Arthur Barker Ltd., 1954.

Wilson, C. F. *A Century of Canadian Grain: Government Policy to 1951*. Saskatoon: Western Producer Prairie Books, 1978.

Wilson, Dick. *Chou: The Story of Zhou Enlai, 1896–1976*. London: Hutchinson, 1984.

Winnipeg 100. 100 Year Pictorial History of Winnipeg, compiled by Edith Paterson. Winnipeg Free Press, 1973.

Woodsworth, J. S. *My Neighbor*. Toronto: University of Toronto Press, 1972.

Wright, Richard Thomas. *In a Strange Land: A Pictorial Record of the Chinese in Canada 1788–1923*. Saskatoon: Western Producer Prairie Books, 1988.

Wright-Nooth, George. *Prisoner of the Turnip Heads, Horror, Hunger and Humor in Hong Kong, 1941–1945*. London: Leo Cooper, 1994.

Xu Youchun and Wu Zhiming, eds. *Sun Zhongshan feng'an da dian* (The great ceremony of Sun Yat-sen's interment). Beijing: Huawen chubanshe, 1989.

Yardley, Herbert O. *The Chinese Black Chamber: An Adventure in Espionage*. Boston: Houghton Mifflin Company, 1983.

Yates, Robert L. *When I Was a Harvester*. New York: The Macmillan Co., 1930.

Ye Jianying. "Sun Zhongshan xiansheng de jianjun sixiang he da wuwei jingshen" (Mr. Sun Yat-sen's ideology of military construction and fearless spirit). In Shang Mingxuan et al., ed., Sun Zhongshan shengping shiye zhuiyilu (Recollections of Sun Yat-sen's life and work). Beijing: Renmin Chubanshe, 1986, pp. 323–29.

The Year Past, 1986. Report of the City of Winnipeg Historical Buildings Committee, Department of Environmental Planning, Winnipeg, 1987.

Zhou Daochun. *Zhonghsan lingyuan boji* (Various notes on the Sun Yat-sen Mausoleum Park). Jiangsu renmin chubanshe (1989).

Index